A History of
American Diplomacy

A HISTORY OF

American Diplomacy

ARMIN RAPPAPORT
University of California, San Diego

MACMILLAN PUBLISHING CO., INC.
New York
COLLIER MACMILLAN PUBLISHERS
London

MACMILLAN PUBLISHING CO., INC.
866 Third Avenue, New York, New York 10022

COLLIER-MACMILLAN CANADA, LTD.

Library of Congress Cataloging in Publication Data

Rappaport, Armin.
  A history of American diplomacy.

  Includes bibliographies and index.
  1. United States—Foreign relations. I. Title.
E183.7.R29   327.73   74–7711
ISBN 0–02–398400–7

Printing: 6 7 8   Year: 4 5

ISBN   0-02-398400-7

TO

Thomas Andrew Bailey

Samuel Flagg Bemis
(1891–1973)

Oron James Hale

PREFACE

In the pages that follow I have narrated the history of American diplomacy and foreign policy from the beginning to the present. My objective has been to tell not only what happened but why it happened. Therefore, I have examined not only the relations between the United States and other powers through the notes exchanged, the treaties negotiated, or the conversations held, but also the factors that went into the formulation of policy, such as public attitudes, domestic political considerations, pressures from interest groups, and aims, aspirations, and ambitions of the principal policy makers as well as their characters and personalities. Further, because a nation's foreign policy cannot be separated from its domestic concerns, I have referred, frequently, to the country's political, economic, and social institutions and to its national traditions.

The study of American diplomacy and foreign policy is useful in that it provides several excellent lessons for the citizens of a democracy. First, it demonstrates that the desirable is not always possible and when the desirable is not possible, the public must not permit the frustrations to generate a scapegoat. Second, one learns that events have multiple causes; rarely is there a single or simple explanation for a complicated event. Hence, one must be wary of only plausible or circumstantial or even reasonable explanations. They may not be the true ones. Third, a decision taken in the past must always be examined in the light of the facts known and the alternatives available at the time of the decision. Hindsight is not a historian's tool. It is easy to win Saturday's game on the Monday following. Fourth, there are rarely simple solutions to complicated problems; hence, one must not succumb to glib or attractive explanations. Fifth, some problems are simply insoluble and those must be left to time. They must be lived with until conditions change. Finally, from a study of our diplomacy, one learns the virtue of patience, of seeing things in the long view, of trading small losses for large gains another day. I have tried, by use of the facts, to illustrate these generalities and deduce these principles.

As for length, I have kept the text short enough to enable the teacher to assign a decent amount of collateral material without putting too great a burden on the student yet not so short as to omit significant aspects of the story.

I have dedicated this volume to three of my former teachers who have had the greatest influence on the development of my ideas and views on diplomatic history. But my indebtedness must also be acknowledged to the several generations of students, undergraduate and graduate, principally at Berkeley but also at La Jolla, who have, by their questioning and challenging, sharpened my perception of men and events. I am indebted, too, to the many excellent histories of American diplomacy that I have used in one way or another—those by Thomas A. Bailey, Samuel Flagg Bemis, Wayne S. Cole, Alexander A. De Conde, Robert H. Ferrell, Richard Leopold, Julius Pratt. A residence at the Rockefeller Foundation's Villa Serbelloni at the time of the conception of this history afforded me unmatched surroundings, physical and intellectual, for calm and reflective thinking. My thanks go to William C. Olson, the director of the Villa. Eunice Konold and Sarah Luft were the typists of the manuscript who must be given credit not only for the excellence of their work but for their courage in wading through my difficult handwriting.

A. R.

La Jolla, California

CONTENTS

x   *Contents*

LIST OF ILLUSTRATIONS

LIST OF MAPS

A History of
American Diplomacy

U.S. State Department.

The Conduct and Control
of Foreign Policy

FOR AN understanding of the diplomatic history of the United States a knowledge of the machinery for the conduct and control of foreign policy is essential. In the constitutional provisions dealing with the formulation and execution of foreign policy, the Founding Fathers applied much the same system of checks and balances as in domestic affairs. The authority and responsibility were to be shared by the executive and the legislature. The president was designated commander-in-chief of the army and navy but to Congress was given the power to declare war, "to raise and support armies, and to maintain a navy." The president was empowered to make treaties and to appoint ambassadors, ministers, and consuls but only with the "advice and consent of the Senate." And any action taken by the president which required the expenditure of funds had to have the concurrence of the House of Representatives where "all Bills for raising Revenue shall originate."

In practice, however, the constitutional provisions for the division of power between the two branches of the government did not lead to a harmonious relationship. They were, rather, an invitation to a struggle for the direction of American foreign policy. Because of the nature of the office of the president and because of the position of the president in the American political system, the chief executive was able, early in the nation's history, to grasp the leadership in foreign affairs and to act independently of Congress. As head of the state and as the voice of the nation, he soon emerged as the sole channel of communication with foreign governments. In 1790, Thomas Jefferson could say, "The transaction of business with foreign nations is executive altogether." And presidents have guarded that prerogative carefully. When in 1793, the newly appointed consul from France requested an exequatur (a document permitting the consul to enter upon his duties) from Congress, he was in-

DEPARTMENT OF STATE

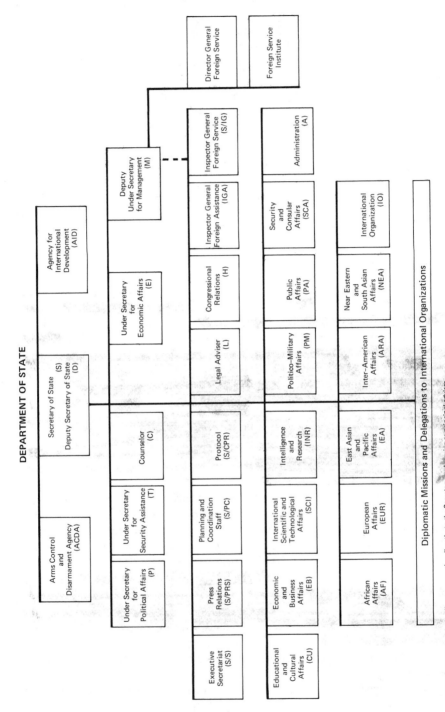

A separate agency with the director reporting directly to the Secretary and serving as principal adviser to the Secretary and the President on Arms Control and Disarmament.

Composition of a U.S. mission

The personnel of an American diplomatic mission may range in number from six, as in Rwanda, to several hundred as in Viet-Nam. The example used below is Venezuela, an important South American country where there is a broad range of official U.S. activities. In addition to the Embassy with its executive, political, economic, consular, and administrative sections, the U.S. mission in Venezuela includes military attachés, agricultural attachés from the Foreign Agricultural Service (FAS) of the Department of Agriculture, Peace Corps representatives, United States Information Service officers, Agency for International Development staff, and two consular posts outside the capital city.

In the two consular posts at Maracaibo and Puerto La Cruz, there are seven consuls and vice consuls. Also at Maracaibo is a public affairs officer directing a branch USIS office. In addition, there are American and local secretarial and clerical employees, translators, maintenance men, security personnel, librarians, and other support staff.

Executive Section

Ambassador
Deputy Chief of Mission
Executive Assistant

Political Section

Counselor for Political Affairs
Two Political Officers
Labor Attaché

Economic Section

Counselor for Economic Affairs
Three Economic Officers
Four Commercial Officers
Transportation and Communications Attaché
Petroleum Attaché

Consular Section

Consul General
Four Consular Officers
Visa Assistant

Administrative Section

Counselor for Administration
Administrative Officer
Two Security Officers
Budget Management Officer
General Services Officer
Disbursing Specialist
Communications and Records Supervisor
Personnel Assistant
General Services Assistant

General Assignment

Foreign Service Officer (a junior officer on
 first tour of duty abroad)

Military Attachés

Army Attaché
Assistant Army Attaché
Naval Attaché
Assistant Naval Attaché
Air Attaché
Assistant Air Attaché

Foreign Agricultural Service (FAS)

Agricultural Attaché
Assistant Agricultural Attaché

Agency for International Development (AID)

AID Representative
Controller
Training Officer
Programs Analysis Officer
Public Safety Adviser
Manpower Adviser
Agriculture Credit Adviser
Industrial Officer
Resources Development Officer
Sociologist
Education Adviser
Reports Officer

Peace Corps

Peace Corps Representative
Deputy Representative
Physician

United States Information Service (USIS)

Counselor for Public Affairs
Information Officer
Cultural Affairs Officer
Executive Officer

---

[1] The Country Team; An Illustrated Profile of Our American Missions Abroad. Department of State, Washington, 1967, page 9.

structed by the American secretary of state to address his request to the president. Similarly, in 1833 President Andrew Jackson found it necessary to instruct American representatives abroad to inform the governments to which they were accredited that communications to the United States must be addressed to the president and not to the president and Congress. In 1877, Secretary of State Hamilton Fish refused to transmit a resolution of the Congress to Argentina thanking that government for congratulating the United States on the centennial of its birth. If there was to be any thanking, said Fish, the president would do it.

More importantly, the president, as the nation's spokesman, can commit the country to a foreign policy simply by announcing the policy, not necessarily after consultation with Congress. In 1823, the famous Monroe Doctrine was enunciated in the form of a message to Congress. In 1899, the policy of the United States in Asia known as the "Open Door" was promulgated by means of diplomatic notes to the great powers. In 1913, President Woodrow Wilson stated American policy toward Latin America in a speech to a meeting of American businessmen, and in 1947 a grateful world first learned of the Marshall Plan from a commencement address delivered by a secretary of state in Cambridge, Massachusetts. In the same way, by a statement from the executive, American neutrality at the time of the outbreak of foreign wars has been made known. Such illustrations of the exercise of presidential power and initiative may be cited for every administration from Washington through Nixon.

Despite the congressional war-making power, no congress has ever voted a declaration of war without a specific presidential request. Presidents have, on the other hand, taken the nation to war without prior Congressional authorization. Thomas Jefferson, acting as commander-in-chief, sent the navy against the Tripoli pirates in 1801, and 113 years later Woodrow Wilson ordered the shelling of Vera Cruz as the executive's reply to an alleged insult by Mexico to the American flag. Between 1811 and 1911, there were fifty landings by American troops on foreign soil at the behest of the executive without prior congressional authorization. But not only minor incidents began on presidential initiative. Two battles were fought in 1846 between Mexican and American troops— the consequence of President James K. Polk's dispatch of soldiers to territory in dispute between the two powers—before Congress declared war. And two major wars in the twentieth century, in Korea and Vietnam, were fought from beginning to end without any declaration of war and as a result of the committing of troops to combat by the president.

In the matter of treaties, the executive found means for circumventing the constitutional check of his power. The executive agreement became the instrument used by presidents to avoid the necessity of senatorial advice and consent. Such an agreement made between the president and his opposite number in a foreign state need not be submitted to the senate and is in force only during the life of the administration that made it—unlike a treaty, which binds the nation until terminated. More than a thousand executive agreements were made between 1789 and 1939 covering all sorts of subjects, mostly of an innocuous nature. On the other hand, some of the most significant diplomatic arrangements of recent times have been incorporated into executive agreement. American relations with Japan in the first two decades of this century were regulated mainly by three such agreements: Taft-Katsura, Root-Takahira, and Lansing-Ishii. In 1940, President Franklin Roosevelt agreed to exchange a number of American destroyers for certain British territory in the Western Hemisphere by an agreement with Prime Minister Winston Churchill. And all of the understandings between the United States and its allies during World War II on the chief political and military questions hammered out at several conferences—Cairo, Teheran, Casablanca, Yalta, Potsdam—were formalized by executive agreements, not by treaties approved by the Senate. Presidents utilized such extraconstitutional means principally to avoid the possibility of senatorial rejection of their actions but also to stave off public discussion of issues considered delicate and sensitive.

As in treaties, so in the matter of representation abroad, presidents have bypassed the Senate on numerous occasions by designating personal agents to treat with foreign nations and to do such other things as the regularly accredited diplomats appointed with Senate approval would normally perform. So, for example, in 1962, President John F. Kennedy sent Dean G. Acheson to Europe to inform the French and British allies of the facts of the Cuban missile crisis and from 1914 to 1918, President Woodrow Wilson used Colonel Edward M. House, one of his closest advisers, repeatedly on missions to the warring nations. Throughout our history, such practices were common. Executive agents, as the personal emissaries are known, have been employed by every president and no constitutional authority has ever questioned the right.

The Constitution says nothing about the recognition of new states or of new governments in existing states, but the president has grasped the power by virtue of certain rights inherent in the office. As commander-in-chief he can order a salute to the flag of the new nation, which is an act of recognition. By inviting the new state to send a minister or by receiving an uninvited minister, he extends recognition. Of course, if a president wishes to associate the Senate with the act of recognition, he need only send up the name of a minister or ambassador for approval. Of equal importance in the matter of recognition is the prerogative of the executive to refuse recognition by taking no action. In a civil war or revolution, the president can take the important step of recognizing the belligerency of the rebels merely by proclaiming his country's neutrality.

So have successive presidents used their "almost royal prerogatives" (to use the words of that sharp observer of the American system in the early nineteenth century, Alexis de Tocqueville) in the area of foreign affairs. It must not be supposed, however, that the Congress has stood by meekly as the executive wielded his authority. In frequent statements and speeches by individual legislators, in resolutions by one or both chambers, and in hearings and reports by House and Senate committees, efforts have been made to redress the balance envisaged in the Constitution but tipped by the executive in his favor. When, in 1864, a resolution passed the House of Representatives suggesting a certain course to be taken relative to the French occupation of Mexico was ignored by the president, the House came back with another resolution proclaiming the right of that body in "prescribing and declaring foreign policy for the United States." More recently, in 1969, the Senate approved a resolution which stated that the "commitment of the armed forces of the United States to hostilities on foreign territory . . . will result from a decision made in accordance with constitutional processes, which in addition to appropriate executive action requires affirmative action by Congress. . . ."

Those legislative expressions did not affect the president's course any more than did the irate statements of senators such as the one by Henry M. Teller of Colorado, who in 1906 said, "I deny the right of the executive department to make any contract, any treaty, which shall bind the United States. It is an assumption on the part of the executive of power that is clearly and unequivocally given to the legislative department of the government." The records of American diplomacy are full of similar examples of the legislative claim for a larger share in the conduct and control of foreign policy that presidents have, for the most part, disregarded.

Those occasions when senatorial expressions, apparently, had an effect on the executive, such as, for example, the Ball-Burton-Hatch-Hill resolution in 1943 on the desirability of the United States joining a postwar international organization or the Dodd resolution in 1963 calling for a nuclear test ban treaty or the report of a Senate Foreign Relations Committee hearing in 1968 urging a de-escalation of the war in Vietnam, it was either because the president's plans coincided with the Senate's suggestions (as in the first two instances) or because the executive saw in the Senate view a reflection of the public mood (as in the third instance).

It should be pointed out that the Congress has, at times, contributed to the erosion of its own constitutional powers by granting to the president, during a period of high emotion, what amounted virtually to a blank check. In 1955, for example, following a request by the president, Congress, in a joint resolution, gave the executive authority to use American forces to defend Taiwan and the Pescadores. Again, in 1957, at the president's suggestion, the legislature approved the Eisenhower Doctrine, which permitted the use of the armed forces to assist any Middle Eastern nation which called for help to resist an "attack from any country controlled by international Communism." Seven years later came the classic example of congressional abdication of its prerogative when, almost without debate, both Senate and House passed a resolution requested by President Lyndon Johnson as a result of an attack on two American warships by North Vietnamese patrol boats in the Gulf of Tonkin. The resolution, which empowered the president "as commander-in-chief, to take all necessary measures to repel any armed attack against the forces of the United States and to prevent further aggression . . . in Southern Asia," became the basis for fighting the war in Vietnam without a formal declaration by Congress. No amount of congressional exhortation could undo the "historic mistake" (to use the words of Senator Wayne Morse); the president continued to interpret the resolution as the "functional equivalent of a declaration of war."

All this is not to say that the Congress is absolutely helpless and powerless in the making of foreign policy. Certain types of legislation have the deepest implications for the nation's international relations and, in a very direct way, set the country's foreign policy. The tariff is one such kind. The Smoot-Hawley Act of 1930 which raised duties on imports to the highest level in American history served notice on the world that this country planned to pursue a course of economic nationalism. On the other hand, the passage four years later of the Reciprocal Trade Agreements Act reversed the nation's economic foreign policy by authorizing the president to reduce rates.

Immigration laws, similarly, can be crucial to the nation's foreign relations. The act of 1924 excluding Japanese nationals from entering the United States (signed by the president despite his disapproval) created a bitter and hostile feeling for the United States in Japan that contributed to the deterioration of relations between the two nations in the years following. Neutrality statutes, too, have their effect. The several acts passed between 1935 and 1939 dictated the nation's policy toward the crisis in Europe preceding the outbreak of war and made impossible any presidential initiative. Finally, there are the bills authorizing the expenditure of funds, which, as Senator Wayne Morse has said, may have the effect of making foreign policy by containing precise instructions or conditions on how the money should be spent. An amendment to a defense appropriation bill in 1970, for example, that was attacked in the Senate, stated, ". . . none of the funds appropriated by this act shall be used to finance the introduction of American ground troops into Laos, Thailand, and Cambodia."

If legislation is a positive way for Congress to make policy, there are negative means only slightly less effective. Congress may refuse to give its consent to appointments and to treaties, to enact enabling legislation necessary for the implementation of a policy, or to appropriate funds for carrying out a program or paying an appointee. It is true, of course, that not infrequently the Congress really does not have the alternative of with-holding funds or denying legislation to carry out a presidential policy when such action would embarrass the president before the world or would tend to punish "innocent" parties. Thus, the most passionate opponents of the war against Mexico in the nineteenth century and in Vietnam in the twentieth regularly joined the war's supporters in voting funds because they could not deny support to the troops in the field.

Two favorite and important devices used by the Congress to increase its participation in the foreign policy-making process and to reduce the executive's role have been the hearings and the investigations conducted by committees and subcommittees of both houses. The Senate Foreign Relations Committee and the House Foreign Affairs Committee have, quite naturally, been the main vehicles of such efforts but, from time to time, Appropriations (and its subcommittee on the State Department), Judiciary (and its subcommittee on the Separation of Powers), and Armed Services (which replaced the separate Military Affairs and Naval Affairs com-mittees in 1947) have considered matters that affected foreign relations. The hearings on legislation and appointments have required the executive to defend and to clarify his position with the attendant publicity not only acting as a brake upon his freedom of action but serving also to permit the congressional point of view to be made known. In hearings before the Senate Foreign Relations Committee on Vietnam in the winter of 1966, senatorial opposition to the escalation of bombing proved so great and so vociferous as to cause the president to call off further raids.

Investigations, similarly, have had the effect of checking the president and of enhancing the role of the Congress. An inquiry into the recall of General Douglas MacArthur in 1951 from his post as commander of the forces in Korea that turned into an examination of the role of the Truman Administration in the defeat of the Chinese Nationalists on the mainland revealed so much hostility toward the Chinese Communists on the part of numerous senators as to make impossible even the contemplation of recognizing the Communists as the rulers of China. It is true, too, that the possibility of an investigation at some future time of a presidential policy has served to cause the executive to think twice before entering on a course of action.

Once only, in the 1950s, did some senators move to curtail the presi-dent's power in foreign affairs by constitutional amendment. It was Sena-tor John Bricker of Ohio who introduced the amendment designed to put an end to the executive agreement as a means for the executive to make arrangements with foreign nations without senatorial "advice and con-sent." The amendment, which contained five sections, provided, basically, that "the Congress shall have the power to regulate all executive and other agreements with any foreign power or international organization." Bricker had great support not only in the Senate but in the country, where many people believed an executive enjoying unbridled power in the area of foreign affairs was dangerous to the nation's safety and might commit the nation unilaterally to all sorts of quixotic adventures. Democratic President Harry S. Truman opposed it as did his Republican successor, President Dwight D. Eisenhower, who claimed the amendments "would make it impossible for us to deal effectively with friendly nations for our mutual defense" and would serve notice "that our country intends to withdraw from its leadership in world affairs." Bricker tried to push his measure through the Senate in six consecutive sessions but without success. When he lost his seat in 1958, the amendment passed with him from the national scene and with it went a threat to presidential power in foreign affairs.

The conflict between the two branches of government has been unfortunate and, in a sense, needless. Despite the constitutional invitation to struggle, the roles of executive and legislature can be complementary instead of competitive. As Secretary of State Cordell Hull said in 1944, "Under our system of government the safeguarding and promotion of the national interest is a joint responsibility of the executive and legislature. Neither can be effective without the other, and the two together can be effective only where there exists between them mutual trust and confidence."

Whether such mutual trust and confidence exist depends in great part upon the position taken by the president. They will not exist if, like Woodrow Wilson, he ignores the Senate in choosing delegates to a major peace conference who will have to be approved by that body or, like Lyndon Johnson, he approves a statement to a Senate Committee to the effect that a Congressional declaration of war is "outmoded phraseology." This latter action caused one senator to exclaim, "This is the wildest testimony I have ever heard. There is no limit to what he [Undersecretary of State Nicholas de B. Katzenbach] says the President can do." In such situations harmony can hardly be achieved. If, on the other hand, the president consults leading senators and representatives at every step of the way in important foreign policy decisions as did William McKinley during the preliminaries of the Spanish War and the peace negotiations and does not usurp or ignore the congressional role as he may because of the nature of the office, then amicable and mutually beneficial relations can result to the country's advantage.

Even those legislators who most jealously guard their branch's prerogatives realize that day-to-day operation of the nation's foreign affairs had best be left to the executive. On the other hand, they insist that Congress and its committees be the accepted and recognized forum and critical testing ground for new foreign policy proposals and for the reappraisal of old ones. The executive, too, must acknowledge the competence of Congress in monitoring his actions and questioning his policies. When Senator J. William Fulbright blasted Lyndon Johnson's intervention in the

Dominican Republic in 1965, the *San Francisco Chronicle* applauded "the highly effective example of the duty of a senator to criticize and lay bare the follies of government." Similarly, the president must not bypass the Congress in the performance of its constitutional and legal responsibilities.

Given the tremendous power and authority of the chief executive in the formulation and conduct of foreign policy, it would be hoped that presidents would come to the office with some experience and interest in international affairs and with some knowledge of the constitutional mechanism. It would be hoped, too, that they would have such qualities of mind and character as would enable them to understand the problems and to choose the courses of action best geared to the national interest regardless of public passions, private pressures, or political consequences. The first six presidents, with the exception of George Washington, entered office experienced in diplomacy—four had served as secretary of state—Thomas Jefferson, James Madison, James Monroe, John Quincy Adams—and of the four, all save Madison had represented the United States abroad. Another, John Adams, had been his country's emissary in several capitals of Europe. After them, only two—Martin Van Buren (briefly) and James Buchanan (extensively) had had prior involvement in external affairs. As for demonstrating wise judgment and making sound decisions, the record is checkered. It included such varied instances as John Adams' stalwart resistance to pressures from the public and his political supporters for war with France in 1798 and William McKinley's collapse in the face of similar pressures for war with Spain in 1898. Harry S. Truman's international programs comprising the Marshall Plan and the North Atlantic Treaty in the late 1940s stand out in sharp contrast to Lyndon Johnson's entanglement in the morass of a ground war in Asia in the 1960s.

From the very beginning of the nation's history, the president has had the advice of a secretary of state in the formulation and execution of foreign policy. That officer has headed the Department of State that Congress established in 1789 as the executive agency for handling correspondence and other communications with the states of the Union and with foreign governments and for conducting the nation's foreign affairs. After the creation of the Department of the Interior in 1849, the State Department concerned itself entirely with foreign affairs (except that it retained the "domestic" functions of housing the Great Seal of the United States that is affixed to all executive documents and of publishing the laws of the land and other public documents). The role of the secretary of state has been inversely proportional to the ability and interest of the president. Under "strong" presidents, such as Theodore Roosevelt, Woodrow Wilson, Franklin D. Roosevelt, or John F. Kennedy, the secretaries have been relegated to routine administrators of an executive department as the presidents have "made" foreign policy themselves or with the advice of their personal advisors. "Weak" presidents, such as Ulysses S. Grant,

Warren G. Harding, Herbert Hoover, or Dwight D. Eisenhower, have tended to leave their secretaries free to take the lead in formulating and conducting foreign policy. The foreign policies of those administrations have been associated not with the names of the presidents but of their secretaries—Hamilton Fish, Charles Evans Hughes, Henry L. Stimson, and John Foster Dulles. Some chief executives, notably James Monroe, John Quincy Adams, Abraham Lincoln, and Harry S. Truman worked closely with their secretaries and leaned heavily upon them for advice so that policy making in their administration was coordinated.

Fewer than half of the secretaries of state from Thomas Jefferson to Henry A. Kissinger had had any prior diplomatic experience (twenty-three out of fifty-five). Of those who had none, several—Daniel Webster, William H. Seward, Elihu Root, Charles Evans Hughes—turned out to be first rate and highly successful by reason of superior ability, intelligence, and wisdom. Not all who had had experience were necessarily of high quality. Still, not one of the men who held the office was less than competent or discreditable save, perhaps, Elihu Washburne, a fellow townsman of Ulysses S. Grant who was appointed to the post for old time's sake but he lasted only eleven days.

To discharge its responsibilities and functions, the State Department has always maintained personnel at home and abroad. Under the first secretary of state, five were at home and two abroad; 180 years later the number at home had grown to a number slightly under 8,000 and abroad to about 19,000 (of which approximately 12,000 were citizens of foreign countries). From a simple organization housed in a few rooms in the nation's capital, the department at home grew to a complex and complicated bureaucracy occupying several buildings in Washington with personnel stationed also in the major cities of the country in passport, security, and public affairs. Jefferson had a chief clerk, three other clerks, and a translator. Over the years, as the volume of business grew and the number of employees increased, assistant secretaries were added to head bureaus and divisions occupied with specialized tasks. By the mid-twentieth century the department's duties in Washington were divided among five bureaus dealing with the various geographical areas of the world and six functional bureaus (international organizational affairs, economics, administration, public affairs, congressional relations, educational and cultural affairs) presided over by eleven assistant secretaries and supervised by two undersecretaries and two deputy undersecretaries. In addition, there were several special assistants for very special problems such as refugee and migration affairs, fisheries and wildlife, and population matters as they affected foreign affairs.

The importance to American foreign policy of the State Department people stationed abroad, that is, those who are in the foreign service of the United States, is crucial for they are the "eyes and ears" of the department.

It is they who keep the department posted on developments in the countries to which they are accredited. It is their estimates of the situation and their appraisals of conditions that most often form the basis for policy. And it is they who interpret the United States to foreign peoples and governments and who represent the United States in negotiations. In the earliest days, the ablest men served as ministers abroad; men of experience, of learning, and of wisdom—Benjamin Franklin, John Adams, John Jay, Thomas Jefferson, James Monroe, William Short, Rufus King—and much of the success of the diplomacy of the last years of the eighteenth century and the beginning of the nineteenth century may be ascribed to those astute men. Unhappily, that breed died out and was succeeded by party hacks, spoilsmen, and generous contributors to election campaigns. The pay was poor, there were no examinations for appointment or advancement, and there was no training for diplomacy. No wonder that much of the history of the foreign service in the nineteenth century could be related in terms of dilettantes, incompetents, wastrels, and scoundrels.

The need for a professional and competent service led to several attempts during the nineteenth century to effect reforms but none of them succeeded. It was not until after 1900 when America's international responsibilities increased as a result of the war with Spain and of a new Asiatic policy and when there was a remarkable spurt in foreign trade that progress was made. Legislation and executive orders in the first two decades of the twentieth century provided for some salutary changes but the first really significant step came in 1924. The Rogers Act of that year combined two hitherto separate and distinct groups operating abroad—consuls who concerned themselves with trade matters and diplomats who were involved in diplomacy—into one Foreign Service of the United States staffed by officers in ten classes. Admission to the service was to be by examination and promotion was to be made on merit. Salaries were increased and a retirement system begun. From that time, the Foreign Service increased its professional quality attracting able young men who saw opportunities to rise in the career service to the top posts of minister and ambassador. Several subsequent acts made the service even more desirable.

All this is not to say that the Foreign Service did not face formidable problems. For one thing, some of the most prestigious posts, those in the Western European capitals, have demanded such large-scale entertaining that only men of independent and considerable wealth could afford to hold the post. It was reported that one ambassador to France spent all of his annual allowance for entertaining on one July Fourth reception. At the same time, too many ambassadorial appointments are still made outside the career service. Where the person chosen has a very special skill or training—Edwin Reischauer, expert in Japanese language and history to Tokyo; John Badeau, experienced in Near Eastern affairs and fluent in Arabic to Cairo; Lincoln Gordon, distinguished economist to Rio de Janeiro—the consequences have been excellent. Most often, however, the selection has been as a reward for political or pecuniary services rendered the party in power with results far from salutary and, occasionally, disastrous. Irrespective of the quality of the appointee, such a practice narrows the possibilities for career officers in attaining posts as chiefs of mission.

Foreign Service officers have suffered, also, from a bad public image. They have been characterized as "effete cookie pushers," "striped-pants boys," and "an inbred clique." In short, they have been viewed as un-American types, not the heroic, strong, masculine he-men so beloved in the cowboy tintypes of movies and television. And in the 1950s, they underwent much maligning as traitorous and disloyal stemming from the infamous accusations of Senator Joseph McCarthy that large numbers of State Department people were communists and from the opinion held by many Americans that the defeat of the Chinese Nationalists in 1949 was the result of deliberate efforts by certain American diplomats to insure a Red victory. As a consequence, many loyal, able, and experienced officers were investigated, hounded, harassed, and dismissed from the service. Those who remained were jittery, intimidated, and nervous. Five distinguished retired ambassadors voiced concern (in a letter to the editor of the *New York Times*) that the attacks on the diplomats might cause them to send home from the field reports and recommendations "which are ambiguously stated or so cautiously set forth as to be deceiving" fearful lest anything franker might return to haunt them years later. Happily, the dire predictions of a timid and conformist corps did not materialize, and by the 1960s confidence reigned once again in the ranks.

Another situation in the period after World War II threatened the equanimity of the Foreign Service—the integration of large numbers of State Department personnel into the Foreign Service between the years 1954 and 1957 as a result of recommendations by a committee headed by Henry M. Wriston, president of Brown University. The lateral entry of some 1,500 persons into classes in the Foreign Service (almost doubling the total number) commensurate with their training and experience and position, making them at once senior and superior to many officers with long service, and their assignment to attractive and responsible positions abroad led to sharp resentment in the career service. Again, happily, the ill effects were short-lived and soon the "Wristonees" took their places alongside the other officers in the service and were indistinguishable from them.

There have been other sources of dissatisfaction in recent years as reflected in a 600-page State Department publication entitled *Diplomacy for the Seventies* which appeared in December of 1970 after a year-long inquiry by 250 career diplomats: lagging promotions, lack of opportunities to achieve responsibility before reaching middle age, "strong pressures toward conformity," reliance by recent presidents upon special White House staff members (McGeorge Bundy, Walt W. Rostow, Arthur Schlesinger, Henry A. Kissinger) in foreign policy making, relegating State Department experts to preparing option papers, and the steadily diminishing number of foreign service officers in missions abroad in relation to representatives of other federal agencies such as Defense, Treasury, Commerce, and Agriculture. To allay the dissatisfaction and remedy the evils, the State Department is prepared to embark on a major reorganization program designed to develop a "new breed of diplomats–managers," officers trained in management techniques and skilled in new facets of foreign affairs—agriculture, labor, commerce, finance, development economics, information, and science. Greater opportunities will be provided for "innovative thinking" and chains of command will be loosened to enable officers to present ideas and recommendations directly to the policy makers.

A revamping of the foreign service of the United States comes none too soon because this country's position in the world of the 1970s and beyond will be vastly different from what it was in the period between the end of the war in 1945 and the late 1960s. To guide the nation safely through those difficult and transitional times will require that "our watchmen overseas" have the flexibility, imagination, and skills to understand and to deal with the changing forces. The days when the two superpowers reigned supreme in their spheres and could determine the destinies of their satellites are coming to an end. America's options in Europe and in Asia are narrowing as the Western European countries and Japan, strengthened and revived, strike out on their own independent courses. The American military presence, so necessary in the post-World War II for the safety and security of the free nations of Asia and Europe, diminishes as the free nations' new prosperity and, indeed, affluence, make possible their providing for their own defenses. In the Western Hemisphere, there is evidence of the reduction of American influence and control in the imminence of the recognition of the Castro regime by several Latin American republics, and the vote in the United Nations in 1970 on the admission of Red China offers further evidence of the erosion of the American position.

As the Pax Romana and the Pax Britannica passed, so the Pax Americana is passing, and the task of the diplomat in the years to come will be to recognize and accept the changes and to adjust American policy to them.

BIBLIOGRAPHY

Gabriel Almond, *The American People and Foreign Policy* (1960).
Thomas A. Bailey, *The Art of Diplomacy: The American Experience* (1968).
H. B. Carroll, *The House of Representatives and Foreign Affairs* (1958).
E. S. Corwin, *The President: Office and Powers* (4th ed., 1957).

D. N. FARNSWORTH, *The Senate Committee on Foreign Relations* (1961).

JOHN E. HARR, *The Professional Diplomat* (1969).

LOUIS HENKIN, *Foreign Affairs and the Constitution* (1973).

WARREN ILCHMAN, *Professional Diplomacy in the United States, 1779–1939* (1961).

ELMER PLISCHKE, *The Conduct of American Diplomacy* (3rd ed., 1967).

SMITH SIMPSON, *Anatomy of the State Department* (1967).

RONALD J. STUPAK, *The Shaping of Foreign Policy: The Role of the Secretary of State As Seen by Dean Acheson* (1969).

FRANCIS O. WILCOX, *The Congress, the Executive, and Foreign Policy* (1968).

Benjamin Franklin.

The Nation Is Formed

On October 19, 1781, a British army of 7,000 seasoned regulars commanded by Lord Cornwallis, a veteran of twenty years of military service, surrendered to a combined force of 9,000 American and 8,000 French troops at Yorktown in Virginia, bringing an end to the War of the American Revolution (except for some desultory engagements in the succeeding months) and an assurance of American independence. As His Majesty's soldiers stacked their arms, a band played "The World Turned Upside Down." The tune was apt for the world seemed, indeed, turned upside down when an army of the world's most powerful empire capitulated to a poor and weak rebel government.

The outcome of that battle and of the war itself, however, would have been very different had France not been a cobelligerent with the United States since 1778 and, for two years before, given secret aid to the Americans. At Yorktown, it was not only the French ground forces but also the presence of a French fleet in adjacent waters, which made impossible Cornwallis' escape or reinforcement, that helped make victory possible. And throughout the war, it was French aid in the form of men, equipment, arms, ammunition, and money that enabled the colonials to keep going and, ultimately, to win. In short, French assistance was crucial to the winning of American independence.

To understand why an autocratic monarchy with vast colonial dependencies should have been willing to come to the aid of insurrectionists dedicated to the principles of liberty, democracy, and republicanism requires an examination of Anglo-French history between 1688 and 1763. Such an examination would reveal that during that time the two powers fought four great wars for mastery of the North American continent and that at the end the British emerged victorious. By the Treaty of Utrecht that closed the second war in 1713, France retained possession of the valley of the Mississippi River and of Canada but gave up Newfoundland, Nova Scotia, and the territory bordering on Hudson's Bay to England.

By the Treaty of Paris of 1763, which marked the termination of the fourth and last war, France was forced to surrender the rest of Canada and all the land east of the Mississippi to England, thereby spelling the doom of the French empire in the New World except for some small (albeit valuable) islands in the West Indies and in the Gulf of St. Lawrence. The British had achieved their purpose, which the eminent French statesman Cardinal Fleury had seen clearly in 1713—"to drive us entirely out of the continent of North America . . . and crush our power." And the French now had a purpose of their own—to undo the disaster and recover their lost territories.

The difficulties that broke out between England and her American colonies after 1763 provided a welcome and superb opportunity for France to wreak her revenge upon her ancient enemy. The colonies would be the instrument of French vengeance. Encouragement of their dissatisfaction and support of a movement for independence appeared to French statesmen as an economical and relatively painless means for hurting and humbling Britain and for wresting political and commercial advantages for France from a grateful America. The French foreign minister, the duke de Choiseul, sent secret observers to the colonies in 1764 to keep him posted on the course of the rift, and as the several measures passed by Parliament widened that rift, Choiseul was convinced that a break would soon come. Upon leaving office in 1770, he prepared a memorandum for the king urging that when the break came, help be given the colonies although not at the risk of open warfare with Britain.

His successor, the count de Vergennes, pursued the same aim, even more insistently. When in 1774, Parliament passed the Intolerable Acts, Vergennes realized that war between mother country and colonies was imminent. Quickly, he dispatched an emissary to Philadelphia, where the Continental Congress was meeting, to make known the French king's good will. At the same time, he outlined to the king the policy France ought to pursue: neutrality in the coming struggle, secret aid to the colonies, no military alliance with them, no hostilites with Great Britain. The king was not entirely convinced of the wisdom of aiding the colonies. He thought the cost too great for the weakened treasury and the risk of war with England, even if aid were secret, too dangerous. Equally unconvinced was the shrewd finance minister, Anne Robert Jacques Turgot, who believed that the French treasury could not withstand aid to the colonies. Furthermore, he believed that even without French assistance, the colonies would eventually become independent—a prelude to the freedom of all colonies everywhere. Nor was he certain that a British defeat in the struggle would be best suited to French interests. Might it not be better, he argued, for England to beat the colonies after a long and exhausting war and then to weaken herself ruling a rebellious and obstreperous colony over the next century?

After much deliberation and hesitation the King's decision, made in May of 1766, was to offer the Americans assistance, secretly. Crucial to the decision was a cogent and closely reasoned memorandum by Vergennes in April 1776 pointing out again the value to France of a British defeat in America—a diminution of British power and trade with a commensurate enhancement of the French position, achieved without the risk of war, and the possibility of recovering lost territory. Interestingly, he assured the king that an independent America would be republican and therefore weak, thus posing no threat to France. Important, too, in the royal decision was a paper prepared by the noted French dramatist Pierre Augustin Caron de Beaumarchais, who had taken a great interest in the American cause, which suggested that a reconciliation between England and her colonies might lead to an assault on the valuable French sugar islands in the West Indies. One other factor, not easily susceptible to proof, may have influenced the king—the attitude of the group of intellectuals in France known as the "philosophers," which included the philosopher and encyclopedist Denis Diderot, the naturalist Georges Buffon, Jean Jacques Rousseau, the jurist Baron Montesquieu, and Voltaire. Those men whose ideas of a rational and scientific world and whose confidence in human reason, natural law, and universal order made the eighteenth century known as the "Enlightenment" or the "Age of Reason," saw in the New World and in the revolution there the ideal place and occasion to test their views. Precisely to what extent they affected the monarch's decision cannot be determined. It is reasonable to believe, however, as some historians have suggested, that their sympathies were known at court and that they counted.

Meanwhile, across the seas in Philadelphia, where the leaders of the rebellion were gathered, nothing was known of the crucial decision made in Paris that was to contribute so heavily to American success in the war. On their part, the leaders knew that the struggle against the mother country could not be continued without arms, ammunition, and other military supplies from abroad. With that in mind, the Continental Congress had, in November of 1775, appointed a secret committee of correspondence "for the sole purpose of corresponding with our friends in Great Britain, Ireland, and other parts of the world." At once, letters went out from the committee to Arthur Lee, a Virginian representing the colony of Massachusetts in London, and to Charles F. W. Dumas, a friend of Benjamin Franklin's living in The Hague, soliciting information on the attitude of the European powers toward the revolution. In March of 1776, encouraged by the visit of Vergennes' agent, Congress decided to send Silas Deane, a wealthy Connecticut lawyer and merchant and a member of Congress, to Paris to procure military equipment and to sound the French government out on the possibility of direct military assistance.

Deane arrived in the French capital early in July of 1776 and learned, to his surprise and pleasure, that not only had the king decided on aiding the colonists, but he had already set up the machinery for funnelling supplies to them—a fictitious company called Roderigue Hortalez et Cie. That company, headed by Beaumarchais and financed by a grant from the royal treasury of 1 million *livres* (about $200,000) plus an equal amount from the king of Spain, who was no less pleased than his royal nephew in France to contribute to the injury of Britain, would purchase military equipment and furnish it to the colonies without compromising French neutrality. Losing no time, Deane and Beaumarchais signed an agreement for the delivery of equipment and for payment by the Congress, and the flow of life-saving material started across the Atlantic—cannon, ammunition, powder, medicines, clothing, muskets, and tents. The French contribution was decisive. It made possible the great victories at Trenton, Princeton, and Saratoga.

In three other significant ways France helped the American cause—by loans of money, by permitting American privateers to fit out in French ports and to dispose of their prizes there, and by use of her fleet to make difficult British capture of American vessels near French waters.

Meanwhile, the American colonies were moving in the direction of declaring their independence from the mother country. So pregnant a step was not taken lightly by men who, as their forebears before them, had prided themselves on being Englishmen and who had wished only to be permitted to enjoy the full fruits of British citizenship. Yet they realized that no assistance from foreign countries could be expected so long as their struggle with the Crown was merely a family affair which might terminate in a reconciliation. What enemy of Britain would expend one penny to help Englishmen secure their rights or to preserve the Empire? There were, of course, other motives behind the decision to make the break such as the use by the British government of mercenary troops and Indians and the British failure to respond to colonial petitions, but the main reason was the need for foreign aid.

On July 2, 1776, Congress adopted a resolution "that these United Colonies are, and, of right, ought to be free and independent states; that they are absolved from all allegiance to the British crown, and that all political connection between them and the state of Great Britain is, and ought to be, totally dissolved." That was the official act of separation. The document known to mankind as the Declaration of Independence was a justification of the resolution prepared by a committee chaired by Thomas Jefferson and approved by Congress on July 4. Some three months later, on September 26, Congress appointed the first American diplomatic mission, consisting of Benjamin Franklin, Arthur Lee, and Silas Deane, and charged it with gaining a recognition of independence and negotiating treaties of commerce.

Although the mission was instructed to approach Spain and other nations, France was the first and chief objective and it was there that Franklin landed in December 1776 to join Deane and Lee who had been in that country for some time. No better choice than Franklin could have been made. Seventy years old, experienced in politics—having long been active in colonial affairs and most recently member of every important committee of the Continental Congress—and in diplomacy—having represented several colonies in Europe—he was famous abroad as an inventor (stove, harmonica, lightning rod, bifocal spectacles), scientist (significant experiments with electricity), and author (of the widely read *Poor Richard's Almanac*). In France, he was loved for his humble and modest qualities and for his homey and rustic air. The fur cap he wore became the model for a women's hair style and his benign face was reproduced on medallions, snuff boxes, rings, and other ornaments. He was lionized and no social event could be a success without him. Shrewdly, he played up the role of the representative of a simple and virtuous people battling against a tyranny.

Despite his brilliant personal diplomacy, Franklin was not successful during the year 1777. Vergennes would neither make a treaty of commerce with the new nation nor recognize its independence. Such acts, he rightly feared, would invite war with England, which France did not want. Indeed, London, aware of the secret aid to the rebels, was even then demanding that it cease under threat of reprisals. The most the foreign minister would do was continue the secret and indirect aid. Franklin and his colleagues could hardly have expected anything more in view of the fact that the war was going badly for the United States in the summer and fall of 1777 and its newly proclaimed independence seemed an empty boast. Defeats at Brandywine and at Germantown and the loss of Philadelphia in September cast doubt on the outcome of the war. What was needed was some stunning victory to make independence "established and notorious" (to use the words of Vergennes in a memorandum to the king).

Fortunately, such a victory came in October of 1777 when, after a series of engagements in Vermont and upper New York, British General John Burgoyne surrendered his entire army to the Americans at Saratoga, marking the collapse of a bold plan designed to split New England from the rest of the country. The defeat galvanized the British cabinet into action. Early in December, the prime minister sent an agent across the channel to offer Franklin peace on the basis of home rule in the Empire (and a high political position for Franklin himself). Franklin did not for one moment consider seriously the British terms, but he kept up the talks for Vergennes' benefit. The talks with the British emissary were secret but the wily American diplomat made certain the French foreign minister knew of the "generous" terms by the British and of the possibilities of reconciliation. As was to be expected, Vergennes could not accept that possibility lest the whole effort of French diplomacy since 1763 come to naught. In the hope of ending the Anglo-American negotiations, he informed Franklin on December 17, 1777 of French readiness to recognize American independence. But Franklin held out for more—for a treaty of commerce and of alliance. Vergennes finally acquiesced but not without first having to convince the king that the Americans had to be helped openly even at the risk of war with England. Reconciliation, he argued, would be followed by a joint Anglo-American attack on the French West Indian islands and, probably, on France. Furthermore, he stated, an alliance with the new republic would "be an act of magnanimity that would reflect glory upon the King's reign." On January 8, 1778, the American diplomats sat down with their French opposite numbers to hammer out the terms of the two treaties.

It should be noted that the Continental Congress in instructing the Franklin mission did not stipulate a treaty of alliance—only a treaty of amity and commerce. That is not to say that the Congress did not consider making alliances with the world powers. It debated the question ardently but in the end, the opponents, led by John Adams, prevailed. Their reasoning was persuasive. It was based on the proposition that "we ought to lay it down, as a first principle and maxim never to be forgotten, to maintain an entire neutrality in all future European wars." An alliance, argued Adams, would inevitably involve the country in a future European war because of the reciprocal obligations a treaty of alliance must necessarily contain. Hence, his advice was "no political connection; no military connection; only a commercial connection." France and other powers, he suggested, would be willing to aid the new nation in exchange for trading rights in American ports which had been prohibited under England's rules. Why, then, the change in the American position? The answer is to be found in the dark days of military reversals in the summer and fall of 1777, which brought the realization that independence could be won only if France were a cobelligerent.

On February 6, 1778, Vergennes and the American representatives signed the two treaties—commerce and alliance. The provisions of the first were almost identical with the recommendations for such a treaty made by a committee of the Congress and adopted in September 1776, known as the "Plan of 1776." They included a most-favored-nation clause, that is, each signatory would grant to the other any commercial concessions given to other nations, and certain articles concerning the right of neutrals on the high seas in wartime. There were four of these articles: (1) should one of the signatories be at war and the other neutral, the citizens of the neutral could trade with the enemies of the belligerent in all items not contraband of war and contraband was limited to arms, munitions of war, and horses (food and naval stores were specifically listed as noncontraband); (2) the citizens of the neutral could trade with the enemies of the belligerent in noncontraband not only from enemy ports to neutral ports but between port and port of an enemy (a practice forbidden by the British); (3) free ships would make free goods (enemy noncontraband on neutral ships not liable to seizure by the belligerent); (4) neutral goods on enemy vessels would be liable to seizure by the belligerent.

The treaty of alliance was to come into force should England go to war against France. At that time both nations would fight together and neither would make peace without the consent of the other. They pledged to fight until American independence "shall have been formally or tacitly assured" by the treaties ending the war. The king of France guaranteed the independence of the United States and its possessions, whereas the United States guaranteed the possessions of France in America (the reciprocal obligations so feared by Adams). The treaty was unlimited as to time, containing the words "from the present time and forever."

Two days after the treaties were signed, the British government received copies sent by the secretary of the American mission, who for years had been a spy in the British employ and had kept London informed on every aspect of Franco-American relations. To forestall the ratification of the treaties by the American Congress, the British government sent a commission headed by Lord Carlisle to America offering reconciliation and peace on what it considered exceedingly favorable terms (but short of independence). Then ensued a race across the Atlantic between the British commission and the treaties. The treaties beat the commission, arriving on May 2, and were ratified promptly by Congress on May 4. On June 17, 1778, hostilities broke out between France and England when their fleets met in battle, thereby setting in operation the treaty of alliance. The French absolutist monarchy and the American democratic republic were now cobelligerents.

France had, of course, already officially recognized the independence of the United States with the signing of the treaty of commerce. On February 25, a French vessel had returned the salute of an American ship commanded by Captain John Paul Jones. On March 20, Franklin, Deane, and Lee had been received at the French court as envoys of the United States and four months later, the first French minister to the United States, Conrad Alexandre Gérard, landed in the United States and presented his credentials. The British mission never even got to see the Congress. Arriving in the United States on June 6, 1778, the Britons sought a conference with Congress only to be met with a refusal unless the subject would be the withdrawal of British forces from America and a recognition of independence. After vain attempts to bribe several congressmen and a futile threat to the American people to abandon the French alliance or face destruction, the mission left for England on November 27, 1778.

The failure of the Carlisle mission and the entry into the war by France marked the transformation of the Anglo-American civil strife into a world war. By 1780, England was standing alone and facing the rest of the Western world. Spain was to join the fight in 1779 and the Netherlands in 1780. In that year, too, Denmark, Sweden, and Russia joined in armed neutrality (to which other neutrals soon adhered) to challenge Britain.

Spain was just as eager as was France to see Britain humbled and, in the bargain, coveted Florida and Gibraltar, which had been lost to England in previous wars. She would not, however, join France in the alliance with the United States despite Vergennes' urging. Her reasons were not hard to discern. For one thing, she could not assist a revolution so long as she was mistress herself of vast colonial possessions. Second, she feared an independent and successful United States which might well push into Spanish land west of the Mississippi River. Indeed, there was no telling what ambitions might drive the new nation. As one Spanish diplomat suggested with remarkable prescience after American independence was won, "This republic has been born as it were a pigmy. But a day will come when it will be a great, a veritable awe-inspiring colossus in these regions." In fact, so much did Spain fear an American victory that after Saratoga she cut down on the secret aid which had begun in 1776.

Only when Vergennes held out the bait of the recovery of Gibraltar did Spain show interest and a willingness to enter the war. But first she tried to get Gibraltar from England as the price for remaining neutral. Failing that move, she signed an agreement with France in April 1779 at Aranjuez which pledged the two nations to fight together against England until Gibraltar was won. Spain refused to accept a French suggestion that no peace would be made until American independence was secured. Because the whole matter was kept secret, the United States did not know that France's commitments to Spain had "chained American independence . . . to the rock of Gibraltar." In view of the fact that France would make no peace without Gibraltar and the United States would make no peace without France, the United States would have to fight on even if it gained independence before Gibraltar were won.

Spain entered the war in June 1779 but her contribution was never very great. She did distract British forces by attacking Gibraltar but little else. Her participation had a moral effect but even that was weakened by a continuous flirtation with Britain for Gibraltar as a price for withdrawing from the war. The United States derived practically no benefit from Spain's belligerency. Interpreting her action as evidence of sympathy for the American cause, the Congress, in October 1779 dispatched John Jay to Madrid to obtain recognition of independence, a loan of $5 million, and an alliance. Jay met with no success except for a loan of $174,000 given chiefly for the effect on England. At one point when Spain suggested the possibility of an alliance in return for American renunciation of the right to navigate the Mississippi River and Jay agreed, the Spanish foreign minister raised the price and Jay quit Spain in disgust.

It was almost inevitable that the Netherlands be drawn into the war against England because of the Dutch position as a prime trading nation. When hostilities broke out between England and America, the Dutch moved to furnish supplies to both sides. To avoid antagonizing Britain, their merchants sent war materiel to the colonies by way of France and their own island of St. Eustatius in the West Indies. In the single month of April 1776, 85,000 pounds of powder went from Amsterdam to France, from whence it found its way to America and between January 1 and May 15, 1776 eighteen ships carrying powder made the voyage to the West Indies and then past the British fleet to the mainland. The profits made in the American trade were very considerable, and when France joined in the war in 1778, the opportunity was at hand to add to those profits by supplying belligerent France.

The Dutch could not expect to ship arms and ammunition to France without grave risk of their being seized as contraband by British war vessels. Naval stores, however, which France needed desperately for keeping her navy up to strength, were not contraband according to an Anglo-Dutch treaty of 1674 and so were not subject to confiscation by English ships. Britain, at any cost, had to halt that traffic and found the opportunity in an Anglo-Dutch Treaty of 1678 which required Holland to go to war on England's side if that power were attacked by a third party, in this case, France. Aware of Dutch reluctance to abandon the lucrative role of a neutral for the thankless state of a belligerent, the British were prepared not to invoke the Treaty of 1678 if Holland would surrender the treaty right to trade with France in naval stores. The Dutch reply was to continue sending ships to France loaded with naval stores, many of which the British seized. It was not long before the Dutch used armed convoys in the traffic and when the British sought to halt the trade, the Dutch resisted. By the end of 1780, a shooting war was in progress.

In the same year, Catherine II, empress of Russia, chafing under restrictions imposed by Britain on her country's neutral commerce in the Baltic Sea, called upon Denmark and Sweden to band with her to defend the rights of neutrals to trade with the enemies of England under certain conditions. The conditions were identical with the maritime principles set forth in the American "Plan of 1776"—free ships make free goods; neutrals have the right to trade between port and port of the belligerents; arms and ammunition constitute contraband with food and naval stores specified as noncontraband—with one addition: a blockade to be considered legal must be effective. The three nations, constituted as a League of Armed Neutrality and joined in 1781 by Prussia and Austria and in 1782 by Portugal, actually did not, at any time, vigorously press their contentions against Britain chiefly because they lacked the naval strength. They did, however, harass her with protests and vex her with complaints, causing a not inconsiderable diversion of the British war effort.

The diplomatic and military alignment against England by the end of 1781 plus severe reverses in the West Indies, a mounting public war debt, and the stunning defeat at Yorktown led many people in Britain to demand an end to the war and to the effort to hold the American colonies. When the news of Yorktown reached London in February 1782, defenders of the war in Parliament could hold out no longer. On February 27, a motion was adopted "renouncing all further attempts to subjugate the colonies" and on March 5, a bill passed authorizing the Crown to make peace. A resolution on March 15 "that the House [of Commons] could no longer repose confidence in the present ministers [headed by Lord North whose measures led Americans to revolt]" lost (by nine votes) but threat of its being reintroduced caused the government to resign on March 20. Two days later, the king called upon the opposition Whigs under the Marquis of Rockingham to form a government which would be pledged to making peace. On April 12, 1782, Richard Oswald was sent to Paris to open negotiations with the American peace commission.

The commission consisted of five people—John Adams, Thomas Jefferson, John Jay, Henry Laurens, and Benjamin Franklin—appointed by Congress in June 1781 to replace a single negotiator, John Adams, who had been designated two years earlier when plans for peace were first considered. The change was engineered by the count de Vergennes, and it was a part of a grand scheme designed to bring about a peace treaty calculated to benefit France. Three principles guided the foreign minister's diplomacy for achieving his objective: help Spain but not too greatly; sow discord between Great Britain and the United States; and prevent the new American republic from emerging from the peace negotiations so strong that she could become "mistress of the whole immense continent" and be free of French tutelage. If the Americans were to get too favorable a treaty, he said to the British ambassador in Paris, "they would immediately set about forming a great marine and as they have every possible advantage for ship-building, it would not be long before they had such fleets as would be an over-match for the whole naval power of Europe. With this superiority they might, when they pleased, conquer both your islands and ours. . . . They would not stop here but would in process of time advance to the southern continent of America and either subdue the inhabitants or carry them along with them and in the end not leave a foot of that Hemisphere in the possession of any European power." So spoke the "friend" of the colonies as he proclaimed his fears for the future.

Vergennes' chief tactic was to control the American peace delegation— choose its members, write their instructions, and supervise their negotiations. Adams had to be gotten rid of as sole commissioner. He was too independent and Vergennes found it hard to manage him. So Vergennes, through his able minister in Philadelphia, Chevalier de la Luzerne, worked on the Congress to add the four other commissioners—Jefferson and Franklin notoriously Francophile; Laurens and Jay of French descent. That Congress readily acquiesced was not surprising for by the liberal sprinkling of money among its members Luzerne had created a sizable pro-French group ready to do his master's bidding. Luzerne was able, also, to put Thomas Paine, the pamphleteer of the American Revolution and, at that time, secretary to the Committee on Foreign Affairs of the Congress, on his payroll at $1,000 per year for which Paine was to keep him posted on the Committee's activities and to write articles favorable to France.

Vergennes moved next to have Congress modify the terms for peace it had drawn up in 1779. Those had included independence and evacuation of American territory by British troops, a boundary which stretched from the Atlantic to the Mississippi and from Canada to the 31st parallel on the south, and full navigation of the Mississippi for the citizens of both nations. Such terms, for Vergennes, were too fixed (and too favorable to America). He needed more flexibility to enable him, in the words of Samuel Flagg Bemis, author of the classic work on the diplomacy of the American Revolution, "to modulate the progress of the negotiations among the several belligerents and mediators until the moment came when French interests were fully satisfied. . . ." Again, Congress submitted to the wishes of the old ally by amending the instructions so that only independence remained essential. Other matters were left to the discretion of the commissioners. Then came Vergennes' masterstroke: Congress instructed the commissioners "to make the most candid and confidential communication upon all subjects to the minister of our generous ally, the king of France; to undertake nothing in the negotiations for peace or truce without their knowledge and concurrence and ultimately to govern yourselves by their advice and opinion."

Having thus secured his objectives on the side of the Americans, Vergennes turned to the British, to convince them that magnanimity to the United States was neither necessary nor desirable. On September 7, 1782, he sent his private secretary, Joseph de Rayneval, to London to talk to the prime minister about Gibraltar and took that occasion to leave with Shelburne (who had succeeded Rockingham on July 1, 1782) the distinct impression that he would not support any American claims beyond independence, neither those concerning the boundaries nor those affecting the right of Americans to fish off the Canadian coast. As Shelburne reported to the king, the French seemed "more jealous than partial to America."

Meanwhile back in Paris, Franklin and Oswald had been talking terms. Franklin was the only member of the American commission in Paris from

April to June when John Jay arrived from Madrid to take up his duties. John Adams was in The Hague negotiating for a treaty of commerce and a loan both of which he secured in early October after which he joined his colleagues in Paris. Henry Laurens, who had been captured by the British, was released in time to be present in the last days of the negotiations. Jefferson, for various personal reasons, did not even get to France and played no role in the making of the peace.

Franklin's demands to Oswald were divided between "necessary" and "desirable" terms. The first category included independence and evacuation of troops, boundaries identical with those in the congressional instructions of 1779, and freedom to fish off the Grand Banks. Those articles considered "desirable" were an indemnity for towns ruined, a treaty of commerce, and the cession of Canada. Oswald, an old friend of Franklin's, was agreeable to the "necessary" demands and urged the prime minister to accept them as the basis for a treaty. That wise and far-sighted statesman was agreeable, too, for he had come to the realization that Britain's interests would best be served not by humiliating and opposing the Americans but by satisfying their needs and by gaining their friendship. Britain needed customers and good friends would make good customers. He saw, also, an opportunity to drive a wedge between the Americans and their French allies, having heard reports from Paris that John Jay had become suspicious of Vergennes' assistance in gaining a good treaty for the Americans. Generous terms, quickly offered, reasoned Shelburne, would, at one stroke, put America in Britain's debt and cause Britain to replace France as America's friend.

Shelburne's estimate of the situation in Paris was correct. Soon after arriving in Paris on June 23, 1782, Jay had, indeed, become uneasy as a consequence of some strange experiences with the French. When he and Franklin refused to treat officially with Oswald because his commission instructed him to treat with representatives of the "colonies or plantations" instead of the United States, Vergennes made light of their concern and advised them to meet with Oswald. To Jay, it appeared that the foreign minister did not rate highly American independence. Next, Jay got a copy of an intercepted letter from the French chargé in the United States urging Vergennes not to support the United States in their bid to gain the right to fish in Canadian waters. Then there was the remarkable suggestion by Rayneval as a compromise to the Spanish claim for all the land from the Appalachians to the Mississippi. It was that great Britain be given the portion north of the Ohio River, with Spain and the United States dividing the area to the south of the river. The last straw was Rayneval's trip to London which Jay viewed as the ultimate evidence of a French plan to divide the west between Spain (as compensation for Gibraltar which Vergennes could not deliver) and England and to get for France instead of for the United States the fishing rights.

The United States After the Peace of Paris, 1783.

Jay was now convinced that he must act on the advice he earlier had given Franklin: "Let us be grateful to the French for what they have done for us, but let us think for ourselves. And, if need be, let us act for ourselves." To get the best treaty, he believed, demanded eliminating Vergennes from the negotiations. Accordingly, he sent word to Shelburne that the Americans stood prepared to hammer out the terms with Oswald if his commission would be altered to "treat with commissioners of the United States." Shelburne complied readily and early in October Jay and Oswald began specific and official talks. Soon Franklin joined them, on recovering from an illness, as did John Adams and Henry Laurens. On November 30, 1782, terms having been agreed upon, the representatives of both sides signed a preliminary peace treaty to become definitive after France and England made peace in conformity with the stipulation in the Franco-American Treaty of Alliance that neither side make a separate peace.

The terms were magnificent for the United States. Besides gaining recognition of independence in the first article, the new republic received an imperial domain stretching from the Atlantic to the Mississippi and from Canada to the 31st parallel and extensive fishing privileges off the Grand Banks. Canada was not acquired, but then Britain would never have given it up. To Jay must go the major share of the credit for the treaty, for it was he who first saw through Vergennes, had the courage to transgress the instructions of Congress on consulting France, and grasped the initiative in moving to the conference table without France. Shelburne, too, must be given praise for correctly analyzing the Franco-American situation and for taking the long-range view of Britain's interest, which was reconciliation with the former colony. He did, after all, secure for his country two important objectives: a promise that British creditors would be aided in recovering prewar debts and a pledge to help the Loyalists get compensation for property confiscated or have it restored.

And what of Vergennes? He could hardly be blamed for his role. His first thoughts were for France and, in view of the tremendous aid rendered the United States, he might well have expected that country to be beholden to its benefactor. He had no choice but to appear pleased upon learning of the favorable terms of the treaty for, after all, he had been pledged to securing that kind of treaty for the United States. Privately, he chided Franklin for acting alone but that seasoned diplomat turned the foreign minister's displeasure away by urging him not to give the British the satisfaction of seeing the allies fall out. Indeed, Vergennes might well be pitied for, in the end, his diplomacy had not succeeded despite the prodigious and devious schemes. To be sure, England lost her important colonies but she was not humbled or rendered powerless, and the liberal terms she gave America presaged good relations between them. Spain was alienated since France delivered neither Gibraltar nor any part of the territory west of the Appalachians Spain claimed. France recovered none of the land lost in 1713 or 1763 and got, for her pains, only a depleted treasury and an exhausted army and navy.

On January 20, 1783, France and Spain signed articles of a preliminary peace with England, and the way was paved for the sealing of the definitive peace which occurred on September 3, 1783. The United States now took its place among the independent nations of the world, and a very different nation it was from the others—republican and confederated instead of monarchical and centralized. Could such a nation survive in such a world? The next two decades would prove years of severe testing for the fledgling nation as it faced various problems arising out of the peace treaty, boundary disputes, and, above all, a world at war.

BIBLIOGRAPHY

SAMUEL F. BEMIS, *The Diplomacy of the American Revolution* (1935).
FELIX GILBERT, *To the Farewell Address: Ideas of Early American Foreign Policy* (1961).
RICHARD B. MORRIS, *The Peacemakers: The Great Powers and American Independence* (1965).
MAX SAVELLE, *The Origins of American Diplomacy: The International History of Angloamerica, 1492–1763* (1967).
WILLIAM C. STINCHCOMBE, *The American Revolution and the French Alliance* (1969).
GERALD STOURZH, *Benjamin Franklin and American Foreign Policy* (1954).
RICHARD W. VAN ALSTYNE, *Empire and Independence: The International History of the American Revolution* (1965).
PAUL A. VARG, *Foreign Policies of the Founding Fathers* (1963).

John Adams (courtesy of the National Portrait Gallery, Smithsonian Institution, Washington, D.C.).

Redeeming the Peace

THE DIPLOMATIC problems that faced the American republic at the beginning of its existence as an independent and sovereign nation were very grave. One foreign nation occupied strategic areas on its northern and western frontiers; another laid claim to a vast portion of its southwestern lands; to still another, it was tied by an alliance which presented the danger of its being entangled in the affairs of the old world. It had a negligible army and no navy, was without financial resources or public credit, and was governed by a constitution that proclaimed the states to be sovereign, free, and independent and limited severely the powers of the national Congress in dealing in international affairs. It is no wonder that many people, both at home and abroad, predicted the early dissolution of the union and the ignominious failure of the twin experiments in federalism and republicanism.

Those dire predictions did not, however, come true. For by the time the eighteenth century ended, the young republic had not only survived the vicissitudes and uncertainties of its infancy, but had resolved all the major diplomatic difficulties with remarkable success. The national territory had been cleared of foreign occupants; the southern boundary problem had been satisfactorily settled; the alliance which had shackled the country to European concerns had been abrogated; and from the great war which had raged in Europe at that time, the nation had been able to remain aloof. Also, a new government had been created that gave the central authority adequate powers for dealing with international affairs.

Of all the problems facing the new nation, those with Great Britain were most serious and vexing. The treaty of 1783 had ended hostilities between England and her late colonies but it did not presage good relations between them. The fighting had left a legacy of bad feeling, and conditions in the immediate postwar years had intensified the animosity. Chief among the conditions was the continued occupation by England of seven strategic forts lying within the boundaries of the United States as

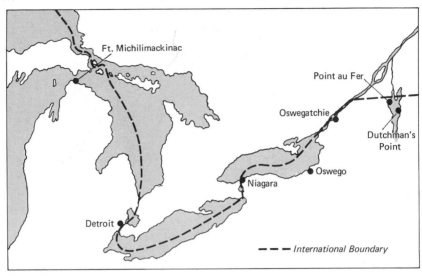

Ft. Michilimackinac

Point au Fer

Oswegatchie

Dutchman's Point

Oswego

Niagara

Detroit

— — — International Boundary

American Posts Held by the British After 1783.

defined in the treaty. They stretched along the Canadian-American frontier from northern Michigan to Lake Champlain and controlled a vast area drained by the Great Lakes and the St. Lawrence River. The treaty stipulated that British forces would withdraw from "every Post, Place, and Harbour" of the United States with "all convenient speed" and so they did except for the seven posts.

The stated British reason for retaining the posts was the failure by the United States to fulfill certain of its obligations under the treaty relating to the recovery by British creditors of debts owed them by Americans from before the revolution and to the restitution of property of Loyalists confiscated during the war. But that was not the true reason. The United States, in fact, had not carried out those provisions of the treaty (the Congress did not have the power under the government of the Articles of Confederation), but neither did the British intend to evacuate "with all convenient speed." On April 8, 1784, one day before the treaty was to go into effect, the decision was made in London to hold the forts because of their importance to the security of the settlements in Canada and to the fur trade. Furs sold in London were obtained from the American northwest by British trappers who needed the forts for protection and for bases of supplies. At the same time, frontier officials in Canada feared the effect of surrendering the posts on Britain's Indian allies living in American territory. It was from those posts that the tribes had gotten their supplies and presents before and during the revolution, and their abandonment might have been viewed by the Indians as a betrayal of their .

British connection, leading to attacks upon Canadian settlements in retaliation. Indeed, in June of 1783, two prominent chiefs visited the governor of Canada to inquire into the rumor that the British were turning the territory over to the Americans, their long-time enemies.

In addition to the posts, there were other problems between the two countries—a disputed boundary separating Maine from New Brunswick, a British failure to return slaves carried away by the evacuating forces as provided by the treaty, and, above all, the matter of trade relations. Shortly after peace was proclaimed, Parliament, by statute, established the conditions of commerce with the United States. American raw materials (food, tobacco, and naval stores needed to feed British factory hands and supply the navy) could be shipped to England in American vessels; manufactures (to compete with British industry) were prohibited. No American ships could enter the ports of British North America or the British West Indies; American products for those colonies had to go in British bottoms. Such one-sided terms angered American merchants who had expected to regain all the rights and privileges in British ports they had enjoyed as colonials before the Revolution. Instructions to the peace commissioners had included a stipulation to secure equality of treatment with British traders in British dominions and possessions and when they failed, John Adams was dispatched to London in 1785 to negotiate a favorable commercial treaty similar to those signed with Sweden (1783) and Prussia (1785). Americans were hoping to lure the British into granting concessions with privileges for British merchants in American ports.

The British, however, would not take the bait and Adams was rebuffed. They did not, they believed, have to give the Americans any preferential treatment in order to attract their trade. As Lord Sheffield observed in his famous paper *Observations on the Commerce of the American States* (1783), "The solid power of supplying the wants of America, of receiving her produce belongs almost exclusively to our merchants." That is to say, the Americans were so accustomed to buying British and selling to Britain for reasons rooted in tradition, experience, language, and custom that no amount of discrimination would divert them. Further, argued Sheffield, "They are becoming foreign states" and why permit them to enjoy the privileges they had had as Englishmen? Nor did the British fear retaliation from the United States government, which was powerless under the Articles of Confederation to regulate international commerce. Some states did levy extra duties separately against British goods landed in their port, but the action was so sporadic and uncoordinated as to be virtually ineffective.

Gouverneur Morris was sent in 1789 to London to settle outstanding differences, but he fared no better than Adams had. A possibility of Britain relenting appeared in 1790 as a consequence of an Anglo-Spanish dispute in Nootka Sound on the Pacific Coast of North America. Fear of hostilities caused English political leaders to think better of pushing America too far, even, perhaps into the arms of Spain. Also, the new constitution of the United States, in force since 1789, gave the government the authority to retaliate commercially. Not surprisingly, London condescended to accredit Britain's first minister to the United States, George Hammond, a young career diplomat, who arrived in Philadelphia in October 1791. Secretary of State Thomas Jefferson sought at once to open discussions with him on the major issues, but Hammond had no instructions from the Foreign Office to negotiate. Thus, by the end of the first decade after independence, the new American republic had failed to come to terms with Britain.

Equally unsuccessful was the American effort to settle outstanding differences with Spain. The problems with that country concerned a disputed boundary and the navigation of the Mississippi River. The Anglo-American treaty ending the war had set the southern and western boundary of the United States at the 31st parallel and the Mississippi River. Spain, however, claimed, as part of the territory of Florida ceded to her by England in 1783, all the land up to the Ohio River and was in occupation of several key forts in the area along the Mississippi. Because she physically controlled both banks of that river up to Natchez, Spain could and did in 1784 bar Americans from its use. Her purpose, of course, was so to discourage American settlers in Tennessee and Kentucky, to whom the river was a lifeline, as to lead them to give up their homes and go back east, thereby weakening the American hold on the territory.

It was one thing, however, to issue an edict closing the river and quite another to expect the Americans docilely to obey it. To them, the river provided the only cheap and speedy route for sending their produce to market, the course over the Appalachian Mountains being tortuous and expensive. Spanish authorities at New Orleans rightfully feared a descent of the river by tough, determined, and fast-shooting American frontiersmen for whom the handful of Spanish troops would be no match. Diplomacy seemed to be the only answer to the Spanish dilemma, and in 1785 Madrid sent Don Diego de Gardoqui across the ocean to deal with the problem. On its part, the Congress designated John Jay, the secretary for foreign affairs, as negotiator. Jay's instructions were to secure the free navigation of the Mississippi and the 31st parallel as the southern boundary. Don Diego would not yield, however, on both points. He was willing to fix the boundary at the 31st parallel and give American merchants certain valuable commercial concessions in Spanish ports provided Americans "foreswore" the use of the Mississippi.

Jay advised the Congress to accept the terms. For him, the country's greatest need was trade without which it could not prosper. As for the river, he argued that "the time was soon coming when Americans would not submit to seeing a fine river flowing before their doors without using

it as a highway to the sea for the transportation of their productions";
meanwhile, "Should we not (for a valuable consideration, too), consent to
forebear to use what we know is not in our power to use?" Delegates from
northern states thought Jay's reasoning sound. Representing mercantile
constituencies, they viewed commerce as crucial. Southerners, on the other
hand, sympathizing with the needs of the settlers south of the Ohio and
representing states with claims to land west of the mountains which
would be worthless without the use of the Mississippi, charged Jay with
wishing to sacrifice southern interests for those of the northeast. They
even accused him of designs to prevent the growth of the country westward so that his section could retain control of the government.

Because Gardoqui would not relent on the river and because the southern states would not approve a treaty surrendering the navigation of the
river, Jay considered it useless to continue negotiations. Under the Articles
of Confederation, five negative votes would kill the treaty, and Maryland,
Virginia, North Carolina, South Carolina, and Georgia stood ready to
oppose it. Frustrated in his efforts to achieve his ends by diplomacy,
Gardoqui turned to intrigue. His plan was to promise the frontiersmen the
right to navigate the Mississippi if they would detach themselves from the
United States by either joining with Spain or erecting an independent
republic. To lead the conspiracy there was James Wilkinson, a young
veteran of the Revolution who had emigrated to Kentucky after the war.
Wilkinson had had a remarkable career in the war and an unsavory one.
A brigadier general at age 20, he had been involved in several shady transactions, but his charm and glibness had saved him from punishment. In
1787 he went to New Orleans, swore allegiance to the king of Spain, contracted for an annual subsidy of $2,500, and began operations. His advice
to the Spanish governor was to bait the frontiersmen with a generous concession on the use of the river and to frighten them by encouraging his
Indian allies to attack their settlements. The first would demonstrate the
advantages of Spanish allegiance and the second would show the futility
of American citizenship. But despite Wilkinson's blandishments, his
liberal use of Spanish gold, Indian attacks, and a Royal Decree in 1788
permitting Americans to bring their produce down the river, the westerners
did not succumb to the intrigue. Instead, the men in Kentucky and
Tennessee retained their loyalty to the United States and looked to their
own country to secure them their rights.

By this time, the new constitution was in operation and the new
secretary of state, Thomas Jefferson, sought to reopen negotiations in
Madrid on the questions at issue. In 1790 he instructed the American
chargé in the Spanish capital, William Carmichael, to approach the
Foreign Office but Carmichael could make no headway. Three years later,
Jefferson ordered William Short, the Minister to the Netherlands, to join
Carmichael in Madrid, but the two fared no better than the one. As a

matter of fact, the time was not propitious for exacting concessions from Spain. On February 1, 1793, war broke out between France and England, as a consequence of the French Revolution, and Spain joined England to contain and destroy the revolutionary forces which threatened her from the other side of the Pyrenees. Faced by a life and death struggle, Spain found more important things to do than negotiate with the Americans and, nestled under the protection of the powerful British lion, she felt no compulsion to yield to American claims.

For the United States, the war in Europe created problems of the gravest nature. Most immediately, they concerned the country's relationship to France under the treaties of 1778 and its role in the war. To his cabinet, President Washington posed thirteen questions designed to guide administration policy. Three were crucial: Should a proclamation of neutrality be issued? Should a minister from the new French Republic be received? Were the treaties with France still in force or did the change in government by the revolution render them void? On the first point, there was unanimity that the United States ought to stay out of the war and on April 22, 1793, four days after submitting the questions, the president issued a proclamation enjoining Americans "to pursue a conduct friendly and impartial" toward the two belligerents and warning them against aiding either side under pain of forfeiture of their government's protection and of prosecution in the courts. The better to safeguard neutrality, Congress, on June 5, 1794, passed a statute, the first of its kind by any country, which laid down specific rules of conduct for Americans and penalties for their violation. Americans could not accept commissions or serve in the armed forces of the belligerent, fit out and arm vessels for the belligerents in American ports, set on foot hostile expeditions on American soil against either side, nor repair a belligerent warship in an American port.

On the other matters raised by the president, the cabinet divided. Secretary of State Thomas Jefferson supported by Attorney General Edmund Randolph believed the treaties still in force on the ground that treaties were concluded between nations and were not affected by changes in government in those nations. As to their "interpretation and application," he counseled postponing a decision "for the future according to circumstances." Although a friend of France, he did not think it to the best interests of the country to spring to the aid of the old ally and to be involved in the war. Secretary of the Treasury Alexander Hamilton backed by Secretary of War Henry Knox, on the other hand, took a more cautious approach to the question of the treaties. In view of the fact that they had been made with a government that no longer existed, he recommended suspending them until the direction of the revolution could become clearer and renouncing them "if such changes shall take place as

[margin, handwritten, rotated] Britian had a problem with impressment

can *bona fide* be pronounced to render a continuance of the connections which result from them disadvantageous or dangerous. . . ."

On the matter of receiving a minister from the French Republic, Jefferson counseled receiving one without qualification, thereby extending legal recognition to the new government while Hamilton advised that the minister be accepted with a carefully worded reservation on the treaties and on recognition. In the end, Washington accepted the Jeffersonian position. The treaties were considered to be in force but a decision on their applicability postponed, the new government would be recognized, and Edmond Genêt, the newly appointed minister, would be received unreservedly.

Not all Americans were pleased by Washington's policy. Some opposed it on purely constitutional grounds claiming that the president's proclamation, in dealing with a question of war and peace, went beyond the competence of the executive. Only the Congress, by Article I, Section 8, could declare war and, by inference, keep the nation out of war. A greater number, by far, viewed the matter more emotionally than legally. Recalling French aid in their own struggle for freedom, they believed that simple gratitude now dictated helping France in its fight. Clear evidence of the widespread feeling of sympathy was in the enthusiastic reception given the new envoy from France when he landed in Charleston early in April 1793. As Genêt made his way from that South Carolina port to the capital in Philadelphia to present his credentials to the president, he was feted and cheered to the accompaniment of the warmest sentiments for the success of his country in the war against the former enemy.

His journey was not only a pleasure trip. All along the way, he busily took measures to translate the public acclaim into concrete assistance for France. He fitted out privateers to raid British commerce and set up prize courts to condemn the captured vessels and cargoes, enlisted American crews, plotted with Americans to outfit expeditions against the possessions of England's ally, Spain, in Florida and Louisiana, and handed out commissions in France's service to Americans, most notably to General George Rogers Clark of Revolutionary War fame.

Little wonder that President Washington received Genêt most cooly, for the Frenchman was compromising the neutral position which he and his cabinet had decided upon. But Genêt was not to be daunted. Encouraged and emboldened by the "hugging and tugging . . . addressing and caressing . . . mountebanking and chanting . . ." by the Francophile citizens of Philadelphia, he continued his violations of American neutrality chiefly by fitting out more privateers which brazenly seized British ships in American territorial waters (that is, within three miles of American shores). Even the most ardent friends of France became disgusted with Genêt's conduct. Not only was he defying the government's wishes and endangering its position but he was, also, as Jefferson, who was at one time full of praise for him, noted, "disrespectful and even indecent towards the P[resident] in his written as well as verbal communications, taking of appeals from him to Congress, from them to the people, urging the most unreasonable and groundless propositions. . . ." By August, his antics could no longer be suffered and Washington requested his recall. Actually, Genêt never did return to France for the government that called him home also ordered his arrest. Facing the strong possibility of execution by the guillotine, Genêt chose to remain in the United States. He married an American, became a citizen, and lived the remainder of his life in his adopted country.

Happily, Washington never had to make a decision on the "interpretation and application" of the treaties with France, for the French government did not invoke the agreement. It was not from sentimental consideration for the young republic's interest that France acted, but rather because Paris believed that the United States could be more useful as a neutral than as a cobelligerent. With a negligible army and a meager navy, the Americans would hardly contribute significantly to the fighting war but as possessors of a large merchant fleet, they could be of the greatest value carrying much-needed American supplies, chiefly foodstuffs and naval stores, to France and French products between the colonies in the West Indies and the mother country. French expectations did not materialize, however, for everywhere on the seas were British warships which picked up American vessels en route to France and took them into British ports where prize courts condemned their cargoes.

Deeply chagrined, the French government urged the United States to resist British action, but, as a matter of fact, there was no legal basis for an American remonstrance. In the absence of treaty relations with the United States specifically defining neutral rights, England had every right to treat food and naval stores as contraband, seize those items if destined for an enemy port, and to take enemy goods found on neutral vessels. To make matters worse, the French could not, legally, prevent American food and naval stores from reaching England nor seize British products carried on American ships because the Franco-American Treaty of Amity and Commerce of 1778 excluded food and naval stores from the list of contraband and accepted the principle that "free ships make free goods." Little wonder that the French felt cheated and frustrated by the ironic turn of events whereby the old ally was deprived of aid while the former enemy received a full measure of it. Less wonder that they felt outraged when they learned that on November 19, 1794 John Jay signed a treaty with the British foreign secretary, that, in effect, permitted the British to continue their maritime practices.

The treaty came about as a result of a serious deterioration of Anglo-American relations in the months following the outbreak of war. Both countries believed that failure to resolve differences would surely lead to hostilities. The principal threat to peace between the two nations stemmed from British captures of American vessels engaged in trade with France. Within one year after war began, several hundred American ships had been seized and their cargoes condemned. The fact that legally there was no basis for complaint did not prevent American shippers and merchants from being incensed at British interference in their profitable activity. Added to that grievance was the British practice of removing deserters from the Royal Navy from American merchant vessels on the high seas. That in itself was not objectionable. What rankled, however, was that British captains, desperate for seamen, took American sailors when they could find no Britons on board.   *Impress-ment*

The British conduct at sea plus the unresolved problems connected with the execution of the Treaty of Peace of 1783 were enough to raise loud cries in the United States for retaliation against England. In January 1794, Congress, in a fierce mood, began considering measures for punishing England. The pro-French Republican party was in the forefront of the agitation, as was to be expected, but even the Federalists, usually ardently favorable to the British cause, clamored for reprisals. In April, spurred by reports of an inflammatory speech by the governor of Canada to some Indian chieftain who had come over from the American side of the border asking for military aid against the Americans, Congress placed an embargo on all American shipping for one month and soon extended it for a second month.

Such a measure, however, was only a stopgap and did nothing to solve the basic problems between the two countries. Indeed, it may even have exacerbated the bad feelings and made war more likely. And a war, Washington and his advisors believed, had to be avoided at almost any cost. Hamilton stated the reasons convincingly in a letter to the president: "We are but just recovering from the effect of a long, arduous, and exhausting war. . . . We are vulnerable both by water and land; without either fleet and army. We have a considerable debt in proportion to the resources which the state of things permit the government to command. Measures have been recently entered upon for the restoration of credit which a war would hardly fail to disconcert, and which, if disturbed, would be fatal to the means of prosecuting it." There was only one way to resolve the dilemma, Hamilton went on to say—send a mission to London to settle the differences with England. Washington agreed and selected John Jay for the task.   *chief Justice of Supreme Court at the time*

Jay was an excellent appointment. No one in the country had had greater diplomatic experience. He had been minister to Spain during the war, had served on the Peace Commission in Paris where he had outsmarted Vergennes, had dealt with Gardoqui in 1786, had acted briefly as secretary of foreign affairs under the Confederation, and was now chief justice of the United States. Still, his nomination met a difficult time in the Senate from Republicans who claimed he was too Federalist and Anglophile to be expected to force concessions from Britain. For three days there was sharp debate but, finally, on April 19, Jay was approved. Soon thereafter he sailed from New York for London, where he arrived in June.

Lord Grenville, the British foreign secretary, received the American envoy cordially. Grenville was most eager for a settlement. A war with the United States could be extremely perilous for England not only because it would impede the fight against the real enemy, France, but because America was Britain's best customer. Spurred by these considerations, he opened negotiations with Jay. On November 19, 1794, a treaty was signed. It provided for evacuation by the British of the posts in the northwest and the granting of certain trading rights to American vessels in the ports of Great Britain and of the British East and West Indies. It also provided for an Anglo-American commission to arbitrate three important problems— the disputed Maine–New Brunswick boundary, the debts owed by Americans to Britons from the Revolution, and the claims by Americans for compensation resulting from seizures by British warships of American vessels in 1793.

In March 1795, the treaty reached Philadelphia. The president presented it to the Senate for approval at a special session on June 8. When the Senators read the terms, they were shocked. Federalists and Republicans both could not believe that so one-sided an instrument would have been accepted by Jay. Southerners and northerners, farmers and merchants alike were disturbed. True, the British had agreed to arbitrate claims for seizures of American vessels, but what about the whole question of attacks on American neutral commerce? Nothing was said about impressment, the right to trade in noncontraband, or "free ships, free goods." The treaty had provided for the settlement of the pre-Revolutionary debts but contained nothing on the matter of the slaves carried off by British troops in 1783. As for commercial privileges, the British concessions were meager. In their West Indian ports, the most important in the Empire for Americans, ships of only 70 tons or less could trade, and for this privilege Jay had promised that American vessels would not carry from those ports molasses, sugar, cotton, coffee, or cocoa to any part of the world other than the United States.

Washington shared the Senate's consternation but still urged the treaty's approval. With all its obvious faults and inequities, it did accomplish its major purpose—the maintenance of peace and the removal from American territory of the last of British occupying troops. Reluctantly and mostly because of the president's vast prestige, the Senate on June 24 voted in favor of the treaty but by 20–10, the minimum two-thirds majority. The vote was even more of a personal victory for Washington when it is realized that it was taken against the backdrop of a violent public outcry. The president had hoped to keep the exact terms of the treaty secret, but inevitably they became known and the passions they aroused shook the country. Mobs attacked any American who dared speak for the treaty and tore down any British flag they found flying. The treaty was denounced as an abject surrender to England and a cowardly desertion of France, but it was John Jay personally who was the chief objective of the popular displeasure. He was labelled a traitor and burned in effigy. People were urged to "Damn John Jay! Damn every one that won't damn John Jay!! Damn every one that won't put lights in his windows and sit up all night damning John Jay!!!" *Talk of impeaching Washington over this incident.*

The calumny heaped on Jay was patently unfair. He had done his best and had only followed instructions which had been to do nothing to jeopardize the peace with Britain. If anyone deserved blame it was Hamilton, who had been responsible for the instructions and who had insisted that the continuance of trade with England and the evacuation of the posts were worth a temporary surrender of the American principles of the freedom of the seas. It was Hamilton also who deprived Jay of a possible lever in the negotiation by assuring the British minister in Philadelphia privately and secretly that the overtures then being made by Denmark and Sweden for the United States to join a coalition against Britain to protect the right of neutrals would be rejected. Not even Hamilton should be reproached for the shortcomings of the treaty. Nothing anybody could have done or have said would have extracted greater concessions from Grenville. He wanted peace with America but not at the expense of weakening his country in the war against France. Had Jay made any excessive demands or had he threatened to join with Denmark and Sweden, negotiations would most likely have come to a speedy termination.

Jay's Treaty meant the end of foreign occupation of the American west north of the Ohio River. It meant, also, greater security for the settlers there from Indian attacks, for the departure of the British from the border forts deprived the Indians of the supplies (and encouragement) they needed to war against the American frontiersman. And that departure plus a stunning victory by General Anthony Wayne over the Indians at the Battle of Fallen Timbers (near present-day Toledo, Ohio) in August 1794 led to the Treaty of Greenville, which was signed one year later by which the tribes ceded large tracts of land in Ohio to the Americans and gave up the British connection.

South of the Ohio River, however, the American west was still in the shadow of Spain. That power continued to claim the land between the Gulf of Mexico and the Ohio and had soldiers stationed as far north as the mouth of the Yazoo River. In addition, the Spanish authorities in Florida were inciting the Indians to raid American settlements. Since

1790, American ministers in Madrid had sought to get Spain to settle the problems of the Southwest but without success. It was not until news of Jay's Treaty reached the Spanish capital in the summer of 1795 that Manuel de Godoy, the Spanish prime minister, appeared willing to negotiate. Fearful that the treaty presaged a joint Anglo-American descent upon Spanish Louisiana or Florida, he hastened to make his peace with the United States. The possibility of an attack seemed very real at the time because Spain had just made a separate peace with France and had left England to fight the war alone. There was another reason for Godoy's change of heart. He knew very well that Spain could not forever resist American demands backed by fierce and well-armed frontiersmen. Better to capitulate and make concessions than stand the chance of losing everything in a war.

A special American envoy, Thomas Pinckney, had just arrived in Madrid from London where he was minister. With him, Godoy negotiated a treaty in which he surrendered to every American demand. Navigation of the Mississippi and the right to deposit goods at New Orleans pending reshipment were granted, the boundary was set at the 31st parallel and Spanish troops were evacuated south of the line. In addition the Spanish promised to restrain the Indians from attacking the frontier settlements. The treaty was a magnificent victory for the United States and cleared the Senate unanimously. The accomplishments of Jay and Pinckney had given the United States undisputed possession of the territory it had got by the peace of 1783.

Jay's Treaty frightened Spain but it angered France and for good reason. Although no part of the treaty violated the Franco-American agreements of 1778, the maritime articles did, in fact, give England an advantage over France on the high seas on the definition of contraband, on the carriage of enemy goods, and on the trade between enemy ports. The French foreign minister considered the treaty tantamount to a declaration of war against France and French agents in America made strenuous efforts to block the approval of the treaty in the Senate and the appropriation measure in the House. Failing in those attempts, the French government announced on July 2, 1796, that its warships would treat American vessels by the same rules as the British which, of course, would lead to a violation of the Commercial Treaty of 1778. At the same time, it moved to engineer the defeat of President Washington, whom they held responsible for the anti-French treaty, in the coming election in the fall. If only his opponent, Jefferson, the friend of France, would be chosen, all the wrongs would be righted they believed.

Washington, however, deprived the French of the opportunity to defeat him by withdrawing from the race. He had hoped to retire in 1793 and had, at that time, prepared some farewell remarks but had been persuaded to serve another term for the good of the country. Now, nothing

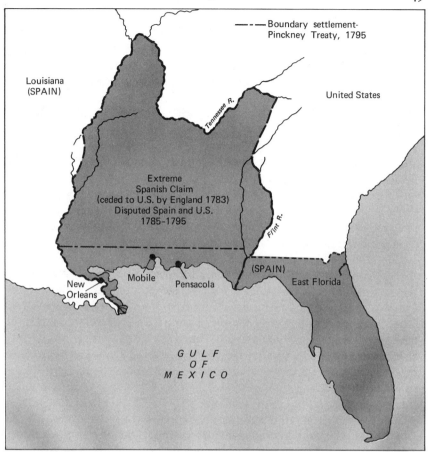

The Boundary Dispute with Spain, 1783–1795.

could alter his decision to leave public life. The painful experience during the struggle over ratification of Jay's Treaty when he was so harshly treated made him long for refuge in the serenity of his plantation at Mount Vernon. To Alexander Hamilton he sent the draft he had composed three years earlier with a request for help as to style and ideas. Hamilton's reply with but slight changes by the president became the famous Farewell Address, which was first presented to the country in the pages of the *American Daily Advertiser* for September 19, 1796.

To his fellow citizens, Washington gave sound advice, which sprang from his sagacious assessment of the national experience. He urged them to act as one people without reference to party or section. Unity to him was the "pillar of independence." He warned the nation to eschew "permanent, inveterate antipathies against particular nations and passionate attachments for others" and to guard against "the insidious wiles of foreign influence . . . since history and experience prove that foreign influence is one of the most baneful foes of republican government." Finally, he suggested that the United States take advantage of its distance from Europe. That distance, he said, enabled the country to remain unaffected by "the ordinary vicissitudes of her politics or the ordinary combinations and collisions of her friendships or enmities." "Why," he pleaded, "by interweaving our destiny with that of any part of Europe, entangle our peace and prosperity in the toils of European ambition, rivalship, interest, humor, or caprice? . . . It is our true policy to steer clear of permanent alliances with any portion of the foreign world." His words did not, at the time, make a great imprint, but as the years went on, they assumed an importance which would have astounded their author. They became one of the articles of faith of the American republic and were widely quoted by succeeding generations as the justification for a policy of isolation.

Hard though they tried, the French could not influence the election. John Adams, the choice of the Federalist party to succeed Washington, received seventy-one electoral votes to the Republican standardbearer Jefferson's sixty-eight, making Adams president and Jefferson vice-president. The French reaction was to intensify their attacks on American shipping and to announce a new policy—any American found serving on a British ship, even though he might have been impressed, would be treated as a pirate. As the French depredations on the high seas increased (316 American ships were seized between June 1796 and July 1797), Adams sought means to come to an understanding with the government in Paris. In May of 1797, he sent to the Senate the names of three envoys who would be sent to France to arrange a settlement. Wisely, the president nominated a bipartisan and bisectional commission—John Marshall, Federalist from Virginia, Charles C. Pinckney, Federalist from South Carolina, and Elbridge Gerry, Republican from Massachusetts. Although Federalists both in the Cabinet and in the Senate balked at the inclusion of Gerry, the nominations received confirmation and the envoys proceeded to France.

They arrived in the French capital in October, where they were received unofficially by the foreign minister, Talleyrand. The success of French arms on the Continent since the early days of the Revolution had led their diplomats to expect bribes in return for ending hostilities. Portugal had paid 1 million francs to ward off an invasion, and even Britain was considering making a substantial payment as the price of peace. Now Talleyrand, by means of three agents who were designated X, Y, and Z, approached the American commissioners suggesting that for a gift to the foreign minister and a loan to the government, a satisfactory settlement of outstanding problems could be arranged. The Americans were outraged and flatly refused to give "one cent for tribute." Marshall and Pinckney departed for home, with Gerry staying in Paris in the hopes of improving conditions.

News of Talleyrand's demands reached Adams in March 1798, and his reaction matched that of his envoys. At once he informed Congress of the rupture of negotiations and the danger of hostilities and recommended that the country be placed on a war footing. Congress responded with dispatch and enthusiasm. Between April and July, a series of acts was passed to strengthen the national defense. Merchantmen were armed, privateers were commissioned, the army and navy were increased, a marine corps was created, a Department of the Navy was added to the cabinet, and a $5 million war loan was authorized. At the same time, Congress voted to abrogate the treaties of 1778.

Federalist party leaders now urged the president to go further and ask Congress for a declaration of war. Here was a chance to enhance the party's popularity in the country for the people were in a very excited state and were demanding that France be punished. All the correspondence relative to the X, Y, Z affair had been made public, and the full story of Talleyrand's insulting treatment of the American mission was known. Rallies and mass meetings urging war were being held in every state. Adams refused to succumb to party pressure or public passion. Peace, he believed, was necessary for the young nation while war might well be disastrous. While the president remained calm, the Federalists became infuriated with him for letting an opportunity slip to enhance the Federalist image and discredit the Republicans who were counseling moderation.

The leading members of the Cabinet, Timothy Pickering at State, Oliver Wolcott, Jr., at Treasury, and James McHenry at War turned away from the president and looked to Hamilton for leadership. The former Secretary of the Treasury was the most ardent proponent of war. He had been instrumental in gaining larger increases for the army than Adams had wished, and he had sought and gained, over the president's objection, appointment as senior major general in the army and second-in-command to Washington who had been called back to active service to head the increased military establishment. He was thinking not only of fighting France but of a grand design for conquest of Florida and Louisiana and for aiding South Americans working for freedom from Spain. He was also in intimate contact with the British minister in Philadelphia on the possibility of joint Anglo-American action. As was to be expected, the English were eager to see America embroiled with France and were holding out all sorts of enticements such as commercial concessions and protection against French privateers in exchange for a declaration of war.

Despite hostility and intrigue, Adams remained unperturbed. To his wife he wrote, "John Adams must be an intrepid to encounter open assault of France and the secret plots of England in concert with all his treacherous friends and open enemies. Yet I assure you, he never felt more serene in his life." He continued to resist all pressure for war and to explore every possible path to peace. He made clear that he was prepared to send a new envoy to France as soon as he had assurances that he would be received with respect. He maintained the peaceful posture in the face of large-scale engagements at sea between French and American ships. For two years, 1797–1799, a "quasi-war" went on involving hundreds of encounters between the ships of the two nations.

Adams' patience was rewarded. In the autumn of 1798, he began hearing from several sources that France was willing to treat with the United States on an equal and honorable basis. From William Vans Murray, the American minister in the Netherlands, from his son, John Quincy Adams, representing his father in Berlin, and from Talleyrand himself, the assurances reached the president in Philadelphia of the French desire for a settlement. The president asked the Cabinet's advice. When it opposed sending an envoy, he ignored the advice and presented to the Senate in February 1799 Murray's nomination as special emissary to Paris. The Federalists were thunderstruck. They wanted war, not peace. "Surprise, indignation, grief, and disgust" was the way one Federalist senator described the reaction of his colleagues. "Embarrassing and ruinous measures," said another. Adams stood firm, making only one change, that of adding the names of Oliver Ellsworth and William R. Davie to that of Murray, thus enlarging the mission. This move, which he suggested to assuage the Federalists, they accepted in the hopes thereby of delaying the mission's arrival in Europe, since both Ellsworth and Davie were in America.

That the Senate confirmed the nominations may be ascribed to moderates in the Federalist councils: George Washington, John Jay, and John Marshall. They joined Adams in rising above party politics, and their influence overcame the machinations of Pickering and Hamilton, who tried in every way to block the appointments. The three envoys reached Paris in April of 1800 and found Talleyrand eager to negotiate. Conditions had recently changed in France with Napoleon Bonaparte in power as a result of a *coup d'état* in November 1799. For him, the real enemy was England, and he did not wish to add America's resources to the enemy's strength. Further, he coveted Spanish Louisiana and feared it might fall to the United States in a war. With these considerations in mind, Napoleon's representative sat down with the Americans in September; the result was the Convention of 1800. By its terms, the French consented to an abrogation of the entangling alliance of 1778, while the United States assumed the claims of its citizens against the French government for French spoliations since 1793. The hostilities at sea between the two nations came to an end. In February 1801, the Senate approved the treaty without serious discussion. The Federalists had already met defeat in the presidential election the previous fall, and much of the steam of the Hamiltonians had been let off. For Adams the settlement with France was the proudest achievement of a long life. He wished nothing more to appear on his gravestone than: "Here lies John Adams, who took upon himself the responsibility of the peace with France in the year 1800."

BIBLIOGRAPHY

SAMUEL F. BEMIS, *Jay's Treaty: A Study in Commerce and Diplomacy* (1923; rev. 1962).

SAMUEL F. BEMIS, *Pinckney's Treaty: America's Advantage from Europe's Distress, 1783–1800* (1926; rev. 1960).

A. H. BOWMAN, *The Struggle for Neutrality: Franco-American Diplomacy During the Federalist Era* (1973).

GERARD CLARFIELD, *Timothy Pickering and American Diplomacy, 1795–1800* (1969).

JERALD A. COMBS, *The Jay Treaty: Political Battleground of the Founding Fathers* (1970).

ALEXANDER DE CONDE, *Entangling Alliance: Politics and Diplomacy Under George Washington* (1958).

ALEXANDER DE CONDE, *The Quasi-war: Politics and Diplomacy of the Undeclared War with France, 1797–1801* (1966).

PETER P. HILL, *William Vans Murray, Federalist Diplomat* (1971).

FREDERICK W. MARKS, III, *Independence on Trial: Foreign Affairs and the Making of the Constitution* (1973).

ARTHUR P. WHITAKER, *The Spanish-American Frontier, 1783–1795* (1969).

Washington's Farewell address - "there should be no entangling alliances." "we might safely trust temporary alliances but avoid long term ones."

Stalin had the same ideology
Washington said we should be an example and not become involved.

Thomas Jefferson (courtesy of the U.S. State Department).

Jeffersonian Diplomacy

Thomas Jefferson came to the presidency on March 4, 1801 with broad experience in public affairs—domestic and foreign. Before independence, he had served in the Virginia House of Burgesses and in the Continental Congress and afterward he had been governor of his state, minister to France, secretary of state, and vice-president. He took office, also, with a number of cherished principles he had developed over the years—among them not only opposition to "entangling alliances," a large army and navy, and war but support of the strict construction of the constitutional powers of the president, economy in government, and friendship with France. It was ironic that before he left the White House in 1809, he had had to sacrifice almost every one of these principles. Yet it was vastly to his credit that he surrendered those ideals when they conflicted with what he considered to be the national interest.

The first compromise Jefferson had to make resulted from his policy toward the Barbary "pirates." For centuries, the rulers of the north African countries of Morocco, Algiers, Tunis, and Tripoli had exacted tribute from the principal maritime nations for the privilege of using the Mediterranean. Before 1776, American merchants had been covered by British "presents." After independence, they had to look to the United States. In the 1790s, the new American government had negotiated treaties with the four states providing for the payment of protection, and Washington and Adams had paid heavy sums. Soon, however, the pirate countries, except for Morocco, demanded more money and treated American commerce with wanton recklessness. The Dey of Algiers, for example, seized an American naval vessel in 1800, replacing the American standard with his own, and ordered the captain to take his ambassador to Constantinople. Tripoli, not content with harassing American trade, actually declared war against the United States in May 1801. Jefferson did not hesitate to take up the challenge. He dispatched a strong squadron to the Mediterranean with orders to fight and, over the next two years, he added to the navy and pushed the war with vigor. Jefferson did not call on Congress for a formal declaration of war as the Constitution stipulated but carried on hostilities by executive authority as commander-in-chief.

The war went on until 1805. It was highlighted by several daring naval engagements and one remarkable act by Lieutenant Stephen Decatur who boarded and destroyed the American frigate *Philadelphia*, which had been taken by the Tripolitans. Peace, however, did not come until another heroic and bizarre military expedition took place. It was executed by the American consul in Tripoli, William Eaton, at the head of a motley army consisting of Americans, Greeks, and Arabs that marched westward from Egypt with the brother of the ruling Pasha of Tripoli, who aspired to take over the country, in tow. Eaton hoped to seat the pretender on the throne and exact a favorable treaty from him for the United States. By the time Eaton reached the eastern border of Tripoli, the Pasha consented to make peace and to end the tribute system. Thus had the antiwar and antinavy president waged a war and enlarged the navy to defend the honor of the United States without authorization by Congress.

The acquisition of Louisiana offers even better evidence of Jefferson's abandonment of principle. On November 20, 1801, the president received news from the United States minister in London that a Franco-Spanish treaty had been signed the previous year providing for the transfer of Louisiana territory from Spain to France. This information unnerved and distressed him. For years before becoming president, he had confidently prophesied that the United States would grow beyond the borders set by the Treaty of Peace of 1783. In 1786, he had written, "Our confederacy must be viewed as the nest from which all America, north and south, is to be peopled." In 1801, he stated, "However our present interest may restrain us within our limits, it is impossible not to look forward to distant times when our rapid multiplication will expand it beyond those limits and cover the whole northern, if not the southern continent." As president he designated as his immediate objectives Louisiana (which included the land between the Mississippi and the Rockies and between Canada and the Gulf of Mexico) and Florida (which consisted of the territory south of the 31st parallel between the Mississippi and the Atlantic), particularly Louisiana into whose fertile areas Americans were already moving in considerable number and through whose port of New Orleans American commerce was passing in large volume. So long as it was in the possession of Spain, "it could be in no better hands," said the president in July 1801. Weak Spain would serve as the perfect guardian of the vast region until the United States was in a position to wrest it from her. In the hands, however, of powerful France and her ambitious ruler, Napoleon, it not only was placed outside America's reach but actually became a menace to American security. There was every reason to believe that the French ruler would withdraw the right granted by Spain to Americans in 1795 to use the port of New Orleans. For the farmers living west of the Appalachians such action would amount to economic strangulation.

To Robert Livingston, the American minister in France, Jefferson sent his troubled thoughts in a letter dated April 18, 1802: "The cession of Louisiana . . . works most sorely on the United States. . . . It completely reverses all the political relations of the United States and will form a new epoch in our political course. . . . There is on the globe one single spot, the possessor of which is our natural and habitual enemy. It is New Orleans, through which the produce of three-eighths of our territory must pass to market, and from its fertility it will ere long yield more than half of our whole produce and contain more than half our inhabitants. France, placing herself in that door, assumes to us the attitude of defiance. . . . The day that France takes possession of New Orleans fixes the sentence which is to restrain her forever within her low-water mark. It seals the union of two nations who in conjunction can maintain exclusive possession of the ocean. From that moment we must marry ourselves to the British fleet and nation." So Thomas Jefferson, friend of France and hater of entangling alliances, was ready to join with France's enemy in an alliance for his country's benefit.

In the hope of avoiding such drastic action, he instructed Livingston in the same letter to get France to give up New Orleans and Florida. Such a surrender, he wrote, would ease the problem immeasurably. Then, in October, came word that the Spanish had suspended the "right of deposit" at New Orleans, a right Spain had granted in Pinckney's Treaty in 1795. Convinced that this action was instigated by the new owners and fearful that it presaged even more dangerous moves by France after she took possession of the territory, Jefferson redoubled his determination to acquire the mouth of the Mississippi without which the American West could not exist. In a curious way, political partisanship helped to force Jefferson's hand. His Federalist opponents, noting western agitation for a solution to the Mississippi question, began to shout for action, thereby hoping to endear themselves to the pioneers in the trans-Allegheny area. Hamilton urged the seizure of New Orleans by force, and a senator from Pennsylvania offered a resolution in the Senate to call on 50,000 militiamen for that purpose.

Ignoring these bellicose rantings, Jefferson, in January 1803, sent James Monroe to Paris to assist Livingston in his task. Monroe carried the additional charge of offering Napoleon up to $10 million for New Orleans and Florida. The choice of Monroe was a wise one politically, for his concern

Treaty of San Ildefonso

about the well-being of the farmers in the west was well-known. It was astute diplomatically as well, since Monroe was a long-time and ardent admirer of France.

Monroe arrived in France in March but before he reached Paris, French policy toward Louisiana had undergone radical change, the consequence of two colossal crises in French diplomacy. The first was the decision by Napoleon in March 1803 to go to war against Britain. The Anglo-French war which began in 1793 had ended in 1802 in a truce, but all the world knew that the rivalry between the two giants could not be resolved unless one of the two achieved total victory. They would have to fight again and to the finish. For such a war, Napoleon needed money; in such a war the superior British fleet could easily take New Orleans and all of Louisiana; and in such a war, American animus toward France over New Orleans could result in an Anglo-American alliance.

The second crisis resulted from the situation in Santo Domingo. The attempt by Napoleon to suppress the uprising against French rule on that island led by the Negro general Toussaint L'Ouverture was, by the fall of 1802, proving unsuccessful. Time after time, Toussaint defeated the French forces. When, in November, General Charles Leclerc, one of France's ablest generals and Napoleon's brother-in-law, was defeated and shortly thereafter succumbed to yellow fever, the French ruler was ready to abandon Santo Domingo despite the great wealth it yielded from sugar and coffee. "Damn sugar, damn coffee, damn colonies," he exploded at dinner one night in January 1803. Having lost Santo Domingo, Napoleon found no use for Louisiana as its chief value had been to feed Santo Domingo. As Henry Adams put it, "The colonial system of France centered in Santo Domingo. Without that island, the system had hands, feet, even a head, but no body. Of what use was Louisiana when France had clearly lost the main colony which Louisiana was meant to feed and fortify."

When on April 10, 1803, Livingston made one of his usual calls at the French foreign office to urge the cession of New Orleans, he was met not by the usual negative response but by an offer to take New Orleans and all the rest of the territory of Louisiana. Livingston must surely have blanched at the prospect of adding so vast a region to the United States. Then there was the problem of exceeding his instructions. He had been authorized to buy a city, not half a continent. Two days later, Monroe arrived, and the two made the momentous decision to accept Napoleon's offer. On April 30, the treaty exchanging Louisiana for $15 million was signed.

For Napoleon, the sale was most welcome. He now had money for the war and not only had headed off an Anglo-American rapprochement but gave "Great Britain a maritime rival that sooner or later will lay low her pride." For Jefferson, the sale raised grave problems. Although elated that the Mississippi now flowed from source to mouth between American banks, and that more than 800,000 square miles of new land were to be made available for American settlement, exploitation, and for the spread of republican institutions, he saw nowhere in the Constitution any clause giving the president the power to buy land or to incorporate the inhabitants of that land into the Union as citizens. Further, France did not yet have title to Louisiana, as the Spanish minister in Washington pointed out, because she had not delivered to Spain the territories in Europe that she had pledged in exchange for Louisiana. He mentioned, too, that Napoleon had promised the king of Spain never to cede or sell Louisiana to another power. What was Jefferson, strict constructionist of the Constitution and man of principle, to do? The French right to sell did not disturb him as much as the American right to buy. To assuage his conscience on that score he suggested an amendment to the Constitution that would expressly permit the purchase of land. Warned that Napoleon might change his mind during the long process, he decided to cast his scruples aside and sent the treaty to the Senate "to secure a good which would otherwise probably be never again in reach." Metaphysical subtleties "would have to be left behind," he wrote; "a strict observance to the written laws is doubtless one of the *high* duties of a good citizen, but it is not the *highest*. The laws of necessity, of self-preservation, of saving our country when in danger, are of a higher obligation."

In the Senate, Federalists at once challenged the Administration on the issue of the constitutionality not only of acquiring territory but of bringing it into the Union as states on equal footing with the others. They argued that new states could be made and admitted to the Union only from land which the United States possessed in 1789. More important than the question of legality was the real fear that the addition of many new agricultural states in the west would end forever the influence in the Union of commercial New England. All the Federalist senators save one voted against the treaty. John Quincy Adams, son of the former Federalist president, alone rose above party and joined the twenty-three Republicans to insure ratification in October of 1803.

Twenty-five years later, two years after Jefferson's death, his act was given constitutional sanction. In the case of *American Insurance Company* v. *Canter*, which concerned the legality of the acquisition of Florida, Chief Justice John Marshall, Jefferson's cousin and one-time bitter political enemy, decided that the government did, by the treaty and war-making powers of the Constitution, "possess the power of acquiring territory [which] . . . becomes a part of the nation . . ." and that the inhabitants of the territory may be "incorporated into the Union of the United States." In 1804, a territorial government was organized for Louisiana and in 1812 the first state to be carved out of the territory, appropriately

Marbois

named Louisiana and with its present boundaries, was admitted into the Union.

Well might Jefferson have congratulated himself on his good fortune in acquiring Louisiana. It was true that his stretching of the Constitution alienated certain Republican leaders and led to a serious schism in the party, but that was balanced by the strength the party gained among western farmers grateful for the final solution of the Mississippi question. It was true, too, that Jefferson suffered twinges of conscience in stretching the Constitution but such pangs were nothing when pitted against the great significance of the purchase for the nation. Robert Livingston grasped that significance when he remarked at the time of the signing of the treaty of acquisition, "We have lived long but this is the noblest work of our lives. From this day the United States take their place among the powers of the first rank."

Livingston surely had in mind the size of the territory added to the national acreage. The precise boundaries were not known for the treaty said only "the same extent it now has in the hands of Spain and that it had when France possessed it [before 1763]." And when Livingston investigated the boundaries under Spanish and French rule, he found a considerable difference. He appealed to Talleyrand for a more precise definition of "extent" but got only the wry observation: "I can give you no direction. You have made a noble bargain for yourselves and I suppose you will make the most of it." But accepting even the narrowest limits, the acquisition at least doubled the territory of the United States at one stroke. And Livingston must have had in mind, too, the gigantic economic and commercial potential of the area. Crossed by rivers, dotted with mountains, and possessing broad plains, the land gave great promise of riches in minerals, metals, livestock, and agricultural products. Two expeditions sent by the president in 1804 and 1806 to investigate the resources of the region—one led by Meriwether Lewis and William Clark that explored the northern part, and the other headed by Zebulon Pike that scouted the southern portion—brought back reports that added to the feeling of confidence in the territory's possibilities. It was significant that Lewis and Clark pushed beyond the boundaries of the territory to the Pacific Ocean, which gave Louisiana yet more significance as a jumping-off point for further expansion to the western-most border of the continent.

Jefferson could not for very long enjoy contemplating the pleasures afforded by the vast new lands on the other side of the Mississippi River for the great war then in progress between France and Great Britain was beginning to affect American life in the harshest way. For its first two years, the struggle had not worried Americans. Their economy had not only not been deranged but had actually been stimulated by the profits of supplying goods to the belligerents and their security had not been

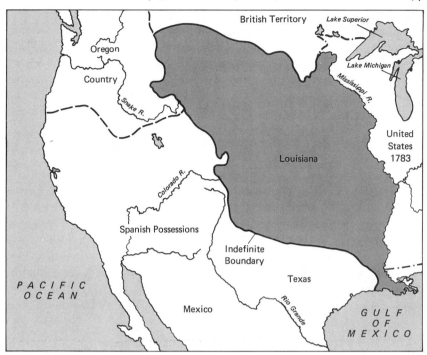

The Louisiana Purchase, 1803.

endangered. By mid-1805, however, the war was reaching an intensity and assuming a character which would before long undermine American prosperity, threaten its security, embroil it in European rivalry and ambition, and divide the people on the wisdom of the measures taken to defend America's neutral commerce.

The war which broke out on May 18, 1803, was the second and final phase of the Franco-British conflict which had started in 1793. It was a titanic struggle between the two great powers for mastery of Europe and may be considered the capstone of the rivalry which began in 1688 for dominance of the New World colonies. As a contest for supremacy, it takes its place alongside those other decisive struggles which have determined the course of history—those between Athens and Persia, Rome and Carthage, and Germany and Great Britain.

Not too long after the war started, it became clear that neither belligerent could inflict upon the other a final defeat because each had supremacy in one of the two phases of military combat and decided inferiority in the other. France had an army that England (together with her allies) could not match; England possessed a navy that Napoleon could not rival. In 1805 at Austerlitz, in 1806 at Jena, and in 1807 at Friedland, the French emperor inflicted defeats on his enemies, converted them into allies however reluctant, and gained control of the continent, but without a superior navy, he could not invade Britain to deliver the knockout blow. In 1805, Horatio Nelson crushed the French navy (at the expense of his life) and routed it from the sea, but England did not have the land force to conquer France. The "Colossus of the Land" and the "Leviathan of the Sea" were at a virtual stalemate, fighting, as it were, on different levels. To achieve victory, the two belligerents would have to resort to measures other than direct attacks, and this they did by means of an economic duel.

Napoleon knew well that Britain's capacity to fight a war stemmed from the revenues derived from her extensive commerce. Wreck that trade and the financial base of British power would crumble. He could not destroy that commerce on the sea convoyed as it was by the mighty British navy, but he could end it by closing the ports of the continent and those of the continental nations' colonies in America to English goods. He could also try to starve the British by cutting off their food imports. These objectives the French Emperor achieved by means of two decrees whose names are derived from the places where they were announced— Berlin in November 1806 and Milan in December 1807. The first prohibited "all commerce and correspondence with the British islands" and forbade "the trade in English merchandise" and the reception of English ships in continental ports. It also set up a blockade of the British Isles. The second declared that any vessel that had touched a British harbor or otherwise traded with England would be considered an English vessel and treated as an enemy. Taken together, these decrees constituted the Continental System constructed by Bonaparte to subdue his adversary.

The British, on their part, realized that France could be humbled only by preventing the sinews of war from reaching her armies in ships of her own nationals, of her allies, or of the neutrals. Halt the importation of food and materiel into France and the invincible Napoleon's military machine would be powerless. In July 1805, the first step in this grand design was taken in the form of a decision in a prize case concerning the American ship *Essex* picked up by a British man-of-war en route from Salem (Massachusetts) to Havana (Cuba) carrying a cargo of goods of Spanish origin, which had come from Barcelona to Salem, where it had been landed and duty paid. The court held that the merchandise had not lost its Spanish character by the landing at an American port and that the carriage of the goods must be considered as continuous from Barcelona to Havana despite the break at Salem. Because such a voyage between mother country and colony by a foreign vessel was not permitted by Spain in peace time, it was declared illegal in war time according to the British Rule of 1756, and the goods, therefore, were confiscated. The

British had decreed that rule to prevent an enemy from using neutral carriers in a trade too dangerous for her own vessels. The decision, of course, set the precedent for prohibiting the carriage of goods from the French West Indies to France in American ships, and since French vessels could not safely engage in the trade because of the superior British navy, France was effectively cut off from her colonies, which supplied much needed articles.

Then, in May 1806, a blockade of Europe from the Elbe River to Brest was announced (called Fox's Blockade after Foreign Secretary Charles James Fox), and two Orders-in-Council, published in January and November 1807, extended the blockade to "all ports and places of France and her allies" and prohibited all trade to ports from which the British flag was excluded. So by the end of 1807, the two mighty contestants had erected their systems of economic warfare calculated to destroy the enemy by indirection, by striking at his only vulnerable spot. Each power relied on its specialized weapon to enforce its peculiar system. Napoleon's army, by keeping the continental nations under subjection, could force them to cease trading with Britain; England's navy, by maintaining supremacy on the sea, could prevent vessels from carrying goods to France and her allies.

Between French decrees and British Orders-in-Council, the neutral nations were caught as in a vise. Forbidden by each belligerent from trading with the other, they stood to suffer great economic losses. The hardest hit of all nations was the United States because, far and away, it was the world's leading neutral carrier. Hundreds of American vessels were seized by the navies of the two warring nations, and the losses in cargo confiscated reached into the millions of dollars. Because the British navy commanded the seas and the French navy was conspicuously absent from the ocean except for an occasional frigate that escaped British vigilance, Britain was the greater offender against American commerce. Everywhere, it was an English warship that halted American vessels and not only to search for contraband or for goods of enemy origin but also for deserters from the Royal Navy. It was this practice of impressment of seamen from American ships that constituted the chief source of controversy between the two countries.

Each year about 2,500 men deserted from the Royal Navy largely because of the hard life and the low pay, and many found refuge in the navy of the United States where a sailor's life was only slightly better but where the wages were three times greater. To recover these deserters, whose number reached 10,000 in the decade 1800–1810, British warship masters boarded American vessels. The difficulty of identifying the deserter was often very great since in dress, speech, manner, and physique there was not a great deal of difference between the British tar and the American gob, and, further, British sailors could very easily obtain forged birth certificates attesting to their United States nationality. Hence, British naval officers frequently removed as many seamen as they needed to fill their crews by arbitrarily selecting anyone suspected of being English. Between 1808 and 1811, 6,000 Americans were impressed. As British captains acted more boldly and more arrogantly, American ire mounted. The height of British insolence and American anger was reached in June 1807 when the British warship *Leopard* hailed the American frigate *Chesapeake* ten miles off the Virginia coast and sent a party aboard her ostensibly to search for contraband but really to remove a British sailor suspected of being in her crew. When the American shipper refused to surrender the sailor, *Leopard* opened fire, killing three and wounding eighteen of the crew. After *Chesapeake* struck her colors, four seamen were taken off—one Briton and three Americans who had formerly served in the British navy.

The American public was outraged by this English presumption. Had Jefferson wished to fight, the Congress would have eagerly declared war and popular support would have been universal, but Jefferson did not choose to fight, nor would he meekly submit. He retaliated at once by ordering all British warships out of American waters and demanding an apology and reparation. Not wishing to add the United States to its roster of enemies, the British government made every effort to atone for *Leopard's* actions. It was prepared to relieve the captain, return the American sailors, make apology and pay an indemnity, and renounce the right to search a warship. What England would not surrender was the right to remove British nationals from American merchant vessels, nor would she relax the strictures on American commerce.

To force her to submit, the president, in December 1807, turned to economic coercion, a weapon which had been used back in the 1760s and 1770s by the colonies against the Crown and which Jefferson himself had had a hand in shaping. Britain needed American products which she was getting because of loopholes in the Napoleonic system. If she were deprived of those necessities, she would surely relent Jefferson believed. Secretary of State James Madison neatly summed up the situation when he remarked, "We send necessaries to her. She sends superfluities to us. Our products they must have. Theirs, however promotive of our comfort, we can to a considerable degree do without." On the 22nd of the month, Congress, at the president's request, passed an Embargo Act which forbade any American vessel from leaving port except for coastwise trade and such a vessel had to post a bond twice the value of the cargo as a guarantee not to take off for a foreign harbor.

Federalists who had voted against the bill in House and Senate immediately accused Jefferson of wishing to aid France by the measure, and it was, of course, true, that the embargo would operate almost solely against Great Britain, for the Franco-American traffic had long ago been brought to a virtual standstill by the British navy. To accuse Jefferson, however, of acting from Francophile motives is to miss the point. Unquestionably, he had England in mind as the object of his retaliation but only because he considered her, not France, the great threat to his country's security and well-being. It was England that was inflicting the principal damage on America's commerce and scarring her honor by the impressment practice.

Jefferson and others in his cabinet and in the country fully expected the embargo to bring Britain to her knees, and there was evidence that she was feeling the pinch. Despite a bumper harvest in 1808 and the opening of sources of supplies in Latin America occasioned by the revolutions on that continent, serious shortages of numerous commodities were frightening Englishmen. Especially affected were the West Indian islands, which depended on importation of American foodstuffs. The embargo was not given a fair chance to work. On March 1, 1809, it was repealed.

The demand for the repeal of the act began at the moment of enactment, and it centered in Federalist New England. The opposition was based on constitutional and economic grounds. The government, said the Federalists, did not have the power to halt commerce, only to regulate it. In addition, they claimed, the embargo was destroying the nation's economy. It was true, of course, that hard times resulted from the stoppage of trade. Exports which, between 1803 and 1807 had risen from $55 million to $108 million, dropped in 1808 to $22 million (although to that figure should be added the not inconsiderable but unknown amount smuggled out of the country by way of Canada and Florida). There was unemployment, prices of agricultural products dropped, and imported items became dearer. Henry Adams described the stark conditions in memorable prose: "As the order [embargo] was carried along the sea coast, every artisan dropped his tools, every merchant closed his doors, every shop was dismantled, American produce—wheat, timber, cotton, tobacco, rice—dropped in value and became unsalable; every imported article rose in price; wages stopped, swarms of debtors became bankrupt; thousands of sailors hung idle around the wharves; a reign of idleness began and the men who were not already ruined felt that their ruin was a matter of time."

It is also true, as Albert Gallatin's *Report on American Manufacturers* (1810) indicated, that much idle commercial capital was channelled into industry, and many new factories were established for the manufacture of glass, textiles, hats, iron, gunpowder, and other articles. Still, this economic activity could not compensate for the losses generated by the embargo. Resolutions by town meetings and state legislatures castigating the presi-

dent and demanding repeal attested to the widespread public dissatisfaction.

The agitation for repeal of the "dambargo" must also be ascribed, in
a large part, to purely political considerations. However conciliatory
Jefferson was and although he followed many Federalist policies and practices, to the arch-Federalists of New England he was anathema and
would always be the radical revolutionary and the slavish admirer of
France. They were determined to undermine him at any opportunity and
found it could best be done at the moment by destroying his embargo.
To their votes were added those of Jefferson's enemies in the Republican
party, led by John Randolph, whose hatred of the president led the
Republicans into an uneasy alliance with the Federalists. It is worth
noting that economic factors did not determine attitudes in the south and
the west. There loyal old-line Jeffersonian Republicans gave the president
unqualified backing although their distress was unrelieved by any com-
pensating diversions of idle capital.

Jefferson, himself, was saddened by the uproar over the embargo and
especially by the personal vituperation directed against him. He had the
satisfaction of judicial approval of the embargo arising out of a case in
the United States District Court of Massachusetts but did not welcome the
harsh and restrictive measures that he had to take to enforce it. The
devices for ferreting out offenders, which were subsequently incorporated
in the Enforcement Act of January, 1809, were uncomfortably reminiscent
of British practice in the 1760s and 1770s against which he had railed in
his youth. By the time the election of 1808 came around, he was more
than ready to be released from the "shackles of power." He was "panting
for retirement" and for escape to his hilltop retreat at Monticello, where
he could indulge his intellectual interests and oversee the establishment
of the University of Virginia. To his successor, James Madison, who took
office three days after the repeal of the embargo, was left the problem
of finding a new solution to the dilemma of American neutral commerce.

BIBLIOGRAPHY

Henry Adams, *History of the United States in the Administrations of Jeffer-
son and Madison* (9 vols., 1889–1891).
Irving Brant, *James Madison, Secretary of State: 1800–1809* (1953).
A. L. Burt, *The United States, Great Britain, and British North America
from the Revolution to the Establishment of Peace After the War of
1812* (1940).
Lawrence Kaplan, *Jefferson and France: An Essay on Politics and Political
Ideas* (1967).

E. WILSON LYON, *Louisiana in French Diplomacy, 1759–1804* (1934).
DUMAS MALONE, *Jefferson, the President, 1801–1805* (1971).
ARTHUR P. WHITAKER, *The Mississippi Question, 1795–1803* (1934).

James Madison (courtesy of the National Portrait Gallery, Smithsonian Institution, Washington, D.C.).

The War of 1812 and
the Settlement with England

JAMES MADISON was one of the ablest men ever to hold the office of president of the United States. He came to the White House with more experience in public affairs than any predecessor or successor. He had served as a member of many of the most important deliberative bodies of his state and of the nation and working closely with Jefferson as Secretary of State, he had played an important role in the formulation of the policies of the Administration. Yet all of the knowledge, ability, experience, and good intentions could not help him keep the United States neutral. Three years and three months after his inauguration the country was at war with England.

The reasons for Madison's failure to carry out the pledge of his inaugural address, "to cherish peace and friendly intercourse with all nations . . . [and] to maintain a sincere neutrality" has been ascribed by some historians to his ineffectual and inept diplomacy and to the patchwork quality of his politics. It must be admitted that the two chief pieces of legislation designed to preserve peace and to force the belligerents to relax their restrictions on American commerce were not parts of a carefully thought-out plan of action but were, rather, desperate gropings for something that would work much as a boxer stabs and jabs aimlessly at his opponent, hoping to land a lucky blow. It is true, too, that on two occasions the president did permit himself to be taken in by both France and England.

The first legislative measure, the Non-Intercourse Act, which replaced the repealed Embargo Act, went into effect three days before Madison entered office, but it had the incoming president's complete approval and must be considered his Administration's policy. Like the old law, the new one was rooted in the Jeffersonian concept of "economic and peaceful coercion" but with a different twist in the method of application. It restored commerce with all the world except France and England but provided that trade would be reopened with those nations as quickly as they repealed their obnoxious orders and decrees. For a moment, this inducement seemed to be the solution to the problem when David M. Erskine, the British minister in Washington, under instructions from London to negotiate a settlement with the United States that would insure the flow of food and raw materials to the hard-pressed British, approached Madison with an offer to repeal the Orders-in-Council in exchange for the lifting of nonintercourse against England but keeping it in effect against France. The president eagerly accepted the terms and in April 1809, the Erskine Agreement was signed.

Two months later, trade was reopened with Britain and 600 American ships at once left American ports for England. What appeared a victory for Madison turned to defeat when the Foreign Office in London repudiated its minister for violating instructions. In his eagerness to reach an understanding, Erskine had failed to include in his terms London's insistence that British warships be permitted to help enforce nonintercourse against France to extend even to capturing American ships engaged in commerce with France. Madison had acted hastily and now, in August 1809, had to invoke nonintercourse with Britain, an act which not only dried up the recently revived commerce and dashed the hopes of American shippers but worsened Anglo-American relations.

The Nonintercourse Act expired with the close of the second session of the Eleventh Congress in 1810, having done the country more harm than good. The Administration, having no better plan, adopted a new variety of "economic coercion" hoping it might work. This was Macon's Bill Number 2 enacted in May 1810. It opened trade with both France and England but provided that should one nation repeal its restrictive measures, commerce would be interdicted against the other power. The renewal of American trade with the two belligerents worked greatly to Napoleon's disadvantage in view of the preponderance of the British fleet. He, therefore, moved to turn Macon's Bill to his advantage by seeming to comply with its provisions. In August 1810, he informed Madison that he was revoking his decrees as of November 1, 1810, and, consequently, expected the United States to invoke nonintercourse against Great Britain. Madison did not wait to ascertain whether the decrees had actually been repealed any more than he had waited to ascertain whether the British government had accepted Erskine's agreement. Instead, he precipitously issued a proclamation in November halting trade with England at the end of three months if by that time she did not cancel her Orders-in-Council. When Britain took no action within the allotted time on the ground that there was no proof that Napoleon had repealed the decrees, Congress, on March 2, 1811, renewed nonintercourse against her.

Napoleon had not, as a matter of fact, revoked his decrees and they still operated against American commerce. Madison had been outwitted and the result was that the United States became, in effect, a party to the French Continental System, thus further exacerbating relations with Great Britain.

There is no doubt that Madison's measures and his gullibility did nothing to solve America's problems; on the other hand, his policies and actions cannot be said to have caused the breakdown of the peace. The president could have gone on improvising legislation and even blundering without war resulting. Indeed, he might have continued in that way until the end of the Franco-British conflict and thereby escaped involvement. To understand why the war came one must turn from the White House to the American frontier—the states west of the Appalachians and the western fringes of the states east of those mountains. From there, a new breed of men came to the Twelfth Congress, which assembled in November 1811. They were passionately patriotic and militantly nationalistic, belligerent and bellicose. These were the men called "War Hawks." They viewed the administration's policy as timid, weak, and negative. They demanded action, and their target was England.

Their leader was Henry Clay of Kentucky. He had been a senator in the preceding Congress and now at thirty-four years of age, was a representative and had been elected Speaker. Prominent among his followers, all in their mid- or late twenties and early thirties, were Richard M. Johnson of Kentucky, Felix Grundy of Tennessee, William Lowndes, Langdon Cheves, and John C. Calhoun of South Carolina, Peter Porter of the frontier area in western New York, and John A. Harper of Western New Hampshire. Why should these men, living so far from the seacoast, feel so deeply about British conduct on the high seas and British restrictions on American sea-borne commerce? For one thing, they believed *their* economic well-being was affected by the Orders-in-Council as much as that of their coastal brethren. The market for their produce was overseas, and they claimed that the British strictures virtually destroyed it. A depression the western farmers suffered in 1810 and 1811 was attributed entirely to Britain. As the *Lexington* (Kentucky) *Register* noted one day in December 1811, "It appears that our government will at last make war to produce a market for our tobacco, flour, and cotton." These inland areas gave no sons to the United States navy, nonetheless their inhabitants considered impressment an affront to their country's honor and a desecration of the flag, which, as a report by the War Hawk chairman of the House Foreign Affairs Committee insisted, "ought to be resisted by war."

The British, too, were blamed for Indian unrest on the frontier and for the renewal of warfare there in the winter of 1811–1812. It all started sometime in 1805 when two Shawnee chiefs and twin brothers, Tecumseh and Tenskwautawa (called the Prophet), moved to organize a great confederacy of all the tribes living between the Appalachians and the Mississippi to resist the advance of the whites. They were impelled to action at that time because of the aggressive conduct of William Henry Harrison, governor of Indiana territory since 1800 and a veteran of the Indian wars. As governor, Harrison had obtained millions of acres from Indian tribes whose chiefs frequently negotiated while in a drunken stupor or when sober were uncertain of the precise nature of the treaties they signed. In 1809, he wrested about 3 million more acres along the Wabash River from some chiefs who had no right to sell and who were in no condition to know what they were selling. Tecumseh, thereupon, journeyed to Harrison's headquarters at Vincennes to urge him to give up the land. The governor, of course, refused and to forestall an attack, he led about 1,000 men to Prophetstown, capital of the Confederacy, some 150 miles north where Tippecanoe Creek flows into the Wabash. Arriving on November 6, 1811, he set up his camp with a view to having a conference. At dawn the following day, he was attacked by a party of braves, thus beginning the Battle of Tippecanoe. Harrison fought back and finally destroyed Prophetstown, suffering a loss of 61 killed and 127 wounded. When Tecumseh, who had been on a tour of the south to raise support, returned and learned of the battle, he went on the warpath and once again the frontier was aflame.

To the western settlers, there was no doubt that the Indians were incited by the British and supplied by them. Captured guns, ammunition, and blankets with British markings offered incontrovertible proof of the latter suspicion. Incitement was harder to prove, but it was nonetheless firmly believed. "The war on the Wabash is purely British," proclaimed one Kentucky newspaper, while a prominent Tennessean named Andrew Jackson cried, "The blood of our murdered countrymen must be revenged" and called on the government to destroy the hostile bands "excited to war by the secret agents of Britain." Quite naturally and logically, this view of British complicity led to demands for the acquisition of Canada, which was the base from which British encouragement and gifts flowed to the Indians. At the same time, the cry for taking Florida from Britain's ally, Spain, was raised, for from that territory came support for Indian raids on the southern frontier.

All through the winter and spring of 1811–1812, the War Hawks maintained an incessant clamor for war which, they claimed, "with all its calamities and desolations" was preferable "to the tranquil and putrescent pool of ignominious peace." The precise effect of this campaign upon the president is difficult to measure. It seems reasonable to assume that were it not for the War Hawks, Madison would not have taken the step he took on June 1, 1812, when he sent his war message to Congress. Indeed, he might never have made the fateful move had it not been for the excitement they created. This is not to say that he was the tool of the war party or meekly followed their bidding or succumbed to their pressure. It is known that he was angry with the British and resented their conduct. While clinging to a policy of peace, he did contemplate stronger retaliatory measures and did not shrink from the possibility of military reprisals.

His replacement of Robert Smith by James Monroe as secretary of state in April 1811 is evidence of his inclination. Smith opposed action; Monroe, who had been subjected to considerable humiliation in the capitals of Europe, favored strong action. His sanctioning of the American occupation of West Florida (to the Perdido River) in October 1810 provides further proof of his mood. In November 1811, in his third annual message, the president talked of British measures "which under existing circumstances have the character as well as the effect of war on our lawful commerce" and went on to say, ominously, "with this evidence of hostile inflexibility in trampling on rights which no independent nation can relinquish Congress will feel the duty of putting the United States into an armor and an attitude demanded by the crisis, and corresponding with the national spirit and expectation." He then recommended building up the land and sea forces. All of this demonstrates that the president stood prepared to defend American trade by force if necessary and that the War Hawks acted only as a catalyst, albeit an important one. If in the war message Madison repeated the War Hawk complaints—Indians, impressment, trade restrictions—it was not that he was a parrot but only that they were the grievances.

Congressional Voting on the Declaration of War, by States

| | House of Representatives | | Senate | |
	For	Against	For	Against
New Hampshire	3	2	1	1
Vermont	3	1	1	0
Massachusetts (including Maine)	6	8	1	1
Rhode Island	0	2	0	2
Connecticut	0	7	0	2
New York	3	11	1	1
New Jersey	2	4	1	1
Delaware	0	1	0	2
Pennsylvania	16	2	2	0
Maryland	6	3	1	1
Virginia	14	5	2	0
North Carolina	6	3	2	0
South Carolina	8	0	2	0
Georgia	3	0	2	0
Ohio	1	0	0	1
Kentucky	5	0	1	1
Tennessee	3	0	2	0
	79	49	19	13

The vote on the war resolution in the House of Representatives re-flected accurately the national mood and the sectional divisions in the country. The measure passed the House on June 4 by a vote of 79–49. (The Senate approved on June 18, 19–13.) Those voting "aye" were all Republicans who represented districts in the three states west of the mountains and on the frontier of the eastern states stretching in an arc from Vermont and New Hampshire to Georgia. There was not a single opposition vote recorded from Kentucky, Tennessee, Ohio, South Caro-lina, or Georgia. Of those voting "nay," twenty-six were Republicans from coastal districts in Virginia, North Carolina, Maryland, Pennsylvania, New York, and New Jersey. The remainder were New England Federalists. Rhode Island, Connecticut, and Delaware voted solidly against war. Obvi-ously, the frontier wanted to fight. Just as clearly, people living on or near the seacoast opposed war and chiefly because they stood to receive the brunt of British naval attacks. As for New England, the merchants there pre-ferred trading with England even under harsh and arbitrary restrictions to no trade at all, while the politically conservative people in the area viewed Britain as the bastion of orderly government and the defender of constitu-tionality against the tyranny and despotism of Napoleon. Interestingly, the presidential election of 1812 also reflected the country's position on the war. Madison received 128 electoral votes representing the west, the south (including the new state of Louisiana admitted in the same year), and Pennsylvania to Federalist candidate, De Witt Clinton's 89, which came from New England (except Vermont) and the middle states.

So the United States and England went to war. It was a war Britain did not want, the real enemy was not America but Napoleon, and it seemed foolhardy and dangerous to add to the roster of enemies, especially the country which supplied so many necessities and took so much manufac-tured goods. Englishmen were hurt and saddened that their cousins across the sea did not appreciate the nature of the war in Europe or recognize the stakes for which the conflict was being waged. In a last-minute effort to avert war (and end a serious depression), the Orders-in-Council were revoked on June 16, 1812, but, of course, it was too late, for on the 19th, long before the news could cross the Atlantic, Madison proclaimed the existence of a state of war. Had there been a cable, the report of the revocation would have reached Washington before the Senate voted and the outcome might have been different, and if there had been adequate American representation in London in the spring of 1812, Madison would have been informed that the tide of opinion in Britain was running in favor of repealing the Orders and of easing the tension with the United States. He might well have held off the war message in the hopes of settling the impressment issue, which would have remained the only major obstacle to peace. Unfortunately, the minister, William Pinkney, had left his post in February, disgusted with British intransigence. Two other interesting "ifs" figure in the road to hostilities in 1812. If King George III had not gone mad in November 1811, and if Spencer Perceval, the prime minister, had not been assassinated in May 1812, the Orders-in-Council might have been revoked earlier and war might have been averted.

The beginning of the fighting in America found the United States in a state of unpreparedness. The regular army numbered only 10,000 men, and it was ill trained, ill equipped, and ill disciplined. The commanders were aged veterans of the Revolutionary War, who since 1781 had had no field experiences. One historian called the general officers "the worst military leaders in United States history." Their incompetence, bad judgment, and ignorance of tactics and logistics were appalling. Throughout the whole war only two really capable men emerged, Jacob Brown and Andrew Jackson. Throughout the war, there never was an adequate fighting force. In July 1812, Congress authorized the addition of 25,000 men to the regular army for five-year terms and 50,000 for one-year periods, but never were there more than 35,000 regulars under arms at any one time. As for the state militia, theoretically 700,000 men were available for duty. Madison called out 100,000 in 1812, but only one tenth that number responded. Worse still, state troops frequently refused to serve beyond their own borders.

The navy was, similarly, small in size, there being only 16 sea-going vessels in commission in 1812—six forty-four-gun frigates, three twenty-two-gun sloops, and seven smaller ships—to face almost 100 British warships in American waters, eleven of which were great seventy-four-gun ships-of-the-line. Unlike the army's senior officers, however, the naval commanders were young and aggressive and had seen much action during the quasi-war with France and against the Barbary corsairs. They won several striking victories over the British, which made them popular throughout the country at the time, and their names have come down in American history as heroes. Stephen Decatur, William Bainbridge, Thomas McDonough, Oliver Hazard Perry, and James Lawrence provided the few occasions for rejoicing and satisfaction in a war characterized by defeats, reversals, and humiliations.

In fighting the war, the United States was handicapped not only by inferior forces and leadership but also by inadequate finances and by disunity at home. The New England Federalists did not accept the decision of the majority. Instead, they continued their opposition in various forms. Governors and legislatures issued proclamations urging their people to withhold support from a "war against the public interest" and on several occasions refused to heed the president's call for militia. Derisively, the Federalists referred to the conflict as "Mr. Madison's War" and as a plot by Virginia to destroy New England. Worse still, they trafficked traitorously with the British forces in Canada and in adjacent waters, supplying provisions and military supplies as, at the same time, they loaned money to the English government. This disaffection seriously affected the American financing of the war. To raise money, Congress doubled the tariff, levied a direct tax on the states, and legislated excise and stamp taxes. None of the devices, however, provided sufficient funds, and the government had to resort to borrowing. Because most of the fluid capital was in the hands of New England commercial people, who opposed the war, bond issues did not find a ready market, and what bonds were purchased had to be heavily discounted to attract buyers.

The military campaign that the Administration launched one month after the declaration of war was a disaster from start to finish. It was directed against Canada, the only vulnerable British target within reach, in a three-pronged attack through the three natural gateways to British North America—Lake Champlain, Niagara, and Detroit. All three failed miserably and ignominiously (two of the three armies surrendered to the British) as a result, chiefly, of the incompetence of the commanders. Another attempt to take Canada in the following year was no more successful and for the same reason. Fortunately, the disasters on land were relieved in part by a series of victories at sea. In four engagements in scattered parts of the world, four British warships were forced to strike their colors in the face of superior American seamanship and fire power. And then there was the stunning victory of Oliver Hazard Perry on Lake Erie in September 1813. His report at the end of the battle—"We have met the enemy and they are ours"—was a modest account of his success for he destroyed every one of the enemy's ships. Another important naval victory was won by Captain Thomas McDonough on Lake Champlain in September 1814. He thereby frustrated a British attempt to split New England and New York from the rest of the country.

That effort was part of a larger plan undertaken by Britain after the final defeat of the French in April of that year released veteran troops for service in America. Moving troops across the Atlantic and landing them on the American coast presented no problem to the British for their navy had undisputed command of the seas. American naval strategy emphasized single-ship action and commerce raiding (500-odd American privateers that roamed the seas destroyed over 1,000 British merchant vessels), and so there never was an American fleet to challenge England's maritime supremacy. In fact, all through the war, the British easily maintained a blockade of American ports and raided the coast from the mouth of the Mississippi to New England and into Chesapeake Bay and the Delaware and Susquehanna rivers. So bold and successful were the British that panic spread up and down the coast and a scarcity of goods created hardship for many families. In the early summer of 1814, 14,000 seasoned soldiers from Wellington's army arrived in American waters without mishap.

The British plan was to strike at the United States through four gateways—Niagara, Lake Champlain, Chesapeake Bay, and New Orleans.

The able generalship of Jacob Brown frustrated the Niagara expedition. McDonough foiled the Lake Champlain venture. The move up the Chesapeake Bay had Baltimore for its objective, and it failed when the fortifications in the harbor held out against an all-night bombardment by a British fleet, a feat which led an American prisoner on one of the British ships, Francis Scott Key, to enshrine his pride that "the flag was still there" in the stanzas of "The Star Spangled Banner." The only satisfaction the British derived from the campaign came from the burning of the Capitol, the White House, all the public buildings, and a few homes in Washington on their way to attack Baltimore. The assault on New Orleans turned out to be a series of engagements lasting two weeks and ending on January 8, 1815 with a decisive victory by General Andrew Jackson at the head of a motley army of militia, regulars, Negro slaves, French from Louisiana, and local river pirates totalling 3,500 over a British force of 5,000 regulars, veterans of the Napoleonic War under General Sir Edward Pakenham. The Americans suffered only twenty-one casualties while British losses numbered 2,000 killed or wounded. Unfortunately, the triumph did not affect the outcome of the war, for two weeks earlier the representatives of England and the United States had signed a treaty of peace at Ghent in Belgium.

The negotiations at Ghent climaxed a long effort to make peace that had begun almost at the moment the war had broken out. Eight days after the declaration of war, Madison had opened a bid for peace on the basis of Britain ending the practice of impressment. But the foreign secretary, Lord Castlereagh, would not "suspend the exercise of a right upon which the naval strength of the empire mainly depends." A British initiative in October foundered on the same issue. Meanwhile in September, the Russian czar, having turned against France in favor of England, sought to end the war which was diverting his new ally from the main theatre of warfare in Europe. His offer to mediate was quickly accepted by President Madison, who sent Albert Gallatin and Senator James A. Bayard of Delaware to St. Petersburg to assist the American minister, John Quincy Adams, in the negotiations. Castlereagh rejected the suggestion, but when the Russians renewed it in September 1813, he replied by informing the American commissioners of his willingness to treat with them directly rather than through an intermediary.

The opportunity came at a propitious time for the United States. American fortunes were low while the British were marching from victory to victory on the European continent. Furthermore, the disaffection in New England was mounting, and a continuation of the war might easily have brought about rebellion. Already there was a growing demand by northeastern Federalists for a convention to act on their complaints. Such a convention did, in fact, meet in December of 1814, and, were it not for the fact that the moderates prevailed over the extremists, what might have been a secessionist movement turned out to be only a call for certain amendments to the Constitution to safeguard the rights of the states.

The negotiations for peace held at Ghent opened on August 14, 1814. The American delegation consisted of Adams, Gallatin, and Bayard augmented by Henry Clay, Speaker of the House of Representatives, and Jonathan Russell, the minister to Sweden. Representing Britain were Lord Gambier, a naval officer; Henry Goulburn, a minor official in the government; and William Adams, an admiralty lawyer. That the Americans were superior in every way to their British adversaries was clear to everyone and may be explained by the simple fact that all the talent the English could muster was at Vienna settling the more important questions attendant upon the defeat of Napoleon.

The British, learning of the successes in the Chesapeake Bay and expecting their veteran troops to win even greater victories, proposed extraordinary terms. They demanded the creation of a buffer Indian state between Canada and the United States (carved out of American territory); the cession of the part of Maine which they then occupied and a portion of New York state for a military road to connect St. John's (New Brunswick) with Quebec (useful because the St. Lawrence route to Quebec was frozen part of the year); free navigation for Englishmen of the Mississippi and the Great Lakes; and the surrender by the United States of the fishing rights off the Grand Banks guaranteed by the Treaty of 1783. The American delegation was aghast at this catalogue of terms that only a victor would dare impose on a humbled and humiliated foe. Adams, proud nationalist and quick to anger, prepared to pack his bags, but Gallatin, who turned out to be the peacemaker within the delegation, reconciling conflicting views and assuaging personal differences (chiefly between the Puritan and straight-laced Adams and the flamboyant, card-playing, hard-drinking Clay), persuaded him to remain. After all, the American demands were no more acceptable to Britain. They included Canada, the renunciation of the impressment practice, the acceptance of the traditional American position on blockade and contraband, compensation for confiscations of cargoes and vessels under the Orders-in-Council, and the return of Negro slaves taken away by the departing British.

What might have easily been a stalemate leading to a halt in negotiations developed rapidly into an amiable meeting of minds and an agreement. For this happy turn of affairs, Americans can thank the distresses that confronted Britain in the fall and winter of 1814. In Vienna, the victorious allies were bickering over the distribution of the spoils of war; in France, there were stirrings of sentiment for a restoration of the defeated Emperor; in America McDonough's victory on Champlain and the British repulse before Baltimore so changed Britain's position as to cause the Duke of Wellington to remark, "I think. . . . [England has] no right from the state of the war to demand any concession of territory from America." The prime minister, Lord Liverpool, agreed with the Iron Duke, and Castlereagh at once instructed the delegation to come to terms with the Americans. Madison, on his part, was no less anxious to conclude peace.

In November and December, each delegation removed from its lists of demands all the features that the other side deemed objectionable until by December 24 nothing remained and a treaty was signed. The treaty simply stated that hostilities would cease and all captured territory would be restored. No mention was made of those controversial issues that had caused the war. Nothing was said about Canada, impressment, neutral rights, or Indians (except that both sides pledged to stop fighting Indians as well as each other).

The treaty reached the United States on February 14, 1815, and three days later the Senate unanimously advised ratifications. On the 18th, the war was declared at an end. Jubilation was universal, and celebrations were held all over the country. For some, the joy was diluted by the feeling that the war was fought in vain and that the sacrifices had been for naught. They agreed with Adams' pessimistic observation, "Neither party gave up anything, all the points of collision which had subsisted between them before the war were left open. . . . Nothing was adjusted, nothing was settled—nothing in substance. . . ." On the other hand, there were people who saw the war as productive of substantial and significant results for the United States. They noted the great increase in manufacturing in New England caused by the difficulty of importing finished products from abroad during the conflict. They knew that while their armies and navies had suffered several defeats, there had been some stunning victories, which had led Europeans to view the United States with a new respect.

Indeed, in the eyes of the great powers, the United States had come of age in the war; in that sense, the war could justly be called the Second War for Independence. Those same people were aware that while the conflict had not settled the issues between the two nations, it had not raised any new ones, as wars so often do. (They would have been even more pleased had they been able to see into the future that some of the old issues which had bothered the two nations would cease to have relevance in the peaceful nineteenth century.) Finally, they saw the war as a great stimulator of nationalism. The exploits of Perry, McDonough, and Jackson had filled the whole nation with pride. Federalists and Republicans, northerners, southerners, and westerners all thrilled to the achievements of the heroes. Albert Gallatin put the matter neatly when he said, "The war has been productive of evil and of good, but I think the good preponderates. . . . The war has renewed and reinforced the national feelings and character which the Revolution had given, and which were daily lessening. The people have now more general objects of attachments, with which their pride and political opinions are connected. They are more Americans, they feel and act more as a nation; and I hope that the permanency of the Union is thereby better secured."

If the war had settled none of the differences between the two countries, at least some issues were resolved in the years immediately following Ghent in a series of agreements. There were several Anglo-American problems that had to be adjusted if peace were to continue—commercial relations, fisheries, the Canadian-American boundary, and rivalry on the Great Lakes. By 1818, they were all settled thanks to the conciliatory policy of Lord Castlereagh, the British foreign secretary. Castlereagh sought repose for his country: England needed time to recover from having defeated Napoleon in the greatest war in her history, and war with another power was to be avoided. Least of all did Castlereagh want a conflict with the United States, Britain's best customer and a threat to Canada. He was, as his biographer noted, "the first British statesman to recognize that the friendship of the United States was a major asset to Britain"; he, therefore, approached the problems across the Atlantic in a spirit of generosity and with a willingness to compromise. His magnanimity was all the more remarkable in view of a certain amount of hostility felt by Englishmen for Americans in the postwar period that was compounded from jealousy over America's growing economic strength and fear of being dislodged from their worldwide pre-eminence. As the British Prime Minister warned shortly after the war, "The views and policies of North Americans seem mainly directed toward supplanting us in navigation in every quarter of the globe. Let us recollect that as their commercial marine is augmented, their military marine must be proportionately increased."

As for the United States, settlement with Britain would have been difficult, even if it were possible, had there been, after the war, a political situation similar to the 1790s. At that time each of the two parties was linked with either France or Britain, and the pro-French Republicans obstructed every Federalist effort to come to an understanding with Britain while pro-English Federalists viewed Republican suggestions to assist France as traitorous. Now, however, the postwar period was characterized by Jefferson's observation in 1801, "We are all Republicans, we are all Federalists." There were no obstructionists.

The first matter approached related to the rivalry of the two powers on the Great Lakes. Immediately after the war had ended, the British began to rebuild their fleet on Lake Erie and Lake Ontario. A strong patrolling force was needed to prevent Americans from smuggling goods into Canada and British soldiers from deserting to the United States army. Although Congress had authorized the president in February 1815 to reduce the American navy on the lakes, there seemed to be no choice in the face of British rearmament but to follow suit. Soon, a naval race was in progress. In London, John Quincy Adams, the American minister, acting under

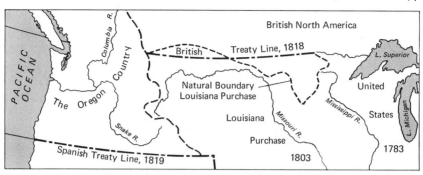

The Agreement of 1818 with Great Britain.

instructions from Washington, urged upon Castlereagh the wisdom of ending the competition, which was not only costly but a threat to peace.

Pressure on the foreign secretary from Canadians who maintained that only by a large force on the lakes could their territory be safe from an American invasion stood in the way of an agreement. When, however, Adams suggested that eventually the United States would be in a position to outbuild Britain on the lakes and that the surest protection for Canada lay in the mutual reduction of armament, the Canadians yielded, and the path to an understanding was opened. The result was an agreement signed in Washington by Richard Rush, the Acting American Secretary of State, and Charles Bagot, the British minister, on April 29, 1818, which provided that each power keep only four vessels on the lakes—one on Champlain, one on Ontario, and two on the others. No ship could exceed 100 tons or carry more armament than one 18-pound cannon. At Castlereagh's instigation, Monroe submitted the agreement to the Senate for approval so that it would have the force of a treaty. As negotiated, it was an "executive agreement" and not binding on succeeding administrations. Demilitarization on the lakes was the prelude to the abandonment of land fortifications along the border. As the years went on and peace became the norm between the United States and England, the need for strong places diminished and finally disappeared. By the 1870s, the Canadian-American boundary became the world's longest "unguarded frontier."

On October 20, 1818, another important treaty was signed that laid to rest the problems of the fisheries and the delimitation of the Canadian-American boundary and renewed a commercial convention signed in 1815 and due to expire in 1819. With peace restored in 1815, Yankee fishing vessels went back to those areas off the Newfoundland Grand Banks that had been assigned them by the Treaty of 1783. The British, however, maintained that those "privileges" had been abrogated by the War of 1812, and their warships proceeded to bar Americans from the fishing grounds. In London, Adams presented to Castlereagh every conceivable

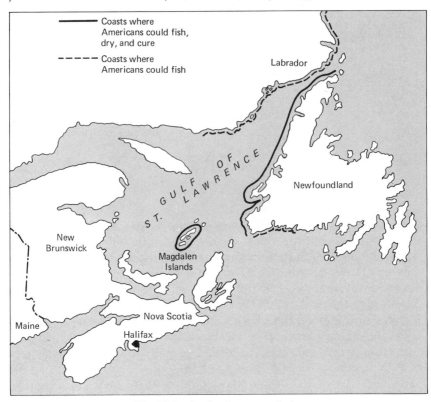

Coasts where
Americans could fish,
dry, and cure

---- Coasts where
Americans could fish

The Fisheries Settlement, 1818.

argument for restoring the "privileges." He pointed out that New England depended on fishing for its livelihood, that deprived of this source of revenue it could buy no British goods, and, finally, he hinted that the hardy fishermen might well use force to protect their "rights." Once again, Castlereagh fended off the Canadians, who wished to retain the industry for themselves, in favor of good relations with the United States and indicated his willingness to restore the "privileges" to American fishermen. This was accomplished in the Convention of 1818, which also included the rectification of the boundary. The Treaty of 1783 had settled the boundary from the Atlantic to the Lake of the Woods; now the 49th Parallel from that lake to the Rocky Mountains was designated the northern limit of the United States. West of the mountains lay the territory known as Oregon (from the Columbia River on the south to 54° 40′ on the north), which both nations claimed. Because neither power would yield and because the area was not considered important enough to fight over, it was decided to push a settlement of the issue into the future. Thus, the treaty provided that the area would be "free and open" to the citizens of both countries. This situation, which was loosely termed "joint occupation" was, technically, an "unorganized condominium."

The extension of the commercial agreement of 1815 for a ten-year period without modification reflected the single failure by the United States to extract a concession from Castlereagh. It will be recalled that the provisions of Jay's Treaty concerning trade between the two countries had lapsed in 1807. As a result of conversations in London in 1814 during the peace negotiations, a treaty was signed in July 1815 that granted Americans commercial privileges in the ports of Great Britain. Clay and Gallatin had tried to include the ports of Canada and the British West Indies but had failed because Castlereagh could not afford to alienate the powerful merchants in England who did not wish to have American vessels compete with theirs in the profitable carrying trade to those places. Equally unsuccessful had been the attempt to get Castlereagh to renounce the rights of impressment. Then it had been the influential navalists who refused to surrender so formidable a weapon in any future war. In 1818, these same strictures operated on the foreign secretary so that the American negotiators could effect no change in British policy. There was no disputing the fact, however, that, all in all, the postwar settlements were important in laying to rest some of the principal causes for disagreement between the two English-speaking peoples.

BIBLIOGRAPHY

IRVING BRANT, *James Madison, the President: 1809–1812* (1956).
ROGER BROWN, *The Republic in Peril, 1812* (1964).
W. H. GOODMAN, "The Origins of the War of 1812: A Survey of Changing Interpretations," *Mississippi Valley Historical Review*, 28 (1941), 171–186.
REGINALD HORSMAN, *The Causes of the War of 1812* (1962).
JOHN K. MAHON, *The War of 1812* (1974).
BRADFORD PERKINS, *Prologue to War: England and the United States, 1805–1812* (1961).
JULIUS PRATT, *Expansionists of 1812* (1925).

War stimulated U.S. productively

John Quincy Adams (courtesy of the National Portrait Gallery, Smithsonian Institution, Washington, D.C.).

The Achievements of
Monroe's Administration:
A Treaty and a Doctrine

IT WAS during James Monroe's administration that the important settlements with England were made after the war, and it was during his administration, also, that two other notable events in the diplomatic history of the United States took place—the treaty with Spain in 1819 and the enunciation of the famous doctrine which bears his name.

The Spanish-American treaty was a great achievement. It gained for the United States the strategic peninsula of Florida and delimited the country's western boundary giving it, for the first time, a foothold on the shores of the Pacific Ocean. Florida had long been coveted by Americans. A Spanish province for most of the eighteenth century, it was ceded to England in 1763 and returned to Spain twenty years later as part of the general settlement following the American Revolutionary War. In British hands, it was divided into East and West Florida at the Appalachicola River, a division the Spanish retained after 1783 for administrative purposes. In the instructions to Robert Livingston to purchase New Orleans, Jefferson had included one or both of the Floridas. When Livingston bought all of Louisiana, the question was whether Florida was a part of it. His only clue as to the eastern boundary of the territory lay in the language of the treaty, "with the same extent that it now has in the hands of Spain, and that it had when France possessed it; . . . ."

Investigation revealed that Florida was never a part of Spanish Louisiana but the western part of it, from the Mississippi River to the Perdido, was definitely a part of French Louisiana. It was up to Jefferson to make good America's claim to that portion of Florida as against Spain.

Quite naturally, Spain would not think of surrendering West Florida.

The entire Louisiana transaction was, in her view, illegal and immoral. Nonetheless, Jefferson was sanguine. "We shall certainly obtain the Floridas, and all in good time," he said in 1803. At his request, Congress, on February 24, 1804, authorized him to annex the land bought from France east of the Mississippi and erect there a customs district. That the president did some three months later by proclamation although he was careful to designate as the port of that district a fort on the Mobile River north of the 31st parallel, clearly in American territory.

When Spain in 1804 entered the recently resumed Franco-British war on the side of France, Jefferson sought to take advantage of Spain's predicament. He suggested an agreement by which Madrid would give up both Floridas in exchange for the assumption by the United States of various claims its citizens had against Spain. When Spain refused, the president turned to intrigue with France. The French foreign minister let it be known that if Spain were offered $7 million, money that the French government needed desperately and that it planned to take at once from Spain, Spain would be prevailed upon to hand Florida to the United States. Jefferson jumped at the opportunity and at once sought and obtained from Congress an appropriation of $2 million to begin negotiations. Unhappily for the president, they did not progress very far because Napoleon, fresh from a series of stunning victories, found his treasury replenished and his ideas about Spain changed. He now placed his brother, Joseph, on that ancient throne and coveted the country, with its possessions undiminished, for himself. So came to an end Jefferson's last hope for gaining the Floridas before leaving office in 1809.

His successor, James Madison, was no less certain that "the manifest course of events" would result in the annexation of the Spanish provinces. Nor was he backward in hastening the course of events. In October of 1810, following the seizure of Baton Rouge by some Americans and their proclamation of a "free and independent" West Florida, Madison announced the extension of American jurisdiction over West Florida up to the Perdido River as a part of the territory of Louisiana. Unwilling, however, to clash with Spanish troops garrisoned in Mobile, the president authorized American soldiers to occupy only the area west of the Pearl River. At the same time, fearful that chaotic conditions in Spain might lead to a foreign power taking possession of Florida, Congress at the president's request, passed a resolution on January 15, 1811 declaring that the United States "cannot, without serious inquietude, see any part of the said territory [Florida] pass into the hands of any foreign power."

To forestall that possibility and in accordance with authorization by Congress, Madison moved to take over East Florida. With a former governor of Georgia named George Mathews, he plotted to effect an uprising in that province as a prelude to its incorporation into the United States. In 1812, Mathews succeeded in capturing Amelia Island and several places on the mainland but so blatant was American official connivance that Madison had to disavow the entire adventure. He did, however, legalize the hold on West Florida by getting Congress to annex formally West Florida between the Mississippi and the Pearl Rivers to the new state of Louisiana on April 14, 1812 and the remainder between the Pearl and the Perdido Rivers to the Territory of Mississippi on May 14, 1812. One month later, the United States was at war with Great Britain.

It was no secret that East Florida, owned by Britain's ally, was considered by southern and southwestern Americans as an objective of the war, and one week after the war message, Congress authorized the president to take possession of the province. But no conquest was made in the course of the war. Indeed, military operations in the Floridas were minimal. General Andrew Jackson made an abortive stab at Pensacola and General James Wilkinson captured Mobile. By the end of the war, the prewar situation was unchanged—the United States in possession of West Florida; Spain still holding East Florida. There was one difference, however, and an all-important one. The policy-makers in Madrid were aware of their inability to hold East Florida much longer. Weakened by the war and faced with a formidable revolution in their South American colonies, they were powerless to defend the Crown's possessions in Florida. Thus, the decision was made to surrender that territory to the United States in exchange for a favorable boundary separating the United States from New Spain.

The Spanish minister to Washington, Don Luís de Onís, so informed Secretary of State James Monroe in 1816, proposing that the two Floridas become American, that pecuniary claims against Spain by American citizens be funded by the United States, and that the Spanish-American boundary in the west be set at the Mississippi River. This last stipulation was, of course, an impossible one for the United States. It would have meant renouncing the vast territory bought from France where many Americans had already settled and out of which one state, Louisiana, had already been carved. Madrid, apparently, did not expect Washington docilely to accept the proposal and had provided de Onís with alternate instructions to push for the best boundary obtainable.

The negotiation of that boundary for the American side fell to John Quincy Adams, who took over as President Monroe's secretary of state in September of 1817. Adams believed it would be a difficult task to secure for his country the best bargain, given the qualities of his adversary. De Onís was a seasoned and experienced diplomat, scion of a distinguished and noble family of Moorish stock, and, in Adams' words, "Cold, calculating, wily, always commanding his own temper, proud because he is a Spaniard, but supple and cunning, accommodating the tone of his pretensions precisely to the degree of endurance of his opponent, bold and overbearing to the utmost extent to which it is tolerated, careless of what he asserts and how grossly it is proved to be unfounded, his morality appears to be that of the Jesuits as exposed by Pascal. He is laborious, vigilant, and ever attentive to his duties; a man of business and of the world."

Yet, Adams was a match for de Onís. Himself seasoned and experienced, having served in numerous posts abroad, and of an equally distinguished lineage, he was no less wily, cunning, supple, and proud. Indeed, it could be said that he enjoyed an advantage in that he spoke for a restless, aggressive, and vigorous country whose people were voracious for land and determined to let no obstacle bar their march across the continent, while the Spaniard represented a waning and exhausted nation facing the dissolution of its three hundred-year-old empire and struggling to salvage whatever might be salvageable.

For a time, de Onís and his superiors in Madrid hoped that they could enlist the European powers against the grasping ambition of Americans to possess all of North America. In June of 1818, de Onís urged his opposite numbers in Paris and London to warn the French and British foreign offices that "If all of Europe or its principal governments do not take steps in time against the scandalous ambition of this Republic and obstruct the well established schemes of conquest which she has set for herself, it may well be too late and she may be master of Cuba, Mexico, Canada, and whatever regions suit her." But the powers did not take up the challenge. England had just finished the long and arduous struggle against Napoleon and had no stomach for more controversy. At that moment, too, her diplomats were engaged in negotiations for the settlement of differences with the United States and to have jeopardized them on Spain's account would have been folly. Not even the possibility of gaining Florida in exchange for support moved Castlereagh. Two months earlier, he had made his position perfectly clear in an instruction to the British minister in Washington: "The avowed and true policy of Great Britain . . . in the existing state of the world [is] to appease controversy . . . and to secure, if possible, for all states a long interval of repose." His advice to Spain was to give up Florida and "secure, on the side of Mexico, the best frontier that circumstances will admit of her obtaining in exchange for so serious a concession on her part."

Nor was France any more inclined to help rescue Florida for Spain. Whatever feelings of guilt Paris may have felt for the shabby and dishonorable treatment of Madrid on Louisiana were offset by a reluctance to clash with the United States. An offer by Spain of Santo Domingo as the price for support could not alter the French decision to stand aloof from the controversy. France's American policy was publicly stated some months earlier in a toast by the French minister at a July 4 celebration to "the perpetuity of the assured blessings of the United States."

So de Onís found himself facing Adams in Washington without foreign backing as he had hoped. There was no question about Florida becoming

American territory; the negotiations concerned the boundary in the west. The Spaniard was willing to retreat from his former stand at the Mississippi River to a new line marked by the Sabine River to its source, then northward to the Missouri River and along that river to its source. But Adams would not accept the proposal since it left Texas to Spain and countered with the line of the Rio Grande River as a maximum and the Colorado River (of Texas) as a minimum.

As the two diplomats discussed their differences in the spring of 1818, an event occurred which renewed de Onís's hope of British support. In March, General Andrew Jackson in pursuing some Indians who had attacked American settlements in southern Georgia crossed the border into Florida and seized two British subjects, whom he suspected of aiding and inciting the Indian marauders. After a court martial, he shot one of them and hanged the other. The British public was outraged at Jackson's conduct. In London, the American minister, Richard Rush, reported, "excitement seemed to rise higher and higher" and the temper of the country was so bellicose that Castlereagh believed "war might have been produced by holding up a finger." But the foreign secretary did not hold up a finger and de Onís' hopes faded.

There was, however, a serious domestic repercussion from Jackson's expedition into Florida that might have helped Spain except for Adams' handling of the situation. The general's political enemies, notably Henry Clay, seeking to embarrass him, introduced resolutions in Congress censuring him for invading foreign territory without authorization. Whether, in fact, Jackson had orders to invade Florida and to capture the two Spanish towns, St. Marks and Pensacola (the latter the seat of government of West Florida), is debatable. He insisted that he had received the president's approval through an intermediary; Monroe denied it. Secretary of War John C. Calhoun, to whom Jackson had reported his victory, urged the president to reprimand the general, and Calhoun's colleagues in the Cabinet supported him, save one—the secretary of state.

It was not Jackson who ought to be censured, said Adams, but rather Spain, which was bound by the Treaty of 1795 to restrain the Indians in her territory. Jackson had every right to pursue the invaders into Spanish territory, he argued, and his action ought to be supported. The spirited defense of Jackson plus the tremendous popularity of his cause in the country led the president to accept Adams' position. At the same time, the resolutions of censure in Congress failed. Thus was averted a sharp division in the government and in the nation that might have tied Adams' hands in the negotiation.

To mollify de Onís who in his anger at the infringement of Spanish sovereignty had broken off conversations with Adams, the secretary of state informed the minister that the two places Jackson had taken would be restored. De Onís, thereupon, returned to the bargaining table; the time was October 1818. For the next four months, the two diplomats haggled over the western boundary—de Onís insisting on the Sabine; Adams holding to the Rio Grande on the Colorado. But so eager was Spain to make a treaty (de Onís realized that without one, Florida would be lost to the United States with no compensation on the western boundary) that Adams probably could have gotten all of Texas or part of it had Monroe not intervened and instructed him to accept the Sabine.

Monroe's decision to surrender Texas, which had the support of the cabinet, was based on the view that Florida mattered much more than Texas and holding out for the former might jeopardize the latter. But there was, also, a political coloration to the decision at least as far as William H. Crawford, the secretary of the treasury, was concerned. As an aspirant for the presidency, he saw a rival in Adams. Were Texas to be obtained by the treaty, it would add to Adams' popularity and enhance his chances in the upcoming election; were it to be lost, Adams' support in the country would be seriously diminished for, in either case, the responsibility would rest with the secretary of state. And Adams was, indeed, later blamed, particularly by westerners, for having given up Texas.

Restricted to the Sabine by the president, Adams' objective was to secure the best possible boundary north of the Sabine. So he set out to push de Onís from the Missouri River line to one that would run across the continent westward to the Pacific Ocean for that was now Adams' great dream. "After a long and violent struggle" (to use his own words), he succeeded, and on February 22, 1819, the two negotiators signed a treaty that set the boundary between the two countries west of the Mississippi at a line running along the Sabine to the 32° degree of latitude, north to the Red River, along that river to the 100th meridian, north to the Arkansas River, along that river to the 42° degree of latitude, and along that line to the Pacific. The treaty also transferred to the United States East and West Florida and provided that the United States would assume the valid claims of its citizens against Spain up to $5 million.

The country was elated by the treaty and it passed the Senate by unanimous vote in two days. The only sour note was registered by Henry Clay and some of his western friends who blamed Adams for not holding out for Texas. But for the vast majority of Americans, Texas and the trans-Mississippi west were not nearly as important as Florida and, indeed, the treaty was known popularly as the Florida Treaty. Adams himself, however, considered Florida less important than the transcontinental gains and for those he took the credit. "The acknowledgement of a definite line of boundary to the South Sea [Pacific Ocean] forms a great epocha in our history," he noted in his diary on the day he signed the treaty. "The first proposal of it in this negotiation was my own, and I trust it is now secured beyond the reach of revocation."

For a time it appeared that the great diplomatic victory would slip out

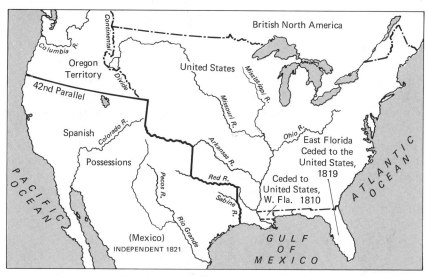

The Adams-Onís Treaty Line, 1819.

of Adams' hands. The treaty called for an exchange of ratifications within six months, but that limit passed without any action by Spain. It seems that the authorities in Madrid had second thoughts about the treaty. Too much territory had been surrendered without commensurate concessions, they believed. They demanded, too, that before ratification Adams promise not to aid or recognize the rebellious Spanish colonies in South America, which he refused to do. Adams was vastly upset by Spain's failure to ratify the treaty, and he was prepared to recommend to the president that force be used to enforce the treaty. Many people in the country shared his view and were ready to follow Andrew Jackson who suggested "the mouth of the cannon" as a suitable means.

Force, however, proved unnecessary. America's bellicose stance was enough to convince the Spanish who really were not in a position for a showdown. On October 24, 1820, the king ratified the treaty. At once, President Monroe resubmitted it to the Senate, which approved it on February 18, 1821. So Adams got his victory after all. Florida was secure and the boundary of the country ran all the way to the Pacific. The loss of Texas was still an issue in the west, where, as Henry Clay said, "Texas was worth ten Floridas" and four western senators had voted against the treaty because Texas was not included. But Adams did not mourn its loss. His views on Texas and, indeed, on expansionism in general were undergoing a radical change. The violent debate on the question of slavery in Missouri in the winter of 1819–1820 had shown him how dangerous to the well-being of the country the issue of slavery in newly acquired land could be. Had Texas been gained, it would have generated such a problem. In his diary entry of April 13, 1820, he noted ominously, "Since the Missouri debate, I considered the continuance of the Union for any length of time as very precarious, and entertained serious doubts whether Louisiana and slavery would not ultimately break us up. . . ." Clearly, expansionism had a price which Adams had come to believe was too high.

In the other diplomatic milestone of the Monroe administration, the Monroe Doctrine, John Quincy Adams also played a significant part. That notable policy had its origin in the revolutions of Spain's colonies in the New World and in a presumptuous declaration by the czar of Russia. The invasion of Spain by Napoleon Bonaparte in 1808 led to the dethronement of King Ferdinand VII and the weakening of Spain's rule in her New World colonies. As a consequence, separatist movements took form all over South and Central America. When the news of the uprisings reached the United States, sympathy for the revolutionists was immediate and overwhelming. The Latin Americans seemed to be repeating the stirring days of 1776, and Americans felt responsible for their ardor. Traders and merchants from North America had, indeed, carried copies of the Declaration of Independence and the Constitution southward and had pointed out the advantages of independence while Latin American leaders, such as Francisco Miranda and Simon Bolívar, had on visits to the United States imbibed the lessons of the Revolution. Some years later, Henry Clay gave expression to this attitude when he said, "We are their great example. Of us they constantly speak as brothers. They adopt our principle, copy our institutions, and in many instances employ the language and sentiment of our revolutionary papers."

Sympathy, however, was one thing, aid and recognition of independence was quite another. Thomas Jefferson, president at the time, followed a wary course. Although he was drawn ideologically to the revolutionists and saw great economic possibilities for the United States in a Latin America free of Spanish rule, he wisely abstained from interfering in the struggle, at least until the revolutions gave reasonable promise of success. (Premature recognition would have been, according to international law, a gratuitous insult to the mother country.) James Madison continued his predecessor's careful policy lest brashness offend Spain from whom, it was hoped, Florida would be obtained. He exchanged unofficial emissaries with several of the revolutionary governments, opened American ports to their privateers, and permitted them to purchase supplies but refused to give direct aid (as France had given in 1776) or promise recognition of their independence.

When Monroe succeeded to the White House, there were even more compelling reasons for moving cautiously. Negotiations with Spain over Florida and the west were in progress; the rebel fortunes appeared to be waning and the likelihood of their making good their independence seemed to be dimming. Finally, European nations (Russia, Prussia, Britain, and Austria) that had defeated Napoleon and were now joined in a Quadruple Alliance (a fifth country, France, under the restored Bourbons was added in 1818) to suppress any revolutions in Europe that threatened the peace and the postwar settlement were talking of crossing the ocean to help restore Spanish rule in the Americas. Were the United States to extend recognition to the new republics and were they reconquered for Spain, the Alliance might well retaliate against Washington. The president, therefore, made certain that America would not become involved by having Congress enact two neutrality statutes in 1817 and 1818 and by engineering the defeat in the House of Representatives in 1818 of a resolution, supported by western congressmen hostile to Spain, to recognize the independence of the republics.

Soon, however, the basis for the cautious policy of nonrecognition crumbled. The Spanish-American settlement was finally made in 1821; the rebel fortunes improved greatly between 1819 and 1822 and their independent existence appeared secure. The European concert, moreover, seemed unable to agree on mounting an invasion of South America. Seeing no reason for withholding recognition any longer, Monroe, in March 1822, asked Congress to appropriate $100,000 to send diplomatic missions to "the independent nations of the American continent." Still there were complications, and serious ones. At a congress held in Verona, Italy, in 1822, the allied powers authorized France to send an army into Spain to liberate King Ferdinand VII, who had been held a virtual prisoner by rebel forces since 1820. The French succeeded in freeing the king and restored him to power, after which Ferdinand urged the Allies to reassert his rule in his former colonies in America. Early in 1822, rumors reached the United States that a large Franco-Spanish force might soon be en route to America and that Spain would cede Cuba to France as a reward for her aid. Fear and alarm spread in the United States at the prospect of an invasion of the western hemisphere by European troops and the transfer of territory that many Americans themselves coveted.

These same reports were heard in England, too, and caused equally great consternation there. The British had much to lose by a restoration of Spanish rule in the Americas. One of the first acts of the revolutionary governments had been to open to ships of all nations their ports that had under Spanish law been closed to all foreigners, and the result had been a tremendous increase in British trade in Latin America. A reassertion of Spanish control would surely mean the reimposition of the exclusive commercial system and the end of the lucrative traffic for Englishmen. It was essential for Britain's economic well-being that European intervention in the New World be forestalled. To achieve that end, George Canning, the foreign secretary, turned to the United States for support. On August 20, 1823, he proposed to Richard Rush, the American minister in London, that their two governments unite in "a joint disapprobation of such projects [intervention]." Since both countries opposed the recovery of the colonies by Spain and the transfer of any part of them to another power why, he said, "should we hesitate mutually to confide them to each other; and to declare them in the face of the world?"

One may well wonder why the world's greatest empire, possessing a navy capable of thwarting any maritime expedition, should feel the need to solicit the cooperation of a nation only forty-two years in existence and possessing virtually no fighting ships. Two theories have been advanced that, taken together, provide an adequate answer. One is that Canning stood absolutely alone facing all the other European powers and any ally, even one weak and relatively inconsequential, was welcome and would help in creating a balance of power. A second is that the foreign secretary really was not interested in America's military assistance or in the European balance but rather in the American market. As "the unconscious servant of . . . British spindles and furnaces," he was courting American good will in the hopes of increasing the number of overseas customers.

Whatever Canning's true motivation may have been, to Minister Rush the significance of the proposal was at once apparent. He saw in it the means for insuring the defeat of the allied schemes, and he was prepared, even without instructions, to join Britain in a statement provided Canning first acknowledge the independence of the new republics. Because neither king nor cabinet were yet willing to sanction rebellion against lawful authority (England had an empire full of potential rebels), Canning could not accept Rush's terms, whereupon the minister sent the proposal home. President Monroe was inclined to accept the British offer, and his two predecessors in office, whose advice he sought, both urged him to join Canning. Jefferson even went so far as to sanction "fighting once more, side by side, in the same cause" doubtlessly recalling the eighteenth-century wars against France.

There was, however, one powerful voice raised against a joint Anglo-American declaration. At a cabinet meeting on November 7, the secretary of state raised strong objections to accepting Canning's proposal. He believed "It would be more candid, as well as more dignified to avow our principles explicitly to Russia and France than to come in as a cockboat in the wake of a British man-of-war." Adams' ardent nationalism could not accept a subordinate position for his country, but it was not only pride and honor that underlay his disapproval. Canning had included in his proposition the words, "We aim not at the possession of any portion of them [Spanish possessions] ourselves," which Adams perceived at once as a subterfuge designed to prevent the acquisition of Cuba by the United States. Did the United States really want to sign such a self-denying ordinance, he asked, when it was commonly expected that someday Cuba would become part of the Union? Monroe and the Cabinet accepted Adams' argument and the decision was made for a unilateral declaration.

At another Cabinet meeting later in the month, the president presented the draft of a proposed declaration. It contained a warning to the European allies not to interfere in the affairs of the republics in the New World or in the revolutions then taking place in Greece and Spain. Once again Adams protested, this time against Monroe's intrusion into purely European matters. The United States, he claimed, ought not concern itself with extra-hemisphere problems; "the European as well as the American systems should be kept as separate and distinct from each other as possible." Further, he urged that Monroe include a reference to the ominous advance of Russia down the west coast of North America. From its headquarters in Alaska, the Russian-American Company had gradually been extending its operations southward. In 1816, a trading post had been established at Fort Ross, a short distance north of San Francisco Bay in Spanish California, and in 1821, the czar issued a pronouncement prohibiting foreign vessels from approaching within 100 miles of the coast from Alaska to 51° north latitude, which included a sizable portion of the Oregon territory claimed by the United States. Both these suggestions Monroe accepted, and in the Doctrine which bears his name the ideas of his secretary of state are prominent.

On December 2, 1823, the president sent Congress his seventh annual message. As in all such documents, the president spoke of many things—domestic and foreign. He reported on the nation's financial condition, the state of the army and navy, the progress of road and canal construction and of exploration in the west, and mentioned the efforts to settle disputes with certain foreign powers. Imbedded, rather unobtrusively and in two widely separated paragraphs in the message, were two statements: (1) "The American continents, by the free and independent condition which they have assumed and maintain, are henceforth not to be considered as subjects for the future colonization by any European powers;" (2) "The political system of the Allied Powers is essentially different . . . from that of America. . . . We owe it, therefore, to candor and to the amicable relations existing between the United States and those powers to declare that we should consider any attempt on their part to extend their system to any portion of this hemisphere as dangerous to our peace and safety."

These two passages constitute the Monroe Doctrine—the first directed against Russia and known as the noncolonizing clause; the second aimed at the European powers contemplating intervention in South America and called the two-hemispheres idea. As time went on, Monroe's words became one of the most important of America's foreign policies accepted by Americans of every class, section, and party as incontrovertible. Typical of the American view was the full-page advertisement in the *New York Times* in 1823, at the time of the centennial celebration, which announced that "the Monroe Doctrine is as binding upon Americans as our God-inspired Constitution." As time went on, too, the powers of the world came to respect the determination and the power of the United

States to enforce the ideas of the Doctrine. By the beginning of the twentieth century, few of them were prepared to challenge America's guardianship of the western hemisphere.

At the time of the Doctrine's enunciation, however, it did not make a very great imprint either at home or abroad. In America, it certainly was not considered a momentous statement of far-reaching and long-range significance. It was both praised and criticized—"an empty menace" and "wise . . . [and] magnanimous." But soon, it fell from view and for the next quarter century, the principles were inoperative. Several French escapades in South America and Mexico were not even protested by the United States, and the British annexation of Argentina's Falkland Islands in 1833 and extension of the boundaries of British Honduras were uncontested.

Abroad, Monroe's statement was received with scorn. The Russians considered that it "merits only the most profound contempt." The Austrian premier called it "an indecent declaration." A leading French newspaper remarked, "Mr. Monroe, who is not a sovereign, has assumed in his message the tone of a powerful monarch, whose armies and fleets are ready to march at the first signal. . . . Mr. Monroe is the temporary President of a Republic situated on the east coast of North America. This republic is bounded on the south by the possessions of the King of Spain, and on the north by those of the King of England. Its independence was only recognized forty years ago; by what right then would the two Americas today be under its immediate sway from Hudson's Bay to Cape Horn?"

Certainly, the plans of the powers were unaffected by Monroe's warning. It was true, of course, that there was no invasion of South America, but that achievement was Canning's. It was he who, in October of 1823, had, in a series of conferences with the Duke de Polignac, French ambassador in London, exacted a pledge, incorporated in the Polignac Memorandum, whereby France renounced any intention to intervene in Spanish America. It was true, too, that Russia retreated northward from the 51st parallel and made no effort to enforce the prohibition against foreign vessels, but the cause lay in difficulties inside Russia.

As for Latin America, the most striking reaction was in the request by emissaries from Colombia, Brazil, and Mexico in 1824 and 1825 for an explanation of the means to be taken by the United States to implement the Monrovian principles. Rumors of an expedition sailing from Cadiz to Peru led to the question of precisely how the United States planned to resist the enemy. After expressing his government's great pleasure over the Message, the representative of Colombia, Don José Maria Salazar, asked Secretary Adams, "Will [the United States] enter into a Treaty of Alliance with the Republic of Colombia to save America in general from the calamities of a despotic system?" Adams reply was not encouraging, but it represented honestly the American view of the scope of the Message.

Having first dismissed the dangers from Europe as unreal, he went on to say that should a crisis arise, "The United States could not undertake resistance . . . by force of arms without a previous understanding with those European Powers, whose interests and whose principles would secure from them an active and efficient cooperation. . . ." To Salazar and the other South American diplomats it was clear that American leadership could not be expected. For their protection they would have to look to Britain and to the Polignac Memorandum, which Canning, cannily, had made public in March of 1824. The British foreign secretary, irked by Monroe's having "stolen a march" on him by the Message, was not displeased to stand revealed as the true protector of the Latin Americans.

All this is not to say that Monroe's statement was without contemporary importance. It was important for what it said of the American dream and of the American spirit and because it summarized the ideas and attitudes that had been taking shape since the beginning of the Republic. In it could be seen the deep-seated yearning to steer clear of European affairs that Washington had voiced in his Farewell Address and succeeding presidents had expressed in various ways. It was a statement of the passion for republicanism and for the rights of nations to govern themselves. South Americans, no less than North Americans, should be permitted to choose the forms of government under which they best could achieve happiness. It was an expression of confidence in the country's future expansion. Neither Russia nor any other power would be free to found new colonies on the continents. The United States would fill in all those places not already in a colonial status. It was, also, and, above all, a manifesto of nationalism, an act of defiance hurled at the "conquerors of Bonoparte, with their laurels still green and blooming on their brows." It was an announcement that the destiny of the western hemisphere would be determined by the United States. The "young republic, whose existence, as yet, cannot be measured with the ordinary life of man," alone would be mistress of the American system and the center of a new mercantilist empire.

BIBLIOGRAPHY

Samuel F. Bemis, *John Quincy Adams and the Foundations of American Foreign Policy* (1949).

C. C. Griffin, *The United States and the Disruption of the Spanish Empire, 1810–1822* (1937).

Bradford Perkins, *Castlereagh and Adams: England and the United States, 1812–1823* (1964).

Dexter Perkins, *The Monroe Doctrine, 1823–1826* (1927).

Edward H. Tatum, Jr., *The United States and Europe, 1815–1823* (1936).

Arthur P. Whitaker, *The United States and the Independence of Latin America, 1800–1830* (1941).

James K. Polk (courtesy of the Bettmann Archives).

Texas and Mexico

THE CONFIDENCE in the country's future expansion as implied in the Monroe Doctrine reflected a widespread popular mood at the time and was to be very much a hallmark of America during the next three decades. Vast numbers of Americans—Whigs and Democrats; northerners, southerners, and westerners; farmers, merchants, and manufacturers; opponents and supporters of slavery—seemed to be in the grip of a fervent expansionist spirit. They wanted to expand in every direction —into Canada, Texas, California, and Oregon; to Cuba, Mexico, and Central America. There was a passionate desire to see the American banner planted in the most distant places. One Kentuckian reflected the national sentiment when he described his conception of the limits of the country as, "On the east we are bounded by the rising sun, on the north by the aurora borealis, on the west by the procession of the equinoxes, and on the south by the Day of Judgment."

A variety of motives underlay this expansionist urge. Many southerners frankly wanted more land southward and southwestward for cotton cultivation (as the soil in the old or upper South became exhausted) and for additional states to bolster their political power in the national legislature. Northern and western farmers sought additional acreage farther west to grow their corn, wheat, barley, oats, rye, and vegetables and graze their sheep and cattle as the fields and meadows in their old homes lost their fertility. They found it easier and cheaper to abandon depleted land than to cultivate it intensively and scientifically. Merchants and manufacturers in New England and in the middle Atlantic states craved the harbors of California and Oregon as vital to their mastery of the trade with the Orient which they considered their most important future market. Strangely enough, many men who lived in the interior of the country and were not at all involved in the Asian traffic supported the acquisition of the Pacific slope because they saw the inland rivers as the highways on which eastern manufacturers would be carried to the Pacific ports and thence across the ocean to the Far East. Senator Thomas Hart Benton of landlocked Missouri talked of a continuous waterway—"short, direct, safe, cheap, and exclusively American" made up of the Ohio, Mississippi, Missouri, Platte, Snake, and Columbia rivers—the ancient dream of a northwest passage through the American continent come true.

Not all the impulses to expansion were economic and material. Many Americans advocated expansionism as the means for carrying out a divine mission to spread democratic institutions and "regenerate the enthralled." They believed themselves to be a people, described by one Charleston editor, as "chosen by the Lord to keep burning the vestal flame of liberty, as a light unto the feet and a lamp unto the path of the benighted nations who yet slumber or groan under the bondage of tyranny." "Free the despot-ridden masses of Canada," cried a magazine editor," add Mexico to the United States to save her downtrodden serfs, and carry the ballot box and republicanism to other unfortunate peoples." Walt Whitman was expressing a widely held view when he wrote,

> Have the elder races halted
> Do they droop and end their lesson?
> Wearied over there beyond the sea
> We take up the task eternal.

When Commodore Robert F. Stockton addressed a meeting in Philadelphia in 1847 called to celebrate his return from the conquest of California, he reflected this attitude with the stirring words: "I care not for the beautiful fields and healthful skies of California. I care not for her leagues of land and her mines of silver. The glory of the achievements there . . . is in the establishment of the first free press in California—in having built the first school house in California—in having established religious toleration as well as civil liberty in California—May the torch grow brighter and brighter, until from Cape Mendocino to Cape St. Lucas, it illumines the dark path of the victims of religious intolerance and political despotism." He then went on to urge that the war against Mexico be continued "for the express purpose of redeeming Mexico from misrule and civil strife . . . [and gathering] these wretched people within the fold of republicanism." It was a solemn duty, he said, from which "we dare not shrink" for "the priceless boon of religious and civil liberty has been confided to us as trustees."

Then, there were those in the United States whose demands for increased territory were rooted in their feelings of nationalism and patriotism. The period, indeed, was one of high nationalism and patriotism, of pride and optimism, of conceit and ambition, and of a boundless faith in the country's future. People were exuberant as they pointed to the great achievement of the United States in its relatively short history. "Where shall we turn to find a parallel to our progress, our energy, and our increasing power," said James Fenimore Cooper in 1835. Daniel Webster could write, with perfect aplomb, to the chargé d'affaires of Austria–Hungary in Washington, "The power of this republic, at the present moment [1850], is spread over a region, one of the richest and most fertile on the globe, and of an extent in comparison with which the possessions of the House of Habsburg are but as a patch on the earth's surface."

Historians like Jared Sparks, George Bancroft, and Mason Weems were writing about the American past as though it were the unfolding of a divine plan in which a providential hand guided a chosen people from triumph to triumph. In such an emotional climate, it was not strange that there was a clamoring for more land and for an increase in the country's greatness. One orator at a state political convention in 1844 brazenly announced, "Make way, I say, for the young American Buffalo—he has not yet got land enough; he wants more land as his cool shelter in summer—he wants more land for his beautiful pasture grounds. I tell you we will give him Oregon for his summer shade, and the region of Texas for his winter pasture. Like all his race, he wants salt, too. Well, he shall have the use of two oceans—the mighty Pacific and the turbulent Atlantic shall be his. . . . He shall not stop his career until he slakes his thirst in the frozen ocean."

Whatever their particular motivation, all proponents of expansionism shared a common watchword and slogan that characterized the movement. It was "manifest destiny," a term coined by John L. O'Sullivan and first used in the July 1845 number of the *Democratic Review*, which he edited. Referring to the question of the annexation of Texas, he wrote of "the manner in which other nations have undertaken to intrude themselves into it, between us and the proper parties to the case, in a spirit of hostile interference against us, for the avowed object of thwarting our policy and hampering our powers, limiting our greatness and checking the fulfillment of our *manifest destiny* to overspread the continent allotted by Providence for the free development of our yearly multiplying millions." The phrase was greatly appealing in that it identified expansionism with inevitability and with some higher authority and it caught on very quickly. Thereafter, it was widely used in the press, in the public forum, and in the Congress during the crisis over Oregon and in the movements to acquire all of Mexico, Cuba, and parts of Central America.

Relations with Mexico in the 1830s and 1840s provide an excellent illustration of the operation of "manifest destiny" as well as, it must be said, of the opposition to expansionism and to the acquisition of new lands, which was considerable. The key to Mexican-American difficulties was Texas, its revolution and subsequent annexation by the United States. The revolution of Texans against the Mexican parent may be said to have been predictable from the moment the Mexican government in 1823 (two years after gaining independence from Spain) confirmed to Stephen F. Austin the grant of land in Texas made three years earlier by Spain to Moses Austin, his father. This act brought to Texas an alien, Protestant, Anglo-Saxon, and largely slave-holding people, who by 1835 numbered 35,000 and dwarfed the indigenous Mexicans. Understandably, the Catholic, Latin, antislave government in Mexico City looked fearfully upon the enterprising and aggressive settlers, all of whom were Americans and had a worldwide reputation for coveting and seizing other people's territory.

As the population increased in the twenties and early thirties (men were attracted by the cheapness of the land: 4,428 acres could be bought for about $200 payable in several installments as compared to a price of $1.25 an acre payable in cash for land in the United States), Mexico sought by various devices to discourage immigration. Restrictions were placed on Protestant worship; a law in 1830 prohibited the further introduction of slaves; there were continuous threats of abolition; and another law in the same year forbade any settlements in the frontier states of Mexico. Texans chafed under these restraints and their leaders made frequent attempts in Mexico City to seek redress. Their efforts were in vain (Austin was put in prison on one of those visits and kept there for eight months). When, in 1834, Antonio López de Santa Anna became dictator, suspended the constitution, and sent troops to Texas to chasten the *gringos*, the Texans rose in revolt.

Their aim at first was, as is usual in revolutionary movements, modest. Like the American revolutionists in 1774 who at the outset looked for home rule within the British Empire, the Texans wanted only certain constitutional adjustments and the organization of Texas as a separate Mexican state (it was part of the state of Coahuila). The Mexicans did not have the foresight or wisdom, any more than the British had, to accept a small loss for a large gain, and the Texans were forced to the next step—independence, which they declared in March 1836.

Meanwhile desultory fighting had taken place. Bands of Texans in the fall of 1835 had taken two towns, San Antonio de Bexar and Goliad, which were recaptured by the Mexicans the following March in the cruellest and bloodiest actions. At San Antonio, the 187 Texans who had sought refuge in the Alamo, an old mission building, were assaulted by a force of 3,000 Mexicans, who took the place after eleven days and massacred the entire garrison. At Goliad, the Texans, hopelessly outnumbered, surrendered, but after being taken prisoner, they were led out of town where the Mexicans proceeded to shoot them. Only 100 of the 400 men escaped. After that, Santa Anna overran all of southeast Texas, scattering the rebels before him. In April, however, as he was camped at San Jacinto, Sam Houston, a former governor of Tennessee, member of Congress from that state, and an immigrant into Texas in 1829 who had been given command of all Texas troops, attacked Santa Anna's army.

After a bloody battle, in which Houston lost only two killed and twenty-three wounded, he drove off the Mexican force and took Santa Anna prisoner. At that moment, the war for independence ended.

From the very beginning of the war, the sympathies of the majority of the American people were, quite naturally, on the side of their fellow Americans in Texas. Their desire to see Texas in American hands had a long history dating from Adams' efforts in the negotiations of 1819. In speeches, resolutions, and articles, they clamored for Texas and expressed approval of the offers made by President Adams of $1 million in 1827 and Andrew Jackson of $5 million in 1829 to purchase the land. Now, the prospect of wresting Texas from Mexico by force of arms and bringing it into the Union seemed the fulfillment of a cherished dream. Calls by the rebels for men and money met with generous response, and in all parts of the country volunteer forces and financial contributions were raised.

All this is not to say that the administration in Washington played a role in fomenting and abetting the revolution as some Americans, many Europeans, and all Mexicans believed. It was true that President Jackson ardently favored the Texan cause. Houston was his friend and had fought under him with distinction in the Indian wars in the southwest in 1814 but there is no evidence to substantiate the claim made by northern antislavery Whigs that the president along with "slave-holders, smugglers, Indian killers, foul-mouthed tobacco spitting men swearing upon sacred fourth of July principles to carry spread eagle supremacy from the Atlantic to the Pacific, who were willing to lay aside all notions of right and wrong and to take unblushingly whatever could be secured safely on the principle of might" instigated or even encouraged the revolt.

A charge of unneutrality is more difficult to rebut. The president did order army commanders and district attorneys to enforce the neutrality statutes of the United States, yet men moved out of the country with obvious intent to "join in a hostile expedition against a friendly power" in violation of the statutes. The protests of the Mexican minister were met with pleas that convictions were difficult to obtain because of the sympathies of judges and juries and that the neutrality laws were inadequate. Such excuses do not, however, absolve a country from the responsibility of observing its obligations as a neutral. It is curious, indeed, that a minor insurrection in Canada in 1837 brought a quick change in the American neutrality laws to prevent volunteers from crossing the border to aid the rebels. One historian considered it "noteworthy that the relatively slight commotions in the adjacent territory of the most powerful empire in the world brought a prompt improvement of hitherto inadequate domestic laws, but that a formidable revolution in the neighboring province of a weak and disorganized Latin-American republic had not brought the necessary amendments."

That the leaders of the Texas revolt would seek to join their republic to the United States, their native land, was to be expected. Once the war ended, a representative was sent to Washington to gain recognition of independence and annexation. President Jackson would have liked nothing better than to fulfill the twin Texas desires, but he feared the consequences for his country and his party. To recognize and annex would, he believed, lead to a war with Mexico and to a likelihood of a split in the Democratic party between proslavery and antislavery elements that might endanger the election of his protegé, Martin Van Buren, to the presidency and even, perhaps, destroy the party. Even after Van Buren's election in November of 1836, Jackson hestitated to act and, in a special message to Congress in December, recommended that Texas be neither recognized nor annexed. It was only several months later and one day before leaving office that he relented on recognition, which he had always considered less dangerous to party and country than annexation. On March 3, 1837, following a resolution by the Senate that Texan independence be recognized and an appropriation by the House for a diplomatic representative to the new Republic, Jackson nominated Alsée La Branche of Louisiana as chargé d'affaires.

One of the first acts of the new minister of Texas in Washington was to request annexation of his country to the United States. President Van Buren, continuing the policy of his predecessor, rejected the suggestion and for much the same reasons. He feared war with Mexico and the alienation of northern antislavery elements from the Democratic party. Following that rebuff, on August 25, 1837, nothing more was heard from the government of Texas on that matter for five years. Then, in 1842, the issue was raised once more by Sam Houston, the Texan president, as a means of solving his country's problems—financial insolvency and a war with Mexico. This time, the response from Washington was not the same as before and the reason for the change is to be found in the occupant of the White House—John Tyler.

Tyler, a life-long Democrat from Virginia, had split with his party in 1840 and had joined the Whig ticket as the vice-presidential candidate. Elected along with William Henry Harrison, he succeeded to the presidency upon Harrison's death in April of 1841. Before long, he fell out with the Whig leaders and soon found himself a man without a party. His political future appeared bleak, and only some spectacular and popular act would put him in the running in 1844. Texas seemed the perfect vehicle for there was wide support in the country for its annexation. Large numbers of southerners saw in Texas an ideal place for the extension of cotton culture and a superb source for the increase of the political representation of the south in the national legislature. They feared, too, that an independent Texas might eventually be persuaded by England to free its slaves (it was well known that British abolitionists had such a plan in mind, using the prospects of loans as bait) and a free Texas would have an evil effect upon the slave institution in the United States by providing a haven for runaway slaves and an example of freedom. On the other hand, many northerners and westerners were concerned that an independent Texas might lure the southern states out of the Union to form a great slave empire from the Gulf of Mexico to California and weaken the United States. They suspected, also, that if Texas did not join the Union, it might be taken by Britain.

Tyler lost no time in negotiating a treaty of annexation. He directed Abel P. Upshur, his secretary of state and a proslavery Virginian, to open talks with the Texas representatives in Washington in the summer of 1843. When Upshur was killed in February of the next year by an exploding cannon on board the U.S.S. *Princeton*, John C. Calhoun, his successor and an ardent annexationist, took over and completed the negotiations on April 12, 1844. Ten days later, Tyler sent the treaty to the Senate with a strong plea for "approval and ratification" on the grounds that Texas was really American territory (a part of the Louisiana purchase), was American in population, laws, customs, and institutions, was valuable agriculturally and commercially, and that its incorporation into the Union would benefit every section of the country. In addition, he warned darkly that "if the boon now tendered be rejected Texas will seek for the friendship of others."

Whatever the merits of the president's arguments they counted for little alongside the impression created by a letter Calhoun directed to the British minister in Washington on April 18. It concerned an exchange between two members of the British House of Lords on the desirability of abolishing slavery in Texas but disclaiming any intent by London to pressure Texas into freeing its negroes. Calhoun's letter was a vigorous defense of slavery as a beneficent institution good for both master and slave and for the well-being of the South. It was, as well, an unabashed statement that the principal purpose of annexing Texas was to thwart any effort by the British to end slavery there. That was all the antislavery elements in the country needed to defeat the treaty. To the votes of antislavery senators were now added those of northern and western expansionists, who, despite the great appeal of Texas, refused to be party to what was boldly stated to be a slave conspiracy. In the vote taken on June 8, the count stood 35 against (28 Whigs and 7 Democrats) and 16 (all Democrats) for.

It was not only Calhoun's letter and proslavery sentiments that caused the treaty to be lost in the Senate. Another important factor was the political situation. The year 1844 was a presidential election year, and it could hardly be assumed that so exciting an issue could be kept out of the cauldron of national politics. Both Henry Clay and Martin Van Buren, who expected to be nominated by Whigs and Democrats, respectively, came out against annexation in letters published on the same day, April 27.

On May 1, the Whigs met at Baltimore and, as anticipated, unanimously nominated Clay. The platform said nothing about Texas.

On the 27th, the Democrats convened in the same city, but Van Buren did not win the prize. Annexationists, led by Calhoun and wishing to have an annexationist head the ticket, pushed through a new rule that required a two-thirds majority for nomination that ended Van Buren's chances. In fact, no one seemed able to get that many votes until a "dark horse" compromise candidate, James K. Polk, was suggested. He was an annexationist and had the blessings of Andrew Jackson, the party's elder statesman. The platform came out unequivocally for "the reannexation of Texas." Thus, by the time the vote in the Senate was taken, party lines had been drawn. Whig senators following their party and their leader cast their ballots against the treaty; Van Buren Democrats stood by their leader and opposed the treaty; loyal Democrats voted for it.

The campaign of 1844, as were other presidential campaigns, was fought on many issues, but one of them clearly was Texas. Polk and the Democrats kept firmly to their demands for Texas (which they coupled with a cry for Oregon then in dispute with Great Britain). Clay and the Whigs changed position as the campaign progressed in the face of what appeared to be a national excitement for expansionism. But instead of taking a clear-cut stand Clay announced that he had no objection to annexation and would, indeed, "be glad to see it, without dishonor, without war, with the common consent of the Union, and upon just and fair terms." Whether such equivocation affected his cause—lost Whig and antislavery votes or gained western and southern support—cannot be determined. The fact is he did lose the election. Polk received 1,337,243 votes to his 1,299,062 and in the Electoral College the count stood 170 to 105.

In view of the fact that Texas was only one issue in the campaign and the margin of victory so slight (a third-party antislavery candidate in New York pulled 5,082 votes away from Clay in New York, which threw the state's thirty-six electoral votes to Polk, the margin of victory in the Electoral College), it could hardly be said that the election constituted a mandate to take Texas. Yet that was exactly how John Tyler interpreted the result. He announced that "a controlling majority of the people and a large majority of the states have declared in favor of immediate annexation" and promptly recommended to the "lame duck" second session of the twenty-eighth Congress, which met on December 2, 1844, that it pass a joint resolution inviting Texas to join the American Union. He suggested that device rather than a treaty because the latter required a two-thirds senatorial vote for approval that Tyler did not think obtainable, but the former demanded only a simple majority of both chambers.

On January 25, 1845, the measure passed the House, 120–98, and on February 21, the Senate approved 27–25. On March 1, the president affixed his signature and the Texas drama, begun nine years earlier, came to an end. It remained only for the people of Texas to accept the proffered hand of the United States, which they did in a series of acts over the next several months. On July 4, a convention voted 55–1 for annexation and drew up a state constitution which was approved by popular referendum in October. On December 29, President Polk signed a resolution by Congress admitting Texas as the twenty-eighth state.

That annexation would bring a crisis in Mexican-American relations was plain to all but the most obtuse observer. Mexico had made perfectly clear that any legislation to incorporate Texas into the Union would be "equivalent to a declaration of war." The Mexicans did not go to war when the annexation act was passed, but their minister did close his legation in Washington four days later and went home. Shortly afterward, the American minister left Mexico City, and diplomatic intercourse between the two nations was suspended.

Polk, the new president, was eager to come to a settlement with Mexico. The termination of relations had left unsettled two very serious problems—the Texan boundary (Mexico having never admitted the facts of Texas independence claimed the Sabine and the United States the Rio Grande) and unpaid claims (amounting to $2,026,119, which a Mexican-American commission in 1842 had awarded to American citizens for property damaged during several Mexican revolutions). Then there was California, which Polk wanted very badly and which he preferred to get peacefully by negotiation.

Like Texas, California was only loosely governed by Mexico and, like Texas, it was extremely attractive to Americans. Stretching almost 1,000 miles from south to north, it was covered by great forests, blessed with fertile valleys, and possessed of three splendid harbors (San Francisco, Monterey, San Diego). Americans began moving there in increasing numbers beginning in the early 1830s. The first to glimpse the promised land were those engaged in the sea otter trade off the coast. They put into Monterey for food and supplies before setting out for China, where they sold their furs and on the way home by way of Cape Horn. Next came the whaling vessels, which also stopped for provisions for the voyage home. Finally there were the Yankee traders who came to California to sell manufactured goods and buy hides and tallow that the great cattle herds produced (the lean, long-horned Spanish cattle were not good for beef). From those visitors, as well as from fur trappers who had entered California after overland voyages from the east, Americans back home learned of the wonders and the potential of California and soon merchants and farmers came to settle permanently. Thomas O. Larkin, who opened a store in Monterey in 1832, and John A. Sutter, who in 1839 established a farm in the Sacramento Valley, were the most prominent of some 900 immigrants who had swept into the towns and the countryside by 1845 (and constituted about one tenth of the population).

Even before the influx, American presidents had been interested in acquiring California. Andrew Jackson who, according to John Quincy Adams, had a "passion" for San Francisco Bay, in 1835 offered Mexico $500,000 for that place or $3.5 million for all of California north of the 38th parallel. But Mexico would not sell to the country that it believed was at that very moment involved in a conspiracy to rob it of another province. John Tyler fared no better in his efforts to purchase California in 1842 despite his scheme to entice Britain to put pressure on Mexico in exchange for America giving up a portion of the disputed Oregon territory. Now, it was Polk's turn and he was determined to succeed where his predecessors had failed. When, in the summer of 1845, he took soundings in Mexico City on the possibility of reopening relations and settling outstanding differences, California was very much one of the "differences."

In view of the reaction by Mexico to annexation, it was surprising that to Polk's query as to whether an American envoy would be received, the Mexican foreign minister replied that "although the Mexican nation is deeply injured by the United States, . . . my government is disposed to receive the commissioner of the United States who may come to this capital with full powers . . . to settle the present dispute in a peaceful, reasonable, and honorable manner. . . ." The president lost no time in taking advantage of the apparent thaw and at once appointed a minister, John Slidell of Louisiana, to discuss all the issues with Mexico. His instructions, dated November 10, 1845, were to obtain the Rio Grande boundary in exchange for assuming the unpaid claims and beyond that to offer $5 million for New Mexico, $25 million for New Mexico and all of California, or $20 million for New Mexico and California north of Monterey. Slidell left at once for the Mexican capital, arriving there on December 6, 1845.

In close connection with his plan to negotiate the differences with Mexico and to acquire California, Polk took several important precautionary measures in the summer, fall, and winter of 1845. In July, at the same time that he took soundings in Mexico City, he ordered General Zachary Taylor with 4,000 troops to take up a position on the west bank of the Nueces River (in disputed territory) and at its mouth where there was a Texan settlement to prevent an invasion of Texas by Mexico. For the same reason and in the same month, he dispatched a naval squadron to the Gulf of Mexico. Next, he moved to provide an alternative to acquiring California should negotiations fail. In October, he appointed Thomas D. Larkin, who had been named United States consul in Monterey eighteen months earlier, his confidential agent charged with encouraging native Californians to separate from Mexico as a prelude to uniting "their destiny with ours." Finally, he moved to thwart the possibility of a foreign power seizing California before he could acquire it.

That possibility seemed very real in 1845. For some years, reports had circulated of England's interest in possessing California and, if that could not be accomplished, in keeping it out of American hands. One rumor had it that Mexico would cede California to Britain in repayment of a loan made earlier; another hinted at a new loan to be secured by a mortgage on California that would not be paid, resulting in a foreclosure and a transfer of title to England; still another concerned orders to the British fleet in the Pacific to take California in the event of a Mexican-American war. So prevalent and plausible was that rumor that in 1842, the commander of the American squadron in the Pacific, Thomas Ap Catesby Jones, upon hearing, incorrectly it turned out, that Mexico and the United States were at war, hastened from his base at Callao in Peru to Monterey and planted the American flag there before the British had the chance to take possession of the capital city of California. Needless to say, he hauled it down as quickly when he learned the truth.

The instrument Polk chose for the warning to foreign nations was his first annual message to Congress on December 2, 1845. In it he reaffirmed Monroe's principle of noncolonization stated 25 years earlier "in the annual message of one of my predecessors" (thereby being the first president since then to refer to the doctrine of Monroe) and let it be known that ". . . . the people of this continent alone have the right to decide their own destiny. Should any portion of them, constituting an independent state, propose to unite themselves with our Confederacy, this will be a question for them and us to determine without any foreign interposition."

Meanwhile, in Mexico City, the government refused to receive Slidell ostensibly because his credentials were too broad (he was empowered to settle all differences; Mexico would talk of the Texas boundary alone) and his title too exalted (Mexico would accept only a commissioner, not a minister), but really because Mexican public opinion was so outraged at the prospect of treating with the nation that had wrenched away the province of Texas that no government could accept Slidell and stay in power. After waiting vainly for several months, Slidell left Mexico City in March of 1846, convinced, as he wrote Polk, that "nothing could be done with these people until they shall have been chastized."

Polk was fully in accord with his emissary and, indeed, seemed ready to chastize the Mexicans if they would not be reasonable. He had gotten the first word of the Mexican government's refusal to accept Slidell in January 13, 1846 and reacted by instructing General Taylor to advance the 150 miles from the west bank of the Nueces to the eastern shore of the Rio Grande and occupy the territory claimed by the United States. Then on April 7, he received the information that Slidell had been finally

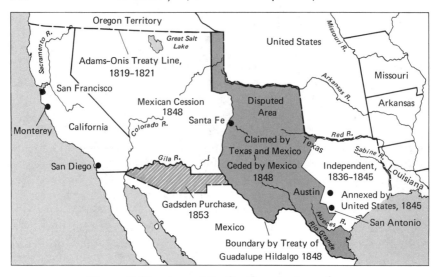

Texas, California, and the Southwest, 1845–1853.

rebuffed and had left Mexico, which led him to decide on war. He took no concrete steps, however, until Slidell reached Washington on May 8 and reported fully to the president his view of the story of Mexican intransigeance and hostility. Now Polk was ready to act. The next day, he called his cabinet together to tell them of the failure of the mission and of his decision to ask Congress, on May 12, to declare war. The causes were ample, he said. Mexico refused to pay just claims and to negotiate other differences; the country was "excited and impatient"; and his duty was clear. He had no other course. The cabinet was in complete agreement with the president save Secretary of the Navy George Bancroft, who urged waiting until a hostile act by Mexico.

Whether the president would have waited beyond the 12th for the hostile act will never be known, because on that very evening he received word that a Mexican force had attacked Taylor on April 24 and had killed or wounded sixteen American soldiers. On April 12, the Mexican commander, at the head of 5,700 Mexican soldiers stationed across the Rio Grande opposite Taylor, had ordered Taylor to withdraw east of the Nueces and evacuate the disputed territory. Taylor not only refused to budge but began to build a fort at the mouth of the Rio Grande to blockade the Mexican city of Matamoras situated there, whereupon the Mexican president on April 23 declared a defensive war against the United States. On the next day the Mexican army crossed the river and attacked.

Polk's path was now greatly eased. He did not wait until the 12th, a Tuesday. On Monday, May 11, he appeared before Congress with a lengthy recital of Mexican wrong-doing, of the rebuff of Slidell, of the refusal to negotiate, of the failure to pay the claims, and of the dastardly assault. "Mexico," he said, "has passed the boundary of the United States, has invaded our territory, and shed American blood on American soil." The fact that the soil was not clearly American and that American soldiers might not have had the right to be there did not alter the impact of the message. Congress reacted with passion and promptness, voting war on May 13 by 174–14 in the House and 40–2 in the Senate.

The overwhelming response to the president should not obscure the fact that the country was not nearly as unanimous as the Congress in approving the war with Mexico. There was considerable opposition, which, while concentrated in New England and in the Old Northwest, was not restricted to those sections. Men in all parts of the country voiced their concern and for a variety of reasons. Many thought the war unjustified in that Mexican conduct hardly warranted armed reprisal. They blamed Polk for provoking Mexico by stationing American troops in the disputed territory. Congressman Abraham Lincoln of Illinois demanded to be shown the exact spot where American blood had been shed and if it was, indeed, on American soil. His colleague from Kentucky, Garret Davis, exclaimed, "It is our President who began this war." The Massachusetts legislature, in a blunt resolution, labelled the war, "a gigantic crime . . . unconstitutionally commenced by the President."

Others considered the president's action immoral, a transgression of cherished American principles and a façade for aggression. Whig Senator Thomas Corwin of Ohio, perhaps the most persistent and hostile critic of the Administration, spoke of "this uneasy desire to augment our territory [which] has depraved the moral sense and blunted the otherwise keen sagacity of our people. Our young orators cherish this notion with a fervid but fatally mistaken zeal. They call it by the mysterious name of destiny. Our destiny they say is onward and hence they argue with rapid sophistry the propriety of seizing upon any territory and any people that may be in the way of our fated advance." Democratic Senator John C. Calhoun of South Carolina was no less outspoken when he scoffed at the "mission of this country to spread civil and religious liberty overall the globe . . .—even by force, if necessary." He called it "a sad delusion" and suggested that the American spirit was "to avoid war when it can be avoided" and "to adopt a course of moderation and justice to all nations." The most vociferous and the greatest opposition to the conflict came from the antislavery people, who insisted that it was precipitated by the southern slaveowners who wanted to annex all of Mexico with "the triple object of extending slavery, of strengthening the slave power, and of obtaining control of the free states." James Russell Lowell put the case more graphically in his *Biglow Papers* with the quatrain:

They jest want this Californy
So's to lug new slave states in
To abuse ye, an to scorn ye
An to plunder ye like sin.

Some of the most prominent names in the country—Charles Sumner, William Jay, Albert Gallatin, Joshua Giddings, Daniel Barnard, and Ralph Waldo Emerson—were ranged against the administration and relentless in their criticism of the president as the creature of the southern slaveocracy.

This division in the ranks of the American people gave Mexicans hope and encouraged them to think they could beat the divided Yankees. They drew confidence, too, from several other expectations: That America might get into a war with England over Oregon, that the slaves might revolt, and that the American army would fail in Mexico as dismally as it had in Canada thirty-odd years before. Also their army was five times larger than their enemy's. Still their enthusiasm came to naught. The slaves did not revolt, the British settled the Oregon question amicably, and the internal division in the United States did not prevent the Congress from appropriating whatever funds were needed to prosecute the war.

Dissident legislators felt patriotically bound to support the armies in the field. As for the size of the military forces, the smaller American regular army was quickly augmented by a large number of volunteers, which raised the total number of soldiers to two and a half times that of Mexico—100,000 to 40,000. Furthermore, the Mexican army was poorly trained, saddled with incompetent leadership, and equipped with obsolete weapons. The Americans, on the other hand, although weak in communication, transportation, and sanitation, were better equipped and trained and had excellent officers, both senior and junior. The leaders of both Northern and Confederate forces in the Civil War—Grant, Sherman, Meade, Hooker, McClellan, Pope, Thomas, Lee, Longstreet, Jackson, the Johnstons, the Hills, Beauregard, Bragg—were manifesting as young men in the war against Mexico those military skills and proficiencies which were to make them distinguished in the next war.

The Mexicans never even came close to winning. They lost every battle and frequently were routed from the field. Their losses in killed and wounded were always many times greater than those suffered by American forces. Even before war was declared, Taylor had already beaten them in two engagements in the disputed territory—on May 8 at Palo Alto and the next day at Resaca de la Palma. As the Mexican army fled across the Rio Grande in disarray, Taylor pursued it, and when it evacuated Matamoras, at the mouth, he occupied the city on May 18. After getting reinforcements, he pushed deeper into enemy territory, capturing Monterrey on September 24. In February of the following year, he pitted his 5,000 troops against 15,000 Mexicans at Buena Vista and routed them, thus ending all fighting in northern Mexico.

Meanwhile, American naval and land forces were being successful in New Mexico and California. On orders from Polk, Colonel Stephen Kearny, in May of 1846, proceeded from his base at Fort Leavenworth, Kansas, to take Santa Fe, the capital of New Mexico province. After occupying that city, he advanced into the province of California, capturing San Diego in December. Monterey, the capital, had already been won by Commodore John D. Sloat in July when he raised the United States flag on the governor's palace and declared California annexed to his country. In August, Commodore Robert F. Stockton had entered Santa Barbara and Los Angeles. Farther north, in the Sacramento Valley, restless American settlers, in collusion with Captain John C. Frémont of the United States Topographical Corps, in June had attacked the Mexican authorities and had declared the independence of the Republic of California with a grizzly bear and a star on a field of white cloth as its standard. California by the end of 1846 was completely in American hands, as were New Mexico and northern Mexico.

There remained only the conquest of the Mexican capital. Polk had hoped that Taylor would proceed south after his victory at Monterrey, but the general had instead settled down to an unauthorized armistice with the Mexicans. His popularity in the United States stemming from his victories was so great that Polk could not replace him as commander and was perhaps too great to permit him to become the victor of Mexico City for, after all, Taylor was a Whig. The president, thereupon, turned to General Winfield Scott and a new plan of attack. Scott, a hero of the War of 1812 and general-in-chief of the army, was also a Whig. Polk was no more eager to enhance his political stature than Taylor's, but there was no other choice. The capital had to be taken and Scott was the only man to do it. The plan, hatched in October of 1846, was to carry Scott's army by sea from Tampico to Vera Cruz and then march overland to Mexico City. On March 9, 1847, the army of 14,000 landed on the beach at Vera Cruz mounting the first large-scale amphibious operation in American history. On the 27th the city fell. Mexico City now lay only 260 miles away but the route to the capital presented serious difficulties, for it rose into mountains 8,000 feet high, whose passes invited ambush, and through populous territory where guerrilla operations could harass the forces. The capital itself was not easily accessible once reached, for it was situated in marshland and could be approached only by crossing causeways.

Undaunted, Scott began his march from Vera Cruz on April 8. All along the route he encountered opposition but always he was victorious, and by May 15 he had come within 80 miles of Mexico City. There he awaited reinforcements and supplies. Early in August he set out again and by the end of the month and after fierce fighting was five miles from the capital. On September 8, he launched his attack on the city at Chapulte-pec Park, a 200-foot hill that guarded two of the approaches to the city. It took six days of fighting before Scott's troops with ladders and pickaxes could storm Chapultepec, but on the 13th, they reached the top. The next day, they marched on the capital and raised the American flag over the National Palace.

The story of the treaty of peace with Mexico is a curious and interesting one. Negotiations were in the hands of Nicholas P. Trist, the chief clerk of the Department of State, who had been sent to Mexico by Polk as soon as Vera Cruz fell. Trist quickly clashed with Scott and acted so strangely and arrogantly that Polk recalled him on October 6, 1847. Trist, however, ignored the president and met the Mexican authorities at Guadaloupe Hidalgo, a small village near Mexico City, where he concluded peace on the basis of his earlier instructions from Polk: The Texas boundary fixed at the Rio Grande; California and New Mexico (which included the present states of Arizona, Nevada, Utah, California, and parts of New Mexico, Colorado, and Wyoming—in all, 500,000 square miles) ceded to the United States; the payment of $15 million to Mexico; and the assump-tion by the United States of the claims of American citizens against Mexico. When the treaty reached Washington, the president's first inclination was to reject his repudiated agent's work, but on second and sober thought, he realized the terms fulfilled all his territorial ambitions. Despite the rising clamor on the part of militant expansionists in his own party for all of Mexico, he submitted the treaty to the Senate, which approved it on March 10, 1848, by a vote of 38–14. Twenty-six loyal Demo-crats supported their party chief, and twelve Whigs voted "aye" because they feared the defeat of that treaty would result in the annexation of all Mexico. Seven Democrats would not accept any treaty which did not include all of Mexico, and seven Whigs would accept no treaty connected with "Mr. Polk's War."

So the United States fulfilled its "manifest destiny" by wrenching from Mexico two fifths of that country's territory. After a relatively painless and inexpensive war, a huge new land was gained which Polk predicted would be "productive of vast benefit to the United States, to the com-mercial world, and the general interest of mankind." It was to be the final addition to the American land mass (except for a small purchase in 1854 from Mexico); territorially, it completed the development of the Ameri-can nation except for the acquisition of Alaska. It also gave the United States an extensive Pacific coastline from San Diego to the 42nd parallel, which when combined with the shoreline from 42° to 49°, gained as a result of the settlement with England two years earlier and with the treaty with China four years before, thrust the country into a new destiny as a Pacific power.

BIBLIOGRAPHY

EPHRAIM D. ADAMS, *British Interests and Activities in Texas* (1910).

K. JACK BAUER, *The Mexican War* (1974).

FREDERICK MERK, *Manifest Destiny and Mission in American History: A Reinterpretation* (1963).

DAVID M. PLETCHER, *The Diplomacy of Annexation: Texas, Oregon, and the Mexican War* (1973).

JOHN H. SCHROEDER, *Mr. Polk's War: American Opposition and Dissent, 1846–1848* (1973).

HENRY N. SMITH, *Virgin Land* (1959).

JUSTIN H. SMITH, *The War with Mexico* (2 vols., 1919).

ALBERT K. WEINBERG, *Manifest Destiny: A Study of Nationalist Expansion in American History* (1935).

S. V. CONNOR AND O. B. FAULK, *North America Divided: The Mexican War, 1846–1848* (1971).

Daniel Webster (courtesy of the National Portrait Gallery, Smithsonian Institution, Washington, D.C.).

The Settlements with England:
Maine and Oregon

THE DECADE of the 1840s was significant for American diplomacy not only because it saw the rectification of the Texas-Mexican border and the acquisition of vast lands in the west and southwest but also for the settlement with England of two troublesome disputes over the Maine–New Brunswick boundary in 1842 and the Oregon territory in 1846.

The problem of the boundary was a legacy of the peace settlement that ended the Revolutionary War. The treaty had described the boundary between the United States and British North America as the St. Croix River and had marked it on copies of the official map used by the negotiators, the work of the eminent cartographer, John Mitchell, dated 1755. The maps disappeared soon after the signing of the treaty and the boundary, therefore, had to be ascertained from the language of Article Two of the Treaty that described it. That language, however, was imprecise and when officials of the two countries sought to locate the principal landmarks mentioned in the treaty—the St. Croix River and the "Highlands which divide those Rivers that empty into the River St. Lawrence, from those which fall into the Atlantic Ocean, ..." they could not agree. There were two rivers which might have been the St. Croix; the British claimed the westernmost, while the Americans insisted on the one to the east. A mixed commission, set up by Jay's Treaty, made a survey in 1798 and supported the British contention. As to the "Highlands," there were two heights of land either of which might have been the one designated in the treaty depending upon the rivers selected. The British considered the St. John and the Penobscot as determining the "Highlands," but the Americans used the large rivers flowing into the Atlantic and the small ones emptying into the St. Lawrence as the guides for identifying the "Highlands."

Because the treaty stipulated that the boundary was to be a "Line drawn due North from the source of Saint Croix River to the Highlands," the precise location of the Highlands was crucially important in that it would determine the amount of land for each claimant. The "Highlands" according to the British interpretation was 40 miles from the source of the river; the American view placed it at 115 miles. Thus, about 12,000 square miles or 7 million acres were actually in dispute—valuable timber and farm land and, for the British, of strategic importance in that it provided a route for a military road from St. John and Halifax to Montreal and Quebec that could be used in the winter when the St. Lawrence River was frozen.

Several attempts to reconcile the different positions failed. In 1803, a mixed Anglo-American commission arrived at a line but it was rejected by the United States Senate. Another survey, made in 1821 by a commission created by the negotiators at Ghent in 1814 could not agree on the location of the "Highlands." Thereupon the king of the Netherlands was called to act as arbitrator. In 1831, that monarch recommended that the disputed land be divided equally, which both the London and Washington governments were willing to accept, but when the state of Maine objected, the United States officially refused.

Meanwhile, settlers from Maine and New Brunswick had been moving into the disputed area and inevitably they clashed. Late in 1838, a party of Canadian lumbermen began operations along the Aroostook River, whereupon the Maine authorities sent an agent with 200 men to oust them. A fight ensued and the Canadians seized fifty Americans. Passions on both sides flared. Maine and New Brunswick called out their militia and dispatched the soldiers to the area. Nova Scotia voted war credits to assist her sister-province, and the United States Congress authorized the raising of 50,000 soldiers and the expenditure of $10 million to defend Maine. Fortunately, neither side really wanted war, and when President Van Buren sent General Winfield Scott in May 1839 to negotiate with the lieutenant-governor of New Brunswick, a truce was arranged ending the "Aroostook War" but both parties retained their claims to the territory, pending a diplomatic settlement.

Unfortunately, the boundary question was aggravated by the existence of a deep reservoir of Anglophobia in the United States and of Yankee-phobia in England resulting from ancient grudges and from more recent issues and situations that plagued relations between the two nations. For Americans, there was the recollection of the colonial controversy and the war that followed; the refusal by Britain after the war to surrender the frontier forts, cut the connection with the Indians, and return the slaves carried away; the harassment of American commerce in the years following the outbreak of the Franco-British war; and, finally, the second war highlighted by the burning of Washington. For Britons, there was the harsh historic fact that twice when they had been fighting a life-and-death

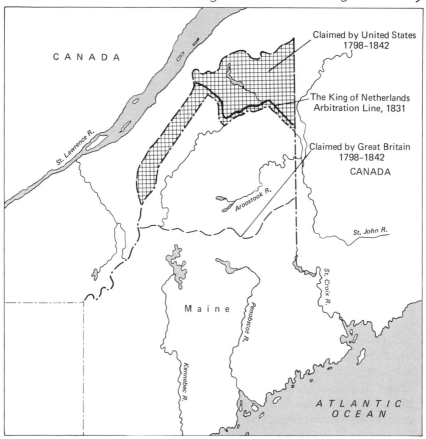

CANADA

Claimed by United States
1798–1842

The King of Netherlands
Arbitration Line, 1831

Claimed by Great Britain
1798–1842

CANADA

St. Lawrence R.

Aroostook R.

St. John R.

Maine

St. Croix R.

Penobscot R.

Kennebec R.

ATLANTIC
OCEAN

The Maine Boundary Settlement, 1842.

struggle the Americans were ranged against them alongside the French foe.

After 1815, there were numerous and varied irritating problems, some of which brought the two countries dangerously close to hostilities. The question of American trading rights in British North America and the West Indies was for fifteen years one of those problems. At the end of the War of 1812, trade was reestablished by treaty on a basis of reciprocity in all places except Canada and the West Indies from which Americans were barred. In the relatively relaxed diplomatic climate in the years immediately following the war, which generated the agreements on disarmament on the Great Lakes and on the boundary between the Rockies and the Lake of the Woods, the British government made some slight concessions by opening the ports of St. John and Halifax to American vessels and by permitting American vessels to carry certain American products to Bermuda for transshipment to the West Indies in British ships.

Americans were not satisfied, however, with such minor privileges. They wanted direct access to the West Indies for their ships and cargoes, and Congress sought to force the British to open those ports by legislation curtailing British rights in American ports. A law in 1820 barred from American ports all British vessels coming from a British colony in the western hemisphere, and all British goods that did not come directly from the place where they were produced (which served the purpose of preventing the importation of West Indian products by way of British North America). British planters in the islands soon felt the effect of the restrictions on their commerce, and their pressure on Parliament led to a further concession two years later. In 1822, American ships were permitted to carry certain American products to the West Indies on the same basis as British vessels except that on livestock, foodstuffs, and lumber a duty had to be paid that similar products of British origin did not pay. Also, American ships could take from the islands any products save arms and naval stores.

The Americans responded at once to the British move by means of a presidential proclamation in 1823 (under congressional authority) opening American ports to British vessels carrying British colonial goods. In retaliation, however, for the preferential treatment given British goods in West Indian ports, the higher tonnage dues levied on foreign ships and the higher duties imposed on goods imported in foreign ships were not removed for England's benefit.

Now began a period of acrimonious and stubborn haggling. The British refused to eliminate the preference accorded British goods on the grounds that it was a purely domestic arrangement; the Americans, on their part, would not remove the alien dues and duties until the British ended the preferential treatment. An act of Parliament in 1825 stipulated that American vessels would be barred from the West Indies if the alien duties and dues were continued. John Quincy Adams was now president and that unbending patriot and nationalist would not yield. The result was that the British closed their colonial ports to American ships, whereupon the Americans reciprocated by closing their ports to British colonial goods carried in British vessels. Trade between the United States and the West Indies had ceased and both sides felt the pinch. West Indian planters depended heavily on American foodstuffs and lumber and on American purchases of their sugar, and American merchants and farmers drew much profit both from supplying and carrying those necessities. And each party blamed the other for obduracy and intransigence.

The problem was resolved in 1830 by President Andrew Jackson, who owed his election two years earlier, in part, to the issue of the West Indian trade and to a popular dissatisfaction with Adams' handling of the matter. On October 5, he declared the ports of the United States open once again to British ships on an equal footing with American vessels without demanding that Britain end preferential treatment. At once, the

British reciprocated by admitting American vessels to West Indian ports and retaining the right to levy such duties as deemed desirable.

The decade of the 1830s saw several more serious difficulties between the two nations. One concerned the suspension of payment of interest and principal on investments in canals and turnpikes by Englishmen in the United States by several states after the Panic of 1837 and during the depression that followed. Large numbers of Britons suffered greatly by the default and were infuriated by the cavalier treatment of a just obligation. A memorial to Congress by one investor summed up the general view: "Your petitioner lent to the state of Pennsylvania a sum of money for the purpose of some public improvement. If their refusal to pay (for which a very large number of English families are suffering) had been the result of war, if it had arisen from civil discord, if it were the act of a poor state struggling against the barrenness of nature, every friend of America would have been contented to wait for better times; but the fraud is committed in profound peace, by Pennsylvania, the richest state in the Union. It is an act of bad faith which has no parallel and no excuse. The Americans who boast to have improved the institutions of the Old World have at least equalled its crimes. A great nation, after trampling under foot all earthly tyranny, has been guilty of a fraud as enormous as ever disgraced the worst king of the most degraded nation of Europe."

Not only investors had cause to feel hostile toward the United States and toward Americans. Writers and publishers, for example, resented the pirating of British literary works. In the absence of an American copyright statute, British writings were freely printed in the United States without payment of royalties to authors. Remonstrances were of no avail. A petition to Congress in 1836 by fifty-six English writers for relief was rebuffed. More importantly, the British ruling classes were violently anti-American. They were jealous of the increasing wealth and strength of the United States and apprehensive over its aggressive territorial and commercial policies. On the North American continent, the British were threatened by a loss of their land in the face of the relentless march westward of the American pioneer and of the insistent cry of "manifest destiny" by the American politician. In almost every part of the globe, American merchants were challenging British mercantile supremacy. Above all, there was an abiding fear of American democracy and republicanism and of their impact on the restless masses of the Old World. Those institutions were viewed as a standing menace to the established order.

This hostility was manifested in a steady stream of caustic and carping articles and essays in the British newspapers and journals. Typical was the observation jeeringly made in a London literary magazine in 1823: "The experiments . . . which our brethren in America are trying is to see with how little government, with how few institutions, and at how cheap a rate men may be kept together in society. Is this a safe experiment? Can it possibly be a successful one?"

Hostility was also apparent in the accounts written by Britons of impressions of their travels in the United States. In the years following the end of the War of 1812, large numbers of English men and women journeyed to America for all sorts of reasons. They came to investigate opportunities for investment of capital or for setting up businesses, to hunt buffalo, to paint landscapes, or to lecture. Invariably, upon their return home they recorded their views of American society and institutions in books and articles. Because they came to their subject with prejudice and bias and, frequently, with a deliberate intent to discredit the nation's achievement and damage its image, their accounts, most often, turned out to be unkind and even scurrilous. People such as Basil Hall (*Travels in North America*), Francis Trollope (*Domestic Manners of Americans*), Frederick Marryat (*A Diary in America*), Fanny Kemble (*Journal of a Residence on a Georgia Plantation*), and Charles Dickens (*American Notes*) had very little good to say about America and Americans. They grudgingly admitted that the resources of the United States were very extensive and that the country was tremendously rich. They marvelled at the network of roads and canals and at the growth of the nation's population and wealth. They conceded that Americans were industrious and energetic, but at the same time they found them to be coarse, crude, rude, boastful, pugnacious, ill mannered, and uncultured. They were revolted by the American propensity for chewing tobacco and spitting out the juices and excessive drinking. They were repulsed by the institution of slavery and by the moblike quality of the democratic process.

The Reverend Sydney Smith, an English divine, acidly summed up the majority opinion in a review of several travel accounts in the *Edinburgh Review* in 1820 with the words, "The Americans are a grave, industrious, and acute people. But they have hitherto given no indications of genius, and make no approaches to the heroic, either in their morality or character. . . . During the thirty or forty years of their independence, they have done absolutely nothing for the sciences, for the arts, for literature, or even for the statesmanlike studies of politics or political economy. . . . Where are their . . . [Edmund] Burkes . . . their [James] Watts . . . their [Adam] Smiths . . . their [Walter] Scotts. . . . In the four quarters of the globe, who reads an American book? Or goes to an American play? Or looks at an American picture or statue? What does the world yet owe to American physicians or surgeons? What new substances have their chemists discovered? Or what old ones have they analyzed? What new constellations have been discovered by the telescopes of Americans? What have they done in the mathematics? Who drinks out of American glasses? Or eats from American plates? Or wears American coats or gowns? Or sleeps in American blankets?"

Basil Hall put the matter another way when he wrote, "The wisdom of a learned man cometh by opportunity of leisure and he that hath little business shall become wise. How can he get wisdom that holdeth the plow, . . . that driveth oxen and is occupied in their labors and whose talk is of bullocks." There were very few who were willing to acknowledge such virtues of American society as one British immigrant recounted after an extensive journey: ". . . an absence of human misery . . . a government taking away a very, very small portion of men's earnings . . . ease and happiness and a fearless utterance of thoughts . . . laws like those of the old laws of England, everywhere obeyed with cheerfulness and held in veneration . . . no mobs, no riots, no spies . . . a debt indeed, but then it was so insignificant a thing; and, besides, it had been contracted for the peoples' use . . . as to the manners of the people . . . unostentatious and simple. Good sense . . . everywhere, and never affectation; kindness, hospitality, and never-failing civility."

Americans resented deeply the harsh and unfriendly assessments made by their British cousins. They had hoped for sympathetic understanding of a new and inexperienced nation from a more ancient and mature people. In chagrin and anger they lashed out in the pages of their own journals against their critics. Typical was "An Appeal from the Judgment of Great Britain Respecting the United States," which appeared in the *North American Review*. The author's purpose was to demonstrate that England was as wicked a nation as any—guilty of barbarism (in the interest of her people in cockfighting) and of oppression (in treatment of Catholics) and of social injustice (in exploiting the working classes). As expected, the British journals replied in kind and soon a war of words was raging across the ocean that heightened the animosity between the two peoples.

A minor rebellion in Canada in 1837 was another occasion for intensifying the ill-feeling between Britain and America. Americans, viewing the uprising as a repetition of the events of 1776, a prelude to annexation, and an opportunity to rid North America of its last monarch, sympathized wholeheartedly with the rebels. When British regulars crushed the insurgents and their leaders, and some followers fled to Buffalo, American arms and money helped them to establish a base at Navy Island on the Canadian side of the Niagara River from which to continue the fight. To supply the rebels, an American steamer, *Caroline*, was hired, and soon it was making trips between the New York shore and the island headquarters. To cut the supply line, a party of British soldiers on the night of December 29, 1837 attacked the *Caroline* and burned her in American waters. In the melee, an American sailor was killed and others were wounded. Americans clamored loudly for revenge "not by simpering diplomacy—BUT BY BLOOD." Passions were heightened when the British government refused to apologize or to indemnify the family of the deceased or punish the perpetrators of the act on the grounds that the ship was engaged in an illicit traffic.

Happily, President Van Buren dampened the ardor of the extremists by refusing to be stampeded and by issuing a stern warning in January of 1838 of punishment for those who "interfere in an unlawful manner with the affairs of the neighboring British provinces." Still, throughout the year 1838, tension continued on the border. In May Americans destroyed a Canadian vessel in retaliation for the *Caroline*; in the summer, a number of organizations, called Hunter's Lodges, were formed with the avowed purpose of ending British rule in North America; and in the fall, there were several armed forays across the border from the American side.

The most dangerous episode connected with the rebellion came in 1840 when a Canadian deputy sheriff, Alexander McLeod, was arrested in New York and charged with the murder of the American sailor aboard the *Caroline* and with arson. The British government demanded his release on the grounds that even had he been in the raiding party (which was not certain), his participation, even to the extent of causing a death, was not a personal act, having been done under official orders. The United States secretary of state conceded the point but was helpless to secure McLeod's release because he could not interfere in the judicial proceedings of a state. McLeod was duly tried in the court of the State of New York. Fortunately, a jury acquitted him, but during the trial the British mood was ugly and there might well have been a war had McLeod been convicted and executed.

One month after the acquittal, in November of 1841, the affair of the *Creole* provided another opportunity for an angry exchange between the two countries. On that American ship, 135 slaves being transported from Virginia to Louisiana mutinied and forced the captain to put into Nassau in the Bahama Islands. There the British authorities freed all the blacks except the leaders of the insurrection, whom they hanged. The American owners of the slaves demanded their return but the British refused. That refusal must be viewed as part of a larger problem that for about 25 years had disturbed Anglo-American relations. In 1807 England had ended the slave trade in her empire and in 1833 had abolished the institution of slavery. Determined to stamp out the hateful traffic in human lives throughout the world, treaties were negotiated with the maritime nations permitting British warships to search vessels suspected of carrying slaves. The United States alone refused to enter into similar treaty arrangements, for although it, too, had made the slave traffic a crime (except in the coastwise trade) and wished to see it universally abolished, the idea of visit and search by English officers was, in the words of John Quincy Adams, "so obnoxious to the feelings and recollections of this country" as to make impossible ratification by the Senate.

To the British, the exclusion from surveillance of vessels flying the American flag was frustrating and reduced measurably the success of their mission since many slavers falsely flew the flag they knew would not be molested. And the United States government would not even permit a search of a vessel under the American flag to determine its true nationality.

Such was the harsh diplomatic climate which the statesmen of England and America faced as they wrestled with the problem of the northeastern boundary. It was, therefore, amazing that their representatives came together in June of 1842, negotiated amicably and briefly, and signed a treaty settling that question and others as well that gained the prompt and overwhelming approval of the United States Senate. The role of Secretary of State Daniel Webster in the settlement was crucial. He came to office in March of 1841 in the new Whig administration of William Henry Harrison and John Tyler committed to reaching an understanding with Britain. His motives were mixed. Closely linked to New England business and commercial interests, which constituted an important segment of the leadership of the Whig party, quite understandably he wished to have harmonious relations with the country's chief trading partner. At the same time, he wanted desperately to become his nation's minister to England. And what better prelude to such an appointment could there be than a successful resolution of the problems between the two powers under his direction? In September of 1841, he informed the British minister in Washington that he was prepared to discuss a compromise solution of the thorny northeastern boundary.

Fortunately for Webster, an election in England in the same month brought in a new government receptive to his overture. The quarrelsome and difficult Lord Palmerston was replaced at the Foreign Office by the conciliatory and agreeable Lord Aberdeen, who quickly dispatched a special envoy to Washington, Lord Ashburton. A better appointment could not have been made. Alexander Baring, Lord Ashburton, sixty-seven years of age, had a long and distinguished career in British politics as a member of Parliament for thirty years. More importantly, he was very well disposed to the United States. The great international banking house, Baring Brothers, that he headed had extensive investments in America and he himself had lived in Philadelphia during the 1790s and had married the daughter of a United States senator. He knew and admired Webster, having dealt with him three years earlier when Webster visited London to market securities and land in the wake of the depression following the Panic of 1837. To many Americans, the selection of Ashburton was welcomed as a gesture of British friendship and a sincere desire to settle differences.

It took Webster and Ashburton only two months to settle their differences. Brushing aside the historic claims and counterclaims, the two statesmen agreed to split roughly the disputed territory and on August 9, 1842 signed a treaty by which the United States received 7,015 and Canada 5,012 square miles. At the same time, the two men disposed of three other boundary questions. One concerned the line between the St. Lawrence and the Connecticut rivers, which had been inaccurately surveyed at one place so that it ran three fourths of a mile north of the 45th parallel, the true boundary. There the United States had built a fort and Webster did not wish to give it up. Ashburton accepted the old line. He acknowledged, too, the American position on the source of the Connecticut River that netted the United States 150 miles there. Finally, regarding a difference of opinion on the precise border between Lake Superior and the Lake of the Woods, the British envoy agreed to the American claim that gave to the United States about 6,500 square miles of territory, which years later was found to contain some of the world's richest deposits of iron ore.

Clearly, Ashburton had presented no problem for Webster. Maine and Massachusetts (which retained half-interest in Maine's public lands when in 1820 Maine separated from Massachusetts) were the obstacles to a settlement. They seemed no more willing to accept a division of the disputed territory in 1842 than they had in 1831. But in the end, they gave way, and it was Webster's shrewd tactics that won the day. First he assuaged the two states by a payment to each of $150,000 and the promise of free navigation of the St. John River where it formed the boundary between Maine and New Brunswick. His masterstroke, however, was to convince them, by the use of two maps, that they had better be contented with part of the territory because all the land was legally Britain's. The maps, which Webster claimed were copies of the Mitchell maps used by the negotiators at Paris, had clearly marked in red the exact boundary line and it supported the British position. One of the maps Webster had purchased from the heirs of Revolutionary War General Von Steuben; the other had been found in the French archives by Harvard historian Jared Sparks. Neither Webster nor Sparks were certain of the authenticity of the maps; still, Webster did not hesitate to use them for, at that particular moment, he valued peace above truth.

Ashburton, too, valued peace above all. Webster had shown him the maps supporting the British position, but not only did he not thereupon demand more territory, he actually financed the trip Sparks made to Maine to convince the state authorities of the wisdom of compromise. The British public learned of the existence of the maps shortly after the ratification of the treaty, and some attacked Ashburton for his apparent capitulation. Ashburton, however, was unperturbed. "Upon the defense of my treaty," he wrote, "I am very stout and fearless. It is a subject upon which very little enthusiasm can be expected. The truth is that our cousin Jonathan is an aggressive, arrogant fellow in his manner. By nearly all of our people he is therefore hated, and a treaty of conciliation with such a fellow, however considered by prudence or policy necessary, can in no case be very popular with the multitude. Even my own friends and masters who employed me are somewhat afraid of showing too much satisfaction with what they do not hesitate to approve."

Ashburton's analysis of the state of British opinion was correct, and it was equally applicable to the United States. The territorial compromise did not generate enthusiasm but there was satisfaction in that the treaty cleared the air between the two nations by disposing of those outstanding differences which had been disturbing their relations. In addition to the several boundary settlements, the matter of the *Caroline* was laid to rest when Ashburton expressed "regret" that "some explanation and apology for this occurrence was not immediately made." Although the *Creole* case was not mentioned, the treaty did make an arrangement relating to the slave trade. Each country was to keep a squadron off the African coast to maintain surveillance over ships of its own nationals, but provision was also made for acting "in concert and cooperation, upon mutual cooperation, as exigencies may arise." Finally, the treaty stipulated seven nonpolitical crimes that were to be extraditable between the two countries, thus ending the dangerous situation of each country serving as a refuge for the criminal fugitives of the other.

One issue between England and the United States was not even discussed by Webster and Ashburton—Oregon. It will be recalled that both nations laid claim to that vast territory lying between the Rocky Mountains and the Pacific Ocean and between 54° 40′ and 42°—a land rich in timber, furs, and fertile soil and possessing a great harbor (at San Juan de Fuca near present-day Seattle). Neither power was willing to surrender its claim nor fight for it. The result was an agreement in 1818 by which both renounced exclusive jurisdiction over the territory and threw it open to the citizens of both countries on an equal basis. For the next half dozen years all was quiet in the area and the rival claimants paid it little attention. Settlers of both nationalities moved in to trap the furs, till the soil, and fell the timber but in small numbers and they were mostly English. The most prominent feature of this period was the purchase, in 1821, of the assets of the Northwest Company, a British fur-trading organization operating in the territory, by the mighty Hudson's Bay Company, since 1670 the relentless exploiter of Canada's wealth. Under its indomitable chief agent, Dr. John McLoughlin, the company quickly came to dominate the economic life of Oregon and to exert unofficial political control over the area.

Then, in 1824, conditions changed. Oregon became an issue in the American election that year as manufactured by the opponent of John Quincy Adams to discredit his candidacy in the West. They said that he cared nothing for the interests of that section, having consented, when he served on the Peace Commission in 1814, to give Britain rights on the Mississippi River in exchange for concessions in the North Atlantic fisheries and having weakened American claims to Oregon during the negotiations of 1818 when he was minister to London again for fishing advantages for New Englanders. Now these men began to reassert the exclusive claim to Oregon. Led by Thomas Hart Benton in the Senate and John B. Floyd in the House, pressure mounted in Congress to occupy Oregon by Ameri-

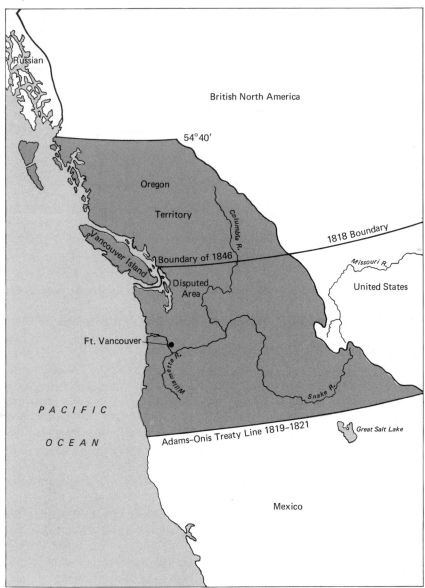

Oregon Territory Boundary Settlement, 1846.

can military forces and to take possession of all of it. Violent British reactions and threats from London to resist any aggressive move by the United States cooled tempers in Washington. Hot heads were impressed by Foreign Secretary George Canning's determination not to "have my name affixed to an instrument by which England would have foregone the advantages of an immense direct intercourse between China and what may be, if we resolve not to yield them up, her boundless establishment on the northwest coast of America." Wisely, Adams, upon taking office in March of 1825, sent Albert Gallatin to London to assure the British of America's intention to respect the "free and open" agreement of 1818. In 1827, it was officially extended for an indefinite period.

The Oregon question did not disappear after 1827 as it had after the settlement of 1818. The agitation during the election of 1824 had so aroused the public interest that in the years immediately following, missionaries, farmers, and trappers started the trek to Oregon to see what was so desirable about the place. Between 1832 and 1836, Methodists established a mission under Jason Lee in the Willamette Valley, Presbyterians led by Marcus Whitman erected another at Walla Walla, and Anglicans and Roman Catholics founded others. In 1828, Jedidiah Smith and his men of the Rocky Mountain Fur Company entered Oregon from California to begin fur-trapping operations, and four years later, Nathaniel Wyeth took a party overland from the east for fur trading and salmon canning. Meanwhile, farmers in increasing numbers were following the Oregon Trail from Independence in Missouri, along the Missouri, Platte, Snake, and Columbia rivers to find new homes in the lush valleys of the Willamette and the Columbia. The largest single caravan, consisting of 1,000 persons, left Independence in 1843, and additional thousands migrated in 1844. By that time, the Trail had become "a deeply rutted highway [worn] by the pioneers in their covered wagons."

It was inevitable that Oregon become an issue in the upcoming presidential election. Agitation had been mounting in the press and in Congress to organize a territorial government there and to occupy it with troops. After the Webster-Ashburton settlement over Maine, there was a good deal of concern in the country that Webster might be sent to London to offer a compromise solution involving the surrender of the land north of the Columbia in return for British pressure on Mexico to yield northern California. A convention of 120 delegates from six states that met in Cincinnati in July 1843 resolved that it was "the imperative duty of the General Government forthwith to extend the laws of the United States over said territory." By the time the national nominating conventions convened in May of 1844, Oregon (and Texas) were on everybody's lips.

The Whigs met first, on the first day of the month. Although the mercantilist interests in the party were attracted to Oregon because of its fine harbor and its potenial as a nexus for the Pacific trade, the delegates decided to play it safe. The party platform made no mention of Oregon (or of Texas). Apparently, the leaders preferred not to run the risk of losing the conservative antiexpansionist vote rather than capitalize on the expansionist spirit. The Democrats, meeting on the 27th and led by ardent expansionists, took the opposite tack. Oregon and Texas were seen as superb bait for the voters in all sections. The platform boldly stated "our title to the whole of the Territory of Oregon is clear and unquestionable; that no portion of the same ought to be ceded to England or any other power; and that the re-occupation of Oregon and the re-annexation of Texas at the earliest practicable period are great American measures which this Convention recommends to the cordial support of the Democracy of the Union." The party's standardbearer, James K. Polk, wholeheartedly concurred in these sentiments and joined, during the campaign, in the popular cry "54° 40' or fight" (the northern limits of the territory).

When elected, Polk continued the demand for all Oregon. In his inaugural address he proclaimed, "Our title to the country of the Oregon, is 'clear and unquestionable' and already are our people preparing to perfect that title by occupying it with their wives and children. . . . To us belongs the duty of protecting them adequately. . . . [and] the jurisdiction of our laws and the benefits of our republican institutions should be extended over them. . . ." At the end of the year, in his first annual message, he recommended that Congress enact legislation to terminate "joint occupancy" of Oregon with Great Britain (permitted under the Convention of 1827 upon giving one year's notice) and to extend to the Americans there "our laws and our jurisdiction, civil and criminal." Several paragraphs later, he warned England away from Oregon by reiterating "the principle avowed by Mr. Monroe [in 1823] and to state my cordial concurrence in its wisdom and sound policy . . . especially in reference to North America . . . [that] 'the American continents . . . are not to be considered as subjects for future colonization by any European powers.' "

The British were not intimidated by Polk's bellicosity. They did not plan to yield to Yankee bluster. The foreign secretary announced in Parliament that the British had rights which "we are fully prepared to maintain" while the *London Times* more bluntly described the method of maintaining them "by WAR." Across the Atlantic, Americans were as obdurate. One editor exclaimed, "*Oregon is ours*, and we will keep it, at the price, if need be, of every drop of the nation's blood." The president told a congressman "that the only way to treat John Bull was to look him straight in the eye." In April 1846, Congress passed a resolution terminating "joint occupancy." The way seemed paved for an American takeover.

The diplomatic climate in the spring of 1846 was harsh as hot tirades crossed and recrossed the ocean, and the prospect of a rupture between the two countries was not remote. Yet, curiously enough, in June 1846, the British minister in Washington was authorized by London to offer a compromise settlement at the 49th parallel, which Polk, with the Senate's consent, accepted. Within a few days, a formal treaty was drawn up dividing Oregon at the 49th parallel from the Rockies to the Pacific that the Senate promptly approved, 48–14. What had happened to transform lions into lambs and eagles into doves? What factors had changed truculence to tranquility?

One cardinal factor on the British side was a political crisis in late 1845 that caused the Whig party to call a truce on baiting the Tory party (in power) on foreign policy matters. Until that time, any concessions the foreign secretary might have made in Oregon to America would have been political suicide. After that, Aberdeen, who had long favored a compromise settlement, could suggest one with impunity. Second, the business and commercial interests in England were just recovering from a depression and needed the trade of the United States. Hostilities would have destroyed any hopes for large sales overseas as well as jeopardized the considerable British investment in America. Oregon was simply not worth the risk. Third, there was a rising feeling in Britain that distant colonies were not really crucial to the survival or prosperity of the Empire. This "Little England" view maintained that of greater importance was an increase in the quantity and quality of manufactures, which alone would form the basis of Britain's wealth and power. The salesman would henceforth be the consul. It was this movement which led to the repeal of the age-old protective tariff and to the destruction of the once deeply intrenched mercantilist system, on which the glory of the eighteenth-century empire had rested and which had been instrumental in the loss of the American colonies. A new imperial concept was in the wind to which the navigation acts would be anathema. Finally, of crucial importance was the fact that the Hudson's Bay Company had moved its operation north of 49°, having trapped out the area south of the line.

As for the American stand, it is clear that Polk's adamant posture was a façade, and his bellicosity was geared to a political advantage. He had never considered the territory north of the 49th parallel worth fighting for. Indeed, on several occasions he had privately offered to compromise on that line while publicly holding out for 54° 40′. Similarly, except for a handful of extreme expansionists in the Democratic party, no one really wanted, or expected, all of Oregon. What was important in Oregon, the rich agricultural land of the Willamette and Columbia River valleys (where most of the Americans had settled) and the magnificent harbor at Puget Sound, lay south of the compromise line. More crucial in Polk's consideration was the fact that he knew all along of the unavoidability of a war with Mexico if California were to be gained and he could not face conflict with England at the same time.

BIBLIOGRAPHY

ALBERT B. COREY, *The Crisis of 1830–1843 in Canadian-American Relations* (1941).

NORMAN A. GRAEBNER, *Empire over the Pacific* (1955).

WILBUR D. JONES, *Lord Aberdeen and the Americas* (1958).

FREDERICK MERK, *The Oregon Question: Essays in Anglo-American Diplomacy and Politics* (1967).

CHARLES SELLERS, *James K. Polk, Continentalist, 1843–1846* (1966).

FRANK THISTLEWAITE, *America and the Atlantic Community: Anglo-American Aspects, 1790–1850* (1959).

Matthew Perry (courtesy of the U.S. Navy).

Manifest Destiny Continued: Overseas

THE EXPANSIONIST movement that was so prominent a feature of American history in the several decades before the Civil War concerned itself not only with acquiring territory on the North American continent but also with projects for adding land and increasing influence and contacts in noncontiguous areas, such as the Far East, Central America, and the Caribbean. In the 1840s and 1850s, the United States negotiated important commercial treaties with China and Japan, made strenuous but futile efforts to bring Cuba under the American flag, and took steps to gain special rights in Nicaragua and in the Colombian state of Panama for building a transoceanic canal.

In the Far East, American interests and activities dated back to the close of the Revolutionary War. At that time, ships made idle by the war's end and by the restrictions on trade in British colonial ports sought new channels of commerce and found them in traffic with China. It was in 1784 that an American vessel, *Empress of China*, out of New York, first touched a Chinese port, Canton. The profit on that voyage was comparatively small but the potential was believed to be very great. Soon more ships engaged in the traffic and profits rose—sometimes as high as 1500 per cent on a single voyage. Exchanging ginseng (a medicinal root highly prized by the Chinese), furs (mink, beaver, fox, and sea otter much in demand by wealthy mandarins), cotton goods, beer, snuff, candles, soap, tobacco, shoes, sugar, pitch, tar, and sandalwood (from Hawaii) for tea and silk, merchants from New York and New England made fortunes. Many of the great families—Astor, Perkins, Higginson, Cabot, Delano, Lawrence, Lowell—trace their wealth and prominence to the China trade.

By the turn of the century, twenty to thirty ships each year were engaged in the China trade. Those ships (and the ships of every other nationality as well) could use only one Chinese port, Canton. Furthermore, the merchants had to conduct their business according to the whim and caprice of the port authorities. In the absence of a Sino-American treaty of commerce, they had no legal rights and no fixed rules. Tonnage and tariff dues varied from day to day, warehouse rates fluctuated, and delays were frequent. American merchants were beginning to demand that their government take measures to terminate what John Quincy Adams, a member of Congress from Massachusetts, in a speech in 1839 termed "the arrogant and insupportable pretensions of China that she will hold commercial intercourse with the rest of mankind not upon terms of equal reciprocity but upon the insulting and degrading forms of relations between lord and vassal."

The conduct of the Chinese may have appeared to Adams as arrogant and insupportable, but to the Chinese it was a logical and reasonable extension of their view of the world. Treaties and "equal reciprocity" presupposed sovereign equality among nations. The Chinese, however, never accepted that theory of international relations. What was a commonplace to Westerners was to them strange and foreign. For them, the world consisted of China, the superior state, and all the others were tributaries who were treated as supplicants required to perform the "kowtow" (three kneelings and nine knockings). Furthermore, the Chinese had little desire to treat with Westerners whom they considered barbarians and whom they looked upon with deep distrust. It would take a war and a defeat before China would be willing to adopt the Western theory of international relations and become party to a treaty.

As the value and volume of the China trade increased in the first three decades of the nineteenth century, American merchants increased the pressure on Washington to negotiate a treaty of commerce with China. A petition to Congress in 1839 requested that a strong naval force be sent to protect American nationals, that official diplomatic relations be instituted, and that a treaty open additional ports, fix tariffs and dues, guarantee compensation for losses suffered by stoppage of lawful trade, and insure that punishment for offenses committed by Americans in China be no greater than for the same offenses in the United States.

Added to the demands of the traders were those of the missionaries. It was in 1830 that the first American—Elijah Bridgman—arrived in China to preach the gospel and convert the heathens. Thereafter, clergymen came in increasing numbers until by the end of the decade there was a sizeable contingent of several denominations operating schools and missions. They, too, sought government intervention to safeguard their work and to protect it from arbitrary treatment by the Chinese.

In response to the twin pressures, the Whig administration that took office in 1841 was prepared to act. Daniel Webster, the secretary of state, a devoted New Englander and conscious of the fact that the greatest number of merchants and missionaries involved with China came from his section, called on Congress in 1842 "to make appropriation for the compensation of a commissioner to exercise a watchful care over the concerns of American citizens." As commissioner, he selected Caleb Cushing,

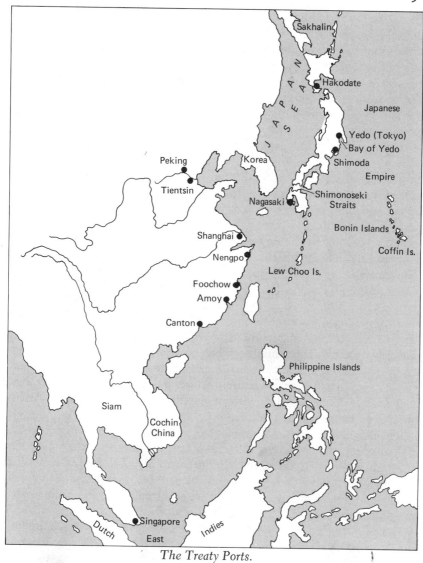

The Treaty Ports.

a brilliant lawyer and Whig politician from Newburyport, Massachusetts and son of a shipowner in the China trade. In instructions dated May 8, 1843, Cushing was charged with negotiating a most-favored-nation treaty. He was to convince the Chinese authorities that his mission was peaceful and commercial and that, unlike England, the United States had no Asiatic colonies and coveted none. He was to perform the "kowtow" but without conveying an impression of inferiority.

In July 1843, Cushing left Boston accompanied by a surgeon, a secretary, a number of young men who paid their own way, and two interpreters in four warships loaded with a wide variety of gifts for the Chinese officials. He arrived in Macao, near Canton, early the following year, and, after several amusing adventures, made the Treaty of Wanghia on July 3, 1844. By that instrument, four ports—Ningpo, Amoy, Foochow, and Shanghai—were opened to American traders in addition to Canton; dues, duties, and other charges were fixed and certain other commercial concessions were granted; any rights China might in the future give to a foreign power would be extended to the United States as well (most-favored-nation principle); and extra territoriality was conceded by the Chinese (the practice whereby Americans accused of crimes would be tried according to the laws of the United States by an American consular official).

Clearly, the terms were excellent and seemingly fulfilled all the wishes of the American traders, but, as a matter of fact, they were not completely pleased by Cushing's success. For one thing, the treaty had not been necessary since the Chinese government the year before had granted to the American merchants all the concessions it contained. In an edict dated November 15, 1843, the Emperor had extended to all foreigners the rights embodied in an Anglo-Chinese Treaty of 1842 (following a British victory in the Opium War, 1839–42), which were identical with the American demands. Indeed, as early as the fall of 1842, Americans in China knew they would get what they wanted when in an exchange of letters between Laurence Kearny, commanding the East Indian Squadron, and the governor of Canton, the latter had virtually promised equality of opportunity for all foreigners. Such magnanimity was not surprising in view of the fact that in Chinese eyes all foreigners were deemed barbarous and all were to be treated in the same way.

The concessions having been granted, Americans were riding a high tide of prosperity under the new dispensation many months before the treaty was signed, and they questioned the need for a diplomatic agreement. As one merchant noted, "we are now on the very best possible terms with the Chinese and as the only connection we want with them is a commercial one, I cannot see what Mr. Cushing expects to do. He cannot make us better off." Indeed, it was feared that Cushing, who deported himself in an "imperial and flourishing" way, might, in the course of the negotiations, "sacrifice the good will of the Chinese and lose all." Once the treaty was made, the chief concern of the merchants was that the substitution of a legal relationship between the United States and China for the former nonlegal and personal arrangement might work to their disadvantage. Future disagreements between the Chinese and themselves would be subject to diplomatic negotiation. The process would be lengthy and involved and would be conducted by diplomats and consuls in China and by officials in Washington who, most probably, would have no knowledge of China or of the Chinese and could not be expected to succeed. Furthermore, such disagreements might be viewed as "affronts to national dignity" which could lead to a rupture in relations and cessation of trade.

All those concerns notwithstanding, the years after 1844 were marked by an increase in American commercial activity, particularly through Shanghai, which was closest to the tea and silk-producing areas of China and to the Pacific ports newly acquired in California and Oregon. As had been anticipated, there were difficulties with Chinese officials who treated Americans, and all other foreigners, with contempt and frequently violated the terms of the treaty, but the problems were not so grave as to affect seriously the position of the merchants. A new treaty, signed on June 18, 1858 at Tienstin, provided new and greater opportunities for them and enabled them to do a large and more profitable volume of business. The treaty also gave the missionaries more rights and privileges and they, too, prospered.

The Treaty of Tienstin was closely related to a fierce and violent rebellion which broke out in China in 1849. At the outset, Americans in China tended to sympathize with the rebels, called Taipings. Missionaries wished for their success because the movement had a quasi-Christian quality. Its leader, who had been greatly influenced by a Baptist missionary, viewed himself as a brother of Jesus Christ on a mission to liberate his people from Manchu misrule. Merchants and traders hoped that the replacement of the Manchus by the Taipings would lead to better treatment and more privileges. Some held the view, also, that if victorious, the Taipings might be incapable of ruling China, leading to the dismemberment of that empire and to the seizure of political control in certain parts by Western powers.

Washington, reflecting the interests of Americans in China, adopted a policy of neutrality while awaiting a rebel victory. Meanwhile, in China, the American commissioner, Humphrey Marshall, was becoming suspicious of British and Russian diplomacy. Both powers, it appeared, were working behind the scenes in an effort to influence the outcome of the rebellion and strengthen their position with the victorious faction. The British, although professing neutrality, were aiding the rebels, and the Russians were helping the Manchus. Marshall warned his government that "If the avarice and the ambition of Russia or Great Britain succeed, the fate of Asia will be sealed and the future Chinese relations with the United States may be considered closed for ages unless now the United States shall foil the untoward result by adopting a sound policy."

The sound policy he recommended was to support the legitimate government and the territorial integrity and administrative entity of China. Only a strong central authority in China could guarantee equality of opportunity and of treatment (an "open door") for all foreigners. What Marshall was suggesting did in fact become the official position of the United States as enunciated in the famous "Open Door" notes at the end of the century that were to underlie America's China policy in the twentieth century.

Fortunately for Marshall and for the United States, Britain came around to realizing the wisdom of supporting the legitimate government and abandoned the rebel cause. The seizure of control by the Taipings of parts of China which they ruled from Nanking led to the conviction that "the dissolution of the Chinese Empire and the separation of its provinces could not fail to be accompanied by the interception of communication, the diminution of wealth, the destruction of industry, by all the calamities which check the power of production and consumption. Such a result would be prejudicial to the interests of Great Britain."

Having decided to back the Imperial government, the British now moved to force it to provide better treatment to British traders. A short war in 1857 ended in a decisive victory for England, followed by a new treaty that opened eleven additional ports and extended several other privileges and rights. Acting on the most-favored-nation principle, China at once extended the terms of the treaty to the United States by an agreement signed at Tienstin.

At the same time, the United States was moving to open the Japanese islands. Those islands had been closed to western traders, except for a single Dutch vessel permitted to enter Nagasaki annually, since the seventeenth century when a warrior clan, the Tokugawa, gained control of the country and at once cut off what had been an active commerce with the Western nations. As American merchants became more involved in the China trade in the early years of the nineteenth century, it was natural for them to wish to extend their profitable operations to the Japanese markets. More urgently and more immediately, they, and also the whaling vessels operating in the Pacific, wanted the right to put into Japanese ports for supplies and fresh water and the assurance that crews of American vessels wrecked on the Japanese coast would receive decent treatment. The practice at the time was to imprison them and to treat them cruelly and as criminals.

In 1832, an effort by Edmund Roberts, a New Hampshire merchant with trading experience in the Indian Ocean, to open contact with the Japanese failed. Fourteen years later, Commodore James Biddle sailed into Yeddo Bay (present-day Tokyo) with two ships on a similar mission but was promptly chased away. Eight years after that episode, Commodore Matthew C. Perry succeeded where the others had failed. On March 31, 1854, he signed the first treaty ever made by Japan with a Western nation. There were several reasons for Perry's success in extracting an agreement from the Japanese. For one thing, Japan was beginning to feel pressure from many nations, particularly Britain and Russia, to abandon isolation. News of the capitulation of China to Western demands seemed to indicate that further resistance would prove futile. News of events in America had also reached the island kingdom: It was revealed that the United States had achieved a sensational military victory over Mexico and had, as a result of that war and of an agreement with Great Britain, gained a vast coastline on the Pacific. As a consequence, it now had to be accepted as a

[handwritten: Emperor lived in Yedo / Shogun- Tokugawa]

Pacific power. Finally, credit must be given Perry for bold and audacious conduct which went a long way toward convincing the Japanese of the wisdom of entering into relations with his country.

[handwritten margin: Became Tokyo]

Perry had arrived in Yeddo Bay on July 8, 1853 in four vessels, two of which were steamers. The dense black smoke emanating from their funnels, and their ability to sail in the face of the wind caused consternation among the Japanese lined up on the shore. They were not so impressed, however, as to accept Perry's demands which were, following instructions from President Millard Fillmore, to secure some permanent arrangement for protecting shipwrecked sailors and to gain access to several ports for trade and for the purchase of supplies. Instead, they urged him to leave, but Perry did not frighten easily. When the port officials refused to accept a letter from the president addressed to the emperor, he went ashore with 400 sailors and marines and delivered it. Then he announced his intention to depart but to return the following year with a more powerful squadron for the Japanese answer.

Six months later, on February 12, 1854, he once again entered Yeddo, this time with seven vessels and a determination to get his treaty. The size of his fleet was enough, apparently, to influence the Japanese to treat with him and six weeks later he had his treaty. By its terms, two ports— Shimoda and Hakodate—were to be opened for trade and for the purchase of supplies; one of them was to be a haven for shipwrecked mariners; and an American consul was to be permitted to reside in Shimoda. The treaty also included a most-favored-nation clause. Within a few months, President Fillmore appointed Townsend Harris, a merchant with considerable experience in the Asiatic trade, to the consular post and in August 1856 he took up residence at Shimoda.

[handwritten margin: Hong Kong]

Immediately, Harris set about to get greater concessions from the Japanese. He had a difficult time in the face of hostility and intimidation by Japanese officials, who seemed to have regretted opening their doors to foreigners. They even asked him to return home. But Harris stayed on and persisted in his efforts. By a combination of tact, patience, and shrewd diplomacy, which included a reminder of the naval attack on China by Britain and other powers, he won his objective. A new treaty, signed on July 29, 1858, opened four more ports for trade and residence (with two *[handwritten: Yedo]* additional places made available a short time later), provided for extraterritoriality, established fixed tariffs and harbor dues, and inaugurated diplomatic relations between the two countries. To Harris went the honor of being his country's first minister to Japan.

If it can be said that the United States sought its objectives in Asia with a maximum of tact and moderation and a minimum of pressure and force, the same does not apply to its Cuban policy in the same period. There the policy was reckless and provocative. It was characterized by frank statements of the desirability and inevitability of the acquisition of the island, by the sanctioning (if not instigation) of armed attacks there, and by a

[handwritten right margin, vertical: Extraterritoriality— British conduct trials of British citizens of to]

[handwritten bottom: Wanghia treaty / Burlingame / Meiji— now Emperor / Parliament (French) / Cabinet (Prussia) / Legal System]

bold and thoroughly reprehensible scheme for wresting Cuba from Spain.

The importance of Cuba to the well-being of the American republic was widely acknowledged in the United States. Few Americans would have disagreed with Thomas Jefferson when he candidly confessed that "I have ever looked upon Cuba as the most interesting addition which could be made to our system of states" or with John Quincy Adams when he stated his belief that "Cuba, almost in sight of our shores, from a multitude of considerations has become an object of transcendant importance to the political and commercial interests of our union." And Adams was certainly reflecting an American consensus when he calmly and confidently predicted, in a letter to the American minister in Madrid in 1823, that Cuba would "eventually belong to us . . . by laws political as well as physical."

Americans coveted the "Pearl of the Antilles" for a variety of reasons. One was strategic. People commented upon Cuba's "commanding position" in relation to the Gulf of Mexico and the Caribbean. It lay directly in the path of American commerce as it passed from the Atlantic ports of the United States to those of Central and South America and of the west coast of America by way of the Isthmus of Panama. Further, it was a perfect springboard for the launching of an attack on Florida and the Mississippi River. The *London Times* recognized Cuba's significant location when it noted that the island was "a station from which the British navy would have complete command over the southern and eastern coasts of the United States." As the Lowlands were to England, so Cuba was to the United States—a pistol cocked at its heart. Clearly, Cuba was a menace as long as it was in the hands of a foreign power.

Economically, the link with Cuba was strong. Since colonial days, there had always been a brisk trade with the island, and by the early nineteenth century this trade had reached a significant figure. Americans sold fish, foodstuffs, lumber, flour, lard, hardware, and manufactured articles and bought sugar, rum, and molasses. There was also an increasing investment of American capital in the island in plantations and in the transportation network. The awareness of the possibility that the trade could be cut off and the property confiscated at any moment by the mother country was enough of a motive for putting the island under the American flag.

The trade with Cuba was in the hands chiefly of Northerners. The products came principally from that section as did the merchants who handled the arrangement, the bankers who provided the capital, and the shipowners whose vessels carried the goods. But Southerners had their own reasons for desiring Cuba. One was the constant fear of a revolt of slaves in that island that might easily spread to the South. Another was the danger of the liberation of slaves there by the Spanish government—called "Africanization"—and its effect on American slaves. As one Southerner put it: "If the slave institution perishes in Cuba, it perishes here." Finally, Cuba offered new soil for growing cotton as well as new territory for carving out slaveholding states that would add to the political power of the South in the national councils.

Despite the strong interest in Cuba, no move was made for acquiring it in the first 45 years of the nineteenth century. Expansionists were preoccupied with projects closer to home—California, Texas, Oregon—and the government was engaged in negotiations with England on various matters that could easily have been jeopardized by a play for Cuba. Britain was vigorously opposed to Cuba falling into American hands and was reported prepared to fight to prevent it. American policy was, therefore, restricted to frustrating any effort by a great power to take Cuba—meaning, of course, Great Britain, whose interest in the island was well known. Rumors were constantly floating around the world of the imminence of British acquisition of Cuba in exchange for Gibraltar, in payment of the debt contracted by Spain for assistance against Napoleon, or as balancing the transference of Florida to the United States. So long as Cuba was Spanish, there was little to fear from that island for Spain offered no threat. Indeed, Spain would serve perfectly the role of trustee until the time was propitious for America to act. On the several occasions when Cuban patriots proposed to Washington that the United States annex the island if a revolution were to be mounted successfully, the State Department politely but firmly refused the offer.

A change in American policy came with the accession to the presidency of James K. Polk in March of 1845. His was a frankly expansionist administration. Having campaigned unabashedly on a platform calling for the annexation of Texas and of Oregon and known widely for his determination to take California from Mexico, Polk surprised no one when he went after Cuba. It was expected, too, that for the Southerners who controlled the Democratic party, Cuba would be crucial politically. Up to 1845, new states had entered the Union in pairs—one slave and one free—and an equilibrium in the Senate had been maintained. But by 1845, with the admission of Texas and Florida, it was clear that the source of slave states had been exhausted while there still existed almost limitless territory in the north and west from which free states would be carved unless Cuba could be had. And after the war with Mexico and the decision not to annex all of Mexico, Cuba became even more important as the sole opportunity for an increase in the number of slave states.

In June of 1848, Polk, after receiving authorization from Congress, instructed the American minister in Madrid to offer Spain up to $100 million for Cuba. At the same time, a wave of excitement was sweeping the country in favor of purchasing Cuba. In speeches and resolutions by senators and congressmen, toasts at banquets (including one made by the vice-president of the United States), letters to editors, and articles in newspapers and magazines, one read and heard all the usual "manifest destiny" slogans and arguments used so recently and successfully in relation to Texas, California, and Oregon. A revolution in Cuba at that moment accompanied by a stirring proclamation by the revolutionaries earnestly petitioning annexation by the United States and enumerating the advantages to Cuba of such a union stoked the passions of the country. Certain groups, unwilling to await the outcome of diplomatic negotiations, were making plans for mounting filibustering expeditions in Cuba and were openly recruiting volunteers, raising money, and holding target practice as societies such as the Order of the Lone Star and the Knights of the Golden Circle were organized to help the cause.

Spain was neither intimidated nor impressed by the popular outburst for Cuba. Indeed, it seemed to stiffen the resistance to the offer to purchase in that it appeared to be a crude threat. The reply to the official tender to negotiate was a flat refusal. "Sooner than see the island transferred," said the foreign minister, he would "prefer seeing it sunk in the Ocean." Thus, Polk left office in 1849 without achieving that objective.

The Whigs who succeeded the Democrats in 1849 did not press for Cuba. Although the Whig party contained many people actively engaged in the trade with Cuba and heavily involved in investments there, the antislavery elements were so strong, particularly in New England and the Old Northwest, as to make impossible the party's support for the acquisition of the island. Indeed, President Millard Fillmore did all in his power to halt the several filibustering expeditions undertaken by General Narciso López, a Cuban refugee, from American ports in 1850 and 1851. What Fillmore did not do, however, and what no administration could have done, was engage in any promise never to take Cuba. When Britain and France in 1852 sought to exact such a promise, Secretary of State Edward Everett replied that his government some day would wish to acquire Cuba in view of its supreme importance to the security of the United States. Furthermore, he added, the question of Cuba and its future should be of no concern to those two countries for it was purely an American question. To point up the absurdity of their suggestion, he compared it to a similar one that the United States might make concerning two hypothetical islands situated at the mouths of the Seine and Thames rivers and owned by Spain.

The return of the Democrats to office in 1853 marked the renewal of an aggressive Cuban policy. President Franklin Pierce was easily as passionate an expansionist as Polk. Although a Northerner from New Hampshire, he had very decided Southern sympathies and inclinations and his appointments to important administration posts went mainly to Southerners. Jefferson Davis, his secretary of war, was his closest political associate, and three other members of his cabinet were from the South. Indeed, his Southern affinities were to culminate in his opposition to the Civil War. There was no question that he supported the Southern desire to possess Cuba and he lost no time in making it known. In the Inaugural Address he announced that "our attitude as a nation and our position on the globe render the acquisition of certain possessions not within our jurisdiction eminently important for our protection." No place was mentioned but everybody knew the president was referring to Cuba.

Southerners, encouraged by the government's expansionist position, now laid plans for a large-scale expedition against Cuba. Under the leadership of a former governor of Mississippi, ships and men (reports ran as high as twelve ships and 50,000 men) gathered at New Orleans preparing to sail in the summer of 1854. But before they could move, the government withdrew its support and the scheme collapsed. It was not that the president disapproved the idea; it was, rather, that the tense domestic situation created by the debate over the Kansas-Nebraska Bill was tearing the Democratic party to pieces, and Pierce feared exacerbating conditions by a semiofficial assault on Cuba. Any disappointment Southerners may have felt was allayed, however, by the more daring project then under consideration: to offer to purchase Cuba from Spain and, if Spain refused, to take it by force.

This most unusual and undiplomatic step had its beginnings in instructions in April, 1854, to Pierre Soulé, the American minister in Madrid, to offer Spain $130 million for Cuba and, Secretary of State William L. Marcy continued, should Spain not be agreeable, "you will then direct your efforts to the next most desirable object, which is to detach the island from the Spanish dominion. . . ." Such a charge was bad enough but it was made incalculably worse because of the nature of the recipient. Few men were more injudicious and imprudent than Pierre Soulé. A Louisianan who had fled his native France after involvement in republican plots, he established a successful law practice in New Orleans, served in the Senate, and emerged as a leader of the States Rights group. He was one of the earliest supporters of the Cuban filibusters and his yearning for that island was widely known. Indeed, Europe interpreted his appointment to the Court of Madrid as an announcement of the Administration's intention. Upon leaving New York for his post, Soulé had the audacity to say, "I hope when I return to see a new star shine in the celestial vault of young America."

In Spain, his indiscretions were monumental. He duelled the son of a leading Spanish duke over an alleged insult to Mrs. Soulé, and he crippled the French minister in another duel. When he was advised by Washington to seek a settlement with the Spanish foreign office over the seizure of an American vessel, *Black Warrior,* in Havana harbor, he proceeded in the brashest manner and had the bad taste to press his claim during the holy days of Easter week. Happily, the foreign minister ignored the impetuous diplomat.

As was to be expected, Spain would not give up Cuba, whereupon Soulé, following instructions, travelled to Ostend in Belgium in October 1854, to confer with his two colleagues, John Y. Mason, the minister to France, and James Buchanan, the minister to Great Britain, both strong expansionists. Out of this meeting emerged one of the most curious documents in international history. Called the "Ostend Manifesto," it was merely a report sent secretly to Washington recommending that if Spain continued to resist an offer to purchase Cuba, then "by every law, human and Divine, we shall be justified in wresting it from Spain, if we possess the power."

By the time the suggestion reached Washington by confidential messenger in November, it had been already leaked to the press and was known all over Europe and the United States. People were amazed at the crassness of American policy that, according to one newspaper, "planned a burglary of great proportions and published a prospectus in advance." The outcry was so great that Pierce and Marcy had no course but to repudiate their emissaries and shelve the quest for Cuba. Marcy felt relieved. He was from New York and, although an expansionist, opposed the extension of slavery and had only reluctantly succumbed to the blandishments of the Southern wing of the Democratic party in its wish for Cuba. The end of the Cuban affair would, he believed, keep Northern Democrats from defecting from the party.

It was, indeed, the end of the Cuban affair. The Democratic party platform in 1856 called for acquiring Cuba, President James Buchanan in his first inaugural address listed its acquisition as an objective of his administration, and in 1858, he asked Congress for $30 million to begin negotiations for the purchase of the island. The Senate Committee on Foreign Relations reported favorably on the bill. The chairman, John Slidell of Louisiana, noted that the annexation of Cuba was a fixed purpose of American policy "resulting from political and geographical necessities." But Congress did not even vote on the measure for by that time the slavery question was the nation's sole preoccupation, and such violent passions were aroused by it that only the most foolhardy legislators would have widened the problem by introducing one more point of controversy.

Unlike Cuba, Central America did not figure significantly in American diplomacy until 1848, when gold was discovered in California. A favorite route from the east coast to the west went by way of the Isthmus of Panama and of Nicaragua, both of which offered the shortest land crossing of the continent. The desirability of a canal at one of those two places to facilitate the transit led to a movement to acquire the necessary territory or, at least, the right to build a waterway. In 1846, a treaty with New Granada (present-day Colombia) gave the United States the right of way across the Isthmus of Panama (which lay in New Granada), but the United States had not sought it. Benjamin Bidlack, the American diplomat who negotiated the treaty, had sought only to gain certain commercial rights for American vessels, but New Granada, at that moment fearful of British activity on its northern border, would grant the American wishes only if Bidlack would accept the right of way and guarantee the sovereignty of New Granada over it. The Senate approved the treaty and President Polk ratified it.

Americans were really more interested in the right of way across Nicaragua which because of the existence of two bodies of water—Lake Nicaragua and the San Juan River—presented less formidable obstacles than Panama in the building of a canal. There, however, the British had a firm foothold which they were unwilling to share with the United States. They had been in the area since the sixteenth century, when they began log-cutting operations on the coast of Honduras. From there, British settlements and authority spread southward into Nicaragua. A protectorate over the Mosquito Indians on the Atlantic coast of Nicaragua and the seizure and occupation of the town of Greytown at the mouth of the San Juan river gave Britain, by 1848, the predominant position vis-à-vis a canal site.

To offset the advantage and following a call for help from Nicaragua, Polk sent Elijah Hise to establish an American presence. In 1849, Hise negotiated a treaty that gave the United States exclusive control over the site for a waterway and obtained a concession for an American company to build a canal. In the same year, another American agent, Ephraim Squier, obtained from Honduras Tigre Island, which lay on its west coast and guarded the approach to a canal from that direction. Meanwhile, the British, on their part, were actively engaged in extending their authority and in frustrating the American advance. A treaty was signed with Costa Rica that protected that country's sovereignty over the northern bank of the San Juan River, and a British warship occupied Tigre Island. The United States government was notified it could not utilize the San Juan River since it belonged to the Mosquito Indians, and the American construction company was similarly advised it had no right to build on Mosquito land.

Not to be outdone, Squier, aggressive, vigorous, and youthful (twenty-one years of age) signed a new treaty with Nicaragua, gaining greater rights to a canal site and set out to organize a Central American federation under United States protection. By the end of 1849, a dangerous rivalry had developed between the United States and England in Central America as their representatives jockeyed for position and sought to gain greater influence with the republics there. Neither Washington nor London was anxious for a fight and both governments took measures to cool the situation. President Zachary Taylor did not send the Squier and Hise treaties to the Senate, and the British Prime Minister, Lord John Russell, repudiated the seizure of Tigre Island and the treaty with Costa Rica. Both sides were prepared to come to an accommodation that would give neither exclusive control over the canal site and thus avoid a collision. The result was the Clayton-Bulwer Treaty signed on April 19, 1850 in Washington.

By that instrument, both nations agreed "that neither the one nor the other will ever obtain or maintain for itself any exclusive control over the said Ship Canal." Both pledged not to erect fortifications in the area, establish colonies there, or exercise "dominion" over the republics in any part of Central America. They also guaranteed the neutrality of any canal to be built. In short, they exchanged their rivalry for cooperation. The treaty did not, however, mark the end of Anglo-American difficulties in the area. When Britain retained her protectorate over the Mosquito Indians and continued her dominion over her settlements in Honduras and in the islands off the coast, which she converted in 1852 into a Crown colony, the United States claimed violation of the treaty. An incident at Greytown in 1854 involving an injury to the American minister, a refusal by Britain to apologize, and a bombardment of that port by an American warship created an extremely tense situation between the two nations. And when William Walker, the American adventurer, embarked on his expedition to Central America, the British were convinced that it was with the connivance of the United States government and was designed, in disregard of the treaty, to achieve American hegemony over the canal site.

Walker, a conspicuous failure as physician, lawyer, and journalist at the age of twenty-five, turned to filibustering as an outlet for his restlessness. His first effort, in Sonora province in Mexico in 1852, ended in failure and in a trial in a United States court for violation of the law prohibiting the launching of a hostile expedition against a friendly power (for which he was acquitted when intent could not be proved). A revolution in Nicaragua and competition between American companies engaged in carrying freight and passengers across the country en route to the gold fields of California gave him a second chance. He was at that time editor of a San Francisco newspaper owned by Byron Cole, a capitalist interested in starting a transportation company in Nicaragua. When one of the revolutionary factions called on Cole for help, Cole asked Walker to lead an expedition there. In July 1855, Walker set sail for Central America with fifty-eight men. He captured the important city of Granada on Lake Nicaragua, defeated the opposing faction, accepted "election" as president of Nicaragua, and set up a government. He quickly granted to Cole the right to control the traffic across the country that had hitherto been enjoyed by Cornelius Vanderbilt.

The reception in the United States of the news of Walker's success and the policy of the government toward the new republic worried the British. Large numbers of Americans were elated. Mass meetings were held in various parts of the country at which resolutions were passed applauding Walker and damning the British. Walker's move was seen, joyously by Southerners and with revulsion by Northerners, as the prelude to the annexation of Nicaragua to the United States and to its eventual incorporation into the Union as a slave state. That view was reinforced when Walker, in September of 1856, proclaimed the re-establishment of slavery in Nicaragua and the imminent revival of the slave trade with the object, he declared, of binding "the Southern states to Nicaragua as if she were one of themselves." As for the government, in May of 1856, President Pierce received an emissary of Walker's in Washington and, at the same time, extended recognition to the new republic. Further evidence, if any were needed, to confirm British suspicions, was the inclusion in the platform of the Democratic party in 1856 expressions of sympathy with "the efforts which are being made by the people of Central America to regenerate that portion of the continent which covers the passage across the interoceanic isthmus."

As a matter of fact, the British had little to fear. Incorporation of new slave territory into the American union was not possible in the late 1850s. Northerners would never have permitted it. In any event, Walker's regime did not last long enough to consummate any plans he, or Southern sympathizers, may have had. Within one year, he was toppled from power by a group headed by Cornelius Vanderbilt. He tried one more adventure, this time to Honduras, where conditions were chaotic as a result of the transfer of certain British-held islands to Honduras. Initial successes frightened the British, who again looked on his campaign as a means for the extension of American dominion. When an opportunity came in September 1860 for a British naval patrol to seize Walker, it did so promptly. He was turned over to Honduran authorities, who put him against a wall and shot him.

By that time, the shadow of the Civil War was looming over the United States and with its eruption came the end of any plans for extending the American dominion to Central America, or any place else for that matter. The British could rest content that the equilibrium in the area covered by the Clayton-Bulwer Treaty would not be disturbed by Washington. On its part, the United States was satisfied by British treaties with Honduras and Nicaragua in 1859 and 1860 whereby England gave up the privileges and dominion it had retained after the treaty. The spirit of that agreement had been achieved at last.

BIBLIOGRAPHY

Tyler Dennett, *Americans in Eastern Asia* (1922).

Foster R. Dulles, *Yankees and Samurai: America's Role in the Emergence of Modern Japan, 1791–1900* (1965).

James A. Field, Jr., *America and the Mediterranean World, 1776–1882* (1969).

Kenneth S. Latourette, *The History of Early Relations Between the United States and China, 1784–1844* (1917).

Basil Rauch, *American Interests in Cuba, 1848–1855* (1948).

Te-kong Tong, *United States Diplomacy in China, 1844–1860* (1964).

Mary W. Williams, *Anglo-American Isthmian Diplomacy, 1815–1915* (1916).

William H. Seward (U.S. Signal Corps photo, Brady Collection, the
National Archives).

Civil War Diplomacy

I N THE great Civil War that broke out in 1861 as a result of the secession of the Southern states following the election to the presidency of Abraham Lincoln, diplomacy played a crucial role. Had the South been successful in its foreign policy, the outcome of the war might have been very different. Had the European powers contested the maritime practices of the United States, had they recognized the independence of the Confederacy, had they insisted that the North halt the war and admit the right of the South to become a nation—Confederate objectives all—there might have been no Appomatox. There is no doubt that the United States would never have accepted mediation nor tolerated attempts to restrict its freedom of action on the high seas. It was prepared to fight rather than submit, to convert the war into "a war of continents—a war of the world," as Secretary of State William H. Seward said in July 1862. If that had happened, it is entirely possible that the Union would have been defeated by a European coalition with Southern independence being the price of peace. As it turned out, no European nation intervened in the struggle nor seriously opposed the Union's conduct of the war at sea, thus permitting Washington to fight without interference and rely on its preponderant resources to win eventually.

Both North and South made strenuous efforts to influence the policies of the neutrals. Their diplomats pleaded the cause in every capital of Europe but in reality only three powers were important—Russia, France, and England. For England, the war had, from the very beginning, posed a dilemma. The country was divided in its reaction to the conflict. Political conservatives and the upper classes—nobility and gentry—loathing the democratic experiment across the ocean and fearful of its effects on British institutions, welcomed the disruption of the Union. They felt an affinity for the Southern patrician slaveholder and despised the money-grubbing and mercenary Yankee businessman. Typical of their attitude was the sardonic and caustic comment in a leading magazine on the presidential election of 1860. "Every four years the constitution is in travail; and the latest result is Mr. Abraham Lincoln. The great achievement in self-government of this vaunted democracy, which we have been so loudly and arrogantly called on to admire, is to drag from his proper obscurity an ex-rail splitter and country attorney, and to place its liberties at his august disposal. It would have been impossible for him or any of his cabinet to have emerged, under British institutions, from the mediocrity to which nature had condemned them and from which pure democracy alone was capable of rescuing them." By the time the war drew to an end, many Englishmen had changed their opinion of Lincoln and some of his sharpest critics came to appreciate his superior qualities. Typical was the poem which appeared in *Punch* at the time of his death:

> Yes, he had lived to shame me from my sneer,
> To lame my pencil, and confute my pen—
> To make me own this hind of princes peer,
> This rail-splitter a true born king of men.

Shippers and manufacturers, also, preferred a Southern victory expecting that the new nation would adopt a free-trade policy, which would insure a steady flow of cotton to feed the British textile factories and a ready and tariff-free market for British manufactured goods. Military and naval people and diplomats who thought in terms of power politics and national prestige saw in Southern independence the breakup of the great American nation that had already done so much to threaten and diminish British ascendancy in the New World and its replacement by two relatively weak countries.

On the other hand, political liberals and the plain people—workers, farmers, shopkeepers, artisans—sympathized with the American working-man in his struggle to end the competition of slave labor. They were, also, sufficiently influenced by the long antislavery tradition in England to wish for the destruction of the slave system in the New World. And because they themselves aspired to a greater share in their government, they wished the democratic experiment in America nothing but success.

It was the divided opinion that explains, in some measure, the contradictions and vacillations in British policy until mid-1863. The first official act of the government toward the war in America was to proclaim British neutrality. That policy accorded the Confederacy belligerent status by acknowledging the existence of a legal war between two sovereign states and clothed the South, as far as Britain was concerned, with certain crucially important rights such as, the right of its captured soldiers and sailors to be treated not as pirates and rebels but as prisoners of war, of its warships to visit and search neutral merchantmen on the high seas suspected of carrying contraband to the enemy, of sending representatives to foreign countries, and of buying supplies and borrowing money abroad.

Washington at once protested on the grounds that Britain had acted precipitously and was manifesting a partiality for the Southern cause; that the war was, in fact, a rebellion and an insurrection undertaken by individuals who were still citizens of the United States against the duly constituted authority. It was true, of course, that the United States government itself had already recognized Confederate belligerency when it instituted a blockade of Southern ports on April 19, 1861, for, according to the international law of the day, belligerent status flows automatically from a blockade. It is true, too, that early in the war, the crew of the Confederate ship *Savannah*, captured by a Northern vessel, was acquitted in a United States federal court of the charge of piracy and, throughout the war, federal courts in various decisions acknowledged the belligerent status of the South. But those actions were not taken to accord the enemy an exalted international status but rather for convenience. It was more efficacious to close Southern ports by blockade than by municipal decree and to treat the Southerners as pirates and rebels would not have been realistic. The British, however, had no such compelling reasons for according belligerent status and by doing so were, in effect, bolstering the cause of the South. They might just as well have taken no action.

In still another way Britain helped the South—by permitting its citizens to violate the spirit, if not the letter, of the domestic neutrality statutes in the matter of supplying vessels for the Confederacy. To gain an instant navy, the Confederates, at the outset of the war, had sent James D. Bulloch to England to buy warships. He knew that the neutrality laws of the country made it illegal to "equip, fit out, or arm in British jurisdiction a ship whose intent is to cruise against the commerce of a friendly power." Legal experts, sympathetic to the cause, advised Bulloch that it was, however, no violation of the letter of the law to build a vessel in England, buy equipment there separately, and join the ship and the equipment outside British jurisdiction.

Bulloch sprang to action. He had a ship built in Liverpool, bought guns, ammunition, and other warlike equipment, and when the ship, named *Oreto* and flying the British colors, sailed away one day in March 1862, it was followed by *Prince Alfred* with Bulloch's supplies. Some weeks later, the two vessels met off a deserted island in the Bahamas where *Prince Alfred* loaded the goods on *Oreto*, which promptly hauled down the British flag and raised the Stars and Bars as seamen painted her new name, C.S.S. *Florida* on her bow and stern. For twenty-one months, she roamed the seas until sunk by the U.S.S. *Wachusett* off Brazil in October 1864 after taking forty Yankee prizes. Responsibility for *Florida* was disclaimed by the British government although everyone in Liverpool knew that *Oreto* was being built for the Confederacy, that she was being fitted out as a warship, that equipment was being bought for her, and that *Prince Alfred* was carrying it for her. When the American minister in England, Charles Francis Adams, presented these matters to Lord John Russell, the foreign secretary, Russell had refused to halt *Oreto's* sailing.

Two other ships followed *Florida* to sea in exactly the same way. One was *Alabama*, the most notorious of all Confederate raiders. Built as *Enrica* in Liverpool and renamed after being joined in the Azores by the vessel *Agrippina* carrying guns and ammunition and gun carriages, she sailed 75,000 miles in two years in every ocean taking seventy American prizes valued at $675 million before being destroyed by U.S.S. *Kearsarge* off Cherbourg in June 1864. The other was *Shenandoah*, which, in a short fifteen-month career, captured forty prizes. Every time Adams protested, Russell rebuffed him, becoming so irritated once as to "express my hope that you may not be instructed again to put forward claims which Her Majesty's government cannot admit to be founded on any grounds of law or justice." The foreign secretary disclaimed any responsibility for "vessels, which may be fitted out in a foreign port, because such vessels were originally built in a British port."

Although a learned English lawyer informed Adams that the building in British ports of vessels that later became Confederate raiders was, in his opinion, a violation of the country's neutrality laws, a British court supported Russell's position. In the spring of 1863, upon Adams's insistence that the *Alexandra*, under construction in Liverpool, was known by everybody to be destined for Confederate use, the British government seized the vessel on the ground that its building violated the neutrality statutes. The builders sued for recovery of the ship claiming she was being built for a private British subject and, therefore, perfectly legal. An overwhelming amount of circumstantial evidence was presented to the court by the Queen's counsel indicating that the ship, by her design, by the interest in her shown by James Bulloch, and by reports of conversations between Bulloch and the builders, was to be a Confederate warship. Yet the judge, in charging the jury, pointed out that the building of a ship in a British port, if it were not armed, could not be considered a violation of neutrality even if destined for use by a belligerent. Such a vessel, he said, was in the same category as any other commodity that a neutral may sell to a belligerent. It was not surprising that the jury held for the plaintiff and the ship was released to embark on her marauding course as *Shenandoah*.

It was not until September 1863, when Bulloch contracted for two powerful ironclads, clearly warships, that Russell changed his course by purchasing the ships for the Royal Navy and letting it be known that no further vessels of questionable destination would be permitted to be built in British ports. It was at that time, too, that Russell called a halt to other evasions and infringements of neutrality. Confererate ships had been allowed to remain in British ports longer than 24 hours and to return to the same port before three months had elapsed, to enlist seamen in British ports, and to take on coal in British ports in excess of the amount necessary to carry them to their own closest port—all violations of British domestic statutes. These practices were stopped.

It was in the matter of mediation in the war and recognition of the independence of the South that Britain most clearly demonstrated her uncertainty. Cherished Southern objectives came close to being achieved. From mid-1861, many prominent Britons, several leading newspapers, and many members of Parliament and the government, including the prime minister, Lord Palmerston, considered diplomatic intervention in the war. A number of motions for mediation were introduced into the House of Commons only to be lost by narrow margins as a result of the votes of Northern sympathizers. The most serious effort came in the late summer of 1862 following the second Battle of Bull Run. That Southern victory caused Palmerston to feel that the time had come to acknowledge that Jefferson Davis had, in the words of William E. Gladstone, "made a revolution and was about to make a nation." Gladstone had uttered those words in a memorable pro-Confederate speech in October, 1862, that ended with: "We may anticipate with certainty the success of the Southern States as far as regards their separation from the North." Lord Russell agreed and suggested that if the United States refused the offer of mediation, England ought to recognize the independence of the Confederacy unilaterally.

All that changed at the end of September when London received word that General Robert E. Lee's bold scheme to carry the war onto Northern territory was crushed at Antietam Creek in Maryland and that he had withdrawn his army into Virginia. Gladstone seemed to have been contradicted and on October 22, Palmerston instructed Russell to drop the matter. It would have been folly to have intervened in favor of the belligerents whose forces were in retreat and appeared incapable of maintaining their own existence on the field of battle. In the following year, a second attempt by Lee to invade the North, his last, ended in failure again when, in July, he was repulsed at Gettysburg.

Never after that did Britain seriously consider interfering in the struggle. Backing the wrong horse was a dangerous diplomatic game. But there were other reasons for England's "hands-off" policy. One was her dependence on American trade for a measure of her prosperity. Although her factories supplied both Northern and Southern needs, her commerce with the Union was by far greater. The probability of war with the United

States as a consequence of mediation would have destroyed that lucrative revenue as well as endangered Britain's large investments in America. War would also have threatened England's merchant marine with destruction at the hands of the federal navy swollen in size and strength by the exigencies of war. And war, too, might well have meant the loss of Canada. Garrisoned but lightly by British troops and so distant from the mother country that no amount of reinforcement could ever hope to match the number of soldiers America could muster, an attack from the south of the border could hardly have failed to succeed. Nor was there any doubt that an American assault on Quebec and Montreal would have been the first move in an Anglo-American war. Canada was, indeed, a hostage in the relations between the two countries.

Another cause of British neutrality lay in the powerful impact of the Emancipation Proclamation of 1863. It strengthened pro-Northern sentiment among the plain people in England and in the ranks of the liberal members of Parliament. A war which had appeared to many Britons to have had the purely political objective of saving the Union and of throttling the nationalist aspirations of the South for freedom was now viewed as a crusade to free the enslaved and the degraded. Palmerston would have found it difficult to have gained support for a war on the side of those who wished to perpetuate the slave system. One must consider, also, the role of cotton as a cause for British inaction. At the beginning of the war, Southern leaders were certain that Britain's hunger for raw cotton to feed the Lancashire textile mills would prove a crucial factor in British policy toward the war. Deprived of Southern cotton, said one Southerner, "England would topple headlong." Effort was made, indeed, to withhold the vital material from Britain by embargoing its export and even burning some 2.5 million bales. But the tactic failed for two reasons. One was that, quite by chance, there was an overbundance of cotton in British warehouses at the outset of the war and a halt in its importation was welcomed. Another was that when cotton was needed in the later years of the war, England found excellent sources in Egypt and in India. King Cotton reigned no more, if it ever had.

Finally, credit for British refusal to mediate must be given to the superior diplomatic skill of President Lincoln and his Secretary of State, William H. Seward. Even if it was to England's self-interest to abstain from intervening in the struggle, coarse and crude diplomacy by American leaders might well have irritated and exasperated the English government and public to the point of their taking retaliatory action, however detrimental to their country's well-being. But both Lincoln and Seward acted with the greatest caution and circumspection, always careful not to push their case and cause too hard. Seward, who was responsible for the day-to-day conduct of American diplomacy, particularly deserves credit.

He was not expected to be a good foreign secretary, quite the reverse. Lord Lyons, the British minister in Washington, expressed to Lord Russell in a letter in January 1861, his fears that "Seward will be a dangerous Foreign minister. His view of the relations between the United States and Great Britain has always been that they are good material to make political capital."

Lyons's analysis seemed to be substantiated a few months later when Seward, on April 1, 1861, offered "Some thoughts for the President's consideration." He suggested that the best means for averting the domestic crisis brought on by secession was immediately to launch a war on foreign nations: "I would demand explanations from Spain and France, categorically, at once. I would seek explanations from Great Britain and Russia, and send agents into Canada and Mexico, and Central America, to rouse a vigorous continental spirit of independence on this continent against European intervention. And if satisfactory explanations are not received . . . would convene Congress and declare war against them." Faced by a common enemy, North and South would be reunited in a great surge of patriotism. Tactfully, President Lincoln turned aside the rash and belligerent advice, a decision that Seward gracefully accepted and thereafter he settled down to a career marked by the most artful diplomacy.

Superbly illustrative of Seward's subsequent skill was his handling of the *Trent* affair. That episode grew out of the seizure by Captain Charles Wilkes, commanding U.S.S. *San Jacinto*, of two Confederate envoys en route to Europe on the British steamer *Trent*. Wilkes carried them to Boston as "contraband of war." The whole nation was thrilled by what it considered a bold and heroic act. Wilkes was feted, memorialized, and praised. The British, on the other hand, were furious and rightfully complained that Wilkes had acted illegally. He had every right to take the entire ship into a United States port for a prize court to decide whether it was carrying contraband and thus subject to seizure but to take two passengers off was impressment and an insult to the flag. Britain was ready for war and, whatever the risk, would most probably have fought had not Seward (backed by Lincoln), with tact and forebearance and no little courage in the face of public clamor to defy England, handed the two envoys back to British authorities with an apology.

To Seward, too, goes much of the credit for the British acceptance of American maritime practices during the war, practices which stretched the rights of belligerents at sea at least as far as any nation had up to that time. They were practices, too, that violated principles the United States had vehemently and piously promoted from the beginning of its existence as an independent nation. In the matter of contraband, America had always supported the narrowest definition of the term to include only material used in the actual waging of warfare—arms and ammunition.

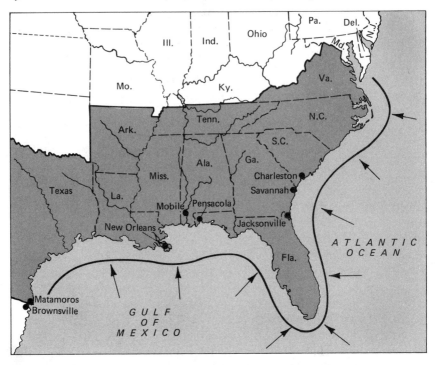

The Civil War Blockade of the Confederate Coast.

Food, clothing, naval stores, and other such items of importance to a war were specifically excluded from the first American list which appeared in the Plan of 1776 and when the belligerents in the wars of the French Revolution and Empire made them contraband, the neutral United States objected strenuously. Now, herself a belligerent, America abandoned her historic position and named as contraband the widest variety of items including food, clothing, naval stores, coin, and bullion.

As for the blockade, the American contention, as first stated in the Plan of 1784, was that a blockade to be legal must be effective; that is, ingress and egress to a port declared under blockade must be made difficult and dangerous by an adequate number of vessels stationed at the mouth of the port. That view the United States successfully incorporated in bilateral treaties made at the end of the eighteenth century with several European powers. That position, too, the United States defended when it was violated repeatedly by France and Britain during their war in 1793–1814. Yet, when on April 19, 1861, President Lincoln "set on foot" a blockade of the Confederacy, there were not enough American ships to blockade effectively the entire Southern coast. To cover a coastline of 3,600 miles including 189 bays, inlets, and rivers, the United States navy had only 90 vessels, of which only 40 were steam. True, the navy was increased tremendously as the war progressed but never to the point of providing a sufficient number of ships for effective blockade duty.

To make up the deficiency, the United States navy resorted to several devices, all used by the British before and all the subject at one time of strong protest by the American government. A flying squadron of speedy vessels patrolled the shipping lanes in the Atlantic in order to pick up neutral vessels far from the blockaded coast that were suspected of intent to land at a port of the Confederacy. American warships stood at the entrance to neutral ports, chiefly those in the British Isles and in the Caribbean, ready to capture any emerging vessel whose destination was believed to be the Confederacy. Finally, neutral ships plying between two neutral ports were seized if their ultimate destination or the ultimate destination of their cargo by any other vessel was thought to be a place in the South. And American prize courts upheld the seizures on the ground that the voyages between the neutral port of origin and the ultimate belligerent port in fact constituted one continuous voyage even though it may have been broken at the second neutral port indicated on the manifest.

The reason for the drastic revisal of America's historic position is not difficult to discover. The old principles befitted a nation which envisaged for itself the role of neutral or of small-navy belligerent. But for a nation fighting a war and possessing a large and powerful navy, they were unsuitable. They benefited the neutrals and the enemy and to observe them would have severly hampered the Union war effort. Expediency alone dictated the change. The abandonment of the long tradition was not lost upon foreign observers. The *London Times* expressed world opinion when it noted, "You see the morally righteous United States which stood as guardian of neutral rights—now when it is a preponderant belligerent is ready to trample on the toes of the neutrals."

As the neutral with the largest merchant fleet, it was Great Britain whose toes were most trampled upon. It was principally English vessels that American warships seized and American prize courts condemned. In Parliament and in the press voices were raised damning American practices—the blockading of Nassau and Liverpool, the capture of ships plying between two British ports, the extension of the contraband list. They accused the British government of surrendering the country's rights at sea and insisted that reprisals be taken even at the risk of war. Protests were, indeed, made by London and they were strong, but they always stopped short of demands that America halt her practices at the risk of war. In effect and despite the lengthy diplomatic remonstrances, Palmerston and Russell rather docilely accepted the American position on belligerent rights. To the claims of British consuls in the Confederacy that so much goods were getting through the blockade that Britain had every right to consider it ineffective and, hence, illegal, Russell replied, "Legality does not require that a blockade make access to the port impossible but only it must create an evident danger of entering or leaving it."

Russell's reasoning was indicative of the British reaction to the war at sea. Britain, in the foreign secretary's words to a session of the House of Lords, had a duty "to remain calm and make remonstrances." Orders were sent out to the admiral commanding the North Atlantic station to avoid any collision with American naval forces in the discharge of their orders and, in general, to exercise restraint. Clearly, the British were willing to permit the United States to exercise their belligerent rights as wartime needs dictated with a minimum of interference.

It was not love for America or sympathy with her cause that underlay British policy. It was chiefly a matter of the dissolution of the Union not being worth a war and of establishing precedent. The latter consideration was of supreme importance in British thinking for, after all, no nation was more interested than Britain in maintaining to the utmost extent belligerent rights at sea. And, noted the *London Times*, if "America had pushed the rights of belligerents on the high seas . . . beyond anything that have ever been claimed in their behalf . . . we of all people in the world are the least interested in opposing the innovation. American precedent may be very precious to England at some future crisis." Particularly important to Britain was the precedent of the blockade, which was described by one observer as "by far the most formidable weapon of offense we possess. Surely we ought not to be over ready to blunt its edges or injure its temper."

Although precedent was crucial to an explanation of Britain's tolerance of American maritime practices, Seward's role was of extreme importance. During every war, the fighting arms—navy and army—consider it their mission to win at any cost, even that of alienating the neutrals. However, it is the task of the diplomat to keep the neutrals neutral. The American Civil War was no exception. The Navy Department stood prepared to cut off neutral traffic with the Confederacy at whatever cost to America's foreign relations, and it was Seward who held it in check. It was he, with the president's full support, who continually urged Gideon Welles, the secretary of the navy, to order his commanders to act with moderation and caution and never in so extreme a manner as to goad the British into striking back. Russell found Seward's conduct assuring, and he was often able to calm tempers in England by citing Seward's memoranda to Welles urging restraint and fairness in the treatment of neutral vessels.

As Britain went, so went France. From the earliest days of the war,

Emperor Napoleon III favored the cause of the Confederacy for a variety of reasons. An independent Southern nation with a free trade policy would have measureably benefited the French textile industry. Similarly enhanced would have been the emperor's ambition to play a dominant role in Mexico and the Caribbean. A single strong United States promised to offer much greater resistance to his pretensions than an independent South and a weakened North. For his Southern sympathies, Napoleon found support among the upper classes who, like their British counterparts, loathed American democracy and republicanism and felt an affinity for the "lords and ladies" of the plantation. The plain people and the intellectuals—Victor Hugo, Alexis de Tocqueville, Adolphe Thiers, and Louis Blanc—were pro-Union because of their antipathy to slavery and their attachment to republicanism, but they carried no weight in the councils of the Second Empire.

French policy, therefore, reflected the imperial inclination. The press, which was officially inspired, was hostile to the Union and friendly to the Confederacy. Southern victories were highlighted and Northern successes slighted. Napoleon received the Southern envoy, John Slidell, cordially, but William L. Dayton, the American minister, was treated coolly. Cruisers for the South were built and equipped in French yards with very little attention paid to the country's official status as a neutral. Above all, Napoleon sought to intervene in the war to gain the South its freedom. His first effort came in October of 1861 and his second in February of 1863. Neither attempt succeeded because the British, whose cooperation he sought, refused to take part. Without England, Napoleon dared not budge. After the Northern successes at Gettysburg and Vicksburg in 1863, Napoleon abandoned all thoughts of interfering in the struggle because of the South's uncertain future. By that time, too, he was deeply involved in his Mexican adventure and could not take on another obligation. He halted the construction of several vessels destined for the South, sent home the Confederate representative, and thereafter virtually ignored the war in America.

As for Russia, there was never any question about its pro-Northern policy. The basis of Russian action was fear of British power as recently enhanced by her victory in the Crimean War. A strong United States was the best means of keeping England in check. It was perfectly reasonable for the *St. Petersburg Journal* to write one day in 1862 that "Russia considers the prosperity of the Union necessary to the general equilibrium." Besides that pragmatic political consideration was an ideological one. Czar Alexander was a great admirer of President Lincoln and fancied himself a liberal statesman of Lincolnian stance. He viewed himself, too, as an ally of Lincoln since both were engaged in suppressing rebellions— Lincoln in the South, he in Poland. Finally, he followed Lincoln's precept by himself issuing a proclamation liberating the serfs in the Russian Empire.

It was little wonder that throughout the war, Russia did everything possible within the limits of neutrality to help the Union cause. Southern belligerency was not recognized, and the Southern envoy was not received at Court. On the other hand, the American minister, Cassius M. Clay, was accorded warm treatment and, at the same time, official American circulars and favorable news of the Union effort were given wide publicity. Russian ports were opened to both Northern and Southern prizes, but life was made very difficult for the latter. A number of Russians journeyed to the New World to join the Union armies and one of them, Colonel John Turchin, rose to command an Illinois regiment.

Taken together, such manifestations of sympathy for the North strengthened Seward's position in Europe and tended to dampen the ardor of those in other countries who favored intervention. Indeed, Russian refusal to join in a mediation proposed by Napoleon in 1862 seemed to have influenced Britain's decision to reject the suggestion. Russia made another important contribution to the Union cause in Europe, although inadvertently. In September and October of 1863, elements of the Russian Baltic fleet visited New York and San Francisco. The reason for their crossing the ocean to America, as revealed in Russian archives, was to prevent their being bottled up in the Baltic in the event of a war with Great Britain. To Europeans and Americans, however, the visit was taken as a gesture of friendship and solidarity and a demonstration of Russia's intent to stand by the United States in its hour of need. Parties and receptions were held for the officers and men, and toasts were drunk to the czar and the president and to the two peoples. Nor did the Russian government disturb the impression by revealing its true motives.

The diplomatic problems of the war did not end with the coming of peace. The question of British responsibility for the losses American citizens incurred by the action of Confederate cruisers built in English yards had not been settled by 1865. During the war, Seward had demanded compensation, but Russell had steadfastly refused to admit Britain's liability. In August of 1866, the secretary of state pressed the American claims once again but this time added to the direct losses of private persons the indirect losses suffered by the United States government which were calculated by Senator Charles Sumner to be $2.125 billion. They stemmed from the cost of tracking down the cruisers, of fighting a war prolonged by the encouragement given the South by the British proclamation of neutrality, of increased insurance premiums for American vessels made necessary by the presence of the cruisers on the seas, and of compensating for the flight of American ships to foreign registry in fear of the cruisers.

By this time a new government had come into power in England, and the new foreign secretary was willing to discuss the question of liability for the direct losses, without admitting that liability beforehand, but refused flatly to consider the indirect losses. Seward next proposed that the whole question of damages be considered as part of a general settlement of other problems between the two countries that involved claims. An agreement was, in fact, negotiated by the American minister in London in January of 1869 providing for the arbitration of all claims by both sides arising from all disputes since 1853. The United States Senate, however, refused to give its consent to the convention because it failed to include any statement of responsibility for the cruisers and did not provide for the indirect damage.

So matters rested until 1870 when the outbreak of a war between France and Prussia in July and the repudiation in October by Russia of a clause in a treaty of 1856 limiting the size of her fleet on the Black Sea caused a change in the British position. The possibility of Russia, under cover of the European war, making a move toward the Dardanelles and the Sea of Marmora seemed real, in which case Britain would find herself fighting Russia. In such a war, the prospect of Russian commerce raiders built in American ports preying on British merchant ships loomed large especially since the United States House of Representatives had four years earlier unanimously amended the neutrality law to permit the sale of naval vessels to belligerents. The time seemed propitious for an admission of responsibility for the Confederate cruisers as a means of avoiding possible Russian *Alabamas*. Already, a new neutrality statute had been enacted that repaired the loopholes of the older law, whose loose language permitted the escape of the Confederate ships.

In January 1871, London sent a seasoned diplomat, Sir John Rose, to Washington to open negotiations leading to a general treaty of arbitration of all claims and other problems outstanding between the two nations. Talks began in February and after thirty-seven meetings, an agreement, the Treaty of Washington, was signed on May 6, 1871. It covered several subjects—fisheries, navigation of the St. Lawrence River, the boundary in the Pacific Northwest (a remnant of the Oregon settlement), and the Confederate raiders. On the latter, it was provided that a tribunal of five arbitrators would meet in Geneva in December to assess damages. It was no longer a question of British responsibility, for in the treaty London expressed regret "for the escape, under whatever circumstances, of the *Alabama* and other vessels from British ports, and for the depredations committed by those vessels."

Three rules were established to guide the arbitrators. The first stated that a neutral was bound to use "due diligence" to prevent the departure from its ports of vessels that it had "reasonable ground to believe" would cruise against the commerce of a friendly power. The second provided

Compromise how the arrangements will be reached

that a neutral must not permit its ports to be used as a base of naval operations or for obtaining recruits and supplies. The third required neutrals to exercise "due diligence" in its ports and over persons in its jurisdiction to prevent the violation of the first two rules.

On December 15, 1871, the tribunal met. The American agent presented his country's case, which included a long and detailed account of the beginnings of the Civil War, of British partiality toward the South, of the building and equipping of the cruisers, of Britain's failure to carry out her neutral duties in the light of the three rules of "due diligence" and concluded with a request for a sum to cover both direct and indirect damages with interest at 7 per cent from July 1, 1863. The British were incensed at the American presumption and lack of civility. London had already admitted culpability and a willingness to be judged, ex post facto, by rules that were not in force when the acts were committed. The least the Americans could have done, they believed, was to drop the claim for indirect damages. A rupture of the proceedings seemed imminent and, indeed, on both sides of the Atlantic tempers were short and a break in relations appeared possible. Fortunately, the tribunal, at the suggestion of Charles Francis Adams, an American member and the very successful wartime American minister in London, disallowed the indirect claims, a decision that Washington accepted and that mollified the British, who then presented their case.

They defended their neutrality and impartiality during the war, pointing out that they had tried to halt the departure of one vessel only to be defeated in the courts. As further evidence of their policy they recalled the purchase of the ironclads reportedly destined for the Confederacy. As for the use of their ports for recruiting and supplying Southern ships, they denied that anything of the sort had transpired. After hearing the arguments, the tribunal ruled, 4–1 (one Briton dissenting), that England had not been sufficiently diligent and had to accept responsibility and pay for the losses to American cargo and vessels and the national expenditure for pursuing and destroying the cruisers. The sum awarded was $15 million. It was a cheap price for England to pay to escape American retaliation at some future time when she would be a belligerent and the United States a neutral.

BIBLIOGRAPHY

Ephraim D. Adams, *Great Britain and the American Civil War* (2 vols., 1925).

Stuart L. Bernath, *Squall Across the Atlantic: American Civil War Cases and Diplomacy*, 1970.

Lynn M. Case and W. F. Spencer, *The United States and France: Civil War Diplomacy* (1970).

PAUL CROOK, *The North, the South, and the Powers* (1973).

GEORGE W. DALZALL, *The Flight from the Flag,* 1940.

MARTIN DUBERMAN, *Charles Francis Adams* (1961).

FRANK OWSLEY, *King Cotton Diplomacy* (rev. ed. by Harriet Owsley, 1967).

GLYNDON VAN DUSEN, *William Henry Seward* (1967).

Hamilton Fish (U.S. Signal Corps photo, the Brady Collection, the National Archives).

11

The Legacies of the War

THE CIVIL War left several diplomatic legacies. One, the claims by the United States against Great Britain for the depredations of the Confederate cruisers, was treated in the preceding chapter. To another, the establishment of a monarchy in Mexico by Emperor Napoleon III, Secretary of State William H. Seward turned his attention immediately as the war came to an end. Developments in Mexico had caused the United States deep concern ever since October 1861 when France, Spain, and Great Britain agreed to a joint expedition against Mexico to collect debts owed them by that country. The debts resulted from long-term obligations of successive Mexican governments as well as from damages arising out of the War of the Reform, as the struggle for control of that country between 1858 and 1861 was called. Out of that war, Benito Juárez, a Zapotec Indian, emerged victorious and became president of Mexico in January 1861. Several months later, he announced a suspension of payments on the foreign debt which led to the Franco-British-Spanish decision. Losses to U.S. & European investors

Following the October agreement, troops of the three powers landed on Mexican soil in December of 1861 and January of 1862. Although each of the powers had specifically renounced any "designs on Mexican territory," it was no secret that Napoleon had very definite plans to tie Mexico to France by erecting a monarchy in that country whose ruler would be beholden to France. Napoleon's interest in extending French hegemony to Mexico is not hard to understand. It stemmed from a mixture of motives: to add to the glory of France, to lay the basis for a new Napoleonic empire, to benefit France commercially, to thwart the expansion of the United States southwestward, to gain the favor of French Catholics whom he had recently alienated by opposing the Pope in the struggle over Italian unification and who would be attracted by a Catholic monarchy in Mexico.

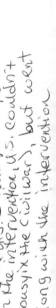

should participate in the intervention. U.S. couldn't (busy w/ the Civil War), but went along with the intervention

161

Napoleon could depend upon considerable Mexican support for his bold scheme. There were people in that country who believed that only a monarchy could bring order and stability out of the chaos and turmoil that was Mexican political life. In the forty years since independence, there had been seventy-three presidents and thirty-six changes of government. Further, they were convinced that only the support of a great power allied to their monarch could save Mexico from the rapacious clutches of the United States. Only two years earlier, President James Buchanan had asked Congress for authorization to send troops to Mexico to end the turmoil there and, at the same time, had made efforts to buy parts of the country. Finally, the party that had been defeated by Juárez was conservative, Catholic, aristocratic, and monarchist and looked naturally to a king or emperor who would institute a government and a society according to those precepts.

As Napoleon's intent became clearer to his allies in the adventure, they drew back and finally withdrew, true to their self-denying pledge. Thereupon, the French emperor sent 30,000 fresh troops across the seas and on June 7, 1863, they entered Mexico City. The French commander summoned an "assembly of notables"—monarchists all—that promptly elected Maximilian, younger brother of the Austrian Emperor, to the throne of Mexico. The new monarch and his consort, Carlotta, daughter of the king of the Belgians, arrived in their adopted country on May 28, 1864.

The whole affair caused considerable consternation in the United States, where the establishment of a monarchy on the ruins of a republican government was viewed as a flagrant violation of the Monroe Doctrine. Typical of the American reaction was the resolution that the House of Representatives passed unanimously that stated that "the Congress of the United States are unwilling by silence to leave the nations of the world under the impression that they are indifferent spectators of the deplorable events now transpiring in the republic of Mexico, and that they therefore think fit to declare that it does not accord with the policy of the United States to acknowledge any monarchical government erected on the ruins of any republican government in America under the auspices of any European Power."

The United States government did not recognize the new monarchy but continued to maintain relations with the Juárez regime through the deposed president's minister in Washington. On the other hand, Secretary of State Seward resisted all efforts by the Mexican minister to draw him into an intervention to unseat Maximilian. Not only was the United States "too intent on putting down our own insurrection" to interfere; it ran the risk of pushing Napoleon into the arms of the Confederacy if it affronted and opposed the French emperor. Hence, Seward's policy was caution and moderation. Until a more propitious moment, he contented himself with lodging a strong protest in Paris. Meanwhile, as he wrote his minister in France, "We have compromised nothing, surrendered nothing, and I do not propose to surrender anything."

The propitious moment came, of course, in the spring of 1865 when Lee surrendered to Grant and more than half a million blue-clad troops were released to concentrate on the new enemy south of the Rio Grande. Napoleon knew that his time had come. His envoy in Washington had kept him completely informed of American sentiment. He was aware of the warnings in the *New York Herald* published early in 1864: "As for Mexico, we will, at the close of the rebellion, if the French have not left there before, send 50,000 Northern and 50,000 Southern troops, forming together a grand army to drive the invaders into the Gulf." And he could recall the words of Andrew Johnson, Lincoln's running mate in 1864: "The day of reckoning is approaching. It will not be long before the Rebellion is put down. . . . And then we will attend to this Mexican affair. . . . An expedition into Mexico will be a sort of recreation to the brave soldiers who are now fighting the battles of the Union. . . ." Now with the war ended, powerful voices of important military leaders, including General Grant, could be heard urging an attack on Maximilian.

But that threat was only a part of the reason Napoleon decided to liquidate France's role in Mexico. There were other factors—the cost, the opposition of liberals at home, the unpopularity of Maximilian in Mexico, the harassment of French forces by Juárez's guerrillas, and above all, the fact that his involvement in Mexico distracted him from concentrating on affairs in Europe, where the real action was taking place and where the German chancellor, Bismarck, was posing a major threat to France.

Meanwhile, Seward had become blunter and more insistent in stating his country's displeasure. In November 1865, he instructed the minister in Paris to register "the serious concern to the United States" at the "presence of the French army in Mexico and its maintenance of an authority there resting upon force and not the free will of the people of Mexico." The French intervention, he said, was "disallowable and impracticable." And on February 12, 1866, he finally demanded "definitive information of the time when French military operations may be expected to cease in Mexico." Ten days later, Napoleon announced the withdrawal of all French troops in three stages, to be completed in November 1867. The delay was designed, as he wrote his commander in Mexico on January 31, 1866, to permit Maximilian "every chance of maintaining himself with his own forces." Actually, the evacuation was completed nine months ahead of schedule and Maximilian never did achieve viability. When the last of the French soldiers sailed away in March of 1867, the

Mexicans put their Emperor against a wall and shot him. He had the chance to flee with the departing troops but, foolishly or nobly, he chose to consider himself a Mexican and to remain with his people.

The third legacy of the war concerned the need for naval bases in the Caribbean and in the Pacific. During the war, the navy's role in hunting down the Confederate commerce raiders and in intercepting neutral traffic to the enemy was made more difficult by the absence of strong places for repairs and supplies. The task of acquiring such sites fell to the Secretary of State and it was not an uncongenial one for William H. Seward was a long-time expansionist. Before the war, first as a young Whig politician and then as a free-soil Republican, he had been one of the apostles of manifest destiny. To a firm belief in the mission of the American people to carry democracy to the benighted peoples of the hemisphere, he added the geopolitical concept of the United States gaining outlying possessions for strategic and commercial advantage. And true to the tradition of those other great expansionists, Thomas Jefferson and John Quincy Adams, Seward's dreams encompassed the entire continent. "I know," he said in 1867, "that nature designs that this whole continent, not merely these 36 states, shall be, sooner or later, within the magic circle of the American Union." There were some who believed that the secretary's passion for adding to the American territory had a rather crass basis, as well, which they labeled "presidential fever."

Seward had some support in the country for his expansionist ideas from sections of the press and from members of Congress. There was talk of "taking up where we left off now that the nasty business is over." *Harper's Weekly*, for example, in a cartoon pictured Uncle Sam in the act of hoisting an enormous flag while saying, "My hands are free now and I'm going to hyst [sic] a flag so big that it'll cover most of the land and a good bit of the sea." The *New York Herald* and several other Northern newspapers suggested that Canada and the British West Indian islands might be adequate recompense for the damages done by the British-built Confederate ships. Meanwhile, grandiloquent phrases by Congressmen echoed sentiments familiar from the stirring days of the Mexican War and the Oregon Treaty. "I regard it as destiny," said Senator O. H. P. T. Morton of Indiana, "that we shall acquire Santo Domingo and Puerto Rico," and Representative Nathaniel Banks of Massachusetts noted that "the West Indies belong to us by their position and the laws of nature." Powerful Thaddeus Stevens of Pennsylvania, leader of the radical Republicans in the House, served warning on the world with the words, "We rise from the rebellion conscious of our power, full of hope and confidence. Such a Nation cannot shrink from her destiny. She does not shrink; she welcomes it."

Yet, there was, on the other hand, a strong antiexpansionist current in the country; so strong, in fact, that it overshadowed the proponents of expansionism and, indeed, may be said to have been the dominant theme in the country so far as foreign relations were concerned. Seward himself acknowledged that fact in 1868, remarking that American attention "continues to be fastened upon the domestic questions which have grown out of the late Civil War. The public mind refuses to dismiss these questions even so far as to entertain the higher but more remote questions of national extension and aggrandizement." The domestic questions alluded to by Seward were regularly referred to in speeches and articles as reasons for resisting expansion of the nation's boundaries. They included reincorporation of the South into the Union and restoring its devastated economy, settling the status of the freedmen, repaying the staggering war debt, developing the country's resources that were neglected during the fighting, completing the transcontinental transportation network, and settling the West. All those things must be achieved, said the *New York Tribune,* before the United States "casts again a covetous eye on fresh possessions." And the *Chicago Tribune* suggested, after observing that "we already had more territory than could be peopled in fifty years," that it was time "we had fulfilled our obligations to the people we have, by diffusing among them the blessings of peace, universal education, and business prosperity and by winning them all over to an affectionate loyalty to our institutions instead of wasting their energies in crusades to foist upon Canada and Mexico institutions which those countries do not desire or appreciate." Given such sentiment, it is no wonder that in the thirty years following the end of the Civil War, of the numerous projects for annexing territory proposed by Seward and his successors, only one, the purchase of Alaska, succeeded (if the acquisition of tiny Midway Island in 1867 is ignored).

Alaska, along with Canada, Hawaii, and islands in the Pacific and in the Caribbean, made up the expansionist ambitions of William H. Seward. The interest of Americans in that vast Russian territory antedated the Civil War. In 1860, Senator William M. Gwin of California approached Baron de Stoeckl, the Russian minister, concerning his country's willingness to sell Alaska. But the outbreak of the war quickly ended the conversation. The end of the conflict found Seward searching for bases, and Alaska seemed a likely one situated strategically in a commanding position in the North Pacific. And the Russians were ready to sell. For some years, the Russian-American Company, charged with exploiting Alaska, had been failing as the supply of sea otter, the chief source of revenue, was becoming exhausted. The Russian government had the choice of pouring in subsidies to keep the company solvent or giving up the territory. Clearly, the financial factor war crucial, but there was also a strategic consideration—Alaska's indefensibility in event of war with a strong naval power like Great Britain. By December 1866, the Russian decision to sell Alaska for $5 million was reached. Stoeckl, who was then in St. Petersburg, was instructed to return to America and make the sale. Upon his arrival in Washington he learned of Seward's keen interest in the possibility, and on the evening of March 29, 1867 called on the Secretary in his home offering to arrange a meeting to discuss the matter. In his haste and pleasure, Seward suggested they begin their negotiations at once. The two thereupon roused their respective staffs and marched to the Department of State offices. Before the new day dawned, a treaty had been signed exchanging Alaska for $7.2 million. The following day, March 30, President Andrew Johnson sent the treaty to the Senate for its approval.

That the treaty had smooth sailing in that chamber, gaining rapid approval by a vote of 37–2, may be ascribed to a safe Republican majority and to the masterful leadership of the chairman of the Foreign Relations Committee, Charles Sumner of Massachusetts. In a three-hour speech on April 6, Sumner marshalled an imposing and convincing body of reasons for the purchase. He enumerated advantages calculated to make universal appeal—natural resources, commercial prospects chiefly in relation to the China market, ousting a European monarch from the hemisphere, repayment for Russia's friendship during the late war, frustrating any British designs, and carrying civilization and republicanism to benighted peoples.

Senate approval should not obscure the rancorous debate in the House of Representatives on the appropriation of funds and in the public forum. In both arenas, there was much hostility to the purchase. Opponents spoke derisively of "Seward's Icebox," "Seward's Folly," and "Walrussia." They poked fun at Alaska's inhabitants—Eskimos, polar bears, and walruses, and listed as attractions cows that gave ice cream instead of milk and a superb ice crop. Underneath the raillery, however, were more serious considerations such as the cost of the purchase and of the upkeep, the barrenness of the land and the absence of cash crops, the possibility of offending Great Britain by boxing in Canada, the distraction of the American people from their real problems, and the danger inherent in absorbing natives not yet ready for the blessings of republican institutions. There was also a political element involved—the unpopularity of the president among the members of his party and in the nation at large because of his Reconstruction policies, which were considered too lenient. Indeed, at the same time that the treaty was being debated, the president's impeachment proceedings were in progress.

Nonetheless, the funds to pay Russia were passed by the House, 113–43, on July 14, 1868. As Sumner was the catalyst in the Senate, so Baron de Stoeckl smoothed the way in the House. The one succeeded by force of leadership; the other by a liberal sprinkling of funds in the right places.

Although an investigation could not substantiate charges of corruption, there seems little doubt that Congressmen and newspaper editors were recipients of de Stoeckl's generosity. The course of the legislation in the House was helped, too, by the fact that the American flag had already been raised at Sitka on October 10, 1867, and the House had the choice of either voting the money or seriously embarrassing the nation. Whatever the contemporary opposition to the purchase, it became clear, as time passed, that the United States had struck a valuable bargain. Alaska has proved a profitable source of minerals, furs, and lumber and a key element in the defense of the United States—all at a cost of 2 cents an acre.

Emboldened by his Alaskan success and by a spurt in expansionist sentiment it had generated, Seward moved quickly to revive an earlier scheme—the purchase of the strategically important West Indian possessions of Denmark. There were three principal islands involved—St. Thomas (with its excellent harbor at Charlotte Amalie), St. John, and St. Croix—and the Danes were willing to sell two of the three. Although Seward wanted all three, he accepted St. Thomas and St. John, and a treaty transferring those islands to the United States for $7.5 million was initialed on October 24, 1867. In the following January, the Danish parliament gave its approval but the United States Senate balked. In December of that year, after only slight debate, the treaty was tabled. More than a year earlier, the House had registered its opposition by a resolution, 93–43, which held "any further purchases of territory are inexpedient" and denied the obligation to vote money for "any such purposes unless there is a greater present necessity . . . than now exists."

The failure of the Danish scheme may be attributed, in part, to a series of natural disasters in those islands that seemed to make patently clear the folly of annexing them. In rapid order, they suffered an earthquake, a tidal wave, and a hurricane, all made the subject of a hilarious and biting tale by Mark Twain. He described the adventures of his uncle at St. Thomas, where he contracted seven kinds of fever and had one of his farms washed away by a great storm and two others destroyed by an earthquake and a volcano. When he later returned to the island in a ship of war given him by Seward, a tidal wave hoisted the ship out of the water into one of the two interior counties. But, more fundamentally, was the general opposition to adding more territory to the Union. Always there was the same refrain—"we have enough to do at home." Indeed, there was mounting anger directed at Seward for his ventures. A Bostonian demanded of Senator Sumner what right had Seward "to commit the government and the people of this country in the purchase of territory they do not want and to pledge the peoples' money for impracticable schemes? How does the Secretary of State get this power? Is there no way to stop him?"

Similarly, Seward's hope to annex the Dominican Republic failed.

That country which occupied two thirds of the island of Hispaniola had had a checkered history. Independent of Spain since 1821, it spent the first twenty-three years of its national life governed by Haiti, whose territory lay in the other third of the island. Spain reannexed the republic in 1861 but surrendered it four years later. Seward had had his eye on the excellent harbor of Samaná Bay which commanded the approaches to the Caribbean and in 1864 offered $2 million for it. Nothing came of the negotiations but in December of 1868, the Dominican president offered his entire country to the United States. Seward jumped at the occasion and President Johnson gave the project his warm support in his annual message delivered the same month. "The time has arrived," he stated, "when so direct a proceeding as a proposition for annexation . . . would not only receive the consent of the people interested but would also give satisfaction to all other foreign nations." The plea was useless; Congress had no interest in the idea. A resolution by Representative Nathaniel P. Banks on January 13, 1869 to extend protection over the Dominican Republic and Haiti was defeated 36–126. The following month, a proposal for the admission of the Dominican Republic as a "territory of the United States with a view to the ultimate establishment of a state government republican in form" failed in the Senate. One heard the same arguments in both chambers—the danger of admitting negroes into the Union, the increase in the public debt, the unwisdom of venturing into foreign fields.

Seward did not omit Hawaii from his roving ambition. American interest in the Sandwich Islands, as Hawaii was then called, was an old story. It dated back to the end of the eighteenth century, when traders first entered the islands' ports. Whaling vessels began dropping anchor there in the 1820s and by 1842, it was estimated that four fifths of all foreign vessels in that country's ports were American. Inevitably, the missionaries arrived, in the early 1820s, and met with very great success in converting the native Polynesians. Their descendants engaged in cultivating sugar, and before long they owned large plantations and controlled the production of sugar. Because of its location and of the prominent role of Americans in its economy, it was not surprising that the United States formed a quick attachment with Hawaii and by 1842 let it be known that any European attempt to annex the islands would be opposed. In effect, the policy constituted a Monroe Doctrine for Hawaii. For its part, the United States made no serious effort to take the islands. In 1854, the Pierce administration did negotiate a treaty of annexation but it was never sent to the Senate. The Civil War diverted attention from Hawaii, as it did from every other thing not directly connected with the outcome, but shortly after it ended, in 1867, Seward entered into a reciprocity agreement with the Hawaiian monarch. He left office, however, before Senate action could be taken and was convinced that there was no "popular sentiment for annexation." One other expansionist victory was gained by Seward—the right to build a canal through Nicaragua. In 1867, he signed a treaty with that country that granted the United States transit rights across the Isthmus, but the treaty did not get to the Senate. Thus, the great postwar expansionist dreams of William H. Seward netted but one success, albeit a significant one. The failure to achieve more may be ascribed to the temper of the people who opposed such schemes.

Seward's tenure at the Department of State marked the high point of official projects for annexation of foreign territory and of an expansionist spirit in administration circles until the administration of Benjamin Harrison in 1889. Save for Ulysses Simpson Grant, the succession of presidents and their secretaries of state followed a policy of abstention from overseas adventures and counseled "minding our own business." Rutherford B. Hayes in 1878 noted with pleasure that the country was steering clear of European problems. Frederick T. Frelinghuysen, Chester A. Arthur's secretary of state, in 1882 advised "the American Eagle . . . not [to] strain his naturally fine voice by shrill and prolonged screaming on small occasions." Grover Cleveland in 1885 counseled "scrupulous avoidance of any departure from that foreign policy commended by the history, the traditions, and the prosperity of our Republic . . . [and concentrating] on development of the vast resources of the great area committed to our charge, and to the cultivation of the arts of peace within our own borders."

The nation could heed such counsel with impunity, for world conditions were such as to offer no threat to American security, and bases abroad did not seem necessary or even useful in an era of international peace. Further, there was no need to go abroad in search of economic opportunities. Sources of raw materials, outlets for investment capital, and markets for manufactured goods and agricultural products could be found at home in the demands and the yields of the burgeoning postwar economy. The building of the transcontinental and other railroads as well as the telegraph lines and the cables, the increase in the output of farm and factory, the mining of copper, coal, gold, silver, and the production of oil, the growth of cities, and the rush of immigrants into the country all tended to provide limitless challenges at home.

Grant, like Seward, had territorial ambitions, but, unlike him, he had no grand vision of a destiny for his country; no large concept of the extension of his nation's influence; nor, indeed, any intellectual or philosophic rationale. He was certainly no Jefferson or Adams. Parochial and narrow, he thought in terms of military needs alone, and his avid interest in pursuing Seward's project for Santo Domingo may have been motivated by his wish to have a Caribbean base. There is some evidence, as well, that he wanted to use that island as a haven for the recently freed American negroes. A treaty of annexation was signed in November of

1869, but it could not gain the Senate's approval. Grant lobbied personally on behalf of the treaty, but even the revered hero of Appomattox could muster no more than twenty-eight votes out of twice that number cast. In great part, he failed for the same reason Seward's efforts had been unsuccessful—the strong opposition to expansionism in the country—but there was one added factor. As was so typical of Grant's administration, unsavory characters—jobbers and shady businessmen—who surrounded the president had been entrusted with the diplomatic negotiations, thus imparting to the affair a sinister and scandalous taint, enough to sicken some would-be supporters.

In Grant's administration, two other sallies in extranational affairs were made. One was an agreement with Hawaii in 1875 that permitted Hawaiian sugar to enter the United States free of duty. The treaty had great economic importance for the island producers in that it gave their product a marked advantage over foreign sugar, thereby boosting the industry tremendously. But its real significance was political for two reasons. First, it strengthened the ties between the white American planters and the United States, and second, it contained a clause prohibiting the alienation of any of Hawaii's territory to a foreign power. The other Grant gesture in overseas affairs concerned the question of a Central American canal. The transit rights Seward had received across Nicaragua in 1867 had not been exclusive; they merely gave the United States equality with other powers. Grant seemed determined to go beyond that state and gain sole rights across an isthmus. Such an objective, of course, involved an abrogation of the Clayton-Bulwer Treaty of 1850, whereby the United States and Great Britain pledged to share in the control of any future isthmian canal. Grant took no steps toward ending the treaty, knowing well that the British would not consent to a surrender of their rights. He did, however, appoint a commission to survey various possible routes. In 1878, the commission reported unanimously in favor of Nicaragua.

The lack of concern with foreign affairs by Grant's successors must not be taken to mean a complete ignoring of everything outside the country's borders. Rutherford B. Hayes was conscious of the importance to the United States of a Central American canal and quite boldly, in a speech on March 8, 1880, called for a canal under American control, thus inferring an end to sharing responsibility with the British. Congress caught up his challenge with a resolution in the House the following month that called for the abrogation of the Clayton-Bulwer Treaty. Hayes also encouraged American participation in the international trade fair held in Paris in 1878 in which 1,229 firms from the United States exhibited their wares. Similarly, James A. Garfield gave his secretary of state, James G. Blaine, complete support in Blaine's plan for calling a conference of all of the republics of the Americas to meet in Washington in November 1882.

Blaine had been guilty of some rather maladroit diplomacy in regard to Latin America early in his administration and hoped to compensate for it by demonstrating United States' friendship for and solidarity with the neighbors to the south. There were, also, more pragmatic and concrete aims. Blaine had in mind the extension of American commercial opportunities in those places and the promotion of peace by a series of arbitration and conciliation treaties. The invitations went out on November 29, 1881. By that time, President Garfield had been assassinated, bringing Chester A. Arthur to the White House. Arthur kept Blaine on for several months but in December appointed as his replacement Frederick T. Frelinghuysen, who, with Arthur's blessings, withdrew the invitations.

The reasons for the change in policy are numerous and complicated. Politics surely played a role. The Republican party was split between two factions—Stalwarts and Half-Breeds—who were bitter enemies. Arthur and his new secretary represented the former, and they gladly killed their opponents' scheme to discredit them. It was true, also, that the Stalwarts had little stomach for a vigorous foreign policy. They were political descendants of the postwar Republican antiexpansionists and Blaine's plan smacked of too outward a thrust. Yet Arthur was interested in the canal idea, and in 1884 signed a treaty with Nicaragua giving the United States exclusive rights over the isthmus in return for American protection of Nicaraguan territory. Similarly, he was responsible for the renewal, in 1884, of the reciprocity treaty with Hawaii with an added clause that assigned Pearl Harbor to the United States for the navy's use.

Grover Cleveland, who succeeded Arthur in 1885, was, of all the presidents of the period, the most reluctant to exercise American power abroad. Soon after entering the White House, he withdrew the Nicaraguan treaty that Arthur had sent to the Senate, and toward the end of his administration in 1888, he vetoed a bill to reissue the invitation for a conference of American states. Apparently, he recognized the importance of Hawaii to the United States as evidenced by his expression in 1886 of his "unhesitating conviction that the intimacy of our relations with Hawaii should be emphasized; . . . the paramount influence we have there acquired, once relinquished, could only with difficulty be regained, and a valuable ground of vantage for ourselves might be converted into a stronghold for our commercial competitors." But he made plain, at the same time, that he had no intention to pursue any political connection with the islands.

In assessing the period that closed with Cleveland's departure from office in 1889, one might well cite the *New York Sun's* observation, made in the same year, that reflected the nation's attitude toward foreign affairs: "the diplomatic service has outgrown its usefulness. . . . It is a costly humbug and sham. It is a nurse of snobs. It spoils a few Americans every year and does no good to anybody. Instead of making ambassadors, Congress should wipe out the whole service." Equally significant was Henry Cabot Lodge's comment in 1889 that foreign affairs fill "but a slight place in American politics, and exert generally only a languid interest." Europeans also were struck by the same phenomenon. The young British diplomat, Cecil Spring-Rice, who one day would be England's ambassador to Washington, regretted in the 1880s that he was being posted to the United States because it was "off the main line" in international affairs, and James Bryce summed the whole matter up most succinctly when, in his acute study of the *American Commonwealth*, published in 1889, he stated, "the only principle to which people have learned to cling in foreign policy is that the less they have to do with it the better."

Times were changing, however, and even as the observations were being made about American lassitude in foreign affairs, certain transformations were taking place that would revolutionize the country's approach to overseas adventures, imperialism, colonialism, and expansionism. They were of great magnitude and resulted in "a new consciousness of strength and with it a new appetite, the yearning to show our strength. Ambition, land hunger, pride, the mere joy of fighting, whatever it may be, we are animated by a new sensation. We are face to face with a new destiny. The taste of empire is in the mouth of the people even as the taste of blood is in the jungle. It means an imperial policy: the Republic renascent, taking her place with the armed nations."

The words were those of the *Washington Post* in 1898, and they reveal the transformation of the American temper that took place in the single decade. It was a transformation that made the American people ready to fight Spain over Cuba and to acquire vast overseas territories.

BIBLIOGRAPHY

HENRY BLUMENTHAL, *A Re-appraisal of Franco-American Relations, 1830–1871* (1959).

ALLAN NEVINS, *Hamilton Fish: The Inner History of the Grant Administration* (1936).

DEXTER PERKINS, *The Monroe Doctrine, 1826–1867* (1933).

MILTON PLESUR, *America's Outward Thrust: Approaches to Foreign Affairs, 1865–1890* (1971).

DAVID M. PLETCHER, *The Awkward Years: American Foreign Relations Under Garfield and Arthur* (1963).

GOLDWIN SMITH, *The Treaty of Washington, 1871: a Study in Imperial History* (1941).

C. C. TANSILL, *The United States and Santo Domingo, 1798–1873* (1938).

WILLIAM A. WILLIAMS, *American-Russian Relations, 1781–1947* (1952).

Alfred T. Mahan (U.S. Office of War Information photo, the National Archives).

The New American Spirit

THE TRANSFORMATION that took place in the temper and spirit of large numbers of Americans in the last 15 years of the nineteenth century from little interest to great interest in foreign affairs and from a pacific to a bellicose disposition had many roots—economic, strategic, intellectual, and emotional. Central and basic to the change was the Darwinian theory of the survival of the fittest as it was applied to human affairs. From it sprang the idea that the Anglo-Saxons were the fittest of all people and had as their duty the elevation of the less fit. It was this sense of mission, in great part, that impelled large numbers of Americans to fight a war to free Cuba from the yoke of Spain and to take up the burden of empire.

It was in the *Origin of Species*, published in 1859, that Charles Darwin proposed his theory of evolution through natural selection. Simply stated, he maintained that the continuous struggle for existence among biological forms resulted in the elimination of the unfit and the survival of higher types. The leap from the plant and animal world to the society of humans was easy to make and some philosophers, historians, and political scientists soon were arguing that only the higher types of people could be expected to survive. Further, they insisted, in the human arena, the more advanced nations had every right to hasten the process whereby they would supplant the backward peoples. And there seemed to be no question of identifying the higher types. Darwin himself unblushingly, in his *Descent of Man* (1871), singled out the Anglo-Saxons, especially the American branch, as the most talented of peoples. "There is apparently much truth," he wrote, "in the belief that the wonderful progress of the United States as well as the character of the people are the results of natural selection; the more energetic, courageous, and restless men from all parts of Europe having emigrated during the last ten or twelve generations to that great country and having there succeeded best. The United States is the heir of all ages, in the foremost files of time."

Clearly, large numbers of Americans did not read Darwin, but his ideas reached them, nonetheless, by way of the writings of Americans who, in the process of transmitting them, popularized them and transformed them into a program for action and a mission. Among them was John Fiske, popular orator and widely read historian whose many books on American history reflected a superpatriotic point of view. Writing in *Harper's Weekly* in 1885 on "manifest destiny," he extolled the virtues of Anglo-Saxons and their institutions, predicting their ulti- mate success in the struggle for the world. Their destiny, he said, was to go on colonizing until their language, religion, customs, and political habits would "cover every part of the earth's surface that is not already the seat of an old civilization" and they would be supreme in commerce and on the sea. In the same year, Josiah Strong, a prominent Protestant clergy- man, published *Our Country: Its Possible Future and Present Crisis,* in which he announced that the Anglo-Saxon, who was the chief representa- tive of civil liberty and pure spiritual Christianity, was to be the victor in the "final competition of races" and that the United States would be the "home of this race, the principal seat of his power, and the great center of his influence" destined to spread over the earth—"down upon Mexico, down upon Central and South America, out upon the islands of the sea, over upon Africa and beyond."

Five years later, a distinguished political scientist at Columbia Uni- versity, John Burgess, issued his major work called *Political Science and Comparative Constitutional Law* which served as the vehicle for assigning world dominion to Teutons and to Anglo-Saxons. It was those people, he wrote, who would carry political civilization to the barbaric races. To achieve that noble objective, he said, was "not only a right but an obligation."

It is difficult, if not impossible, to measure the effect and the influence of such men in shaping the public view. It is known that Fiske not only wrote books and articles carrying the message but lectured as well to large numbers of adults in forums and lyceums. An indication of his popularity may be seen in the fact that his *Destiny of Man Viewed in the Light of His Origin* (1884) went into nineteen printings. As for Strong, his book sold 170,000 copies in a few years after its appearance, while Burgess taught the gospel of Anglo-Saxon superiority and destiny to a generation of Columbia University students, one of whom was Theodore Roosevelt. President Nicholas M. Butler of Columbia, himself, attested to the pro- found impression made by Burgess' book.

Politicians and journalists, as well as writers, propagated the word. Most prominent of the journalists were Whitelaw Reid of the *New York Tribune,* Albert Shaw of the *Review of Reviews,* and Walter Hines Page of the *Atlantic.* Those men seized every opportunity, as editors, to use the pages of their newspapers and magazines for instilling into the readers the ideas of their country's destiny. Not untypical of the material featured was the editorial in a Pacific Coast journal that called upon Americans to take up their responsibilities. "The subjugation of the continent," wrote the editor, "was sufficient to keep the American people at home for a century. But now . . . we are looking for fresh worlds to conquer . . . the colonizing instinct which has led our race in successive waves of emigration is the instinct which is now pushing us out and on to Alaska, to the isles of the sea—and beyond."

Of the politicians who used the floor of the Senate and the House as vehicles for urging a strong foreign policy, there were Cushman K. Davis of Minnesota, John T. Morgan of Alabama, Hernando Money of Mississippi, and, pre-eminently, Henry Cabot Lodge of Massachusetts. Enthusiastically and aggressively imperialistic, an able parliamentarian, an effective speaker, a Harvard doctor of philosophy in history, a prolific author of filio-pietistic biographies of leading Americans, including Washington and Hamilton, dapper and with a grand manner, Lodge made a deep imprint on his contemporaries. His appeals to his countrymen were stirring as evidenced by his article in the *Forum* in 1895 entitled "Our Blundering Foreign Policy." In that piece, he set out a blueprint for the United States: annex Cuba and Canada, build a canal in Nicaragua, control the Hawaiian Islands, maintain influence in Samoa, eliminate England from the West Indies, take at least one strong place there ourselves, build a great navy, and become a colonial power. "The tendency of modern nations," he counseled, "is toward consolidation; small states are of the past and have no future. The great nations are rapidly absorbing for their future expansion and their present defense all the waste places of the earth. It is a movement which makes for civilization and the advancement of the race. As one of the great nations of the world, the United States must not fall out of the line of march."

Lodge played a role in the campaign to enlarge the country's boundaries and influence not only as a political figure but in a quite different context as well. He was a member of a small select coterie of intellectuals who were, at the same time, men of wealth, of social position, of old American stock, easterners, and firm believers in Anglo-Saxon-Teuton superiority and in the idea of mission for their country. Henry Adams was among them, as was his brother Brooks. Shy, sensitive, unable (because of personality) and unwilling (because of the low state of American politics) to participate actively in the governance of the country as had his great-grandfather (John Adams) and grandfather (John Quincy Adams), Henry stood on the sidelines as "stableman to statesmen." Brilliant, albeit biased, historian of the early years of the American republic, he had flung himself "obediently into the arms of the Anglo-Saxon in history." Therein lies the source of his racist views. They stemmed from no soft, sentimental attachment to his English forebears but were rooted firmly in his conception of history. He was a member of a school of historians which numbered many of the greatest of the day—Herbert Baxter Adams, Moses Coit Tyler, John Burgess, Albert Bushnell Hart, Andrew Dickson White—who subscribed to the "germ" theory as an explanation of the origins of American democracy and political institutions. They traced the origins of our system back to the organization of the Teutonic tribes in the German forests in the days of Tacitus, which by evolutionary stages developed through British institutions into the American political institution. Thus, the United States emerged as the final and highest stage of the Darwinian theory.

Henry's brother, Brooks, also brilliant and racist, feared for the future of his country. He considered America to be on the threshold of retrogression and deterioration unless it embarked on a bold course of expansion commercially and politically. For that objective, he was prepared even to abandon the precepts of the Founding Fathers and enter into an Anglo-Saxon front with Great Britain. John Hay, although Indiana born, was in every respect part of the eastern establishment. Educated at Brown, he remained in the New England mold all of his life. Poet, biographer, private secretary in his youth to Abraham Lincoln, destined to fill high diplomatic office in the McKinley administration, Hay was an ardent member of the group. Theodore Roosevelt was part of it, too. His Darwinism was a dominant theme of his life. Dedicated to the strenuous and vigorous life for individuals, he believed the same held true for nations. He believed that nations must grow to live and by growth he meant, of course, vigorous expansion. All of his historical works—chiefly, the multivolume *Winning of the West* and *Naval War of 1812*—were paeans of praise for the aggressive, virile policy of early Americans and a lesson for the future.

Drawn together by their common beliefs and their social, economic, and intellectual bonds, this group met frequently (usually in the homes of Hay and Henry Adams who had connecting houses on 16 and H Streets in Washington across from the White House) for dinners and discussions about their country's foreign policy and wielded an unobtrusive but firm influence on public opinion and on policy.

Alfred Thayer Mahan, too, played a crucial role in the transformation of the American temper. It was he who planted the strategic root for the new imperialist adventures. In articles, books, and lectures, he preached the doctrine that the United States was destined for greatness as the reward for its industry, efficiency, discipline, and character. And the foundations of greatness, he said, are in a flourishing commerce, a large merchant marine, a strong and modern navy, and colonies to serve as bases and coaling stations. Those views appeared in an article entitled "The United States Looking Outward," printed in 1890. His most important work, however, was *The Influence of Sea Power Upon History, 1660–1783*, published in

1890 and based on a series of lectures he gave in 1888 at the Naval War College in Newport, Rhode Island. In the book, he demonstrated that the ultimate victory of Great Britain over France in their titanic 100-year struggle for world dominance was the result of British command of the sea, which made it impossible for France to supply her overseas forces and gave Britain, at the same time, unrestricted access to her armies in the distant theatres of war. Sweep the enemy warships from the sea, Mahan said, and our ports will never be menaced and our coasts will be secure.

The impact of the book, supplemented by another published two years later dealing with the wars of the French Revolution and empire, was very great. The German kaiser had it placed in every wardroom of his navy. In the United States, it led to a revolution in naval doctrine of the widest significance. Hitherto, and since Jefferson's day, American naval theory was rooted in the twin concepts of destroying the enemy's commerce by a fleet of swift, heavily armed but lightly armored vessels and of protecting the coasts with fortifications and slow shallow-draft gunboats. There was no concept of a sea-going capital ship navy that could engage and defeat the enemy's fleet and take command of the sea. Mahan's lesson was clear and converted men in high places in the government like Benjamin F. Tracy, Secretary of the Navy in the Harrison administration. It must be said that Mahan was not the first person to urge the "command of the sea" theory on Americans or to plump for a modern navy and for bases. Rear Admiral Stephen B. Luce and others proposed those ideas much before Mahan, but it was Mahan who gave the idea currency, immediacy, and coherence.

The churches of all denominations in America contributed to the alteration of the American temper and provided the religious root for expansionism and imperialism. Quite expectedly, the missionary arm of the churches saw superb opportunities for saving souls of dark savages living in distant places and in the grip of primitive religious beliefs. Hence, they preached to their congregations and communicants the Christian duty of acquiring control over native peoples. "Woe to any nation," wrote one minister, "brought to a pass where it is called to guide a weaker people's future and hesitates for fear its own interests will be entangled and its own future imperilled by the full discharge of its unmistakable duty."

Finally, there was an economic root that underlay the alteration of the American temper and provided an impetus for expansionism. In the closing years of the century, the American economy was in high gear and production of factory and farm jumped significantly—beyond the capacity of the American market to absorb, many people feared. The prospect of a glut of goods and produce led to the demand that trading posts be established throughout the world as distributing points for American goods and that colonies be acquired as markets. Already, exports were an important outlet for the farmer and manufacturer. Wheat sales overseas by the 1880s accounted for between 30 to 40 per cent of the gross income of the growers, and the shipment of cattle to Europe and other places rose steadily in the same decade. Similarly, companies like Standard Oil, McCormick Farm Machinery, and Pullman were becoming more and more involved in foreign trade and investment. There was also a geopolitical and missionary aspect to the economic root. As put by Senator Albert Beveridge some years later, the exportable surplus would be the means by which the United States would corner the trade of the world. "American factories are making more than the American people can consume," he said. "American soil is producing more than they can consume. Fate has written our policy for us; the trade of the world must and shall be ours. . . . We will cover the ocean with our merchant marine. We will build a navy to the measure of our greatness. Our institutions will follow our flag on the wings of our commerce. And American law, American order, American civilization, and the American flag will plant themselves on shores hitherto bloody and benighted, but by those agencies of God henceforth to be made beautiful and bright."

The avalanche of books, articles, editorials, and speeches advocating a vigorous policy of expansion descended upon the American people at a crucial period in their history, which made them susceptible and receptive to the blandishments of the imperialists. The early 1890s were a time of great stress, of discontent, of frustration, and of social protest. The causes seem clear enough. For one thing, there was the severe economic depression in 1893 that gave rise to strikes and violence and presented the threat of radical solutions to the country's problems. Then there was the foreboding interpretation by Frederick Jackson Turner of the census report of 1890. The report had stated, "Up to and including 1880, the country had a frontier settlement, but at present the unsettled area has been so broken into by isolated bodies of settlement that there can hardly be said to be a frontier line." Around that observation, Turner developed his famous thesis that it was the existence of a frontier that had made possible the development of American democracy and institutions and accounted for the country's marvelous growth and development. The conclusion seemed inescapable that if there would no longer be a frontier, what would America's future be like? Woodrow Wilson was only one of many thoughtful Americans who feared greatly the consequences of the Turnerian hypothesis. "The days of glad expansion are gone," he said, "our life grows tense and difficult." Although millions of acres of undeveloped and virgin land remained, men felt symbolically hemmed in and were struck by a sense of claustrophobia and strangulation. The country's prosperity and well-being were linked with the expanding frontier. With that outlet gone, where would the people turn for opportunity? The imperialists supplied the answer—turn overseas. Important, too, to an understanding of the stress of the 1890s was the rise of the giant corporation as the unit of American industrial life with its juggernaut tactics designed to eliminate competition and squeeze out the independent businessman. Finally, there was the rapacity and corruption of civic officials on every level of government, which generated a feeling of uneasiness and desperation.

All these factors, wrote historian Richard Hofstadter, came together to create a "psychic crisis" in the 1890s and as a remedy for the crisis the American people turned to populism and jingoism. Both sprang from the same roots—frustration and discontent. Both served the same needs. The teachings of Darwin, Fiske, Strong, Mahan, and the other expansionists were most welcome.

In the same period, there was a series of diplomatic crises that played an important part in the transformation of the American spirit because they served both to whet the new imperialist appetite and to provide it with an outlet. The first crisis was in far-off Samoa. Consisting of fourteen islands, chief of which were Savaii, Upolu, and Tutuila, the archipelago lay in the South Pacific astride the trade route to New Zealand and Australia. Because of the excellent harbor at Pago Pago on Tutuila, American shipping interests were eager to secure a coaling station there. There was also pressure on the United States to extend American political influence in the islands from the Polynesian Land Company, a San Francisco firm, which in 1868 had acquired a large tract of land in Tutuila. In 1872, an American naval officer negotiated a treaty giving the United States exclusive rights for a naval station in return for protecting the native regime. Given the state of opinion at the time, the Senate Foreign Relations Committee not surprisingly never reported it to the floor of the Senate. In the following year, President Grant, in his search for naval bases, sent an emissary to Samoa on a reconnoitering mission that ended with the emissary becoming premier of the native government for a brief time. In 1878, a new treaty was written in Washington on the occasion of a visit to that city by a Samoan chief. The United States received a coaling station on Pago Pago in exchange for a promise to use its good offices in any future dispute between Samoa and another nation. Because there was no political involvement implied in the treaty, the Senate voted approval.

Meanwhile, both England and Germany had shown great interest in the islands, and their consuls, as well as the American representative, were busily jockeying for concessions and influence. The Germans were particularly active in shipping and land exploitation by Hamburg firms and they seemed to have received, at the Congress of Berlin in 1878, support from Britain for their ventures. As the years went on, the Germans became more aggressive. Finally, in 1886, the German consul deposed the native ruler in Apia (on Upolu) and replaced him with his own choice, at the same time raising the German flag over the government house. The American consul, at once, sought to reinstate the former monarch and substitute the American for the German standard. The consequence was

good offices

Pago Pago

turmoil on the island. To ease the tension, Secretary of State Bayard called a conference at Washington, but his efforts to bring some order out of the chaos failed when he insisted that Samoan autonomy be the basis for an agreement, and Germany, backed by Britain, plumped for direct control by the powers.

The American people had been following events in Samoa in their newspapers and were becoming excited and angry at German machinations and demands. A clamor was raised in the press for protecting American interests in the islands and resisting German encroachments. President Cleveland's dispatch of three vessels to Apia on Upolu island to balance the three that Germany had there was stoutly supported. Congress responded by appropriating $500,000 to safeguard American lives and $100,000 to develop the harbor at Pago Pago. The presence of the warships at Apia, plus a rising emotionalism in the United States, led the German government to seek an accommodation. A terrific hurricane in the harbor at Apia on March 16, 1889 that wrecked all six German and American warships also had a sobering effect on the crisis. On April 29, 1889, the three interested nations met in Berlin and agreed on a tripartite protectorate over Samoa. The native king was restored, but the real rulers were the three powers operating through a chief justice.

As might have been expected, such an arrangement had built-in difficulties, and problems over the islands' governance continued all through the following decade. Finally, in 1899, the protectorate was replaced by a division of Samoa between Germany and the United States with the latter receiving Tutuila and the harbor at Pago Pago as well as several smaller islands. The ownership of colonies by the United States would not have been possible in 1889 when the appetite for expansion and imperialism was nascent, but the experience in that year and the agitation to stand firm against Germany on the matter of remote and distant islands may well have been, as one prominent historian put it, "the overture to imperialism."

The Samoan settlement in 1889 had taken place some five weeks after the inauguration of President Benjamin Harrison. The conference had been characterized by a mild and conciliatory attitude on the part of the participants. No bluff and no bluster—which caused some surprises in view of the fact that Harrison and his Secretary of State, James G. Blaine, were known to be aggressive and inclined to pursue a spirited foreign policy. The president was a veteran of the Civil War and a stalwart champion of American rights. He had been opposed to what he considered Cleveland's timidity in foreign affairs and gave every indication of a reversal of that approach. Blaine, called "Jingo Jim," never lost an opportunity to stand up to foreign nations if only for the domestic political capital to be gained. One American newspaper had predicted that his dispatch to his representatives at the conference would be like "fast approaching thunder."

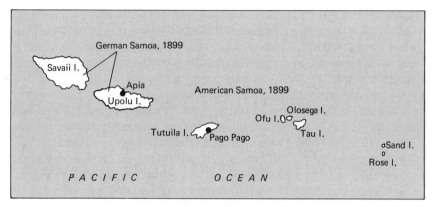

The Partition of Samoa, 1899.

That neither he nor the president acted rashly or impetuously may be laid to the fact that they were confronting two major powers. But there seems to be no doubt that they had no plans to play a reticent or retiring role in foreign affairs.

One of Harrison's earliest acts was to support his secretary of the navy, Benjamin F. Tracy, in his determination to get Congressional approval for a fleet of battleships that could carry out the Mahan theories and give American foreign policy muscle. In 1889, Tracy's *Annual Report* recommended the construction of twenty battleships to be up to date in speed, armor, and armament—twelve for the Atlantic and eight for the Pacific and, in justification, he emphatically pararphrased Mahan's argument about command of the sea versus commerce raiding and passive coast defense. The following year, Congress did authorize building three vessels equipped with heavy armor and ordnance and capable of long-range operations designed to search out and destroy an enemy fleet of warships. It was the first time in American history that a naval building program conformed to the most modern concept in doctrine and equipment. At sea, at least, the United States now had the beginnings of a capability for implementing an aggressive foreign policy.

Harrison also gave encouragement to Secretary of State James G. Blaine in his program for drawing the American republics closer to the United States. President Cleveland had vetoed, in 1888, a congressional bill to reissue the invitations to the Latin American nations for a conference to meet in Washington that Blaine had sent out in 1881 and that President Arthur had cancelled in the same year. When Congress overrode the president's veto, Cleveland's secretary of state, Thomas F. Bayard, dutifully called the nations to meet. They assembled in the American capital on October 2, 1889, there to be greeted, in a strange historical coincidence, by Blaine, the father of the scheme. All the republics, save the Dominican

New Manifest Destinies - 1880's + 90's
Anti-Imperialist League
Spineos Survival of the fittest

Republic, sent representatives and they sent their ablest people. For the United States, there were Andrew Carnegie; William H. Trescott, a career diplomat; and Clement Studebaker, a businessman.

Blaine's opening remarks, as host, were conciliatory and friendly and used such words and terms as would allay any suspicion that the United States was assuming the role of "big brother." He talked of "friendship and not force; the spirit of just law, and not the violence of the mob, should be the recognized rule of administration between American nations." The agenda for the conference was a bold one encompassing the widest variety of subjects of common interest designed to draw the republics together in a bond that would make a reality of the ancient concept of the "doctrine of the two hemispheres" that Jefferson had promoted to keep the Western hemisphere distinct and separate from Europe. The conference went on until April 19, 1890 (interrupted, however, by a lengthy transcontinental tour for the delegates that involved visits to forty-one American cities and inspections of numerous factories and farms and receptions and dinners) but achieved very few concrete results. The two most important items discussed, a customs union and treaties of arbitration, failed to be adopted because of sharp differences on technical aspects. The only accomplishment was the establishment of a bureau, the direct ancestor of the present-day Pan-American Union, that served as a clearing house and center of information for the republics. With headquarters in Washington and with an American, William Curtis, as first director, it published a monthly bulletin, maintained a library, and housed a staff to handle inquiries.

But if the tangible results were negligible, the intangible consequences were considerable. A Mexican delegate felt that the sentiment of mutual confidence, respect, and trust spread among the delegates was the really significant achievement of the conference. The *New York Tribune* saw the meeting as the first step of a new development in the relations of the American republics. "From this day," wrote the editor, "the Monroe Doctrine passes by processes of diplomatic evolution into a stage of higher development. There is an American continental policy to be worked out and consummated." The *Tribune* was overly optimistic, as events in the next decade and a half were to show. Viewed from another perspective, the conference might well have been a manifestation of a new vigorous thrust of American foreign policy in a southerly direction.

In the fall of 1891 there arose a crisis with Chile that gave the Harrison administration an occasion to flex its muscles and the Americans a cause for testing their developing aggressive spirit. On October 16, 1891, 117 sailors from the U.S.S. *Baltimore* went ashore on liberty in Valparaiso. At the True Blue Saloon, where some of them went for refreshment and entertainment, a riot began when a mob attacked them. In the melée, two Americans were killed and sixteen injured. Several more wound up in jail where, it was reported, they were beaten. News of the event printed in the American press aroused a storm of wrath. The situation was exacerbated by another crisis that had taken place in May of the same year. At that time, the American warship *Charlestown* had almost clashed with a Chilean vessel that had escaped from San Diego, California, where it had been impounded on the grounds it was carrying arms to rebel forces at home. One other difficulty between the two nations further aggravated the problem. The U.S.S. *Yorktown*, in Valparaiso harbor, had been harassed by Chilean torpedo boats on maneuvers and had threatened to fire on them.

Harrison's reaction was to wait for an apology through the fall and early winter and when one did not come by the time of his annual message to Congress on December 6, he included in the message a threat of strong action. The Chileans responded with an insulting statement by the foreign minister that touched off a really serious possibility of hostilities. Secretary of the Navy Tracy provided the president, at his request, with figures on steaming time to Valparaiso, and leading Democrats in the House of Representatives let Harrison know that party politics would be set aside if the president wished to lay the matter before Congress.

Harrison did precisely that. On January 21, 1892, he sent Chile a strong note demanding an apology for the offensive remarks by the Chilean foreign minister. If one was not forthcoming, said the note, the president "will have no other course open to him except to terminate diplomatic relations." Four days later, with the Chilean apology on the way to Washington, Harrison laid before Congress a detailed account of the imbroglio and in language that smacked of a war message left to Congress the decision "for such action as may be deemed appropriate." Before Congress could act, the apology was officially received and accepted and the crisis ended. A $75,000 indemnity paid to the families of the deceased sailors closed the episode. But the whole world had watched the excited and bellicose reaction of the people and the administration and wondered, as did a member of the British legation in Washington in a dispatch to London, "what will the U.S. be like when their fleet is more powerful?" As a matter of fact, the American navy was not as strong as Chile's in 1891 and 1892, but its growth was keeping pace with the rising tide of imperialist thought.

While Chile was occupying the attention of Americans, conditions in Hawaii were becoming equally absorbing. In January of 1891, Queen Liliuokalani succeeded her brother on Hawaii's throne. Strongly anti-American and nationalist, her plan was to wrest power from the white Hawaiians, who in 1887 had, as a result of a successful revolution, come to dominate the legislature. Two years later, on January 14, 1893, she proclaimed a new constitution designed to restore power to the natives. Two days later, the whites rose up in revolt. They had all along opposed annexation to the United States for fear that would cut off their supply of cheap contract labor. Even the passage of the McKinley Tariff Act of 1890, which had ended Hawaiian sugar's preferential place in the American market and had brought on serious economic problems, did not change the views of the whites on annexation. Now the queen's new constitution forced the decision on them. The only way for them to retain their political power was by nestling under the wing of the American eagle.

Their revolution succeeded but only because the American minister, John L. Stevens, supported it with 150 marines and sailors from the U.S.S. *Boston,* which was in Honolulu's harbor. He landed the troops ostensibly to protect the legation and the consulate, but they never got close to American property. Ardent annexationist that he was, Stevens, on February 1, raised the American flag on Government House and proclaimed Hawaii a protectorate of the United States. Meanwhile, on January 19, by which time the revolution had ended, a delegation representing the newly established provisional government and consisting of four Americans and one Englishman, journeyed to Washington to consummate annexation. A treaty was signed on February 14 and the following day President Harrison sent it to the Senate. At the same time, annexationist newspapers kept up a steady drumbeat of expansionist copy. The *San Francisco Call,* for example, printed a cartoon showing Uncle Sam sitting under a tree catching a ripe fruit labeled Hawaii; other fruit still on the tree represented Cuba, Canada, Haiti, Mexico, and Samoa. With only two weeks remaining in Harrison's term, the treaty could not possibly be shepherded through the Senate so quickly, especially since the incoming Democratic administration of Grover Cleveland was known to be opposed to the whole idea.

Five days after his inauguration, Cleveland formally withdrew the treaty from the Senate on the grounds it needed re-examination. He believed, as did many other Democrats, that American collusion had been dishonorable and thereby the treaty was tainted. To ascertain the facts surrounding America's role, he sent James H. Blount to Hawaii to investigate. Blount's report, rendered in the summer of 1893, bore out Cleveland's suspicions. Stevens had clearly abetted the revolution; it was decidedly a minority revolution; and the mass of Hawaiians were loyal to their queen. Cleveland thereupon tried to convince the president of the newly created republic, Sanford B. Dole, to turn the government over to the deposed queen. Dole and the American Hawaiians in control refused, whereupon Cleveland extended recognition to the new nation, but annexation was out of the question. Hawaii would have to wait four more years before being brought within the American orbit. Only because of the high emotion during the war with Spain and in order to secure Admiral Dewey's Pacific Ocean operations did the joint resolution for annexation gain the approval of Congress in July 1898. The Democrats all through the Cleveland regime were able to block any Republican move to consider the treaty.

If Cleveland was a "dove" on Hawaii, he proved to be a "hawk" on the

anti-expansionist

by 1893 - 3 new battleships commissioned
By the end of 1890's - 20 new battleships + support craft

crisis that erupted in 1895 over the boundary between British Guiana and Venezuela. Indeed, he outdid the most jingo expansionists in his position on the question. The boundary problem had a long history dating back to the early nineteenth century. A Briton surveyed the boundary in 1840, but Venezuela refused to accept the line. Discovery of gold in the disputed territory in the 1880s brought to the matter a new importance and a sharpening of the issue. President Cleveland offered the good offices of the United States in 1887 but Britain rejected them. Seven years later, in his second administration, Cleveland renewed the offer and again was refused. Meanwhile, the former American minister to Venezuela, William L. Scruggs, published, in August of 1894, an account of *British Aggressions in Venezuela, or the Monroe Doctrine on Trial,* in which he pressed Venezuela's case and accused England of belittling the Monroe Doctrine.

The book achieved instant popularity—a tender chord had been hit in the collective sensibility of Americans. To them, the Monroe Doctrine had over the years grown to unexpected proportions—had, indeed, become something of a sacred object bracketed with such basic Americana as the Declaration of Independence and the Constitution. Now, there was talk in the press and in Congress of forcing England to arbitrate the dispute. Feelings, which were already running high, got a boost from the British seizure in April of 1895 of the Nicaraguan port of Corinto, where disorders had damaged the property of some Englishmen. A resolution passed unanimously by Congress in February 1895 urging Britain to arbitrate was indicative of the state of American opinion and of the political agreement on the question. Then on July 20, 1895, the administration, in a note to London, forged ahead of the public and the Congress. It was the work of Secretary of State Richard Olney and dubbed "a 20-inch gun" by Cleveland. Bluntly, Olney ascribed to the United States the paramount right of dominating affairs in the Western hemisphere. "Today," he wrote, "the United States is practically sovereign on this continent, and its fiat is law upon the subjects to which it confines its interposition." He implied, conversely, that Britain had no such right. By the Monroe Doctrine, indeed, Britain was required to keep "hands off." Hence, arbitration was Britain's only recourse.

The British clearly were not intimidated. Lord Salisbury, the prime minister, and foreign minister as well, took four months for his reply although Olney had asked for an answer before the opening of Congress in early December. And when it arrived it was not, by American standards, satisfactory. It might even be said to have been arrogant; it was certainly unrelenting. Salisbury denied that the Monroe Doctrine was binding on England or that it was applicable to the matter at hand, which was "simply the determination of the frontier of a British possession which belonged to the throne of England long before the Republic of Venezuela came into existence." He could see no reason to accept American interference

1896-McKinley

or to acknowledge the special right of the United States to interpose itself in the dispute. He would not arbitrate.

Cleveland wasted no time getting back at Salisbury. He was, according to a friend, "mad clear through." On December 17, 1895, less than two weeks after the receipt of Salisbury's note, he asked Congress to appropriate $100,000 for a commission that would determine the boundary that the United States would then defend. That both houses of Congress unanimously voted the money and endorsed the plan did not escape Salisbury nor did the warlike spirit in the American press and in the country elude him. "*War If Necessary*," ran a headline in the *New York Sun*. Was some distant territory in a South American jungle worth a war to Britain? Decidedly not, concluded London especially in view of the complications she was facing in the world. In South Africa, a war was imminent with the Boers, and in Europe there was a hostile Germany. In early January 1896, the British got a fright when the German kaiser sent a telegram of congratulations to President Kruger of the Republic of the Transvaal on his defeat of a raid led by a British subject in his land. It seemed important to keep peace with America, especially considering the vulnerability of Canada. Salisbury quickly changed his tune; he now equated the United States' relation to Venezuela with England's to Holland and prominent Britons spoke of the Stars and Stripes joined with the Union Jack. In March, Salisbury accepted American good offices; in February of the following year, Venezuela and England signed a treaty of arbitration; a panel of five arbitrators decided the case in October 1899 and thus the matter came to a close. Although Venezuela received some valuable land at the mouth of the Orinoco River, her lifeline, the settlement was not appreciably different from what Britain had offered on several occasions.

So Grover Cleveland had gained his point and brought Britain to heel. It did seem strange that the moderate, antijingo, antiexpansionist Democrat who had resisted taking Hawaii should have been so stern and insistent over Venezuela. Numerous explanations of his conduct have been advanced. It has been said that he sought to distract the country from the depression it was undergoing; that he had to demonstrate that Democrats were as patriotic and nationalistic as Republicans; that he had in mind the strategic importance of the area and the ill effect upon the United States of British expansion there; that he was really doing Olney's bidding. Whatever Cleveland's motives, the significance of the confrontation lies in the fact that it forced Britain to take a fresh look at her relations with the United States. Indeed, the crisis marks a milestone in the relations between the two nations. For England, the prospect of facing enemies on many fronts made friendship with America attractive and essential. For the United States, the closeness of hostilities brought a fright. The two powers, hitherto rivals and antagonists on many scores from the days of the War of Independence and the War of 1812, through the numerous disputes

Olney - Pauncefote Treaty

over Oregon, the Maine boundary, the canal site, and Britain's neutrality during the Civil War, were able to enter the twentieth century as friends as a result of the clearing of the air over Venezuela. Indeed, that century would prove to be very much an Anglo-American century.

BIBLIOGRAPHY

G. R. Dulebohn, *Principles of Foreign Policy Under the Cleveland Administrations* (1941).

Richard Hofstadter, *Social Darwinism in American Thought* (1945).

Walter LaFeber, *The New Empire: An Interpretation of American Expansionism, 1860–1898* (1963).

Harold and Margaret Sprout, *The Rise of American Naval Power, 1776–1918* (1944).

Charles C. Tansill, *The Foreign Policy of Thomas F. Bayard, 1885–1897* (1940).

Alice F. Tyler, *The Foreign Policy of James G. Blaine* (1935).

William A. Williams, *The Roots of the Modern American Empire: A Study of the Growth and Shaping of Social Consciousness in a Market Place Society* (1969).

1887- Treaty (?) didn't get approval

1898 - Joint Resolution -
It was pigeon-holed in committee

Treaty- 2/3 in the Senate (for approval)
Joint Resolution - 1/2 in the House + Senate (for approval)

William McKinley (courtesy of the National Portrait Gallery, the Smithsonian Institution, Washington, D.C.).

The War with Spain

THE WAR with Spain, the shortest, most popular, and least painful war in United States history was the logical outcome, the capstone, of the new spirit which had permeated the American people in the last fifteen years of the nineteenth century. It may be likened to a marriage after a courtship. It was the fulfillment after years of preparation. It also seemed to have satisfied the passion for a vigorous policy, for shortly after war ended the spirit appeared spent and interest in overseas adventure waned.

It was the situation in Cuba that precipitated the war. That "Pearl of the Antilles" had been restive under Spanish rule ever since the early years of the century and sporadic uprisings punctuated relations between colony and mother country. A bitter and cruel revolution erupted in 1868 that lasted ten years with no appreciable results. The United States had remained aloof from the struggle despite a deep interest in the fortunes of an island so close to our shores and so intimately linked by commerce and finance and by feelings of sympathy for people striving for freedom. Even a provocative incident in 1873 involving the execution of fifty-three crewmen and passengers of a vessel flying the American flag that was captured by the Spanish did not lead to intervention. There was simply no will to fight. Twenty-five years later there was a will and it was galvanized by a renewal of the rebellion.

On February 25, 1895, the Cuban insurrectionists rose up once more against Spain. They fought doggedly and ruthlessly, burning and plundering wherever their forces could strike. Their objective was to sap Spain's strength and determination and force an exhausted mother country to grant independence. They had expected, too, that the United States would spring to their aid in view of the extent of American investment on the island ($50 million) and of American trade ($100 million annually). Indeed, the rebels were not careful to spare American-owned plantations and other property as they practiced their scorched-earth policy.

Their expectations, however, were to be frustrated. President Cleveland, true to his instincts and to his inclinations, took a cautious course. On June 12, 1895, he acknowledged the existence of an insurrection and proclaimed his country's neutrality, all the while carefully avoiding extending the status of belligerents to the rebels. He warned his countrymen to observe strict impartiality and to give aid to neither side. In his annual message in December, he voiced sympathy for the struggles of the patriots fighting for liberty and expressed hopes for an early peace but reiterated his determination to keep America out of the fray. To the leaders of the Republican-dominated Congress, he made clear that he would ignore any resolutions designed to enmesh the United States in the war. One such resolution, indeed, was passed in February of 1896 by Senate (64–6) and House (246–27) granting belligerent status to the rebels and providing for the use of American good offices in a Cuban-Spanish negotiation leading to independence. Another Senate motion, in December of the same year, directing the president to recognize Cuban independence, was favorably reported out of the Foreign Relations Committee but Cleveland's opposition forestalled a vote. All this is not to say that the president was oblivious to the problem at his doorstep. By quiet and unobtrusive diplomacy, he was making efforts to get Spain to make reforms in Cuba and grant the islanders autonomy, and he did warn of the possibility of intervention if concessions were not forthcoming. The latter point he proclaimed publicly in his annual message of December 7, 1896. If Spain does not pacify the island, he said, "Our obligations to the sovereignty of Spain will be superseded by higher obligations, which we can hardly hesitate to recognize and discharge."

Cleveland's successor, William McKinley, did not depart notably from his predecessor's course of action upon coming into office in March of 1897. He was by no means a jingoist or an annexationist. He knew little and cared less about foreign affairs. As two-time governor of Ohio and long-time (thirteen years) member of the House of Representatives, his interests were domestic and internal. It is true that his party's platform in 1896 called for a "firm, vigorous, and dignified" foreign policy and for a navy "commensurate with [the nation's] position and responsibility" and mentioned, specifically, such rather expansionist projects as the construction of a Nicaraguan canal, the purchase of the Danish West Indies, and the acquisition of Hawaii. As for Cuba, it supported the exertion of American influence to bring peace and independence to the island. Yet, McKinley did not even refer to Cuba in his Inaugural Address, and what clearer indication of his administration's direction could there be than his words: "We want no wars of conquest; we must avoid the temptation of territorial aggression."

As did Cleveland, he ignored a Senate resolution passed by 41–14 on May 20, 1897 directing him to recognize Cuban belligerency and kept it off the House floor. But, like Cleveland, he did not remain aloof. Privately and quietly he instructed his minister in Madrid, W. L. Woodford, on

September 23, 1897, to let the authorities there know that Cuba must be pacified and that the United States stood ready to help. Continued turmoil in Cuba may, he warned, make American intervention necessary and unavoidable.

The president believed his cautious and modest policy would be profitable in view of the establishment in Spain of a new liberal ministry in October headed by Mateo Sagasta and pledged to making such reforms as would mollify and satisfy the rebels. In November, Sagasta recalled General Valeriano Weyler, who had been sent out in February of 1896 to quell the insurrection. It was Weyler, called the "Butcher," who had outraged the American sensibilities by his "reconcentration" policy, which placed the entire population (men, women, and children) of cities and towns in certain areas within barbed wire to separate them from the insurrectionists. Two hundred thousand of them were reported to have died because of unsanitary conditions, famine, and disease. Sagasta also granted the islanders the same rights Spaniards enjoyed at home and took steps to create an autonomous government in Cuba. He really could not do very much more, reported Woodford, without threatening the very existence of the monarchy. It was, therefore, with some degree of satisfaction that McKinley, in his annual message of December 6, 1897, could report of the progress being made in settling the Cuban problem and urge that Spain be given a reasonable chance to succeed. He continued to oppose recognition of independence or of belligerent status for the rebels but did not rule out American intervention should Spain founder.

Unhappily, events in the next several months—some beyond the president's control and one, at least, that could have been avoided—created such a furor in America as to force McKinley's hand and cause him to take the plunge for war.

The American consul in Havana, Fitzhugh Lee, who had been calling for United States warships to anchor in Havana to protect American property and evacuate American citizens, changed his mind early in January of 1898 following an outbreak of riots in the city. He now urged the president to keep naval vessels away lest they provoke reprisals. McKinley, however, decided to send a cruiser as a means of demonstrating American good will and as an indication of improving relations between the two powers. That move proved to be a cruel and crucial mistake. On February 15, 1898, three weeks after *Maine* dropped anchor in Havana harbor, it lay a ruined hulk—the result of an explosion that took the lives of 260 officers and men.

The effect on the country was electric. It had just about recovered from the revelation of an indiscretion by the Spanish minister in Washington, Dupuy de Lôme, who had, in a private letter to a friend, made some extremely unseemly remarks about McKinley. He had called the president "a would-be politician who tries to leave a door open behind himself while keeping on good terms with the jingoes in his party." The *New York*

Journal had gotten hold of the letter and printed it on February 9, 1898. De Lôme had resigned at once, but the bad taste lingered in the mouths of Americans who had been shocked by the affair. Now, the sinking of *Maine* seemed further proof of Spanish perfidy and treachery, for no one doubted that the explosion had been the work of Spanish agents. An American court of inquiry report, published on March 21, 1898, ascribed the sinking to an "explosion of a submarine mine, which caused the partial explosion of two or more forward magazines" but did not identify the perpetrator of the deed. Consul-General Lee and the captain of *Maine* positively acquitted Spain of responsibility. Still, Americans were convinced of Spain's guilt. "THE WARSHIP MAINE WAS SPLIT IN TWO BY AN ENEMY'S SECRET INFERNAL MACHINE" headlined the *New York Journal* and the assistant secretary of the Navy, Theodore Roosevelt, wrote a friend that "the *Maine* was sunk by an act of dirty treachery on the part of the Spaniards."

All over the country, parades and mass meetings were decrying "hesitation, delay, diplomacy, and idle talk" and proclaiming the need to punish Spain. "Remember the Maine" became the watchword and slogan for those demanding intervention in the Cuban crisis. The sinking, according to the *New York World*, was itself "an act of war." McKinley tried to head off the public stampede for war. He had on March 8 asked for and received by a unanimous vote of Congress, $50 million to bolster the country's defenses, but beyond that he would not go. The pressure on him was very great. Congress was demanding he recognize Cuban independence, but the press, led by William Randolph Hearst's *New York Journal* and Joseph Pulitzer's *New York World*, was crying for even stronger action.

The two newspapers, locked in a titanic struggle for circulation in New York City, had, for some years, been exploiting the Cuban situation. Each outdid the other in lurid, sensational, and, often, untruthful accounts to excite and satisfy the American appetite for gore. They seemed unconcerned by the fact that their journalistic efforts might be creating a climate that could lead to war. Indeed, Pulitzer admitted he was not averse "to the idea of war. Not a big one but one which would arouse enough interest to give me a chance to gauge the reflex in my circulation figures." Moderates were rightfully shocked by the antics of Pulitzer and Hearst. The respected editor of the *Nation*, E. L. Godkin, wrote of the coverage by the press of the *Maine* tragedy, "Nothing so disgraceful as the behavior of two of these newspapers this week has been known in the history of journalism. Gross misrepresentation of facts, deliberate invention of tales calculated to excite the public, and wanton recklessness in the construction of headlines, have combined to make the issues of the most widely circulated newspapers firebrands scattered throughout the country. It is a crying shame that men should work such mischief simply in order to sell more papers."

Missionaries and other religious groups were also clamouring for strong action against Spain, Baptist minister Poindexter S. Henson blamed the *Maine* sinking on "the procrastinating policy of those at the head of our nation who have failed to deal honestly and courageously in behalf of an oppressed people." Methodist Bishop McCabe believed "there are many things worse than war. It may be that the United States is to become the Knight Errant of the world. War with Spain may put her in a position to demand civil and religious liberty for the oppressed of every nation and of every clime." The feeling was general in spiritual circles that "the United States would go to Cuba with a loaf of bread at the end of its bayonet, with its warships laden with flour and shot. Its banners have been preceded by the Red Cross flag and will be followed by Bibles and school books."

Standing solidly athwart the public clamor was the business community. Since the beginning of the Cuban crisis, it had counselled moderation. Leading business men like Marcus Hanna, John D. Rockefeller, Andrew Carnegie, Mortimer Schiff, Thomas Fortune Ryan, James J. Hill, and Edward Harriman, boards of trade, chambers of commerce, and the commercial and financial press joined in condemning the drift to war and all had similar reasons. War, they claimed, disrupted prosperity, imperiled currency stability, interrupted trade, and endangered commerce and ports. As the Boston financier, S. M. Weld, informed Senator Henry Cabot Lodge, "You were sent to Washington to represent one of the largest business states in the country. The business interests of the state require peace and quiet, not war. If we attempt to regulate the affairs of the whole world we will be in hot water from now until the end of time." The proponents of vigorous action were appalled by what they considered the weakness and cowardice of the business people. They likened them to Benedict Arnold, traitors to the country. They indicted them for lack of courage and patriotism, for valuing profits above noble deeds.

On March 17, 1898, an event occurred that had a profound effect on the country and virtually made untenable McKinley's moderate stand. It was a speech by Senator Redfield Proctor, conservative, dispassionate, and moderate Republican from Vermont. Proctor had tended to disbelieve the stories of the wretchedness of the Cubans and of their sufferings so he went to the island for a first-hand view. What he saw shocked him and he conveyed that sense to his listeners. He described the horrors of the concentration camps, of the miseries of the 400,000 people incarcerated in them, and of the deaths of large numbers. He placed no confidence in Spain's reform efforts and urged American intervention to end Spain's misgovernment and mismanagement of the island. That single speech, it was said, turned opponents of intervention into proponents, including the business community. The *Wall Street Journal* said as much when it reported that Proctor had "converted a great many people in Wall Street."

The *Literary Digest* reflected the prevailing national mood with the words: "Intervention is the plain duty of the United States on the simple ground of humanity." From that point on, Spain and peace were doomed. The course to war was unalterable.

On March 26, McKinley acted. Instructions went out to present an ultimatum to Spain—an armistice to October, during which time peace negotiations were to be undertaken; an end to the concentration camps; "full self-government for Cuba," which meant, of course, independence. The terms were difficult and compliance would be a serious blow to Spanish pride. Minister Woodford reported from Madrid a rift in the mother country on the question of war and peace. The lower and middle classes were for capitulation to American demands and for cutting Cuba loose from its Spanish moorings, but the army, the aristocracy, and the political leadership wanted to fight. Out of the struggle came compromise. On March 31, Woodford cabled the Spanish reply: revocation of the concentration camp order in the western provinces (where the fighting was greatest) but as for an armistice, the rebels would have to request it. Nothing was said about independence.

Meanwhile, Spain appealed to the European powers for help in saving the remnants of her empire in the New World. Shades of the past. Seventy years earlier, at the time of the Adams-de Onís negotiations, Madrid had made a similar plea against the rapacious Americans who were bent on dispossessing the European powers from their American holdings. Spain had been rebuffed then and was rebuffed now. After some half-hearted remonstrances, she was left to face the United States alone. No one seemed bold (or foolhardy) enough to challenge America.

McKinley was not satisfied with Spain's reply. He warned Woodford on April 4 that tension in Congress was mounting and he did not know how long he could resist the clamorings for intervention if Madrid did not give way. Woodford, on his part, was working fervishly to get an armistice and on April 5 informed McKinley that he believed he would succeed. He did, finally, on April 9 but it was too late. The pressure on the president was too great and whatever his good intentions and his wish to give Spain more time, he gave way to the prevailing passion. On April 11, 1898, he presented to Congress a war message that he had prepared six days earlier. In it he reported the diplomatic stalemate and the futility of further negotiations. The only way to restore peace, end the bloodshed, protect American citizens, and prevent further injury to American trade was by the "forceable intervention of the United States. . . . The issue is now with Congress," he said. "It is a solemn responsibility. I have exhausted every effort to relieve the intolerable condition of affairs which is at our doors. Prepared to execute every obligation imposed upon me by the Constitution and the law, I await your action." At the end of his message, he noted that the Spanish government had authorized the general commanding in Cuba to suspend hostilities—almost as an after-thought.

Whether McKinley had, in fact, exhausted every effort for peace is debatable. Clearly, Spain was on the way to acceding to America's demands by a timetable commensurate with her national pride. It seems likely that had the president held off for another month, Cuba would have been freed. But, perhaps, that would have been asking too much in view of the fierce pressure on McKinley from nearly every segment of the American public and from the Congress and in view of the danger to the future of the Republican party if he ignored the public mood. Whatever the verdict of history, the die was cast for war.

There was no doubt as to the course of Congress. "Excitement was at fever heat," reported the *London Times* correspondent, referring to the House of Representatives. The result was a joint resolution passed on April 19, 1898 authorizing the president to use force to eject Spain from Cuba and give the islanders their independence. An amendment proposed by Senator Teller of Colorado renounced any intent on the part of the United States to annex Cuba. McKinley affixed his signature to the bill on the 20th and on the same day, the Spanish minister was handed his passport. On the 25th, Congress declared a state of war to have existed between the two countries as of the 21st of April.

It was, in the words of John Hay, a "splendid little war." Admiral Mahan had predicted it would last three months. He was wrong by one month; it took four to lick the enemy. On paper, Spain had the edge both as to land and sea forces, but that was only part of the story. The decrepit state of her army and navy was matched by the defeatist attitude of her officers and men. The cause was hopeless and they knew it. The American army was not in much better shape as to equipment and training but the enthusiasm of the soldiers and their leaders was great. Indeed, they marched to war confident of victory. As for the navy, it was in splendid condition, the result of a modern building program in the 1890s, which yielded some superb battleships, and increasingly effective fleet maneuvers in the years preceding the war.

The theater of war was in both the Caribbean and in the Pacific, and in the two places the outcome was never in doubt. On April 24, Admiral George Dewey, commanding the Asiatic squadron, had received orders to proceed to the Spanish-owned Philippine Islands from his Hong Kong base and destroy the Spanish fleet there. On May 1, he carried out his instructions literally by sinking every enemy ship in Manila Bay. To take possession of the capital city of Manila, McKinley dispatched an army under General Wesley Merritt. The first three troopships left San Francisco on May 25; others followed and by July 31, 11,000 soldiers had landed on the island of Luzon. On August 14, Manila fell. On the other side of the world, an American fleet under Admiral William T. Sampson an-

The Spanish Atlantic Fleet put in at Santiago to help the land forces but was defeated.

198   *A History of American Diplomacy*

nihilated a Spanish flotilla of seven vessels trying to escape into open sea from the harbor of Santiago, thus ending Spanish sea power in the Caribbean as it had been ended in the Pacific. That was on July 3. On the 16th, General William R. Shafter occupied Santiago; on the 25th, General Nelson A. Miles captured Puerto Rico. The Madrid government's position was hopeless and on July 26, it was ready to give up. On August 12, an armistice was signed in Washington by which Spain freed Cuba and ceded to the United States Puerto Rico and Guam in the Marianas, which General Merritt had taken en route to Manila. The United States was to hold Manila pending a definitive peace treaty to be negotiated in Paris on October 1.

the Rough Riders— Roosevelt stormed San Juan Hill

The question confronting McKinley on the eve of the peace was precisely how much of Spain's empire would fall to the United States. Cuba had been ruled out by the Teller Amendment. Puerto Rico and Guam would undoubtedly be retained by the treaty. But what of the Philippines, that vast archipelago inhabited by strange people—strange in color, language, culture, custom, and outlook? And, if the islands became American territory, could they be incorporated? Would they become states of the Union, taking their places alongside Virginia and Massachusetts, and would their people become citizens on an equal footing with mainlanders? Or would the islanders be ruled, frankly, as colonies and dependencies? At stake was nothing less than the future of the American system—was it to be an empire like Britain or Rome or remain a continental republic? The fact that Hawaii had already been annexed (by joint resolution in July of 1898) did not affect the problem of the Philippines for although it numbered among its inhabitants nonwhites—Orientals and Polynesians—there was a considerable base of whites of American ancestry, sufficient to give a familiar cast to the structure of society and politics.

Clearly, McKinley had not, at the outset of the war, contemplated holding territory in Asia. The conflict with Spain had purely western hemisphere origins. The dispatch of Dewey to the Philippines had as its purpose the elimination of the Spanish fleet there lest it be free to cross the Pacific and attack the American West Coast. It was, also, simply sound strategy to strike the enemy wherever he could be found. There were, to be sure, people like Roosevelt, Lodge, Mahan, and Beveridge, who from the very beginning and for reasons of national pride, considerations of strategy, and as a base for commercial penetration of the China market, desired the Spanish possessions in southeast Asia. But there is no evidence that McKinley thought in these terms. Yet by the time the war came to an end he had certainly moved in the direction of annexation.

The change in his position was gradual. The composition of the peace commission provided the first clue. It consisted of five men, three of whom were avowed expansionists: Senator Cushman K. Davis, Republican of Minnesota and chairman of the Foreign Relations Committee; Senator William P. Frye, Republican of Maine; and Whitelaw Reid, Republican and editor of the influential *New York Tribune.* Of the other two, Secretary of State William R. Day, who headed the delegation, could be considered a moderate and Senator George Gray, Democrat from Delaware, was definitely opposed to expansionism. The instructions to the commission, dated September 18, 1898, may be viewed as the second step on McKinley's road to Damascus. They demanded that Spain give up Cuba and cede to the United States Guam, Puerto Rico, and the island of Luzon in the Philippines with free entry for American vessels in all other parts of the archipelago. Then came the third and final stage—revised instructions on October 28 that demanded all of the Philippines.

What had caused McKinley's change of heart? Much like the president's road to war, his path to empire was the result of acute pressures from all sides. There were missionaries who longed for souls to save (they seemed to have ignored the fact that most of the Filipinos were Catholics), steamship operators who visualized vast profits on the transport of goods and people, naval planners who dreamed of bases and coaling stations and an enlarged naval establishment to defend the far-flung possession, businessmen who wanted the Asian markets, and the imperialists for whom the great attraction was planting the flag on distant shores and fulfilling the mission of civilizing native races. All those interests were summed up superbly by Senator Albert Beveridge in a stirring speech on January 9, 1900. Mission, trade, destiny, civilization, chosen people, power, Christianize, educate—all the clichés of Manifest Destiny rolled off his lips that day in the Senate. "We will not," he said, "repudiate our duty in the archipelago. We will not abandon our opportunity in the Orient. We will not renounce our part in the mission of our race. . . . And we will move forward to our work, not howling out regrets like slaves whipped to their burdens, but with gratitude for a task worthy of our strength and thanksgiving to Almighty God that he has marked us as his chosen people."

Beveridge's speech was greeted by loud applause from the Senate galleries that gave some indication of the state of public opinion. There was no question that the war and its easy victories excited the American people and fed their cupidity for empire and power. McKinley learned of that sentiment on a two-week tour of the country in early October of 1898. He addressed fifty-seven audiences and was impressed by the enthusiastic support for empire which he encountered. Six days after his return to Washington he had made up his mind to revise the instructions to the peace commission and demand all of the Philippines. To a group of visiting clergymen a year later, he recalled the steps leading to his decision and the reason behind it. He did not want the Philippines. They came "as a gift from the gods . . . [they] dropped into our laps." The president did not know what to do with them. Then, after several nights of prayer, "It came to me this way—I don't know how it was, but it came (1) that we could not give them back to Spain—that would be cowardly and dishonorable; (2) that we could not turn them over to France or Germany—our commercial rivals in the Orient—that would be bad business and discreditable; (3) that we could not leave them to themselves—they were unfit for self-government—and they would soon have anarchy and mis-rule over there worse than Spain's was; and (4) that there was nothing left for us to do but take them all, and to educate the Filipinos, and uplift and civilize and Christianize them, and by God's grace do the very best we could by them, as our fellowmen for whom Christ also died." The God McKinley communed with did not sound very much different from Beveridge and He certainly would not have felt uncomfortable in the company of Lodge, Mahan, Roosevelt, and the others

The definitive articles of peace were signed on December 10, 1898 in Paris and sent up at once to the Senate. The terms were not surprising—Guam, Puerto Rico, and the Philippines to the United States; $20 million to Spain. Spain had balked at surrendering the archipelago but the choice was not hers to make. What was surprising was the extent of the opposition to the treaty in the Senate and in the country. Now were marshalled all the anti-imperialist and antiexpansionist sentiment that had existed throughout the post-Civil War period but had lain dormant in the exciting time leading up to the outbreak of the war. It had been submerged by the stirring victories of Dewey, Sampson, Merritt, and Miles but the acquisition of the Philippines and its meaning for America brought the spirit to the surface and gave it new vigor.

The opponents of the treaty waged a powerful and determined campaign to defeat it. In their ranks were to be found representatives of all parties and factions—Mugwumps like Carl Schurz and Charles Francis Adams, old-line Republicans like George F. Hoar and Thomas B. Reed, Silver Democrats like William Jennings Bryan and Gold Democrats like Grover Cleveland. There were reformers of every stripe—single-tax advocates, freetraders, descendants of abolitionists, municipal reformers, social welfare workers, pacifists, and prohibitionists. Distinguished intellectuals were among them, too—David Starr Jordan, president of Stanford and Charles W. Eliot, president of Harvard, the historian Hermann E. Von Holst, E. L. Godkin, editor of the *Nation*, writers Mark Twain and William Deane Howells, sociologist William Graham Sumner, psychologist William James, poet William Vaughn Moody, and humorist Finley Peter Dunne. Labor was represented by Samuel Gompers and capital by Andrew Carnegie.

Theirs was no haphazard effort; it was highly organized. By June of 1898 many cities throughout the country had each its own Anti-Imperialist League, from which emanated brochures, broadsides, cartoons, books, and pamphlets. Speakers went out to address meetings and monitor discussions. The arguments were powerful and persuasive and centered about a few basic themes. One was the difficulty of governing territory so distant from home; another involved cost; still another touched on strategy. Andrew Carnegie argued that the possession of outlying, noncontiguous

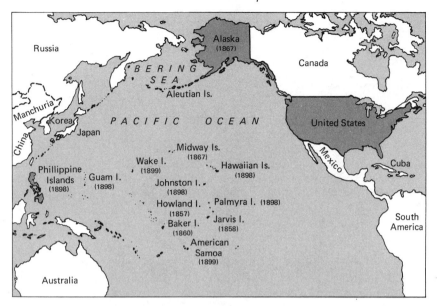

The American Empire in the Pacific, 1900.

islands would be difficult to defend, would make us vulnerable, and would draw us into the highly competitive and dangerous Far Eastern political and diplomatic vortex. But, above all, were stressed certain basic principles—constitutionality, democracy, morality, tradition. Has Congress the power to conquer and govern a people, queried Senator George F. Hoar, and, more importantly, has Congress got the moral right to do those things against the will of the inhabitants? William Graham Sumner warned of the effect of imperialism upon traditional American democracy. Imperialism leads to wars, creates debts, requires vast armies, generates pomp, and promotes vanity—all of which are destructive of democracy. The United States, the traditional leader of the revolt against imperial states, now itself succumbs to the lure. The ultimate victory was Spain's, Sumner claimed, for the United States adopted her ideals and policies. The platform of one Anti-Imperialist League lamented the extinction of the Spirit of 1776 in substituting "might" for "right" by attempting to subjugate the Filipinos, while William Jennings Bryan noted "Our guns destroyed the Spanish fleet but they cannot destroy that self-evident truth that government derived their just powers, not from superior force but from the consent of the governed." Wittily but bitingly, Finley Peter Dunne defined the American concept of liberty as the "indulgent parent kneeling on the stomach of the adopted child."

The most powerful indictment of imperialism came from the pen of William Vaughn Moody, whose "Ode in Time of Hesitation" had a wide circulation.

> Lies, lies. It cannot be! The wars we wage are
>   noble and our battles are won by justice.
> We have not sold our loftiest heritage.
> The proud republic hath not stooped to cheat
> And scramble in the market place of war.
> Ah—no, we have not fallen so.
>
> We are our father's sons; let those who lead us know
> We charge you, ye who lead us
> Breathe on their chivalry no hint of stain
> Turn not their new-world victories to gain.
> Tempt not our weakness, our cupidity!
> For save we let the island men go free,
> Those baffled and dislaureled ghosts
> Will curse us from the lamentable coasts
> Where walk the frustrated dead.
> O, ye who lead, take heed
> Blindness we may forgive, but baseness we will smite.

Assuming all ninety senators were present for the vote, the Administration needed sixty "ayes" to gain approval for the treaty. Of the fifty-seven Republicans, only forty-one could be counted on to stand by the president; the others were anti-Administration or antiannexation. Of the thirty-three Democrats, some were in favor of retaining the Philippines but, in any case, the decision would be close and the administration was not confident of success. The president worked hard to influence the vote. It was said that he put pressure on recalcitrant senators with the mighty weapon of the patronage, but he used, also, all the charm and powers of persuasion he had. In the Senate, Lodge, Davis, and Frye carried the burden of the argument in favor of the treaty. On the other side, the leader was the stalwart Republican from Massachusetts, George F. Hoar, whose sharp wit and impeccable logic carried much weight.

The debate was passionate and the air in the legislative chamber was charged. The Administration forces were able to beat down several resolutions designed to keep the Philippines out of American hands, but they were not so certain of mustering enough votes to cinch the treaty. That they finally succeeded on February 6, 1899 in getting a two-thirds majority was the result of aid from two unexpected sources. One source was William Jennings Bryan, who was titular leader of the Democratic Party and the defeated standardbearer in 1896. He opposed annexing the Philippines, yet he urged Democratic senators to vote for the treaty as the only means of ending the war. The question of retaining the islands, he said, could be handled once peace was assured. He swayed 11 Democrats, who with the forty-one safe Republicans and five Populists and Independents provided one vote more than necessary to carry the treaty. The final score was 57–27.

Help came, too, from Emilio Aguinaldo, the noted Filipino patriot. He had been a long-term exile from his homeland and an indefatigable fighter against Spain for the independence of his people. In April of 1898, after war was declared, he had been brought to Luzon in an American vessel to organize his followers and help the United States forces defeat the Spanish army there. He had, indeed, fought valiantly expecting to be rewarded with independence. He had not bargained on trading one master for another. Disillusioned and dismayed by the terms of the treaty that placed the American flag over the islands on January 5, 1899, he proclaimed himself head of the Filipino Republic (that he had actually created in August of 1898). Such a move led inevitably to a clash of arms with American forces for the United States did not plan to surrender what it had just acquired. On the night of February 4, 1899, the insurrection began that was to last until July 1902 at the cost to the United States of $600 million and 4,000 lives and the use of certain devices that were not unlike Spain's methods in Cuba and of which the United States might well have been ashamed. Still, the fighting coming one day before the vote did cause some doubtful senators to "rally round the flag."

So, the United States emerged from the war possessor of an imperial domain stretching far into the Pacific and at Asia's door. The continental republic had been transferred into a maritime empire. The cherished principle of the Founding Fathers to steer clear of extracontinental involvement was abandoned; the doctrine of the two spheres was set aside. Samuel Flagg Bemis labelled the move "The Great Aberration," and he dated America's international difficulties from that time. Whether for good or for evil, the United States entered the twentieth century much changed.

BIBLIOGRAPHY

ROBERT BEISNER, *Twelve Against Empire: The Anti-Imperialists, 1898–1900* (1968).

PHILIP FONER, *The Spanish-Cuban-American War and the Birth of American Imperialism* (1972).

DAVID HEALY, *United States Expansionism: The Imperialist Urge in the 1890's* (1970).

MARGARET LEECH, *In the Days of McKinley* (1959).

ERNEST R. MAY, *Imperial Democracy: The Emergence of America As a Great Power* (1961).

JULIUS PRATT, *Expansionists of 1898: The Acquisition of Hawaii and the Spanish Islands* (1936).

DANIEL B. SCHIRMER, *Republic or Empire: American Resistance to the Philippine War* (1972).

E. BERKLEY TOMPKINS, *Anti-imperialism in the United States: Great Debate, 1890–1920* (1971).

John Hay (U.S. Signal Corps photo, the Brady Collection, the National Archives).

In Asia—Retreat

THE UNITED STATES entered the twentieth century heavily enmeshed, for the first time in its history, in Asian affairs with commitments and interests that were to lead directly and inexorably to a great Pacific war and to a test of strength with Japan. The Philippine Islands constituted one link to the Orient. Over that archipelago the American flag flew—thus creating the responsibility to defend the islanders. Second, there was the obligation, if only moral, to stand behind the two notes emanating from Washington in 1899 and 1900 that, taken together, came to be known as the "Open Door" policy.

The notes had their origin in the fear in many quarters in the United States that the scramble for a favored position in parts of China by the European powers and by Japan would lock American businessmen and financiers out of a fruitful and lucrative market for goods and capital. The race for concessions in China was touched off by the apparent ease with which Japan defeated China in a six-month war in 1894–1895. Between August and February, Japanese military and naval elements had swept the Chinese troops from Korea and Manchuria, occupied Port Arthur at the tip of Manchuria and Wei-Hai-Wei in Shantung, and destroyed a Chinese fleet off Shantung peninsula. By the Treaty of Shimonoseki of April 17, 1895 that terminated the conflict, Japan had extracted from her beaten opponent considerable privileges. China ceded to Japan Formosa and the Pescadores, giving the Rising Sun a superb jumping-off point for exploiting the mainland, the Liaotung peninsula at the tip of Manchuria and containing the major ports of Dairen and Port Arthur, and temporary occupation rights of Wei-Hai-Wei.

Japan did not, however, enjoy the fruits of her victory, for the major European powers—France, Russia, and Germany—at once forced her to surrender the most important acquisition—Liaotung. It was not that the powers were taking China's part. It was that they did not wish to see Japan strengthened by so great a foothold in China. Indeed, appreciating that country's weakness in the last war, they moved in promptly to share the plunder. In March 1898, Germany demanded and received as indemnity for the murder of two missionaries a ninety-nine-year lease of the port of Tsingtao in Kiaochow Bay as a coaling station and railroad and mining privileges in Shantung. In the same month, Russia gained a seventy-five-year lease of Port Arthur and Dairen on the Liaotung peninsula and the right to build a railroad from the latter city to Harbin in central Manchuria where the Russian-owned and -operated Chinese Eastern Railroad crossed on its way from its junction with the Trans-Siberian Railroad to Vladivostok. In April, France got a ninety-nine-year lease of Kwangchow and mining and rail rights in three adjacent provinces.

Britain joined in the scramble, negotiating in August a lease of Wei-Hai-Wei (for as long as Russia would hold Port Arthur) and Kowloon opposite Hong Kong but the British were not happy. They stood to lose much by the intrenchment of the powers in parts of China, for in those parts preferences would be given to nationals of the occupying nations and British merchants would be at a disadvantage. For half a century they had enjoyed a monopoly of the Chinese market because trade was open to all nations on an equal basis and, given England's advanced position industrially, her merchants outsold the competition. The British objective, therefore, was to get the powers to maintain equality of treatment in their leaseholds for the citizens of all nations.

For assistance, London turned to the United States in March of 1898 proposing a joint statement to the powers. Shades of Canning's overtures to Richard Rush in 1823! Washington, however, was not interested. Preoccupied with the Cuban question and confident that the policy of open trade in China would be maintained, President McKinley replied to England with a polite "no." Yet one year and six months later, the United States sent, on its own accord, precisely the kind of statement Britain had suggested. The reasons for the change in policy were simple. With the victory over Spain won and the Philippine archipelago annexed, many Americans began to dream extravagant reveries of penetrating the China market. Given the huge industrial and agricultural surplus at the end of the century resulting from increased mechanization, businessmen looked eagerly to the 400 million Chinese as customers for tobacco, cotton goods, flour, wheat, and the like. They were particularly interested in the Oriental market in view of the efforts by certain European nations to exclude American goods from their countries in retaliation for the high United States tariff of 1897. Financiers, cotton spinners, railroad promoters, mining companies, tobacco growers, and other business interests joined in associations such as the American Asiatic Association, the Committee on American Interests in China, and the American China Development Company to put pressure on the government to take steps "for the prompt and energetic defense of the existing treaty rights of our citizens in China and for the protection and preservation of their important commercial interests in that Empire." Letters, telegrams, and memorials poured into the State Department urging action.

Added to the pleas of businessmen were those of the missionaries. China was the goal, the lodestar of the American Protestant missionary effort. The challenge of saving 400 million souls was the magnet which drew the great majority of missionaries to China. There were 1,500 of them there at the end of the century and their numbers were growing. There would be 3,000 in 1905 (out of a worldwide 3,800). And they feared exclusion from the leased territory and spheres of influence. The occupying powers would surely give preference to their own faiths and denominations. Russian Orthodox, Roman Catholics, Lutherans, and Buddhists would replace Baptists, Methodists, Presbyterians, and Congregationalists in Russian, French, German, and Japanese areas.

There were also the voices of the imperialists and expansionists—of Lodge, Mahan, Beveridge, and the Adamses—in support of government action to prevent the United States from being elbowed out of a place in the Oriental sun. The Stars and Stripes must fly where other flags flew.

The pressure converged on three persons charged with making policy—President McKinley, Secretary of State John Hay, and William W. Rockhill, chief of the Latin American Division of the State Department but also Hay's principal advisor on Far Eastern affairs. Rockhill was not hard to convince. Long a resident of China and widely travelled there, he loved and was an expert on Chinese art, language, and literature and did not wish to see that great civilization ruined and polluted by western contamination. He cared not a whit for the businessmen or the missionaries. He wished to preserve China from foreign encroachment for China's sake. As for Hay, he willingly went along with his imperialist–expansionist friends. McKinley resisted longest not wishing to participate too actively in international affairs and not convinced that American interests would suffer by the leaseholds (having been assured by the Russians of their intent to maintain equality of opportunity in Manchuria). What changed his mind was the report brought back by Jacob Gould Schurman, president of Cornell University, whom McKinley had sent to Asia to investigate conditions and in whose wisdom he had great confidence. Returning in August of 1899, Schurman warned the president of the danger to American interests in China from the European powers, especially Russia, and urged action to prevent the dismemberment of China and to maintain equality of treatment for nationals of all countries.

Convinced, McKinley instructed Hay to prepare a remonstrance to the European powers. Hay gave the task to Rockhill. The date was August 24, 1899. Rockhill went to work at once aided by a close friend of long standing, Alfred Hippisley. A Briton who had lived forty years in China and who was a highly placed employee of the Chinese Customs Services, Hippisley was, like Rockhill, a Sinophile and also an authority on Chinese art and ceramics. To save China from foreign domination was his dream and he eagerly joined Rockhill in drafting a state paper on the subject. The result of the combined effort was handed to Hay on August 29, 1899. Eight days later, after a polishing by Assistant Secretary of State Alvey A. Adee, it was put on the cable to Berlin, Rome, St. Petersburg, London, Paris, and Tokyo.

The circular note, dated September 6, 1899, did not seek to disturb the leasehold arrangement. It sought only assurances that there would be no discrimination practised in those leaseholds regarding harbor dues and rail charges, that the Chinese tariff in the treaty ports in the leaseholds and spheres of influence apply equally to all, and that the tariff be collected by the Chinese government. One can easily imagine the reception of such a plea in the foreign offices of the powers. The whole point of the leaseholds and the spheres was discrimination and it would have been foolhardy for the European powers to surrender such an advantage. Their replies, therefore, were, not surprisingly, evasive and equivocal. Not wishing to offend the United States, they accepted the principle of equality of opportunity piously but with such reservations as to emasculate it.

A second note received a similar reception. It was occasioned by the response of the European powers to a revolt by the Boxers, a Chinese secret society. Antiforeign and ardently nationalist, the Boxers, in June of 1900, attacked Christian missionaries in Shanghai and then proceeded to Peking, which they occupied on June 13th and where they placed the foreign legations under seige. An allied relief force of 18,000 (including 2,500 American troops) fought their way into the city and rescued their nationals beseiged in the legations. Concerned lest the punishing of the Boxers and of the Chinese government that had supported them serve as a pretext for extending political control over parts of the Empire, Hay on July 3, 1900, urged the nations to concur in the American policy "to seek a solution which may bring about permanent safety and peace to China and preserve Chinese territorial and administrative entity." The European powers neither dissented from the principle nor opposed it. They did not even reply (no reply was requested by Hay). They did strengthen their position in their leaseholds, a change the presence of such large numbers of their troops facilitated.

Hay was not fooled. Despite his assurances to the American public that the European powers' reply to his first note contained "adequate assurances" and was "final and definitive," he knew that he had not changed their views or altered their plans. The best indication of his true assessment of the situation was his own effort, at the insistence of the Navy Department, to join in the scramble. In November, 1900 he sought from the Chinese government a lease of a base at Samsah Bay. Imagine his embarrassment when the Japanese reminded him of his note on preserving Chinese territorial integrity. The deal did not go through. It was blocked by Japan, in whose sphere of influence, Fukien province, Samsah Bay was situated.

For Hay, as well as for Rockhill, the notes had failed to achieve their objective. Rockhill, who went to Peking as minister late in 1900 and witnessed the activity of the European powers in extending their influence, was "sick and tired of the whole business. I trust it may be a long time before the United States gets itself into another muddle of this description," he wrote. The only possible way for Hay's principles to be maintained and to prevent the dismemberment of China was by a balance of power. As one historian put it, "the mutual jealousies and rivalries of the powers became so strong that they could not agree as to how the quarry should be dismembered. Each of the potential partitioners feared a first move that might set off a chain reaction and then a world war." Certainly, the principle of the "Open Door" would not be maintained by American force of arms. There was neither the will nor the wherewithal. Hay knew it and so did Theodore Roosevelt, who came to the White House in September of 1901 following McKinley's assassination. Hay told the new president, "We will not fight for Manchuria for the simple reason that we cannot," and Roosevelt lamented, apropros of the spirit of the American people after the Spanish war and the question of the security of the Philippine Islands, "It is very difficult to awaken any public interest in providing any adequate defense of the islands."

Clear to American policy-makers was the fact that Russia seemed to be the power most likely to disturb the balance in Asia. She was most aggressive in closing the door in Manchuria and in transforming that province into a protectorate. That she had ambition to extend her influence beyond Manchuria into some or all of the other 18 provinces of China was universally suspected. Operating from home territory in contiguous Siberia and diplomatically supported by her European ally, France (whose Chinese interests were far to the south), Russia was relentless in making demands on the Chinese government and in building railroads and exploiting the mines in Manchuria. Once she succeeded in erecting a stronghold in that place, there was justifiable expectation of a next move.

Of all the nations interested in China, Japan appeared the most likely antagonist of Russia. It was that nation that had engineered the move after Shimonoseki to deprive Japan of the Liaotung peninsula and had herself taken over the area in 1899. It was that nation, too, which was hamstringing Japanese development in Manchuria and was eyeing Korea, which Japan considered her preserve and necessary to the security of the home islands. And if Russia had French support, Japan could call on even more powerful backing from Great Britain with whom an alliance had been made in 1902. To halt Russia and to thwart her ambition became the basis of Japanese foreign policy.

Japan had, late in 1903, offered to reach an understanding with Russia —mutual recognition of Chinese sovereignty over Manchuria and acceptance of a privileged position for Russia in Manchuria and for Japan in Korea. Russia refused, leaving Japan no choice but to bridle her rival. On

February 6, 1904, Japan severed relations with Russia. Two days later, her fleet launched a surprise attack on the Russian naval squadron at Port Arthur—destroying it. That stunning victory was followed by a Japanese declaration of war. Then came the relentless advance of Nippon's armies on the mainland. By March, there were 100,000 soldiers in Korea; on May 1, they crossed the Yalu into Manchuria; on May 30, they occupied Dairen; in January of the next year, Port Arthur fell; on March 10, Mukden was captured. Manchuria was in Japanese hands. The Russians had been routed. The final blow came in a great two-day naval battle, May 27–28, in Tsushima Strait, where the Japanese fleet sunk all thirty-two ships of the Russian squadron.

Russia had been annihilated on land and on sea. Japan had achieved an astounding and unexpected victory, but the effort had exhausted her resources. She could fight no longer and, secretly, a proposal was made on May 31 to President Roosevelt that he end the war by mediating between the two belligerents. The president eagerly grasped the opportunity. He had followed the course of the war with greatest interest. Japan's early victories had delighted him. To his son, he wrote two days after the attack on Port Arthur, "I was thoroughly pleased with the Japanese victory for Japan is playing our game." He believed he could depend upon Japan to respect the twin principles of the "Open Door" and Chinese territorial integrity; but not if she grew too strong and preponderently powerful in eastern Asia. To Henry Cabot Lodge, he revealed his fears. "While Russia's triumph," he wrote on June 16, 1905, "would have been a blow to civilization, her destruction as an eastern Asiatic power would also in my opinion be unfortunate. It is best that she should be left face to face with Japan so that each may have a moderating action on the other."

At Portsmouth, New Hampshire, on an American naval base, the president convened the peace conference in the summer of 1905 and on September 5, a treaty was signed. By its terms, Japan regained what had been lost at Shimonoseki—the Liaotung peninsula with Port Arthur, Dairen, as well as the South Manchurian Railroad, with the right to station guards along the right of way. She got also recognition of her paramount economic, political, and military rights in Korea and the southern half of the Sakhalin Islands. Russia had by no means been eliminated as an Asian power. Holding the northern half of the Sakhalins and entrenched in northern Manchuria with control of the Chinese Eastern Railroad, she was very much in evidence. And for that, Roosevelt was grateful. Still, the war had demonstrated Japan's strength and appetite and had enhanced her position in China immeasurably. Indeed, a subtle transformation had taken place in Roosevelt's estimate of the situation. It was now Japan, not Russia, that presented a threat to American interests and to the concept of the "Open Door." Furthermore, the president felt, even the Philippines might be endangered by Japan's new-found confidence in her prowess. And there was no doubt that the victory over

Russia marked a milestone in the development of Japanese nationalism. The war had proved, one Japanese pointed out, "that there is nothing westerners do which Asians cannot do, or that there is nothing westerners try that Asians cannot also try." The war had proved, too, that a yellow people could whip a white nation. Politics and diplomacy in Asia would never be the same.

Carefully and deliberately, the Japanese moved to solidify and legalize their gains in eastern Asia. First, Korea, by a treaty negotiated in November of 1905, acknowledged Japan's suzerainty over that ancient kingdom. Already, Great Britain had recognized Korea as a Japanese protectorate, in August of 1905, when the alliance of 1902 was renewed. In December, China, by the Treaty of Peking, accepted the terms of the Portsmouth settlement. Two years later, France's assent was gained (in exchange for Japanese consent to that country's paramount position in south China), and, in the same year, Russia formally agreed to the partition of Manchuria—south to Japan; north to Russia. The network of treaties and agreements also recognized Japan's interest in Inner Mongolia and Fukien province (which lay opposite Formosa).

Meanwhile, President Roosevelt, aware that he had neither the force nor the public support to keep the door open in China or to safeguard the Philippines (which he called "our heel of Achilles") had come to the realization that American interests in eastern Asia had to depend, in the final analysis, on Japan's good will. It became his policy, therefore, to assuage Japan and to make clear he would not stand in the way of her exploitation and enjoyment of what she had gained and what she considered her preserve. He had made beginnings in that direction after Tsushima and before the war with Russia ended (sensing intuitively the dawn of a new era) when he approved a conversation, held in Tokyo on July 27, 1905, between Secretary of War William Howard Taft and Japanese Prime Minister Taro Katsura. Taft had stopped off at the Japanese capitol on his way to the Philippines as directed by the president and exchanged views with Katsura. Taft noted, in opening the talk, that the president was worried over the safety of the Philippines and also that he believed that the Japanese protectorate over Korea would be good for peace in the Far East. Whereupon, Katsura replied that Japan harbored no aggressive designs on the Philippines. History has termed the talks the Taft-Katsura agreement. It was not, strictly speaking, an agreement; nor, as some have made out, a quid pro quo or a bargain. It was, rather, to use the technical term, "an agreed memorandum" and reflected the concerns of the two nations. It certainly fit into Roosevelt's new concept of America's Asian policy. Taft had received, if not a pledge, an assurance concerning the Philippines and had satisfied Katsura on Korea. Little wonder the president, upon receiving the text of the memorandum, told Taft, "I confirm every word you have said." Similarly, when in November of 1905, Tokyo announced that Korea's foreign affairs would be handled in the Japanese Foreign Office, Roosevelt at once closed the American legation in Seoul (the first nation to do so). It was a gesture of confidence in Japan and consistent with the Taft position in the memorandum.

As can happen only in the United States, given its federal system of government and the autonomy of municipalities in certain matters, a purely local and domestic situation threatened to upset the nation's foreign policy. It concerned the presence of Japanese on the West Coast. They had been immigrating in increasing numbers since about 1870 and by 1905, about 100,000 Japanese had settled in the three Pacific coast states, chiefly in California. Their emigration from the home islands was encouraged by their government as an element in the Empire's peaceful expansion. Overseas settlement would siphon off excess population, require additional ships to carry the settlers, thereby increasing the navy, provide a source of income in the money settlers would send home, and create a market abroad for Japanese goods. Americans, however, viewed the immigrants only as undesirables and feared that the large influx of orientals constituted a "yellow peril." There was large-scale agitation in California for their exclusion, and the state authorities there demanded action by the federal government. San Francisco went beyond agitation when, on October 11, 1906, the school board of that city passed a resolution segregating ninety-three Japanese schoolchildren in a special school. The reasons were flimsy. It was said that the students were too old and too mature for their American fellows. Actually, of the ninety-three, twenty-eight were girls, thirty-three over fifteen years of age, and the two oldest were twenty years old. Twenty-five were American citizens.

The Japanese government and people were humiliated and outraged by the insulting treatment of their nationals across the ocean. They had already been irritated by reports of boycotts and discrimination against Japanese in California. The intensity of popular feeling and the demand for action was reflected in anti-American riots in many Japanese cities and in a raft of articles in the Tokyo and provincial press. A typical outburst appeared in the *Japan Weekly Mail:* "Stand up Japanese nation! Our countrymen have been humiliated on the other side of the Pacific. Our poor boys and girls have been expelled from the public schools by rascals of the United States, cruel and merciless demons. At this time we should be ready to give a blow to the United States. Yes, we should be ready to strike the Devil's head with an iron hammer. Why do we not insist on sending ships?"

President Roosevelt was no less upset than the Japanese—for different reasons. It was not that he disagreed with his countrymen on the nature of the Japanese menace. He worried greatly about the prospect of Japanese coming to the United States by the hundreds of thousands and turning the West Coast into a zone of alien nonwhites incapable of being absorbed into the American mainstream. What troubled him was the possible effect of Japanese ill will upon America's interests in Asia. "They [the

Philippine Islands] are all that make the present situation with Japan dangerous," he wrote to Taft in August of 1907 and to his son, he confided, "I am being greatly bothered about the Japanese business. The infernal fools in California and especially in San Francisco insult the Japanese recklessly and in the event of war it will be the nation as a whole which will pay the consequence."

War talk was very much in the air in 1907 on both sides of the Pacific and a clash was considered inevitable by many Americans and Japanese. Roosevelt went so far as to alert the governor-general of the Philippines, directing him, in code, to prepare to defend the Islands against a momentarily expected attack and to ask the Navy Department for a ship-by-ship comparison of the two countries' navies. In Tokyo, the Navy staff, for the first time, drew up plans for an American war that began with an attack on the Philippines. But Roosevelt's task was to avoid war—a war he did not think he could win. The Pacific had been denuded of battleships in July 1906 when they had been transferred to the Atlantic (there were fears of a war with Germany) and even the four new armored cruisers that had replaced them were scheduled soon to be withdrawn to the West Coast. Further, there was no adequate naval base in the western Pacific. He made every effort, therefore, to get the San Francisco authorities to rescind the segregation order, and he succeeded with the pledge to halt the flow of immigration.

Accordingly, he began negotiations with the Japanese for a face-saving formula whereby the Japanese would be kept from coming to the United States without specifically excluding them. An arrangement was reached in February 1908 in an exchange of notes (termed the Gentlemen's Agreement) that placed upon Tokyo the responsibility for regulating Japanese movement to the United States. The Japanese agreed to issue passports only to former residents of America and to relatives of those presently resident. Thus, Japan was spared humiliation. But the president, meanwhile, took other measures to meet the crisis in Japanese-American relations. One was to send the American fleet on a world cruise. The Japanese naval attaché in Washington viewed the cruise as a means of impressing Japan with America's might and that was probably in Roosevelt's mind. It seems more nearly true, however, that the cruise of the fleet was designed primarily to impress Americans and to instill in them a sense of pride in their navy so as to cause them to support large appropriations for the fleet. The president planned to ask Congress for two battleships a year beginning in 1908 instead of the one he had been recommending and for that public backing was needed.

On December 16, 1907, sixteen white battleships escorted by numerous auxiliary craft left Hampton Roads (Virginia) on its round-the-world adventure by way of Cape Horn, the Pacific, the Indian Ocean, Cape of Good Hope, back into the Atlantic, and home. The highlight of the voyage was the stopover in Japan by invitation of the Japanese government.

The reception was warm, cordial, and heartfelt. For three days, officers and men from the ships enjoyed Oriental hospitality. Everywhere, there were evidences of friendship and touching ones at that—for example, Japanese schoolchildren singing the Star Spangled Banner in English and waving little American flags. Unquestionably, the visit cleared the air. Clearly, the Japanese were not ready for a showdown. The dates were October 18–21, 1908.

One month and one week later, Roosevelt took a second step in meeting the crisis with Japan. It was incorporated in an agreement following a conversation between Secretary of State Elihu Root and Ambassador Kogoro Takahira on November 30, 1908 in Washington. The two statesmen pledged their nations to maintain the status quo in the Pacific, which, plainly translated, meant that the United States would not disturb the Japanese where they were at the time: Manchuria and Korea. They resolved, too, "reciprocally to respect the territorial possessions belonging to each other," which, plainly translated, meant that Japan would not disturb the Philippines. Additionally, both powers promised to support the "independence and integrity of China and the principle of equal opportunity for commerce and industry."

The Root-Takahira agreement was the last move made by Roosevelt in his Asian policy before leaving office ten weeks later. It was also the final element in the elaborate diplomatic structure erected by the president to safeguard American interests in eastern Asia while remaining within his military capabilities and consistent with the public attitude. The American people would not fight to defend the "Open Door" or the Philippines nor did the United States have the necessary force. The only alternative to surrendering the country's interests was to appease Japan—to give her free rein to pursue her objectives in return for guarantees to respect America's stake. The corollary was to give no offense to the Japanese and run no risk of retribution. Taft-Katsura, Gentlemen's Agreement, Root–Takahira were, thus, all of one piece.

Roosevelt's policy in Asia was wise and cautious; it was rooted in a realistic assessment of the situation in that part of the world. It was rooted, too, in his philosophy of statecraft that he outlined to a friend in 1905: "I never take a step in foreign policy unless I am assured that I shall be able eventually to carry out my will by force." There was one supreme irony for the president in the policy he pursued. He had ardently backed the acquisition of the Philippines in 1899 as a place from which the China market could be exploited. Now to protect those islands, he had, tacitly, to acquiesce in the closing of the markets in those parts of China, chiefly Manchuria, that Japan considered her own and that were most important to American business. Did Roosevelt miscalculate the Japanese threat to the Philippines? He may have overrated their capability to attack and capture the Islands. They were, in fact, deeply distracted by several problems, chiefly the incessant revolts in Korea. But the president played a safe game and he was convinced he was right, so much so as to warn his successor, William Howard Taft, of the wisdom of continuing his policy. "It is peculiarly to our interest," he wrote, "not to take any steps as regards Manchuria which will give the Japanese cause to feel, with or without reason, that we are hostile to them or a menace—in however slight a degree—to their interests," and, he went on, as regards the "Open Door" in Manchuria, "if the Japanese chose to follow a course of conduct to which we are adverse, we cannot stop it unless we are prepared to go to war, and a successful war about Manchuria would require a fleet as good as that of England, plus an army as good as Germany. The Open Door in China was an excellent thing, and I hope it will be a good thing in the future, as far as it can be maintained by general diplomatic agreement, but, as has been proved by the whole history of Manchuria, alike under Russia and under Japan, the Open Door policy, as a matter of fact, completely disappears as soon as a powerful nation determines to disregard it, and is willing to run the risk of war rather than forego its intention."

Those words written on December 22, 1910 were occasioned by Roosevelt's distress with Taft, who had revised completely his Japanese policy. Instead of keeping out of Japan's way, Taft, from the moment he entered the White House in March of 1909 made every effort to thwart Japan's unilateral exploitation of Manchuria. He believed the way to protect American interests in Asia—the Open Door, Chinese territorial integrity, and the security of the Philippines—was to weaken Japan's hold on China and keep her from strengthening her position in Asia. The means of achieving that objective was not bullets but the dollar. He agreed with Roosevelt that the United States could not win a war against Japan nor would the American people be willing to fight such a war. American capital would be the instrument that would "smoke Japan out," as Taft's secretary of state, Philander C. Knox put it. Willard Straight, one of the principal architects of the new policy, described it as "the financial expression of John Hay's Open Door policy." Straight, as a young foreign service officer in Seoul at the time the legation was closed, had disagreed violently with Roosevelt's abandonment of Korea. From there, he was posted to Mukden, where he watched the Japanese strengthen their hold in Manchuria. By the time he was returned to Washington in March of 1908 to serve in the newly created Far Eastern Division of the State Department (whose chief he was to become in September), he had come to despise and distrust the Japanese. "They certainly seem less human than others," he noted, "[they] will have to change a good deal before they cease to cause one to look for the tail." His idea was to make American investment the means for extending American political influence and diminishing that of Japan. In June of 1909, he left the government service to represent a group of American bankers interested in investments in

China. He worked closely with the railway magnate, E. H. Harriman, who had a grandiose plan to construct a globe-encircling transportation system involving ownership of railroads in China.

The new Administration's first step in its positive and aggressive policy of "dollar diplomacy" centered on China's agreement with British, French, and German bankers signed in June of 1909 to borrow money for a new railway project in the southern and central part of the country. Taft demanded entry into the consortium and joined it in May of 1910. The following year, Japan and Russia entered the group which came to be known as the Six Power Consortium. The whole business did not advance the American strategy very much because only a small amout of new trackage was constructed. Taft's second step was bolder. It involved a proposal to the major powers in November of 1909 that China be loaned money to buy the Manchurian railroads from Russia (Chinese Eastern) and Japan (South Manchuria). Should that venture fail, the alternative would be to build parallel and competing lines with American and British capital to divert and bankrupt the foreign-held railroad. The scheme was imaginative and, if successful, would have achieved the desired objective— put the United States squarely in the center of Chinese economic and political affairs, weaken Japan's unilateral grip on Manchuria, and strengthen China's sovereignty over the province.

The only trouble was the plan failed. Japan and Russia, who had recently signed an agreement partitioning Manchuria, refused to relax their hold on the province to suit the United States. France and Britain, as was to be expected, supported their allies, Russia and Japan, respectively, whose assistance they needed on the broader stage of world diplomacy.

A third opportunity to carry out the Taft policy came in 1912 when the government of the new Republic of China, which replaced the Manchu regime after a successful revolution, asked the Six Power Consortium to advance it $300 million for general purposes. By the time the request could be acted on, Taft had left office. He could hardly look back with satisfaction on his Asian policy. It had had no effect on Japan's course in Manchuria. It had succeeded only in antagonizing and irritating her and in arousing her suspicions and enmity. Japan had not expected Taft to reverse Roosevelt. She had looked for a continuation of the tacit approval of the United States in her quest for preponderance in Manchuria, Korea, and Fukien.

Taft's successor, Woodrow Wilson, came to the White House in March of 1913 without any great interest in foreign affairs. He concentrated his efforts on domestic reform and on putting into practice the program known as the New Freedom. It would be ironic, he said, were his administration to be involved in international matters. This repugnance to become involved was one reason why Wilson withdrew from the Six Power Consortium so avidly favored by his predecessor. Another was Wilson's hesita-

The Far East, 1898–1919.

tion to enhance the power of the banking interests of the country, which he thought too monopolistic already and too closely linked with the government. Third, he considered a loan to China with its conditions for repayment "to touch very nearly the administrative independence of China itself and this Administration does not feel that it ought . . . to be a party to those conditions."

Wilson reversed Taft not only on the loan; he overturned the very foundation and assumption of his predecessor's Asian policy and returned to Roosevelt's position. It must be said, however, that although Roosevelt had acted out of conviction, Wilson acted out of necessity. The problems of Mexico and of neutrality in the World War that erupted in 1914 lay at the bottom of his treatment of the Japanese question in China. Once those two distractions came to an end, Wilson pursued the Taft concept.

The outbreak of the great war in Europe gave Japan a superb opportunity to pursue with greater intensity her primary purpose of reducing China to a state of virtual vassalage. With the European powers engaged in a titanic struggle thousands of miles away and the equipoise in Asia shattered, Japan had no fears of European objections to a program of advancing her influence in China. There would be no repetition of her humiliation at the hands of the European states as after Shimonoseki. Indeed, the reverse happened. Eager to sap German strength wherever it was, France and Britain encouraged Japan to attack her holdings in Asia. Dutifully, a Japanese expedition moved against the German base at Tsingtao in November of 1914, capturing it and taking over, as well, the German concessions in Shantung. At the same time, a Japanese fleet occupied the German insular possessions in the Pacific: the Marianas, Carolines, and Marshalls (a move which was to prove costly to American marines a quarter of a century later).

Japan expected her move would have the approval of the Allies, but what of the United States? Would there be a protest from Washington or, at the least, a reminder of the need to respect the "Open Door" in Shantung and China's territorial integrity? The Wilson administration remained silent, and its position was clearly stated in an instruction to the American minister in Peking relative to a request by the Chinese government for help: "While the State Department desires, of course, to safeguard all American rights in China," wrote Acting Secretary of State Robert Lansing to Minister Paul S. Reinsch on November 4, 1914, "it is at the same time anxious that there shall be no misunderstanding of its aims by the Chinese government. The United States desires China to feel that American friendship is sincere and to be assured that this government will be glad to exert any influence to further *by peaceful means* the welfare of the Chinese people but the Department realizes that it would be quixotic in the extreme to allow the question of Chinese territorial integrity to entangle the United States in international difficulties." So the pattern was set for America's Far Eastern policy for the duration of the war.

Japan's next move in China was met with the same determination to steer clear of getting enmeshed. On January 18, 1915, the Japanese ambassador in Peking handed the Chinese Foreign Office a memorandum in which twenty-one demands, arranged in five groups, were made. They touched upon Japan's position in Shantung, southern Manchuria, Inner Mongolia, the Yangtze Valley, and Fukien province. Taken together and if acceded to by China, they would have entrenched Japan's position in large areas of China and reduced that power to the status of a Japanese protectorate.

The Chinese cry for help and support for the twin principles enumerated in 1899 and 1900 met with no great enthusiasm in Washington. Although the chief of the Far Eastern Division of the State Department and an old China hand, E. T. Williams, urged stern and resolute resistance, the Administration backed down. In a note of March 13, Secretary of State William Jennings Bryan pointed out that the demands did, indeed, violate the Open Door and the territorial integrity of China but, at the same time, he admitted that "territorial contiguity creates special relations between Japan and those districts" mentioned in the demands. Such a rejoinder must surely have satisfied the Japanese for it, clearly, recognized that they had preponderant, if not exclusive, rights of exploitation in those places. Bryan's inclusion of a fervent hope that Japan would not press upon China the acceptance of the proposals did not add to the message's strength as a deterrant to Japan.

Japan was, in fact, pressing the demands on China, albeit in modified form and pointing out in Peking that no help could be expected from the United States or Europe. Resignedly and reluctantly, China had no choice but to capitulate, on May 9. The American reaction to the fait accompli caused Japan puzzlement but no pain. On May 11, Bryan, in identical notes to Tokyo and to Peking, stated that his government would not recognize any agreement between the two Oriental nations "impairing the treaty rights of the United States and its citizens, the political or territorial integrity of the Republic of China, or the international policy relative to China commonly known as the open door." The incongruity between the notes of March 13 and May 9 was baffling. How can one enjoy "special relations" in an area without abridging someone's rights? How can one reconcile China's territorial integrity with Japanese control over certain functions and places? Just which of Bryan's two messages was to be taken as American policy? In any case, there was no cause for concern in Tokyo. Washington was all words and no threat.

The inconsistency was, however, bothersome; enough so for the dispatch of a mission to Washington to seek clarification and assurance. On June of 1917, two months after America's entry into the war, Kikujiro Ishii, veteran diplomat and former minister of foreign affairs, arrived in Washington for conversations with Secretary of State Robert Lansing. Ostensibly in Washington to coordinate belligerent activities against the common enemy, Ishii's real interest was China. He talked to Lansing about his concern over the fact that American bankers were lending money to China for various purposes. Was there a political purpose behind the economic activity, he wondered? But basically, he wanted Lansing's signature on a document like the one Root had signed in 1908 that would put to rest any uneasiness over Bryan's nonrecognition principle.

Such an assurance, Ishii believed he got in the exchange of notes between the two statesmen on November 2, 1917. Both powers pledged to respect China's territorial integrity and equality of commercial opportunity. They also recognized that "territorial propinquity creates special relations between countries and, consequently. . . . Japan has special interests in China. . . ." Ishii triumphantly reported home his victory. "Special interests" were "paramount interests," he said, and political as well as economic. Lansing explained to the Chinese that Japan had gotten only what was natural for them to have—a special economic relationship with a nation so close geographically and, he added, he had gotten a pledge on Chinese territorial integrity.

An impartial examination of the Lansing-Ishii agreement must conclude that Ishii got the better of the bargain and that his interpretation was more nearly correct. The Chinese certainly thought so and told Lansing as much in a reply to Lansing's explanation. Paul Reinsch, the American minister in Peking, was of the same opinion. Upon leaving his post in June 9, 1919, he regretted the agreement as playing into Japan's hands and abandoning China. He predicted that ten years hence, Americans would be wondering why nothing had been done to stop the Japanese while there was time. He was prophetic albeit a decade or so off on his chronology.

So, it may be seen, the Wilson policy marked a return to that of Theodore Roosevelt—but only for the duration of the war. Once the conflict came to an end, the president took measures reminiscent of Taft—designed to curb and bridle Japan. Unhappily, they all ended in failure. The first revived the consortium idea for lending China funds to buy back public works alienated over the years to foreigners. As before, so now, Japan flatly refused to permit any changes in the status quo in Manchuria or Mongolia. The second took the form of an American force of about 7,500 men joining an international brigade, which included about 70,000 Japanese soldiers, sent to occupy Vladivostok in Siberia. The purpose was to prevent a large amount of Allied war supplies stored there from falling into German hands. The withdrawal of Russia from the war in March of 1918 after the Bolsheviks overthrew the czarist regime and the ensuing peace with Germany made that a possibility. Another purpose of the expedition was to help a Czech army, liberated from Russian prison camps, fight its way through Bolshevik lines to Vladivostok to take ship for Europe to rejoin the war.

Wilson had another purpose—to keep his eye on Japan and frustrate any plan to make Siberia into another Manchuria. There was no question of Japan's intent to take advantage of the chaotic conditions in Russia following the revolution just as she had derived benefit from China's weakness in wresting concessions and privileges. Wilson tried several times to get the Japanese to sign self-denying agreements but never succeeded. They refused to let themselves get boxed in. When the United States and the Allies withdrew their forces from Siberia in April 1920, the Japanese army remained and did not leave until October 1922 and after Japan had gained special rights in northern Manchuria and in parts of Siberia. The army also continued to occupy the northern half of the Sakhalins. *Islands*

At the peace conference ending the great war in 1918, Wilson turned his efforts to ousting the Japanese from Shantung. They refused to budge and had the support of the Allied nations. But even without that support, they held a whip hand over Wilson by threatening to quit the conference and refusing to sign the treaty and adhere to the League of Nations. They refused, too, to evacuate the islands in the Pacific they had taken from Germany.

The end of the war found Japan solidly entrenched in Shantung, Manchuria, Mongolia, and Siberia. Wilson failed, as had Taft, to dislodge the Japanese. Like Taft, he had succeeded only in irritating the Japanese and in presenting the United States as the sole power which seemed to stand in the way of their expansion on the mainland. In the course of the next two decades, the Japanese were not to lose sight of that fact.

Non-recognition of any Japanese territory taken by Japan during this time.

BIBLIOGRAPHY

HOWARD K. BEALE, *Theodore Roosevelt and the Rise of America to World Power* (1956).

CHARLES S. CAMPBELL, JR., *Special Business Interests and the Open Door Policy* (1951).

HERBERT CROLY, *Willard Straight* (1924).

ROY W. CURRY, *Woodrow Wilson and Far Eastern Policy, 1913–1921* (1957).

TYLER DENNETT, *Roosevelt and the Russo-Japanese War* (1925).

RAYMOND ESTHUS, *Theodore Roosevelt and Japan* (1966).

A. WHITNEY GRISWOLD, *The Far Eastern Policy of the United States* (1938).

AKIRA IRIYE, *Pacific Estrangement: Japanese and American Expansion, 1897–1911* (1972).

JERRY ISRAEL, *Progressivism and the Open Door: America and China, 1905–1921* (1971).

TIEN-YI LI, *Woodrow Wilson's China Policy, 1913–1917* (1952).

ROBERT MCCLELLAN, *The Heathen Chinee: A Study of American Attitudes Toward China, 1890–1905* (1971).

THOMAS MCCORMICK, *China Market: America's Quest for Informal Empire, 1893–1901* (1967).

CHARLES NEU, *An Uncertain Friendship: Theodore Roosevelt and Japan* (1967).

EUGENE P. TRANI, *The Treaty of Portsmouth: An Adventure in American Diplomacy* (1969).

PAUL A. VARG, *The Making of a Myth: The United States and China, 1897–1912* (1969).

CHARLES VEVIER, *The United States and China, 1906–1913* (1955).

MARYLIN B. YOUNG, *The Rhetoric of Empire: American China Policy, 1895–1901* (1963).

Theodore Roosevelt (courtesy of the National Portrait Gallery, Smithsonian Institution, Washington, D.C.).

In Latin America: Preponderance

IN THE Western Hemisphere, there was no Japan to contest American policy as there was in Asia. But even had there been, there would have been neither retreat nor compromise but conflict and combat and victory at any price. For in that hemisphere lay the nation's security and lifeline. There could be no equivocation and no hesitation. The story of American policy in the Americas in the two decades after the end of the Spanish war was one of erecting an international system in which the United States' influence and power would be paramount. Propinquity did, in fact, create special interests no less in the western hemisphere for the United States than in Asia for Japan.

The first step in erecting the system was to build an interoceanic canal under exclusive American control. That project, which was almost as old as the republic, became a necessity after 1898. As a consequence of the war with Spain, the United States found itself a Pacific as well as an Atlantic power with interests and responsibilities in the two oceans but with only a one-ocean navy. To move elements of the fleet rapidly from one ocean to another demanded a maritime short cut between the two continents. The lesson had been learned during the war when the battleship *Oregon* required sixty-six days to make the voyage around Cape Horn after being ordered from Puget Sound on the Pacific coast to the West Indies. The idea received executive approval in President McKinley's annual message to Congress on December 5, 1898. Said the president, "the construction of such a maritime highway is now more than ever indispensable."

Gaining exclusive control of the canal posed a serious problem. By the Clayton-Bulwer Treaty of 1850, still in force, the responsibility for a canal was shared by Great Britain and the United States. The question was would England voluntarily relinquish her rights and at what price. Given her isolated diplomatic situation at the turn of the century and her conflict with the rebellious Boers in South Africa plus her desire to have America as a friend, there seemed every reason to expect that the United States would get its way. As for price, Britain expected to gain an advantage in the Alaska boundary dispute then being adjudicated. But when the United States would not yield on the border question, England capitulated without a quid pro quo.

The result was a treaty initialed by Secretary of State John Hay and the British Ambassador, Lord Pauncefote, on February 5, 1900. By its terms, the United States gained the right to build, regulate, and manage a canal but could not fortify it and had to keep it open in war as well as in peace to vessels of all nations. Magnanimous as Britain was in thus modifying the agreement, she did not go far enough to suit the Senate and a large part of the American public. Without the capability to defend the canal and to prevent an enemy from using it in wartime, such a waterway was worse than useless—it was dangerous and even suicidal. No wonder the Senate tacked on a series of reservations before approving the treaty, the principal one giving the United States the right to use armed force to defend the canal and to maintain order in the area. That principle, however, England would not accept. Still, London well knew that eventually and inevitably the United States must get its way. So why not accept the unavoidable gracefully? On November 18, 1901, a new treaty was negotiated which superseded the Clayton-Bulwer Treaty and, while giving the United States the right to construct, regulate, and manage a canal, made no mention of a ban on fortification or a requirement that it be kept open in wartime. The absence of the restrictions in the treaty was, as the British foreign secretary admitted in a note dated August 3, 1901, permissive. Such an instrument passed in the Senate handily, 76–6 on December 16, 1901. The United States thus took the first step on the road to predominance in the Americas.

Having gained exclusive control over a canal, the next consideration was the site—Nicaragua or Panama, which was a state in the Republic of Colombia. The United States had the right to build in both places by a treaty in 1867 in the former country and by one in 1846 in the latter (with New Granada, as Colombia was then called). Panama was the shorter route but Nicaragua was the cheaper to construct. The cost was estimated at about $189 million for Nicaragua and $144 million for Panama, but to the latter cost had to be added $109 million demanded by the company, which had been digging there for some years, for its assets and equipment.

Over the years, several commissions appointed to compare the two routes invariably inclined to Nicaragua, mainly for financial reasons. The report of one of them, in 1901, became the basis for a bill passed in the House on January 9, 1902, 308–2, that appropriated $180 million for a canal in Nicaragua. Major stockholders in the Panama company, faced by the prospect of a total loss of their investment, reduced their price to $40

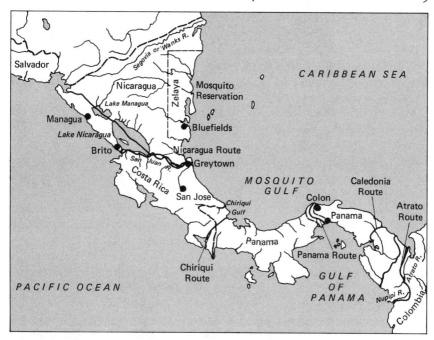

Proposed Isthmian Canal Routes.

million. The Senate, with the new figure in mind and with a copy of a report by a new commission that favored Panama, amended the House bill authorizing the president to purchase the Panama company's assets, obtain whatever rights were necessary from Colombia, and build a canal across the Isthmus of Panama. Supporters of each route now engaged in a battle for their favored site. Astute and relentless propaganda by Philippe Bunau-Varilla, a large stockholder of the Panama company and once its chief engineer, and a judicious use of money by a prominent and politically well-connected American lawyer, William Nelson Cromwell, turned the tide in favor of Panama. The cause was greatly aided by a fortuitous volcanic eruption 100 miles from the Nicaraguan site which Bunau-Varilla graphically put before the Senate's eyes in the form of a Nicaraguan postage stamp depicting the volcano sent to each senator. The vote in the Senate was 67–6 and in the House 260–8. Panama was the place.

Now to come to terms with Colombia. Negotiations between Secretary of State John Hay and the Colombian chargé in Washington, Thomás Herrán, resulted in a treaty on January 22, 1903 by which the United States secured for 100 years, and renewable, the sole right to build, operate, and control a canal in a strip six miles wide in return for a flat payment of $10 million and an annual subsidy of $250,000 beginning in 1912. It was all the United States could ask for and the Senate voted approval, 73–5 on March 17, 1903. Five months later, the Colombian senate rejected it. The reason was chiefly financial. The Colombians wanted more money but there was also a question of pride. It was believed that the provision for a mixed Colombian-American court in the canal zone impaired Colombia's sovereignty.

President Roosevelt was furious with "the contemptible little creatures" who stood in the way of America's destiny. "Anthropoids," John Hay called them. The president could, of course, have upped the ante but he would not succumb to "the inefficient bandits." As a way out, he contemplated asking Congress for authority to build a canal in Panama without Colombia's consent. That move proved unnecessary thanks to Bunau-Varilla, Cromwell, and others interested in the matter. The possibility that Roosevelt would use the Nicaraguan route (as the legislation of 1903, in fact, provided should negotiations with Colombia fail) galvanized them into action. The obvious solution was to separate the province of Panama from Colombia and negotiate separately with Roosevelt. So a revolution was hatched in late October and early November of 1903.

The perpetrators of the revolt would never have undertaken the step had they not been certain of Roosevelt's sympathy and willingness to see it succeed. It is equally clear that his dispatch of warships to the Isthmus in October and his instructions to prevent the Colombians from engaging the Panamanians insured a rebel victory. The standard of revolt was raised on November 3. Colombian troops had already landed on the Isthmus at Colón on the Atlantic side. The rebels were on the Pacific end at Panama City. The American contribution to the victory was the refusal by the commander of the U.S.S. *Nashville*, which had arrived the previous day in the area, to permit the superintendent of the Panama railroad to transport the government soldiers across the Isthmus. The basis for that action was flimsy, indeed. It lay in the American interpretation of the Treaty of 1846, which bound the United States to keep the Isthmus open. The transit of troops, it was said, would produce conflict and interrupt the free use of the Isthmus.

It was not inappropriate, therefore, that the rebels proclaimed the independence of Panama on November 4 amidst shouts of "Long live Panama! Long live President Roosevelt!" Two days later, the United States entered into relations with the new republic. On November 9, Bunau-Varilla presented his credentials as the country's first minister in Washington and on the 18th the expected treaty was signed between the two nations. A grateful Panama surrendered everything including its recently won sovereignty. A ten-mile strip was deeded to the United States in perpetuity for building, maintaining, operating, and fortifying a canal. In that zone, the United States would be sovereign. In exchange for so munificient a grant, the United States "guarantees and will maintain the independence of the Republic of Panama." It also threw in a lump-sum payment of $10 million and promised an annual subsidy of $250,000. The treaty passed the Senate on February 23, 1904 by a vote of 66–14. The opponents were distressed at their country's role in the whole affair and rightfully so. It was a sordid and shameful collusion. That it was for national security did not diminish its immorality. Years later, Roosevelt brashly boasted "I took the Canal Zone" and, in a sense, he was right. Many people, however, felt remorse and shame and in 1921, amends were made to Colombia in the form of a payment of $25 million. That tacit admission of guilt did not, as some people wished, include a statement of regret.

The United States was now exclusive possessor of the site and proceeded to dig the big ditch. It was clear to American policy-makers, however, that the canal would be not a life-line but an Achilles heel unless its approaches were made secure. To achieve that objective demanded that the Caribbean be made an American lake, that American influence there be preponderant, and that foreigners be prevented from getting a foothold in the republics of the area. Within the next decade and a half, the objective was to be achieved as a result of the use of superior force and of a ruthless policy of intervention.

By the time Panama came into the American orbit, the United States had already made a significant start in dotting the Caribbean with strong places and extending its power. The strategically located island of Puerto Rico was American as a consequence of the treaty ending the Spanish war. Then there was Cuba. By the Teller Amendment, it will be recalled, the United States had promised not to annex that island. There were, however, other ways to exert dominion and those ways were incorporated into an amendment to the Army Appropriation Act of 1901, the work, chiefly, of Secretary of War Elihu Root. This Platt Amendment, named for Senator Orville H. Platt of Connecticut, chairman of the Foreign Relations Committee, who attached it to the Act, gave the United States the right to intervene in Cuba to preserve order and maintain the republic's independence, forbade Cuba from entering into any arrangements with a foreign power that would impair its sovereignty or contract any debt beyond its resources, and permitted the United States to buy or lease naval stations. As a condition for the evacuation of American troops from the island after the war, Cuba had to incorporate the terms of the amendment in an appendix to its constitution of 1900. They became, also, the provisions of a Cuban-American treaty signed on May 22, 1903. So Cuba became a virtual protectorate of the United States and an element in that country's strategic position in the Caribbean. A splendid site, Guantánamo Bay, was taken, in 1903, for a naval base.

Meanwhile, President Roosevelt was confronted with a painful dilemma concerning the European presence in the Caribbean. Chaotic conditions in the republics in the area presented a constant invitation to European intervention. Revolution and civil strife were regular events and defaulting on debts was the norm in financial affairs. The first endangered foreign lives and property; the second threatened foreign investment. To protect their nationals and to seek satisfaction, the European nations frequently landed troops, bombarded ports and forts, occupied territory, and took over custom houses. Clearly, such adventures menaced American security yet, the president could not, legitimately, deny the nations the right to seek redress on behalf of their nationals. Indeed, he sympathized with their plight knowing well that the leaders of the republics were "utterly incompetent" to govern and, indeed, at one time, he believed the European powers should "spank" any Latin American country which misbehaved. But, he could not permit it as a regular practice.

The problem was exacerbated by a decision by the Court of International Justice at The Hague in February of 1904. It related to action by the European powers in Venezuela. In 1902, that country had defaulted on a debt owed the nationals of several European countries. Of all the creditor nations, only Germany, Great Britain, and Italy attempted to collect the debt by force. An Anglo-German fleet blockaded Venezuelan ports from December 1902 to February 1903, bombarded coastal forts, and sank some vessels. Italy joined in a modest way in mid-December. Roosevelt was instrumental in getting the powers to adjudicate the question at The Hague. In awarding a judgment to the creditors, the justices of the court gave first claim on Venezuela's assets to those states that had taken the trouble to send expeditions to the new world. A premium was, thus, put on force and an incentive provided for future action. The situation was ominous.

In the same year, the Dominican Republic which had a debt of $32 million, $22 million of which was owed to European investors—Belgians, Germans, British, Dutch, French, Italians, Spanish, and also American— failed to pay either principal or interest. Following The Hague decision, it could be expected that the powers would race across the ocean to get their claim strengthened by using force. For the president, the alternative was clear. The United States would do the job, would act for the world as policeman in the Western Hemisphere. It would make unnecessary European intervention by itself maintaining order and guaranteeing payment of the debt. The new policy was announced in a message to Congress on December 6, 1904 when the president said, "Chronic wrong-doing . . . may in America, as elsewhere, ultimately require intervention by some civilized nation, and in the western hemisphere the adherence of the United States to the Monroe Doctrine may force the United States, however reluctantly, in flagrant cases of such wrongdoing or impotence, to the exercise of an international police power."

So was enunciated the famed Roosevelt Corollary to the Monroe Doctrine. The Doctrine had said, "Europe, Hands Off"; the Corollary said, "America, Hands On." The idea was not a new one. It was foreshadowed as early as 1853 by Senator Sam Houston, who claimed that the United States could not expect Europe to honor the Monroe Doctrine unless the United States assumed responsibility for the conduct of the Latin American countries. Similarly, in 1895, Britons accused the United States of protecting Venezuela without accepting responsibility for its actions. Said the *London Chronicle*, "If the United States proposed to enforce the Monroe Doctrine, it ought to take the responsibility for the foreign policy of all the petty and impetuous states." Roosevelt, himself, had been thinking along the same lines. To his son, he had written on February 10, 1904, "Sooner or later [we must] assume an attitude of protection and regulation in regard to all these little states." And to Elihu Root, he had addressed a letter made public in May 1904 in which he assured those nations that acted decently—paid their debts, kept order—that they had nothing to fear from the United States. But "brutal wrongdoing resulting in loosening the ties of civilization" could not be ignored by the United States. Its duty was to intervene.

The president, implementing his policy, entered into an agreement with the Dominican Republic on January 20, 1905 by which the United States took over collecting the customs, assigning 55 per cent to the retirement of the debt and the remainder to operating the country, and guaranteed the republic's independence. American bankers floated a loan to begin funding the debt, and American warships patrolled Dominican waters to discourage European action and maintain order. Two years later, on February 8, 1907, the agreement was formalized in a treaty that omitted the guarantee of independence. Nor did it mention the right to lease a naval station. Nonetheless, there was no question that the Dominican Republic was safely in the American orbit—a protectorate, and a satellite answerable for its conduct to the giant northern neighbor.

Nicaragua was next and it fell to Roosevelt's successor, William Howard Taft, to extend the protection of the American eagle to that strategically located Central American republic—the alternate site of the canal. For Taft and his secretary of state, Philander C. Knox, the Roosevelt philosophy was perfectly sound. Knox reiterated it approvingly in a speech toward the close of the administration. "The logic of political geography and of strategy," he said, "and now our tremendous national interest created by the Panama Canal, make the safety, the peace, and the prosperity of Central America and the zone of the Caribbean of paramount interest to the government of the United States. Thus the malady of revolutions and financial collapse is most acute precisely in the region where it is most dangerous to us. It is here that we seek to apply a remedy." The remedy had, by that time, been successfully applied.

Roosevelt had hoped to bring order to Central America, not by American arms but by an agreement among the five republics there. In 1907, he had sponsored a conference in Washington that had set up a miniature international organization with the machinery for ending disorders. The nations pledged to settle their disputes by arbitration, to withhold recognition from revolutionary governments, to surrender revolutionists who sought refuge in their borders, and to cease fomenting revolutions one against the other. Honduras, the traditional battleground, was neutralized. Unhappily, the Nicaraguan dictator, José Zelaya, doomed the scheme to failure. His arrogance and belligerence, his continuous forays against his neighbors, his hatred of the United States, his refusal to pay the debt owed foreign investors, his dreams of a Central American empire with himself at the helm, kept his country and the other republics in constant turmoil and agitated foreigners in Nicaragua. When a revolution broke out in 1909 against Zelaya, Taft threw American support behind his opponent. In the fighting, two American citizens on the insurgent side were killed by the Zelaya forces, which further alienated Taft. Marines were landed to protect life and property but were soon withdrawn.

The revolution succeeded and with the new government, Knox concluded a convention on June 6, 1911 by which American bankers advanced money to begin retirement of the huge debt. The United States took over the customs house, collected the revenue, and assigned the proceeds. Civil war broke out again in July of 1912, causing Taft to send in 2,500 marines and sailors and eight warships. The force supervised and policed elections and maintained the government in power. Order was restored, leading to the removal of the troops in January 1913 except for a legation guard of 100 marines and one war vessel. The final act of the Nicaraguan drama was a treaty, the drafting of which was begun by Taft in 1913 and completed by the Wilson administration's secretary of state, William Jennings Bryan, on August 5, 1914. The Bryan-Chamorro Treaty made of Nicaragua a protectorate like Cuba, Panama, and the Dominican Republic. In exchange for a payment of $3 million, the United States received a ninety-nine-year lease of two strategic islands (Great Corn and Little Corn), a naval base in the Gulf of Fonseca, and perpetual right to build a canal. The Senate approved the treaty on February 28, 1916.

It was not surprising that, by the time Woodrow Wilson entered the White House on March 4, 1913, the image of the United States in Latin America was tarnished. The interventions of Roosevelt and of Taft created in the South American republics ill-feeling, hostility, and fear. The Colossus of the North, as the United States came to be known, was viewed as the threat, the danger, and the menace to the independence and the sovereignty of the nations of the western hemisphere. It did not matter that Washington justified its actions in terms of increasing the security of the whole hemisphere and pointed out that in the wake of its interventions came prosperity, order, peace, and improved sanitation. Nor were the recipients of American benevolence and munificence assuaged by assurances such as given by Elihu Root on his good will tour in 1906, that "We wish for no victories but those of peace, for no territory except our own, for no sovereignty except over ourselves." Philander C. Knox's expressions of good will on his visit to ten Caribbean countries in 1912 were equally unconvincing. His statement, "that my government does not covet an inch of territory south of the Rio Grande" must have sounded ironic. American control over certain republics was as complete as though they were part of the Union.

Anti-United States feeling was strongest among students and intellectuals. The former reflected distrust of the northern neighbor at meetings of the various student federations—local, national, and continental. In manifestoes and resolutions, they depicted Americans as rude, pugnacious, boastful, and money-grubbing and Yankee civilization as crass and materialist and lacking in subtlety and sentiment. They looked to Europe, particularly to "fragrant, Catholic, poetic Spain" for their cultural and intellectual sustenance. The Monroe Doctrine was viewed as a sinister unilateral vehicle for exploitation and not as a force for solidarity.

Much the same sentiments were expressed by poets, essayists, dramatists, and novelists such as Ruben Darío of Nicaragua, Manuel Ugarte of Argentina, José María Vargas Vila of Colombia, Rufino Blanco-Fombona of Venezuela, José Rodo of Uruguay, Fernando Garcia Calderón of Peru and others. Typical was Darío's bitter "Ode to Roosevelt" written in 1905 in which he compared the "men with Saxon eyes and barbarous souls" with "Our America [which] lives, and Dreams and loves and is the child of the Sun." Ugarte called the Mexican frontier more than a political convenience. It was, rather, a boundary between two civilizations. He went on to detail the affinity between Latin Americans and their European forebears "but to the United States we are united," he said, "by no bonds unless they be fear and dread." He urged his compatriots to reject the Pan-American movement as an instrument of absorption by the United States of all Latin America. The Pan-American Union he labelled a ministry of colonies.

There was, in fact, much suspicion and mistrust evident at the three regular Pan-American conferences which met in the period, at Mexico City in 1901, Rio de Janeiro in 1906, and Buenos Aires in 1910 and at the dozen or so special conferences dealing with a wide variety of topics such as sanitation, communications, finance, aviation, science, child welfare, coffee, administration of justice, and the like. At all of the meetings, the delegates from the other countries were wary and suspicious and operated always in the shadow of American marines and warships intruding their presence somewhere on the continent.

The accession of Woodrow Wilson to the presidency in 1913 raised hopes in Latin America of a change in American policy toward the southern neighbors. Known as a reformer, a liberal, and a man of high moral principle, he was expected to end the policy of military and financial intervention and to establish, in its place, an atmosphere of trust and confidence between the two parts of the hemisphere. Upon his election, Manuel Ugarte addressed a plea to him urging the righting of all the wrongs inflicted by his predecessors to Cuba, Nicaragua, Colombia, Panama, and Mexico. Latin Americans desire, he wrote, "that the United States abstain from officiously intervening in the domestic politics of our countries and that they discontinue the acquisition of ports and bays on the continent; we desire that measures of sanitation shall not serve to diminish the sovereignty of the nations; we ask, in short, that the Star Spangled Banner cease to be a symbol of oppression in the New World."

Judging by his public statements, Wilson could hardly have been more satisfying to the Latin Americans. Time after time during his eight years in office he pledged his country's determination to treat the southern neighbors on a plane of equality and to respect their sovereignty and independence. In the week of his inauguration, he announced the purpose of his administration "to cultivate the friendship and deserve the confidence of our sister republics." In October of the same year he gave his famous Mobile address in which he heralded a new era in western hemisphere relations. The United States, he vowed, "will never again seek one additional foot of territory by conquest; nor will it, any longer, act the role of big brother, a role which protected Latin America from aggression from Europe but left it open to attack from the United States." To guarantee the new dispensation, the president proposed an arrangement "by which we will give bond . . . that all of us will sign, of political independence and territorial integrity. Let us all agree that if any one of us, the United States included, violates the political independence or territorial integrity of any of the others, all the others will jump on her." In the same vein, Wilson continued in other speeches throughout the remaining years of his term of office to renounce "the claim of guardianship" and speak the language of "a full and honorable association as of partners . . . upon a footing of genuine equality and unquestioned independence."

There could be no question that the president's views were revolutionary in that he was turning his back on Roosevelt's unilateral interpretation of the Monroe Doctrine—so far, that is, as words were concerned. An examination of his deeds must lead to an opposite conclusion for he outdid both Roosevelt and Taft in the number of interventions undertaken by American forces in the internal affairs of the sister republics. And the paradox of Woodrow Wilson was just that—he spoke one way and acted another. In his eyes, there was no inconsistency. His interference and meddling did not nullify his stated aim to achieve friendship and partnership with the neighboring countries. Quite the reverse; the former made the latter possible. The purpose of the interventions was to establish constitutional government and insure democracy because only when such conditions obtained could hemispheric solidarity become a reality. And it was America's mission, he believed, to lead people to democracy and constitutionalism. But to those countries that felt the weight of America's might and to their sympathizers, Wilson's lofty aims provided little consolation. The consequences for them were the same had his motives been as crass as had Roosevelt's. Bayonets were no less lethal weapons just because they carried at their tip the banner of democracy and constitutionalism rather than the slogans of security. "Missionary diplomacy" seemed not very much different from "gunboat diplomacy" to those at the receiving end.

Conditions in Haiti drew Wilson's attention early in his administration. That that republic was in a constant state of chaos and instability could not be denied. Seven presidents held office between August 1911 and March 1915, and none achieved office by the normal political process. Accompanying revolution was corruption. Both constituted the island republic's normal condition. Wilson tried, unsuccessfully, in July of 1914 to force a treaty upon Haiti to permit the United States to supervise the customs collection, thereby insuring a retirement of the national debt. One year later, the situation grew so violent that Wilson took unilateral action. At that time, an angry mob had dragged President Guillaume Sam from the French embassy where he had taken refuge and hacked him to pieces. Riot followed but, fortuitously, on the same day, July 28, 1915, an American warship dropped anchor in the harbor of the capital. Marines were landed, the custom house was seized, and the naval officer in command prepared to hold elections for a new government that, in the words of President Wilson, would be one "which we can support." The electoral process was so closely supervised that the American naval officer could confidently cable Washington on August 7, 1915, "Next Thursday, . . . unless otherwise directed, I will permit Congress to elect a president."

The Haitian Congress did exactly that and on September 16, the new president signed a treaty which reduced his country to a state of vassalage to the United States. By its terms, Haiti could not alienate any territory nor increase its indebtedness without American consent. The United States gained the right to control the collection of the country's revenue and determine the allocation of the income, direct the constabulary and the program of public works, nominate certain government officials, and take whatever measures necessary to preserve Haitian independence. A new constitution was written by Americans in 1918 that operated with the help of American marines who continued in occupation.

The Dominican Republic fared somewhat differently at Wilson's hands. In that country, there was a period of peace and prosperity following American intervention in 1905 and the agreement in 1907. In 1911, however, the good times came to an end with the assassination of President Ramón Caseres. Riot and civil strife now raged for several years until Wilson sent in marines in 1914 who held an election, organized a new government, and paved the way for negotiating a treaty similar to the one with Haiti. Curiously, the new Dominican president balked at the prospect of surrendering his country's sovereignty, which led Wilson "with deepest reluctance" to place the Dominican Republic under American military rule. For four years, from 1916 to 1920, a naval officer acted as president and legislature with subordinates discharging the duties of cabinet ministers.

It was in Mexico that the heavy hand of the Wilson administration was most prominently displayed and where the president put into practice all his ideas on the role and the mission of the United States. Accompanying his interference in the domestic affairs of that country were the proclamation of the loftiest principles and the disclaimer of any low motives. "Mexico means more to us than commerce," he informed Congress, "it means the enlargement of the area of self-government." America's purpose, he stated on another occasion, was to secure peace by insuring that the process of self-government is not interrupted. He preferred doing it peacefully but would use force if necessary. All his efforts were directed "to help Mexico save herself and serve her people."

Mexico was easily as important to the United States as were the countries of Central America and the Caribbean. American investments had grown greatly since 1877 when Porfirio Díaz came to power and introduced stability and order into Mexican political life. By 1908 half of Mexico's wealth, including 80 per cent of her railroads, were in American hands and five years later statistics revealed that 50,000 Americans had a billion dollar stake in the country. In addition to economic considerations, there was always the strategic importance of the republic not only because of its contiguous border but for the Yucatan peninsula and its potential as a canal site. Unquestionably, any disturbance south of the border was bound to have severe repercussions to the north. In May 1911, the disturbance occurred in the form of a revolution. Francisco Madero overthrew Díaz, thus ending a thirty-four-year dictatorship. President Taft at once extended recognition to the new government. Not only did it fulfill the traditional American criteria for recognition—that it, in fact, existed, was in control of the machinery of government, and was in no danger of being overturned—but it also appealed to Americans in its sworn objective to restore constitutional liberties to the Mexican people.

Unhappily, Madero had little time to carry out his reforms for on February 18, 1913 one of his most trusted generals, Victoriano Huerta, unseated him. In the same month, the deposed president was shot dead by an unknown assailant believed universally to have acted under Huerta's orders. Taft, within one week of leaving office, took no steps to recognize Huerta, thereby leaving the problem to be faced by Wilson. The new president quickly reached a decision. It was to deny recognition to the Huerta regime, and it was based upon a position he took publicly on March 11, 1913, one week after his inauguration. New governments, he said, would be recognized "only when supported at every turn by the orderly processes of just government based upon law, not upon arbitrary or irregular force." Since Huerta had achieved power by force and bloodshed ("a government of butchers," he labelled the regime) and not by constitutional procedures, it could not expect recognition. Here were new criteria applied by Wilson to the diplomatic problem of recognition, different from those laid down more than one hundred years earlier by Thomas Jefferson and consistently followed by his successors. It was not enough for Wilson, as it had been for Jefferson, that a government existed and exercised authority over territory and people; it had to pass the test of legitimacy and morality in the way it came to power. Wilson, the moralist, was not prepared to encourage "government by assassination." "I am going to teach the South American republics to elect good men," he remarked.

Wilson was not satisfied with withholding recognition from Huerta. He was determined to rid Mexico of him. In August, he proposed a plan which provided for free elections in which Huerta would not be a candidate. Huerta's defiant reply was to arrest 110 members of the opposition and seize dictatorial powers. Wilson, next, sought to isolate the dictator diplomatically and succeeded in persuading Great Britain to withdraw the recognition granted earlier. He also lent aid to the forces of Venustiano Carranza, a former lieutenant of Madero who was fighting Huerta, by lifting an arms embargo he had instituted months before. All was to no avail. Huerta clung tenaciously to power.

Wilson's next move was a calamity. It took the form of an actual attack upon Mexican soil and was unpardonable. On April 9, 1914, eight American sailors from the U.S.S. *Dolphin* were mistakenly arrested in Tampico, a port controlled by Huerta. The authorities released them at once with an apology. The American naval commander, however, demanded a twenty-one-gun salute to the American flag, which Huerta refused to do. Thereupon, Wilson, with congressional approval, landed 1,000 marines at Vera Cruz, the principal Mexican port on the east coast. A skirmish ensued which left 400 casualties, mostly Mexicans. The next day, April 22, five American battleships landed 3,000 more marines and bluejackets. By April 30, the American force had reached 6,700 men. There seems to be no doubt that the alleged insult to the flag was not the true reason for Wilson's move. It was rather to deprive Huerta of ports through which he was getting arms and ammunition from abroad. Indeed, the landing at Vera Cruz coincided with the arrival of a German merchantman with war supplies that Wilson's troops prevented from getting ashore.

The outcry raised in Mexico, in the United States, and in Latin America by Wilson's brash act was great, and the president himself quickly realized that he had gone too far. Willingly, he accepted mediation by Argentina, Brazil, and Chile, which permitted him gracefully to withdraw his forces from Mexico and which led, in July of 1914, to Huerta's resignation. In August, Carranza entered Mexico City and assumed the presidency.

Huerta's departure, however, brought no peace to Mexico. No sooner was Carranza installed in the presidential palace, then one of his generals, Pancho Villa, turned against him and drove him from the capital in September. There then followed a most confused situation. Wilson first backed Villa and then Carranza, as the fortunes of war dictated. By October, it appeared that Carranza had gained the day, whereupon the United States formally recognized him as president. Villa retaliated by a series of wanton and cruel acts. In January 1916, he shot sixteen American engineers he had pulled off a train in northern Mexico and in February led a raid on the border town of Columbus in New Mexico, leaving nineteen Americans dead and the town in flames.

Villa's actions outraged Wilson and the reaction of the American people matched his own. Cries for retaliation reverberated throughout the country and Wilson heeded them for they coincided with his own sentiments. On March 13, 1916, he concluded an agreement with Carranza, whereby each nation had the right to cross into the territory of the other in pursuit of bandits. Two days later, an American expeditionary force of 6,000 men under Brigadier General John J. Pershing entered Mexico to track down Villa. It drove deep into Mexico—some 300 miles —failing to capture Villa but thoroughly alarming Carranza, who had envisaged a small detachment operating close to the border. He now took steps to have Wilson recall Pershing's army. There was no question that the presence of so large an American force and a hostile native population constituted an invitation to a clash of arms. Such a fight actually took place at Parral in April between American and Mexican soldiers in which forty Mexicans and two Americans died. Another battle occurred in June at Carrizal with more casualties. War seemed a very likely possibility, especially after Wilson mobilized 140,000 national guardsmen following a Villa raid into Texas in May.

Once again, Wilson seems to have realized that he had gone too far and, confronted with the increasing difficulty of maintaining neutrality in the great European war that had broken out in 1914, he eagerly sought a solution. Carranza was agreeable; hence, in September representatives of both nations met in New London, Connecticut to try to halt the drift to war. The meeting that lasted until January 15, 1917 accomplished nothing

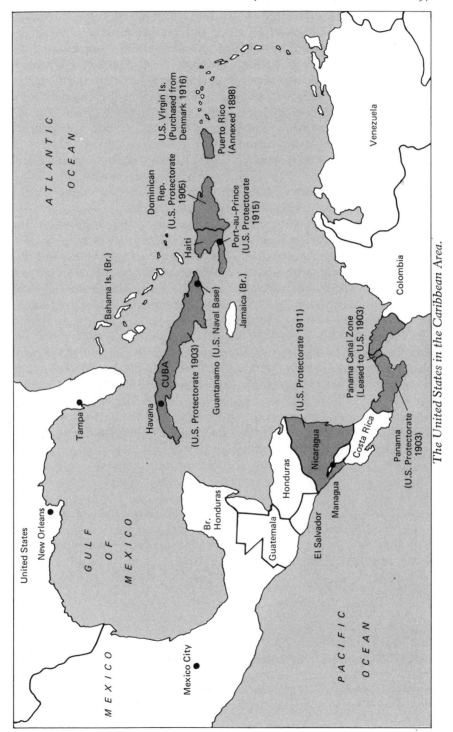

The United States in the Caribbean Area.

concrete. It did clear the air, however, and led to the American delegation advising Wilson that a withdrawal of the punitive force would end the hostility between the two neighbors. Wilson gladly complied and by February 5, no American soldiers remained on Mexican soil. The culmination of the conference was the official recognition of the Carranza government and the accreditation of a minister to it in March of 1917.

So ended Wilson's adventures in Mexico. By every yardstick, it must be deemed a failure. He changed not by one whit the Mexican political situation. He brought that country neither freedom, liberty, democracy, nor constitutionalism. He earned, instead, that country's hostility and suspicion. To Mexicans, as to all Latin Americans, Wilson, for all his high morality and noble sentiments, appeared to be just another in the succession of twentieth-century American presidents who sought to achieve hegemony in the western hemisphere at the expense of the sovereignty and independence of the other republics. It is true, that the idealism reflected in several of his speeches and programs concerning the war in Europe, such as the "Peace Without Victory" address, the Fourteen Points, and the League of Nations, allayed some of the mistrust and aroused a spark of hope. It is true, too, that the threat of Germany forced a kind of solidarity upon the nations of the hemisphere and, indeed, 8 of the 20 countries joined the United States in declaring war on the Central Powers, and five others broke relations with Germany. Cuba and Brazil even took an active part in the fighting. But the inclusion in the League of Nations convenant of a clause protecting the Monroe Doctrine dashed whatever expectations there were of a new deal in inter-American affairs. The southern republics could see no reason for a regional doctrine in a universal organization unless it be to give the United States special rights in the hemisphere.

In assessing America's overall Latin American policy in the first two decades of the twentieth century, one may well judge it a huge success in that its objectives had been achieved superbly. The canal had been built and it was an American canal; the Caribbean had become an American lake; European nations could enter the area only upon American sufferance; and protectorates, naval bases, and strong places were strategically located. Hegemony had been won—but at a high price, the estrangement of the sister republics. The United States was feared and hated, too.

BIBLIOGRAPHY

WILFRED CALCOTT, *The Caribbean Policy of the United States, 1890–1920* (1942).

PETER CALVERT, *The Mexican Revolution, 1910–1914: The Diplomacy of Anglo-American Conflict* (1968).

P. E. HALEY, *Revolution and Intervention: The Diplomacy of Taft and Wilson with Mexico, 1910–1919* (1970).

DAVID HEALY, *The United States in Cuba: Generals, Politicians, and the Search for Policy* (1963).

H. C. HILL, *Roosevelt and the Caribbean* (1927).

GERSTLE MACK, *The Land Divided* (1944).

DANA G. MUNRO, *Intervention and Dollar Diplomacy in the Caribbean, 1900–1921* (1964).

SCOTT NEARING and JOSEPH FREEMAN, *Dollar Diplomacy: A Study in American Imperialism* (1925).

ROBERT E. QUIRK, *An Affair of Honor: Woodrow Wilson and the Occupation of Vera Cruz* (1962).

WALTER V. and MARIE V. SCHOLES, *The Foreign Policies of the Taft Administration* (1970).

Andrew Carnegie.

In Europe—Noninvolvement

THE INTERESTS of the United States in Europe between 1898 and 1914 were neither political nor territorial, only cultural and commercial. Hence, the policy toward that continent followed by Washington was very much different from that directed to Asia and to Latin America. It was restricted to expanding the market for capital investment and for the products of farm and factory, to advancing international understanding by participating in humanitarian and nonpolitical conferences, and to promoting projects for maintaining the peace. From purely political matters, the United States stood aloof. Of the frantic jockeying by the nations of the Old World for a favorable diplomatic position, of their mad race for naval supremacy, of the rivalry for colonies, and of the precarious nature of the European balance of power, the American government and people knew little and cared less. Indeed, in the several crises that gripped Europe in the 16-year period, the United States was affected only once—in 1906 in Morocco.

The American interest in Morocco, although peripheral, dated back at least to 1880 when the United States signed and ratified a convention dealing with extraterritoriality in the country. Twenty-four years later, Morocco figured once again, fleetingly, in American life. In June 1904, Jon Pericardis, an American citizen of Greek origin, was captured by a local bandit named Raisuli. Raisuli had nothing against Pericardis or the United States. Apparently, he wanted only to enmesh the ruling sultan in a difficult situation by antagonizing a foreign nation. Nonetheless, President Roosevelt bristled and, determined to extend the protection of the flag to all citizens, demanded Pericardis' release. Seven warships were dispatched to Tangiers and a handful of marines landed to enforce the president's wish. Needless to say, the sultan was impressed and promptly arranged the American's release. Thus, when a crisis flared up in Morocco as a result of the rivalry of France and Germany for influence there, the place was not exactly unknown.

That France should have a deep concern for Morocco was not surprising. Even a cursory glance at a map of the western Mediterranean conveys sharply the strategic value of that part of north Africa to French security. In 1904, an agreement with Great Britain assigned to France preponderance in Morocco in exchange for French support of Britain's claim to Egypt. Italy and Spain were persuaded to back France in return for territorial compensation elsewhere. Germany, however, contested French pretentions and on March 31, 1905, the German emperor, Kaiser Wilhelm II, dramatically demonstrated his intention to safeguard his country's interests by a personal visit to the sultan. Upon landing in Tangiers, Wilhelm greeted his host with a salutation full of meaning saying, ". . . I look upon the Sultan as an absolutely independent sovereign."

France was alarmed by this show of German bravado and a serious crisis loomed. The sultan, wishing to avoid a fight in which his country would be the battleground as well as the stake, called for a conference. Germany, not yet ready for a showdown, appeared willing to discuss the issue; the French, believing they had nothing to gain and everything to lose by a meeting that would probably result in compromise and partition, balked. Now, the United States stepped into the controversy. President Roosevelt, fresh from his success in settling the Russo-Japanese war, prevailed upon France to accept the invitation. The conference met at Algeçiras in Spain in January of 1906, and in its deliberations Roosevelt, through his delegate, the experienced diplomat Henry White (the ambassador to Rome) exerted a large and salutary influence. The instrument that emerged, called the Act of Algeciras, resolved the rivalry, at least for the time being. It bore White's signature and was duly approved by the Senate, albeit with a reservation that American ratification does not impair the traditional nonentanglement policy of the United States. Thus passed the first and last political involvement with Europe until August 1914 when President Wilson would try to avert the great war about to erupt.

In nonpolitical affairs, however, the United States found itself intimately linked to the old continent. American delegates took part in all sorts of international conferences covering the widest variety of matters. The relationship was not a new one in the twentieth century for Washington had, throughout the preceding century, participated in international gatherings such as the one at Paris in 1856 to codify the law of the sea in wartime, at Geneva in 1882 covering the treatment of the wounded in time of war, and five others between 1883 and 1898 dealing with the protection of industrial property, submarine cables, exchange of official publications, repression of the African slave trade, and customs tariffs. After the turn of the century and up to the beginning of the Great War, American representatives attended 16 international gatherings that produced treaties ratified by the United States. Sanitation, traffic in women, agriculture, public health, pharmaceuticals, and importation of liquor into Africa were some of the matters discussed.

In the same period, the United States government played an active role in promoting and aiding projects to insure world peace. It attended three important conferences on the reduction and limitation of armaments and on the codification of the rules of land and sea warfare and led the way in negotiating treaties designed to substitute peaceful for warlike means of settling international disputes.

Americans took a special pride in their nation's contribution to the idea and practice of the pacific settlement of disputes. They could point to the fact that the earliest modern treaty containing an arbitration clause was the one in 1794 between England and the United States—the Jay Treaty. They could point, also, to frequent statements by their leaders pledging faith in arbitration. A resolution of the Senate Foreign Relations Committee in 1851 proclaimed "the spirit of the age, the genius of our government, the habit of our people, the claims of humanity, the dictates of enlightened reason all require adoption of peaceful means of settling international disputes." Half a century later, President McKinley affirmed that "Arbitration is the true method of settlement of international as well as local individual differences. It has been recognized as the leading feature of our foreign policy throughout our entire history." And in 1910, Secretary of State Philander C. Knox boasted that "Not only has the United States sought thus [by arbitration] to settle its own difficulties by the implements of peace rather than by those of war but it has assiduously exerted all popular pressure to induce the world to adopt the principle of arbitration as a means of settling international disputes."

The United States had, indeed, settled many of its differences with other powers by arbitration beginning in 1794 and continuing throughout the nineteenth century. With Great Britain there were the major adjudications of the *Alabama* claims (1871), the problem involving the hunting of fur seals in the Pacific (1893), and the Venezuelan boundary question (1899) as well as several less important problems concerning claims and boundaries. With Spain there were settlements for damages arising out of Spanish attacks on American neutral commerce in 1793–1812 and out of the destruction to American property during Cuban insurrections. With France, there were settlements of claims stemming from the action of French vessels upon American shipping in the Napoleonic wars, the Civil War and the Franco-Prussian war. There were settlements, too, with lesser powers over the years.

After the Spanish-American war, the United States intensified its efforts to provide for the amicable settlement of disputes. In the 16 years that remained before the eruption of war in Europe, 67 bilateral treaties were negotiated by the administrations of Roosevelt, Taft, and Wilson that included provisions for either arbitration or conciliation (the latter, unlike the former, involves a commission of inquiry, which after investigation renders a nonbinding opinion on the merits of the case. The decision of the judge in an arbitration that is based on the legal aspects of the case must be accepted by the litigants). In 1904 and 1905, Secretary of State John Hay signed 11 treaties that stipulated that differences of a legal nature would be arbitrated. The Senate approved them, but President Roosevelt refused to exchange ratifications with the cosignatories because the Senate attached a reservation requiring that each specific arbitration under the treaties be submitted for its consent. The Senate placed the same stricture on 24 treaties arranged by Hay's successor, Elihu Root, in 1908–1909. This time the president accepted the limitation and ratified all but three. In 1911, President Taft's secretary of state negotiated agreements for compulsory arbitration with Great Britain and France but senatorial opposition to them was very great because they did not exclude, as all earlier treaties had, questions of vital interest, honor, and independence and Taft withdrew them from senatorial consideration.

The final effort was made by the Wilson administration in 1913–1914. That consisted of thirty conciliation treaties, providing for a commission of inquiry of five people chosen by the two nations concerned that would conduct an investigation and make a recommendation. They were called "cooling-off" treaties because the signatories pledged to take no warlike action for a certain period of time. All but ten of the treaties received the Senate's approval.

Despite the spotty record of the treaty effort, the United States between 1898 and 1914 engaged in several important arbitrations. Two were with England and they concerned a boundary dispute between Alaska and British Columbia and the question of the rights of Americans to fish in Canadian waters. The first, which had its origin in the days of Russian ownership of Alaska and became crucial after the discovery of gold in the Klondike in 1896, was decided by a panel of six jurists—three Americans, one Briton, and two Canadians—in America's favor. The second, which went back to the peace settlement of 1783, had been a continuous source of friction between the two countries and had brought their fishermen to the brink of hostilities on several occasions. Temporary agreements from time to time only deferred the problem. Finally, under the terms of the Anglo-American treaty of 1909, a final solution was reached by arbitration in 1910. Five judges, one of whom was American and another Canadian, handed down a judgment in favor of the United States. It is worth noting that these two arbitrations put an end to all the main differences between the United States and Great Britain that had haunted them since American independence, save one—the matter of the rights and duties of neutrals and belligerents on the seas in time of war. One other problem arose when Congress in 1912, in preparation for the opening of the Panama Canal, passed a law exempting American coastwise vessels from paying tolls. Such legislation violated the Hay-Pauncefote treaty, which specified that ships of all nations would be treated "on terms of entire equality." Britain protested and President Wilson heeded the protest. He asked Congress to repeal the objectionable and illegal act, which it did.

With Mexico one settlement was reached by arbitration, the Pious Fund case. It concerned the question of the payment from a Mexican fund of a subsidy to Franciscan missions in California that had been halted when California came under the American flag. In 1902 five arbitrators decided that a lump sum of $1.5 million had to be given by Mexico to the missions.

In the movement to limit and reduce armaments, the United States participated fully. A conference called by the Russian czar in 1899 to halt the race in military preparations that met at The Hague found an American delegation among the twenty-six nations represented. From the meeting nothing in the way of limitation or reduction of weapons emerged. It seems that the principal powers were not seriously interested in weakening their defenses. Some salutary results did, however, come from the deliberations in the form of regulations designed to diminish the barbarity of war. Thus were outlawed poison gases, dum-dum bullets, and projectiles dropped from balloons. Rules were also drawn up concerning the treatment of prisoners of war, flags of truce, and the Red Cross. One important achievement of the conference was the establishment of a Permanent Court of Arbitration, which was not a court but a panel of 100 jurists drawn from many countries from which nations wishing to arbitrate their differences might draw judges. It is doubtful that the panel's existence encouraged the use of arbitration as a means of settling disputes. President Roosevelt utilized it in the Pious Fund case and convinced Germany, Italy, and England to use it in their claim against Venezuela in 1903.

A second conference called, again, by the czar met at The Hague in 1907 and, again, an American delegation was seated among those from forty-three other nations. Like the first, this international gathering did nothing in the way of stopping the piling up of armaments by the powers. Some delegations tried to make arbitration compulsory, but German objections thwarted the effort. The United States sought to write into international law the immunity of private property at sea in time of war but there was opposition from England. In further discussions on maritime rights and duties in wartime, the major issues—definitions of blockade and contraband—were not resolved. An International Prize Court was created, but the details of its operation were left to a future conference to meet in two years.

In 1909, the conference met in London as scheduled and the United States, as a principal maritime power, had a delegation present. The accomplishment of the conference was considerable. Unlike the failure in 1907, this time the major issues were resolved. The nations defined contraband, blockade, continuous voyage, and the status of enemy and neutral property found on the vessels of belligerents and nonbelligerents. The rules adopted were very much like those the United States had pushed for through most of its history. That is to say, they were more favorable to neutrals than to belligerents, and the Senate unhesitatingly approved the results. The British, on the other hand, fearful that their belligerent status in a future war would be greatly hindered by such liberal rules, refused to accept the results leaving the Declaration of London a meaningless document and a pious hope.

The active and vigorous participation of the American government in all projects for peace in this period cannot be understood or properly evaluated without a clear comprehension of the prevailing intellectual climate in the country. It was one of boundless optimism that wars, at least major ones, were no longer a possibility and that the millennium was at hand. The view was rooted in the belief that man was too rational and too civilized to fight and too moral to settle his differences by butchering his fellows. Furthermore, men believed that peace made good sense. Wars were unprofitable, too costly and destructive. There were no victors and no vanquished; no one won; no one lost; everyone suffered. It seemed inconceivable, too, that nations that were so interlocked in their commercial and financial affairs—in trade and in investment—could afford to rupture their relationships by wars. "The era of the brotherhood of man is not coming, it is here now," said William Jennings Bryan in 1912, and President David Starr Jordan of Stanford University wrote in an article in the same year, entitled "Bankers As Peace Guardians," that the web of international finance and business was a sure guarantor of the peace. Dean G. Acheson, writing in the fiftieth anniversary issue of the *Yale Review* in 1961, recalled that in 1911 the world was convinced "it was moving on the great current of progress to the reign of universal peace and universal law."

The manifestation of these sentiments and views and beliefs was in a vigorous movement to promote projects designed to aid the cause of peace and of international understanding and to substitute peaceful settlement of disputes for war. There was, first, the proliferation of activities of the peace societies. They were, of course, not a new phenomenon in American life. It will be recalled that after the War of 1812 the New York Peace Society and a counterpart in Massachusetts were established to propagandize for the abolition of war and by 1860, fifty such organizations were flourishing in the United States. But never were their activities as numerous and varied, their coffers so full, their roster of membership so distinguished, their audience so large and so respectable as after the turn of the century. Several other features differentiated the earlier from the later peace movement. The leadership of the former was drawn largely from the ranks of the clergy, the scholars, and the writers—Channing, Parker, Thoreau, Emerson, Fuller. The guiding spirit of the latter were hardheaded and wealthy businessmen, labor leaders, and editors. As stated by one historian, "The new peace movement had moved from the pulpit under the leadership of men of religion to the public rostrum under the leadership of men of affairs. The basis had shifted from idealism to common sense."

The principal vehicles of the peace societies were lectures, forums, meetings, and publications. By those means, large numbers of people were reached. In 1904, at a congress in Boston, 3,000 delegates representing 200 organizations (churches, women's clubs, boards of trade, labor unions) discussed the progress of the peace movement and hailed the coming of the millennium. Three years later, the first national meeting of the American Peace Society was held in New York with ten mayors, nineteen congressmen, four Supreme Court justices, two presidential candidates, thirty labor leaders, forty bishops, and sixty newspaper editors in attendance. An equally distinguished representation of American leadership was present at two subsequent congresses—in 1909 at Chicago and in Boston in 1911. At the latter President Taft made a major address that imparted to the movement a luster and a kind of official sanction. In one typical year, it was estimated, the New York Peace Society reached 3,500 businessmen, 6,000 lawyers, 5,000 social workers, 2,000 physicians, and 2,500 ministers, sent out 40 speakers who addressed 1,500 meetings, and distributed 3 million pieces of literature.

Alongside the peace societies there were other organizations working for peace. In 1903, a Cosmopolitan Club was established at the University of Wisconsin to promote discussions on the question of avoiding war. Within a decade, branches were founded on other campuses to create a national federation of clubs to advance international understanding. In 1904 an Intercollegiate Peace Association was formed at Goshen College, a small Mennonite school in Indiana, that sponsored literary contests on war and peace. By 1913, more than 100 chapters of the Association were in operation throughout the country. In 1907 three other groups were formed— the American Association for International Conciliation under the presidency of Nicholas Murray Butler, head of Columbia University and a leading peace advocate, which published a monthly bulletin entitled, *International Conciliation,* devoted to accounts of the efforts for peace; the American School Peace League which distributed literature on the subject to teachers; and the prestigious American Society of International Law to promote the study of the legal aspects of international relations. One year earlier, a milestone effort was achieved when John Bassett Moore, a prominent international lawyer, completed a massive eight-volume *Digest of International Law,* which described the policies and practices of the United States on the major international legal and diplomatic questions. It was a work designed to demonstrate the importance of law in the affairs of nations and, by implication, the usefulness of law and diplomacy as pacific means for settling disputes.

Two significant events in 1910 and 1911 constituted a sort of high-water mark in the movement for peace in the period. The first was the creation of the Carnegie Endowment for International Peace financed by a $10 million gift from Andrew Carnegie, the Scottish-born American steel magnate. Its purpose was to publish documents and studies on international law, on the causes of war, on efforts for peace, and on other questions of international relations. The second was the formation of the World Peace Foundation, made possible by a grant of $1 million by Edwin Ginn, the Boston publisher. Its function was similar to that of the Carnegie Endowment. Both institutions exerted an important influence on the flourishing peace movement, which was described in 1912 as "more virile today than at any time since men and women first began to think it possible to substitute judicial settlements for war in international disputes."

It was not only in America that people put their faith in the pacific settlement of disputes but in Europe as well, particularly in England. As W. E. Darby, secretary of the London Peace Society noted in 1911, "Never were peace prospects so promising or peace sentiments so insistent as at the present moment. The cause is flourishing now." And in the 1911 edition of the *Encyclopaedia Britannica* there appeared for the first time an article entitled "Peace." The author, Sir Thomas Barclay, a noted expert on international law, wrote, "Peace, until quite recently, was merely the political condition which prevailed in the intervals between wars. It was a purely negative condition. . . [It] has now become, or is fast becoming, a positive subject of international regulation, while war is coming, among progressive people, to be regarded merely as an accidental disturbance of that harmony and concord among mankind which nations require for the fostering of their domestic welfare."

Yet both in Europe and in the United States, counter voices were being raised. There were men who feared that the enthusiasm for peace was creating an illusion and a dangerous one. They did not believe that wars could be eradicated or that men would settle their disputes amicably. They were deeply concerned that those who did believe it would let down their guard and not make adequate provision for defending the country. Theodore Roosevelt voiced that concern when he wrote President Eliot of Harvard that "the United States navy is an infinitely more potent factor for peace than all the peace societies." Henry and Brooks Adams both saw war and conflict in the future for their country—in Asia with Japan and/or Russia and in Europe with Germany and counseled that not in naive faith in peace but only in alliance with England could the nation's security be guaranteed. Lewis Einstein, a career diplomat, and Herbert Croly, an editor and writer, similarly, urged a British alliance as the best safeguard for the United States. More sensationally in the same vein were the works of Homer Lea, a brilliant student of strategy and diplomacy and a professional soldier of fortune who served as military advisor to the Chinese revolutionary leader, Sun Yat-sen, and who was commissioned a general in the Chinese army. Lea wrote two striking and remarkably prophetic books—*Valor of Ignorance* and *Day of the Saxon*—that foretold a Japanese attack on the United States and a German-American war. Lea also urged adequate preparation.

The warnings had little, if any, effect upon the American public or their governors. They continued to bask in an optimistic and blissful euphoria. Typical was the observation by one United States senator during a debate on a naval appropriation bill in 1909 that "the prospects of the United States becoming involved in a war is as chimerical and unlikely as a descent on our coasts of army from the moon." And another legislator in the same debate saw little use in building a great navy in view of the imminence of a world federation presaged at the Second Hague Conference.

Most Americans were unwilling to accept the realities of international life. Far from putting their faith in peaceful panaceas the European nations were arming to the teeth and girding themselves for a showdown. Armageddon was around the corner while Americans made preparations to welcome the millennium. Men might be intelligent but they were also patriotic and nationalistic, and history was to prove the latter qualities more decisive than the former.

So it came to pass that when in August of 1914 the Great War erupted, Americans were stunned and mystified. All their hopes and dreams had been proven wrong, had been shattered. Had they, then, been wrong? Not entirely, in their view. They had only overestimated the degree of civilization the Europeans had attained. The people of the old world had not, apparently, progressed to the point of rationality and intelligence of being able to settle their differences amicably. As a matter of fact, that ought not have been terribly surprising for if Americans had not kept abreast of European developments they had always had a view of Europe as the place of sordid politics and power-driven statesmen, of rivalries and strife from earliest times. They had, after all, escaped that continent to free themselves from those Old World conditions. So a war was really not so unthinkable and should not have been too surprising. Americans, then, could say upon the outbreak of the war, "that is Europe's way of settling her problems but it is not the American way." Neutrality was but the next logical step.

BIBLIOGRAPHY

PETER BROCK, *Pacifism in the United States* (1968).
MERLE CURTI, *Peace or War: The American Struggle, 1636–1936* (1936).
CALVIN D. DAVIS, *The United States and the First Hague Conference* (1962).
SONDRA R. HERMAN, *Eleven Against War: Studies in American Internationalist Thought, 1898–1921* (1969).
MERZE TATE, *The Disarmament Illusion: The Movement for a Limitation of Armaments to 1907* (1942).
JOSEPH F. WALL, *Andrew Carnegie* (1970).

Woodrow Wilson (courtesy of the National Portrait Gallery, the Smithsonian Institution, Washington, D.C.).

The Road to War, 1917

ON JULY 28, 1914, Austria-Hungary declared war on Serbia when that small Balkan kingdom failed to give the great central European empire satisfaction following the assassination of Archduke Franz Ferdinand. Within one week, in accordance with the network of alliances and alignments worked out in the previous quarter century, every major European power had become involved—Germany on the side of Austria, and Russia, France, Belgium, and Great Britain on Serbia's side. Within one week, too, the United States announced its neutrality in the struggle. On August 4, President Wilson issued the formal proclamation. Fifteen days later, he made a second statement in which he urged his countrymen to be "neutral in fact as well as in name. . . . We must be impartial in thought as well as in action," he warned, "must put a curb upon our sentiments as well as upon every transaction that might be construed as a preference of one party to the struggle before another."

Both his proclamation and his admonition were enthusiastically endorsed by the vast majority of Americans. They wanted no part of the war and had no intention or desire to get involved. They agreed with their president when he said in August of 1914, "it is a war with which we have nothing to do, whose causes cannot touch us," and were fully in accord with his view stated in December of 1914, "there is no reason to fear from any quarters that our independence or the integrity of our territory is threatened."

All this is not to say that Americans, any more than Wilson himself, could avoid some emotional entanglement in the conflict. They were, after all, human and not mechanical and could not help sympathizing with one or the other of the two sets of belligerents. Almost every American had some attachment to the Old World. Of a population of 92 million, 32 million were either foreign born or, if native, had at least one parent born abroad. Few of the remainder did not have some affinity—cultural, social, commercial, ethnic, or familial—with one or another of the warring nations. Still, the overwhelming sentiment could be summed up in the oft-heard statement, "It is not our fight." Sympathy was one thing; participation quite another. The popular position was expressed in slogans such as, "a plague on both your houses," and "business as usual." As it turned out, the crucial question was could business be conducted as usual without the nation becoming involved in the war. Two years and eight months passed before that question was to be answered and, tragically, in the negative.

"Business as usual" meant continuing to carry on trade with the European nations as though there were no war. That, however, was easier said than done for both sets of belligerents bent every effort to prevent the other side from getting the sinews of war from the great neutral arsenal on the other side of the Atlantic. The policies and practices of England and Germany toward the United States (and the other neutrals) between 1914 and 1917 recalled the prodigious contest between France and England a century earlier. Now, as then, the task of American diplomacy was to maintain a neutral course and defend the right of American citizens to trade and to engage in other lawful and peaceful pursuits subject, of course, to the rules of maritime warfare then in force.

The problem for President Wilson was compounded by several factors. One was the absence of any rules of maritime warfare binding on the great powers in 1914. It will be recalled that the rules which had emerged from the conference in London in 1909, as embodied in the Declaration of London, had not been ratified by the maritime nations when Great Britain rejected them (they were considered too favorable to neutrals). Nonetheless, the United States planned to conduct its policy on the basis of certain rules that it had traditionally supported: a blockade to be considered legal had to be effective; contraband goods are divided into two categories—absolute and conditional; absolute contraband consisted of goods exclusively used for war and destined for an enemy country; conditional contraband consists of goods that may be used for warlike or peaceful purposes; "continuous voyage" applies to absolute but not to conditional contraband; visit and search by a belligerent warship of a neutral vessel must be conducted at the point of interception on the seas; the citizens of a neutral state may trade and lend money to a belligerent. Some of those rules were uncontested by the belligerents; others were ignored for expediency's sake or because they seriously hampered the conduct of the war at sea.

A second difficulty facing the president was in the use of the submarine as a weapon to halt neutral traffic with the enemy. The rules of maritime warfare had grown up long before the submarine's appearance on the seas and had concerned only surface ships. The adherance of underseas craft to cruiser (surface ship) rules was problematical. Third, there was the president's deep sympathy and partiality for the Allied course. The Allies, especially England, represented all that was dear to Woodrow Wilson—parliamentary democracy, liberalism, constitutional government. He loved her history, her poets, her novelists, her ballads, her language. "His eyes became moist when he spoke of Wordsworth's sonnets," recorded Sir Cecil Spring-Rice, the British Ambassador in Washington, "he knew them by heart and had them in mind all the time." To colonel Edward House, the president wrote, "If Germany won it would change the course of civilization and make the United States a military nation." And to his secretary, Joseph Tumulty, he confided, "England is fighting our fight."

Not only Wilson but his official family wholeheartedly favored the Allies and wished for their victory—all save William Jennings Bryan, secretary of state from March 1913 to June 1915. Robert Lansing, counselor of the Department of State and Bryan's successor, believed that Germany had to be defeated even if it meant America had to fight. Indeed, he wanted to get into the war in 1916. Walter Hines Page, the ambassador in London, from the very beginning, urged open identification with the Allied cause "as a means of rededicating our faith in democracy" and a manifestation of hatred for the German system. He softened whatever seemed harsh in Wilson's notes to Britain and collaborated with the British foreign secretary in drafting replies. As for Colonel Edward M. House, the President's closest advisor, his preference for the Allies was unreserved. Although he faithfully carried out his chief's instructions in his several missions to mediate in the conflict, there was never any question of his wish to see England triumph.

It ought also be said that the majority of the American people favored the Allies. The image of France and England in the mind of the average American was a favorable one while the reverse was true in the case of Germany. Germany connoted militarism, autocracy, imperialism represented popularly by a swaggering, uniformed, blustering Kaiser "with fierce upturned mustaches." The recent history of German-American relations was punctuated with conflict—in Samoa, the Caribbean, and China—and with rivalry over colonies and markets. Then, too, inept propaganda and certain acts of apparently needless cruelty further alienated most Americans. The attack on small and defenseless Belgium; the sacking of the cathedral and university in Louvain; the killing of Edith Cavell, a British nurse and prisoner of the Germans; the sinking without warning of steamships with the loss of lives of women and children, the attempt on the life of J. P. Morgan, the American banker; the sabotaging of American ships in American harbors; the blowing up of several munitions arsenals in the United States; and the recovery by an American secret service agent of a briefcase left on a New York train by a German official that contained all sorts of scatterbrained plans for inciting strikes, performing sabotage, and perpetrating frauds, all conspired to create loathing for the German cause.

The Anglo-American story was very much different. Relations between the two nations and peoples had been remarkably cordial. By 1914, all the points of conflict between them, save neutral rights, had been resolved. The British had voluntarily relinquished their position in the Caribbean to the United States, leaving it undisputed master of the area. In addition, an astute, efficient, and highly organized propaganda machine exploited all the connections between countries—language, literature, customs, law, common ancestry, and business methods.

Some historians have made the pro-Allied bias of Wilson, his advisors, and the majority of the American people the chief factor in their interpretation of America's decision to fight in 1917. They have claimed that that bias caused the president to be unneutral from the very beginning and to pursue such policies deliberately as would aid the Allies and harm Germany. Those policies drove the Germans eventually and inexorably to the unbridled use of the submarine, which brought America into the war. Those policies, too, formed a bond between the United States and the Allies—economic and emotional—which led to American intervention when the Allied fortunes on the battlefield seemed to be sinking. The thesis is plausible but is not supported by the evidence. It would be more nearly correct to say that although Wilson ardently desired an Allied victory, he followed an absolutely neutral and impartial course, hoping always to keep the nation uninvolved. What eventually took him into the war was the German violation of American rights at sea. Nor did those violations stem from any Wilsonian policies. They grew out of purely internal German decisions.

Within one week of the outbreak of the war, the Administration had to confront the first test of neutrality. J. P. Morgan, whose banking house had already become involved in Allied trade in war goods, asked the State Department if his firm might make loans to Britain to help finance purchases. Bryan, after gaining the president's approval, advised against it. While lending money, he said on August 15, 1914, was perfectly legal, it was "inconsistent with the true spirit of neutrality." Money, he added, "was the worst of all contrabands because it commands all things." Thus, Wilson went beyond the legal obligations of a neutral in an effort to keep the country uninvolved. Soon, however, the policy changed and for reasons unconnected with neutrality. In October, the National City Bank of New York warned the Administration that the Allies were running out of cash and needed credits to continue their purchases. Now the problem took on another dimension. The country's economy was the issue. War purchases had just begun alleviating a serious recession that had gripped the nation. A cessation of the trade might well have led to a depression.

A reversal of policy was inevitable and it was accomplished in two stages. The first, privately made known to the banking community in October, drew a distinction between advancing credit and lending money. The former only was permitted. J. P. Morgan at once granted a $10 million credit to France. Less than one year later, as the Allies stepped up their purchases and began running low on money, the administration removed its objection to loans, and the American financial market soon began absorbing British and French bonds. In September 1915, $0.5 billion were raised by the sale of British bonds in the United States. By the time America entered the war, $2.5 billion were raised for the Allied cause as against $27 million for Germany.

Judging by the loan policy, it would appear that the president placed more importance on the country's economic well-being than upon safeguarding its neutrality. Indeed, Robert Lansing, then counselor of the State Department, said as much when he observed at the time of the reversal, "Can we afford to let a declaration regarding the spirit of neutrality made in the early days of the war threaten the national interest [prosperity] now?" The fact is, however, that Wilson's dominant motivation in conducting the nation's foreign policy regarding the war was the protection of the right of American citizens to follow their normal pursuits. The removal of the ban on loans had to come because the ban denied Americans one of their rights. Never again would the president place strictures upon those rights. In fact, it was in defense of those rights that he eventually intervened. Throughout the period of neutrality, he resisted all efforts by certain Americans to curtail those rights. Agitation to place an embargo on the export of war supplies on the grounds that the Allies, because of their control of the ocean, alone benefited from the trade met with stern opposition from the White House. It was not the duty of the neutral, said the president in reply to a demand by certain Congressmen for an embargo, to redress an imbalance between belligerents caused by their weaknesses or strengths. It was the responsibility of the belligerents, he claimed, to halt the traffic to the enemy by exercising their legal rights to institute a blockade or to intercept the passage of contraband at sea. The executive prestige was sufficient to beat down every attempt to legislate an embargo. Only once did a resolution actually reach the floor of either house—on February 18, 1915 in the Senate and there it was tabled 51–36.

Meanwhile, Germany and England, without waiting for the president's suggestion, had begun erecting systems calculated to halt trade with the enemy. The English began on August 20, 1914, the same day they rejected a suggestion by the United States to be guided by the Declaration of

London, with an Order-in-Council that greatly enlarged the contraband list to include items such as foodstuffs and raw materials hitherto and traditionally on the free list. In the months to follow, the list was increased until it contained every conceivable thing even remotely useful for fighting and at the same time, the doctrine of "continuous voyage" was rigorously applied. Items on the contraband list of neutral origin were captured at sea if destined to ports in Holland or Denmark. Also, on November 3, 1914, London declared the North Sea to be a "military area" and planted mines there in ostensible retaliation for the indiscriminate sowing by Germany of mines in waters around the British Isles. Finally, on March 11, 1915, a sweeping order was promulgated making subject to capture all goods of "enemy destination, ownership, or origin." The word "blockade" was not used but it was, in effect, a "blockade" of Germany, albeit, a "paper" one.

The last measure was avowedly a reply to a German action of February 4, 1915 that had declared a "naval war zone" around the British Isles, effective February 18. After that date, all enemy merchant vessels in the zone would be sunk at sight. Neutral vessels were warned that because of the use of neutral flags by the enemy, visit and search to determine nationality was too risky. Hence, the safety of neutral vessels could not be guaranteed. After all, even small merchant vessels were more than a match for the fragile submarine. If they were armed, their cannon could sink her; if they were unarmed they could ram her. The submarine dared not surface. The deadly torpedo had to be launched underwater.

Again, as in 1793–1812, the United States was caught between the two belligerent systems. This time, it was not a question of the Colossus of the Land fighting the Leviathan of the Seas but the submarine against the blockade. And that was to make all the difference for Wilson as he faced the issues. The British action strained the rights of belligerents to the breaking point. It was, by Wilson's standards, illegal. It was oppressive; it restricted American trade with Germany; it was maddening. But compared to German action, it was mild. The submarine sank ships without warning, giving innocent passengers no chance to escape. If the British were thieves; the Germans were murderers. The president saw the difference clearly and felt it deeply. "Property rights," he said, "can be vindicated by claims for damages when the war is over, and no modern nation can decline to arbitrate such claims, but the fundamental rights of humanity cannot be; the loss of life is irreparable."

The American protests to Britain were severe in tone (too much so for the Anglophile Walter Hines Page). They contained lengthy disquisitions on the illegality of British policy and historical allusions to previous practices of nations. But they never threatened; they never menaced; they never carried portents of retaliation; they were legal and technical. To

Germany, the language was blunt, sharp, and threatening. Six days after the German war zone announcement, on February 10, Wilson replied. If American ships are destroyed or American lives lost, he would hold Germany to "strict accountability," he warned. The United States, he added, may take any steps necessary "to secure to American citizens the full enjoyment of their acknowledged rights on the high seas."

Wilson did not think the Germans would carry out their plan; he hoped they would not. But they did. On March 28, 1915, the British liner *Falaba* was sunk by a submarine in the Irish Sea with the loss of 103 lives including one American. Here was the test of "strict accountability." But Wilson did nothing. He sent no note, made no remonstrance. His failure to act was partly due to a difference of opinion among his advisors. The secretary of state believed that American citizens ought not to travel on belligerent vessels; they ought not to risk involving their country in dangerous controversy; trouble with Germany could be avoided if they did not expose themselves to destruction. Lansing disagreed. It was his view that the responsibility lay with Germany. American citizens had every right to travel and not risk destruction. The president strongly inclined to Lansing's view but held up a note he drafted because he was as yet unsure of his ground.

But certainty replaced uncertainty in May. On May 7, a German torpedo sank the great British passenger vessel *Lusitania* with a loss of 1,198 lives of which 128 were Americans. A wave of rage crossed the United States as the news was relayed across the country. Opinion was inflamed, and had Wilson wished to take the people to war right then, they would have followed willingly. The anti-German sentiment was intensified when five days later the British government published a report of German atrocities in France and Belgium, the veracity of which was vouchsafed by one of the most respected of Englishmen, scholar–diplomat Viscount James Bryce. But the president, like Thomas Jefferson a century earlier after the *Chesapeake-Leopard* affair, remained calm. The awful responsibility of sending American boys to fight balanced his own sense of outrage. Despite the advice of many close advisors and the nagging of political opponents such as Theodore Roosevelt and Elihu Root that he break relations with Berlin, he planned only a protest but a sharp one.

The note, which he drafted in seclusion, went out over the wires to Berlin on May 13. In it, he insisted on the rights of Americans to travel on belligerent merchant vessels and on the duty of German submarine commanders to visit and search ships accosted on the seas to determine their nationality. If found to be an enemy vessel, sufficient time must be given passengers to evacuate before firing the fatal torpedoes. He demanded a disavowal of the sinking, reparation for lives lost, and a pledge against recurrence of the action.

The German reply of May 28 was defensive. Tacitly admitting that a passenger ship ought to be warned before sinking, the Foreign Office maintained that the *Lusitania* was not such a vessel. She was more like a warship—commanded by a naval reservist, armed, carrying a number of Canadian troops, and a considerable amount of ammunition. Furthermore, a submarine could not possibly be expected to practice visit-and-search and warn in view of an order from the British Admiralty to all British vessels to ram submarines at sight. Wilson lost no time in shooting back a rejoinder. On June 9, he again defended the rights of citizens to travel and demanded renunciation of the act. A third note, dated July 21, warned of a rupture of relations if another *Lusitania* occurred.

By that time, two significant events had taken place. The German government had publicly expressed regret over the sinking and admitted liability and secretly issued instructions to submarine commanders to spare large passenger liners. Berlin had no wish to add the United States to its list of adversaries. The second event was the resignation of William Jennings Bryan. He could not, in conscience, sign the second *Lusitania* note for he did not believe Wilson's policy wise or correct. The United States must not, he claimed, pass on German acts concerning non-American ships, and it must discourage Americans from travelling on belligerent vessels in the war zones. The question he posed was not whether Americans had the right to travel but their obligation to deny themselves the right so as to prevent the embroilment of their country in the war.

Bryan was not alone in his position. Sentiment for legislation to make travel on belligerent vessels unlawful was mounting. It came to a head with the introduction into the House and Senate in February of 1916 of a resolution to that effect. Proposed by Texas Democratic Representative Jeff McLemore and Oklahoma Democratic Senator Thomas P. Gore, the motion urged all American citizens "to forebear to exercise their rights" to travel on belligerent ships and provided that no passport would be issued to those who intended to exercise the right. Support in both chambers was great and sufficient, it was believed, to assure its passage. But the president was opposed and that guaranteed its defeat. Using to the fullest the prestige of his office and by personal persuasion, he was able to get the resolution tabled—68–14 in the Senate and 276–142 in the House.

It has been suggested that Wilson stood against the measure because it constituted a legislative challenge to his executive authority in the making of foreign policy. There was, without question, some truth in the allegation, but there was a more fundamental reason for the president's position. It may be seen clearly in his letter to Senator William J. Stone of Missouri, chairman of the Foreign Relations Committee, of February 29, 1916. "For myself," he wrote, "I cannot consent to any abridgements of the rights of

American citizens in any respect. The honor and self-respect of the nation is involved. We covet peace and shall preserve it at any cost but the loss of honor. . . . Once accept a single abatement of rights and many other humiliations would certainly follow. What we are contending for in this matter is the very essence of the things that have made America a sovereign nation. She cannot yield without conceding our own impotency as a nation and making virtual surrender of her independent position among the nations of the world." He had said earlier that "America was too proud to fight." Now he was saying she was too proud to surrender. What Wilson did not seem to realize was that the two contentions may have been incompatible.

By the time the Gore-McLemore resolutions met defeat in March of 1916, another serious crisis with Germany was brewing. On August 15, 1915, another British liner, *Arabic*, had been sunk with the loss of forty-four passengers, including two Americans. Berlin at once expressed regret and on September 1, pledged to Wilson that "Liners would not be sunk by our submarines without warning and without safety of the lives of noncombatants provided that the liners do not try to escape or offer resistance." For seven months thereafter, all was quiet on the Berlin-Washington axes. Then came the sinking of the cross-channel British boat, *Sussex*, without warning on March 24, 1916, and the controversy flared anew. Wilson was angered by the German violation of the *Arabic* pledge. Lansing and House advised an immediate severance of relations. But again, Wilson resisted the pressure of advisors and others and contented himself with a strong protest. On April 16, he handed Count Von Bernstorff, the German Ambassador, a sharp note. Reminding him of the numerous pledges and assurances of his government, he warned that America continued to hold that Germany's use of the submarine was not compatible with the principles of humanity and the rights of neutrals and non-combatants. "If Germany did not abandon its present method of submarine warfare," he stated bluntly and unequivocably, the consequence would be a severance of relations.

Once again, Berlin was not ready for a break and on May 4 offered once more a pledge not to sink merchant vessels without warning and without providing for the safety of noncombatants. Wilson accepted the promise but rejected a proviso attached to it whereby Germany reserved to herself complete liberty of action unless Britain relaxed her blockade. Said the president, "responsibility in such matters is single, not joint; absolute, not relative."

For the next nine months, Germany kept her word providing President Wilson a much-needed breathing spell. There were domestic affairs demanding his attention, problems in the Caribbean and in Mexico needed solution, an election was in the offing, and some action had to be taken against England, whose conduct at sea was becoming unbearable. While Wilson had been occupied with Germany, the British had slowly but surely been tightening the noose around the enemy using every device imaginable to cut off German exports and imports. Additions to the contraband list, applying the doctrine of "continuous voyage" even more stringently, withholding coal and oil and stores from neutral vessels refusing to conform to British practices, examining neutral mail to gain evidence about cargoes, taking neutral vessels into British ports for leisurely visit-and-search, and, by an Order-in-Council of July 8, 1916 establishing a "Black List" of about 100 neutral persons or firms known to be doing business with the enemy. Inclusion on the list earned severe penalties, such as prohibition from trading in Britain, denial of the use of British cables and mail and insurance, credit, and banking facilities. Wilson's reaction was unpredictably sharp. "I am, I must admit, about at the end of my patience with Great Britain and the Allies," he wrote, in the summer of 1916, "This blacklist is the last straw. I am seriously contemplating asking Congress to authorize me to prohibit loans and restrict exportation to the Allies. Can we any longer endure this intolerable course?" And, when in September, he signed the largest peacetime naval appropriation bill in American history, he pointedly remarked, "Let us build a navy bigger than hers and do what we please."

But, of course, it was not likely that Wilson would carry out the threat of an embargo. The effect on the American economy and on the Allied war effort would have been crippling. Further, such action would have run contrary to the president's cherished principle of not curtailing the rights of American citizens. The presidential outburst was a reflection of his exasperation not a blueprint for policy. It was followed by a sharply worded note on July 26, 1916 excoriating the British for using the "Black List" and branding it a subterfuge and an unfair means of supplementing the defective blockade and the onerous visit-and-search procedure.

As for using the navy against England, that was unthinkable. An Anglo-American war was never a viable alternative for the United States and the British knew it hence their frequently cavalier and verbose replies to American protests. The navy bill, far from being a club against England, was a part of a larger program of preparedness that the president had adopted after the *Lusitania* sinking. That act had presented to him the real possibility that he could not remain neutral if Germany persisted in her submarine policy. He had realized the woeful state of the country's defenses and began taking measures to increase the army and navy. In November of 1915, he had drawn up a program and had explained it to the country in a tour in January and February of 1916. The fruit of his efforts, despite strong opposition from pacifists and socialists, was legislation in June to increase the regular army from 105,029 to 219,665 men and to expand the National Guard, and in August, to build, in three years, ten battleships, six battle cruisers, and ten scout cruisers. So, he prepared the nation should it be drawn into the war.

Still, he hoped to escape entanglement. Thus far, he had successfully maintained neutrality and had defended, however precariously, the rights of American citizens to engage in their legitimate pursuits. He had every intention of continuing such a course and in his campaign for re-election, the slogan "He kept us out of war" was true and apt. There had been several crises with Germany that could have led him to war had he wished for it. But how long could he walk the tightrope? For him the "only alternative to entering the war was to end it." That had been in his mind from its very outbreak and he had, in fact, made mediation a cardinal element in his policy of neutrality. His earliest efforts, made at the time of the outbreak, were formal and general. Official notes to the belligerent governments went out in July and, again, in August and September offering the good offices of the United States. Subsequently, his efforts were unofficial and specific.

The winter of 1915 seemed to him an opportune time. Germany had failed in her plan for a lightning victory over France, and the war had settled down to a stalemate with the armies facing each other from the trenches. With the specter of a long and costly conflict in manpower and money, the nations, he hoped, would welcome intercession. Accordingly, he sent Edward M. House to Europe on January 30, 1915. It took him only one week to learn that a compromise plan was not possible. Berlin and London were confident of victory and determined to deliver a knockout blow as a prelude to a dictated peace. Sadly, House reported to Bryan in April, "Everybody seems to want peace but on their own terms and nobody is willing to concede enough to get it. Germany is not willing to evacuate Belgium at all nor even France without an indemnity. The Allies, of course, will not consent to anything else—and there the situation rests." So failed Wilson's first try. He failed, too, to ease the pressure on American shippers by getting the belligerents to relax their maritime warfare. In February a proposal that German submarines practice visit-and-search in exchange for England abandoning the use of neutral flags and permitting food to get through to civilians in Germany had been rebuffed by Berlin. The Germans wanted all raw materials to be made noncontraband.

The president did not give up hope. He could not afford to. As the submarine warfare intensified and the British tightened their "blockade," America's chance of remaining at peace diminished. Wilson now moved to a new plane. He would try armed mediation—a threat of force. To House he revealed his ideas in October of 1915. He would call a peace conference, lay down reasonable terms for a compromise peace, and the side that refused to attend the conference or accept the terms would find the United States in the war on the other side. Off to Europe went House in January 1916 with Wilson's terms: (1) Germany to evacuate Belgium and France; (2) Alsace-Lorraine returned to France; (3) Germany to receive compensation in colonies. In Berlin, House learned that Germany would not surrender her conquests. In Paris, he found France noncommittal. Only in London, he was encouraged. Out of conversations held there in February came the House-Grey Memorandum of February 22, 1916. At a given signal from England and France, Wilson would call a conference and propose terms (agreed to in advance by the United States and the Allies). If the Allies accepted or agreed to negotiate and Germany declined, "the United States would *probably* enter the war against Germany." The "probably" was inserted by Wilson in view of the fact that only Congress could declare war. Whether the uncertainty over the "probably" or the confidence in ultimate victory, London never took up the offer, and by May Wilson knew he had failed again.

The summer of 1916 found the president fearful. At the end of August he had reports from Berlin of a change in the military command that promised to have a profound effect upon the use of the submarine. The new army commander, Paul Von Hindenburg, was known to support the navy's determination to set aside the *Sussex* pledge and renew the policy of sinking at sight all merchantmen in the war zone. To the navy chief, Admiral Alfred Von Tirpitz, that was the only formula for winning the war. Wilson felt the urgency of making peace, because he knew that a resumption of submarine warfare would surely mean war for the United States. But he was not hopeful. The German terms would not be acceptable to the Allies, and the Allied terms would be rejected by the Germans. Nonetheless, he made one last effort after his re-election.

He neither proposed a conference nor offered mediation. He asked only, on December 18, 1916, that both sides state the terms they would accept as a basis for peace. His request was unfortunately timed for it came within one week of a German suggestion to the Allies for a conference to discuss peace terms. To some observers, the juxtaposition of efforts smacked of collusion but, of course, there was none. In any event, the Germans rejected the Wilsonian opportunity to state their aims. The Allies replied with a statement of their war aim, which was the annihilation of Germany.

Meanwhile, in Berlin, the kaiser and his advisors were reassessing grand strategy. The discussion centered on the submarine and reflected a sharp difference of opinion between the chancellor and the foreign minister on the one side and the military and naval people on the other. The latter supported unleashing the submarine as the only way to beat England even at the risk of American entry. They promised victory in six months. That was all the time needed to cut the British off from all exports and imports. Their opponents opposed the "sink at sight" policy on the grounds that it would bring the United States into the war and that would guarantee Germany's defeat. At all costs, they said, a break with America must be avoided. To the kaiser was left the decision and, on January 9, 1917, he made it. On the 31st, Von Bernstorff was instructed to inform President Wilson that unrestricted submarine warfare in a zone around the British Isles would begin on the next day, February 1.

This time there was to be no "strict accountability" response by the president. One could not undo two years of conflict, controversy, and broken promises. The threat levelled in the *Arabic* and *Sussex* exchanges had to be carried out. Von Bernstorff was handed his passports on February 3, and Ambassador Gerard was recalled from Berlin. Relations between imperial Germany and the United States were severed. That did not, however, mean war. Only an attack on American vessels could push Wilson to that decision.

The days following the rupture of relations were tense and difficult. Within two weeks, two American vessels were sunk by torpedoes but Wilson took no action, perhaps because there was no loss of life. Then on February 25, the British liner *Laconia* went down with three Americans. One day earlier, an event occurred that shook the president and, indeed, the whole nation when it learned of it several days later. The British government placed in Wilson's hands an intercepted instruction from Alfred Zimmerman, German secretary of state for foreign affairs, to his minister in Mexico City to approach the Mexican government with an offer of an alliance in the event of a German-American war. Mexico would be rewarded for her efforts with money and recovery of the territory lost in 1848. Wilson was outraged by what he considered German perfidy although Zimmerman acted entirely within legal and moral limits in seeking aid in the event of war. Believing the Germans capable of even worse conduct, he went before Congress for authority to arm merchant ships. He was determined to protect Americans in the pursuit of their rights, by force if necessary. The House approved, 403–13, on March 1, spurred, probably, by the publication of the Zimmerman telegram on that very day. The Senate, however, adjourned on March 4 without taking action. Eleven senators filibustered the measure so that it never came to a vote. They opposed it because it contained, in addition to the provision for arming merchantmen, authority for the president "to employ any other instrumentalities or methods . . . to protect our ships and our people in their legitimate and peaceful pursuits on the seas." That appeared like too much of a blank check to the legislators.

The president was not to be deterred by what he called "a little group of wilful men representing no opinion but their own." Armed neutrality was his only alternative to war or submission. On his own and by virtue of his constitutional powers as commander-in-chief, he ordered naval gun crews assigned to merchant vessels. That occurred on March 9. On the same day, he called Congress into special session on April 16. Five weeks would be enough, he believed, to test his policy and report its results to the nations' representatives.

But, as Henry Cabot Lodge said, the president "was in the grip of events" and they were pushing him inexorably to war. On March 14, news came of the sinking of an American tanker. Four days later, three American freighters were sent to the bottom with a loss of six lives. On March 21, another vessel was torpedoed, taking seven more Americans to their deaths. Events were catching up with Wilson. He had hoped to avert war; he had wanted only to bring Germany to her senses. He had been resisting the advice of Lansing and others to brand Germany an outlaw. Now, he had to admit failure and defeat. After two years and eight months, neutrality could no longer be maintained. On March 21, he changed the date for the special session of Congress to April 2. The decision for war had been made by the president.

On April 2, he addressed the joint session. "The recent course of the Imperial German Government," he said, is "in fact nothing less than war against the government and people of the United States" and he asked the Congress to accept the "status of belligerent which had been thrust upon us." There was no question as to the response. The chamber shook with loud applause and shouts of support and the vote was a foregone conclusion—in the Senate, on April 4, 82–6; in the House, on April 6, 373–50. And, so, the war came.

BIBLIOGRAPHY

EDWARD H. BUEHRIG, *Woodrow Wilson and the Balance of Power* (1955).
WILTON B. FOWLER, *British-American Relations, 1917–1918: The Role of Sir William Wiseman* (1969).
ROSS GREGORY, *Walter Hines Page* (1970).
N. GORDON LEVIN, *Woodrow Wilson and World Politics* (1968).
ARTHUR S. LINK, *Campaigns for Progressivism and Peace, 1916–1917* (1966).
———, *Confusion and Crisis, 1915–1916* (1964).
———, *The Struggle for Neutrality, 1914–1915* (1960).
ERNEST R. MAY, *The World War and American Isolation, 1914–1917* (1959).
BRADFORD PERKINS, *The Great Rapprochement: England and the United States, 1895–1914* (1968).

Horace C. Peterson, *Propaganda for War: The Campaign Against American Neutrality, 1914–1917* (1939).

Daniel M. Smith, *Robert Lansing and American Neutrality* (1958).

Charles C. Tansill, *America Goes to War* (1938).

*Henry Cabot Lodge (courtesy of the National Portrait Gallery, the
Smithsonian Institution, Washington, D.C.).*

The Lost Peace

LONG before he made the decision for war, President Wilson had been thinking of the nature of the postwar world and his country's role in it. By the time he made the decision to fight, he had already fastened on the kind of peace he thought necessary to avoid a repetition of the bloody conflict and on the means for guaranteeing it. The peace was to be a peace without victory, a just and, therefore, a lasting peace guaranteed by an international league in which America would play a leading part. The development of this great and noble dream may be traced in the numerous speeches he gave in 1916 and 1917 as part of his search to end the war and in the war message itself. He rarely lost an opportunity to expose his ideas and to gauge their reception.

There was, for example, the address on May 27, 1916 before the members of the League to Enforce Peace. "We are," he said, "participants whether we like it or not in the life of the world. The interests of all nations are our own also. We are parties with the rest. What affects mankind is inevitably our affair as well as the affair of the nations of Europe and Asia." He talked also of the elements which constituted a just peace—the rights of all people to choose their sovereign, equal rights for small and large nations, guarantee of territorial integrity. Again, on January 22, 1917, in referring to replies from the belligerents to his requests that they state their war aims, he outlined his own. He repeated his earlier proposals with some notable additions, such as limitation of armaments and direct outlets to the sea for all nations, which taken together, "imply, first of all, that it must be a peace without victory." As for the role of the American people, he solemnly pledged "to add their authority and their power to the authority and force of other nations to guarantee peace and justice throughout the world."

The war message of April 2, as well, contained the same thoughts. Said the president, "Our object . . . is to vindicate the principles of peace and justice in the life of the world as against selfish and autocratic power and to set up amongst the really free and self-governed peoples of the world such a concert of purposes and of action as will henceforth insure the observance of those principles." He called for a "partnership of democratic nations" to maintain "a steadfast concert of peace." Here was his concept of a League of Nations.

The most important statement, however, came on January 8, 1918, after the United States had become a belligerent. It took the form of an address to a joint session of Congress and contained detailed and concrete conditions for a lasting and just peace. "What we demand in this war," said the president, "is nothing peculiar to ourselves. It is that the world be made fit and safe to live in; and particularly for every peace-loving nation which, like our own, wishes to live its own life, determine its own institutions, be assured of justice and fair dealing by the other peoples of the world as against force and selfish aggressors." He then went on to enumerate the conditions for achieving such a world. There were 14 of them, and the document has since been known by that number. The Fourteen Points were: (1) open covenants, openly arrived at; (2) absolute freedom of navigation upon the seas; (3) the removal of all economic barriers and the establishment of an equality of trade conditions among all nations; (4) reduction of armaments; (5) adjustment of colonial claims based upon interests of the population concerned weighed equally with those of the Government whose title is to be determined; (6) evacuation of Russian territory and leaving to the Russians the determination of their own destiny; (7) Belgium to be evacuated and restored; (8) restore Alsace-Lorraine to France; (9) readjustment of Italian frontiers along lines of nationality; (10) autonomy for the peoples of Austria-Hungary; (11) evacuation of Rumania, Serbia, Montenegro; (12) autonomy for nationalities of Ottoman Empire; (13) an independent Poland; (14) formation of a general association of nations.

Wilson's proposals were, at once, spread widely throughout the world in the form of millions of leaflets prepared by the American Committee on Public Information and they made a powerful impression on ally and enemy alike. People everywhere saw hope for a new world, a just, open, democratic, free world to replace the secretive, militarist, despotic, oppressive world. To the Germans facing the prospect of American might tipping the balance against them, the Fourteen Points offered a way to end the war without being crushed by a victorious and vindictive foe. Indeed, it was to Wilson, not to France or to England, whom they appealed in October of 1918 for an armistice based on the Fourteen Points, and such an armistice was signed November 11, 1918, bringing the fighting to an end. But not without cracking Allied solidarity. The flush of enthusiasm generated by the nobility of the ideas in the Fourteen Points had evaporated in the Allied capitals as the leaders contemplated the peace that was to come. Wilson's proposals threatened to stand as a barrier to extracting from the enemy the full fruits of victory. British Prime Minister David Lloyd George and French Premier Georges Clemenceau were not prepared to see four years of sacrifice and anguish capped by a settlement

Lloyd George really wanted Germany to suffer

that would have rendered it vain. They owed it to their people to make the Germans pay and suffer. Wilson's proposals stood, also, in the way of the fulfillment of an intricate network of secret treaties made by the Allies during the war that provided for the distribution among the victors of the territory of the vanquished. Autonomy and self-determination for colonial peoples and for nationalities in the Ottoman and Austro-Hungarian Empires, as envisioned in Points five through thirteen, were incompatible with the Allied plans for dividing the spoils of war. Britain and France were to get land in the Middle East, Japan was to be awarded German colonies in the Pacific and part of China, Italy was to receive large numbers of Slavs and Germans, and Russia was to gain parts of the Turkish Empire in Asia Minor. Those pledges were easily as important to the Allies as Wilson's Points were to him.

Wilson finally got the Allies to accept the Fourteen Points as the basis for the peace negotiations, but only after he threatened to make a separate peace with Germany and only after paying a price. He had to make two concessions. Britain was permitted to "reserve complete freedom of decision" concerning the freedom of the seas and coupled with the evacuation and restoration of enemy-held territory was the understanding that Germany must pay for "all damages done to the civilian population of the Allies." Wilson had made his first compromise; it was not to be his last.

The peace conference was scheduled to meet in Paris in January of 1919, and the president decided to attend in person as head of the American delegation. Although such a move was unprecedented and roundly criticized by many Americans, Wilson believed he alone could get the kind of treaty he thought necessary to insure a peaceful world in the future. To charges that, by leaving Washington he lost touch with American opinion and subjected himself to the passions of the bargaining table, one might reply that only his prestige, personally exercised, could guarantee the fulfillment of his dream of a world organization and prevent a Carthaginian peace. And his prestige and popularity were enormous. They bordered on the divine and people, indeed, compared him to Jesus. His saving mankind from Prussian militarism was considered no less an achievement than Christ's sacrifice on the cross. The adulation and wildly enthusiastic reception he received from crowds on his visits to Rome, Paris, and London before the opening of the conference had been accorded no king, emperor, or hero. If anyone could impose his will on a group of negotiators, Woodrow Wilson at that moment was the one.

His prestige, it must be said, was not quite as high at home as abroad. Several events had eroded it before his departure for Europe on December 4. One, already noted, had been his decision to go to Paris. Another had been an appeal made in October to the American people to return to Congress a majority of Democrats in the forthcoming election. Without such a majority, he had said, he could not remain "your unembarrassed spokesman in affairs at home and abroad." The very plea impaired his integrity for he had, during the war, pledged to "adjourn politics," a pledge the Republicans had honored and were continuing to honor. The president had broken his word. Worse still, his plea was rejected making him something less than even an embarrassed spokesman. Ex-President Theodore Roosevelt warned, "Mr. Wilson has no authority whatever to speak for the American people at this time. His leadership has just been emphatically repudiated by them."

Then, there was the president's choice of the delegation to accompany him to Paris. It was an unwise choice that weakened his authority and led to a questioning of his judgment. It was also to affect adversely his subsequent relations with the Senate and with the Republican leadership there. The delegation consisted of Secretary of State Robert Lansing, Colonel Edward M. House, General Tasker Bliss, and Henry White, a career diplomat. No senator was represented despite the important (and constitutional) role the Senate played in the treaty-making power. Nor was a Republican selected (unless White's nominal membership in the party qualified him), thus inviting political recrimination. Why Wilson should have committed such a grievous and costly error is difficult to understand. Some historians and biographers have ascribed it to arrogance, messianic complex, obstinacy, and witlessness. Whatever the reason, he was to pay heavily for what he had done.

On January 12, 1919, the representatives of twenty-eight nations met to draft the peace treaties that, when signed and ratified, would formally and legally end the great war, a war that had exhausted victor and vanquished alike and whose repercussions would determine the future course of world history. They were to sit until August 20, the time it took to complete the treaties for all the enemy nations—Germany, Austria, Hungary, Bulgaria, and Turkey. Fourteen plenary sessions were held but their work was restricted to ratifying the document prepared by the fifty-two commissions of experts. The real decisions were made, first, by the Council of Ten, the heads of state and the foreign ministers of the United States, France, Italy, Great Britain, and Japan. That group by March was whittled down to a Council of Four consisting of the heads of state of the aforementioned countries minus Japan. Finally, by April it was the Big Three when the Italian leader, unable to get all the territory the secret treaties had promised, left Paris in a huff.

Conspicuously absent from Paris were the Germans and their allies and the Russians. The losers did not share in the deliberations or in the drafting of the treaties. For them, the peace was dictated, not negotiated. When the instruments were completed, they were handed to them. Their choice was to accept them or face a continuation of the war and occupation of their territories and destruction. The Russians, too, had not been invited. They were not, of course, the same Russians who had entered the war in August 1914. They were Bolsheviks who had seized control in November of 1917 from the moderates who, earlier in March had overthrown the czarist monarchy. The Bolshevik leaders, Lenin and Trotsky, had pulled their country out of the war (it was a war for imperialism, they believed, with which they had nothing to do) in December of 1917 and signed a treaty with Germany at Brest-Litovsk on March 3, 1918. Since then, the Russians had been treated like pariahs and traitors. The virus of communism was loathed and feared. Its spread was dreaded and efforts were made to destroy it before it enveloped the west. Allied and American troops had joined forces with anti-Bolshevik elements in Russia in the winter of 1918–1919 at Murmansk and Archangel but without success. The failure to include them in the peace arrangements meant that there was no settlement made for eastern Europe.

The treaty that the Germans saw for the first time on May 7, 1919, was not exactly the kind of treaty Wilson had envisaged. In many respects it violated the spirit and the letter of the Fourteen Points. There was nothing in it about the freedom of the seas or the removal of economic barriers among nations. The matter of the reduction of armaments was left to a future conference (the treaty provided specifically, and in detail, for the reduction of armaments for the defeated powers only). The principle of self-determination was twisted out of shape when the Japanese retained Shantung and its millions of Chinese and Italy received the Tyrol and its Austrians. Above all, the reparations issue struck a blow at the Wilsonian concept of a just peace. Points six to thirteen, dealing with the evacuation and restoration of enemy-held territory, were understood to mean that Germany would be held responsible, monetarily, only for damage to the civilian population and their property, and Wilson had, on February 17, 1918 told Congress there would be "no punitive damages." Yet, at the Conference, the Allied leaders demanded payment for all war costs. Punishment was the key. Make them pay "until the pips squeak" said one British official.

Wilson was appalled at the inconsistency with "what we deliberately led the enemy to expect." He finally succeeded in scaling the demands to liability for veterans' pensions in addition to damages to property. The sum was fixed at $33 billion by a commission that met in 1921. The Germans were bitter and felt betrayed not only because the armistice agreement had been violated but also because they were denied the means for paying. They lost all their colonies, their merchant fleet, their property in Allied countries, the coal mines in the Saar region, and many of their sources of raw materials. Then there was Article 231 of the treaty that placed sole responsibility upon Germany for causing the war—"the war imposed upon them [the Allies] by the aggression of Germany and her allies." This "war guilt" clause was soon to be revealed as completely false as historians combed the archives of the nations and found culpability for the coming of the war to have been shared by all the powers. But it stuck in the German conscience and was to be a source of Hitler's strength one day.

There was, to be sure, much that was good about the treaty. Secret diplomacy was tendered a stunning blow by the provision that all treaties must henceforth be registered with an international body and those not so registered would have no force. The mandate system was a reasonable and fair means of settling the colonial question. Former enemy colonies were placed under control (mandates) of each of the several powers with the idea they would eventually become independent when they reached the capacity for self-rule. It was a decent compromise between granting immediate independence and turning them over as outright possessions to the victors. As for the principle of national self-determination, it must be said that in the treaty, it was more honored in the observance than in the breach. There was the creation of Poland, Czechoslovakia, and Yugoslavia, the refusal to turn over large numbers of Slavs in the Fiume area to Italy, and the resistance to French demands for a buffer state east of the Rhine. Winston Churchill's estimate that fewer than 3 per cent of the people of Europe were condemned to live under governments whose nationality they repudiated seems a fair one and is a measure of Wilson's success at Paris. The president, himself, seemed satisfied with the results. "We have made a better peace," he remarked, "than I should have expected when I came here to Paris."

For the president, the greatest victory he achieved at the Conference was in turning his dream for an association of nations into the reality of a League of Nations riveted in the treaty. Its constitution or covenant, as it was called, became the first 26 articles of the treaty. It was to be, in Wilson's vision, the instrument for righting all wrongs, and repairing all injustices, and for overseeing the future course of international affairs. It was the vehicle by which the United States would participate in maintaining the peace. It had been his handiwork. He had pushed for it; he himself had headed the commission that had drafted it, and he had made compromises at the conference to assure its acceptance by the powers. He had, now, only to have it approved by his own countrymen.

The drafting of the covenant was completed on February 14, 1919. The next day, Wilson sailed for home to sign some bills passed by Congress in his absence and to acquaint Americans with the epoch-making document. Before leaving Paris, he cabled all the representatives and senators on the committees dealing with foreign affairs to dine with him on the 26th to talk about the treaty. He asked them, also, not to discuss the covenant publicly until after the dinner meeting. The president touched American soil at Boston and promptly made a speech explaining and lauding the League. It was a foolish and tactless thing to do and only played into the hands of his enemies and of the enemies of the treaty and of the covenant, whose numbers were mounting. Two days after Wilson spoke in Boston, Henry Cabot Lodge, Republican Senator from Massachusetts, gave a public address in which he warned against entangling alliances and urged retaining freedom of action for the United States. Clearly, the League was in trouble in America. Indeed, one might date the Battle of the Ratification of the Treaty and of the Covenant from this Lodge-Wilson exchange. They were to become the two great antagonists in that battle. On February 26, the meeting called by Wilson took place at the White House. It did not bode well for the president. He made no favorable impression upon his guests. One Republican senator left the dinner with the impression he had been "wandering with Alice in Wonderland and having tea with the Mad Hatter."

The Sixty-fifth Congress was due to expire on March 3, 1919. Late that day Senator Lodge fired the first salvo in the Battle of the Ratification. It took the form of a resolution read to his senatorial colleagues: "That the constitution of the League of Nations in the form now proposed . . . should not be accepted by the United States. . . ." He suggested that consideration of the League of Nations be set aside until after the treaty had been disposed of. Thirty-six other Republicans joined in the "round robin" (with two more adhering the following day). This opening gun in the campaign to defeat the League was a mighty one and gave Lodge a decided edge. The president joined the battle the next day in a speech in New York in which he proclaimed the covenant and the treaty inseparable and indivisible. The country could not have one without the other. Rejection of the League meant no peace treaty.

That same day, too, Wilson left for Paris to continue working on the treaty. He also would seek some modification of the League Covenant for some of its supporters warned him that as it stood it had no chance. Certain safeguards would have to be added if it was to have any chance in the Senate. Four changes were made—no member need accept a mandate; all domestic affairs were excluded from the League's jurisdiction; regional understandings, such as the Monroe Doctrine, were not to be impaired; any member may withdraw after two years' notice. Those qualifications, the president hoped, would assuage the opposition. He remained in Paris until the German treaty was completed and signed, leaving for home on June 28, 1919. Immediately upon his return, he sent the treaty, with the covenant of the League of Nations imbedded in it, to the Senate for its "advice and consent." In the accompanying message, the president urged favorable action. "The stage is set, the destiny disclosed," he said, "we can only go forward with lifted eyes and freshened spirits to follow the vision." He was confident that the Senate had no choice but to approve. To a reporter who asked him whether he thought the treaty could be ratified with certain reservations, the president said, "I do not think hypothetical questions are involved. The Senate is going to ratify the treaty."

The Senate, which received the treaty on July 10, had been in session since May 19, the opening day of the Sixty-sixth Congress. With the Republicans in the majority, Henry Cabot Lodge became chairman of the Foreign Relations Committee whose crucial function it was to recommend to the full Senate acceptance or rejection of the treaty. Of his seventeen colleagues on the committee, ten were Republicans and six of them were irreconcilably and irrevocably opposed to American participation in the League. Most prominent among them were William E. Borah of Idaho, Philander Chase Knox of Pennsylvania, and Hiram Johnson of California. They, together with eleven other senators (including one Democrat, James Reed of Missouri) who were unalterably opposed to the League were labelled, aptly "Bitter Enders," "Battalion of Death," and "Irreconcilables."

The basis for their position was their view that the League was a superstate and membership in it would deprive the United States of freedom of action. As Borah wrote to a constituent, "there is too much red blood in your system to subscribe to this treacherous unAmerican scheme. . . . The white-livered cowards who are standing around while the diplomats of Europe are undermining our whole system of *independence* and self-control will have no hearing when the American people come to know the facts." He, and the others saw in Article X of the covenant the trap that would, in Borah's words, send "our boys to fight throughout the world by order of the League." That article stated that "the members of the League undertake to respect and preserve as against external aggression the territorial integrity and existing political independence of all Members of the League." They considered themselves true nationalists and, in support of their position, invoked the hallowed names of Washington, Jefferson, and Monroe and their warnings to avoid involvement in Europe's "woes and broils."

The remainder of the Senate may be divided into three groups on the question of the League: those who favored approval of the Covenant as it stood; those who favored approval with mild reservations; those who favored approval with strong reservations. Henry Cabot Lodge put himself in the last camp. He claimed to be as much a nationalist as Borah, but he stated his belief that strong and specific reservations to the Covenant would protect America's freedom of action and still permit participation in the League for whatever good it might accomplish. Judging, however, by his words and actions, it seems more reasonable to conclude that his real aim was to defeat the treaty and to defeat it because it was the instrument and the achievement of his archfoe, Woodrow Wilson.

His animosity and hostility toward Wilson were unconcealed, intense, and of long standing. It dated back at least to 1914 and surfaced during the Mexican crisis. He thought Wilson's desire to oust Huerta was rooted in the president's colossal egotism. Referring to a speech Wilson made in 1915, Lodge wrote, "the whole speech was not only angry but cheap and the natural cheapness of the man has come out. I live in the hope that he will be found out by the people of the United States for what he really is." The feud broke out in public over the *Lusitania* sinking when Lodge accused Wilson of withholding vital information related to the incident and Wilson replied, not very candidly, and virtually called Lodge a liar. They clashed, too, on Wilson's neutrality policy. Lodge considered it not sufficiently helpful to the Allies. To his friend and fellow-Republican, Theodore Roosevelt, he wrote, "I do not wonder that you feel warlike with this administration. I never expected to hate anyone in politics with the hatred I feel towards Wilson." And when the president, finally, asked for war against Germany, Lodge was not moved. Again to Roosevelt he wrote, "He is a mean soul and the fact that he delivered a good message does not alter his character. . . . The man has changed his policy but the policy has not changed the man." In his account of *The Senate and the League of Nations*, published in 1925, Lodge gave his measured estimate of his opponent, dead by that time: ". . . Mr. Wilson in dealing with every great question thought first of himself. He may have thought of the country next, but there was a long interval, ... Mr. Wilson was devoured by the desire for power."

What motivated Lodge's passionate hatred of Wilson is difficult to determine precisely. Much of it was personal. Lodge thought himself the better man and better suited to occupy the presidency in time of crisis. A Ph.D. and LL.B. from Harvard, descendant of great Boston families, author of numerous biographies of great Americans, Lodge had been the undisputed scholar in politics until Wilson, a Hopkins Ph.D. and a Princetonian, came on the scene to crowd Lodge off his pedestal. Once referring to the League Covenant, Lodge sneeringly remarked, "It might get by at Princeton but certainly not at Harvard." He made no secret of the fact that he thought Wilson the worst president of the United States with the exception of Buchanan.

Lodge would have preferred to see the treaty defeated at once but he did not think it could be done, he told Borah, because of the large amount of public support for the treaty and for the Covenant. And he was right. Support was great. Thirty-two state legislatures and thirty-three governors had endorsed the League. A *Literary Digest* poll found the majority of America's newspapers in favor and Lodge, himself, admitted that all the newspapers in his state were for it. One of the "Irreconcilables," Senator George H. Moses of New Hampshire, reflecting some years later on the matter, recalled his opinion that had a vote been taken in the Senate immediately, the treaty would have been approved. Lodge's tactic, therefore, was to kill the treaty by two devices, delay and amendments. Delay he considered important for two reasons: first, postponement of a vote would tend to diminish public support as the people became more involved in the domestic problems then gripping the nation such as inflation, strikes, race riots, and the menace of Bolshevism and as they became more disillusioned with idealism and world-saving missions; second, the many opponents of the Covenant and of the treaty would become better organized. And there was considerable opposition from liberals who thought the treaty too harsh and objected to Article X as a device for freezing the status quo; from socialists who considered the settlement a triumph of capitalism; from conservatives who believed the Covenant destroyed their country's independence; from Irish-Americans who resented the failure to free Ireland from British rule; from German-Americans who thought their Fatherland had been betrayed; and from various immigrant groups who protested the boundary settlements.

As for amendments or reservations attached to the treaty, Lodge felt he had nothing to lose by that device. If Wilson accepted the treaty with reservations, he and the Republicans would be given much of the credit by the League's supporters, many of whom preferred some reservations; if the president took the opposite course, the onus would fall on him, and Lodge would emerge as the selfless man who tried to save the League by moderate compromise. But he believed Wilson would not accept the amendments. When Senator James Watson suggested that Wilson might accept the amendments, Lodge replied, "But, my dear James, you do not take into consideration the hatred that Woodrow Wilson has for me personally. Never under any set of circumstances in this world could he be induced to accept a treaty with Lodge reservations appended to it." He was, of course, tragically right.

Four days after the treaty reached the Senate chamber and after its referral to the Foreign Relations Committee, Lodge, as chairman, acted on it. Although copies were readily available (and had been since May when Senator Borah got hold of a copy from a Chicago *Tribune* reporter and placed it in the *Congressional Record*), Lodge read all 246 pages of the treaty aloud. That took two weeks. Next, he conducted a public hearing. Beginning July 31, 60 witnesses testified before his committee. Some of them were important participants in the proceeding; many were, however, peripheral. That took six weeks. So much for delay.

While the hearings were in progress, Wilson made a move that turned out to be disastrous. Aware of Lodge's tactics and fearful of their consequences and made uneasy by a visit of the Foreign Relations Committee to the White House on August 19, during which visit the committee questioned him for three hours, Wilson decided to take his case to the people. He would stir up a great groundswell in favor of the treaty and the Covenant that neither Lodge nor the other senators could ignore. He planned a speaking tour of the country to last about one month. It was to be a fatal mistake and end abruptly in his collapse, which made impossible his facing the crucial test of the treaty—the vote in the Senate. He started out on September 3 and moved westward. In twenty-two days his train covered 8,000 miles and made twenty-nine stops. He delivered thirty-two major and eight minor speeches. Sixty-three years of age, in poor health, exhausted by transatlantic crossings and interminable bargaining in Paris, his collapse in Pueblo, Colorado on September 25 was not unexpected. His train hurriedly returned to Washington where he underwent a stroke, cerebral thrombosis, on October 2. For seven-and-one-half months after that, he was helpless, paralyzed on the left side of his face and his speech thickened. His mind was unimpaired and alert but his ability to conduct the affairs of state was impaired. He could communicate only in writing; he held no cabinet meetings. His wife acted as the conduit between her husband and the world outside.

Whether the president had accomplished his mission is open to question. His earnestness and sincerity, his lofty ideas, his impressive rhetoric had moved crowds, but many of his audiences had been equally receptive to Borah and Johnson who had followed Wilson closely wherever he stopped. The real test was in how the Senate voted.

Lodge was ready for a vote by September 10 when the Foreign Relations Committee placed the treaty on the floor of the Senate. To it was attached forty-five amendments and 4 reservations. There was no question of the Senate rejecting so cumbersome and involved a document. The treaty went back to the Committee, emerging on November 6 with fourteen reservations. On the 19th, it came to a vote and failed to command a two-thirds majority. Thirty-nine senators—four Democrats and thirty-five Republicans—voted "aye"; fifty-five voted "no"—forty-two Democrats and thirteen Republicans (the "Bitter Enders"). A second vote on the treaty *without* the reservations, the same day, resulted in a very similar count— thirty-eight for, fifty-three against.

So the treaty with the covenant imbedded in it failed in the Senate, but that was not the end of the story. Important people inside and outside the government demanded another try. Men like William Jennings Bryan, ex-President William H. Taft, Colonel Edward M. House, and Joseph P. Tumulty, Wilson's private secretary, would not accept the defeat of the treaty as final. They, and large numbers of newspaper editors, churchmen, academics, and ordinary citizens saw America's entry into the League as necessary to insure a peaceful future. So another effort was made, a final one, on March 19, 1920. This time fifteen reservations were attached— Lodge's fourteen plus one more, providing for the independence of Ireland. The treaty, again, failed by seven votes to receive the necessary two-thirds majority. There were 49 votes for (twenty-eight Republicans and twenty-one Democrats) and thirty-five opposed (twelve Republicans and twenty-three Democrats).

A close analysis of the vote reveals that of the forty Republicans who voted, twenty-eight loyally supported Lodge and his reservations, and twelve would have nothing to do with the treaty, reservations or no. They were the "Irreconcilables." Of the forty-four Democrats, twenty-one stood with the treaty and the reservations because they believed *a* treaty with reservations was better than *none* while twenty-three Democrats accepted Wilson's view that no treaty was more desirable than a treaty with reservations. It was well known that almost all of the twenty-three would have preferred joining their fellow-Democrats in voting "aye" but remained loyal to their party chief who had exerted extreme pressure on the Democratic senators to defeat the treaty with the Lodge reservations. The decisive element, therefore, seems to be Wilson's refusal to accept the Lodge reservations.

Why did Wilson refuse to accept the reservations? Did they make all that difference? Did they alter the treaty significantly? The answer, after a careful examination of the reservations by competent observers, must be a decided "no." David Hunter Miller, an expert at the peace conference and author of its multivolume history, declared: "As far as the Lodge reservations made changes in the League, they were of a wholly minor character and they would have interfered with its workings not at all." And Herbert Hoover noted, "The reservations do not seem to me to imperil the great principle of the League of Nations to prevent war." Borah thought them "immaterial and irrelevant." Lodge, himself, used the term "It goes without saying" when pressed as to the meaning of the reservations. Even the president could make no great case against the reservations significantly impairing the League's function and purpose. Indeed, at one point, he gave Senator Hitchcock, the minority leader, four reservations to be used as he saw fit and they were virtually identical with Lodge's chief four. Everything points to the fact that, as one historian noted, the reservations were repetitious of what was in the Covenant or in the American constitution.

Did Wilson reject the reservations because he thought the other members of the League would not accept the United States under special conditions? Hardly! It was no secret that America's presence in the League was desperately desired. The view was universal that only her presence would guarantee the League's success. The United States would have been accepted under any conditions. Wilson, himself, explained to his wife his refusal to accept the treaty with the reservations in terms of his obligations to the other signatories. "Can't you see," he said, "that I have no moral right to accept any change in a paper I have signed without giving every other signatory, even the Germans, the right to do the same thing? It is not that I will not accept; it is the Nation's honor that is at stake." Such reasoning, however, does not seem sound or honest for Wilson knew well that the other signatories would not have demanded equal privileges as the price of American acceptance of the treaty.

It seems that the real and fundamental reasons for Wilson's refusal to accept the Lodge reservations must be sought in his qualities of character and personality and in his loathing for Lodge. His revulsion for the Senator from Massachusetts was immense. He viewed him as the principal obstacle to the achievement of his dream. "Accept a treaty with Lodge's reservations?" he said to Senator James Watson, "Never, never. I'll never consent to adopt any policy with which that impossible man is so prominently identified." Does that mean Wilson would have consented to changes sponsored by anyone other than his hated enemy? Unlikely. It was not in his character to compromise. Once before, years earlier, when president of Princeton University he had accepted defeat rather than compromise on a major issue. Obstinate, arrogant, a firm believer in his righteousness, he had to prevail. Supremely egotistical and confident in his own creation, he would brook no modification of his handiwork. "I will consent to nothing," he told French Ambassador Jules Jusserand, "The Senate must take its medicine." He had a propensity for shutting out that which was unpleasant and hence could ignore the realities of the facts surrounding the defeat of the treaty in the Senate. When informed by his wife that the treaty had been voted down, he replied, "All the more reason I must get well and try again to bring this country to a sense of its great opportunity and greater responsibility."

It was tragic and ironic that the creator of the League of Nations, whose fondest wish was that his country become a member, should have been most responsible for keeping his country out. The responsibility, in the final analysis, was his for demanding that the Democratic senators vote against it with the reservations. One of those Democratic senators who refused to obey his chief's instructions, Henry F. Ashurst of Arizona, aptly summed up the judgment of history. "As a friend of the President, as one who has loyally followed him, I solemnly declare to him this morning: if you want to kill your own child because the Senate straightens out its crooked limbs, you must take the responsibility and accept the verdict of history." The final word may well have been said by that shrewd and astute observer of men and morals, William Allen White, famed Kansas editor, in his *On Wilson the Man*: "Tommy Wilson [his given name was Thomas] threw down his bat and left the field. . . . If Tommy had only learned to stand and fight and fail and fight again." Wilson died, broken in heart, spirit, and body in 1924 in his house on S Street in Washington.

BIBLIOGRAPHY

THOMAS A. BAILEY, *Wilson and the Peacemakers* (1947).
RUHL J. BARTLETT, *The League to Enforce Peace* (1944).
PAUL BIRDSALL, *Versailles Twenty Years After* (1941).
JOHN A. GARRATY, *Henry Cabot Lodge* (1953).
LAWRENCE E. GELFAND, *The Inquiry: American Preparations for Peace, 1917–1919* (1936).
HERBERT HOOVER, *The Ordeal of Woodrow Wilson* (1958).
J. M. KEYNES, *The Economic Consequences of the Peace* (1920).
ARNO MAYER, *Wilson and Lenin: Political Origins of the New Diplomacy* (1964).
———, *Politics and Diplomacy of Peacemaking: Containment and Counter-revolution at Versailles, 1918–1919* (1967).
RALPH A. STONE, *The Irreconcilables: The Fight Against the League of Nations* (1970).
SETH TILLMAN, *Anglo-American Relations at the Paris Peace Conference of 1919* (1961).
DAVID TRASK, *The United States in the Supreme War Council* (1961).

Aristide Briand (U.S. Information Agency photo, the National Archives).

The Twenties: In Europe

WRITING to Secretary of State Charles Evans Hughes in March of 1923, John Bassett Moore, the distinguished international jurist and legal scholar, decried the use by certain newspaper editors of "isolation" to describe American foreign policy. "There has never been," he said, "a more shallow absurdity than the talk of the 'isolation' of the United States." He was, of course, correct. Far from being isolated, withdrawn, and apart from the rest of the world, the United States was very much a part of it, constantly "extending commercial and other nonpolitical activities." American products and investment capital went to every corner of the globe, hundreds of thousands of Americans travelled to every continent, and the United States government participated in a multitude of international conferences of every kind. As Edwin L. James of the *New York Times* noted in 1930, "there was no zone where American interests were not involved and where American influence was not felt."

In the same letter, Judge Moore offered his own description of the foreign policy of the United States as "holding aloof from foreign and from particularly European political alliances and intrigues." Again, he was correct for American policy after the First World War and, indeed, right up to 1940, was characterized by nonparticipation in international political affairs, refusals to make advanced commitments of force, and abstention from becoming a party to alliances and alignments. The great rule of conduct was, to use Senator William E. Borah's words, retention of "freedom to do as our people think wise and just; . . . the unembarrassed and unentangled freedom of a great Nation to determine for itself and in its own way where duty lies and where wisdom calls." Secretary of State Hughes gave it official sanction in an address in November of 1923. "We are, as in the days of George Washington, opposed to alliances and to commitments in advance of United States power in unknown contingencies," he said. At the same time, he pledged his country's cooperation in humanitarian matters and in projects to further peace and justice.

There is no doubt that the policy had the support of the vast majority of the American people—labor and capital, liberals and conservatives, farmers, the churches, and the professions. Nor is there any doubt that the policy had its roots in the bitterness, the disillusionment, and the disenchantment with the Great Crusade. It all started when Americans read in their newspapers of the sordid squabbling by the victors at the peace conference for the spoils of war. All of them, with the exception of the United States, vied for the greatest share of the colonies, fleets, and other assets of the losers. Americans learned, too, of secret treaties and agreements made by their allies during the war to partition the empires of the defeated nations among themselves. Poor innocent Americans! They thought they had fought for democracy and self-determination only to discover they had been in a contest for imperialism and aggrandizement. Their Allies sounded no different from the Germans. As the eminent theologian, Reinhold Niebuhr, exclaimed in 1923, "How can we believe in anything again—when we compare the solemn pretentions of statesmen with the secret treaties. The war was simply a contest between two alliances." And Senator George W. Norris of Nebraska was appalled at the dishonesty of the Allied statesmen. "No man," he said, "had more honest and beautiful intentions than I had when the peace conference met at Versailles. . . . I believed that our allies were honest and honorable . . . square . . . and fair." But when "they pulled out those secret treaties at the peace table . . . demanding that those secret treaties be legalized, . . . after proclaiming to us and after we believed you were in earnest and fighting for democracy. . . ." He was determined to have no further dealing with them.

There was yet another awakening when, in January of 1918, the Bolsheviks opened the Russian czarist archives to lay bare the machinations of the capitalist nations in the prewar years. The documents gave evidence of the complicity of the Russian, French, British, and other Allied leaders in bringing on the war. They told a tale of cynical statesmen eager to promote a war to gain more raw materials, more markets, more prestige, more oil, more control over native races. They revealed encouragement of one by the other to provoke Germany and Austria to fight. Soon, there followed a spate of memoirs and recollections by the participants calculated to throw the onus on their opposite numbers and relieve themselves of blame. From the avalanche of revelations, historians and publicists began to reconstruct accounts of the coming of the war completely at variance with what Americans had been told in the prewar years by Allied propagandists and by their own leaders during their belligerency. They had been told that only the Germans were guilty; that only the Germans

Frank B. Kellogg (Experiment Stations photo, the National Archives).

were fighting for gain and profit; that the Allies were forced to fight to protect and defend democracy and freedom against the barbaric Huns. Now they learned, by way of luminous and scholarly articles and books (Sidney B. Fay and Harry Elmer Barnes) and more popular journalistic accounts (Philip Gibbs and John K. Turner) that the Allies were as guilty as the Germans and that their idealism was a hoax. Where was the cause in whose righteousness they had believed? The Great Crusade turned out to have been neither great nor a crusade but just another old-fashioned traditional war. Americans felt duped, sucked in.

Historian Harry Elmer Barnes, whose *Genesis of the War* (1928) made the Germans out to be the victims and the Allies the aggressors, caught superbly the feelings of his countrymen when he wrote, "If we can but understand how totally and terribly we were taken in between 1914 and 1918 by the salesmen of this most holy and idealistic world conflict, we shall be the better prepared to be on our guard against the seductive lies and deceptions that will be put forward by similar groups when urging the necessity of another world catastrophe in order to crush militarism, make the world safe for democracy, put an end to all further wars, etc." Little wonder that Americans faced the 1920s determined that they would not again get themselves involved in "Europe's miseries and Europe's woes." No more saving worlds for them.

In view of the American temper, United States policy toward the League of Nations was wholly predictable. President Warren G. Harding, interpreting his landslide victory in 1920 as a mandate to reject Wilsonism, firmly and unequivocally announced in his first message to Congress that his Administration "definitely and decisively puts aside all thoughts of entering the League. It does not propose to enter now by the side door, back door, or cellar door." George Harvey, wealthy publisher, powerful Republican leader, archcritic of Woodrow Wilson and his ideals, and ambassador to Great Britain, made certain the message got to Europe. In his first address upon arriving in London, he declared, "The United States will not have anything to do with the League or with any commission or committee appointed by it or responsible to it, directly or indirectly, openly or furtively."

For the first six months of its life, the Harding administration kept its word and completely ignored the League. Correspondence from the secretariat in Geneva remained unanswered. A registered letter sent in September 1921 that demanded a receipt forced Secretary of State Hughes's hand. He acknowledged the letter and replied to all the communications received up to that time, albeit perfunctorily. There was no softening of America's stand, however. Hughes refused to transmit invitations from Geneva to American judges of The Hague Court to nominate justices for the new World Court and when one of them, Elihu Root, received a personal inquiry, Hughes advised him to take no part in the proceedings. He refused to permit an American to sit on the Mandates Commission and rejected all offers to send unofficial observers to League conferences dealing with nonpolitical matters such as suppression of the opium traffic and of white slavery. Further, he threatened to bolt the International Office of Public Hygiene if it merged with the League's Health Bureau and to withdraw from the International Convention on Opium if the Dutch government, which administered it, turned it over to the League.

Many Americans were quite distressed by the Administration's treatment of the League. One of them, Raymond Fosdick, reflected a widespread view at the end of 1921 when he wrote that it was "characterized by indirection, deliberate obstructiveness, and bad manners." He called it "a discreditable page in America's diplomatic record," and went on to say "It is all very well for Mr. Hughes to say that we are not a member of the League of Nations and that he has no authority to act as if we were. The point is whether in spite of our nonmembership we must stand like children twittering in a corner and making faces at the League." The pressure from prominent Republicans not in politics—Nicholas Murray Butler, Henry L. Stimson, Elihu Root, Abbott Lawrence Lowell, Herbert Hoover, for example—was enough to cause a change in the Administration's position but not as great a change as to upset the "Bitter Enders" in the party. "New Attitude Toward League," noted the *Literary Digest* in September 1922. The change was slight, from hostility to tolerance, but significant. The president noted it in February of 1923 with the observation, "I have no unseemly comment to offer on the League. If it is serving the Old World hopefully, more power to it. But it is not for us." Nonetheless, the way had been opened for some form of participation.

Soon, Washington was designating "consultative observers" to sit on League commissions and attend League conferences. They were "official representatives acting in an unofficial capacity," according to Hughes. In 1924, the first official delegates acting in an official capacity were representing the United States at certain League-sponsored conferences, and the American consul in Geneva was seen daily in the corridors in the League buildings, a situation which would have been inconceivable one year before. The American minister in Switzerland was in frequent communication with the Secretariat and openly received copies of all notices sent member states. It was a far cry from the earlier days when Joseph Grew, then minister to Switzerland, was in a panic after having run into a *Chicago Tribune* reporter while in the company of a League official. He had asked the reporter not to send news of the encounter to the paper lest "it embarrass me greatly." And he "felt pretty uneasy during the next few days."

Lest anyone get the impression that the United States was moving toward membership, Harding's successor, Calvin Coolidge, quickly dispelled the notion. Said the president in his first annual message, "Our country has definitely refused to adopt and ratify the covenant of the League of Nations. I am not proposing any change in this policy nor is the Senate. The incident, so far as we are concerned, is closed." Yet the scale of involvement grew and was becoming commonplace and useful. By 1928 the Republican party platform could boast of the extent of co-operation with the League and not send shivers down any spines except those of die-hards such as the *Chicago Tribune* owners and some of the "Irreconcilables" of 1919. In 1930 the United States came as close as possible to having diplomatic relations with the League short of joining when a career foreign service officer, Prentiss Gilbert, chief of the Western European Division in the State Department, was appointed consul in Geneva and charged specifically with coordination with the League. Five vice-consuls were designated to devote full time to the League. In that year, President Hoover could report, "We are glad to cooperate with the League in its endeavor to further scientific, economic, and social welfare and to secure limitation of armaments." While he spoke, Americans were sitting on nine committees: opium, arms traffic, slavery, transit and communications, import and export regulations, double taxation, counterfeiting, disarmament, and codification of international law.

So far so good. But what of cooperation in political affairs where it really mattered? The great test came in the fall of 1931 on the occasion of the Japanese invasion of Manchuria. The League council convened in October to consider measures to be taken in this first instance of warfare since 1918. The United States was, of course, deeply affected by the Japanese move for it not only threatened the concept of the Open Door but, also, violated a network of treaties to which the United States was a party. The whole world waited and watched and wondered. What would the United States do? Great expectations for concerted action arose when Prentiss Gilbert was authorized to accept an invitation to sit in at the Council meeting in Geneva. Those expectations, however, came to naught. America's participation was shortlived. Gilbert was quickly pulled out and when the Council reconvened in Paris in November, the American ambassador to Great Britain, Charles G. Dawes, was ordered to the French capital to keep abreast of the deliberations but not to join the Council. Thereafter, the United States acted independently of the League, by-passing it and dealing directly with Japan. There really should not have been much hope of United States cooperation on so political an affair. It should not have been expected that Americans would have forgotten their experience in the so-called and discredited Great Crusade even after more than a decade. The policy of noninvolvement in international political affairs remained firm.

American policy toward the Permanent Court of International Justice (the World Court) created by Article XIV of the League Covenant illustrates the theme of the decade. Just such a tribunal had for many years been a dream of American jurists and statesmen who prided themselves on their support of the resolution of international differences by adjudication and arbitration. At each of The Hague Conferences, in 1899 and 1907, Americans submitted plans for the creation of a court of justice to serve the nations. The League's Court seemed a fulfillment of the American quest. Not unreasonably, President Harding, in February of 1923, proposed to the Senate that the United States join the Court with the understanding, of course, that that step would, in no way, involve American membership in the League. Such a distinction was entirely feasible since the Court was a completely separate and independent institution. The "Irreconcilables," however, would not accept the distinction. They feared it as a subterfuge to drag the country into the League by indirection and they successfully kept the measure bottled up in the Foreign Relations Committee for three years. When it finally emerged in January of 1926, it carried five reservations and two understandings. Thus loaded with safeguards and qualifications touching such matters as withdrawal, expenditures, the Monroe Doctrine, and League relations, it was ready for a vote. In the debate preceding the ballot, the old "Bitter Enders" raised up all the bogeys and skeletons reminiscent of the course of the Treaty in the Senate years earlier. Apropos of the matter of the separation of the League from the Court and the reservations, Senator Hiram Johnson who categorically opposed membership observed, mockingly, "We are wholly out of the League. We are in part of the League. By reservations we are out of the part of the League we are in. The part of the League we are in, and from which by reservations we get out, functions as a part of the League with our assistance.

Despite the scorn and cynicism of the Old Guard, the treaty passed the Senate on January 27, 1926, 76–17 but the other member nations would not accept the United States with the fifth reservation. It was an extraordinarily self-centered one and rightly rejected. It said that the Court would not "without the consent of the United States, entertain any requests for an advisory opinion touching any dispute or question in which the United States has or claims an interest." Aptly, an American described the Senate's conditions for joining as providing the United States with "a bottle of disinfectant and a portable fire escape."

In December of 1930, President Hoover tried once more to push a treaty for membership through the Senate this time with some changes worked out by Elihu Root and agreed to by the other signatories. Once again, the Foreign Relations Committee, pigeonholed it, this time for four years. At President Franklin D. Roosevelt's insistance, it was sent to the floor of the Senate, where on January 29, 1935 it failed by seven votes to get the Senate's approval. Senator Johnson was jubilant. "The Senate," he proclaimed, "has averted a serious danger to our beloved Republic." In that judgment, he was joined by other ultranationalists—Borah, Huey Long, Father Coughlin, Robert McCormick, William Randolph Hearst— all of whom had worked assiduously to defeat the measure.

As the American policy toward the World Court and the League mirrored the temper of the twenties so did the American position regarding the limitation of armaments, a key movement in that decade. Agitation to reduce armaments began even while the war was being fought. Proposals came from all quarters but the most important was Point 4 of Wilson's Fourteen Points that provided the blueprint. It stated that "Adequate guarantees will be given and taken that national armaments will be reduced to the lowest point consistent with domestic safety." Therein lay one of the chief stumbling blocks facing successive disarmament conferences. Who was to judge the needs of "domestic safety?" One nation's defense needs might appear as menacing to another. There were other problems. Measuring and regulating guns, tanks, ships, planes and other "visible" weapons was relatively simple but how assess "invisible" weapons—the mathematician working on a range finder or bombsight, the chemist occupied with poison gas and explosives, the biologist searching for germs and bacteria? The question, "what is a soldier" also presented difficulty. France, for example, refused to consider reserves in counting soldiers. Hence, a million-man French army, by that standard, might mean, in reality, many more millions made up of highly trained and ready reservists. Then there was the differing approaches to limiting naval vessels. France wished each nation to be allotted a total tonnage with freedom to build any type and number of ships up to the allowable tonnage. Other nations supported limitation by category of vessel; that is, maximum tonnage would be set for each type of ship separately.

Finally, there was the crucial division between an American and a European viewpoint on the relationship between disarmament and security. For Europeans, security had to precede disarmament; that is, no European nation would be willing to reduce its armament unless it received a guarantee of military aid in the event of attack. As put by a Belgian foreign minister, "Give us an assurance of safety and we Belgians will gladly dismiss our soldiers." And as a French official noted, "If we could get an understanding in the event of an attack on us, it would be quite simple to work out questions of armaments."

The United States, on the other hand, maintained that disarmament would lead to security. The chief proponent of that idea, Senator William E. Borah, summed up the position neatly in a speech in September 1921. "Disarmament alone," he said, "promises relief from wars; armaments cause wars; an armed world is a fighting world; arms competition engenders hatred, suspicion, and, finally war; disarmament will make political settlement easier."

The sources of Borah's position are not difficult to determine. Acceptance of the European contention would have demanded an American commitment to spring to the defense of a nation attacked. And that was the one thing the political leaders and the American people had rejected in the 1920s.

Part V of the Treaty of Versailles had provided for limiting, drastically, the armament of the vanquished powers. It was left for a future conference to consider the reduction of the armies and navies of the victors. Borah lost no time in calling such an international meeting. He was disturbed by what appeared to be a three-way naval race in the making among Japan, England, and the United States. The crushing financial burden and the danger to peace of the naval increase led him to propose in December of 1920 that the three powers convene to discuss the reduction of naval armaments. Congress approved the idea overwhelmingly, 74–0 in the Senate and 332–4 in the House, in June of 1921, and within two weeks invitations went out from Washington. Symbolically, the conference opened on November 11—three years after the last shot in the great war had been fired.

Nine nations gathered in Washington—United States, Great Britain, Japan, France, Holland, Portugal, Belgium, China, Italy. Only five had navies worth limiting. The other four were present to discuss political questions relating to the Far East, placed on the agenda at Britain's request. That the United States accepted the British suggestion was a tacit admission of the necessity of considering political-security matters alongside of disarmament. Indeed, the United States was to insist at the conference that certain security arrangements be made before accepting cuts in armaments.

Secretary of State Charles Evans Hughes, as chairman and host of the conference, gave the opening address. It was, as tradition and propriety dictated, a cordial welcoming but that was not all. It contained a concrete and startling proposal to halt, immediately, all major naval construction for at least ten years and to scrap sixty-six battleships afloat and under construction—thirty American, seventeen Japanese, and nineteen British. It was, as one shocked and stunned British delegate remarked, "an audacious and astonishing scheme." But it stuck and became the basis for the final ratio of tonnage among the three powers.

For three months, the delegates worked and finally came up with three major treaties. One, the Five Power Treaty, signed on February 6, 1922, dealt with naval armaments. It provided for the scrapping of certain ships following Hughes' proposal, declared a ten-year holiday in the construction of capital ships (above 10,000 tons and carrying guns over 8 inches), limited capital ships to 35,000 tons and 16-inch guns, and set a maximum tonnage for battleships at 525,000 tons for the United States and England, 315,000 tons for Japan and 175,000 tons for France and Italy (5:5:3:1.75:1.75) and for aircraft carriers at 135,000 tons; 81,000 tons; 60,000 tons in the same order. Two crucial observations must be made that illustrate some general problems concerning arms limitation. First, nothing was said about reduction of cruisers, destroyers, or submarines. France, believing that submarines were essential to her domestic safety (guarding the lifeline between north Africa and the homeland), would not consent to limiting that weapon. Hence, destroyers and cruisers, vessels designed to hunt the submarine, could not be regulated. Second, the Japanese would not accept an inferior ratio without gaining a measure of security as compensation. Article XIX of the Treaty satisfied that demand. It forbade the building of new or the strengthening of old fortifications in Asian possessions. For the United States, that meant the status quo in the Philippines, Guam, Wake, Midway, and the Aleutian Islands; for Britain, Hongkong (Singapore, Australia, and New Zealand were not included); for Japan, the Bonins, Formosa, the Kuriles, the Ryukyus. Thus, the security of the Japanese home islands was measurably increased for *they* did not come under the restriction and could be fortified. Article XIX *plus* ratio "3" was adequate for balancing "5."

The two other instruments, the Four Power Pact (December 13, 1921) and the New Power Treaty (February 6, 1922) were political. The former, signed by the United States, Japan, France, and Great Britain, guaranteed the insular possessions of each other in the Pacific and provided for consultation in case of controversy between any two of them. It also abrogated the Anglo-Japanese Alliance. The other treaty, initialed by all the nations represented, pledged them "to respect the sovereignty, the independence, and the territorial integrity of China" and to maintain the Open Door for commerce and industry. For the United States, the political-security aspects of the two agreements were singularly important as preludes to a reduction of armaments. Had the alliance between Japan and England remained in force, American naval strength in the Pacific would have been at a 5:8 disadvantage. The renunciation of aggressive designs on the Philippines by Japan in the Four Power Pact, gave the United States security there without which Washington would not have been able to accept a limitation of the size of the American fleet.

President Harding presented the network of treaties to the Senate on February 10, 1922 with no small measure of pride. American objectives had been secured—naval reduction, pledges on China, guarantees for the Philippines, end of the one conceivably menacing alliance—and without sacrificing or compromising the lodestar of American policy. "I can bring you assurances," he said, "that nothing in any of these treaties commits the

United States, or any other power, to any kind of an alliance, entanglement, or involvement." And, added Senator Lodge, there was not even a moral commitment. Little wonder that the treaties went through the Senate easily except for the Four Power Pact. Borah and others of the old "Bitter Enders" feared that the words *"respect* their . . . insular possessions" really meant *"guarantee* their . . . insular possessions." A reservation to the treaty stating, "there is no commitment to armed force, no alliance, no obligation to join in any defense" satisfied enough of them to assure a safe margin.

The failure to limit cruisers at Washington led to an increased building of such ships by Great Britain and Japan. It was President Calvin Coolidge who took the lead in an effort to halt the incipient race. In June of 1927, he issued invitations to the signatories of the Five Power Treaty to meet in Geneva to consider the application of that treaty's yardsticks to those types of vessels left unregulated. The conference, which opened on June 20, began inauspiciously. Italy, for her own reasons, stayed home. The French were willing to attend only if France could get a guarantee against an attack. When told that matters of security would not be discussed, they saw no use in participating. Shortly after the deliberations began, it became clear that a deadlock was in the offing between England and the United States. The crisis resulted from each nation's estimate of its peculiar needs for insuring "domestic safety." With relatively few naval bases and insular possessions and with interests in every part of the world to protect, the United States had to rely on large, long-range cruisers of 10,000 tons mounting 8-inch guns. Washington believed 21 such ships constituted a minimum. The British, on the other hand, with bases dotting every sea, preferred a larger number, estimated at 70, of smaller cruisers of 7,000 tons carrying 6-inch guns. Each viewed the other's needs as menacing to its own safety. Japan tried to mediate between the two but did not succeed. After six weeks of wrangling, the Conference adjourned on August 4, 1927.

If there were political leaders devoted to the cause of reducing armaments as a means of insuring peace, there were others who believed that peace could be guaranteed only by outlawing war. The movement was set on foot by a wealthy Chicago lawyer, Salmon O. Levinson, who, in December of 1921, organized the American Committee for the Outlawing of War and drew up a "Plan to Outlaw War." To a generation surfeited with war, the attraction of such a movement was immediate and immense. It picked up powerful support among all walks of life and particularly in the intellectual community. James T. Shotwell, Bryce Professor of International Relations at Columbia, and Columbia's president, Nicholas Murray Butler, were among the project's most tireless and fervent promoters. Of great value was Senator Borah's interest in the idea. He had come to believe that force could never be the ultimate arbiter of international affairs; that only public opinion and law could be the determinants of the conduct of nations. Hence, he favored making war "illegal and illegitimate" by international statute and enforceable by domestic courts.

It was Shotwell who brought the idea to outlaw war into the diplomatic arena. He suggested to the French Foreign Minister, Aristide Briand, that he propose to the United States a bilateral treaty renouncing war. Briand, eager to pull the American government into European affairs and to tie it to France, jumped at the idea. American policy-makers, just as eager to stay out of European affairs, balked at the Briand proposal. Briand had, however, cleverly made his overtures to Washington by means of a statement printed by the Associated Press on April 6, 1927, and public opinion was excited by the prospect of an agreement to outlaw war. Secretary of State Frank B. Kellogg had set aside the Briand suggestion when first received but by the end of the year he found the pressure from all sides so insistent that he took the proposal to the Senate Foreign Relations Committee for an opinion. There, Chairman Borah encouraged action but in the form of a multilateral rather than a Franco-American treaty (on the grounds, probably, that there was safety in numbers—meaning there would be less chance of being saddled with obligations). Thus fortified, Kellogg replied to Briand with a counterproposal of a multilateral treaty, which the foreign minister accepted, albeit reluctantly.

On August 28, 1927, in Paris, 15 nations signed the document known as the Pact of Paris or Kellogg-Briand Pact. It contained only two paragraphs. The first pledged the signatories to "condemn recourse to war . . . [and to] renounce it as an instrument of national policy." The second bound them to settle their disputes by pacific means alone. Eventually, nearly all the civilized nations of the world subscribed to the Pact. The United States Senate approved it, 85–1.

It would be a mistake to conclude that the nearly unanimous vote indicated unstinting and unreserved satisfaction with the Pact. It did not. Most senators agreed with their colleagues, Carter Glass of Virginia, who did not think the treaty "worth a postage stamp in the direction of accomplishing permanent international peace" and James Reed of Missouri who called it an "international kiss." They appreciated the fact that the exclusion of wars of self-defense from the renunciation clause rendered the Pact virtually useless since, as Senator Claude Swanson of Virginia pointed out, every war ever fought was in self-defense. Senators gave the treaty their approval because to have voted against it would have been psychologically bad and politically unwise (in view of overwhelming public support) and because its passage created no enforcement obligation for the United States. Its passage, as the distinguished Spanish diplomat, Salvador de Madariaga, noted, also satisfied the image Americans had of themselves as leaders in the movement for moral progress in the world. The best comment on the American estimate of the Pact, and an ironic one, was that the same Senate that so warmly approved the Pact, within one month, joined the House in passing a bill to build fifteen 10,000-ton cruisers at a cost of $274 million.

Still, there was hope of further reducing naval armaments. A conference met in London in January of 1930 following a meeting between President Herbert Hoover and British Prime Minister Ramsay MacDonald the previous October in Washington to tackle the problem of limiting noncapital ships. There were some salutary results. Limits were applied to cruisers, destroyers, and submarines; rules were established prohibiting unrestricted submarine warfare; the holiday on capital ship construction was extended by five years, and provision was made for additional scrapping of capital ships. But there was evidence of jitters, nervousness, and uneasiness among the participants. France and Italy could not agree on cruiser ratios and ratified only part of the treaty; France thought the entire proceedings useless without a security treaty; Japan was angered by being forced to accept an inferior ratio (except in submarines); and, finally, among the United States, England, and Japan, an "escalator clause" was approved, permitting them to build beyond the treaty limits if they felt their security in danger.

London was the last serious effort at arms reduction in the interwar years. Within one year of its closing, the first step was taken on the road to the second great war when the Japanese invaded the Chinese mainland. Thereafter, events moved rapidly to make a shambles of the idea of arms limitation. In 1932, a conference to consider land weapons met at Geneva under League of Nations auspices after long years of preparation in which the United States had participated. It failed, miserably, for all the now-familiar reasons. The question of "adequate defense consistent with domestic safety" arose again and could not be resolved. France demanded an international police force be organized before any attempt was made to reduce armaments. The United States, speaking through President Hoover, responded with a grand proposal to cut all armaments by one third and the abolition of tanks, bombing planes, chemical warfare weapons, and mobile guns. And while the conference was in session, Japan, in 1934, announced her intention to withdraw from the limitations of the Washington and London treaties. The next year, Adolf Hitler served notice of abrogation of the arms strictures of the Versailles treaty, and Italy began her campaign in Ethiopia. It was too late by that time to do anything about disarmament. The nations were interested only in increasing their armaments. Perhaps, something might have been done earlier had the United States been willing to give guarantees of security.

The American approach to international economic problems of the

1920s was based upon the same assumption that conditioned the attitude toward disarmament and toward international organization. Essentially, it was Borah's narrow and self-centered precept that only the interests of the United States mattered.

The problems rotated around the debts the Allies owed the United States and the reparations Germany owed the Allies. By 1920, the United States was owed about $10 billion, of which $7 billion stemmed from cash loaned the Allies during the period of American cobelligerency (and raised by selling United States Treasury bonds to American citizens) and the remainder from loans after the Armistice for relief and recovery granted to victors and vanquished alike. Europeans, quite frankly, expected that they would not be required to repay the loans. They considered the money to have been in the nature of a political subsidy to fight a common enemy and not a purely financial transaction. American dollars had spared American lives, they believed, for it was those dollars that enabled the Allies to fight a war as much America's as theirs. It was pointed out, also that nine tenths of the money was spent in the United States for war goods. To demonstrate that the talk was not idle, Great Britain, herself a creditor nation to the tune of $10 billion, suggested a mutual cancellation of all debts "owed by one associated nation to another."

The idea was not so far-fetched for Americans, themselves, had talked when they were at war about considering the money as a gift. As one senator had remarked, "I am perfectly willing to give to any of the Allied nations the money which they need to carry on our war, for it is now *our* war." Other senators thought it unfair to hold the Allies responsible for repayment of the money when they had bankrupted themselves "fighting our fight." The noted banker, Paul Warburg, favored cancellation on the grounds the United States would never collect anyway; why then, he asked, should the country be placed in the position of being the world userer?

Those sentiments were expressed, however, during the high tide of wartime passion and emotion when the feeling of solidarity and comradeship prevailed. After the war and after the peace conference and after the diplomatic revelations, American sentiment was not nearly as benign. The "common cause" idea was not at all popular. Under the impact of the postwar disillusionment, the money was viewed quite differently, as a straight business loan. "They hired the money, didn't they?" said Calvin Coolidge. All sorts of arguments were advanced to justify the demand for repayment. One heard mention of business ethics, sanctity of contracts, moral obligation, good faith, and the like. People scoffed at the European contention that there was no money with which to pay. There always seemed to be enough, Americans observed, for building armies and navies.

Determined to collect the legal and just debt, Congress, in 1922, created the World War Foreign Debt Commission and charged it to negotiate repayment agreements with each debtor. The terms were generous, as far as financial transactions went. They were based on a capacity to pay and on the premise that "No settlement which is oppressive and retards the recovery and development of the foreign debtor is to the best interests of the United States and Europe." The British debt of $4.5 billion was made payable in sixty-two years and bore interest at 3 per cent to 1932 and 3.5 per cent thereafter. Italy was charged no interest on her $2 billion loan to 1930, after which the rate was minimal and fixed until 1950, when the repayment of the principal was to be completed. France refused, at first, to enter into an agreement but upon the threat of an embargo on future loans, she capitulated and came to terms not unlike those made with England.

The capacity of the Allies to pay was dependent in large part upon their amassing dollars. There were several ways that could be done: profits from carrying American goods in their freighters and from services by their banking houses and insurance companies, cash sent home by relatives in America and dollars left in Europe by American tourists, and income from the sale of their goods in the United States. The last provided the greatest opportunity for earning the largest number of dollars but, alas, American tariff policy made it difficult. Instead of keeping the import duties low as befits a creditor nation wishing to encourage its debtors to ship it goods as payment on the loans, the rates in the postwar period were pegged at all-time highs. Further, not only was the importation of commodities discouraged; the United States pursued an aggressive policy of pushing exports, thereby creating more indebtedness.

An effort had been made at the end of Wilson's second term by the Republican majority to raise the tariff rates to protect American industry at home, but the president vetoed it on the soundest grounds. American industry, he said, need fear no competition from a devasted Europe and, he added, the high tariff would eventually invite retaliation, which would affect the American market abroad and hinder the Europeans in their effort to repay the debt owed the United States. Those were the words of an internationalist who sought to widen not contract contacts with the world. His successors in power were, however, of a different sort. Nationalist, insular, and nation-centered, they revived the measure when Harding came into office and in 1922 the Fordney-McCumber Act became law. Duties at once rose on thousands of items.

Europeans complained, as was to be expected, pointing out the serious impediment posed by the tariff to their economic well-being and to their capacity to pay the debt, but the spirit of the 1920s deafened the American ear and hardened the American heart. Indeed, eight years after the first increase in rates came another tariff which jumped the duties higher. The Smoot-Hawley Act, passed in 1930, alarmed not only Europe but large numbers of Americans, as well. On May 5 of that year, 1,028 professional economists in a memorial to the president urged a veto. Their arguments were cogent and timely: increased duties would raise the price for the American consumer, encourage wasteful means of manufacturing, make difficult the payment of debts, invite reprisals by foreign nations, and retard recovery from the Depression. They also pointed out, poignantly, that "A tariff war does not furnish good soil for the growth of peace."

The president, however, was not moved by the reasoning of the economists nor by the misgivings of certain prominent Republicans such as his own secretary of state, Henry L. Stimson, and Charles Evans Hughes. He agreed, more nearly, with the Undersecretary of State William R. Castle, Jr., who could see no connection between the tariff and the Allied capacity to pay the debt. Exports would have to be stupendous, he claimed, to affect the capacity. Furthermore, he argued, it was not a matter of capacity to pay but of will. The president signed the measure and it became law.

It was not only between the tariff and the debts that the policy-makers in the 1920s claimed no relationship but also between the debts and reparations. Reparations had been fixed at $32 billion in May of 1921 to be paid at the rate of $0.5 billion annually. That sum constituted an important source of revenue for the European nations and affected their capacity to pay the money owed the United States. If the Germans did not pay, the Allies, in turn, would have difficulty paying. That is precisely what happened in 1922 when Germany failed to meet a reparations installment. The Allied capability to pay America was at once impaired, and it suffered further when Germany quit payment altogether following the occupation of the Ruhr Valley by French and Belgian troops in retaliation for the default. The occupation provoked a worker's strike, which led to a serious dislocation of the German economy and to a period of wild inflation.

That there was a real and logical connection between debts and reparations seemed inescapable to Secretary of State Hughes who proposed the creation of a commission to examine means for restoring the German economy and making possible a resumption of reparation payments. Headed by the Chicago banker, Charles G. Dawes, a commission worked out a plan, to take effect in September of 1924, whereby a $200 million loan (chiefly from American sources) would be pumped into the German economy to revive it and permit Berlin to begin making payments. The plan was successful but only temporary and in 1928, the United States took the initiative to arrive at a more permanent, and, indeed, a final settlement. A new commission chaired by the American industrialist, Owen D. Young, reduced the principal by $9 billion and arranged a schedule for amortizing the balance in fifty-nine annual installments at 5.5 per cent interest.

One other American move reflecting an apparent acknowledgement of a close debt–reparations connection came on June 20, 1931 when President Herbert Hoover proposed a one-year moratorium on all intergovernmental debts. The United States, he said, would expect no payments from its debtors in the fiscal year 1931–1932 if other governments followed suit in relation to their debtors. The president then went on to smash any hopes that the moratorium might be made permanent. The suggestion, he added, was no prelude to a cancellation of the war debts. If the European powers chose to terminate the reparations, that was their business. Reparations were a wholly European problem without effect upon the United States, he maintained, and had nothing to do with the war debts.

That categoric position struck Europe as unfortunate for there had been a movement growing for several years to wipe the slate clean of all debts and reparations as a means of recovery from the Great Depression then raging. Yet, despite Hoover's disclaimer, the European nations meeting in Lausanne, Switzerland in June 1932, did link the two in a final effort to settle Europe's financial liabilities. They proposed an end to reparations with a final lump sum payment of $714 million contingent upon a cancellation of the war debts by the United States. But Washington would not hear of it, insisting that one had nothing to do with the other.

Europe made one more effort to get the United States to accept the interrelationship of not only debts and reparations but of the tariff as well at a world economic conference that met in London in June of 1933. The American delegation attended on the understanding that neither debts, tariffs, nor reparations would be discussed, which was, of course, a ludicrous demand since all three matters stood at the root of the world's ills. British Prime Minister Ramsay MacDonald, in opening the conference, alluded to the war debts when he remarked, "While it must not be mentioned, it must be dealt with before every obstacle to general recovery has been removed and it must be taken up without delay."

As a matter of fact, there need have been no great concern about the war debts because the conference broke up over another issue, stabilization of currency. The various national currencies were jumping unpredictably in the world market and seriously hampering international trade. The United States and Britain had gone off the gold standard; France had not. There was a plan to tie the dollar and the pound at the current rate of exchange and then go on to tie them to the gold currencies. A preconference statement by the newly inaugurated Democratic president, Franklin D. Roosevelt, offered encouragement. He had underlined the importance of the conference as the instrument "to establish order by stabilization of currencies. It must supplement individual domestic programs for economic recovery by wise-considered international action." But when the time came for the "wise-considered international action," Roosevelt "torpedoed" it. On July 2, in cabled instructions to the American delegation, he forbade pegging the dollar to the franc or pound or any other currency. It must be left free to float as the state of the American economy demanded. That was enough to put an end to the conference, and it adjourned without much to show for its labors.

The collapse of the conference was, in part, responsible for the debtor nations taking matters into their own hands. Several of them had missed the December 1932 installment because of the state of their economy; fewer paid the June 1933 installment. After the conference broke up, no nation except Finland met the amount due in December 1933. That marked, in fact, the real end of the war debt question. Many Americans were furious at the lack of honor and of responsibility shown by the borrowers, and Congress retaliated by passing an act in 1934, sponsored by Senator Hiram Johnson, that forbade loans to defaulting nations. Such a prohibition served no useful purpose. It did provide an outlet for American frustration and generated a good deal of hostility on Europe's part.

Some historians have maintained that America's policies toward international organization, disarmament, and economic matters contributed measurably to the breakdown of the peace in the late 1930s. They claim that the story would have been different had the United States joined the League, underwritten security treaties, cancelled the debt, and kept the tariff low. One never knows what might have happened, and speculating about it is a fruitless exercise. It seems reasonable to assume, however, that the refusal to become involved in international political affairs and the pursuit of a nationalist economic foreign policy, however much they might be justified by the experience of the war and the peace conference, did not contribute to the maintenance of peace.

BIBLIOGRAPHY

Selig Adler, *The Isolationist Impulse: Its Twentieth Century Reaction* (1957).

Robert P. Browder, *The Origins of Soviet-American Diplomacy* (1953).

L. Ethan Ellis, *Republican Foreign Policy, 1921–1933* (1968).

Beatrice Farnsworth, *William C. Bullitt and the Soviet Union* (1967).

Robert H. Ferrell, *Peace in Their Time: The Origins of the Kellogg-Briand Pact* (1952).

Peter G. Filene, *Americans and the Soviet Experiment, 1917–1933* (1967).

D. F. Fleming, *The United States and World Organization, 1920–1933* (1938).

Betty Glad, *Charles Evans Hughes and the Illusion of Innocence* (1967).

Carl Parrini, *Heir to Empire: United States Economic Diplomacy, 1916–1923* (1969).

Robert Freeman Smith, "Republican Policy and the *Pax Americana*, 1921–1932," in W. A. Williams, *From Colony to Empire* (1972).

WILLIAM A. WILLIAMS, "The Legend of Isolationism in the 1920's," *Science and Society*, XVIIII (1954), 1–20.

JOAN H. WILSON, *American Business and Foreign Policy, 1920–1933* (1973).

Henry L. Stimson (U.S. Signal Corps photo, the National Archives).

In Asia: Retreat from Responsibility

As AMERICAN officials surveyed their country's position in the Far East following the Washington Conference for the Limitation of Armaments, they believed they had good reason to feel satisfied. The twin principles of the Open Door policy—equality of commercial opportunity and integrity of China's territory—had, for the first time since their enunciation by John Hay in 1899 and 1900, been accepted by the other powers and incorporated into formal multilateral treaties. There was a good deal of self-congratulation in the American capital on the success of having placed on eight other backs the burden of enforcing the cherished principles that had been so difficult to maintain without any aid in the first two decades of the century. It was, of course, particularly gratifying and important to have the Japanese signatures on the documents, for it was the island empire that had most menaced Hay's policy. As for the safety of the Philippines, that, too, had been deftly taken care of by the self-denying pledge imbedded in the Four Power Pact. A brilliant diplomatic victory had been achieved, one consistent with the objectives of American foreign policy in the postwar world. American interests had been secured without creating obligations because the several treaties made no mention of force should they be violated.

There were those, however, who did not share the euphoria of the policymakers. Men in and out of the government expressed uneasiness with the naval and political settlement. Elmer Davis, a prominent journalist, called the conference the greatest success in Japanese history. It left Japan supreme in the Far East, he claimed, and free to pursue any course her leaders desired. William H. Gardiner, a prolific and intelligent writer on maritime matters, pointed to Article XIX of the naval limitation treaty that gave the Japanese preponderance in the western Pacific and Admiral Harry Knapp, a scholarly officer interested in the political, diplomatic, and philosophic aspects of navalism, considered Article XIX as gravely impairing the ratios agreed upon and as delivering a fatal blow to American

301

prestige and security. For many Americans, the greatest danger for the United States resulting from the new situation in the Far East lay in the fact that, in the final analysis, American security rested upon Japan's good will. Given Japan's strengthened position and American refusal to use force to chastize a treaty-breaking nation, the only constraint upon Japan's acts was her willingness to honor her commitments and pledges as set out in the treaties.

Such a constraint, however, Administration spokesmen considered adequate. They viewed Japan as a contented, satisfied, and even satiated nation that, once having gained adequate security for the homeland by the Washington treaties and fair treatment at the Conference, harbored no aggressive designs. Further, they argued, the drift of Japanese political and social development gave promise that Japan would pursue a peaceful policy in Asia and take a conciliatory line toward China. Great steps were being taken in the direction of establishing a liberal, democratic, parliamentary system. Cabinet government and party responsibility were instituted and the suffrage was extended to all adult males. Military budgets were cut and social reform instituted. The government was dominated by political figures who supported disarmament, membership in the League of Nations, the peaceful settlement of disputes, and accommodation with the West. They and the great business interests—the Zaibatsu—favored penetration of the China market by peaceful, not warlike, means. The Foreign Minister, Kijuro Shidehara, represented a brand of statesman whose views augured well for the future. Liberal, antimilitaristic, and western oriented (he wrote his state papers in English), he and his colleagues could be depended upon to direct Japanese foreign policy with "the most scrupulous regard for its honor and the fulfillment of its commitments," to use the words of Professor James T. Shotwell of Columbia University, a specialist on international affairs. Encouraging, too, was the apparent inclination by the majority of the Japanese people to support the liberal civilian element in their country as against the military clique, who were the exponents of expansion and imperialism. As one American noted, "The Jingoes have not, by any means, been silenced. But their voices are no longer the voices of Japan. Their ultranationalism is being tempered by contact with a new Japan that feels itself a part of a worldwide movement to end war, to remedy economic injustice, to establish for the good of the common man the institution of democracy." In short, it was believed that the rule of those responsible for the Twenty-one Demands had been replaced by the rule of those responsible for ratifying the Washington treaties.

Administrative leaders pointed out, also, that conditions in China as well as in Japan gave promise that the Washington settlement would be maintained. That populous and sprawling country was in the midst of a nationalist revolution with Sun Yat-sen, father of the republic, and his lieutenant, Chiang Kai-shek, as leaders of the Kuomintang, or Nationalist,

Party. Efforts were being made to modernize the government and to effect social, financial, and judicial reforms. Under Chiang's leadership, after Sun's death in 1925, Chinese armies began a drive to unify the country by unseating the war lords who ruled as independent chieftains, each in his own area. Beginning in Canton, the Nationalist troops moved north, occupying Nanking on March 24, 1927, where the capital of the "new" China was established, and then proceeded to Peiping, which was taken in June of the following year. At the same time, Chiang was continuing Sun's program of liquidating the special rights foreigners had enjoyed for more than a century that had kept China in a weakened state. Of significance, too, was Chiang's break with the Soviet Union in 1927 after years of close friendship and collaboration. Much was made of China's new-found stability and unity as factors in enabling Chiang and his government to help maintain the principles of the Open Door— particularly in keeping Japan at bay.

Unhappily for America's position in the Far East, the estimate of the situation by the defenders of the Washington settlement proved false. China never did (at least not until 1949) achieve sufficient strength or stability to defend her territorial integrity and the principle of equality of commercial opportunity for all foreigners. She was continually troubled by civil strife and internal disorders and her government was shot through with corruption and venality. As for Japan, there was a serious miscalculation made concerning the jingoes. The determination and resolve of the army to capture the government and embark on a policy of expansion and conquest on the mainland was grossly underestimated.

To a passionately patriotic group of junior-grade officers, the Washington settlement was viewed as "the lost-rights conference." There, Japan had been relegated to an inferior position in the assigned ratios which was, to them, characteristic of the treatment of Asiatics by Caucasians. Ignoring the fact that Article XIX more than made up for the smaller ratio in naval tonnage, they concentrated their attention on the humiliating treatment by the western powers. Those powers, they believed, would never willingly permit Japan to enjoy her fair share of the land and the resources of Asia. Hence, their program was frankly to seize that share, and more, by force. Organized into numerous secret societies, they plotted and planned and waited for the propitious moment to strike. They appealed to the Japanese people for support, claiming that the liberals and civilians in the government had betrayed their interests, and that the policy of cooperating with the West would not be fruitful. For evidence to back up their contention, they had only to point to the Immigration Act passed by Congress in 1924 that excluded the Japanese from coming to the United States as immigrants. What better indication was there of American contempt for the Japanese and of unjust and discriminatory treatment! The legislation was, indeed, a needless affront for had the Japanese been assigned a quota along with other foreigners, it would have resulted in no more than 250 of them entering the country. News of the legislation was received with shock in Japan. The day the law went into effect was proclaimed National Humiliation Day, and 15 Tokyo newspapers printed a joint declaration condemning it. That the measure strengthened the case of the militarists and discredited the liberals was indisputable. Japanese pride suffered a wound that was not soon to be healed.

The militarists had been on the watch for an opportunity to overthrow the civilian government since 1921. A coup planned for 1923 was frustrated by a devastating earthquake (whose victims were aided generously by American charity). Four years later, the liberal government fell as a consequence of its failure to punish a Chinese attack on the Japanese consulate in Nanking. General Tanaka, a blustering firebrand and author of a blueprint, the Tanaka Memorial, for Japanese conquest and exploitation of Asia, became premier. He could not, however, carry out his plans because of the opposition to an aggressive policy by the emperor, the Zaibatsu, and important civilians. He resigned in 1929, after the murder in Manchuria of Chang Tso-lin, the Chinese war lord in that place, and was succeeded by a moderate civilian, Yuko Hamaguchi as premier. Kijuro Shidehara once again became foreign minister.

It seems clear enough that by that time the army was becoming more and more restless, and the chances of a move on the mainland were increasing. The shooting of Premier Hamaguchi in November of 1930 by some jingo officers was one indication of the desperate state of the army and a harbinger of coming events. A series of incidents in China in the summer of 1931—a Chinese attack upon Koreans in Manchuria, the death under mysterious circumstances of a Japanese army officer while in civilian clothes, a growing boycott of Japanese goods—gave the military a feeling of confidence that a punitive expedition against the Chinese would receive wide popular support. Most significant in the catalogue of factors propelling the army was the mounting effort by the Chinese government to tighten its hold upon Manchuria. That move the Japanese could not permit because Manchuria was their "lifeline." There, the Japanese had vast rights and interests secured by treaty with China—two major rail nets (the South Manchurian from Port Arthur and Dairen on the water at the tip of the Liaotung Peninsula to Changchun 400 miles to the north; and the Mukden-Antung line connecting the South Manchurian to the Korean rail system) as well as coal and iron mines, hotels, banks, factories, lumber, harbor facilities, and utilities. There was stationed a sizable body of regular troops designated the Kwantung Army, and military guards along the railroads' right-of-way (one every 15 kilometers). As army officers observed the measures being taken by the Chinese to exploit Manchuria—build a port on the opposite side of the

Gulf of Chihli from Dairen to rival that entrepôt, construct a competitive railroad parallel to the South Manchurian, settle Chinese colonists on the land—they came to believe that a strike had better come quickly. They were distressed, too, that the autonomous war lord in Manchuria, Marshal Chang Hsueh-liang, had sworn allegiance to Chiang Kai-shek. All in all, it appeared that the proper moment was at hand in the fall of 1931, especially in view of the fact that the worldwide economic depression was at its worst with the Western powers virtually paralyzed by its evil effects and thoroughly preoccupied with seeking ways to combat it.

The blow did come that fall, on September 18. At about 10:00 P.M., a squad of Japanese railway guards, while patrolling the tracks of the South Manchurian line some three miles south of Mukden, heard an explosion about 500 yards away and saw some Chinese soldiers fleeing from a section of damaged track. The damage, clearly, was inconsequential, for a few minutes later an express train passed over the track. Yet, the Japanese guards pursued the Chinese. At once, as if by prearranged signal, they were joined by large numbers of their fellows who fanned out from their garrisons along the railroad right-of-way and began an assault on several Chinese army units. Within 24 hours, they had occupied Mukden, and a number of other important towns and by the 22nd, Japan was in control of a large part of Manchuria south of the line of the Chinese Eastern railroad.

China's forces were no match for the well-trained and tightly disciplined Japanese soldiers, and they lay helpless before the enemy's advance. If Manchuria were to be saved for its rightful owner, it would have to be done by the Western powers whose signatures appeared at the foot of three great treaties which China claimed had been violated—the Covenant of the League of Nations (specifically Article X guaranteeing the integrity and independence of member states), the Nine Power Treaty (guaranteeing Chinese territorial integrity) and the Kellogg-Briand Pact (outlawing war as an instrument of national policy). So, on September 21, the appeal went out from Nanking to Geneva and to Washington, but any sanguine hopes the Chinese may have had for assistance were to be cruelly dashed.

The League Council, in the midst of a regularly scheduled meeting, responded to the appeal with the utmost caution and reticence. There was no wish to make the Manchurian incident the test of the postwar treaty structure. The risk of war was too great. Hence, the assurances by the Japanese delegate that his country's action must be regarded as a measure of self-defense to protect the railway and not as an aggressive war designed to deprive China of any territory was welcomed and accepted, with relief. The promise that Japanese forces would withdraw to their proper zone as quickly as the situation warranted seemed to satisfy the other delegates. The Council's only act was a resolution on September

Manchuria, 1931–1932.

30 expressing confidence in the Japanese pledge, after which it adjourned until October 13.

In Washington, the reaction to the Chinese appeal was much the same. Secretary of State Henry L. Stimson who, in view of President Hoover's preoccupation with domestic matters, made the nation's foreign policy very much by himself, was no less cautious and moderate than the men in Geneva. His policy was based on the acceptance of the explanation by the Japanese foreign office for the events in Manchuria as detailed by the Mikado's ambassador in Washington. It was that the army had moved without the approval of the civilian authorities in Tokyo and, given time, the civilians would reassert their authority and curb the military. But time and patience were essential and, above all, nothing must be done by the United States or the other powers that might provoke public support for the military. So, Secretary Stimson, while informing the Japanese ambassador of his concern over the bold move by the army, over the fact that Japan was in control of much of Chinese territory, and over the possibility that both the Nine Power Treaty and the Kellogg-Briand Pact may be affected, did nothing to embarrass Foreign Minister Shidehara. "It would be advisable," he told his colleagues, "that nationalist feeling not be aroused against the Foreign Office in support of the Army." His position was to play no favorites. "We have not attempted to go into the question of right or wrong . . . we are not taking sides," he said. To both Japan and China, he expressed the hope that military operations in Manchuria would cease. To make certain there would be no attempt to assess blame for the events, he discouraged a move by the League Council to send the commission of inquiry to Manchuria that the Chinese had requested and the Japanese had opposed. And to demonstrate his confidence in the expectation for a peaceful settlement of the dispute he permitted the American Ambassador in Tokyo to go home on leave.

So the secretary of state dealt with the crisis and there is little reason to doubt that his policy received the approval of the American people. They had made clear their intention to avoid international complications that might require the use of force. They would never condone fighting a war in distant Asia for a piece of remote territory or even in support of a principle. That is not to say that they took no sides—emotionally. Their sympathies were overwhelmingly for the Chinese who awakened images of hard-working laundrymen in America or pitifully paid coolies at home drowned by constant floods and starved by perpetual famine. Almost every Christian American had some connection with the vast missionary endeavor in China, if only to the extent of a few pennies tossed into the collection plate on Mission Sunday. As for the Japanese, there was no such sentiment for them. Considered intelligent, aggressive, vigorous, efficient, and skilled, they were viewed as the aggressors against a defenseless China. However much their rights may have been violated, there was no just reason for launching a brutal and devastating attack, Americans believed. But never were those feelings made grounds for proposing military action against Japan.

Even had there been a wish to pursue such a policy, it would have been impossible in view of the state of the military establishment and of the economy. The Depression had had the severest effects upon the army and navy budgets. Enlisted strength had dropped drastically, one third of the fleet was out of service, and the Asiatic squadron boasted only one heavy cruiser in its major armament. Further, the absence of strong and well-equipped bases in the western Pacific made impossible the effective deployment of the Pacific fleet based in San Diego. Stimson, whatever his inclination, was basing his policies, in good diplomatic fashion, upon his capabilities.

The League Council reconvened on October 13, by which time the crisis had reached a new stage occasioned by the aerial bombing of Chinchow. That city, the headquarters of Marshal Chang Hsueh-liang after his flight from Mukden, was miles away from the Japanese railway zone. There seemed no justification for that attack. It appeared to be simply an enlargement of military operations and either evidence of Shidehara's inability to curb the army or his collusion with the jingos. Stimson was upset. To his diary he confided his fears that "We have got to take a firm ground and aggressive stand toward Japan."

What he did was, in a sense, revolutionary. He authorized the American consul in Geneva, Prentiss Gilbert, to join the League Council in its deliberations when it discussed the Kellogg-Briand Pact. The cooperation, however, was to be short lived and not only because the move had aroused the ire of those in the United States—chiefly Senators Borah and Johnson and the Hearst and McCormick press—who violently opposed participation in the League. More importantly for Stimson was the fact that the Council, on October 24, had issued a virtual ultimatum to Japan demanding an evacuation of Chinese territory and a withdrawal to the railway zone by November 16. With such drastic action, Stimson refused to be associated. He wished "to leave a ladder by which Japan could climb down." He was still willing to give Shidehara a chance to carry out his pledge and still unwilling to sit in judgment on Japan. The most he would do, so as not seem to be leaving the League too far out on a limb, was to reiterate the demand for evacuation and withdrawal but without the deadline.

Meanwhile, news came of a large-scale attack by Japanese infantry, artillery, cavalry, and aircraft on November 3, the day of Stimson's note to Tokyo, against Tsitsihar, a city north of the Chinese Eastern railway line and far from Japan's treaty zone. More and more, it began to appear that the difference between the civilian and military elements in Japan was being blurred. There was almost universal public support for the "brave soldiers" fighting for the emperor in China and no civilian government could possibly have put a brake on the army's operation. On December 11, the liberal Wakatsuki cabinet fell replaced by one frankly promilitary. And the forces in Manchuria continued their advance.

The League Council had met in Paris on November 16. The American ambassador in London, Charles G. Dawes, was instructed to proceed to Paris and report the proceedings to Washington. He was not to take part in the meetings but was, rather, to have private conversations with the Chinese and Japanese delegates in the hope of arriving at a formula to stop the fighting. The council was faced with Japan's defiance of its resolution of October 24. November 16 had come and gone and no withdrawal or evacuation had been effected. Indeed, the reverse was true. Tsitsihar was occupied on the 19th, and reports indicated the imminence of an assault on Chinchow. There was talk of strong action such as economic sanctions but it proved to be only talk. The major powers wanted no part of so serious a measure that could easily have led to war. Further, the United States, without whose cooperation sanctions could not succeed, was strenuously opposed for the same reason. The Council contented itself with setting up a commission of inquiry, following a Japanese suggestion, to investigate, thoroughly and impartially, the events connected with the September 18 incident.

Stimson supported the commission idea but his hope that a peaceful solution was at hand did not materialize. Shortly after the new cabinet took office in Tokyo, the drive against Chinchow began. It was a complete success. There was no Chinese resistance and on January 3, 1932, Chinchow, the last Chinese stronghold in Manchuria, fell. The beaten and broken Chinese army fled south of the Great Wall. Organized resistance in Manchuria had come to an end.

The Secretary felt betrayed. All the promises and pledges from Tokyo upon which he had based his policy of playing no favorites and of patience had proven to be hoaxes. Now, he was determined to take strong and positive action against Japan. Several possibilities existed in varying degrees of seriousness: convene a conference of signatories of the Nine Power Treaty; recall the American ambassador from Tokyo; place an embargo on materiel of war to Japan; level economic sanctions against Japan. None, for a variety of reasons, was adopted. Instead, Stimson chose another alternative, a milder one than any of the foregoing. It was popularly called nonrecognition and was embodied in identical notes to Japan and to China sent on January 7, 1932. The notes informed the two nations that the United States "cannot admit the legality of any situation de facto nor does it intend to recognize any treaty or agreement entered into between those Governments [China and Japan], or agents thereof, which may impair the treaty rights of the United States or its citizens in China . . . and that it does not intend to recognize any situation, treaty or agreement which may be brought about by means contrary to the . . . Pact of Paris." Although directed to both nations, the notes were obviously meant only for Japan, which alone had the power to upset the status quo by force. It was the means adopted by the American government to reproach Japan and to state America's displeasure and disapproval. Force or even measures "short of force" were out of the question. Nonrecognition alone was left to register disgust with a nation that was violating the norms of fair play and international morality.

The action received wide acclaim in the United States. It was hailed as a splendid means of strengthening the treaty structure and contributing a revolutionary idea to the body of international law. The fact that it was ineffectual was mentioned by only a few people. But they were right. It had no effect on Japan's course in Manchuria. It did have an effect on Japanese-American relations in that it worsened them. For Stimson alone had, of all the powers, censured Japan. America alone appeared as the opponent of the Island Empire's advance on the Asian mainland. For historians analyzing the policy in the perspective of time, it must be viewed as an element in the retreat from responsibility in Asia for it did nothing more than shake an admonishing finger in Japan's face. It did nothing to enforce the treaty structure or the cherished principles of the Open Door or America's stake in Asia. The Chinese characterized the policy aptly as having the "head of a dragon and the tail of a rat," a new scrap of paper, useless without a string of battleships in its wake.

Undaunted and unafraid, Japan embarked on a program for integrating Manchuria economically and politically into the Empire. Various devices were used—banks, mines, and industries came under Japanese management; laws were passed preventing purchases from foreign firms; business, in general, was diverted to Japanese firms; Japanese served either as advisors to the Chinese administrations or themselves occupied posts in the government. Whatever the means, the Open Door was being shut tight. The transition to the next step was inevitable—severing Manchuria from China, which was accomplished by fomenting an independence movement there among the Chinese inhabitants. It succeeded and on February 18, 1933, the new state of Manchukuo was proclaimed with the last of the Chinese Manchu emperors, Hsuan-tsung, whom Japanese army officers had dragged from his place of retirement in Tientsin, as ruler. A Japanese-Manchukuo treaty was signed that assigned to Japan great and exclusive rights in the new country.

Now the façade was finally and definitely stripped from Japanese policy. What had been called a temporary police action to safeguard rights had all along been a war fought to tear away part of China's territory. In the process, the Japanese had destroyed the treaty structure and the settlement of 1921–1922. As for the Open Door principles that constituted the basis of America's Far Eastern policy—its heart and its head—they had been made into a shambles by Tokyo. And not only in Manchuria did the Japanese seek to close the door and impair Chinese territorial integrity. In late January of 1933, a large-scale aerial and ground attack was launched against Shanghai. Ostensibly begun to punish the Chinese for an anti-Japanese boycott and to protect Japanese merchants, it was, in reality, the second phase of the Japanese timetable for the conquest of north China. It failed. Tokyo had miscalculated the reaction of the great powers. Shanghai, unlike Manchuria, had a large number of foreign residents and the powers had important and extensive interests there. An international force (as in the days of the Boxer rebellion) was gathered in Shanghai to protect the foreigners and their property and Japan was pressured into halting the operation. Japan was, as a matter of fact, not very anxious to continue the attack. It was proving too costly and the Chinese resistance was considerable.

How was the United States to respond to Manchukuo and to Shanghai? How was America's Far Eastern policy and stake to be safeguarded? The reply to those questions can be summed up by the single word: retreat. That the Japanese acted immorally was unquestioned; that they acted outrageously was almost universally acknowledged; that Americans were upset and troubled was plain to see. But, as President Hoover said, there was no cause for war. Neither obligations to China nor American dignity nor American interests warranted fighting. The controversy, he said, was between Japan and China and the United States had no mandate to preserve order and peace in the world.

The government's policy followed the president's assessment of the situation. Despite the talk in some quarters, particularly among church and peace organizations, for an embargo or for economic sanctions, Stimson did nothing more than make a remonstrance to Japan laying the blame for the Shanghai episode on Japan and exonerating China of any responsibility. He also prevailed upon a reluctant President Hoover to authorize the dispatch of elements of the Asiatic Fleet as well as 1,400 soldiers and marines to Shanghai to protect American lives and property but with another objective, as well. He wanted the fleet to act as a sword suspended over the Japanese. If they could be kept guessing and worried about whether the navy would intervene, the effect might well be sobering. He put great reliance upon "the unconscious element of our great size and military strength. . . . Japan was afraid of that, and I was willing to let her be afraid of that without telling her that we were not going to use it against her."

Acting on the same theory, Stimson addressed an open letter to Senator William E. Borah on February 24, 1932, in which he leveled a veiled threat at Japan. After affirming American belief in the efficacy and wisdom of the Open Door agreements at the turn of the century and of the network of treaties concluded at Washington in 1922, he gave fair warning that the modification or abrogation of any part of the treaty structure by any signatory released the United States from any or all of its obligations under the treaties. The inference was plain. The United States might build beyond the tonnage limited by the treaty and strengthen its Pacific fortifications forbidden by Article XIX in response to a Japanese violation of the treaty.

American policy had no appreciable effect on the Japanese except to irritate them and to lead them to believe that the United States was their real enemy in Asia and the sole power standing in the way of their destiny. Stimson derived from his efforts only the satisfaction that the League of Nations Assembly heeded his urging, in the letter to Borah, that other nations withhold recognition of Manchuria. That action the Assembly took on March 11, 1932. But Japan did not seem phased by the censure. Indeed, Tokyo was becoming less and less interested in what the world thought of Japan's conduct—as evidenced by the reaction to the report of the commission of inquiry on September 4, 1932.

The commission, headed by the Earl of Lytton, distinguished British literary figure and public servant, and consisting of representatives from Italy, Germany, France, and the United States, had spent six intensive months in Japan, Manchuria, China, and Korea searching and sifting the facts and opinions concerning the September 18 incident and the subsequent events. Much effort went into drafting the report and there was much difference of opinion among the members of the commission. The end product reflecting compromises between two extreme positions, was, as described by George H. Blakeslee, an American expert on the Commission, "objective and judicial; its tone was restrained and conciliatory; yet it is positive and definite upon the vital issues of the controversy." It did not recognize the validity of the Japanese conquest, yet it did not advocate a return to the condition prevailing before September 18. It attempted a reconciliation between Japan's rights and Chinese sovereignty. The solution proposed was to elect a special administration for Manchuria under Chinese sovereignty but with autonomy. Troops of both nations would be replaced by a *gendarmerie* that would keep order and monitor a proposed Sino-Japanese treaty of commerce, arbitration, and nonaggression.

The proposed solution to the Manchurian problem seemed reasonable to all the powers save Japan. That Tokyo would reject it was expected and when Japan officially recognized Manchukuo on September 15, 1932, on the eve of the publication of the report, the expectations were confirmed. Japan's next step was also anticipated: withdrawal from the League of Nations. The acceptance of the report by the League Assembly on February 24, 1933 was the signal for Tokyo to give the League the two-year notice of intent to quit the international organization.

Within one month, a new administration had come to power in Washington but the replacement of Republicans by Democrats did not alter America's Far Eastern policy. Both the new president, Franklin D. Roosevelt, and his secretary of state, Cordell Hull, agreed to continue the Hoover-Stimson doctrine of nonrecognition and accept the *fait accompli* in Manchuria without further protest. Even when in February and March of 1933, Japanese forces pushed westward into Jehol and southward into Hopei and annexed Jehol to Manchukuo, Washington took no action. Like Stimson, Hull believed the policy of the United States ought to be "maintaining the independence of China and in preventing Japan from gaining over-lordship of the entire Far East" but, like Stimson, he was aware of the state of American public opinion, which indicated the Americans were not willing to fight in Asia. A bellicose statement by a Japanese

Foreign Office spokesman, Eiji Amau, in April of 1934 which arrogated to Japan the destiny and future of East Asia and defied the world to interfere in Chinese affairs, elicited from Washington only the mildest objection. Still, Hull would not renounce American rights in East Asia and acquiesce in Japanese hegemony there. An attempt by the Japanese Ambassador in Washington in May of 1934 to negotiate an agreement which would have recognized Japan's paramount rights in East Asia (a new version of the Taft-Katsura, Root-Takahira, and Lansing-Ishii agreements) met with a firm rebuff from Hull.

The failure to wrest from the United States an admission of Japan's supremacy in Asia did not affect Tokyo's foreign policy. Manchukuo's affairs were kept under tight control and foreigners were kept from significant participation in that country's economic exploitation. It was plain, also, that Japan was not to stop with Manchukuo. In December of 1934, Tokyo gave notice that the naval limitation treaties of Washington and London, due to expire on December of 1936, would not be renewed, an act that was rightfully viewed by world observers as an indication, along with withdrawal from the League, of Japan's determination to push further for control of China.

It was clear that sooner or later, the United States would have to make a clear-cut decision on Asian matters. To continue the 1920s policy of non-recognition, mild protest, and veiled threat would result eventually in Japanese dominance of China and, possibly, of all of eastern Asia for that policy would never prove effectual in halting the Japanese. Only a program of positive action, economic or military, could affect Tokyo's advance on the mainland. The decision to follow the latter course was finally made in the late 1930s; this made inevitable the great war of the Pacific.

BIBLIOGRAPHY

Dorothy Borg, *American Policy and the Chinese Revolution* (1968).

Thomas H. Buckley, *The United States and the Washington Conference, 1921–1922* (1970).

Robert H. Ferrell, *American Diplomacy During the Great Depression* (1957).

Akire Iriye, *After Imperialism: The Search for a New Order in the Far East, 1921–1931* (1965).

Elting Morison, *Turmoil and Tradition: A Study of the Life and Times of Henry L. Stimson* (1960).

Armin Rappaport, *Henry L. Stimson and Japan, 1931–1933* (1963).

Gerald E. Wheeler, *Prelude to Pearl Harbor: The United States Navy and the Far East, 1921–1933* (1963).

Cordell Hull (courtesy of the National Portrait Gallery, Smithsonian Institution, Washington, D.C.).

In Latin America:
The Good Neighbor

I F IT is true, as most historians believe, that the interventionist policy of the United States between 1900 and 1916 was caused by fears for the security of the Panama Canal, then the reversal of that policy after 1921 becomes intelligible. The war had put an end to the danger to the Caribbean and to the Panama lifeline posed by European powers before the conflict. Four years of fighting and suffering had so weakened them that they had neither the resources nor the will to mount an expedition against the western hemisphere. "Does anybody believe," questioned Secretary of State Frank B. Kellogg in 1928, "that the present governments of Europe are in any position to attack any one of the South American countries. . . ?" He might have questioned, too, whether the European governments were in any position to challenge America's economic hegemony in the area. The liquidation of American imperialism in the southern continent was a luxury that Washington could now afford and the Colossus of the North could be transformed into the Good Neighbor without jeopardizing American security. And, given the revulsion of the American people to foreign adventures as a result of the disillusionment with the Great Crusade, successive administrations in the 1920s and 1930s could expect public support for the policy.

One of the first fruits of the new policy was the willingness of the Senate, on April 20, 1921, to approve, by a bipartisan vote of 69–19, the Treaty of Bogotá with Colombia that had failed in that body in 1914. The treaty ended the long dispute occasioned by the Panama revolution in 1903. By its terms, Colombia received a payment of $25 million and certain rights in the canal area in exchange for the recognition of the Republic of Panama. The United States did not express regrets for any part it may have played in the rebellion, but the indemnity was, in itself, an expression of guilt to be expiated.

Thereafter, successive Republican administrations took measures to disengage the United States systematically from involvement in the domestic affairs of the republic to the south. In 1922, Washington ended the control of the government of the Dominican Republic by the United States navy preparatory to its holding national elections in two years. When the newly elected government took office in 1924, American marines left the country. A treaty, replacing that of 1907 signed on December 24, 1924, ended the protectorate but left the collection of the customs under American control.

In Nicaragua, similarly, the 100-man marine legation guard, which had been protecting American property and lives and maintaining American-favored governments in power over the years, was withdrawn by President Coolidge in August of 1925 leaving the destiny of that country to its own people. The departure of United States troops came after the election of a new government under Carlos Solórzano in February and following a conference of Central American nations held in Washington that stabilized that region. Thirteen treaties had emerged from that international gathering covering such subjects as the maintenance of peace, arms limitation, liberalization of trade, and reciprocal citizenship. Important agreements were reached forbidding intervention by any one state in the domestic affairs of another and pledging nonrecognition of governments achieving power by coup d'etat or by revolution. Commissions of inquiry and machinery for settling disputes by arbitration or conciliation were created.

The outbreak of a bitter civil war in August of 1926 brought back a force of 4,500 leathernecks. In ordering them to Nicaragua, Coolidge cited the need to protect American lives and property. He might, also, have indicated his fears that the pro-American regime of President Adolfo Díaz was in danger from strong rebel forces lead by Juan B. Sacasa. Hoping to bring order and peace to the country and cut short American involvement, the President sent Henry L. Stimson, former secretary of war in the Taft administration, to Managua in April of 1927 "to clean up the mess." His orders were to mediate between the rivals for the presidency and after intense and careful negotiations, he succeeded, in May, in bringing the antagonists together in the Truce of Tipitapa. By its terms, Díaz was to retain the presidency but take members of the opposition into the government with new elections to be held in 1928. Meanwhile, the Nicaraguan army was to be replaced by a National Guard, trained and temporarily officered by Americans. The elections, conducted under American supervision, brought to the presidential office José M. Moncado of the Liberal Party, which was, normally, anti-American. That fact, however, was not the reason for the marines remaining in the country. It was, rather, because of the guerrilla warfare carried on by Augusto Sandino, who had refused to accept Stimson's terms. After three years of jungle warfare, American marines succeeded in subduing Sandino, making possible their gradual withdrawal beginning February of 1931. Two years later the last of them left Nicaragua. So ended a quarter of a century of military occupation.

A revolution in Honduras in 1923 and Washington's reaction to it reflected the Republican administration's determination to reverse the prewar policy of the United States in Latin America. Warships were sent to Honduras and marines were landed but there was no occupation of the country nor was a treaty forced upon the nation's leaders creating a protectorate. President Harding sent a seasoned diplomat and expert in South American Affairs, Sumner Welles, to a conference in Honduras attended by representatives of the other four Central American republics. Pursuant to several of the treaties agreed to at Washington in the same year, the conference set up a provisional government, supervised an election, provided for the funding of the outstanding debt whereupon the American military and naval contingent sailed away. It does not take much imagination to guess how Roosevelt, Taft, or Wilson would have behaved in a similar situation.

In Mexico, conditions in the years immediately following the end of the war were such as would have, under the old dispensation, invited swift and cruel interference in that country's domestic affairs. But, President Coolidge held his hand and approached the problem in an entirely different way.

The situation resulted from a reform movement that was pursued with vigor and zeal after the war. It concentrated on land reform and on nationalization of the sub-soil resources such as oil and minerals. Land taken from foreigners for distribution to the peasants was adequately compensated for and raised no serious problems. It was the sub-soil question that raised difficulties between the two nations. Article 27 of the Constitution of 1917 nationalized the sub-soil—that is, the oil and minerals that lay below the surface of privately owned land belonged to the state. That the constitutional provision was legal could not be denied. What was contested was its retroactive application by the Mexican government. Pressure from Washington resulted in a compromise embodied in the Bucareli agreements in 1923 whereby foreigners who owned property before 1917 and performed some "positive act" of improvement would retain the subsoil rights.

In 1924 a new Mexican president, Plutarco Calles, refused to abide by the compromise and supported legislation that limited the ownership of subsoil rights on property acquired before 1917 to fifteen years. That policy, quite expectedly, raised a demand in the United States by the oil interests for some sort of reprisal. The situation became tense when Roman Catholic elements in the United States, angered by a virulent anticlerical crusade in Mexico (which meant, practically, an anti-Catholic crusade), joined the oil people in calling for action by the American government. There was also a belief, widely spread north of the border, that Communist agents, both Soviet and American, were behind Mexico's secret aid to rebel forces in Nicaragua then battling American marines. The soil for intervention was fertile, but the spirit of disengagement prevailed as evidenced by a unanimous Senate resolution passed on January 27, 1927, urging President Coolidge to settle differences with Mexico not by force but by arbitration.

President Coolidge did exactly that. He dispatched to Mexico City in September of the same year his Amherst College classmate, the wealthy banker, Dwight W. Morrow, with instructions to come to terms with the Mexicans. Morrow was extraordinarily successful in arriving at an amicable and reasonable settlement with Calles that resulted in a new Petroleum Code drawn up by the Mexican Congress in December of 1927. The code, in effect, restored the Bucareli agreements and the "positive act" doctrine.

It is not surprising that Latin Americans were pleased and impressed by what appeared to be a significant change in America's western hemisphere policy from the days of Roosevelt, Taft, and Wilson. As the decade of the 1920s advanced and evidence of Washington's resistance to armed intervention as a solution to the problems of the hemisphere piled upon evidence, leading statesmen of the republics to the south were willing to believe that the United States had, indeed, turned a corner and was prepared to treat its fellow American nations not as clients but as sovereign equals. The numerous policy statements issuing from Washington proclaiming such a view were accepted not as pious mouthings but as bases for policy. Secretary of State Charles E. Hughes' remarks to a group of Americans in Rio de Janeiro in September of 1922 were impressive. "You . . . know full well," he said, "how sincerely we desire the independence, the unimpaired sovereignty and political integrity and the constantly increasing prosperity of the peoples of Latin America. . . . There is no imperialistic sentiment among us. . . . We covet no territory; we seek no conquest; the liberty we cherish for ourselves we desire for others; and we assert no rights for ourselves that we do not accord to others. We sincerely desire to see throughout this hemisphere an abiding peace, the reign of justice and the diffusion of the blessings of a beneficent cooperation." And again, in November of 1923, he spoke of the equality of all the American states and the respect for the territorial integrity of each. Significant, too, was the acceptance by the United States of the Treaty to Avoid or Prevent Conflict Among the American States adopted at the Fifth Inter-American Conference, which met at Santiago (Chile) in 1923. That agreement, commonly called the Gondra Treaty after Manuel Gondra, a former Paraguayan president was, in effect, a "cooling-off" treaty requiring an investigation by an impartial commission into the facts of a dispute before the parties resorted to fighting.

The supreme test, however, of the new policy was not action or words, important though they were, but, rather, would be a pledge—a binding pledge enshrined in a multilateral treaty—in which the United States would promise never, under any circumstances, to intervene in the affairs of any American state. Only such a guarantee could satisfy completely the southern republics. Only such a renunciation, permanent and irrevocable, could give the neighboring countries the assurances they needed and eradicate the suspicion, hostility, and fear that had been the hallmark of the hemisphere's international history for a century.

Latin American diplomats, led by men of the stature of Carlos Calvo and Luis M. Drago, both eminent Argentinians, had for years striven to extract such a declaration from the United States but always without success. Always the United States had been able to keep that and other controversial subjects from being included in the agenda of hemispheric conferences and meetings. In 1928, however, substantive diplomatic and political issues found their way into the agenda of the Sixth Inter-American Conference, which met in Havana in January. It seems that Washington, as part of its new policy, had interposed no objection. For that reason, the Conference was expected to be of real significance. The composition of the American delegation reflected that importance. Ex-Secretary of State Charles E. Hughes headed the delegation that included a senator, a distinguished authority on international law, a university president, and a seasoned diplomat. President Coolidge himself journeyed to Cuba's capital to make the opening address.

The crucial item to be considered was the report by the Commission of Jurists, which had been set up at the Third Inter-American Conference at Rio de Janeiro in 1906 to propose codes of international public and private law. Drafts of several codes were on the floor. One of these concerned "States: Existence, Equality, Recognition" and contained the clause, "no state has the right to intervene in the internal affairs of another." The supreme test was at hand. The United States, however, was not yet ready to meet it. Despite the fine words and selfless acts, Washington was not willing to take the next and final logical step in the development from Colossus of the North to Good Neighbor—the pledge never in the future to intervene.

Hughes made plain to the conference the reasoning behind the refusal to make the pledge. It was not fear of European encroachment, he said, that might necessitate intervention. "The difficulty . . . is not of any external aggression. It is an internal difficulty, if it exists at all. . . . What are we to do if government breaks down and American citizens are in danger of their lives? Are we to stand by and see them killed because a government . . . can no longer afford reasonable protection?" To assuage bruised feelings, Hughes went on to coin a phrase. Such interference, he noted, must not be viewed as "intervention" but only as "interposition" of a temporary character . . . to protect its citizens." In a talk to the Havana Chamber of Commerce he amplified the assurances. "We have," he said, "no desire to stay. . . . We enter to meet an imperative but temporary emergency, and we shall retire as soon as possible."

Disappointment at Havana was deep and the suspicion and distrust of former times flared up anew. The recent dispatch of troops to Nicaragua and their presence there while the conference was in session exacerbated the resentment. All the Latin American republics save four—Panama, Cuba, Peru, and Nicaragua—which were at the moment and for one reason or another beholden to their giant northern neighbor—voted solidly against the United States on a substitute resolution proposed by Hughes. It was one of the worst diplomatic defeats ever suffered by the United States at an international gathering.

At home, too, there was dismay and chagrin. The policy of nonintervention and disengagement was extremely popular, and to many Americans it seemed logical and wise to legalize and institutionalize the practice in treaty form. William Green, the president of the American Federation of Labor, said as much in a letter to Secretary of State Kellogg. "The working people of the United States," he wrote, "are firmly convinced that cordial and friendly relations can only be established and maintained between all countries represented in the Pan-American union through the development of a perfect understanding that the government of the United States will not at any time interfere in the affairs of any Latin American nations, and will not, either directly or indirectly, encroach upon their sovereign or territorial rights. Such a guarantee should be absolute, without reservations. . . ." Walter Lippmann, the noted political columnist and commentator, expressed a widely held view when, referring to the Havana meeting, he wrote, scornfully, "We endorsed our own solitary obligation with our own solitary praise. We indulged ourselves in a unilateral vote of confidence in our unilateral policy. We had to do it. No one else was prepared to endorse our policy, or praise it, or give it a vote of confidence. . . . We proceeded as we saw fit, consulting only our own interests and our own consciences, subject to no limitations except those we impose on ourselves, accountable to no one but ourselves."

The failure at Havana to commit the United States to nonintervention must not obscure the achievements of the conference. Certain salutary changes were made in the reorganization of the Pan-American Union (the permanent "secretariat" of the twenty-one republics) and treaties were adopted on a host of important subjects: aliens, asylum, consular agents, diplomatic officers, maritime neutrality, private international law, and rights and duties of states in event of civil strife. This last was designed to discourage revolutions by prohibiting the contracting states from giving aid to rebel forces. But all those useful and welcome accomplishments provided bare solace to the Latin Americans when measured against their futile effort on intervention. To them, all the good works of the Coolidge administration in Mexico, Central America, and the Caribbean were marred.

Coolidge's successor in the White House, Herbert Hoover, continued his predecessor's policy in every respect. He spoke the language of the Good Neighbor, resisted intervention, practiced disengagement, and would make no commitment for the future. Shortly after his election, he embarked on a seven-week good-will tour of Latin America, visiting more than half the countries there and making a number of reassuring speeches. He expressed his unhappiness with the military interventions of his predecessors and with the interpretation of the Monroe Doctrine by Theodore Roosevelt. He admitted the unpopularity of his country in the western hemisphere and pledged to alter the image. Speaking in Honduras' capital, on November 26, 1928, he used the felicitous term "good neighbor" in describing his conception of America's role in the Pan-American system. "We have a desire," he said, "to maintain not only the cordial relations of governments with each other but also the relations of good neighbors." And after returning home and taking office, he continued his assurances. In the Inaugural Address he said emphatically, "We have no desire for territorial expansion, for economic or other domination of other people." Again, in Washington on April 23, 1929, he announced his opposition to intervention by force "to secure or maintain contracts between our citizens and foreign States or their citizens."

True to his words, he did not send marines to Haiti in 1929 when civil war broke out there and when the government defaulted on payment of interest on bonds. Instead, he sent a commission of inquiry to Port-Au-Prince to determine the causes of the unrest and the financial collapse. Finding the seat of trouble in the high-handed conduct of the Haitian president, the commission recommended new elections which were held promptly. A new government was installed that negotiated a treaty with the United States in September of 1932. It provided for the transfer of the public services of Haiti from American to native control and the removal of the American military from control over the National Guard. Because the treaty approved continuation of supervision by the United States of the country's finances, the Haitian legislature withheld its approval. The following year, however, the new Democratic administration of Franklin D. Roosevelt came to an understanding with Haitian leaders that resolved that problem.

Just as Hoover did not send troops to Haiti, so he did not intervene in Panama during a revolution there in 1931, in Cuba in the same year when there were uprisings against President Gerardo Machado, and in El Salvador in the following year when there was unrest. Secretary of State Henry L. Stimson's remarks when announcing his government's policy toward the Cuban difficulty are significant. "The situation in Cuba," he noted, "is an internal political situation in a sovereign state, and it would be intermeddling imperialism of the most flagrant sort to intervene therein."

There were other means the Hoover administration used to strengthen its nonintervention policy. One was a new and restricted approach to the practice of protection of the lives and property of Americans in Latin America. The president let it be known that troops could no longer be expected to respond immediately and indiscriminately every time an American believed his life or property to be menaced. Local legal remedies would first have to be exhausted in the matter of property and intelligent action, such as evacuating the country, would be expected in the matter of personal danger. Another was the President's position on the question of recognizing new governments in the Americas. It will be recalled that Woodrow Wilson had reversed the historic and traditional practice of the United States instituted by Thomas Jefferson that recognition be extended to a government which was in de facto control of the land and the people. Wilson applied the completely novel and extraneous yardstick of legitimacy and constitutionality. If a government came into power by unconstitutional means, recognition was refused. That practice was, in effect, "indirect intervention" in the internal affairs of a country for it denied self-determination. Hoover, on June 6, 1932, in response to a revolution in Chile, announced the return to the Jeffersonian policy and extended recognition to the revolutionary government in that country on the grounds that it exercised de facto control and was willing and able to fulfill its international obligations.

Still, like his predecessor, President Hoover consistently refused to renounce formally and officially the *right* to intervention. He would do nothing to alter those bilateral treaties that conferred upon the United States the legal right to intervene—with Panama, 1903; Cuba, 1903; Haiti, 1916; Dominican Republic, 1924. Nor could he give up the inherent right of a nation to interfere in the domestic affairs of another in certain situations as "generally recognized by the law of nations." Clear and resolute evidence of that position may be found in the publication by the Administration in March of 1930 of a memorandum on the Monroe Doctrine. Prepared in 1928 by Undersecretary of State J. Reuben Clark, the 236-page document was an account of the historical meaning of the Doctrine and had for its chief purpose the correction of the widely held view that American military intervention in the Americas had been carried out pursuant to the terms of the Doctrine. Such a view was responsible for the low estate into which Monroe's famous declaration had sunk in the eyes of Latin Americans. According to Clark, the Doctrine had nothing to do with the relations between the United States and Latin America and, hence, had no connection with American policy toward the southern republics. It related solely to the relations between "European states on the one side, and, on the other side, the American continents . . . [it] states a case of United States versus Europe, not of United States versus Latin America." If there was any document, he went on, that sanctioned intervention, it was Roosevelt's Corollary, but that had nothing to do with the Monroe Doctrine and should not have been bracketed with it.

Thus, Clark purged the Doctrine of the stigma of military intervention but in doing so, he carefully avoided either remorse for past interventions or promises that they would not be repeated. Indeed, he upheld the right of intervention that "originates in the necessities of security or self-preservation." And that position, written during the Coolidge Administration, was adopted by Hoover as his own when he made the document public.

It remained for the next administration of Democrat Franklin D. Roosevelt to take the final logical step from Colossus of the North to Good Neighbor that Latin Americans had looked for over the years by committing the United States to the doctrine of nonintervention. Roosevelt's accession to office gave hope to people all over the Americas that a new day would come to the hemisphere. He had endeared himself to them during the presidential campaign by his social conscience and his sincere concern for the common man. He was looked to as the bearer of a new spirit in hemisphere affairs and as a welcomed relief from twelve years of Republican rule always identified with the "Big Stick" of an earlier Roosevelt. It was known that as a young assistant secretary of the navy in Wilson's cabinet he had condoned intervention and had even boasted that he had written the constitution of Haiti in 1914 but it was also known that he had matured since that day. In 1928, while governor of New York, he had, in an article in an authoritative journal, *Foreign Affairs*, condemned intervention whether by Democrats or Republicans and had urged the renunciation "for all time" of "arbitrary intervention in the home affairs of our neighbors." If there were to be a need for "a helping hand . . . to bring back order and stability" to a sister nation that "may fall upon evil days," he wrote, "it is not the right or duty of the United States to intervene alone. It is rather the duty of the United States to associate itself with other American republics, and, if the conditions warrant, to offer the helping hand or hands in the name of the Americas. Single-handed intervention by us in the internal affairs of other nations must end." Here were articulated the two main elements destined to be the core of Roosevelt's Latin American policy—renunciation of unilateral intervention by the United States and the multilateralization of the responsibility for the maintenance of peace, order, and stability in the hemisphere.

Roosevelt's election in 1932 was hailed by Latin America as "a beautiful episode" in democracy and his speeches in the first months in the White House added substance to the idea. The most significant of them was delivered to the Governing Board of the Pan-American Union meeting in Washington on April 12, 1933. To them, Roosevelt laid down the principle that "the essential qualities of a true Pan Americanism must be the same as those which constitute a good neighbor, namely, mutual understanding, and through such understanding, a sympathetic appreciation of the others' point of view. It is only in this manner that we can hope to build a system of which confidence, friendship, and good will are the cornerstones." Eight months later, at Montevideo, a major step in the achievement of true Pan-Americanism was taken.

It was in Uruguay's capital that representatives of all the American republics, save Costa Rica, gathered early in December to attend the Seventh Inter-American Conference. Few of them failed to recall that the previous conference had been a disaster and that it had foundered on the rock of United States intransigence on the question of intervention. There were better hopes for success this time, and they were not to be betrayed. The American delegation, as at Havana, was a distinguished one headed by Cordell Hull, the secretary of state, who was admired and trusted by Latin Americans, and included a prominent diplomat experienced in hemisphere affairs, a leading financier with extensive dealing in South America, J. Reuben Clark, the author of the memorandum on the Monroe Doctrine, and a woman professor of sociology. That it would behave very differently from Charles Evans Hughes's group was a foregone conclusion.

The test came on the vote on the Convention on the Rights and Duties of States whose Article 8 stated, "No state has the right to intervene in the internal affairs of another." This time, the test was met. Hull, the first to vote on the treaty, said "aye," marking the first occasion in hemispheric history that the huge and powerful northern republic was willing to take the pledge. That the momentous step did not elicit applause was not because the significance was lost on the delegates but because Hull had qualified his country's approval with a reservation—the right to intervene "by the law of nations as generally recognized." The United States stood glaringly alone in its qualification. All the other states voted affirmatively each adding, pointedly, some phrase such as "without reservation," "with all my heart," "heartily and unconditionally," and "for United and Free America." Those statements received thunderous responses from the galleries as well as from the floor.

Nonetheless the United States had turned a corner in its Latin American policy and that was what counted. That enormously important fact should have been enough to temper disappointments. After more than a century of absolute freedom of action, it may have been too much to have expected the United States to tie itself unreservedly and unconditionally in one grand leap. A second step would have to be awaited. Meanwhile, satisfaction could be drawn from Hull's earnest remarks to the conference concerning his country's support of the "absolute independence, the unimpaired sovereignty, the perfect equality, and the political equality of each nation large and small, as they similarly oppose aggression in every sense of the word." Each of those principles was incorporated in the articles of the convention signed at Montevideo. Two days after the meeting ended, President Roosevelt put his stamp of approval upon the work of the conference in remarks made before the Woodrow Wilson Foundation. "The definite policy of the United States from now on," he said, "is one opposed to armed intervention." He made no mention of the reservation. It was just as well, for three years later at the special Inter-American Conference for the Maintenance of Peace in Buenos Aires, the qualification was removed, leaving nonintervention categoric and absolute.

Roosevelt himself had suggested the meeting in the face of the mounting tension in Europe resulting from the actions of Germany and Italy. Steps ought to be taken, he wrote his fellow chief executives in January of 1936 "to determine how the maintenance of peace among the American republics may best be safeguarded." And he, himself, travelled to the Argentine capital to open the conference on December 1, 1936. Fresh from a smashing victory at the polls not one month earlier, he arrived in Buenos Aires full of confidence and buoyancy and received a tumultuous welcome. More than a half a million people jammed the streets to hail him. It was as much a testimonial to a new image of the United States as to the president personally. One would hardly have guessed that Argentina had been and was at the time the great and jealous rival of the United States for hegemony in the hemisphere. Her distinguished and learned foreign minister, Carlos Saavedra Lamas was elected permanent chairman of the Conference (at the nomination of Cordell Hull).

The new image of the United States stemmed in part from the epoch-making events at Montevideo and in part from the events in the three years which followed. Those years saw the American government take giant steps in implementing the policy of nonintervention. On May 29, 1934, not six months after Montevideo, Sumner Welles, the American Ambassador in Cuba and one of Roosevelt's closest advisors on Latin-American matters, signed a treaty in Havana which abrogated the one of 1903—the instrument which had made Cuba an American protectorate. The odious Platt Amendment was now exorcised from Cuban-American relations, restoring to the Pearl of the Antilles her sovereignty and self-respect. In November of the same year, the last marines were withdrawn from Haiti and the treaty of 1915 that had reduced that country to the status of an American dependency was allowed to expire in 1936, as provided for by its terms.

Panama, which was tied to the United States by the umbilical treaty of 1903, became truly independent for the first time since her successful revolution against Colombia. A new treaty, signed in March of 1936, deprived the United States of its rights of intervention in that isthmian republic. With the Dominican Republic, the treaty of 1924, which gave the United States significant privileges, was not due to terminate until 1945. It was under review in the light of Rooseveltian policy but before any measures could be taken to modify or abrogate it, the action of the United States at Buenos Aires virtually nullified it (it was formally ended by a new treaty negotiated in 1940).

President Roosevelt's opening remarks to the Conference set its tone. He referred to the twenty-one republics as "the American family" united in "common purpose" and in the "glories of interdependence." He warned that the "madness of a great war in other parts of the world would affect us and threaten our good in a hundred ways." To avoid that catastrophe, he urged that the hemisphere be "wholly prepared to consult together for our mutual safety and mutual good." It was the fulfillment of that plea which turned out to be the Conference's greatest achievement. The Convention for the Maintenance, Preservation, and Re-establishment of Peace provided for the joint action Roosevelt had suggested. In the event of a threat to peace from inside or outside the hemisphere, the "American Republics . . . shall consult together. . . ." Thus was the protection of the peace of the hemisphere which, more than 100 years earlier, Secretary of State John Quincy Adams had insisted was solely a responsibility of the United States, made the responsibility of all of the republics. And thus was the Monroe Doctrine continentalized and multilateralized.

Of only slightly less importance was the Additional Protocol Relative to Non-Intervention by Article I of which "the High Contracting Parties declare inadmissable the intervention of any one of them, directly or indirectly, and for whatever reason, in the internal or external affairs of any of the other Parties." To that instrument, Cordell Hull affixed his signature without reservation, qualification, or inhibition. Thus was swept away the last vestige of an American right to intervene. So was Buenos Aires the great landmark in the relations of the two parts of the hemisphere; so was the principle of equality fastened onto Pan-Americanism; and so did the Colossus of the North finally become the Good Neighbor.

BIBLIOGRAPHY

J. REUBEN CLARK, Memorandum on the Monroe Doctrine (1930).
ALEXANDER DE CONDE, Herbert Hoover's Latin American Policy (1951).
DONALD DOZER, Are We Good Neighbors? Three Decades of Inter-American Relations, 1930–1960 (1961).
EDWARD GUERRANT, Roosevelt's Good Neighbor Policy (1950).

J. LLOYD MECHAM, *The United States and Inter-American Security, 1889–1960* (1961).

ROBERT F. SMITH, *The United States and Cuba: Business and Diplomacy, 1917–1960* (1960).

————, *The United States and Revolutionary Nationalism in Mexico, 1916–1932* (1972).

JOSEPH S. TULCHIN, *The Aftermath of War: World War I and United States Policy Toward Latin-America* (1971).

BRYCE WOOD, *The Making of the Good Neighbor Policy* (1954).

Franklin Delano Roosevelt (courtesy of the National Portrait Gallery, the Smithsonian Institution, Washington, D.C.).

The Road to War, 1941: Germany

s AMERICANS followed the course of events in Europe and in Asia in the 1930s, a deep uneasiness gripped them. Certain nations seemed to be going wild. Brute force seemed to be replacing law. Cherished values—decency, democracy, and liberty—were under attack and the norms of conduct that long had separated civilized states from barbaric peoples were being breached.

In Germany, Adolf Hitler had erected a totalitarian state—nationalist, chauvinist, aggressive and antidemocratic. He was in the process of ridding his country of Jews by incineration and of liquidating his political opposition by means only slightly less cruel. As a prelude to the carrying out of his bold-faced plan for world conquest, as blueprinted in his book *Mein Kampf*, the German *Führer* withdrew from the Geneva Disarmament Conference and from the League of Nations in 1933; reinstituted compulsory military service and increased the army from 150,000 to 500,000 men in 1935, both acts in violation of the Treaty of Versailles; repudiated the entire Versailles settlement in 1936; and, in the same year, marched his army into the Rhineland and occupied it in repudiation of the Treaty of Locarno of 1925 that guaranteed the frontiers of Germany's western neighbors. Americans knew a good deal of what was going on in Germany. Newspaper reports, magazine accounts, newsreel films, and eyewitness reports all kept the public well informed. The effect could be best described by the words "shock" and "dismay." Hugh Johnson, director of the National Recovery Administration, reported in 1935, after a visit to Berlin, "I have seen something of that sort in Mexico during the Villa ravages and among semi-civilized people or savages half-drunk on marijuana—but that such a thing [murder by Hitler of a group of his associates in the Nazi Party] should happen in a country of some supposed culture passes comprehension." And, more soberly, Douglas Miller, a member of the American

embassy staff in Berlin, wrote home, in 1934, that the "fundamental purpose" of German policy was "to dominate the entire globe" by force of
arms, if necessary.

In Italy, Benito Mussolini, self-styled Duce and a cardboard copy of his
northern counterpart, had ruled since 1922 and had created a fascist state,
repressive at home and aggressive abroad. In the 1930s, he, no less than
Hitler, dreamed dreams of world conquest and of restoring the grandeur
of ancient Rome. As the first step, his "legions" launched an invasion of
Ethiopia in 1935 that was marked by the indiscriminate bombing from
aircraft of helpless civilians and by the hurling of tank columns against
spear-wielding tribesmen. Wide publicity was given in America of the
statement by Mussolini's son, pilot of an Italian bomber, that strafing
Ethiopians was "good sport." Equally well publicized was the dramatic
and moving personal plea by the bearded and dignified emperor of
Ethiopia before the League of Nations for help against the invader. In
1936, Mussolini announced the annexation of that ancient kingdom to
Italy. In the same year, he withdrew from the League of Nations and
joined Hitler in intervening in the Spanish Civil War on the side of the
fascist rebels and against the democratic government in power. In 1936,
too, the two European dictators made a pact, the Rome-Berlin Axis,
cementing their collaboration in Spain and sanctioning each other's
policies.

As for Japan, Manchuria proved to be only the beginning. An attack
against Shanghai in 1932 was followed two years later by a renunciation
of the network of naval treaties that limited Japan's tonnage and by the
withdrawal from the League of Nations. Three years later came the major
assault upon China precipitated by an "incident" on the Marco Polo
bridge outside Peking. In rapid succession came the occupation of Nanking, Hankow, and Canton and soon every coastal city, every important
port, and all the main railroad lines were in Nippon's hands. The conquest was accompanied by bombings, strafings, looting, and other bar-
barities all plainly recorded by American cameramen and shown in
thousands of theatres across America. "Insane imperialism" and "beyond
the pale of civilized warfare" were among the more common epithets used
by Americans to describe Japanese action. Particularly galling was the
sinking by Japanese aircraft in 1937 of the American gunboat *Panay* while
on patrol on the Yangtse river and the wanton machine-gunning of sailors
in the small boats used to escape the wreckage. One year earlier, Hitler
and the Japanese emperor had formed an anti-Comintern pact, to which
Italy adhered in 1937. Thus the three predators came together in an unholy
alliance.

Americans were distressed and disturbed. Of that there was no question.
But greater than those feelings was the conviction that they must not

permit themselves to become enmeshed in the miseries of Europe and Asia. Sympathy was one thing; involvement was something else. Much as their hearts went out to Ethiopians, Chinese, Spanish loyalists, German Jews, and other victims of the dictators, they were determined to take no action on their behalf. The recollection of the last war, of the futility and the sense of betrayal was too fresh. "It must not happen again," said the collective voice of American people. The call to aid the oppressed must be resisted was the almost universal sentiment in the country. The liberal *New York Nation* accurately caught the spirit of the time in an editorial on October 16, 1935 which said, "As a people we have little sympathy for the inhumanity of Italian fascism. We are shocked and indignant at Mussolini's brazen invasion of Ethiopia. But the experience of one war fought for what we believed to be the highest of idealistic principles has convinced us, rightly or wrongly, that the harm resulting from the Il Duce's mad adventure will be slight compared with the havoc that would be wrought by another world conflict. Whatever may happen we are determined that American youth shall not again be sacrificed. . . ." And, in the same year, there appeared a brilliant account of America's *Road to War, 1914–1917* by Walter Millis which described, according to the dust jacket, the "Frenzied years . . . when a peace-loving democracy muddled but excited, mis-informed and whipped to a frenzy, embarked upon its greatest foreign war." The lesson was plain. "Read it and blush; read it and beware," continued the advertising blurb.

Words and sentiments were not enough, it was believed, to stave off a repetition of 1917 and people called for legislation to make impossible any future involvement. Senator Bennett Champ Clark of Missouri reflected a strongly held view when, in May of 1935, he urged Congress to avoid the next war by taking certain measures before war began. And that was precisely what Congress did. The legislators isolated, one by one, what they considered to have been the causes of America's entry into the war of 1914–1917 and in each case proceeded to make its recurrence illegal. The economic reason appeared paramount. It was almost universally accepted that the United States had gone to war to protect the stake of the munitions makers and bankers who had loaned vast sums to the allies and who had supplied them with the sinews of war. A Senate subcommittee had, under the chairmanship of Senator Gerald P. Nye of North Dakota, been investigating the munitions industry and had come to that premise as an inescapable conclusion. The lure of profits, warned Nye, had gotten the country into war once and would again unless the "merchants of death" were prevented from plying their trade. In the summer of 1935 Congress took up the challenge and passed a neutrality statute, on August 31, making it unlawful to export arms and ammunition to nations at war. Recalling that another of the grievances against Germany in 1917 involved the loss of American lives on belligerent merchant vessels sunk by submarines, the act warned American citizens not to travel on the ships of the warring nations.

Thus, the Congress wrote into legislation the determination that "it shall not happen again." And the law was passed speedily that, according to the *Nation*, "dramatized the American peoples' passionate abhorrance of war." When Mussolini sent his soldiers into Ethiopia in October and the president proclaimed neutrality, the embargo went into operation. The following year, Congress added loans to the category of embargoed items and in 1937, when the legislation expired a new law extended the embargo indefinitely, forbade (rather than warn) American citizens from travelling on belligerent vessels, and put all trade with belligerents (other than arms and ammunition) on a "cash and carry" basis. The law also extended the provisions to civil war to cover the conflict in Spain.

One other attempt was made to keep America out of war. It was in the form of a constitutional amendment proposed by Representative Louis Ludlow of Indiana in 1937 that would have given to the people of the country, by means of a referendum, the war-making power. The measure was extremely popular. A poll showed that 80 per cent of those questioned favored the idea, and 218 congressmen were prepared to approve it. People hailed it as a guarantee that the will of the people alone could decide the country's policy in so crucial a matter as life and death. For 267 Congressmen (a bare majority) to be able to drag 127 million people into war seemed to many people undemocratic. Despite the widespread support, the measure never reached the floor of the House. A motion to take it out of committee failed by only twenty-one votes. The chief cause for the failure seems to have been a reluctance by many legislators, as well as by the president, to surrender the power of those entrusted by the Constitution to make war and the feeling that the mass of people could not really be trusted with so weighty a responsibility.

Not all Americans approved of the neutrality legislation. There were those who considered it unrealistic in that it dealt with conditions that obtained 20 years earlier and that might not be repeated. The *New York Herald Tribune* called the 1937 law, "An Act to Preserve the United States from Intervention in the War of 1917–1918." And one Congressional opponent of the law complained, "We have been trying to cut a suit out of the whole cloth to fit whom? To fit the man designated as 'the World War of 1917.' Always we have before us the terms, conditions, and circumstances under which that war was fought. But we disregard the fact that in years to come, perhaps 5, 10, or 15 years from now, a war will be fought under totally different terms and conditions, and the suit of cloth that we shall have so carefully built in those days will be found unfitted for the use of the man designated as 'the World War of 1950.' "

Then there were those who did not believe America could stay out of a great international war despite the neutrality laws and that the only sure way to keep the country unembroiled in a conflict was to cooperate to prevent war from breaking out anywhere. The great problem, said ex-Secretary of State Henry L. Stimson, was the prevention of war. Furthermore, claimed Stimson, the neutrality laws were amoral in that they made no distinction between the aggressor and the victim. Indeed, the embargo favored the former in that he generally was better prepared for war than his opponent. It disturbed him that the American people, even the liberals, ignored the moral issue in the Italo-Ethiopian conflict. "I have heard T[heodore] R[oosevelt] say," he wrote in a prophetic and widely quoted letter to the editor of the *New York Times* on October 7, 1937, "that he put peace above everything except righteousness. Where the two came into conflict he supported righteousness. In our recent efforts to avoid war, we have reversed the principle and are trying to put peace above righteousness. We have, thereby, gone far toward killing the influence of our country in the progress of the world. . . . Such a policy of amoral drift by such a safe and powerful nation as our own, will only set back the hands of progress. It will not save us from entanglement. It will even make entanglement more certain." And the *Times* agreed wholeheartedly with Stimson. "We have an inescapable interest in the future of other nations," wrote the editor, "We are certain to be affected by the decisions they make between democracy and dictatorship, between peace and war." He then went on to urge that the United States accept "the share of responsibility which falls naturally to a great world power."

There were others who took the Stimson position—William Allen White, nationally known editor of the *Emporia* (Kansas) *Gazette*; Hamilton Fish Armstrong, the editor of the influential quarterly, *Foreign Affairs*; Walter Lippmann, the noted columnist and commentator; Max Lerner and Lewis Mumford, academicians; and, most importantly, the president of the United States and his secretary of state.

Neither President Roosevelt nor Secretary Hull, anymore than the vast majority of the American people, wished to become enmeshed in the morass of European politics. Both of them sedulously maintained a careful and cautious policy of noninvolvement and noninterference as a random scanning of the diplomatic correspondence for the year 1938 makes clear. In January, Hull, referring to the Spanish Civil War, cabled Ambassador William C. Bullitt in Paris, "all told, the possibility of mediation in a conflict between ideologies holds out little hope of success and would eventually be regarded by public opinion in this country as injecting us into the European picture." The following month, he instructed the American minister in Vienna, "You should carefully avoid . . . making any statements which can possibly be construed as implying that your government is involving itself, in any sense, in European questions of a purely political character or is taking any part, even indirectly, in the determination of such questions." And in March, Undersecretary of State Sumner Welles recorded a conversation with the Czechoslovkian minister concerning German claims on his country's territory. Said Welles, "with regard to the immediate situation in Europe . . . this government had taken no action, had made no representation, and intended to make none . . . the policy of the United States . . . as supported by the majority of the people of this country was to remain completely aloof from any involvement. . . ."

But both Hull and Roosevelt opposed the neutrality laws because they treated dictatorships and democracies alike, because they drew no distinction between aggressors and their victims and because they made impossible giving aid to the forces defending the values Americans cherished. As Hull said, they tied "the hands of the Administration just at the very time when our hands should have been free to place the weight of our influence in the scales we should have been morally supporting." Roosevelt signed the act of 1935 and the two that followed reluctantly because in the event of war he could offer the democracies no help.

That a war would come eventually seemed to the president certain and what seriously concerned him was the widespread feeling of confidence in the country that the United States could and would remain untouched if the world were in flames. He believed the opposite and in several key speeches he warned the American people of the dangers confronting them. At Chautauqua, New York, on August 14, 1936, he said, "I hate war. We shun political commitments which might entangle us in foreign wars. . . . Yet we must remember that so long as war exists on earth there will be some danger that even a nation which most ardently desires peace may be drawn into war." And on October 5, 1937, in Chicago, he told his audience, "We are determined to stay out of war. We are adopting such measures as will minimize the risks of involvement. . . . but we cannot insure ourselves against the disastrous effect of war and the danger of involvement; we cannot have complete protection in a world of disorder in which confidence and security have broken down."

At Chicago, the president went beyond giving warning; he proposed a means for dealing with the aggressor nations. "When an epidemic of physical disease starts to spread," he said, "the community must quarantine the patients." And, he continued, there was an epidemic of lawlessness in the world which demands quarantining those responsible for it to prevent its spreading. He left no doubt that he believed the United States should join the movement. "Those who love freedom," he declared, "must work together. . . . Peace-loving nations must unite."

The quarantine speech raised a furor in the United States. While men like Stimson and Hull were heartened by the president's remarks, opponents of involvement denounced it as a violation of the spirit of the neutrality acts and the charting of a dangerous course. Editorials in the Hearst press and in the *Chicago Tribune* led a nationwide chorus of condemnation. A poll of congressmen conducted by the *Philadelphia Inquirer* found them to be 2–1 against any common action with foreign nations. James Byrnes recorded in his diary that the president "was disappointed by the failure of the people to respond to his Chicago speech."

As the president had predicted, the epidemic of lawlessness was spreading. Not six months after he spoke in Chicago, in March of 1938, Adolf Hitler added Austria to the German Reich. Seven months later, in October, he absorbed the Sudetenland, the part of Czechoslovakia inhabitated by 3.5 million Germans and in March of the next year, the rest of that unfortunate republic came under Nazi rule. Not to be outdone by his northern neighbor, Mussolini annexed Albania to the Italian kingdom in April.

The ominous turn of events frightened the president. Each of Hitler's moves had been bloodless. The western European powers had opposed his acts but were not willing to stop him by force. Yet, it seemed clear that his appetite had not been satiated and that the powers would not permit his gobbling up other parts of Europe. A showdown had to come. Somewhere the line had to be drawn. War was bound to come. Confronted by that certainty, Roosevelt, on January 4, 1939, urged Congress to change the neutrality statutes. "We can and should," he said, "avoid any action, or lack of action which will encourage, assist, or build up an aggressor. We have learned that when we deliberately try to legislate neutrality, our neutrality laws may operate unevenly and unfairly—may actually give aid to an aggressor and deny it to the victim. The instinct for self-preservation should warn us not to let it happen."

The warning not only went unheeded, it was viewed as downright dangerous. Senator Robert A. Taft of Ohio issued his own warning: that the neutrality laws must not be changed; that the president must not be given discretion to favor one nation over another; that the experience of 1917 taught that such executive power leads to war. And he scoffed at the president's alarmist position that American security would be endangered by a European war. And joining Taft was an imposing battery of senators, led by William E. Borah of Idaho, stalwart defender of the right of Americans to be isolated.

In the summer of 1939, it appeared certain that war would come. In April, Hitler had made demands on Poland for the cession of the port of Danzig and the surrender of the strip of Polish land separating East Prussia from the rest of Germany. Poland would not yield and her resistance received the support of her allies, France and England. The line was being drawn. No one expected Hitler to take "no" for an answer. Hurriedly, in July, Roosevelt summoned half a dozen senatorial leaders to the White House. War was imminent, he said, offering to show them cables from American diplomats abroad as proof, and urged that the embargo on arms and ammunition be lifted. Borah, loftily, claimed that he had his own sources of information; that they were more reliable than the president's; and that they indicated there would be no war. That was in July. Six weeks later, on September 1, Hitler, fortified with a Soviet nonaggression pact signed in August, hurled his mechanized columns and his air force against Poland. Two days later, Britain and France declared war.

So war came to Europe for the second time in 25 years. Like his predecessor a quarter century earlier, Franklin D. Roosevelt proclaimed his country's neutrality. Unlike Wilson, however, he did not ask his countrymen to remain neutral in thoughts as well as in deed. No one could "close his conscience," he noted. His certainly was not closed and had not been since 1935, at least. In that year, speaking in San Diego, he had expressed his "great concern when ideals and principles that we have cherished are threatened." Thereafter, he had consistently sought changes in the neutrality laws for the benefit of the allies. Now, with the threat against them transformed into action, he returned to the fray. On September 21, 1939, he proposed to a special session of Congress a formula that he hoped would satisfy all sections of opinion. The embargo on war goods would be lifted thus enabling the western democracies to get their much-needed materiel but, to insure noninvolvement, sales would be on a "cash and carry" basis; combat zones would be designated from which American citizens and ships would be barred; travel of American citizens on belligerent vessels would be barred; loans would be forbidden. Once again, there was strong opposition in Congress. Borah, Taft, Nye, and other senators saw the measure as a prelude to American military participation. Borah ridiculed the idea that the struggle was between the forces of good and of evil. It was nothing more, he said, than an old-fashioned power struggle for territory and none of America's business. Where would the "cash" come from in "cash and carry," he queried? From the American taxpayer was his own prompt reply. And following arms and ammunition, he warned, would be men.

For six weeks the Congress debated the president's proposal. In the end, the Borah-Taft forces lost. To the majority of legislators (and the public, as well) Hitler represented evil and those who were fighting him deserved American aid. The issue was moral and strategic. American security would be endangered by a German victory but the Führer's triumph would also be a blow to international morality. By 243–172 in the House and 63–30 in the Senate, a new neutrality law was passed that the president signed on November 4. It enacted, in toto, the measures Roosevelt had proposed, thereby toppling the neat structure erected between 1935 and 1937 to insulate America from the "broils of Europe" and to prevent a repetition of 1914–1917. It had taken only four years (and some startling and frightening moves by Hitler) to convince Americans that their destiny was inextricably interwoven with other parts of the world however distant and that they could not stand on the sidelines as disinterested observers. The new statute was not, of course, a complete return to the 1914–1917 situation. There were the built-in safeguards: "cash and carry", prohibition on loans and on travel, designation of combat zones. Still, the commitment had been made to aid the Allies and large quantities of war goods began at once to cross the Atlantic paid for and carried away by the French and the British.

The winter of 1939–1940 was a curious one in terms of the European situation. It was termed the *Sitzkrieg* (sitting war) and the "phony war." Nothing much happened. Having conquered Poland handily, Hitler seemed completely preoccupied with governing it. But the inactivity did not last long. In April 1940, the German Führer turned his troops westward. In a campaign appropriately labelled *Blitzkrieg,* or lightning war, he conquered Belgium, Holland, Norway, and Denmark and in June France fell before his *Panzer* units. All of western Europe, save Britain, was now in German hands and that country, all through the summer and fall, was in great peril. German aircraft subjected the British Isles to a merciless and relentless pounding, destroying large sections of London and other major cities and it was questionable whether England could survive the Battle of Britain.

Americans were horrified and frightened. The president expressed the mood of large numbers of his countrymen in a speech on June 10 at the University of Virginia in which he pledged more aid to "the opponents of force" and a build-up of the defenses of the United States. Congress eagerly accepted the president's proposals for the latter measure. In July, there was passed the largest defense appropriation act in the nation's history—$5 billion to beef up the army from 280,000 to 1.2 million men, to add 18,000 planes to the army and navy airforces, and to build 1.325 million more tons of naval vessels. In September, Congress enacted a compulsory military service act—the first in peacetime. How far Congress would have gone in increasing aid to the last surviving member of the anti-German coalition will never be known because the president took the next step without legislative action. On September 2, 1940, he gave the British government fifty destroyers (veterans of the last war) in exchange for ninety-nine-year leases on certain British possessions in the Western Hemisphere.

The announcement of the "destroyer deal" had an electric effect on the country. Condemnation of the act was loud and vociferous from many quarters. A headline in the *St. Louis Post-Dispatch* neatly summed up the basis of the opposition. "Dictator Roosevelt Commits Act of War," it read. Thus, some people maintained that the transfer of the ships had, in fact, made the United States a cobelligerent and by executive instead of legislative action as the constitution provided. Furthermore, there were those who questioned the president's right to give away American property without Congressional approval. Still, all the evidence points to the conclusion that the act received the approbation of the majority of Americans and their representatives in Congress. There was satisfaction, that, in one stroke, the president had given Britain much-needed aid and had strengthened America's defenses. The destroyers were desperately needed to protect convoys from submarine attack while the leased land would serve as bases for warding off any sea or air attacks on the United States.

One may rightfully ask why the president did not seek Congressional approval for the exchange. It seems reasonable to suggest that Roosevelt feared, rightly or wrongly, that the Borah-Taft forces might have succeeded in defeating the plan, or, at best, so delaying its passage as to impair its usefulness.

The presidential election in the autumn of 1940 gave incontrovertible proof that the Administration's twin policy of aid to Britain and abstention from war had wide support. Both Republican Wendell Wilkie and Democrat Franklin Roosevelt campaigned on an "all-out aid—no foreign war" platform. Roosevelt was most emphatic in his pledge, made "again, again, and again. Your boys are not going to be sent into any foreign war." There is every reason to believe his profession sincere. He had no thought, in 1940, of leading the country to war. What he hoped and expected was what the majority of Americans hoped and expected—that all-out aid would be enough to swing the balance in favor of the democracies making active participation unnecessary. That view constituted the philosophy of the Committee to Defend America by Aiding the Allies founded in May of 1940 by William Allen White. Its 600 branches scattered throughout the country hammered home the message that the more aid extended, the less likelihood of war for the United States. What neither Roosevelt, nor White, nor the Committee's membership nor the average American faced was the possibility that the "all-out aid—no war" slogan contained mutually exclusive and incompatible elements. What if "all-out aid" so provoked Germany and so enmeshed the United States in the fortunes of the democracies as to make impossible the avoidance of war? Would the American people then choose halting aid over going to war? The gradual realization by the president in the spring and summer of 1941, based on numerous polls and narrow majorities on legislation, that his countrymen might choose that course provides the key to an understanding of why the really significant steps taken in 1941 that brought the United States into the war against Germany were by executive action without the prior consent of the Congress or of the American people.

The president won a third term handily although his majority was less than in 1936. Nonetheless, he took his victory as a mandate to continue his policy of aid to Britain and to the other Allied governments that were in exile. With the cares and distractions of campaigning behind him, he turned at once to working out the next step in his program of supporting the democracies. It was previewed in a "fireside" chat on December 29, 1940. The United States, said Roosevelt, must become the "arsenal of democracy" and must give, not sell, the sinews of war to those resisting aggression. He wanted to do away with "the silly, foolish old dollar sign." A few days later, he proposed legislation to implement the plan. The bill, known as H.R. 1776, at once drew the fire of those who saw in such deep involvement with the Allies a sure road to war. The opposition, led by Senator Burton K. Wheeler of Montana who predicted that the act "will plow under every fourth American boy," consisted of notable and reputable people. Charles A. Lindberg was among them as were Robert M. Hutchins, president of the University of Chicago, General Robert E. Wood, head of Sears, Roebuck and Company, and several key members of the Senate, notably William E. Borah, Robert A. Taft, and Hiram Johnson. The Hearst press and the *Chicago Tribune* served as the opposition's chief publicity vehicles blanketing their columns with admonitions not to get sucked into a war. At the same time, the America First Committee, founded by General Wood in September of 1940, sponsored large public meetings at which prominent speakers railed against the president's plan to turn the country into a supplier of war goods for foreign nations. They urged, instead, that America's great productivity be used to strengthen the country's defenses by building a "Fortress America." Such action alone, they insisted, would keep the nation independent and secure.

There were, however, strong supporters of the measure. The *New York Times* warned that the United States would never be safe if Hitler defeated the British. The country could not long remain the only democratic nation in the world. Only by helping England resist the Nazi tyranny could America assure her continued existence and that of western civilization. In the Senate, men like Carter Glass of Virginia, Alben Barkley of Kentucky, and J. W. Bailey of North Carolina spoke for the bill. Its object, said Bailey, was to head off war. And so the arguments ran, for and against, in the halls of Congress and in the public forum for two months until the vote was taken in the second week of March. The count was 60–31 in the Senate and 317–71 in the House and "an Act to Promote the Defense of the United States" became law on March 11. By its terms, the president was authorized to sell, exchange, lease, lend, or transfer war goods and food to the value of $1.3 billion to any country whose defense the president deemed vital to that of the United States. Eventually, "lend-lease" goods worth $50 billion went to Britain, Russia, and the other countries joined in the grand alliance against Germany. Forbidden under the act were the convoying by American warships of "lend-lease" goods and the entry of American vessels into combat areas. Thus did America's legislators make provision for "having their cake and eating it"—for aiding Britain while avoiding those acts that might bring on war.

The war, meanwhile, raged on several fronts. On the Atlantic, the German navy, using submarines in "wolf-packs" and pocket battleships, engaged in destroying British, Norwegian, and other Allied shipping carrying goods from America to Europe. Millions of tons of vessels were sent to the bottom of the ocean loaded with precious cargo designed to bolster Britain's defenses. Between February and May of 1941, the Battle of the Atlantic, as the contest between British warships protecting Allied convoys and German attackers was called, was at its greatest intensity. On land in North Africa, German and Italian troops under General Erwin Rommell, the "Desert Fox," were pushing British forces steadily westward toward Egypt. In the Balkans, German army units conquered Greece and Yugoslavia in April and occupied Crete in June. On June 22, Hitler turned against his ally, Joseph Stalin, whom he called "the Mongol halfwit," and invaded the Soviet Union.

To those events, President Roosevelt responded in the winter, spring, summer, and fall of 1941 with the drastic and daring moves that brought on war with Germany. Between January and March, at his direction, the joint chiefs of staff conducted secret talks in Washington with their British opposite numbers laying plans for coordinated military action should the United States enter the war against Germany. It was agreed, too, that should there be a war with Japan, the main effort would be directed toward defeating the enemy in Europe first. In March, the President authorized the repair of British ships in American yards. In the same month, he seized German vessels in American harbors and turned them over to the Allies. On April 9, he announced the occupation of Greenland by American soldiers, following an agreement with the Danish government-in-exile, to prevent it falling into Nazi hands and threaten the United States. On the same day, he informed the public he had removed the Red Sea from the list of combat zones into which American vessels were forbidden to sail under the 1939 Neutrality Law. Thus American suppliers were able to carry American goods directly to British forces fighting in North Africa. In April, too, Roosevelt authorized the use of American naval craft and airplanes for spotting and reporting to the British the presence of German submarines threatening their convoys. In

June, the president declared frozen all the assets of Germany and Italy held in American banks. In the same month, he ordered the closing of German and Italian consulates in the United States. In July came the announcement of the dispatch of American troops to Iceland to keep that country from becoming a German base. At the same time, the president told of the convoying of American merchant vessels by United States warships and planes as far as Iceland, which was only 700 miles from the coast of Scotland. Then, in August came the dramatic meeting between President Roosevelt and British Prime Minister Winston S. Churchill in an American warship off Newfoundland.

From that four-day conference, which began August 9, there emerged the Atlantic Charter, an 8-point program designed to create "a better future world." It pledged no territorial aggrandizement; no territorial changes without the consent of the people concerned; the right of all peoples to choose their own form of government; the free access to trade and raw materials; the improvement of labor standards, social security, and economic advancement; the security for all peoples of freedom from fear and want; the right to freedom to travel the seas; the abandonment of the use of force in settling international disputes and the establishment of a permanent system of general security. The meeting dealt also with important immediate needs in the agreement reached that American warships would join the British in convoying the vessels of all nations carrying goods across the Atlantic.

By this time, the United States and Britain had so linked their war effort that it was only a matter of time before Germany and America clashed at sea. It happened on the night of September 4 when a German submarine fired two torpedoes at the American destroyer *Greer*, which had been tracking the U-boat. The *Greer* replied with depth charges. Neither vessel was hit but the effect was warlike. The president took to the air waves on September 11 to reveal details of the attack. It was piracy, he told the American people and its aim was to end freedom of the seas and dominate the Western Hemisphere. He called the German ships "rattlesnakes of the sea," and he gave orders that they be shot at sight if they entered America's defense zone. Six weeks later came a second and more serious encounter. On the night of October 16–17, the destroyer *Kearny* on patrol duty off Iceland was hit by a German torpedo with the loss of 11 American lives. Again, the president went before the people to castigate the Nazis and their designs on the Americas. The shooting war had begun, he said, and the United States had joined Britain and the other democracies to stop Hitler and make a better world. Four days later, on October 31, the destroyer *Reuben James*, on convoy duty 600 miles west of Iceland, was sunk by a German submarine with the loss of

115 lives. The United States could hardly be said to be an innocent neutral bystander in the Battle of the Atlantic.

Indeed, only one impediment remained to make American participation in the Battle of the Atlantic complete—the Neutrality Law of 1939. As long as it remained on the statute books, the United States was an ally with one hand tied. On October 9, the president proposed its repeal so that American ships could carry goods anywhere in the world. For five weeks the measure was debated in the Congress between those who saw in the repeal the prelude to undesirable full cobelligerency and those who saw no hope for a German defeat without all-out American aid even at the risk of war. The final vote came on November 7 in the Senate and in the House on November 13. It stood 50–37 and 212–94. The last vestiage of neutrality was now gone. American merchantmen were to be armed and would go wherever those of the belligerents could go. There was now no real difference between America and Britain. Both nations were fighting side by side at sea, and the legal recognition of the fact could hardly be avoided. It came on December 11, 1941 when the German government recognized the existence of a state of war with the United States. America was now involved in a two-ocean war for, three days earlier, Congress had, at the request of the president, declared war on Japan following the attack on Pearl Harbor by Japanese aircraft on December 7.

BIBLIOGRAPHY

Mark L. Chadwin, *The Hawks of World War II* (1968).

Wayne Cole, *America First: The Battle Against Intervention, 1940–1941* (1957).

James V. Compton, *The Swastika and the Eagle: Hitler, the United States and the Origins of World War II* (1967).

Robert Dallek, *Democrat and Diplomat: The Life of William E. Dodd* (1968).

Robert A. Divine, *The Illusion of Neutrality* (1962).

———, *The Reluctant Belligerent: American Entry into World War II* (1965).

Alton Frye, *Nazi Germany and the American Hemisphere, 1933–1941* (1967).

Lloyd Gardner, *Economic Aspects of New Deal Diplomacy* (1964).

Walter Johnson, *The Battle Against Isolation* (1944).

Manfred Jones, *Isolationism in America, 1935–1941* (1961).

William L. Langer and S. E. Gleason, *The Challenge to Isolation, 1937–1940* (1952).

———, *The Undeclared War, 1940–1941* (1957).

ARNOLD OFFNER, *America's Appeasement: United States Foreign Policy and Germany* (1969).

JULIUS PRATT, *Cordell Hull* (2 vols., 1964).

Kichisaburo Nomura and Saburo Kurusu (Wide World Photo).

The Road to War, 1941: Japan

T
HE SURPRISE attack on the Pacific fleet at Pearl Harbor on December 7, 1941, was the way of resolving a situation the Japanese considered hopeless. They could not, by peaceful and diplomatic means, convince Washington of the fact that the domination of the Asian mainland and the great chain of islands to the southeast was necessary for their security and economic well-being. They failed to get American leaders to appreciate the simple geographical fact that Asia was to Japan as Latin America was to the United States and that a Monroe Doctrine for Asia was as valid as one for the Western Hemisphere. Thus, the United States emerged as the prime obstacle in the fulfillment of their destiny and force was the only way to remove it.

It had not always been that way, of course. Every president before Franklin Roosevelt had admitted Japan's special interest in areas adjacent to her home islands and acquiesced in the Japanese assuming the leading role in their exploitation. Even Roosevelt, upon assuming office in 1933, while subscribing to the nonrecognition doctrine regarding Manchuria, certainly did not take any steps to force a Japanese retreat. But as the decade of the 1930s moved on, the Roosevelt administration seemed to undergo a change in policy. It was, apparently, coming to the position that Japan could not be permitted to ride roughshod over China or extend her control to other parts of the continent.

The Japanese assaults upon Peiping at the Marco Polo bridge in July of 1937 and upon Shanghai the next month may be seen as the point at which the administration made the decision to contain Japan. It was not that Roosevelt and Hull wished to ignore the Island Empire's legitimate needs for raw materials, markets, and security. It was only that they wished Japan's requirements to be met by peaceful means and not at the expense of China's sovereignty and independence. Four months before the attack on China, Hull, in a speech, let Japan know that the United States would not turn its back on the Far East. American moral, cultural, and commercial interests in China, he said, were too great to permit any power to gain exclusive control over that country. In short, he made clear that the principles of the "Open Door" would be defended and maintained.

Japan, of course, was not deterred by Hull's words. Nor, on the other hand, was the United States intimidated by Nippon's move. Ambassador Joseph Grew advised from Tokyo that Administration policy ought to be strict noninvolvement in the conflict. American property should be protected, he said, but no sides should be taken. The president followed Grew's suggestion only in part. He did not intervene. Indeed, military action was out of the question in 1937. He did, however, take sides. His sympathies, as well as those of the vast majority of the American people, were wholeheartedly with China and he gave them concrete form in not invoking the neutrality statute, which made possible the export of war materiel to that beleaguered country. It was lucky for him that Japan had not formally declared war, for he then would have had no choice but to put the statute into operation.

As the fighting on the mainland continued, Roosevelt lost no opportunity to demonstrate his displeasure with Japan. In his "Quarantine" speech in Chicago on October 5, 1937, it was to Japan he referred when he spoke of lawbreaking nations and aggressors. And on the following day he announced his concurrence in a resolution by the League of Nations Assembly branding Japan as the violator of both the Kellogg-Briand Pact and the Nine Power Treaty. In early November, he joined 18 other nations meeting at Brussels to deal with the Asian crisis. Convened by the Belgian government at the suggestion of the League, the conference proved a failure. Japan, as was to be expected, refused to attend and, in any event, no power, least of all the United States, was willing to take drastic action.

The Japanese, meanwhile, were continuing their drive in China. Aerial bombings of major cities were followed by their capture and occupation: Nanking in December of 1937 and Hankow and Canton the following October. By the end of 1938, the Japanese were in control of most of the important coastal cities and railways and had created, at Nanking, a Reformed Government of the Chinese Republic as the legitimate government of China. Chiang Kai-shek, retreating before the enemy, had removed the really legitimate Chinese government to Chungking, deep in the interior of the country. Tokyo was now ready to announce the "new order" in eastern Asia based on "a tripartite relationship of mutual aid and co-ordination between Japan, Manchukuo, and China in political, economic, cultural, and other fields." Proclaimed in an official Foreign Office statement on November 3, 1938, it established the Greater East Asia Co-Prosperity Sphere—the vehicle for the exercise of Japanese hegemony in the area. There followed, slowly but surely, the closing of the "Open Door." The operations of foreign firms were curtailed and, in many cases, they were forced out of business by severe restrictions and discriminations. Asia was for the Asians under Japanese direction. The day of Caucasian supremacy had passed.

There was not very much Washington could do to thwart Japan short of war or economic sanctions, and neither course was viable given the state of the public attitude. Even the wanton sinking in December of 1937 of the American gunboat *Panay*, on patrol in the Yangtze River, with two Americans dead and thirty wounded, did not arouse the public ire sufficiently to warrant strong reprisal. Roosevelt did, however, take several measures that should have left no uncertainty in the minds of the Japanese as to his position. In July of 1938, he placed a "moral" embargo on airplanes to Japan by urging American manufacturers to withhold their sale. At the same time, he extended a loan of $25 million to China through the Export-Import Bank for the purchase of tung oil. In February of 1939, he gained an appropriation from Congress to strengthen the fortifications at Guam, Samoa, and Alaska; and on July 29 of the same year, he gave Tokyo the required six-month notice of his intent to terminate the Treaty of Commerce of 1911. This last move was ominous, for it implied a threat of greater economic reprisal. And for the record, strong protest was lodged in Tokyo by Ambassador Grew on instructions from Washington on the closing of the "Open Door" and the establishment of the "new order." The United States, said Grew, could not accept an infringement of the treaty rights of its citizens nor the unilateral rearrangement of sovereignty in eastern Asia. Considered together, the several measures taken by the Administration were correctly interpreted by Grew as "a hardening of the American position." In a speech in Tokyo before the American-Japan Society on October 19, 1939, shortly after returning from leave in the United States, Grew warned his audience that Japanese policy was driving a wedge between the two peoples and could lead to a dangerous confrontation.

Grew was seriously worried about the possibility of a collision and so apparently, were the Japanese. They continued, nonetheless, doggedly on their course of conquest and expansion oblivious of any baneful consequences. In fact, they were in the process of widening their sphere of operations beyond the Chinese mainland. Already, in the winter of 1939, they had occupied two islands in the French sphere of influence—Hainan, off China's south coast, and Spratly in the South China Sea. There was no question of their designs on French, Dutch, British, and American territory in Indochina, the Netherlands East Indies, Malaya, and the Philippines. A conference of cabinet ministers and army and navy officers on September 19, 1940, drew up a program of conquest which went beyond those lands to include Thailand, Burma, New Zealand, Australia, and India. A document discovered by American army personnel in Tokyo archives after the war and dated December 1941 made provision for the occupation and governance of territory even in the Western Hemisphere—Central America, parts of the West Coast of the United States and Canada, and several islands in the Caribbean.

Japan's opportunity to act was greatly enhanced in the spring of 1940 when Germany's victories in Europe weakened the hold of mother countries on Asian colonies. France's capitulation in June and the creation of a German-dominated government in Vichy ruling over part of the country not in Hitler's hands provided a superb opportunity. Tokyo lost no time in demanding of the French authorities access to certain key places in northern Indochina which the aged French leader, Marshal Henri Pétain, granted on September 22, 1940. In the same month, a Japanese delegation, taking advantage of the German occupation of the Netherlands, went off to Batavia to secure concessions in the Dutch East Indies but was meeting firm resistance. Meanwhile, diplomatic fences were being mended and flanks protected. On September 27, 1940, in Berlin, Japan entered into a pact with Italy and Germany that provided for mutual recognition of each signatory's "new order." It guaranteed, too, the benevolent neutrality of each of the powers in the event a cosignatory became involved in war. A final and crucial step in the international jockeying was achieved in April of 1941 when Tokyo and Moscow initialed a five-year treaty, each pledging neutrality should the other go to war.

To all these maneuvers, the United States responded vigorously and unequivocally. Immediately upon the collapse of the lowland countries, Secretary Hull issued a plain warning to Japan that any move to grab Asian territory of the conquered nations would threaten the peace and security of the "entire Pacific area." Not content with words alone, Washington in July moved to deprive Japan of much-needed raw materials. Petroleum, petroleum products, and scrap metal were forbidden to be exported without license and licenses were denied to shipments destined for Nippon. Similarly, aviation gasoline could not be sent outside the Western Hemisphere except for use by American aircraft in the service of a foreign country. Some time later, chemicals, machine tools, and other vital raw materials were embargoed. Roosevelt's policy was unmistakable. It was to apply pressure on Japan to keep her in line. She was to be denied vital material as a punishment for wrongdoing. Repentance and good conduct would be rewarded by a restoration of the flow of the things she needed. The irony of the situation was that the withholding of the crucial items caused Japan to seek them, and by force, in the very places the president sought to keep out of her clutches.

The Japanese were not eager for a confrontation with the United States. They hoped an accommodation could be made for a recognition of Tokyo's needs and interests in eastern Asia. They would have preferred an American blessing to their enterprise. Had not Theodore Roosevelt admired their pluckiness and courage and had he not sanctioned, in two significant executive agreements, their special rights on the mainland? Why would not his distant cousin, Franklin, follow suit? Despite the president's apparent hostility to Japan's pretensions and his lack of sympathy with her aspirations, Tokyo did make an effort, in the spring of 1941, to seek an accommodation, on its own terms, of course.

It came about through the medium of two American Roman Catholic priests who were in Asia on a mission for their order. When they were ready to return home, Prince Fuminaro Konoye, the prime minister, entrusted them with a series of terms to be submitted to President Roosevelt as a basis for discussion and resolution of the impasse between the two countries. The terms were strangely liberal and generous, providing for an evacuation of Japanese troops from China, respect for the principle of the "Open Door," and modification of the Tripartite Pact—all as a prelude for a review of Japan's economic needs. Roosevelt and Hull were certainly interested and it was agreed that serious conversations would await the arrival of the newly appointed ambassador, Kichisaburo Nomura, in April.

When Nomura arrived, it was found that his version of the terms differed markedly from that the clerics had brought back. It represented the views of the foreign minister, Yosuke Matsuoka, and the military clique. Their position was very much different from that of Konoye and the civilian element in the government. It was harsher, tougher, more unyielding, more nationalist, more belligerent. It reflected the historic disagreement the military had with the civilians who were considered too soft, pliable, and peaceful. The conflict between the two component parts of the leadership was, of course, not new. It was a perennial conflict in Japanese politics, but never before was it so dangerous and threatening for relations with the United States.

Nomura's terms were not very likely to serve as a basis for an agreement given the American position. They called for the recognition of the Japanese puppet regime in Nanking as China's legitimate government and demanded that Chiang Kai-shek accept a place in it; that Japanese troops remain in North China and in Inner Mongolia; that the United States restore normal trade relations with Japan and help Japan gain raw materials from southeast Asia. Nomura promised that Japan would agree to pursue its policy in Asia by peaceful means and end any thought of conquest on the mainland. As was to be expected, the terms were unacceptable to the United States. Hull retorted with his own version of what a settlement ought to entail and it was very different from Nomura's. He demanded the evacuation of all Japanese troops from China, the unseating of the Nanking government and the recognition of Chiang's government, and the disavowal of the treaty with Germany and Italy. He insisted, also, on a pledge to respect the principles of the "Open Door."

Clearly, an impasse had been reached. Two such diametrically opposed sets of terms could not be reconciled and by June, it was clear that to continue the conversations would be useless. The talks came to an end formally on July 24 when Japanese troops, with the reluctant consent of Vichy France, landed in southern Indochina and occupied several airfields and Saigon harbor. Such a move the United States could construe only as an indication of Tokyo's aggressive intentions. Nor need Washington have been greatly surprised for, having cracked the Japanese code in August of the previous year, it was known that at an Imperial conference on July 2 the Emperor had sanctioned an advance into Thailand and Indochina even if it meant war with England and America. Approval had also been given for attacks eventually on the Dutch East Indies and Singapore. Any American hopes for a peaceful settlement seemed slender indeed.

Washington responded sharply to the newest Japanese move. On July 26, President Roosevelt froze the assets of the Japanese in the United States, barred their commercial vessels from the Panama Canal, and halted all sales of petroleum to them (88 per cent of their oil was imported, of which 80 per cent came from America). At the same time, he recalled from retirement an experienced soldier and former chief of staff, Douglas MacArthur, and placed him in command of a newly formed Far Eastern headquarters located in the Philippines. In August, he warned Ambassador Nomura that should Japan take any further steps against neighboring countries, the United States would be "compelled to take immediately any and all steps which it may deem necessary" to safeguard American rights and security. There was no mistaking Roosevelt's intent or meaning. A Japanese attack on British or Dutch possessions in Asia would bring the United States into the war. That much the president had agreed to in his conference with Winston Churchill earlier the same month off the coast of Newfoundland.

Roosevelt was running the risk of war with Japan by his firm stand, but there was no alternative save assigning Asia to Japanese exploitation. Americans, following the course of events in the press, seemed, for the most part, willing to support the president. There were strong feelings that the Japanese should not be permitted to take over the continent. Particularly strong was the view that China must not be sacrificed. The president, of course, hoped that a war would not be necessary to bridle Japan. The tightening of the economic screw plus an unequivocal and unmistakable warning that America would not stand by passively while the forces of Nippon enveloped Asia ought to be enough, he believed, especially in view of the fact that he was prepared to take a hard look at the overall economy of the western Pacific region and to find a way to fulfill Japan's needs.

Prince Konoye was still hopeful for a settlement and he was prepared to make another stab at negotiating. His task was eased by the departure from the Cabinet of the firebrand ally of the militarists, Foreign Minister Matsuoka, in July and by Roosevelt's willingness to resume talks if there were a halt to further expansionist moves. The premier had in mind no ordinary conversations conducted by ambassadors and foreign ministers. He proposed that he and Roosevelt meet somewhere in the Pacific and thrash out their difficulties. Ambassador Grew at once advised the president to accept the proffered hand. Japan was in real trouble, he said, and was ready to make concessions in return for economic assistance. The cost of the China war, the economic squeeze by the United States, disillusionment with the German ally—all conspired to weaken the aggressive spirit and make Tokyo more amenable to compromise. Roosevelt was impressed by his ambassador's analysis and seemed ready to grasp the opportunity especially when Konoye, on August 28, disavowed the use of force by Japan upon her neighbors. Hull, however, was wary and distrustful. He did not believe that Japan would retreat from her position and he advised the president to consent to no meeting unless general lines of an acceptable basis for negotiating were agreed upon beforehand. The president, with some reluctance, accepted his secretary's suggestion and so informed the prime minister on September 3. That decision, in effect, ended the chances for a conference for as Konoye told Grew on September 6, he could not possibly have made advance commitments. The military clique would never have countenanced it.

It was on September 6 that another Imperial conference was held in Tokyo where, in the presence of the emperor, the decision was taken to pursue negotiations with the United States but with the clear understanding that if no progress were made by October, "we shall immediately make up our minds to get ready for war against America (and England and Holland)." It would be a war to break free of the economic straitjacket that the policies of the three countries was placing upon Japan.

Such a decision did not please Konoye. He feared its finality. He genuinely wished to avoid war at almost all costs and, indeed, at a Cabinet meeting on October 12, he even suggested that America's terms be accepted in principle as a basis for negotiating. His efforts to reverse the decision of September 6 caused his downfall. The militarists could not permit someone with so little backbone to head the government. On October 16 he was ousted from the premiership and replaced by a fierce militant, General Hideki Tojo. On instructions from the emperor, Tojo made plans to continue negotiations with the United States, but his announcement that

Japanese policies were "immutable and irrevocable" boded ill for their success.

On November 5, at an imperial conference, terms for the renewed conversations were considered. Two sets were prepared, Plan A and Plan B, the latter to be presented only in the event of the rejection of the former by the United States. A deadline of November 25 was set, later extended to the 29th, for America to accept the proposals, after which, if there was no agreement, "things are automatically going to happen." At the same time, it was decided that war preparations would be completed by early December. The new Japanese government was eager to meet the crisis. Delay was bad for them. Time was on the side of the enemy. They could use it to build their defenses.

Washington, of course, knew every Japanese plan and intention from the messages they intercepted between the Foreign Office in Tokyo and the embassy in Washington. Roosevelt and Hull were aware of the two plans, of the deadline, and of the war preparations. *They* were *not* eager to meet the crisis. Delay was crucial to them. They needed time to build the defenses of the Philippine Islands, a project that was proceeding at a slow pace. The first nine B-17 bombers had arrived at Clark Field on Luzon in the Philippines on September 12; a second group of twenty-five landed there on November 6, and more time was needed, as the chiefs of staff pointed out. There was also the fact that Roosevelt was completely preoccupied with the war in Europe—supplying the British and fighting off German submarines attacking American convoys. Japan, for him, was secondary. The master plan was to "baby the Japanese along" until Hitler was defeated.

On November 7, Ambassador Nomura presented Plan A to Secretary Hull. It was a vague and general proposal and Hull rejected it summarily. Thirteen days later, the Japanese representative, now joined by a seasoned career diplomat, Saburo Kurusu, sent expressly from Tokyo to assist the ambassador, handed the secretary Plan B. It was designed as a temporary measure to halt the drift to war and lay a basis for further negotiations. It provided that (1) neither government was to make further advances in southeast Asia (Japanese forces to remain where they already were); (2) Japanese troops were to leave French Indochina after a general Asian peace was effected; (3) the two nations were to cooperate to secure from the East Indies the resources they needed; (4) Japanese-American commerce was to be restored as before the freeze on July 25; (5) the United States was to sell Japan "a required quantity of oil"; (6) the United States was to take no action to prejudice the termination of hostilities between China and Japan (which meant, of course, no further aid to Chiang Kai-shek).

Hull could not accept Japan's terms. Even without the minute study to which they were later subjected, he saw them as "virtually a surrender." Agreement with Tokyo's position, he and the president concluded, "would mean condonement by the United States of Japan's past aggressions, assent to future courses of conquest by Japan, abandonment of the most essential principles of our foreign policy, betrayal of China . . . and abetting Japan in her effort to create a Japanese hegemony over the Western Pacific and eastern Asia." It was decided to make a counterproposal for a permanent settlement that would be tied to a temporary agreement lasting three months. During that time, there would be opportunity to reach an understanding based on the American proposal and if that failed, at least time would have been gained for the army and navy to strengthen the Philippines, where a Japanese attack was expected.

Hull's terms for the truce period provided for mutual pledges for peace, renunciation of further expansion in the Pacific area by force, withdrawal of Japanese forces from southern Indochina and a reduction to 25,000 of her army in northern Indochina, free flow of Japanese exports to the United States, the proceeds of which to be used for Japanese purchases in America to include raw cotton, food and medical supplies, and petroleum for civilian use, and included an affirmation that any settlement between Japan and China should be based on "the principles of peace, law, order, and justice."

The secretary did not believe Tokyo would accept the truce proposals. They were too different from their own suggestions. But that was not the reason he did not present them to Nomura and Kurusu. There were other factors. One was that the Chinese interposed strong objections. They saw nothing in the terms to prevent the Japanese from invading China during the three months. Furthermore, they opposed the stationing of 25,000 Japanese soldiers in Indochina and the resumption of Japanese-American trade. The British also voiced concern over the terms. They thought it unwise to supply the Japanese with oil and believed some pledge ought to be extracted from Tokyo to suspend operations in China for the truce period. Then there was the danger that a publication of the truce terms would be viewed by Americans as a capitulation to Japanese ambitions. So, Hull decided, reluctantly and with Roosevelt's approval, to set aside the truce proposals and hand to the Japanese emissaries a "comprehensive basic proposal for a general peaceful settlement." That was done on November 26.

The proposal was in two sections. The first dealt with general principles such as that both powers had no aggressive designs and that they sought peace in the Pacific. The second contained ten specific points. Distilled to their essence, they demanded that Japan withdraw her armed forces from Indochina and China, abandon the puppet regime in Nanking, recognize Chiang Kai-shek's Nationalist government, and agree to a multilateral nonaggression pact for East Asia in exchange for which the United States would resume trade with Japan on a liberal basis and stabilize the yen–dollar rate to bolster the sagging Japanese currency.

That Japan would reject the terms was a foregone conclusion. Hull advised Nomura and Kurusu to study the proposals carefully and the ambassadors themselves requested two weeks for their government to deliberate and prepare a reply. But at the same time, they spoke "disparagingly" of the document, as Secretary Hull later recorded in his *Memoirs*. And well they might have, for, as the Foreign Office noted in the official rejection on December 7, the proposal "ignores Japan's sacrifices in the four years in China, menaces the Empire's existence itself, and disparages its honor and prestige." It also, clearly, would have altered the course of Japanese history since 1895 when Tokyo first cast eyes on the mainland and launched the first attack on China. Everything that followed—Korea, Manchuria, the Marco Polo Bridge, Indochina—were logical consequences of that first move.

Hull was so certain nothing would come of his efforts that he told Secretary of War Stimson the next day, relative to the negotiations, "I have washed my hands of it . . . [the situation] is now in the hands of you [Secretary of the Navy] Knox, the Army and Navy." The same day he telephoned the same sentiments to the president, who was having a brief holiday in his retreat at Warm Springs in Georgia. He, also, had the chiefs of the armed services alert the commanders in Hawaii and in the Philippines of the breakdown in negotiations and of the possibility of an attack on the Philippines or somewhere in southeast Asia. To the Australian minister in Washington two days later, he reported that the "diplomatic stage is over" and he cautioned the British ambassador to expect a Japanese move "suddenly and with every element of surprise."

Tokyo, indeed, had already set the surprise in motion. At 6:00 A.M. of the day Hull handed Nomura and Kurusu the American proposals, a Japanese fleet consisting of six carriers, with a full complement of bombing planes and their fighter escorts, two battleships, cruisers, destroyers, and submarines, set out on an eastward course from a secret base in the Kurile Islands. Its instructions were to proceed to Pearl Harbor and attack the naval base there—subject to recall, however, should conditions change. In the flagship of the task force, the admiral commanding carried the flag flown at the great victory of Tsushima 36 years before.

President Roosevelt returned from Warm Springs on December 1 and set himself to preparing two messages—one to Congress apprising the legislators of the serious turn of affairs, the other a plea to the Japanese emperor for peace. Meanwhile, events were moving, indisputably, toward war. On November 30, General Tojo in a speech in Tokyo spoke of getting Great Britain and the United States out of East Asia with "a vengeance."

The same day, he telegraphed his ally in Berlin announcing the imminence of war with the Anglo-Saxon countries. On December 1, the cabinet council voted to reject Hull's terms. The next day, the secretary of state was informed of the decision but with a statement that Japan wished to continue negotiations. On December 2, orders went out from Tokyo to the carrier task force to carry out the strike against Pearl Harbor. The following day, the Foreign Office instructed the embassy in Washington to destroy the codes, coding machines, and all records.

Hull and Roosevelt, of course, by the intercept of messages from Tokyo to Nomura, were well informed of Japanese intentions (they did not know of the instructions to the task force). On December 3, commanders in Hawaii and the Philippines were apprised of the supremely important warlike indication contained in the order to destroy the codes. Two days later, Hull himself warned American envoys in east Asia of the possibility of a sudden break in their communication with the State Department, in which event they should burn their embassy codes and files.

December 6 was a day full of reports from varied sources of a huge Japanese fleet of thirty-five transports, eight cruisers, and twenty destroyers moving down the China coast destined for either Singapore, Thailand, the Philippines, or the Dutch Indies. Now the president sent off to the emperor the message he had been planning. Reminding him of the historic friendship of the two countries and noting the threat to all of southeast Asia by the continued concentration of Japanese forces in Indochina, he urged Hirohito to effect their withdrawal. Hull put the message on the cable for Tokyo that same night at 9:00 P.M. but it was too late. The plea did not reach Grew until after the attack on Pearl Harbor. It was, of course, never delivered to the emperor.

Early on the morning of December 7 (December 6, Tokyo time), at 7:55 A.M., the first wave of bombers swooped down on the great American naval base at Pearl Harbor. Wave after wave followed until the last plane winged its way back to its carrier at 9:45 A.M. In the wake of the assault, two American battleships lay totally destroyed, six others badly damaged, almost every airplane a wreck, and 2,400 people dead. The attack had come as a total surprise. Pearl Harbor had been totally unprepared.

On that same day, at 10:00 A.M., Hull and Roosevelt had been handed the intercepted reply to Hull's November 26 Ten Point Plan sent by the Foreign Office to Nomura and Kurusu for delivery to the secretary of state. Parts of it had been decoded the previous night and by 9:30 P.M. they had learned the general nature of the negative response. The Japanese emissaries had been instructed to deliver the reply at 1:00 P.M. on December 7 but because of a delay in the decoding they did not appear at the State Department until 2:05. By the time of their arrival, Hull already had received word of Pearl Harbor and he was inclined not to receive them.

Nonetheless, he did, at 2:20 P.M. He greeted the emissaries coldly, did not ask them to be seated, took the document they offered him, made a pretense of glancing through it, then "put my eye on him [Nomura]" and exploded. "I must say," he said, "in all my fifty years of public service I have never seen a document that was more crowded with infamous falsehoods and distortions—. . . on a scale so huge that I never imagined until today that any government on this planet was capable of uttering them." Without permitting Nomura, who was on the verge of saying something, to speak, Hull showed the two the door. Neither Nomura nor Kurusu knew anything of Pearl Harbor.

Two hours later, Japan declared war against the United States. The next day the Senate, unanimously, and the House, with one dissenting vote, acknowledged the existence of hostilities between the two countries.

Could the war have been avoided? Ambassador Grew believed that Hull and Roosevelt had made errors in their dealings with Japan and had missed opportunities for compromise. Others have maintained that the president had pushed Japan too far and too hard by his economic squeeze and had been unwilling to recognize her legitimate interests. They have even accused Roosevelt of goading the Japanese to fight. It would seem, however, that war could have been prevented only if the United States had been willing to stand aside and remain silent while Japan became mistress of east Asia and made of China a province of the Japanese Empire. Henry L. Stimson put the matter most aptly when he wrote some years later in his autobiography, *On Active Service:* "A careful reading of the diplomatic negotiations that preceded Pearl Harbor can lead to no conclusion but that it was American support of China—American refusal to repudiate the principles of Hay, Hughes, Stimson, and Hull—which proved the final cause of the breakdown of negotiations and the beginning of war. If at any time the United States had been willing to concede to Japan a free hand in China, there would have been no war in the Pacific." The United States was unwilling to sacrifice China and so the war came.

BIBLIOGRAPHY

CHARLES A. BEARD, *President Roosevelt and the Coming of the War, 1941* (1948).
ROBERT J. C. BUTOW, *Tojo and the Coming of the War* (1961).
DOROTHY BORG, *The United States and the Far Eastern Crisis of 1933–1938* (1964).
HERBERT FEIS, *The Road to Pearl Harbor: The Coming of the War Between the United States and Japan* (1950).
JAMES H. HERZOG, *Closing the Open Door* (1973).
DAVID J. LIU, *From the Marco Polo Bridge to Pearl Harbor: Japan's Entry into World War II* (1962).

WILLIAM NEUMANN, *America Encounters Japan: From Perry to MacArthur* (1963).

BASIL RAUCH, *Roosevelt from Munich to Pearl Harbor* (1950).

PAUL SCHROEDER, *The Axis Alliance and Japanese-American Relations, 1941* (1958).

CHARLES C. TANSILL, *Back Door to War* (1952).

ROBERTA WOHLSTETTER, *Pearl Harbor; Warning and Decision* (1962).

*Prime Minister Churchill, President Roosevelt, and Marshal Stalin at Yalta
(Wide World Photo).*

side at the liquidation of the British Empire." Another difference related to political arrangements in southeastern Europe. Churchill seemed to support a frank acceptance of the doctrine of spheres of influence as the basis for reconciling conflicting interests among the leading powers. In a meeting with Soviet Premier Joseph Stalin in October of 1944 in Moscow, he agreed to such spheres in the Balkans. To President Roosevelt and Secretary of State Hull such an approach to international life was abhorrent. They viewed such deals as a violation of the Atlantic Charter and as a return to the sordid practices of power politics that had been, in their eyes, the cause of the breakdown of the peace in 1914 and in 1939.

The two Anglo-Saxon powers differed also on the important matter of military strategy. Both agreed as to the order of priorities—Germany would have to be defeated first and then the full weight of the victorious forces would be turned against Japan. They disagreed, however, on how best to lick the Nazis. The American strategy was to mount a cross-channel invasion of the continent, meet Hitler's armies in northern France, and drive them back to Germany and to defeat and destruction. The Joint Chiefs of Staff envisaged such an assault in a modest way taking place in late 1942 to be followed by a bigger drive the following year as President Roosevelt told Soviet Foreign Minister Vyacheslav Molotov in May of 1942. The British idea was very much different. It was opposed to meeting the main body of the German forces head on. Such a prospect brought back grim memories of World War I when the two armies faced each other across a "no man's land," emerging from their trenches from time to time to fight bloody and indecisive battles. As one Briton told Army Chief of Staff George C. Marshall during a discussion of strategy, "It's no use— you are arguing against the casualties on the Somme [one of the costliest battles of the earlier war]." Instead, Churchill argued for hitting the periphery of the German bastion in Europe, poking away at the more vulnerable points through the "soft underbelly"—The Balkans, the Mediterranean, the Adriatic, Italy, the Ljubljana gap, the Aegean. Then, with Germany weakened by such tactics (as well as by massive aerial bombing), the cross-channel assault might be launched as a coup de grâce. In July 1942, Churchill decisively vetoed a landing in northern France that year.

The debate on the issue between the two allies was bitter and acrimonious. At one point, when Churchill proposed a landing on Rhodes, General Marshall exploded saying, "No American is going to land on that goddam island." Still, it must be said, that that difference, as well as the others, was debated against a broad background of basic confidence, trust, and understanding. Relations between the military and civil leaders of the two nations were close, friendly, and harmonious. Churchill and Roosevelt kept in constant and close touch by personal meetings (eleven from Argentia to Yalta), by letter, and by Harry Hopkins, the president's confidential emissary, acting as intermediary. In January of 1942, there was created a Combined Chiefs of Staff—the American chiefs and deputies of the British chiefs—sitting in Washington and planning strategy, allocating supplies, and generally directing the war effort on the daily level. Later that year, several combined boards were organized to handle specific aspects of the joint war effort such as raw materials, shipping, food, production, and resources.

The upshot of the squabble over strategy was a compromise agreed to at a Churchill-Roosevelt meeting at Hyde Park, the president's family home on the Hudson River, in June of 1942. It provided for an attack upon German forces in North Africa in November (code name: *Torch*). Roosevelt had been opposed to a Mediterranean campaign out of fear of the Spanish dictator, Francisco Franco. Flagrantly pro-Hitler, even to the extent of dispatching troops (the Blue Division) to the Russian front, Franco could have sealed off the Mediterranean at Gibraltar, thus trapping the Allied soldiers. He could have also permitted Nazi reinforcements to cross his country on the way to Africa. Shrewd, if distasteful, courting of Franco by selling him much-needed goods and paying good prices for what he had to sell gave Roosevelt some assurance that *Torch* could proceed without fear from that quarter.

At several subsequent bilateral encounters, the two leaders made other significant decisions. In January of 1943, at Casablanca, they elaborated plans for an expansion of the Mediterranean campaign and also agreed on the "unconditional surrender" formula for the Axis powers. That decision came in for considerable criticism on the ground that it tended to stiffen enemy resistance and to postpone the end of the war. On the other hand, its defenders saw it as an assurance to the Soviet Union that the fight would be to the finish and that there would be no separate peace. It also was calculated to deprive the Germans of a pet contention after World War I—"the stab in the back"—that their leaders had made peace although the military could have gone on fighting. In May of the same year, in Washington, the attack on Sicily and the Italian mainland was approved. Three months later, in Quebec, preparations were made for the surrender of Italian forces and in September, again at Quebec, an understanding was reached on the division of Germany into occupation zones and on a campaign in Burma.

Unhappily, no such experiences can be recorded in Soviet-American relations. That there were agreements reached and compromises made cannot be denied but there was, at the same time, a strong undercurrent of distrust and suspicion—on both sides and for good reason. The history of their recent relations (since the Bolshevik revolution) had been stormy. Russians could not forget the interventions by American soldiers in their country in 1918–1920 for the purpose, they believed, of foiling the revolution, or America's failure, for sixteen years, to grant recognition to the new government. (They seemed not to have recalled that Russia did not recognize American independence until twenty-six years after it was won.) Americans, for their part, had recollections of betrayals of Soviet pledges made at the time of recognition in 1933. Promises to suspend communist propaganda in America, permit freedom of religion in Russia, and negotiate the settlement of debts the czarist regime owed American citizens were never fulfilled. Nor was the great expectation of a giant Soviet-American trade realized. Then there was the series of purges in Russia in 1936–1937 that were so cruel and ruthless as to revolt the American people.

The worst, however, was yet to come. In August of 1939, Stalin made his pact with Hitler that paved the way for the German attack on Poland in September. At once, the Soviet dictator, himself, vulturelike, jumped in for his share of the kill. He grabbed eastern Poland and took the three Baltic states—Estonia, Lithuania, Latvia—into the Soviet empire. In November, he attacked Finland after that little republic resisted his demands for territory. To all those events, Americans reacted with revulsion and disgust. The Russians seemed no better than the Nazis, their partners, or the Japanese, with whom Stalin also made a pact in April of 1941.

Then came June 22, 1941, the day Hitler turned on his ally and suddenly and wholly unexpectedly, Russia was ranged alongside the democracies fighting the common enemy. At once, the Muscovites came in for their share of American aid. "We must give Russia all aid to the hilt," Hull told Roosevelt. "We have repeatedly said we will give all the help we can to any nation resisting the Axis." In July, Roosevelt sent Hopkins to ask Stalin what he needed to fight the enemy and, soon, supplies began to flow eastward—guns, tanks, planes, vehicles. By October, war goods to the value of $41 million had reached Stalin, paid for in cash. On October 30, the president extended lend-lease to Russia to the amount of $1 billion. Thereafter, a steady and seemingly endless stream of war materiel crossed the seas entering the Soviet Union by way of Murmansk, Vladivostok, and the Persian Gulf. By the war's end, the value had climbed to $11 billion.

In the fall and winter of 1941, Russia was in a desperate position. Nazi armies had made deep inroads into the country, sweeping all opposition before them. By early December, they had breached the outer defenses of Moscow. But, like the army of an earlier dictator invading from the west, they were repulsed. The Russians fought valiantly and fiercely, and their courage and bravery aroused the greatest admiration in America. Forgotten were the harsh indictments heard on all sides not half a year before. Now everything Russian was popular. American soldiers watched films of heroic Russian resistance to the Nazis as part of their indoctrination program in their basic training. Millions of ordinary citizens saw the motion picture made from Joseph E. Davies' *Mission to Moscow* and were moved by the benign portrait of "Uncle Joe" Stalin and thrilled by the Red Army chorus singing their cavalry march as accompanying music. Davies' book, a narrative of his tenure as ambassador in the Soviet capital, was immensely popular, passing through thirteen printings in hardcover in 1941–1942 and seven more in paperback in 1943–1944. Many people were willing to accept his portrayal of Stalin as giving "the impression of a strong mind which is composed and wise. His brown eyes are exceedingly kind and gentle. A child would like to sit in his lap and a dog would sidle up to him."

Additional praise came from strange quarters, indeed—the Daughters of the American Revolution at their convention in Washington in the spring of 1942; Thomas Lamont of J. P. Morgan and Company at a Congress of Soviet-American Friendship in New York in November of the same year; Douglas MacArthur on an anniversary in 1942 of the founding of the Red Army; and the *Saturday Evening Post*, long-time arch-foe of the regime. Observers noted many evidences of a new Stalin, a lover of freedom and a supporter of democracy. They pointed to his adhesion to the Atlantic Charter, his signing of the United Nations Declaration, his dissolution in May of 1943 of the Comintern (the party vehicle for international propaganda and revolution), and his pledges in various speeches to refrain from interfering in the affairs of other nations, to seek no territory for Russia, and to liberate enslaved regions, restoring to them their sovereignty and independence.

The euphoric honeymoon quality of the Soviet-American relationship did not, however, conceal or dispel the uneasiness felt by many Americans concerning Russia. They saw Stalin's transformation as more apparent than real and the result not of conviction but of expediency rooted in his need for American supplies. They shared the judgment of Averill Harriman, the Ambassador in Moscow, who believed that "all the Soviets intend to do is to give lip-service and to create certain instances which would give the impression of relaxation without really changing their present practices." Those people did not ignore Stalin's reservation when signing the Atlantic Charter: "Considering that the practical application of these principles will necessarily adapt itself to the circumstances, needs, and historical peculiarities of particular countries." It was viewed as an ominous portent of his intention to place outside the Charter's purview certain territories he deemed essential to the security of his country.

Many acts of the Soviet government seemed to justify the term "strange alliance," which Major General John R. Deane used to characterize the Soviet-American relationship. The Russians consistently refused to provide the Americans with information on their latest weapons and would permit only a handful of American scientists to visit Soviet installations. They were extremely reluctant to permit the United States to use Russian territory as bases for the shuttle bombing of the Balkans, and, when permission was given, American airmen at the bases were subjected to treatment hardly to be expected from an ally. Their insistence that the three Baltic states, eastern Poland, and part of Rumania be recognized as Soviet territory aroused grave apprehension as to Stalin's designs for the postwar world. What else, one wondered, did he covet? What additional land would he claim? The *New York Times* reflected the fears when it editorialized on February 14, 1943, "As Red armies plunge forward they are raising many questions in many minds as to what orders they have written on their banners." And Cordell Hull, writing to British Foreign Secretary Anthony Eden in March of 1943, voiced a common concern in the words "Many people here are stating that at the end of the war Russia will do as she pleases, take what she pleases, and confer with nobody."

As in America, so in Russia, there were many who were sharply critical of the ally across the sea on many accounts. The invasion of North Africa in November of 1942 was deprecated by Stalin. It hardly could be considered a real second front, he claimed. It engaged only ten German divisions while the Soviets were confronted by 280. The failure to open a second front (until 1944) was viewed by some Russians (and publicly presented in a lecture by one, a prominent Soviet theoretician, Professor Yadin, on October 28, 1942) as a deliberate design by anti-Red groups and by capitalists to hold off until the Russians were so weakened as to present no threat to the west. There was, also, dissatisfaction over America's dealing with Franco and with the French Vichy government. The United States had retained diplomatic relations with Vichy not out of feelings of friendship for the puppet rulers, the aged marshal Pétain and Pierre Laval, but for expediency. It was hoped that the American connection would tend to reduce Hitler's influence and prevent the surrender to the Axis of the French fleet and of French bases in North Africa. An ambassador, Admiral William D. Leahy, was sent in January of 1941 and in February, an agreement was signed whereby the United States would provide supplies to Morocco and Algeria. Vichy broke relations when North Africa was invaded, but the connection paid off in that Pétain and Admiral Jean Darlan, his representative in Africa, ordered their troops not to resist the Americans.

It was this web of misunderstanding and suspicion and ill-feeling which caused Cordell Hull to fly to Moscow, despite the fact he was old, sick, and hated flying, to meet with Molotov and Eden and clear the Allied air. The conference lasted twelve days—October 19–30, 1943—and produced some important results. Agreement was reached on the establishment of an international organization after the war to insure the peace of the world, on the creation of a European Advisory Commission to sit in London charged with studying questions concerning political problems arising out of the war, on the partition of Germany amongst the three Allies to govern the country pending a decision on its future status, on setting up an Advisory Council to make recommendations on the governance of Italy, which had surrendered the previous month, on the establishment of an independent Austria, and on the advisability of bringing the Nazi leaders to trial. Of great significance was Stalin's promise to enter the war against Japan after Germany's defeat. The results of the meeting pleased the Soviet dictator, who celebrated by giving a huge reception at its end. And Hull was equally happy with the accomplishments. For him, the chief victory was in Stalin's acceptance of the idea of a postwar international organization. In reporting to a joint session of the House and Senate upon his return, he expressed satisfaction that "there will no longer be need for spheres of influence, for alliances, for balance of power, or any other of the special arrangements through which, in the unhappy past, the nations strove to safeguard their security or to promote their interests."

One month after Moscow, the three wartime leaders had their first meeting at Teheran. On the way, Roosevelt and Churchill stopped off at Cairo to settle with Chiang Kai-shek certain problems relating to the war in Asia. It was Roosevelt's policy to raise China to be the great power in that area and to be the stabilizing Asian force. He had, since the beginning of the Sino-Japanese war in 1937, given the generalissimo financial aid and, somewhat later, had sent a military mission to the capital. He had, also, provided the Chinese air force with an American commander (Claire L. Chennault), American planes, and American pilots (air force personnel retired or on leave). Since joining the war, the president had stepped up aid, which, because the Japanese controlled the seacoast, had to make its way by way of Rangoon and the Burma Road into southwest China. When Japanese forces closed that highway in 1942, supplies had to be flown over the "hump" of the mountains until, in 1944, a new road was opened between India and Yunnan province (the Ledo Road). Things were not going smoothly for Chiang. The truce he had made in 1937 with the Chinese Communists for a united front against the Japanese had broken down and the rivalry between the two groups was very great. He could not get along with the Commander of American forces in China, the tough and tart General Joseph W. Stilwell (aptly nicknamed "Vinegar Joe") whose estimate of the generalissimo was very low (he referred to him as the "peanut dictator"). Eventually, Roosevelt recalled Stilwell but the conflict between the two had weakened their effort against the Japanese. And, finally, there were grave problems at home—inflation, suspicion of corruption and venality, and increasingly repressive politics all tending to arouse dissatisfaction in the population.

Still, Roosevelt put his support behind Chiang. In January of 1943, he took a major step in abrogating the extraterritorial rights and other privileges enjoyed by the United States in China since the mid-nineteenth century, thereby removing from Chinese sovereignty a painful and humiliating servitude. At the end of the same year, he was to have the Chinese Exclusion Act of 1882 repealed and to place China on a quota system for immigration. At Cairo, he further enhanced China's international position. Pledges were given to strip Japan of her conquests and restore to China territory seized from her by Japan—Manchuria and Formosa. Korea, it was agreed, would be given independence. There was no denying that, despite Roosevelt's build-up of China, that country's usefulness in the war in Asia was not very great and diminished as American troops approached closer to the Japanese homeland from the east and from the south by sea.

The Teheran conference, coming two days after Cairo, was a milestone in the diplomacy of the war. It was a cordial and intimate meeting. As Roosevelt described it some weeks later, "We had planned to talk to each other across the table . . . but we soon found we were all on the same side of the table." Crucial issues were settled—the cross-channel invasion (*Overlord*) was set for May or June of 1944; a landing on the southern coast of France was set; aid was to be given to Marshal Tito, leader of the Yugoslavian pro-Communist partisans (in preference to the rightist Chetniks under General Drazha Mihailovich); Stalin promised to enter the Japanese war after Germany's defeat; the Polish boundary was established at the Curzon line (an ethnographic boundary established in 1919) on the east and the Oder river on the west (as compensation for territory lost in the east); an agreement on the "establishment of international peace, security, and prosperity after the war in accordance with the principles of the Atlantic Charter. . . .", and, lastly, plans were made to coordinate the military effort for the final defeat of Germany.

In his study of the relations between the two men, *Roosevelt and Hopkins*, Robert Sherwood wrote, "If there was any supreme moment in Roosevelt's career, I believe that it will be fixed at this moment, at the end of the Teheran Conference." If Sherwood exaggerated, it was not by very much because the president left the meeting in a state of elation. It was not only that he could say, "We leave here, friends in fact, in spirit, and in purpose." It was that he and Stalin had agreed on every issue and especially on the postwar international organization and on Russia's entering the Asian war. He had all along believed that only with Stalin's cooperation would peace be maintained in the world, and he was equally convinced that Stalin would cooperate if treated properly. To William C. Bullitt, a trusted diplomatic advisor, he wrote, "I think that if I give him everything I possibly can and ask for nothing in return, noblesse oblige, he won't try to annex anything and will work with me for a world of democracy and peace." He belittled the view of Stalin as a threat. "I think the Russians are perfectly friendly"; he wrote in March of 1944, "they aren't trying to gobble up all the rest of Europe or the world. . . . They haven't got any crazy ideas of conquest; . . . these fears have been expressed by a lot of people here—with some reason—that the Russians are going to try to dominate Europe. I personally don't think there is anything in it." History, of course, proved him wrong. The Soviets did come to dominate a considerable part of Europe—after his death. What would have happened had he lived and governed into the postwar period, we will never know. He once remarked to Churchill, "I think I can personally handle Stalin better than your Foreign Office or my State Department." Some historians believe that Roosevelt, indeed, knew best how to handle the Soviet Premier, and, had he lived, there would have been no confrontation and no Cold War. Unhappily, such a theory is not susceptible to proof.

The year 1944 was a time of allied success on every front. In Italy, German forces were being pushed relentlessly northward. Rome fell in June and in the same month the long-awaited massive crossing of the channel took place and the battle for mastery of the continent began. The German units defending their positions in France fought hard, but the Anglo-Americans proved too much for them. Mile after mile they retreated before the massed infantry, artillery, and armor supported by tactical aircraft. Paris was liberated in August, and the same month saw the Allied landing on the Mediterranean coast of France. Meanwhile Soviet armies were advancing on their front, driving the Germans before them. The doom of the Third Reich, destined by its founder to last for a thousand years, was imminent. The time had come, Churchill believed, for another meeting of the three leaders to resolve problems which the final victory would raise.

First, there was Germany and its future. Should it remain a single state? If it should, what of its boundaries? Several proposals had been considered. Roosevelt at one time thought it ought to be divided into five separate countries. At another, he favored tearing Prussia away from it. Most serious was the plan advanced by Secretary of the Treasury Henry Morgenthau to give parts of Germany to Poland, Russia, Denmark, and France; divide what was left into two parts and convert them into "primarily agricultural and pastoral" countries, eliminating their war-making industries. The plan was actually formally adopted by Roosevelt and Churchill over the opposition of Cordell Hull and Henry L. Stimson in September of 1944 but dropped not long after that. The danger of leaving an industrial void in central Europe and of relegating the highly industrialized German nation to a rural future quickly became apparent.

Then, there was the French question and it was thorny. After the occupation of one part of France by the Nazis and the creation of a German puppet government in the other, many French patriots fled their country, resolving to carry on the fight from exile or from one of the colonies. Leading the resistance with headquarters in London (where several other governments-in-exile were based) was Charles de Gaulle, a capable and dedicated general officer, a graduate of St. Cyr (the French military academy), and a career soldier. Operating at first through the Free French National Committee, de Gaulle with General Henri H. Giraud, also in exile, created, in June of 1943, the Committee of National Liberation (to which the United States provided lend-lease goods), which devolved into the Provisional Government of the French Republic. Arrogant, vain, and obstinate, de Gaulle got along badly with his associates. He soon fell out with Giraud and in November eased him out of the organization. De Gaulle remained the sole leader. Roosevelt and Churchill actually preferred Giraud to de Gaulle. They had, in fact, selected Giraud to lead loyal French forces in the North African campaign. They had no choice, however, in view of de Gaulle's position of leadership, and on October 27, 1944 recognized de Gaulle as leader of the Free French. The French role in the fighting was minimal and Stalin did not believe that that role warranted treating France as a great power. The other two leaders, feeling a sense of history, could not relegate that country to a minor position in the postwar world. The chief practical question that had to be faced related to France's part in the occupation and governance of Germany. Already, one important decision concerning France's future had been taken in September of 1944 at Dumbarton Oaks (outside of Washington), where a conference was held to draw up a tentative charter of the new international organization. There it had been agreed that France would become, along with the Big Four (United States, Russia, Britain, China), a permanent member of the Security Council.

Dumbarton Oaks proved to be a memorable and significant conference. There, from August 21 to October 7, representatives of the United States, Britain, China, and Russia met to draw up proposals for the charter of the United Nations, the name given to the new organization. The principle that such an international institution be created had already been agreed to by the powers. It remained now for the details to be worked out. The idea had been American from the start. The first reference to it, veiled to be sure because of Roosevelt's fear of arousing opposition at home, appeared in the Atlantic Charter of 1941. Article 8, which talked of the reduction of armaments, included the phrase, "pending the establishment of a wider and permanent system of general security." The president need not have been so apprehensive. There was a mighty groundswell of opinion in the United States that some sort of an association of nations would have to be established to regulate international life and eliminate wars as a means of settling disputes. More importantly, there was a large measure of support from both political parties and in both houses of Congress. On March 16, 1943, the epochal bipartisan B2H2 resolution (named for Republicans Ball and Burton and Democrats Hill and Hatch) calling for the United States to take the initiative in forming an international organization was introduced into the Senate. In June, a resolution by Representative J. William Fulbright of Arkansas for "establishment of international authority with power to prevent aggression and to preserve world peace" was presented to the House of Representatives. It passed in September by a vote of 360–29. A similar proposal (modifying the B2H2 resolution) was given to the Senate by Tom Connolly of Texas and was approved 85–5 in November.

Thus was accomplished a diplomatic revolution in the United States. The American people and their legislators had muffed the first chance after World War I; they were not going to muff the second. One can sense the high drama at the meeting of the Republican Post War Advisory Council in September of 1943 at Mackinac Island in Michigan when the party leadership turned its back on the "Irreconcilables" and "Bitter Enders" of 1919–1920. Much credit must be given to Senator Arthur Vandenberg of Michigan, long an opponent of international political commitments, who led the movement for a United Nations in the party of Lodge, Borah, and Johnson. His, and his colleagues', conversion may be laid to a realization that the security of the country was best achieved by *averting* war and that war could best be averted by some sort of international authority. Yet, recognition must be given the role played by Roosevelt and Hull in the Republican shifts. Avoiding Wilson's mistakes, they, from the very beginning, brought the opposition party's leaders into the planning of the international organization. Hull's Advisory Commission on Post War Policy, created in 1942, included Republicans as well as Democrats and legislators from both houses of the Congress. At every stage of the development, that kind of consultation continued. In May of 1944, Hull took the draft of the UN charter to the Senate Foreign Relations Committee for its comments and suggestions. Some historians have maintained that the course of the League of Nations in the Senate might have been very different from what it was had Wilson been a Roosevelt and Lansing a Hull.

On October 9, 1944, the proposed charter was published for the world to see. It was much lengthier than the League of Nations Covenant but not essentially different. It provided for an Assembly, a Security Council (eleven members; five permanent—the Big Five—six rotating), an Economic and Social Council, and an International Court. Power of enforcement was lodged in the Security Council, with the Assembly serving as the forum for debate. Membership was to be open to all nations. Several important procedural matters could not be agreed upon and had to be left to the meeting Churchill was proposing.

At the coming conference there also would be the question of the future of the nations of eastern and southeastern Europe now liberated from the Germans—their boundaries and their form of government. Stalin had, on several occasions, pledged noninterference in the internal affairs of those countries and support of the principle of self-determination. Still, by the summer and fall of 1944, Red armies were in control of much of the area and leaders of the liberation and resistance movements were frequently communists tied to Moscow. Churchill, fearful of eventual Soviet domination of the countries by local communists to the exclusion of British interests, sought to come to terms with Stalin for a division of the area into spheres of influence. In October, he and the Soviet premier initialed an agreement in Moscow, mentioned earlier, assigning the preponderant influence in Rumania, Hungary, and Bulgaria to Russia and in Greece to England with Yugoslavia divided equally between the two at an east–west line. The United States, in the words of Secretary Hull was "flatly opposed to any division of Europe or sections of Europe into spheres of influence." A final arrangement clearly required consultation among the three nations.

Poland was even more difficult a matter. The problem was two-fold—territorial (where the eastern boundary would be drawn) and political, that is, control of the liberated government. As to the boundary, Stalin made clear his determination to move the pre-1939 line 150 miles to the west, to the 1919 Curzon line, as the necessary buffer for Russian security. But the Polish government-in-exile in London had flatly rejected the move which meant the loss of 40 per cent of Polish territory and 5 million Poles. That was only one issue which split Stalin and the London Poles. There were others—the suspicion that Russia, not Germany, was responsible for the murder of 10,000 Polish officers in April of 1943 in the Katyn Forest, the failure of the Soviet Army to come to the aid of the Polish underground in the Warsaw uprising in August of 1944 although it was only six miles from the Polish capital, and a difference in ideology. London Poles, first led by Wladyslaw Sikorski and then by Stanislaw Mikolajczyk, were anticommunist, and Stalin had created his own resistance group, the Union of Polish Patriots. It was believed that Stalin withheld help from the Poles in their uprising because they were not his brand of Poles (although he claimed his troops had been pinned down by Nazi forces). In any event, when the Soviet armies reached the outskirts of Warsaw in July of 1944, Stalin turned over the land west of the Curzon Line to the Committee on National Liberation, which was the political arm of the Union. On August 15, 1944, the Committee established a temporary capital at Lublin and on January 5, 1945, Stalin recognized the Lublin Poles as the government of Poland.

Both Churchill and Roosevelt believed Russia ought to have the Curzon Line as her western border with compensation for Poland at Germany's expense and so had agreed at Teheran. They were impatient with what they considered the obstinacy of the London Poles regarding the boundary and did not plan to jeopardize their good relations with their powerful ally to satisfy their national pride. Yet they were not willing to accept Lublin as the Polish government. It remained for the projected conference to settle the matter once and for all.

The meeting took place in February of 1945 at Yalta, a lovely, albeit war-torn, resort in the Crimea, site of a magnificent palace of the czars. It was to be the last meeting of the three leaders of the war against Hitler. Roosevelt, recently inaugurated as president for a record-breaking fourth

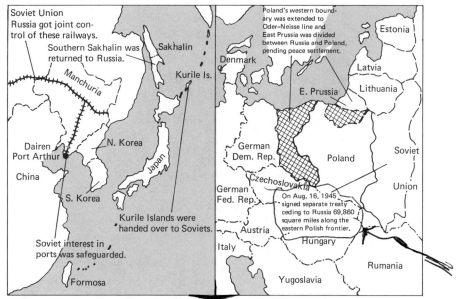

Soviet Union
Russia got joint control of these railways.
Southern Sakhalin was returned to Russia.
Sakhalin
Kurile Is.
Manchuria
Denmark
Dairen
Port Arthur
N. Korea
China
Japan
S. Korea
Kurile Islands were handed over to Soviets.
Soviet interest in ports was safeguarded.
Formosa

Poland's western boundary was extended to Oder-Neisse line and East Prussia was divided between Russia and Poland, pending peace settlement.
Estonia
Latvia
E. Prussia
Lithuania
German Dem. Rep.
Poland
Soviet
German Fed. Rep.
Czechoslovakia
On Aug. 16, 1945, signed separate treaty ceding to Russia 69,860 square miles along the eastern Polish frontier.
Union
Austria
Hungary
Italy
Rumania
Yugoslavia

LEFT: *Yalta Agreement—February, 1945*; RIGHT: *Potsdam Agreement—August, 1945.*

term, would be dead some two months later, and Churchill would soon be driven from office by a Labor landslide. For eight days, beginning on February 4, the Big Three and their military and civil staffs discussed and debated the issues attendant upon the last days of the war. There were disagreements and differences but they were resolved, and the result was a series of far-reaching decisions concerning, principally, the postwar world.

The fate of Germany was central and its destiny was sealed by the decision to dismember it. Pending the working out of details by a London-based committee consisting of the British foreign secretary and the Soviet and American ambassadors in the capital, it was to be divided into four zones of occupation—the one for France over Stalin's objections and carved out of the British and American areas. Close coordination of the zones was envisaged by means of the four commanders constituting an Allied Control Council headquartered in Berlin. For her wanton course of conduct, Germany was to pay—dearly. An estimated $20 billion of reparations were to be levied—in "kind" not cash—half of which was assigned to the war's chief sufferer, Russia. A reparations commission, sitting in Moscow, would determine the precise figure eventually. Meanwhile, payments would be of three "kinds"—forced labor, removal of capital goods (plans and equipment), and annual deliveries of goods from current production.

Poland and the other liberated areas came next on the agenda. The

Occupation Zones in Germany and Austria, 1945–1946.

Polish boundary did not arouse controversy. The Curzon line was adopted for the east with "substantial accessions of territory in the North and West" (left undefined). The nature of the future government caused trouble. Stalin would have nothing to do with the London exiles; Roosevelt and Churchill would not accept Lublin. The compromise reached finally leaned toward Stalin. There would be an "interim" government consisting of the Lublin Poles plus "democratic leaders from Poland itself and from Poles abroad" pending "free and unfettered elections as soon as possible on the basis of universal suffrage and secret ballot." Stalin's view of "free elections" was different from that of the west's (as Harriman had warned in a dispatch from Moscow some two months earlier) and since the Soviet leader would not permit supervision of the elections (his soldiers were in control of the country) there was every opportunity for Stalin to get what he most needed—a government "friendly" to Russia. The same solution for the other liberated areas—"interim" governments "broadly representative of all democratic elements" pending "free and democratic" elections—would provide Stalin the same opportunity.

Then there was consideration of Russia's entry into the Asian war. Stalin agreed to join the fight two or three months after Germany's defeat. In return, Roosevelt and Churchill promised Stalin the Kurile Islands and the southern half of the Sakhalins, restoration of the lease of Port Arthur, the internationalization of Dairen with Russia's preeminent interests there safeguarded, joint operation with China of the South Manchurian and the Chinese Eastern Railroads, and the maintenance of the status quo in the Soviet-sponsored Mongolian Peoples' Republic.

Finally, there were resolved the questions left unanswered at Dumbarton Oaks. Stalin agreed to attend a conference to open at San Francisco on April 25, 1945 to which all nations fighting the Nazis as of March 1 would be invited for the purpose of writing a definitive charter for the United Nations. On voting in the Security Council, unanimity was adopted as the rule on substantive matters and 7 out of 11 on procedure. The two Soviet republics of Belorussia and Ukraine were admitted as independent states and France was confirmed as a permanent member of the Council. The accords on voting and on the Japanese war were secret and not to be revealed for another year.

The conference ended on February 11 and Roosevelt and his delegation left in a mood of "supreme exaltation." Cooperation with Russia had been assured on every major matter—the Asian war, the occupation of Germany, the United Nations, and support for democratic governments in Poland and the other liberated areas. The delegation "really believed that this was the dawn of a new day. We were absolutely certain," wrote Robert Sherwood recording Harry Hopkins' recollection, "that we had won the first great victory of the peace. The Russians had proved that they could be reasonable and farseeing and there wasn't any doubt in the mind of the President or any of us that we could live with them peacefully for as far into the future as any of us could imagine." For the president, "The Conference in the Crimea was a turning point—I hope in our history and therefore in the history of the world. . . . It was a successful effort," he told Congress in a report on March 1, "by the three leading nations to find a common ground for peace. It spells the end of the system of unilateral action and exclusive alliances and spheres of influence and balances of power and all the other expedients which have been tried for centuries and have failed. We proposed to substitute for all these a universal organization in which all peace-loving nations will finally have a chance to join."

Roosevelt was not alone in his exurberance. It was shared by Churchill. "We were all standing on the crest of a hill with the glories of future possibilities stretching before us," he wrote. And to the House of Commons, he optimistically reported, "I know of no government which stands to its obligations . . . more solidly than the Russian government."

The tragedy of the postwar world was that the great hopes were to be falisfied. Cooperation, good will, and unity did not long survive Yalta and the causes for the rupture were laid at Roosevelt's door by many historians. They claimed he surrendered too many advantages to the Soviets in eastern Europe and in China. Some of them believed he had been duped by the wily Soviet dictator who took advantage of the president's failing health and naiveté; others advanced the theory that there were traitors in the State Department who prevailed upon the president to turn over to the Russians large areas for them to exploit and control.

The charge, as made, for example, by John T. Flynn in *While You Slept*, that the State Department was "heavily loaded with friends and agents of Stalin" who planned deliberately to sell out to the Soviets is an allegation without foundation and has not been proven. That the president was ailing was true but that his physical condition led to concessions to Stalin is an hypothesis not shared by other students of the event. Nor, do they believe he was naive. What he "gave away" was either not his to withhold or was necessary to gain Stalin's cooperation in the war still in progress and in the peace to follow.

The Balkans and eastern Europe were in Soviet hands. What bargaining power did Roosevelt have? Indeed, it may be said that the President won a real victory in exacting a promise from Stalin for free elections in the area. That the Soviet dictator either reneged on his promise or never intended to keep it or meant something different by it cannot be cause for blaming Roosevelt.

The massive advantages Russia gained in China were believed by the American delegation necessary as the price of Soviet aid in the Japanese War. Without that help the war could probably have been won, they thought, but at the expense of a gigantic invasion of the home islands and at a cost of one million Americans casualties. The atomic bomb was nearing completion and ready to be tested but as a weapon of war it had, in Februray of 1945, no bargaining power. It was yet an unknown quantity. It is true that Stalin had at Moscow in October of 1943 and at Teheran two months later indicated his intention to join the fight in Asia. It was another matter, however, to pin him down and when that time came he made demands to Ambassador Harriman in Moscow in December of 1944 similar to what he received at Yalta. It must be recalled that Roosevelt got a significant quid pro quo in the bargaining. Stalin recognized China's sovereignty over Manchuria and pledged to deal only with Chiang Kai-shek as the legitimate ruler of China.

And it was not only help against Japan needed by the United States but against Germany, too. The German war was by no means over in February. The attack in the Ardennes forest in December of the previous year may have been the Nazi's last military gasp but no one knew it—in February. The Germans still had 200–300 divisions in the field.

In 1955, during the administration of President Dwight D. Eisenhower, the Department of State published a collection of documents on the Yalta Conference. If Republicans expected the documents to reveal a sell-out at the conference they were to be disappointed. The legend of a failing president misled by traitorous advisors was not substantiated. There was no evidence of a betrayal of Poles and Chinese. The story was only that of a tired but alert president doing the best he could under the circumstances and using as a guiding principle the absolute necessity of retaining Russia's good will and cooperation.

BIBLIOGRAPHY

ROBERT BEITZELL, *The Uneasy Alliance: America, Britain, and Russia, 1941–1943* (1973).

ROBERT J. C. BUTOW, *Japan's Decision to Surrender* (1954).

DIANE S. CLEMENS, *Yalta* (1970).

ROBERT A. DIVINE, *Roosevelt and World War II* (1969).
  Second Chance: The Triumph of Internationalism in America During World War II (1967).

JOHN R. DEANE, *The Strange Alliance* (1973).

HERBERT FEIS, *Churchill, Roosevelt, and Stalin: The War They Waged and the Peace They Sought* (1957).

GABRIEL KOLKO, *The Politics of War: The World and United States Foreign Policy, 1943–1945* (1968).

WILLIAM H. McNEILL, *America, Britain, and Russia: Their Co-operation and Conflict, 1941–1946* (1953).

WILLIAM NEUMANN, *After Victory: Churchill, Roosevelt, Stalin and the Making of the Peace* (1967).

ROBERT SHERWOOD, *Roosevelt and Hopkins: An Intimate History* (1948).

JOHN L. SNELL, *Illusion and Necessity: The Diplomacy of the Global War, 1939–1945* (1963).

Dean Acheson (courtesy of the National Portrait Gallery, the Smithsonian Institution, Washington, D.C.).

The Soviet–American Rift

O N APRIL 12, 1945, just two months after Yalta, President Roosevelt died, unexpectedly, of a massive cerebral hemorrhage. The great wartime leader passed away at his vacation home in Warm Springs, Georgia, where he had gone for a short holiday, and news was telephoned to his widow in Washington. At once, she had the vice-president summoned to the White House where, in her second-floor study, she told him, simply, "Harry, the President is dead." And so, Harry S. Truman, high school graduate, ex-haberdasher, machine politician, county judge, and United States senator, became the nation's thirty-third chief executive. He had none of the education, social grace, or distinguished ancestry of his predecessor, but he made up for those deficiencies in honesty, integrity, good sense, forthrightness, and courage—qualities that were to stand him and the country in good stead in the trying years to come.

Truman came to the presidency ignorant of the military and diplomatic complexities of the war. While vice-president, he had not been kept informed by the president on the crucial international matters. Indeed, in the three and a half months between the inauguration and Roosevelt's death, the two men had talked only two or three times. The new president had much to learn before he could approach the problems confronting the nation but he learned them quickly. If he had come into office sharing the generally held view in the country that the Soviet alliance would hold together for the duration of the conflict and would continue into the postwar world, he soon was disabused of the notion. Eleven days after assuming office, on April 23, he was lecturing Soviet Foreign Minister Molotov at their first meeting, on the failure of Russia to carry out the Yalta agreement on Poland. His words were harsh causing Molotov to complain that he had "never been talked to like that in my life." To which Truman tartly replied, "Carry out your agreements and you won't be talked to like that." At the same time, he was setting out as America's task "to make difficult for her [the Soviet Union] to . . . [build a tier of friendly states], since to build one tier of states implies the possibility of further tiers, layer on layer."

Stalin had, in fact, been building just such a tier of friendly states, which seemed to him to make good sense. "The Soviet Union," he said, "in a desire to ensure its security for the future, tries to achieve that those countries [on her borders] should have governments whose relations to the Soviet Union are loyal." In Rumania, Hungary, Bulgaria, Albania, and Yugoslavia, he had set up "People's Democracies" dominated by communists without the benefit of "free and unfettered" elections as pledged at Yalta in the Declaration of Liberated Europe. In Poland, similarly, he cemented relations with the Lublin government by a treaty of mutual assistance signed on April 21, 1945, and although in the following month he promised to incorporate noncommunists in the government, he continued to exclude them. Nor did he permit elections to be held. And, as for Germany, after the Nazi surrender on May 8, Stalin set out on a course designed to bring his area of military occupation into the Soviet orbit. He begun by building a local communist party and joining it with Social Democrats to form a Socialist Unity Party to run the zone's political life. Economically, he embarked on a program of stripping the area of its industries and exacting reparations payments from current production, violating the agreement at Yalta to defer such action until Germany recovered her economic self-sufficiency.

Despite these evidences of wayward Soviet conduct, Truman had no wish to break with the wartime ally or to view Stalin as an enemy. He resisted Churchill's suggestion that American troops be kept in the Soviet zone of Germany and in Czechoslovakia and Austria, where they had penetrated, as a weapon in bargaining with Stalin. Although the British leader feared that the removal of those forces would leave 200–300 Soviet divisions unopposed and result in the area falling completely under Russian domination, Truman ordered their removal beginning July 1. And in spite of differences with the Soviets at the San Francisco conference to create the United Nations organization, he retained his optimism that the difficulties between the two powers were soluble.

The meeting by the Golden Gate opened on April 25 and lasted for two months. Fifty nations sent delegations consisting of distinguished and important public figures and led, in most cases, by the country's foreign minister. The crucial importance of the conference was apparent to all. The world was being given a second (some believed a last) chance to create a world organization to replace great power combines and substitute the rule of law for the rule of force. Secretary of State Edward R. Stettinius, Jr., brought with him two congressmen, one from each party, a leading woman educator, and a former Republican candidate for the presidency. There would be no repetition of Woodrow Wilson's needless and fatal blunder in 1918 of excluding members of Congress and of the opposition party. Great Britain sent Foreign Secretary Anthony Eden and from Moscow came Foreign Minister Molotov, but only at Truman's insistence. Stalin, at first, had appointed a lesser official in the foreign office to represent the Soviets.

That crude, insulting, and demeaning act was only one cause for uneasiness. Molotov came to San Francisco hostile and suspicious and surrounded by a formidable body guard. In the discussions, he insisted on the right to exercise the veto not only on substantive questions but, also, on whether the Security Council should consider discussing an issue. He also refused to permit the admission of Argentina to the conference and sought to gain entry for the Lublin Polish government. As it turned out, on none of those points did he succeed but the impression his intransigent attitude created was not a pleasant one. There was distress, too, over his cavalier disregard of the small powers and his position that the great nations that won the war ought to run the peace.

The Soviet difficulty aside, the conference proceeded smoothly and achieved its objective. The charter was written substantially as Dumbarton Oaks had recommended. There were only a few changes. A Trusteeship Council was created to supervise the nations charged with administering dependent territories. The Economic and Social Council was raised from a subsidiary to a principal organ. The jurisdiction of the International Court was settled and a lofty and noble preamble was added to the Charter. On June 26, 1945, all the participating nations signed the charter and the United Nations was born. One week later, President Truman submitted the instrument to the Senate, which, after five days of hearings by the Foreign Relations Committee and six days of debate on the floor, gave its approval overwhelmingly by a vote of 89–2 (five abstentions). The significance of the occasion was not lost on Americans or, for that matter, on people all over the world. That the United States Senate, after rejecting one international organization a quarter of a century earlier, had now by so great a margin voted adhesion to another was evidence of a realization that America could no longer stand aloof from the world. It was evidence, too, of a shrewder political hand at the helm than Wilson's.

While the conference was in session, Truman was searching for a way to ease the mounting tension with the Soviet Union and to resolve the problems which threatened to disrupt the alliance. In May, he had sent Hopkins to Moscow to warn Stalin that Soviet conduct was draining the large reservoir of good feeling Americans felt for their brave Russian ally. Hopkins expressed the president's fears that the estrangement would jeopardize cooperation in the postwar period. Poland, particularly, constituted a sore point, he said. Stalin, on his part, complained of the abrupt termination of lend-lease on August 21, 1945 and the grave economic problems that move had created for Russia. Yet he disclaimed any intention to interfere in Poland's internal affairs and promised to adhere faithfully to the Yalta agreements. Before leaving Moscow in early June, Hopkins completed arrangements for a meeting of the Big Three at Potsdam in July.

Hopkins' mission pleased the president. In reporting the results to the press, he remarked confidently, "The Russians are just as anxious to get along with us as we are to get along with them." It must be emphasized again that he wished ardently to get along with them and thought it possible. Vandenberg was correct when he noted in his diary on April 24, 1945 that Russo-American relations would no longer be conducted by the United States on the basis of "all 'give' and no 'take'." He was correct, too, when he observed that "FDR's appeasement of the Russians is over." But the end of appeasement must not be construed to signal the beginning of confrontation. It meant only a firmer and more realistic policy and Roosevelt himself was coming to that position in the spring of 1945. One hour before he died, he had written Churchill, "I would minimize the general Soviet problem as much as possible because these problems, in one form or another, seem to arise every day and most of them straighten out. . . . *We must be firm, however*" (italics mine).

At Potsdam, in full view of the ruins of Berlin, the leaders of the Big Three met for the last time. The war in Europe had ended nine weeks earlier and much had to be done to effect the transformation of the continent from war to peace. The atmosphere was friendly. Stalin invited Truman to preside and Truman played the piano for Stalin. That Soviet troops were in occupation of eastern Germany, Austria, Czechoslovakia, Hungary, Bulgaria, Rumania, Poland, Yugoslavia, and Albania did not seem to mar the benign climate. Nor did the successful testing on July 16, one day before the conference opened, of the first American atomic bomb in the New Mexican desert have an effect on the meeting. Some historians have claimed that Truman's spine was measurably stiffened by the news and that he was made bolder by it as he faced Stalin but there is no hard evidence to support the thesis. That the president was less amiable and more brusque than his predecessor in the White House was true but it was a reflection of personality differences, not the bomb.

The fixing of the details for the occupation of Germany constituted the central task of the conference. The European Advisory Commission had, in 1944, fixed the boundaries of the four zones. Now it was agreed that each power would administer its own zone with supreme authority to be placed in the hands of the military commander. An Allied Control Council to sit in Berlin was charged with coordinating matters affecting the whole of Germany; this coordination was chiefly economic for the decision was taken to treat the divided country as a single economic unit. Also, steps were taken to demilitarize, denazify, and democratize the nation as well as to bring its leaders to trial and punish those convicted of being war criminals. As for reparations, each power was to remove the necessary goods and property from its own zone.

Drawing up peace treaties for Hitler's allies—Italy, Rumania, Bulgaria, Austria, Hungary, and Finland—was referred to a newly created Council of Foreign Ministers representing the Big Four. Finally, the western boundary of Poland was set temporarily at the Oder-Neisse line on the west pending the negotiation of a German peace treaty that would settle that country's borders permanently.

To President Truman, the conference gave indication that cooperation among the Allies was proceeding splendidly. He reported to Congress that the Big Three were more closely bound than ever in their desire for peace. To Secretary of State James Byrnes, however, Potsdam was a "success that failed." He saw too much evidence of an absence of cooperation and of seeds of discord. Too many issues had not been tackled; too many problems had been left unresolved; too many Soviet demands had been made that augured badly for the future. Stalin's wish to control the Dardanelles and to have a trusteeship over Italian colonies in north Africa revealed an ambition too great for comfort. His insistence that the United States and Great Britain extend recognition to the one-party governments in eastern and southeastern Europe gave little hope for the future of democracy there and his refusal to internationalize all European waterways raised the prospect of a closing of Soviet-held rivers and canals to western commerce.

The events of the months following Potsdam reinforced Byrnes' dark forebodings and those of the year 1946 gave them credibility. During that time, Soviet-American relations worsened and disagreements were more frequent than agreements. Each of the two powers became more hostile and more suspicious where the other was concerned until between them there was so much enimity and ill-feeling that a "Cold War" was said to exist. By the spring of 1946, Churchill could say in a speech at Fulton, Missouri, rightfully and ruefully, "That from Stettin in the Baltic to Trieste in the Adriatic, an iron curtain has descended across the continent" separating the democratic part from the communist part controlled by Moscow.

The several meetings of the Council of Foreign Ministers between 1945 and 1947 reflected the growing Soviet–American rift. The first, at London, in September and October of 1945, was an exercise in futility. There was disagreement over Chinese and French participation in the making of the satellite peace treaties and over the terms of the treaties. There was a wrangle, too, over the Soviet demand for a voice in the peace treaty with Japan. At the second at Moscow in December of 1945 and the third at Paris, which met on two occasions between April and July of 1946, the differences were exacerbated and Soviet conduct was such as to elicit from President Truman after Moscow the exasperated comment, "I am tired of babying the Soviets" and to provoke Byrnes at Paris into telling Molotov there would be no more unilateral concessions by the United States. At the second Paris session some progress was made on the satellite peace treaties; the ministers actually agreed upon terms on July 1. Those terms were quickly submitted to a conference of 21 nations, which Molotov, at Moscow, had consented to convening, to debate the drafts. The delegates—representing the Big Four and 16 other countries from both sides of the Iron Curtain that had contributed to the war effort —gathered in Paris on July 29, 1946. For eleven weeks they debated the terms and differed on many matters, chiefly along east-west lines, but finally drew up five treaties—with Finland, Bulgaria, Italy, Romania, and Hungary. They, in turn, were reviewed by the Council of Foreign Ministers meeting in New York in November and December of 1946 and approved but not without more Soviet-American disagreements. Byrnes considered Soviet demands and maneuvers so excessive and obstructionist that he told Molotov that "The United States government was not so interested in making the treaties that it would accept endless delays and new compromises suggested by the Soviet Union." Vandenberg, who was on the American delegation, was pleased that "our 'surrender days' are over." The treaties were finally signed by Byrnes for the United States in Washington on January 20, 1947 and by the other nations in Paris on February 10.

In the United Nations, too, from the very first session in London in January of 1946, the Soviet–American rift was apparent. The two powers differed on the composition of the military forces to be made available to the international organization for enforcement. The United States (and Great Britain) supported the idea of specialized force—Russia, ground troops; America and England, air power and navy—while the Soviet Union insisted on equal and similar forces from both sides. In the absence of agreement, no forces were established. Then there was the question of atomic control. On January 24, 1946, a United Nations Atomic Energy Commission was created to control atomic weapons. To it, on June 14, Bernard Baruch, the American member, presented a plan. It provided for the licensing and inspection of nondangerous atomic energy and the ownership of "all atomic energy activities potentially dangerous to world security" by an International Atomic Development Authority.

Inspection rights were to be unrestricted and no power would be able to veto punishment of any nation breaking the rules. Baruch promised that, once the authority were set up and operating, the United States would destroy its stockpile and cease further manufacture of atomic weapons.

Nothing came of the suggestion because of Russia's rejection of it. The Soviets would not accede to unrestricted inspection nor surrender the veto, yet they insisted that the United States, nonetheless, destroy its pile and manufacture no more. On September 23, 1949, President Truman announced the news of the detonation of an atomic bomb by the Soviet Union.

Disarmament, also, proved to be a source of conflict between the two great powers. On February of 1947, there was formed a United Nations Commission for Conventional Armaments to draft measures for reducing the forces of the victorious nations but 18 months of discussion resulted in failure only. So great was the mutual feeling of mistrust that neither power would accept a cut in their armies, navies, or air forces. There were other differences between the two nations—the admission of new members to the UN, choosing a neutral government for Trieste, and the evacuation of Soviet troops from Iran. At the Teheran Conference, the Big Three had promised to evacuate Iran six months after the end of the war, but when that time came, the Soviet Union retained its soldiers there. They stood in support of the communist Tudeh Party which, in November of 1945, raised a revolt in the Iranian province of Azerbaijan. When the Security Council, at its first meeting in January of 1946, referred the whole matter to direct negotiation between Iran and the Soviet Union, the latter demanded the right to station troops in the country indefinitely (as in eastern Europe), control of a Soviet–Iranian oil company, and autonomy for Azerbaijan (no doubt, as part of the Russian security belt, which was to stretch from the Baltic Sea to the Persian Gulf). When Iran refused, a crisis loomed but the United States put pressure on Stalin in the form, virtually, of an ultimatum and the Russian dictator capitulated. In May of 1946, he cleared his soldiers out of Iran. One historian, at least, dates the true beginning of the Cold War to the confrontation over Iran.

Of all the problems and questions which separated the two wartime alliance and caused them to engage in the Cold War, Germany stood preeminent. Indeed, the German question constituted the core of the Soviet-American conflict. The two nations disagreed on that country's future. Both expected Germany to take its place eventually in the family of nations once again as a sovereign state, but there the agreement ended. Americans envisaged the new Germany a federal republic with all the trappings of democracy—free elections, competing political parties, parliamentary government, ministerial responsibility—purged of Nazism and dedicated to following a peaceful course in international affairs. The Soviets, on the other hand, looked to a Germany not unlike the other nations surrounding Russia—a centralized and unitary one-party state run by local communists and tied to the Soviet Union by treaty and by ideology.

Given such divergent views, it is not surprising that the Allied Control Council found itself in chronic deadlock on the matter of a common policy for the four zones and on the treatment of Germany as a single economic unit. There was no agreement on such important matters as reparations, land reform, foreign and internal trade, education, political parties, and labor organizations. In each of those matters, the Soviets went very much their own way in their own zone, acting unilaterally, secretively and in disregard of the needs of German recovery. They continued to strip their zone of crops, raw materials, finished products, machinery, and factories and to transport Germans to Russia for forced labor.

Byrnes, believing that the source of Soviet conduct was rooted in a fear of a military resurgence of a reunited and strengthened Germany, offered a four-power alliance, guaranteeing German demilitarization as a price for allied cooperation. He made the proposition in September of 1945 at the London Foreign Ministers' meeting, again at Moscow in December and, again, at Paris in April of 1946. Each time, Molotov found some fault with the plan. In exasperation, Byrnes, in May, had halted shipments of reparations to Russia from the other zones. Such shipments had been agreed upon at Potsdam: industrial equipment in exchange for food, coal, and other raw materials from the Soviet zone (which the Soviets had not been providing). Yet Byrnes continued to look for an accommodation. In July he suggested a merger of the American zone with the others and in September, in a speech in Stuttgart, Germany, he pushed the idea again—this time suggesting not only an economic union of zones but a political one organized into a federal government. The zones, he said, were not meant to be and should not be self-contained areas, and he warned the Soviets that the others would join their zones without Russia's. Once again, he proposed an alliance—this time for forty years. Once again, Stalin spurned the offer. Thereupon, Byrnes went ahead with his alternative. Arrangements were made to join the American and British zones and on January 1, 1947, "Bizonia" came into being. Shortly thereafter, the French zone was added to the two to make "Trizonia."

Germany was now divided into two parts and the division reflected the growing rift between the two wartime allies—one almost too great to be mended. Still, George C. Marshall, who in January of 1947 replaced Byrnes as secretary of state, made another effort to work with Russia. It came at the Council of Foreign Ministers' meeting in Moscow in March. The

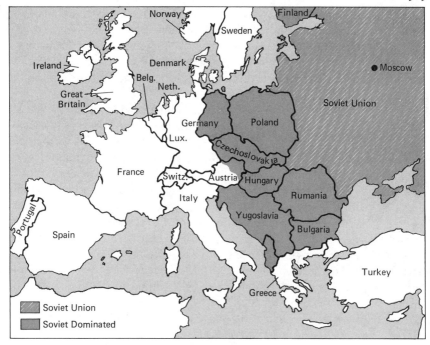

The Cold War Line-up.

Soviet minister was willing to entertain the suggestion of German unity but at a price—$10 billion in reparations, a Russian share in control over the industrial Ruhr area located in the British zone, and a centralized government for a united Germany. For Marshall, the price was too high and he rejected it. The point of no return had been reached. Other efforts were to be made by the United States later in the year but they could not have been expected to bear fruit because the decision had already been made in March by the Truman administration to take such action as would seal the antagonism between the two countries and make them hostile rivals.

The action came on March 12, 1947 when President Truman appeared before a joint session of Congress to request an appropriation of $400 million for military and economic aid to Greece and to Turkey. He was responding to calls for help from those two countries, who were being threatened by the Soviet Union. Ever since December of 1944, the Greek royalist government had been fighting off communist guerrilla forces, which were receiving aid from neighboring communist countries. The British had been sending supplies and money to the Greeks but on February 24, 1947 they informed the United States that, as of March 1, that subsidy would have to stop. They had reached a grave crisis in their economy and were virtually bankrupt. Similarly, their aid to Turkey ended just at the time when the Russians were making demands on that country for land at the eastern end of the Black Sea and a voice in the control of the Dardanelles. Truman was proposing to assume the British burden; the eagle was replacing the lion.

In his message to Congress, the president enunciated a new policy for the United States—one that was to endure for the next twenty-five years. It was "to help free peoples to maintain their free institutions and their national integrity against aggressive movements that seek to impose upon them totalitarian regimes. I believe," he said, "that it must be the policy of the United States to support free peoples who are resisting attempted subjugation by armed minorities or outside pressure." Despite the liberal use of the word *free*, the message ought not be construed in ideological terms. Neither Greece nor Turkey could be considered "free" as the term was used in western democracies. Rather, Truman's position must be viewed as directed against the expansion of Soviet power and territory and influence. It was a call to contain the Soviet Union in its boundaries and permit no further expansion.

The tactic of containment was most lucidly spelled out by George F. Kennan, in an article in *Foreign Affairs* for July 1947, entitled "The Sources of Soviet Conduct." In it, Kennan suggested that "the main element of any United States policy toward Soviet Russia must be that of a long-term patient but firm and vigilant containment of Russian expansive tendencies . . . by the adroit and vigilant application of counter-force at a series of constantly shifting geographical and political points corresponding to the shifts and maneuvers of Soviet policy." And that was exactly what Truman was recommending—counterforce in the eastern Mediterranean. Kennan had for some time been urging strength and firmness by the United States. A close student of Russian language, history, and literature, he had served in the embassy in Moscow from where, in January of 1946, he had warned his superiors in Washington that "The Kremlin's neurotic view of world affairs is traditional." In February of 1947, Secretary of State Marshall brought him back to the Department of State as head of the newly created Policy Planning Staff.

Truman's request for funds (and for approval of his new policy) passed both branches of Congress handily—67–23 in the Senate and 287–107 in the House—but not surprisingly as the president had consulted the leadership of both parties in February. Still, there was rancorous debate in both chambers. From left and right, the policy was assailed. The left scorned the appelation "democracy" to Greece and Turkey, labelling them corrupt and tyrannical and claimed the action would provoke the Soviet Union and weaken the United Nations. The right objected to the deep involvement in international political affairs that the measure would demand. The great majority of legislators, however, saw no alternative. If the Soviet Union was to be halted, the United States would have to do it. A face-saving amendment proposed by Senator Vandenberg that the United States would turn over the task of aiding beleaguered countries to the United Nations as soon as that body proved capable helped assuage some uneasy consciences. President Truman signed the bill on May 22, 1947 and at once sent money, supplies, and military and civilian advisors to the two embattled countries.

In adopting so revolutionary a policy, both president and Congress were satisfied that they had widespread public support. For at least two years, as relations between the United States and Russia were deteriorating, there had been a good deal of public sentiment in favor of a hard line toward the Kremlin. There had, also, been some severe criticism of Truman's stiffening position, voiced most notably by Secretary of Commerce Henry Wallace. In a speech at a rally in Madison Square Garden in New York on September 12, 1946, Wallace castigated the Administration for meddling in eastern European affairs, which area, he said, was rightfully a Soviet sphere. "We must get out of eastern Europe," he stated. Five days later, Truman fired him from the Cabinet. Since that time, the supporters of a "get tough" policy had increased in number and by the spring of 1947 a Gallup poll on the Truman Doctrine, as the new policy came to be called, revealed only 4 per cent in favor of "hands off" in the crisis. What a far cry from the sentiment of the majority of Americans after the first great war when the vast majority *favored* "hands off!"

The road from the Truman Doctrine to the Marshall Plan was short, logical, and inevitable. It was clear to American planners that Truman's aid to Greece and Turkey was, in one sense, a negative measure. That is, it was designed to meet a threat after one had been made. Steps would have to be taken, they believed, to create such conditions that would discourage a threat from being made. Specifically, the president and his advisors had in mind the state of Europe in the winter of 1946–1947. The old continent was on the verge of collapse. Drought, storms, snows, power shortages had brought it to the brink of ruin. Winston Churchill described it as "a rubble heap, a charnel house, a breeding ground of pestilence and hate." Shortages of food, clothing, shelter made for a desperate situation. And Marshall was convinced that Stalin regarded the imminence of Europe's collapse with equanimity. He recalled the Soviet dictator's remark at the Moscow conference in March of 1947 that delays in reaching agreement on European matters were not tragic to his country. Indeed, delay was to his advantage. If Europe continued its decline, its inhabitants, hopeless and hungry, despairing and debilitated, would fall victims to revolution and to communism. Obviously the answer was to strengthen

Europe, to reconstruct it, to restore it to prosperity and well-being, thereby enabling its people to resist the twin menaces of communism and revolution. Such a scheme, Secretary of State Marshall unveiled in a speech at the Harvard University commencement on June 5, 1947.

The idea had been touched on the previous month in a little-noticed address by Undersecretary of State Dean G. Acheson in Cleveland, Mississippi. Acheson, substituting for the president, announced that the United States was ready to give long-range help "to aid free peoples to preserve their independence." The key word was *long-range*. The United States had, since 1943, contributed vast sums through the United Nations Relief and Rehabilitation Association to provide food, clothing, and other supplies to impoverished peoples. That help was, however, for relief, not recovery. The new program, elaborated by Marshall at Harvard, was designed to rebuild Europe's factories and farms, end unemployment, increase production, restore the cities, and make the countries self-supporting again with viable economies. "It is logical," he said, "to assist in the return of normal economic health in the world without which there can be no political stability or assured peace." He then invited the European nations to meet and to detail their needs, to which the United States would respond.

The European reception of Marshall's call was immediate and enthusiastic. British Foreign Secretary Ernest Bevin likened it to "a lifeline to sinking men." At once, he and French Foreign Minister Georges Bidault suggested to Soviet Foreign Minister Molotov that the three meet in Paris for preliminary discussions. The three men did meet in the French capital on June 27 but the Soviet minister stayed only long enough to attack the plan. Calling it a "new venture in American imperialism" and a Trojan horse calculated to extend America's capitalistic tentacles into the European markets, he spurned the offer of help. At the same time, he recommended strongly that the Soviet satellites follow Russia's lead, which they did. The Soviet refusal to participate in so useful a scheme has been ascribed mainly to two factors—the disinclination to reveal economic statistics and the danger of a successful Marshall Plan acting as a magnet drawing the satellite nations from the Soviet orbit. Whatever the reasons, Russia stood aloof, thereby adding one more dimension to the widening gulf between west and east.

Meanwhile, sixteen European nations met in Paris on July 12, 1947 as the Committee of European Economic Co-operation to discuss their needs. On September 22, they passed the estimate to Marshall—$19.1 billion from the United States and $3.1 billion from the International Bank of Reconstruction and Development (created in 1945 at an international monetary conference at Bretton Woods in New Hampshire) over a period of four years. On December 19, President Truman submitted to

Congress a request for an appropriation of $6.8 billion to be funnelled to the European nations in the following fifteen months and $10.2 billion over the coming three years. The Foreign Assistance Act, passed by Congress in March of 1948 by 69–17 in the Senate and 329–74 in the House, provided $5.3 billion for the first twelve months and authorized $13 billion over a four-year period. The president signed the legislation on April 3, 1948.

The vote in Congress reflected accurately the sentiment of the country. To be sure, there was opposition. The left branded the measure "the martial plan" and claimed it was a warlike and provocative action; the right feared the expenditure would bankrupt the country and wondered, further, whether foreigners were worth helping. But to the vast majority of Americans, resistance to the program seemed naive and unrealistic and dangerous to American security in view of the nature of the Soviet response.

The Russian moves to counteract the Marshall Plan were violent and desperate. In a fiery speech, Andrei Zhdanov, a leading party ideologue and a deputy premier, called for a holy war against the Plan and at a meeting in Warsaw of the Communist Parties of Yugoslavia, Bulgaria, Rumania, Hungary, Poland, France, Italy, Czechoslovakia, and the Soviet Union in early October of 1947, a Communist Information Bureau (Cominform) was established to direct the campaign. Plans were laid to forment strikes in western Europe, to cripple industries, and to sabotage Marshall Plan projects. Particular attention was to be paid to France and to Italy, which had large and powerful Communist parties, to force those countries to renounce Marshall Plan aid. Meanwhile, the Soviet Union was tightening its hold on the satellites. In February of 1948, treaties of friendship and mutual assistance were signed with Rumania, Hungary, and Bulgaria and, in April, with Finland. In February, too, a Soviet-engineered coup in Czechoslovakia placed a communist government in power, thereby rounding out the ring of satellites protecting Russia. At the same time, Stalin was moving to clear Berlin of the western powers.

That city, it will be recalled, although lying entirely in the Soviet zone of Germany, was divided among the Four Powers. On March 31, 1948, the Soviet authorities in Germany began to take measures to seal Berlin off from the western zones. The first step was to subject freight, people, and baggage to delays and checks upon entering or leaving Berlin via the Soviet zone. That harrassment culminated on June 24, in an edict halting all surface transportation to or from the city.

The options open to the United States, Britain, and France were two —abandon the Berliners under their jurisdiction to the Russians or fight their way through the Soviet zone to supply them. Fighting was not a really viable alternative; nor was leaving the Berliners to their fate. For, as the American commander in Berlin, General Lucius D. Clay, noted, "When Berlin falls, West Germany will be next. If we mean . . . to hold Europe against communism, we must not budge. . . . If we withdraw, our position in Europe is threatened. If America does not understand this now, does not know the issue is cast, then it never will and communism will run rampant. I believe the future of democracy requires us to stay."

America did stay. By means of a massive air lift, food, clothing, and other supplies were provided to the residents of Berlin. By September, 4,000 tons of goods were being flown in daily and by the spring of 1949, the figure had doubled. The Soviets could have intercepted the air delivery but they were not willing to risk a clash and on May 12, 1949, they ended the blockade. They had tested the resoluteness of the western powers and had found it firm. They capitulated for another reason. The blockade had been, in part, an attempt to frustrate the creation of a federal republic out of the three western zones of Germany. By the spring of 1949, they realized they could not frustrate or impede the movement. The three western powers were determined to form a government for Germany without Russia once they accepted the fact that the Soviets would never join with the others nor treat Germany as a single economic unit.

In June of 1948, representatives of the United States, France, Britain, Belgium, the Netherlands, and Luxemburg reached agreement at a meeting in London to hold elections for a German constituent assembly to meet in Bonn. The assembly convened there on September 21, 1948 and wrote a constitution that the military governors approved on May 12, 1949. On September 1, the new Federal Republic of Germany came into existence. Military government ended and the allied connection was maintained by high commissioners representing the former occupying powers. Konrad Adenauer, distinguished elder statesman, former mayor of Cologne, and long an anti-Nazi, became the new nation's first chancellor.

The end of the Berlin blockade eased the considerable tension that had built up between east and west since the harrowing events of the winter and spring of 1948. It did not, however, reverse or alter the decision by the United States to create a western military alliance capable of resisting or thwarting any Soviet designs on land not already under Russian control. What had crystallized that decision had been the very real war scare in the spring of 1948 following the Czech coup and the cutting off of Berlin from the west. At that time, General Clay had reported ominously from Berlin "A new tenseness in every Soviet individual with whom we have official relations . . . gives me a feeling that war may come with dramatic suddenness." And, in America there was the same feeling. Talk of the need for a western military alliance was heard on all sides. At a Senate hearing on foreign assistance in June of 1948 there was overwhelming agreement that a military pact with Europe was imperative. In the same month, an epoch-making resolution was introduced into the Senate by Arthur Vandenberg, Republican of Michigan, that the United States should associate itself "by constitutional process, with such regional and other collective arrangements as are based on continuous and effective self-help and mutual aid, and as affect its national security." It passed 64–4.

The way was now paved for American adherance to the Brussels Pact, a 50-year defensive alliance created in March of 1948 among Great Britain, France, Belgium, Luxemburg, and the Netherlands. At once, the Brussels states along with Canada, Norway, Iceland, Denmark, Portugal, and Italy were summoned to Washington for preliminary conversations. By September, the general character of a treaty was agreed upon. Negotiations began in December and continued into the winter and spring of 1949. They were completed in April and on April 4, the North Atlantic Treaty was signed. There was no question of its intent and purpose. It was designed to forestall a would-be aggressor by the common pledge in Article 5 that "an armed attack against one or more of them [the signatories] in Europe or North America shall be considered an attack against them all; . . . ." An aggressor could not do what Hitler had done—pick off certain nations one by one. He would have to contend at once with a grand coalition of nations. And that might be sufficient to give him pause. As President Truman noted upon signing the treaty, "If [this document] . . . had existed in 1914 and in 1939, supported by the nations who are represented today, I believe it would have prevented the acts of aggression which led to two world wars."

On April 12, 1949, the treaty was submitted to the Senate for its "advice and consent." There was no doubt of the outcome of the vote. Few questioned the desirability of a treaty. There were some senators who feared that the treaty did violence to the United Nations charter in that it substituted two hostile worlds for the one world envisaged by the world organization. They pointed, also, to the inconsistencies between the treaty and the charter. The charter permitted regional groupings among member states but some of the parties to the treaty were not UN members; nor could the treaty be said to be regional with signatories so widely scattered geographically. Then there were certain senators who were concerned that Article 3, which provided for the build-up of armaments ("maintain and develop their individual and collective capacity to resist armed attack"), would provoke Russia needlessly. Other legislators worried over the huge expenditures that would be incurred in furnishing military aquipment to the allies in accordance with Article 3. Still others were concerned that Article 5 would plunge the United States automatically into war without a Congressional declaration. Three reservations, proposed by Republican senators Robert Taft, Arthur Watkins, and Kenneth Wherry designed chiefly to safeguard Congress's role, were beaten down. When the vote was taken on July 21, the approval was overwhelming: 82–13.

The North Atlantic Treaty along with the Marshall Plan constituted America's reply to the threat believed to be posed by the Soviet Union to the safety and security of western Europe and of the western hemisphere. Each served a different purpose. Marshall Plan money was designed to bolster the economic well-being of the continent, thereby rendering it immune to the blandishments of communism and forestalling revolution. The treaty was to serve to make the continent strong enough militarily to discourage an aggressor or to resist one foolhardy enough to attack. The significance of the treaty in the long perspective of American history must not be lost. It was the second military alliance ever made and the first in time of peace. So radical a departure from tradition may be explained in terms of the degree of danger felt by Americans but it must be viewed, as well, as the consequence of the realization that to *prevent* the conquest of the European continent was cheaper than to have to *liberate* it from an aggressor's domination. For Europeans, it was the fulfillment of a long dream. As the French foreign minister noted when the treaty negotiations were finished, "Today, we obtain what we sought between the two wars. The United States offers us both immediate military aid in the organization of our defense and a guarantee of assistance in case of conflict." Better late than never.

BIBLIOGRAPHY

GAR ALPEROVITZ, *Atomic Diplomacy: Hiroshima and Potsdam, the Use of the Atomic Bomb and the American Confrontation with Soviet Power* (1965).
STEPHEN AMBROSE, *Rise to Globalism: American Foreign Policy Since 1938* (1971).
HERBERT FEIS, *From Trust to Terror: The Onset of the Cold War, 1945–50* (1970).
D. F. FLEMING, *The Cold War and Its Origins, 1917–1960* (2 vols., 1961).
JOHN L. GADDIS, *The United States and the Origins of the Cold War* (1972).
LOUIS HALLE, *The Cold War As History* (1967).
JOYCE AND GABRIEL KOLKO, *The Limits of Power: The World and United States Foreign Policy, 1945–1954* (1972).
WALTER LAFEBER, *America, Russia, and the Cold War, 1945–1966* (1967).

THOMAS G. PATERSON, *Soviet-American Confrontation: Post-War Reconstruction and the Origins of the Cold War* (1973).

JOHN SPANIER, *American Foreign Policy Since World War II* (1968).

Douglas MacArthur (courtesy of the National Portrait Gallery, the Smithsonian Institution, Washington, D.C.).

Containment in Asia

I N ASIA, as in Europe, the United States found itself, in the years
following the close of the war, in the forefront of the fight against
communism. In Europe, it was the Soviet Union that presented the
threat; in Asia, the challenge came from China—the China led by Mao
Tse-Tung who had driven Chiang Kai-shek and his Nationalist government out of the country in 1949 and had erected a communist regime in
its place.

It had been President Roosevelt's hope during the war years that the
Communists and Nationalists could be brought together in the fight
against Japan and, after victory, that they would join in erecting a strong,
stable, and democratic China. Participation of the Communists in the war
and the peace was essential in view of the effectiveness of their army, their
widespread support among the peasants, and their program for reforming
society. Their help was all the more valuable and necessary because, as the
writer George Sokolsky noted in 1944, the Communists ranks contained
"the morally best elements of the nationalist movement in China." And
they were not even considered "real" communists. As one observer, Freda
Utley, put it, "Their aim has genuinely become social and political reform
along capitalist and democratic lines." And Carl Crow, a close student of
China, found, after a summer's study of communism in that country in
1939, "that there are a very large number of Chinese who call themselves
communists but they have no connection with Russia and their so-called
communism is nothing more than a liberal agrarian movement tinged with
a few socialistic ideals." It was true, of course, that they had been repudiated by the Soviet Union. Stalin referred to them derisively as "margarine"
or synthetic communists and said he would not support them. In a treaty
with Chiang signed on August 14, 1945, the Soviet dictator threw his
support to the Nationalist government. Whether the Communists were
"real" or not would, of course, not be known until after they gained
power.

Chiang and Mao had come together in 1937 in a common effort against the Japanese invader but soon had drifted apart. When General Stilwell came to China in 1942 as Chiang's Chief of Staff and Commander of United States forces, he tried to get Chiang to form a united front with the Communists against the Japanese but he did not get very far. Chiang seemed more interested in fighting Communists than Japanese. Vice-President Henry A. Wallace, whom President Roosevelt sent in June of 1944 to effect a union of the two factions, fared no better. He found the Generalissimo too distrustful of Mao and his hostility toward the Communist leader very great.

Patrick J. Hurley, who followed Wallace some two months later (as special emissary until appointed ambassador in November), was somewhat more successful. A blunt and bluff ex-army officer and descendant of Choctaw Indians, he moved vigorously and quickly. He flew to Yenan, Mao's headquarters in North China, and was, apparently, impressed by what he saw and heard. Although he, flippantly and condescendingly, called Mao "Mouse Dung" and Chou En-lai "Joe N. Lie," he concluded that "the only differences between Chinese Communists and Oklahoma Republicans is that Oklahoma Republicans are not armed." In late August of 1945, he got Mao to come to Chungking, Chiang's capital, where he and the Nationalist president had talks that seemed to have gone well. The two agreed on several important matters—the desirability of a coalition government, of a unification of the two fighting forces, and of democratization and reconstruction of their country. But the thaw did not last. Deeply suspicious and distrustful of each other, they disagreed on certain technicalities concerning political and military integrations and shortly after Hurley went home on leave, in mid-September, fighting broke out anew.

The rivalry between Communists and Nationalists was intensified by the competition for control of the territory being evacuated by the Japanese after their surrender in August of 1945. The Japanese had been instructed to surrender only to Nationalist forces, and American aircraft were used to ferry Chiang's soldiers to points of Japanese troop concentration before the Communists got there. To assist in the disarming of the Japanese, 50,000 American marines were brought from the Philippines. With that help, the Nationalists were able to gain control over major coastal cities and over territory south of the Yangtze. In the north, however, particularly in Manchuria, which Soviet armies had overrun after Russia's entry into the war, Communist troops, with some clandestine Soviet aid, were able to beat Chiang's men to the draw. They moved into the area, took possession of about 600,000 tons of arms that Soviet armies left as they prepared to withdraw, and fastened their hold on much of Manchuria.

Hurley never did return to China. In November, after an emotional address to the National Press Club in Washington in which he accused the career foreign service officers in China of undermining his efforts, he resigned. In his letter of resignation, he went into detail complaining bitterly that "the professional foreign service men sided with the Chinese Communist armed party . . . [and] continuously advised the Communists that my efforts in preventing the collapse of the Nationalist Government did not represent the policy of the United States. These same professionals openly advised the Communist armed party to decline unification of the Chinese Communist army with the National army unless the Chinese Communists were given control." That estimate of the situation, although disputed by close students of the matter, was believed widely in the United States to be true and accurate.

It was true that the career diplomats in the field considered Chiang's regime corrupt, inefficient, despotic, and doomed to failure unless major reform were undertaken, and the Communists were seen as efficient and honest and committed to economic and social reforms. Given that assessment, it was not strange that the diplomats believed the Communists would become "the dominant force in China within a comparatively few years." It was not true, however, that the foreign service officers sided with the Communists. Hurley's accusations were gross distortions and exaggerations. Typical of the position of the diplomats was the cable sent to Washington in February of 1945, while Hurley was home for consultation, and signed by the entire staff of the embassy. It urged that the Communists, along with the Nationalists, be given support. It did not counsel abandoning Chiang. It maintained only that supporting Chiang exclusively would make him uncompromising and unyielding and would result in civil war. The career officers wished and hoped for a joining of the two factions.

Hurley's resignation did not end the efforts to bring the two leaders together, for it was clear to Washington that only a coalition government could avoid civil war and solve China's problems. On the day Hurley quit, President Truman asked General Marshall to replace him. Although worn out by his arduous wartime labors and on the threshold of a much-anticipated period of rest and repose in his Virginia home, Marshall accepted the call. On December 15, 1945, he left Washington for Chungking armed with instructions to stop the Nationalist-Communist fighting in North China and to effect a coalition between the two groups as a prelude to forming a unified, democratic Chinese government. There was no question that the Nationalist government would continue to be recognized alone as *the* legitimate government of China (and alone qualified to receive aid) and that the Communists were to be integrated and absorbed in it.

Marshall quickly achieved what seemed to be a phenomenal success. He gained a cease-fire on January 10, 1946, and got Mao to disavow any intention to establish a separate regime and to accept a subordinate position in Chiang's government. Next, he secured agreement by both sides to join in a Political Consultative Conference to meet in January to draft a new constitution and to erect a coalition cabinet to replace the existing one pending the creation of the new government. Finally, he gained a promise of a reduction in the size of the two armies to be effected by September of 1947—to fifty Nationalist and ten Communist divisions—the sixty to constitute the new unified Chinese army. On March 11, the general went home to report his successes to the president.

Those successes, however, did not survive his departure. Not long after he left the country, new clashes broke out between the two armies in Manchuria. Again mutual distrust and suspicion clouded efforts at conciliation. On April 15, Mao's army attacked Changchun, a major city held by the Nationalists. Three days later, Marshall returned to China and on the same day, the Communists occupied the city. Disappointed, Marshall sought to arrange another cease-fire. The two sides agreed to halt hostilities for fifteen days, beginning June 7. The truce was later extended to June 30, but in the absence of any real agreement on principles, the fighting was resumed on July 1. All through July, Marshall tried valiantly to convince Chiang to make concessions on certain political conditions the Communists demanded as the basis for any new government but without success. Even an embargo on aid to the generalissimo that Marshall got Washington to impose made no imprint on the Nationalist leader. In December, Marshall gave up and went home. By that time, full-scale civil war was in progress. Chiang, shrewdly, was operating on two assumptions: (1) That he could lick the Communists in the field and (2) That, if he seemed to be failing, the United States would intervene in his behalf. He was convinced that after all the money and supplies given him and in view of the powerful friends he had in America, notably certain Republican senators and some key newspapers and magazines, he would never be abandoned.

He was wrong, of course, on both counts. Far from beating the Communists, Chiang saw their armies move from victory to victory. By the end of 1947, they were in control of the principal rail network in Manchuria and the connections from that province into north China. By October of the next year, they had cleared Manchuria of Nationalist troops. They then pushed into north China, taking Tientsin on January 18. Peiping fell in March, Nanking in April and Hankow and Shanghai in May. Then they moved south. Canton was occupied in October and Chungking in November. While his armies were taking possession of the country, Mao was creating a Communist government for the new China. In September, a Chinese People Consultative Conference met in Peiping and wrote a constitution for the People's Republic of China. On October 1, the new republic came into existence officially with Mao Tse-tung as president and Chou En-lai as premier and foreign minister. On December 8, Chiang fled with his government and the remnants of his army to the island of Formosa. There the seat of the Republic of China was transferred, and from there Chiang planned to continue the fight against his Communist enemies.

While the Nationalists were reeling, the United States did not intervene nor even provide massive aid to help stave off defeat. The decision had long since been made not to get involved in the civil war. The instructions to Marshall had made that point clear as had the rejection in September of 1947 of the recommendation by General Albert Wedemeyer, who had been sent to China in the summer of 1947 to investigate conditions, to furnish large-scale assistance to Chiang. As Undersecretary of State Dean G. Acheson told Senator Tom Connally on March 10, 1948, any effective help for Chiang would require "an unpredictably large American armed force in actual combat," and the Administration was not prepared to engage in a major land war in Asia.

As the Nationalist defeat appeared imminent and inevitable in the spring and summer of 1949, the Administration took measures to explain its China policy and to parry accusations that that policy was responsible for the "loss" of China to the Communists. On August 5, 1949, there appeared a bulky State Department publication—the China White Paper—containing 1,054 pages of text and documents that sought to prove that China was not America's to "lose." As Secretary of State Dean Acheson noted in his letter of transmittal to the president, "The unfortunate but inescapable fact is that the ominous result of the civil war in China was beyond the control of the government of the United States. Nothing that this country did or could have done within the reasonable limits of its capabilities could have changed that result; nothing that was left undone by this country has contributed to it. It was the product of internal Chinese forces, forces which this country tried to influence but could not. A decision was arrived at within China, if only a decision by default." The plain fact, according to the documents, which were mainly reports from American military and diplomatic observers in China, was that Chiang Kai-shek had lost the confidence and the support of his people. No amount of money or material could have saved him. Between 1937 and 1949, he had received from the United States $4.5 billion in money and supplies to fight first the Japanese and then the Communists. But the problem was on another level and General Wedemeyer saw it clearly as early as 1947 when he prophetically warned the Generalissimo, "The Communist movement cannot be defeated by the employment of force. . . . The central government will have to remove corruption and incompetence from its ranks in order to provide justice and equality . . . and to protect personal liberties." That prescription the Nationalist leader steadfastly refused to follow.

The collapse of the Nationalists signalled the end of American intervention in China's civil war. On January 5, 1950, President Truman announced that the United States would not defend Formosa against a Communist attack nor would American bases be established there. The Nationalists would continue to receive economic aid but not military support. One week later, Secretary of State Acheson in an address to the National Press Club eliminated Formosa and the Asian mainland from America's security perimeter. That perimeter he traced from the Aleutians through Japan, the Ryukyus, and the Philippines. The United States, it appeared, was prepared to accept the new order in China. Whether diplomatic recognition would follow was problematical. Before the end of 1949, some dozen nations, led by the Soviet Union and including Great Britain and other American allies in Europe, had recognized the People's Republic as the government of China. Standing in the way of American recognition were two factors. One was the strong sentiment in some quarters in the United States that the old ally, Chiang, must not be betrayed; another was the harsh and arbitrary treatment of Americans and their property by the Communists in China. Still, there was a reasonable possibility that recognition would be accorded. That it did not come to pass may be ascribed to the events beginning on June 25, 1950. Early in the morning of that day war broke out between North and South Korea. It was a war that would have profound effects on the Far Eastern policy of the United States.

Korea was in two parts as a consequence of military expediency. At the Cairo Conference in 1943, it was agreed that Korea, which had been ruled by Japan since 1908, would become free and independent after the war. As the war came to a close, however, General MacArthur, Commander of American forces in the Far East, feared that Soviet troops, then in Manchuria and North Korea, might overrun the whole peninsula. Hence, he decreed, on August 17, 1945, that the country be divided at the 38th parallel for the purpose of receiving the Japanese surrender. North of the line, the Soviets would disarm the enemy; south of the line, the United States would perform the task. There was no thought of a permanent division. At the conference of foreign ministers in Moscow in December of 1945 and, again, in March of 1946, the Soviet and American military governors of the two zones were directed to take steps to unify the country but unification proved impossible because of the difficulty of agreeing on the several political groups to be included. The problem was, thereupon, laid before the United Nations Assembly which, in November of 1947, appointed a temporary commission charged with holding elections for a constituent assembly. The Soviets, however, who had been organizing their zone along communist lines (as in Germany at the same time) refused to permit UN personnel to cross the parallel. The elections then were held only in the south in May of 1948. In July, a constitution was drawn up and on August 15, 1948 the Republic of Korea came into existence with Syngman Rhee as president. Ten months later, American troops, except for 400 military advisors, left the country. Six months earlier, in December of 1948, Soviet troops had withdrawn from the north following the creation of the Democratic People's Republic in August.

For the next two years, the two republics—one under Soviet and the other under American auspices—glared at each other across the parallel and engaged in frequent skirmishes. No one was prepared, however, for the large-scale crossing by North Korean troops of the border on June 25, 1950. The news was cabled to Washington by the American ambassador from Seoul, the capital, and Secretary of State Acheson at once telephoned President Truman at his home in Independence, Missouri. That was Saturday evening, June 24, Washington time. After being assured that the attack constituted a major Communist move, the president returned by plane to Washington the next morning. That same afternoon, Sunday, June 25, the secretary general of the United Nations, at President Truman's request, convened the Security Council in emergency session. At that meeting, the Council passed a resolution (9–0) declaring the action of North Korea a "breach of the peace," demanding that the attacking troops be withdrawn, and calling upon UN members to assist in carrying out the resolution. Two days later, a second resolution directed UN members to furnish troops to help Korea repel the invaders. On that same day, June 27, President Truman announced to Congress and to the American people the dispatch of American sea and air forces to Korea; three days later, came the additional information that ground forces had been committed and that air strikes were being carried out over North Korea.

The prompt response by President Truman to the invasion should have come as no surprise. It was a logical concomitant of his European policy and an aspect of his general policy of containment of the communist threat. As he had exerted counterpressure in Greece and Turkey three years earlier, so now in Korea. And there was no question that the pressure in Asia was no less a Soviet thrust than in Europe. Public approval was overwhelming. The questioning by Senator Robert A. Taft of the president's right to commit troops without congressional authorization must not obscure his support of the bold move to resist. That the UN had acted so quickly (indeed, had acted at all) may be ascribed to the fortuitous absence of the Soviet delegate Jacob A. Malik. He had walked out of the Security Council some time before in protest over the retention by Nationalist China of its permanent seat. Had he been there that memorable June day, he would, most certainly, have exercised the veto, thereby preventing the passage of the "breach of peace" resolution.

The war went badly for the defenders of South Korea at the outset. North Korean forces, using excellent Soviet equipment, rolled southward relentlessly and by early July had cornered United Nations troops in a small pocket surrounding Pusan, the port on the southeast point of Korea. But soon the tide turned. On September 15, 1950, General Douglas MacArthur, who, pursuant to a Security Council request that an American be

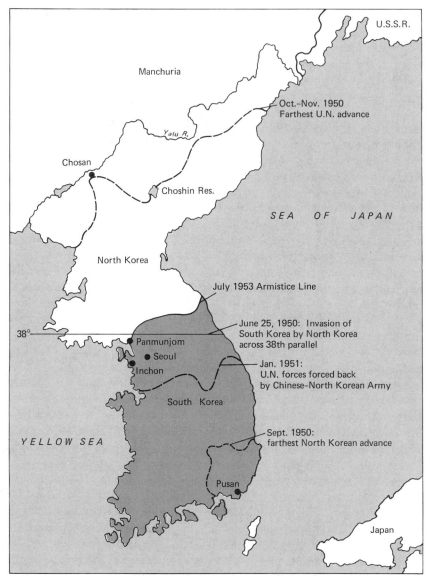

The Korean War, 1950–1953.

named to head the unified UN forces, had been designated on July 8 commander of all UN troops (which consisted of 850,000 men—48 per cent American, 43 per cent Korean, 9 per cent from fifteen other nations), executed a bold amphibious landing at Inchon, on the west coast of Korea a few miles below the 38th parallel. From there, he pushed on to Seoul, which he occupied on September 26. On October 9, his men crossed the border and plunged ahead to take Pyongyang, the North Korean capital, on October 19. On October 26 UN troops were by the Yalu River that separated Manchuria from Korea. Meanwhile, the beleaguered forces around Pusan had broken out of the encirclement and had advanced northward. Then came the deluge in the form of China's entry into the fighting.

Chou En-lai had gravely warned that China would not stand by idly while Communist North Korea was being invaded and mauled. And he was true to his word. On October 26, as UN forces reached the Yalu, a Chinese army crossed the river into Korea. Four days later, it engaged the enemy some 50 miles to the south and began a fierce and massive attack. By early December, UN troops were in full retreat southward. On December 5, the Reds took Pyongyang, crossed the parallel on December 26, and occupied Seoul on January 4, 1951. MacArthur, recovering from the shock of the unexpected Chinese intervention, regrouped his forces and launched a counterattack in late January in which he succeeded in pushing the Communists back across the parallel. UN forces retook Seoul on March 7 and after fighting off two Red assaults in April, grabbed the initiative in May. By that time the Communists seemed to have had enough for on June 23, Soviet delegate Malik, in a UN radio broadcast, hinted at the possibilities of peace. By that time, too, Douglas MacArthur was no longer commander-in-chief having been replaced, on April 11, 1951, by Matthew B. Ridgeway.

The recall of General MacArthur must not be viewed simply as the termination of the services of an unsuccessful military commander. It was true that he had failed to anticipate the Chinese intervention and had had to flee ignominiously down the Korean peninsula but there was more to it. The matter went deeper and it revolved around larger questions—the relationship between the civil and the military, the grand strategy of the war, and the policy toward Nationalist China.

From the very beginning of the conflict, President Truman and his advisors had decided to keep it localized and limited in scope. Two days after it erupted, the president issued orders to the Seventh (Pacific) Fleet to take station in the waters separating Formosa from the mainland for the purpose of preventing each side from attacking the other. The Red Chinese had to be kept out of the war at all costs. General MacArthur had a different idea. He wished to join the Korean conflict with the Chinese civil war. He wished to use Chinese Nationalist troops in the Korean peninsula, bomb Communist troops and supply depots across the Yalu in Manchuria, blockade China's coasts and destroy its industry by sea and air bombardment, and support an invasion of the mainland by Chiang—in short, fight an all-out war in Asia. And those ideas he did not keep to himself. He spread them widely in manifestoes and pronouncements. Orders to clear all statements with the Department of State, he blithely ignored. To the annual convention of the Veterans of Foreign Wars, he cabled, on August 27, 1950 a message suggesting that the United States hold Formosa permanently and said the island was "ideally located to accomplish offensive strategy." Constantly and continuously he referred to the need to bomb the enemy's "privileged sanctuary" in Manchuria and even threatened the Communists directly with such an eventuality, on March 25, 1951, if they refused his offer of an armistice.

The president was growing more and more irritated with the general. He had enough of "open defiance of my orders as President and Commander-in-Chief" and of flouting "the policy of the United Nations." The last straw came on April 5, 1951. On that day House Republican leader Joseph W. Martin read to his fellow congressmen a message he had received from General MacArthur replying to a request for an opinion on the use of Chinese Nationalist troops in the war. The general was emphatic in his view that they should be used but he went beyond the immediate question to criticize the administration's policy of fighting a limited war in Asia. "It seems strangely difficult," he said, "for some to realize that here in Asia is where the Communist conspirators have elected to make their play for global conquest, and that we have joined the issue thus raised on the battlefield; that here we fight Europe's war with arms while the diplomats there still fight it with words; that if we lose this war to communism in Asia the fall of Europe is inevitable, win it and Europe most probably would avoid war and yet preserve freedom. As you point out, we must win. There is no substitute for victory." Six days later he was relieved of command. "I could do nothing else and still be President," Truman said. "Even the Chiefs of Staff came to the conclusion that civilian control of the military was at stake." At stake, too, was the issue of who was to make American foreign policy, the president or the general.

The recall did not come as a great surprise to the American public, who had followed the course of the contest between MacArthur and Truman in their favorite newspaper. Still, to many people it came as a shock that "an ex-National Guard captain fires a five-star general." There was harsh criticism "of the little ward politician . . . from Kansas City" and calls for his impeachment. Even some newspapers that in December of 1950, at the time of the disastrous retreat from the Yalu, thought MacArthur ought to have been dismissed, now sympathized with him. Still, the president had considerable support from those who saw in MacArthur "a threat of Caesarism" and who did not wish to see the Korean war enlarged. The European allies were uniformly pleased by Truman's action. MacArthur's Asia-first policy had posed a serious threat to their security. To have fought an all-out war in Asia would have required concentrating American military strength there and stripping Europe's defenses. His dismissal assured Europe the continued primacy of that theatre in America's plans.

MacArthur's return to the United States after an absence of sixteen years was triumphant. Everywhere he went, huge crowds welcomed him. His long (forty-eight years) military career highlighted by his successful leadership of American troops in the war against Japan and his administration of occupied Japan as well by such dramatic moments as his command of the forces that routed an "army" of veterans in Washington in 1932 and his evacuation of the fallen stronghold of Corregidor in 1941 had made a legendary hero of him. There were parades and receptions and a speech before a joint session of Congress on April 19 watched and heard by 60 million people on television. But soon, the excitement died down and the general, following the prescription of an old barracks song, "Old Soldiers Never Die," faded away (to a luxurious suite in the plush tower of New York's Waldorf-Astoria Hotel). At a rally in his honor held in May in Carnegie Hall in New York, a pitiable handful of admirers showed up. His cause, however, was not so easily eclipsed. It became the subject of an inquiry by the Senate Armed Services and Foreign Relations Committees, which opened as an investigation of the reasons for his recall and wound up in an attack by Republicans on the Administration's policy of making Europe the prime theatre in the struggle against communism to the neglect of Asia.

It was perfectly clear to the Republican Senators that MacArthur had been dismissed because his analysis of the international situation and his view of what the country's policy ought to be differed from the Administration's. It was equally clear to them that the general was right and the Administration wrong. He was right in believing that the main communist challenge was in Asia, not Europe and that the real enemy was China, not Russia. Hence, he was correct in urging that the chief effort should be concentrated in Asia and the all-out war should be fought against China. Spearheading the attack were some of the leading men in the Senate such as Robert A. Taft, William F. Knowland, Kenneth Wherry, and Styles Bridges and they had the support of powerful voices in the House (notably that of the former China medical missionary, William Judd) and among the nation's press, mainly Henry Luce's magazine empire, the New York Daily News, the Scripps-Howard chain, and the Chicago Tribune. The cry was to unleash Chiang Kai-shek in an assualt on the mainland and fight an unlimited war in Korea.

There was no dearth of defenders of the administration, whose ranks included the majority of the nation's press. They insisted that the greatest danger to the United States came from Russia, not China. They warned that the adoption of an "Asia first" policy would necessitate the withdrawal of the bulk of American support from Europe, thereby laying it open to conquest by the Soviets. Possessed of the industry, skills, and manpower of western Europe and of advanced bases on the western edges of the continent, the Russians would be in a superb position to mount a real threat against the western hemisphere. In his testimony, General

George C. Marshall pointed out the extreme urgency of America having access to European bases for the bombers of the Strategic Air Command and to European manpower to counterbalance Russia's superiority in ground forces. General Omar Bradley put the problem neatly when, in appearing as a witness, he said, to follow MacArthur's strategy would "involve us in the wrong war, at the wrong place, at the wrong time, and with the wrong enemy." James Reston, leading columnist of the *New York Times*, characterized the matter in another way when he called Europe the main tent and Asia the side show.

By early June the debate was petering out with the victory clearly on the administration's side. There seemed to be no question that the country was behind the policy of limited war in Korea and of placing the major emphasis on Europe. A final and unanimous report of the committees conducting the hearings issued on June 27, 1951 announced that America's foreign policy remained unchanged. Vindicated was the substantial increase in the number of American troops sent to Europe in early 1951, the appropriation of $6 billion in military aid to the Allies in late 1949 (to be spent over a period of years), the creation of a unified military command for allied forces in December of 1950, and the appointment of General Dwight D. Eisenhower as supreme commander.

It must be said, however, that the victory did not come cheaply. The debates and the hearings were bitter and rancorous, they were filled with accusations and recriminations. Many people suffered and wounds were inflicted whose scars would never heal. Opponents of the Administration were not content to discuss the question of Asia versus Europe. They also rekindled the fires of controversy over Chiang's defeat. In reviewing the reasons for that debacle, they ascribed primary responsibility to the presence of communists or their sympathizers in the Department of State on duty in Washington and in China. Dedicated and devoted foreign service officers like John Carter Vincent were openly accused of traitorous conduct for their praise for Mao and criticism of Chiang. It was their reporting that led the Administration to withhold the aid Chiang needed for victory, their accusers claimed. They deliberately set out to turn China over to the Communists. On the floor of the Senate, William Jenner of Indiana proclaimed "this country today is in the hands of a secret inner coterie which is directed by the agents of the Soviet Union."

The accusations were never substantiated. Not even Senator Joseph R. McCarthy, who devoted almost all his time to uncovering communists in the State Department and who was the most violent and irrational of the witch-hunters, could prove a single one of his allegations. Still, the appetite of the wolves had to be appeased, and several foreign service officers were dismissed on grounds of "doubtful loyalty." The whole business left many Americans with a feeling of uneasiness regarding the integrity and the dependability of their diplomats.

The hearings and the debates tended, also, to cast doubt in many minds regarding the willingness of the European allies to shoulder their fair share of the burden. Former President Herbert Hoover had raised that question in a nationwide radio broadcast in December of the previous year when he urged that not "another man or another dollar" be landed on European shores until the Allies "avail themselves of their own resources." And now, the "Asia firsters," in their endeavor to deemphasize the European theatre, made the same points. The Europeans, they said, were dragging their feet and were expecting the United States to bear the brunt of their defense. That position had led, with a kind of inexorable logic, to a next step—the questioning of the entire containment policy with its vast array of commitments of men and money and the longing to return to the pre-1941 period of the "Fortress America" idea of Charles Lindberg and the American Firsters. Hoover had also touched on that subject in his address when he proposed building a "Gibraltar of the Western Hemisphere." It had been his contention that the United States could never win a land war against the communists and ought, therefore, to concentrate on defending the hemisphere with superior air and naval forces. Now the *New York Daily News* and the *Chicago Tribune* were proclaiming containment "a flop" and a notice to the world that the United States "would bounce to battle anywhere." The Truman policy was leading to "spreading ourselves too thin" and to leaving to others the power to determine America's fate. In an editorial on December 30, 1951, the *Daily News* called for the adoption of the "Gibraltar" concept.

The administration was unmoved by the suggestions that descended on it from all sides and kept to the policy it had inaugurated in March of 1947. Meanwhile, negotiations for a cease-fire in Korea got under way on July 10, 1951 (following Malik's overture on June 23) at Kaesong, a village south of the 38th parallel but in Communist-held territory. The atmosphere did not augur well for the success of the operation. It was charged with hostility and mistrust, which was aggravated by the obtrusive presence of armed Communist guards who patrolled the area ceaselessly. Conditions were somewhat eased after the negotiations were moved to Panmunjom in "no man's land." By November agreement was reached on a demarcation line between north and south that was fixed at the point of contact of the two armies at the time of the cease-fire. The next issue broke up the conference. It concerned prisoner repatriation. The Communists insisted on the repatriation of all prisoners; the UN wished to leave the choice to the prisoners. It was believed that many Communists would, if not forcibly repatriated, prefer to cast their lot in the south. For a year, the wrangling continued until on October 8, 1952, talks were suspended.

Meanwhile, the fighting continued albeit on a limited scale. Still, bloody battles were being fought, casualties suffered, and the country further

devastated. Quite unexpectedly, in March of 1953, the Communists signalled their interest to resume conversations. Whether it was the death
of Stalin in that month that softened them or President-elect Dwight
Eisenhower's veiled threat of a resumption of full-scale military operations
is not known. Nonetheless, talks began again in April and by July 7, terms
had been agreed upon—a new demarcation line was drawn (consistent with
the actual battlefield condition); optional repatriation of prisoners—and
an armistice was signed. To allay the fears of President Syngman Rhee
caused by the expected continued presence of Chinese troops in the North,
the United States signed with the Republic of Korea, in October, a mutual
security treaty to defend the country from attack and agreed to keep two
American divisions in the country as well as to train and equip a Korean
army.

So ended what to many people was, perhaps, the most futile war in
American history. It had changed nothing. The two Koreas yet glared at
each other across a border virtually identical with the one established in
1945. The casualties were staggering: 36,606 dead; 103,327 wounded, and
a deep schism in the country. Suspicion and distrust of loyalties and of
patriotism were aroused by it, and repression of ideas and views was un-
leashed by it. Still, it must be said that had the war not been fought, all of
Korea might have become communist, and one does not know what
might have followed. As President Truman told Congress on January 8,
1951, "If the democracies had stood up against the invasion of Manchuria in 1931, or the attack on Ethiopia in 1935, or the seizure of Austria
in 1938 . . . as the UN had [now] done, the whole history of our time
would have been different."

One positive effect of the war was to fix America's China policy firmly
in one direction. If there were ever a possibility of recognition of the new
regime on the mainland and of supporting its admission to the United
Nations, the intervention in the war in the winter of 1950 put an end to
it. Red China at once became the treacherous enemy and hostility became
the order of the day. Trade and travel were cut off and contact of any
kind was forbidden. Considered a pariah, the regime was to be isolated
and, if possible, overthrown. At the same time, relations with the Nationalists on Formosa took a new turn. Chiang, once abandoned to his fate, was
now to be defended and the island was to be prevented from slipping
behind the "bamboo curtain." Maintaining the integrity and inviolability
of the Republic of China now became an element in the policy of containing communism in Asia. Economic aid was stepped up and military
assistance resumed. It should be noted that the hearings on MacArthur's
recall also accounted for the new China policy. A sure way for the Administration to parry the accusations that it had been soft on Mao and hard
on Chiang was to reverse the roles emphatically. So it may be said that in

one sense the Republican opposition shaped the foreign policy of the party in power.

The Korean war also affected, importantly, American policy toward Japan. The objective of the United States after the surrender on September 2, 1945 on board the U.S.S. *Missouri* in Tokyo Bay was to democratize, demilitarize, and neutralize the former enemy and end the possibility of his being a threat to the peace of Asia. That program was to be carried out by the American occupation forces under the command of General Douglas MacArthur. There was a Far Eastern Commission in Washington (consisting of representatives of 11 nations who fought the war in the Pacific) that was charged with making occupation policy but MacArthur paid it little heed. Similarly, a four-power Allied Council (the United States, China, the Soviet Union, Great Britain) sat in Tokyo to advise the commander but it was rarely used. In short, MacArthur ruled virtually by himself and might properly have been called the American Mikado.

He quickly set about discharging his mission. Japan's armed forces were abolished; the great industrial and commercial combines, which had made possible the great military advances, were dissolved; landed estates were divided; educational reforms were instituted; and trade unionism was encouraged. The capstone of the new dispensation was the constitution adopted on May 3, 1947. Under its terms, Japan became a parliamentary democracy with sovereignty residing in the people. The emperor lost his divine status but remained "as the symbol of the State and of the unity of the people." There was a bill of rights and a judicial system like that of the United States incorporated in the document. And of supreme importance was the clause renouncing war forever and prohibiting rearmament.

Then came, in rapid order, the Communist victory on the mainland, the Korean war, and the Chinese intervention, and American policy underwent drastic change. Japan now was viewed as a bulwark against the Red Chinese and as an element in America's policy of containing the Communists in eastern Asia. It was a quick metamorphosis from "dangerous threat" to "useful ally."

A peace treaty with Japan was one of the prime instruments considered by the United States crucial to bringing that country solidly into the anticommunist camp. With her sovereignty and independence restored and the occupation terminated, it was expected Japan would throw in her lot with the free world. A treaty of peace had, of course, been considered earlier. In 1947, MacArthur had urged it as a means of effecting Japan's economic recovery. All efforts to get the eleven members of the Far Eastern Commission to a preliminary conference were blocked, however, by the Soviet Union, which wished the negotiations left to the Big Four where a veto could be exercised. The United States did not pursue the matter further until the frightening events of 1949 and 1950. In September of 1950, President Truman instructed John Foster Dulles, a Republican and an expert on international matters, to move toward a peace conference without Russia if necessary. Dulles moved and after a year of talks and consultations, he succeeded in getting fifty-two nations to a peace conference in San Francisco. The delegates assembled on September 4, 1951 and, four days later, 49 of them affixed their signatures to the treaty. The Soviet Union, Poland, and Czechoslovakia refused to sign.

The treaty was generous. Japan recovered its sovereignty and independence. Although shorn of all its territory save four home islands, no penalties or disabilities were levied. The question of reparations was left to bilateral negotiations with those nations who had suffered at Japan's hands. All occupation forces were to be withdrawn within ninety days but, Article 6 went on to say, nothing would "prevent the stationing or retention of foreign armed forces in Japanese territory under or in consequence of any bilateral or multilateral agreements" between Japan and an Allied power.

The United States lost not a minute to avail itself of that clause. On September 8, the day the treaty was signed, a Japanese-American security agreement was initialed. Its preamble mentioned the "danger to Japan [of] . . . irresponsible militarism" in the world and stated the treaty's objective to be the defense of Japan. American troops would be stationed in Japan "to deter armed attack" but only until Japan could provide for "its own defense. . . ." Measures to provide for Japan's own defense had, in fact, already been taken. Shortly after the Korean war broke out, a National Police Reserve was created to replace American troops sent to Korea. Careful to avoid the use of the word "rearmament" (prohibited by the new constitution), the Japanese government continued to improve the country's defense capabilities. The National Police Reserve was transformed first into National Security Forces and, finally, into National Defenses Forces equipped with modern weapons, including tanks and artillery, supplied by the United States. There was a naval arm, too, of some seventy vessels provided by the United States under a lend-lease arrangement.

On March 20, 1952, the Senate approved, overwhelmingly, the two treaties of peace and of security. On that day it approved, also overwhelmingly, two other security treaties—one with the Philippine Republic, negotiated on August 30, 1951 and the other with Australia and New Zealand, negotiated on September 1, 1951. Thus, the Senate gave its consent to the collective security of structure in Asia erected by the Truman Administration. The Asian commitments were not precisely like those made to Europe. There was no "attack upon one is an attack upon all" clause. The Asian language was more modest. An attack upon one was viewed as "dangerous to all." Still, the underlying assumption of the policies in both continents was the same—draw the line and hold it against the further advance of the two great communist powers—Russia in Europe and China in Asia.

BIBLIOGRAPHY

RUSSELL BUHITE, *Patrick J. Hurley and American Foreign Policy* (1973).
WARREN COHEN, *America's Response to China* (1971).
HERBERT FEIS, *The China Tangle* (1953).
GEORGE KENNAN, *Memoirs, 1925–1950* (1967).
GLENN D. PAIGE, *The Korean Decision: June 24–30, 1950* (1968).
DAVID REES, *Korea: The Limited War* (1964).
TANG TSOU, *America's Failure in China, 1941–1950* (1963).
BARBABA TUCHMAN, *Stilwell and the American Experience in China* (1971).
ALLEN WHITING, *China Crosses the Yalu* (1960).

President Eisenhower and Secretary of State John Foster Dulles (Wide World Photo).

Containment Continued—
Republican Version

DWIGHT David Eisenhower came to the presidency on January 20, 1953, committed by the Republican party platform to making drastic and dramatic changes in the foreign policy of his Democratic predecessor. The party leaders, in part out of conviction and in part for political reasons (to capitalize on the frustrations and tensions of the American people over the Korean War and the Cold War) pledged to replace what they considered the weak and negative policy of the Truman administration with a new vigorous and firm approach to international affairs. Instead of containing the Soviet Union in its present borders there would be a rollback of its frontiers and liberation of the enslaved satellite states. Instead of conducting a limited war in Korea there would be an all-out fight against communism in Asia that would include sending Chiang against the mainland and bombing the Chinese bases in Manchuria. Europe would become a secondary theatre; American interests and activities there would be curtailed and the North Atlantic Treaty allies would be required to assume a greater share of the burden of their own defense. There would also be a cleansing of the State Department to rid it of the traitors and communist sympathizers who, the Republicans believed, had been responsible for the "loss" of China. Because Republicans believed, too, that Yalta and Potsdam had been the vehicles for delivering eastern European peoples to the Soviet Union, those agreements would be renounced. Finally, steps would be taken to curb the power of the executive to make agreements, such as Yalta and Potsdam, without senatorial approval.

During the campaign, the standardbearer, who had resigned the supreme allied command to run for office, had hit hard at mismanagement in foreign affairs and bungling in Korea by the Democrats. He had alluded to the "red stain" in government and to the "Godless Red tide . . . engulfing millions." He had not been the choice of the Old Guard of the party, who had preferred the tried and true conservative Robert A. Taft. Eisenhower was not even a Republican. As a career army officer, he had been apolitical. If anything, his appointment to high military posts by the Democratic presidents tainted him with the color of the enemy camp. But, he was performing properly. In Ohio he had praised Taft; in Indiana, he had supported Senator William Jenner, although Jenner had called his chief, George C. Marshall, a front for traitors; and in Wisconsin, he had deleted a favorable reference to Marshall in a speech at Senator McCarthy's request. And the man who would serve as secretary of state, John Foster Dulles, was known to be an implacable and inflexible opponent of communism. Grandson of one secretary of state and nephew of another, possessor of a broad experience in foreign affairs dating back almost half a century, and a stern and moral Presbyterian elder, Dulles had been a long-term critic of containment and an advocate of a more aggressive policy. Indeed, he had been responsible for much of the tough language in the platform. Earlier, in an article in *Life* magazine in May of 1952, he had urged the United States "to strike back where it hurts, by means of our choosing."

The early words and acts of the new administration pleased the party leaders. The president, in his inaugural address promised a firm policy in Korea and an unleashing of Chiang. Then in an order, on February 20, 1953, he removed the Seventh Fleet from patrolling the narrow strait between Formosa and the mainland, which presaged, according to the admirers of Chiang, a Nationalist assault on the Communists. Similarly, Secretary of State Dulles, in a radio address on January 27, 1953, told the eastern European peoples "you can count on us" and to the European allies he had issued a warning one month earlier that their failure to increase their share of the defense burden would lead to a reappraisal by Washington of the whole matter of foreign aid. Then there was the "New Look" in military policy heralded by Admiral Arthur Radford, chairman of the Joint Chiefs of Staff on December 14, 1953. It meant a reduction and a streamlining of ground forces and a heavier reliance upon atomic weapons. The purpose was, mainly, to effect economies in the budget for manpower was more expensive than machines—"more bang for a buck," as columnist James Reston labelled it. The president had, in February of 1953, stated his object was "to achieve military strength within the limit of endurable strain upon our economy." To many Republicans, however, the policy sounded new and bold and aggressive and very different from the Democratic approach. An address by Dulles before the Council on Foreign Relations in New York on January 12, 1954, gave credence to the view. He talked of a new strategy that placed "more reliance on deterrent power and less dependence on local defensive power" and that relied on a "great capacity to retaliate instantly by means and at times of our own choosing." One month earlier, the president had announced the withdrawal of two divisions from Korea, which seemed to reinforce the belief that the new administration, instead of leaving the initiative to the communists and responding to pressure by counterpressure on the ground by forces as the Democrats had done, would seize the offensive and carry the fight to the enemy by atomic weapons.

As it turned out, the party leaders were to be proven wrong in their expectations, because the Eisenhower Administration, despite its fine words and bold slogans and pronouncements, pursued a moderate and unwarlike foreign policy. It continued, in the main, its predecessor's emphasis on Europe not Asia and on holding the line on both continents. It practiced containment not "rollback" and "liberation" and strengthened and extended the network of alliance begun by the Democrats as the means of defending the free world against the threat of communism. There was no cleansing of the State Department of the large numbers of officers whom Senator McCarthy claimed were communists or their sympathizers. Nor did the president renounce the Yalta and Potsdam agreements, which the Old Guard Republicans had expected. Nor did he support a constitutional amendment by Senator John Bricker of Ohio to curb the power of the executive in making agreements with foreign powers without senatorial approval. Eisenhower was able to pursue such a course in the face of his party's conservative wing because of his great personal popularity and because Democrats and Republican liberals stood behind him. Indeed, he succeeded in getting the Bricker amendment defeated in the Senate and in obtaining confirmation of his appointment of Charles E. Bohlen, whom McCarthy considered an arch-member of the traitorous Truman-Acheson crowd, to be ambassador to Moscow.

The removal of the Seventh Fleet from the Formosa Straight had no effect on Chiang's mainland ambitions. Without American assistance, particularly in the form of transport and landing vessels, the Nationalists were powerless to mount an assault. And Eisenhower had no intention of supplying the equipment. Unleashing Chiang was no part of his Asian strategy. Indeed, there was every indication that he had accepted the existence of the Communists on the mainland as a fact of international life with which he was prepared to live. The Reds were there to stay and Chiang was in Formosa to stay. There were to be two Chinas, in fact, with neither one to be permitted to disturb the other. When Chou En-lai announced on August 11, 1954 that Formosa must be liberated, Eisenhower came back promptly with the retort that he would have to "run over the Seventh Fleet" to accomplish it.

The Republican administration's China policy was most fully revealed in the crisis over the Nationalist-held islands of Quemoy, Matsu, and the Tachens situated a few miles off the mainland. There was no question that the Communists coveted Formosa. To them it was as integral a part of the People's Republic as, say, Manchuria. To capture it, however, was easier said than done in view of Eisenhower's determination to defend it. The Reds, therefore, contented themselves for the time being with testing America's resolve. That they did by opening, on September 3, 1954, a murderous artillery barrage against Quemoy from the port city of Amoy, six miles away. The president's response was a treaty with the Nationalist government on December 12, guaranteeing Formosa against an armed attack and against Communist subversion and providing for the stationing of American forces "in and about" the island. At the same time, he rejected any suggestion for military action against the mainland or for defending the offshore islands unless the attack on them was a prelude to an assault on Formosa itself. After the Communists occupied one of the Tachens—Yikiangshan—on January 18, 1955, Eisenhower reaffirmed his policy. On January 29, at his request, Congress passed a joint resolution, overwhelmingly, authorizing the president to defend Formosa "and such related positions . . . as he judges . . . appropriate." But, again, the offshore islands were not included in the perimeter and in February, Chiang's forces evacuated the Tachens, still holding to Quemoy and Matsu.

The Communists stopped their shelling in April in part because of Eisenhower's determination to keep hold on Formosa and in part because of a setback at an Asian-African conference held at Bandung in Indonesia in April. There, the uncommitted nations of the two underdeveloped continents had some harsh things to say about Red China's (and the Soviet Union's) tactics in third-world areas. The Chinese were not prepared for criticism when they had expected accolades for standing up to the "imperialist-capitalist" powers.

Three and a half years later, the Reds renewed their assault on the offshore islands. When they opened fire on Quemoy and Matsu in August of 1958, Eisenhower lost no time in reminding Mao of the Formosa resolution. At the same time, he backed away from any commitment to defend the islands or to abet an invasion by Chiang of the mainland. On September 21, 1958, Undersecretary of State Christian A. Herter announced that the islands were not "strategically defensible in the defense of Formosa" and the next day Dulles, himself, reiterated the policy.

The Old Guard Republicans were not pleased with the Administration's China policy. The "two Chinas" concept was anathema to them. To them, Chiang's China was the only China and they expected it to prevail on the mainland with the United States' help. Typical of the group was Senator William F. Knowland of California, sometimes referred to as the "Senator from Formosa" who, although majority leader in the Senate, continually needled the Administration on the obligations to the wartime ally to aid in restoring him to his rightful place. Nor did the group derive much solace from the fact that the Administration would not recognize Mao's government nor relax its opposition to its admission to the United Nations. There were too many contacts and flirtations with

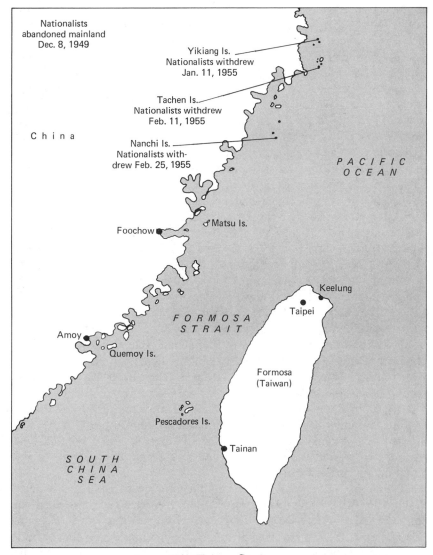

Nationalists
abandoned mainland
Dec. 8, 1949

Yikiang Is.
Nationalists withdrew
Jan. 11, 1955

Tachen Is.
Nationalists withdrew
Feb. 11, 1955

China

Nanchi Is.
Nationalists with-
drew Feb. 25, 1955

PACIFIC
OCEAN

Matsu Is.

Foochow

Keelung

FORMOSA
STRAIT

Taipei

Amoy

Quemoy Is.

Formosa
(Taiwan)

Pescadores Is.

Tainan

SOUTH
CHINA
SEA

The Taiwan Strait.

the Reds to suit them. In February of 1954, the United States indicated a willingness to discuss Asian affairs with the Reds and in April of the following year, conversations got under way in Warsaw. Most disturbing was the president's statement in April of 1955 that the admission of the People's Republic was unlikely *"under present circumstances"* (my italics).

The Administration's position on Korea was no less distressing to the Old Guard than its approach to the problem of China. The firm policy toward the North Koreans promised by the president in his inaugural address quickly turned out to be something very different. At a press conference in April of 1953, Secretary Dulles talked about "peace at the narrow waist." Senator Knowland and his friends were horrified. In a speech at a meeting of the California Dental Association in the same month he demanded unification of Korea as the price of peace. Anything less, he said, would be a betrayal of the Korean peoples. Anything less would have been, as well, a betrayal of the Republican Party pledge. The president, however, stuck to his cautious, moderate, and Trumanlike policy. There was no enlargement of the war. When peace came several months later, it was at the "narrow waist."

Eisenhower's approach to the confused situation in Indochina reflected much the same careful and temperate policy. When the opportunity and the occasion came to widen the war there, he rejected them. The Indochinese problem had its beginnings when the French masters returned to the area after the Japanese surrender and found themselves faced by a revolt. It was a movement for independence led by Ho Chi Minh, a revolutionary trained in Moscow and Peiping, at the head of the Viet Minh (League for the Independence of Viet Nam) party. In 1946, Ho had announced the creation of the Democratic Republic of Vietnam with the capital at Hanoi. France had countered by establishing its own version of an independent state of Vietnam, ruled by Bao Dai, a former emperor of Annam, with the capital in Saigon. The consequence was a bloody civil war between the two Vietnamese states. To the Truman administration, the war was viewed not as a domestic struggle between rival groups nor a war of liberation but as an element of the cold war in Asia. Truman and Acheson had recognized the regime of Bao Dai in Febuary of 1950 and began funnelling aid to the French, who were seen as the instrument for containing communism in southeast Asia. Five hundred million dollars annually were poured into the French effort. The support Ho received from the Red Chinese gave greater credence to the American interpretation of events.

Eisenhower continued Truman's aid program upon coming into office and, as the Viet Minh pushed harder on the French, he stepped up America's contribution. By early 1954, 80 per cent of the French expenditure was American financed. The president considered the money well spent, for he believed that should Indochina fall to the communists, the effect on the rest of the southeast Asia—Burma, Thailand, Malaya— would be fatal. He likened those countries to dominoes, with Indochina the first—push it and the others follow. Soon, however, it became apparent that money would not be enough for a French victory. Ho was gaining control over more and more areas and was sapping French strength by the use of guerrilla tactics. Then on March 14, 1954 came the crucial Viet Minh siege of Dienbienphu, a French fortress in northern Vietnam. Twenty thousand French and Vietnamese soldiers were bottled up and their condition was desperate. The French government let it be known that American military aid was essential to their salvation.

For the Eisenhower Administration the dilemma was cruel. That Indochina was important in the worldwide struggle against communism they did not question. But was it worth sacrificing American lives? Dulles thought so and proposed armed intervention to a group of congressmen from both parties. Vice-President Richard M. Nixon agreed and told an audience of American newspaper editors on April 16 that "we may have to put American boys in." Admiral Radford went so far as to suggest an atomic strike. But the president was opposed to any American participation. So was the majority of legislators and of the people as revealed by a Gallup poll. A hurried trip by Dulles to Europe on April 10 to sound out the allies convinced him that no support could be expected from that quarter. On April 20, he announced that it was "unlikely" American soldiers would be sent to Asia without Congressional approval and on April 28, the final historic decision not to intervene was made public. The French were left to their own defense and Dienbienphu fell on May 7 after fifty-five days of the siege.

That event ended, for the time being, the Indochina drama. A cease-fire followed and a conference at Geneva, convened in April to discuss Korea, took up the Vietnamese problem on May 8. Vietnam was divided at the 17th parallel, the north being assigned to Ho's Democratic Republic and the south to Bao Dai's Republic of Vietnam. At the same time, the conference provided for general elections to be held in July of 1956 as a prelude to unifying the two states. The same year, France granted independence to the State of Vietnam as well as to Laos and Cambodia, which France had carved out of its Indochina holdings.

The United States took no part in the Geneva Conference's settlement of the Vietnamese question. In the face of the Republican party's strong anticommunist and Asia-first component, the Eisenhower administration could hardly afford to put its signature to a document that surrendered 60,000 square miles and 11 million people to the communists. That is not to imply that the president was happy with the arrangement. He realized fully the victory the communists had won and he moved quickly to take steps to hold the line against their future advance. First of all, he sent money, supplies, and equipment to South Vietnam to strengthen the economy and the armed forces. Also, he provided American military personnel as advisors to train the army. That began the introduction of American soldiers into the Vietnamese cauldron. Their number was modest, 800 by the end of 1960, and no one dreamed in 1955 that the figure would grow to half a million by 1968 and the mission would change from training to combat.

The second step was to bring the noncommunist nations of the continent into some kind of organization to present a united front against the enemy and to improve their capacity to resist the Red tide. That was accomplished by the creation of the Southeast Asia Collective Defense Treaty, the handiwork of John Foster Dulles. Eight nations—the United

States, France, Great Britain, Australia, New Zealand, Pakistan, the Philippine Republic, and Thailand—met in Manila on September 6, 1954 and two days later signed the instrument. Dulles had hoped to include Burma, India, Ceylon, and Indonesia in the organization but they chose to remain nonaligned. They did not believe it wise to risk antagonizing the giant dominant power of the continent.

The treaty was not like its European counterpart. It did not say that an attack upon one was to be considered an attack upon all. It said only that an attack would be viewed by each member as endangering its "own peace and safety." Nor did the organization created at Bangkok the following year to implement the treaty provide for a standing army or a joint command. Emphasis was placed, rather, on the nonmilitary aspects of the venture—the promotion of the economic and social welfare, furnishing of technical assistance, and the prevention of subversion. A protocol attached to the treaty extended its coverage to the three Indochinese states of Laos, Cambodia, and South Vietnam, which, by the terms of the Geneva settlement, were forbidden to make alliances. That protocol was to take on great significance as the United States was drawn deeper into the Vietnamese war. It was to become one of the legal basis and justifications, however dubious, for American intervention.

The Senate's near-unanimous approval of the treaty (85–1) came as no surprise. Democrats supported it because it was considered an extension of Truman's containment policy to Asia. "Asia-firsters" in the Republican party hailed it for the attention it focused on their preferred continent where they viewed the communist menace to be greatest, and the liberal wing of the party accepted it as a wise means of holding the line in Asia.

Dulles called the treaty the capstone of the Pacific security system. He was referring, of course, to the fact that it completed the network of agreements that linked the United States to the defense of those Asian states wishing to take a stand against communism's advance. The Democrats in the preceding administration had signed defensive agreements with Australia, New Zealand, the Philippine Republic, Japan, and Korea. The Republicans had added China, Pakistan, and Thailand and had reintegrated Australia, New Zealand, and the Philippines in a multilateral pact. They had also enhanced the Japanese connection. In March of 1954, a mutual defense assistance pact between the two nations was signed that provided for the flow of American military supplies and equipment to beef up Japan's defense forces. Six years later, changing conditions in the island empire necessitated a revision of the 1951 treaty. That agreement had reflected Japan's subordinate position in the relationship. Since then, however, a tremendous growth in the nation's prosperity as well as opposition from ultranationalists to the subservient status caused Tokyo to demand the status of an equal. The new treaty achieved that objective in several ways, chiefly in giving the Japanese a voice in American troop

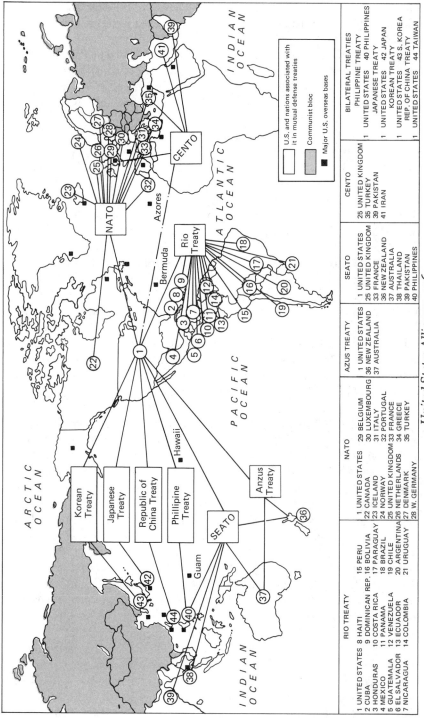

United States Alliances, 1961.

U.S. and nations associated with it in mutual defense treaties
Communist bloc
■ Major U.S. overseas bases

RIO TREATY
1 UNITED STATES 8 HAITI 15 PERU 16 BOLIVIA
2 CUBA 9 DOMINICAN REP. 17 PARAGUAY
3 HONDURAS 10 COSTA RICA 18 BRAZIL
4 MEXICO 11 PANAMA 19 CHILE
5 GUATEMALA 12 VENEZUELA 20 ARGENTINA
6 EL SALVADOR 13 ECUADOR 21 URUGUAY
7 NICARAGUA 14 COLOMBIA

NATO
1 UNITED STATES 29 BELGIUM
22 CANADA 30 LUXEMBOURG
23 ICELAND 31 ITALY
24 NORWAY 32 PORTUGAL
25 UNITED KINGDOM 33 FRANCE
26 NETHERLANDS 34 GREECE
27 DENMARK 35 TURKEY
28 W. GERMANY

AZUS TREATY
1 UNITED STATES
36 NEW ZEALAND
37 AUSTRALIA

SEATO
1 UNITED STATES
25 UNITED KINGDOM
33 FRANCE
36 NEW ZEALAND
37 AUSTRALIA
38 THAILAND
39 PAKISTAN
40 PHILIPPINES

CENTO
25 UNITED KINGDOM
35 TURKEY
39 PAKISTAN
41 IRAN

BILATERAL TREATIES
PHILIPPINE TREATY
1 UNITED STATES 40 PHILIPPINES
JAPANESE TREATY
1 UNITED STATES 42 JAPAN
KOREAN TREATY
1 UNITED STATES 43 S. KOREA
REP. OF CHINA TREATY
1 UNITED STATES 44 TAIWAN

movements in their country, but it did nothing to alter the fact that "democracy's iron chain in Asia from the Aleutians to New Zealand hinges on Japan."

In dealing with Europe, the Eisenhower administration continued very much in its predecessor's path—holding the line against further Soviet advance and maintaining and strengthening the Atlantic alliance.

Strengthening the alliance meant bringing Germany, with its vast potential resources in manpower and material, into it. Dean Acheson had mentioned the possibility as early as September of 1950 at a NATO Council meeting. The French, with the recollection of three invasions from across the Rhine in two successive generations, balked at the prospect of a rearmed Germany. Still, they accepted the fact of the old enemy's indispensability to the defense of Europe. Their own contribution, they knew was seriously impaired by the struggles then in progress in their Algerian and Indochinese colonies. The solution to the dilemma was advanced by Premier René Pleven in October of the same year. It rested on the proposition of "no German divisions, no German general staff, no German minister of war." The idea was to incorporate German units below division size with troops from the other allied countries into an international army controlled by a European Defense Community. Thus, Germany would have no independent military capability and would present no threat. The EDC was envisaged as more than an alliance. It was to be an international community with a governmental structure—council of ministers, assembly, secretariat, court of justice. There would be a European minister of defense and a single military budget.

The EDC was logical and responsible and in tune with the times. The western European nations were scouting ways of forming larger political and economic units. They knew that in the bipolar world of the two giants—the United States and the Soviet Union—the small nations could not survive except as satellites. As a beginning, Robert Schuman, the French foreign minister, had in May of 1950 suggested that France, Italy, Belgium, Luxemburg, the Netherlands, and West Germany create a supernational authority to control the production and distribution of coal and steel. That scheme had the unqualified support of the United States. President Truman called it "an act of constructive statesmanship." According to Washington, an integrated western Europe would be better able to provide for its own defense. The Schuman plan came to fruition quickly. On April 18, the six nations signed a treaty and on July 1, 1952, the European Coal and Steel Community came into existence.

The EDC did not, however, fare as well. The nations concerned—the six of the ECSC—signed the necessary agreements on May 26, 1952 that provided for the rearmament of Germany, bringing the soldiers into the EDC, and the EDC into NATO, but the French had a change of heart and the National Assembly kept delaying ratification of the agreements. The idea of Germans in uniform again less than a decade after the war was too much for them. Dulles and Eisenhower, now in office, were angry. They needed German manpower. They had considered the EDC the cornerstone of their European defense system. On December 14, 1953, Dulles warned France that failure to approve the EDC might result in "an agonizing reappraisal" of American policy and implied the possibility of a unilateral rearming of Germany. Undaunted, the French, eight months later, refused to accept the arrangement. They feared a rearmed Germany some day breaking away from the strictures of the EDC and embarking again on a course of conquest. Dulles' dire foreboding that the whole of the alliance structure "might be undermined and even swept away" had no effect.

Happily, the British came to the rescue. They suggested that the Brussels Pact of 1948 consisting of France, Great Britain, and the "Benelux" states be opened to receive Germany (and Italy, too) to create a Western European Union. Germany would be permitted to rearm and invited to join NATO. To allay French fears, the British promised to commit troops to the continent—for the first time in their history. Thus negotiations began in September of 1954. They were completed on October 23, duly signed and WEU came into existence on May 6, 1955. "A near miracle," sighed John Foster Dulles. Germany, rearmed and her sovereignty regained, became a full-fledged member of the club.

The Soviet Union had, of course, been paying close attention to the German drama on the other side of the continent. Fear of a rearmed Germany was no less a reality there than in France. Russia, too, had suffered, from the invaders. Moscow's reply to WEU then was expected— a counteralliance, called the Warsaw Pact, consisting of the Soviet Union and her satellites, was created on May 14, 1955. But that did not affect the amiable state of relations between east and west which dated from March 6, 1953, the day Stalin died. His passing brought to power a very different breed of ruler, a collective leadership in place of one man, and a much relaxed attitude toward the nations on the other side of the Iron Curtain. Georgi M. Malenkov, the new premier and party secretary, ushered in the new era by declaring, "There is not one dispute or undecided question that cannot be decided by peaceful means on the basis of mutual understanding of interested countries. This is our attitude towards all states, among them the U.S.A." Further, he called for "a peaceful co-existence of the two systems." Nikolai Bulganin and Nikita Khrushchev, who in February of 1955 replaced Malenkov as premier and party secretary, respectively, continued in the same spirit exemplified by Khrushchev's mocking promise "we will bury you." He meant, as he explained, that communism's victory would come not by war but by the example of its overwhelming economic and social success.

Evidence of the "thaw" was on every hand—diminished use of the veto in the UN; lifting of the curb on travel by foreigners in the Soviet

Union; widening of the opportunity for exchanges of journalists, farmers, scientists; consenting to a truce in Korea and a peace treaty with Austria; and expressing a desire for a summit conference. Dulles was opposed to such a meeting. It would, he said, give a certain respectability to the new leadership that ought to be denied it. Nor did he expect anything useful from such an encounter. Similarly, hard-liners in Moscow, led by Foreign Minister Molotov counselled against a conference. They wanted no accommodation with the west. But Eisenhower was for it. He sensed an opportunity to break the decade-long deadlock that had characterized Soviet-American relations since the last summit in 1945. Correspondence with his wartime comrade-in-arms, Marshal Gregory K. Zhukov, now defense minister, convinced him of the sincerity of Russia's leaders. The British, also, were favorable to any effort to improve east-west relations.

So, the meeting was held, in Geneva, from July 18 to 23, 1955. The atmosphere was cordial and friendly. Bulganin stressed peaceful coexistence and drank to toasts of "Down with war." Eisenhower avoided raising thorny questions. Senator Joseph McCarthy had tried to force him to discuss liberation of the satellites at the conference. On the Senate floor, he had read the 1952 party platform and indicted the party leaders for betraying it. They were, he said, as guilty of appeasing the Reds as their Democratic predecessors, and he cited as evidence the Korean truce at the "narrow waist," the failure to halt Ho Chi Minh in Indochina, and the abandonment of the Tachens to Mao. But the Wisconsin Senator could marshall no support for his resolution to place liberation on the agenda. It was smothered by a vote of 77–4. Once again, Eisenhower had succeeded in gaining approval for his policy of moderation and caution and liberation from the reckless promises of the electoral campaign. Even the most die-hard Republicans, like Hickenlooper of Iowa and Capehart of Indiana, had turned their backs on McCarthy.

The big issues at the conference were German reunification, European security, disarmament, and east-west contacts. Some startling proposals were made. Bulganin suggested the prohibition of the manufacture and use of atomic weapons and a reduction of the armed forces of the United States, China, and Russia. Eisenhower responded with a dramatic "open skies" appeal—aerial inspection to guarantee compliance with disarmament provisions. But disagreements ran deep and the heads of governments only defined the problems. Their resolutions were relegated to a foreign ministers conference, which met in the same place in October. There again, differences prevented solutions. Yet, the failure to accomplish concrete gains must not be the sole measure of the conference's achievement. Much was said about the improvement of the international atmosphere and people talked of the "Spirit of Geneva." There was a feeling that the Russian leaders were neither monsters nor brutes but reasonable men who were willing to discuss problems. Observers noted, too, that the western allies had maintained a quite remarkable solidarity.

Unhappily, the next year brought a transformation in the international climate. The western allies had a falling out and the Soviets resorted to a Stalinesque behavior pattern. It was the situation in Hungary that turned the Soviet clock back to pre-Stalin times. The relaxation of the Soviet regime after the old dictator's death affected the satellites as well as the home country. The new leadership talked approvingly of "national communism" and seemed to encourage a show of independence by the client states. Yugoslavia, which in 1948 had been expelled from the Cominform for "doctrinal errors," was restored to favor in 1955. Khrushchev went to Belgrade in May of that year to apologize for Stalin's mistakes and the next June, President Tito returned the visit. That same fall, an anti-Soviet outbreak in Poland did not lead to intervention by the Russians but rather to a treaty that acknowledged Polish equality with the Soviet Union. Riots in Hungary in October elicited from Moscow a very different reaction. When a new government was installed in Budapest that admitted noncommunists into high places, declared Hungary a neutral state, demanded the withdrawal of Soviet troops, and repudiated the Warsaw alliance, Soviet troops and tanks moved in. Independence was one thing; weakening communist solidarity was another. By November, the uprising was ruthlessly crushed and Hungary was back to "normal" governed by a pro-Soviet communist leader.

Hungary provided a test for the Eisenhower Administration. There was the perfect opportunity to "liberate" an enslaved people and to "roll back" the Soviet border and, given the Republican Party's platform, as well as some encouraging words from Voice of America radio broadcast, (a government-sponsored propaganda network) Hungarian freedom fighters expected help. Many Americans believed, too, that Dulles' highly vaunted "instant massive retaliation" doctrine ought to be invoked. But the president and his secretary of state followed a cautious and moderate policy. There was no intent to disturb Soviet–American relations and run the risk of a great nuclear war. Eisenhower contented himself with a plea to Khrushchev to leave Hungary alone.

It was precisely at the time of the Hungarian outbreak that the Suez crisis errupted to affect seriously the solidarity of the western alliance. It began when the Israeli government, disturbed by an Egyptian arms build-up, launched a lightning attack on the Sinai peninsula on October 29, 1956. Britain and France, who were believed to have helped plan and supply the assault, seized the occasion to punish Egyptian President Nasser for his nationalization of the canal the previous June. They issued an ultimatum to both sides to cease operations and to keep ten miles away from the canal. Egypt's refusal led to a joint Franco-British intervention. Their aircraft bombed Egyptian military targets and their soldiers occupied Port Said at the western terminus of the canal. Meanwhile, Israeli forces were destroying the Egyptian resistance.

Eisenhower, in the midst of a presidential campaign that stressed peace and prosperity, acted swiftly. The danger of a large-scale war was very real for the Soviets, who had been supplying arms and equipment to Egypt, threatened to come to Nasser's aid. They talked of sending "volunteers" and of using the most sophisticated weapons. On October 30, the American representative on the Security Council called for a cease-fire and a withdrawal of Israeli troops. When that resolution, and a similar one by Russia, were vetoed by France and Britain, the question was moved to the General Assembly. There, Russia and the United States, acting together, had no trouble getting a resolution passed to end the fighting. Israel, France, and Britain had no choice but to withdraw.

It may well have been true that a major war was averted by America's prompt action, but it was also true that at the same time the Atlantic alliance came close to being wrecked. France and Britain were bitter and resentful that their ally had not supported what they considered a justified effort to right a wrong. Their thoughts turned, quite reasonably, to the importance and desirability of freeing themselves from American domination. Washington, on its part, was worried by the prospect of a weakening of the Alliance. The cornerstone of Eisenhower's foreign policy, as well as Truman's, was NATO. It was the instrument for holding the line against communism's advance and in the principal theater of concern which was still Europe as it had been in 1950. The new Soviet leadership with its more liberal and lenient mien fooled no one. The threat was believed to be as great as ever. That fact was brought out clearly by George Kennan in testimony in February of 1956 before the Senate Foreign Relations Committee. Commenting on a rather cavalier statement by Dulles that the policy changes by Bulganin and Khrushchev were signs of weakness and of collapse, Kennan observed, "The Soviet threat is more serious today than at any time since 1947." The new leniency, he noted, was only tactical and the leadership more flexible, more confident, and more resilient. Khrushchev's famous denunciation of Stalin at the Twentieth Party Congress in 1956 did not, as Hungary had shown, signify an alteration of the basic Soviet approach to international life. Indeed, in the speech, Khrushchev had not ruled out violence. He had said only that in certain areas objectives could be better achieved by nonviolence.

Actually, the estrangement caused by Suez did not last long. Harmony among the allies was soon restored and cooperation was resumed. During 1957, visits to the United States by British and French officials and to Europe by President Eisenhower led to a restoration of confidence and to concrete agreements on bolstering the forces in Europe with tactical nuclear weapons and missiles. Important, too, in 1957 for European-American relations as well as for strengthening the allied defense capability was the creation of the European Economic Community (Common Market). The United States had been pushing for greater unity among the western European countries beyond merely coal and steel. And now it had come to pass by a treaty signed in Rome in March by the six members of the Coal and Steel Community. The objective of the new organization was to integrate all economic activity among the six and, eventually, to achieve a political union. The idea was to eliminate all internal duties among the six and erect a single tariff wall around them for the outside world; to permit the free movement among them of capital, labor, and services; and to achieve common agricultural, transport, and tax policies. All of that was to happen in three four-year stages. One day, no one knew when, the six would speak with one voice in matters of defense and foreign policy—a single state?

The United States knew well the significance of the new organization in relation to the policy of containment. How much better could a unified Europe pooling its resources, manpower, and skills defend its territory and its way of life than six separate, and often warring, nations. In February of 1958, one month after the community came into official existence, the United States accredited an ambassador to it, experienced career foreign service officer W. Walton Butterworth. It was the first nation to do so. It was a disappointment to Washington that Britain refused to join the community. She stood aloof for several reasons: allegiance to the worldwide Commonwealth of British Nations, consisting of her former colonies; a wish to retain a certain special relationship with the United States; an aversion to linking her political and economic destiny with non-Anglo-Saxon continentals (a viewpoint continentals considered supercilious and condescending). Still, aware of the likely deleterious effects of being outside a large trading area, the British sought to create their own, looser, block, which they did in November of 1959. It was called the European Free Trading Area and consisted of England, Austria, Sweden, Switzerland, Norway, Denmark, Portugal (the Outer Seven as against the Inner Six). It established free trade among the seven but permitted each nation its own external tariff system.

The healing of the schism among the allies came none too soon as ominous sounds were coming from the east during 1957 that sent tremors through the western alliance. In August, the Soviets tested successfully an intercontinental ballistics missile and in October there was the brilliant achievement of putting the first man-made satellite in orbit in outer space (*Sputnik*) to be followed by a second in November. Then there was the suggestion by Polish Foreign Minister Adam Rapacki in October that the two opposing alliances—NATO and Warsaw—withdraw their troops and nuclear weapons from the two Germanys, Poland, and Czechoslovakia. It was an attractive proposal for easing tension and for lessening the possibility of a clash of hostile forces. Some Europeans were attracted by it. Veteran diplomat George Kennan, himself, favored such a disengagement. In a series of lectures delivered over the British Broadcasting network in the autumn of 1957, he counseled getting Germany out of NATO and clearing her soil of allied troops as the only way to achieve reunification of the two Germanys. Neutralize West Germany, he said, and the Soviets would vacate the eastern republic, leaving the two parts to come together. But the proposal was not a good one for the west and the allies stood together to resist it. A pullback for them meant the loss of German soldiers and of a place for deploying their own troops. Dean Acheson, Truman's secretary of state and one of the principal architects of containment, made the most telling argument against the whole idea in an article in *Foreign Affairs* for April of 1958 and they were the sentiments of the Republicans as well. He called it an "attempt to crawl into the cocoon of history" by which he meant it would be a prelude to the kind of neutralism practiced in the 1930s. Withdrawal, once begun, would not end until American forces were all back in the United States, he said.

The remainder of the Eisenhower Administration was marked by a renewal of tension with the Soviet Union. The political and diplomatic offensive launched by Khrushchev may be ascribed in part to a new confidence as a result of the *Sputnik* success and in part to hostility toward the new Community whose success posed a threat to Soviet ambitions. In a surprise announcement on November 10, 1958, Khrushchev demanded an end to the occupation of Berlin. Seventeen days later in formal notes to the three western occupying powers, he set a deadline of six months for the withdrawal of their troops from Berlin and for an accommodation with East Germany on routes through that country from West Germany to Berlin. His objectives were clearly to force recognition of the existence of the communist East German state and to turn Berlin over to it. Eisenhower would no more think of abandoning the 2 million noncommunist Berliners than had Truman in 1948. In a reply dated December 14, the allies rejected the Soviet demand. Their rights in Berlin, said Dulles, would be defended "if need be by military force."

The Soviet leader backed down in the face of such determination and consented to a conference of foreign ministers in Geneva to discuss Berlin and the whole question of status of the two German nations. The meeting lasted three months, from May to August of 1959, but nothing concrete came of it. Fundamental east–west disagreements on the relationship of the various European problems killed its chances. The western allies sought to consider Berlin, German unification, disarmament, and European security as inseparable; the Soviets wished to deal with Berlin separately. The impasse led to renewed tension, which was eased by a visit to the United States by Nikita Khrushchev in September. The Soviet premier toured the country for ten days, stopping at several major cities and in farm areas chatting pleasantly with all sorts of ordinary Americans and plugging coexistence. He wound up his stay with an intimate meeting with Eisenhower at Camp David, the presidential retreat in the mountains of Maryland. It was a cordial and amiable encounter and the press began referring to the "Spirit of Camp David." But like the earlier "Spirit of Geneva," the slogan masked the poverty of real accomplishment. Nothing was settled and consideration of the problems was put off to a summit conference to be held in Paris in May of the following year. Meanwhile, the international atmosphere hardened with Khrushchev repeating his demands for evacuation of Berlin and the allies reiterating their determination to remain.

The meeting in Paris opened on May 16, 1960 and closed on May 17. No one had expected a settlement of issues; on the other hand, no one had expected the conference to last only one day. The short duration may be ascribed to the strange case of the U-2. On May 1, 1960, an American high-flying reconaissance plane, model U-2, was shot down in the Soviet Union. Four days later, Moscow announced the capture of the pilot and his photo equipment. Rather lamely, Washington explained the presence of an American plane over the Soviet Union in terms of a navigational error. That was so patently false that the president soon acknowledged the true mission of the aircraft—spying. As a matter of fact, he had no alternative in view of the fact that the pilot had already confessed.

That was all Khrushchev needed as ammunition to show up western perfidy (as though the Soviet Union was blameless of such activity). At Paris he demanded an apology and punishment of the responsible parties. His tone was belligerent, his demand exorbitant. He would do no negotiating, he said, until the United States satisfied him. Since Eisenhower would do nothing of the sort, the meeting broke up at once.

For the seven months remaining in the Republican Administration, Soviet-western relations remained tense and unfriendly, each side suspicious of the other and miles apart on fundamental issues. Eisenhower's term of office closed as Truman's had with containment still the basic assumption of American policy. The line was still being held in Europe at the same place and with the same allies, and in Asia the addition of new allies, in effect, fixed a new line. Indeed, it may be said that the Eisenhower administration extended the NATO line into Southeast Asia by SEATO. Thus, continuity in foreign policy was maintained and was proved more important as a determinant of policy than the Republican party's electoral pledges.

BIBLIOGRAPHY

SEYOM BROWN, *The Faces of Power: Constancy and Change in United States Foreign Policy from Truman to Johnson* (1968).

ROBERT J. DONOVAN, *Eisenhower: The Inside Story* (1956).

DWIGHT D. EISENHOWER, *The White House Years* (2 vols., 1963, 1965).

RICHARD GOOLD-ADAMS, *John Foster Dulles: A Re-appraisal* (1962).

NORMAN A. GRAEBNER, *The New Isolationism: A Study in Politics and Foreign Policy Since 1950* (1956).

TOWNSEND HOOPES, *The Devil and John Foster Dulles* (1973).

EMMET JOHN HUGHES, *The Ordeal of Power* (1963).

Gamal Abdel Nasser (Wide World Photo).

The Middle East

LIKE Europe and Asia, the Middle East served, and serves, as an arena for the two great contestants in the Cold War. It is a vast land and crucially important in a myriad of ways. Stretching from Turkey and Egypt on the west to Pakistan and Iran on the east with Lebanon, Syria, Israel, Jordan, Iraq, Saudi Arabia, and Yemen in between, it bridges three continents and constitutes a highway for the commerce of east and west. Rich in oil (two thirds of the world's reserves lay under its sandy soil), it is indispensable as a supplier of the nutriment for the machines of the industrialized nations. Clearly, neither side could afford to permit the other to gain a preponderant influence there. Their rivalry was, and is, intense and each convulsion in the region provided occasion for a confrontation. Given the conflict between Arabs and Jews and the numerous military coups and political upheavals in the Arab states there never has been a dearth of convulsion.

A principal source of turmoil in the area is the state of Israel created in 1948 over strenuous Arab opposition. The origins of the new nation reached back to 1917. In that year, the British government, eager to gain Jewish support in the war and out of gratitude to Chaim Weitzman, the brilliant Jewish head of the Admiralty's chemical laboratories, issued the Balfour Declaration, which promised "the establishment in Palestine of a National Home for the Jewish people." There was only one trouble with that noble aim. It conflicted with a similar promise the British gave the Arabs one year earlier. In 1916, they had been assured an independent state carved out of the ruins of the Ottoman Empire to include Palestine. The problem was compounded by the fact that the League of Nations in assigning Palestine as a mandate to Britain in 1922 endorsed the Balfour Declaration as did an Anglo-American treaty (albeit indirectly) in 1924. The difficulty of reconciling the two mutually exclusive promises was to plague Britain for 30 years.

As the decades of the 1920s and 1930s moved on, the Jewish population

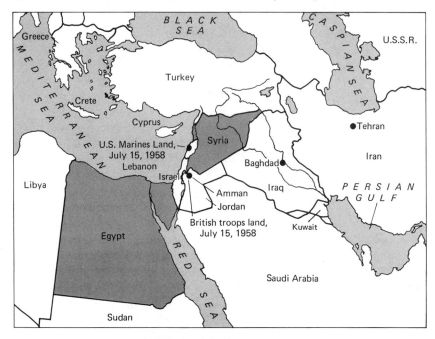

The Middle East, 1958.

in Palestine increased tremendously. Numbering only 55,000 in 1920, it reached almost 500,000 by the late 1930s as Palestine was swelled by Jews who escaped Nazi persecutions to find peace and freedom from oppression and discrimination in the Promised Land. The Arabs, thoroughly alarmed at the prospect of a Jewish avalanche inundating the land, demanded that the British halt the flow of immigration. An Arab general strike and a campaign of terror against the Jews in 1936 frightened London into action. In an effort to placate both sides, a royal commission suggested, in 1937, that Palestine be partitioned between Arabs and Jews with Jerusalem remaining mandated. Arab hostility to the plan put an immediate end to it. More concerned with Arab than Jewish sensibilities, the British next, in 1939, announced that Palestine would be given independence in ten years and that Jewish immigration would be restricted to 75,000 over the next five years. Any further admission of Jews would be subject to Arab permission.

Now it was the turn of the Jews to be alarmed for the British plan presaged the continuation of an Arab majority and the end of the dream of a Jewish homeland. Their response was a resolution, in 1942, by the World Zionist Organization, the international organization of Jews dedicated to erecting a national state which had recently moved its headquarters to New York from London, calling for a Jewish state, a Jewish army, and unlimited Jewish entry into Palestine. At the same time, a terrorist campaign was launched against Arabs and Britons designed to lift the immigration restriction. Meanwhile, Jews were slipping into Palestine illegally.

In the United States, support for the Jewish cause was nearly universal, as might be expected. Sympathy for the victims of Hitler's terror was everywhere and there was a feeling that they deserved their own land and the safety it would provide. Sympathy, alone, does not explain completely the preference by American leaders for the Jewish over the Arab Cause. There was a political factor, too. The Jewish vote, especially in urban centers, was large, significant, and occasionally decisive. An Arab vote did not exist. Of importance, too, was the very different image Americans had of Jew and Arab. The Jew was viewed, generally, as energetic, literate, civilized, modern, and western. The term *Arab* conjured up a white-robed bearded figure riding a camel aimlessly across vast and trackless deserts or a dirty, ill-kempt, uneducated peasant living in squalor in a teeming city. There was, too, a stereotype of the Arab woman that played a role in the formation of the American attitude. Unlike her Jewish sister, she seemed a pitiable figure, veiled, clad in ankle-length black, and in a constant state of bondage to her husband whom she had married at the command of her father. Pity, in this case, generated not support but rather revulsion and disgust with so backward and archaic a culture.

It was not surprising, therefore, that Congress, in 1944, urged President Roosevelt to prevail upon the British to open the gates of Palestine to all Jews who wished to settle there and to aid in the creation of an independent Jewish state and that both Democrats and Republicans incorporated in their platforms in that same year support for the Jewish cause. Roosevelt did, indeed, in 1945, at a meeting with King Ibn-Saud of Saudi Arabia, make an appeal for Jewish immigration but, expectedly, the Arab monarch would hear nothing of it. He was, of course, reflecting the implacable Arab opposition to a Jewish state and to the presence of a large number of Jews in the area.

When the war ended, France quickly gave up its League of Nations mandate in Syria, from which came the two new states of Syria and Lebanon. The British could do no such thing. They had to find some other formula for Palestine. They did not feel they could simply walk away from the problem. Prime Minister Clement Atlee, who had succeeded Churchill in 1945 when Labor defeated the Conservatives at the polls in the first postwar election, hoping to shift some of the burden to the United States, suggested in 1946, the establishment of a joint Anglo-American commission of inquiry to offer a solution to what appeared to be an insoluable conundrum. A report, arrived at in April, recommended that the mandate be continued but that 100,000 Jews be admitted at once. President Truman refused, however, to betray the Jewish hope for an independent state. Now, the British were ready to wash their hands of the whole business. Plagued by a series of postwar difficulties, they were in the process of surrendering a host of obligations that had been the hallmark of a great power. In February of 1947, the Labor government placed the problem at the doorstep of the United Nations. That body at once created a Special Committee on Palestine, which proposed that on August 1, 1948 Palestine be partitioned between Arabs and Jews and that Jerusalem be placed under international control. On November 29, 1947, the General Assembly accepted the proposal.

Jews were elated; Arabs were enraged. Both the United States and the Soviet Union were prepared to aid in the enforcement of the resolution. The British, however, fearful of getting caught in an Arab-Jewish squeeze, announced in December, that they would surrender the mandate and quit Palestine on May 14, 1948. Meanwhile, the Arabs had launched an attack on the Jewish settlements to prevent partition. With heavy fighting in progress and Palestine in turmoil, the United States thought it best that the execution of the plan be put off for a time. In March of 1947, the American delegate to the UN suggested a temporary trusteeship for Palestine under UN auspices. Jewish leaders, desperate at the prospect of their cherished hope being dashed, decided on a bold step. They would, unilaterally, carry out the UN resolution. At 6 P.M. on May 14, the British, true to their word, withdrew from Palestine. One minute later, the existence of the State of Israel was proclaimed in Tel Aviv. Ten minutes later, the United States extended recognition to the infant republic with the Soviet Union following in three days. The Arab response was a pledge to destroy the new state, and the course of events in the Middle East from that day to this has been shaped by the Arab efforts to carry out the pledge. The fighting has never ceased completely whether in the form of pitched battles or border raids. An armistice negotiated in July of 1949 by UN official Ralph Bunche that, in addition to halting hostilities, divided Jerusalem between Israel and Jordan, hardly lasted until the ink on the document dried.

Egypt was the country that spearheaded the drive against Israel. Headed by the dynamic strongman, Gamal Abdel Nasser, who came to power two years after the successful revolution of 1952 that ousted King Farouk, Egypt grasped the leadership of the Arab world. The western powers, noting Egypt's prime position, sought to make that power the fulcrum of the Middle East defense arrangement against Soviet aggression. That Russia had designs on the region was accepted as a fact of international life and not a particularly new one. The czars of Imperial Russia had coveted the region and Stalin and his successors were only dutiful inheritors of that historic tradition. It was no secret that Stalin had ambitions to extend his power southward to the Persian Gulf and into the Indian Ocean. After the war, his demands on Turkey for a voice in the control of the straits separating the Black Sea from the Mediterranean and his retention of troops in Iran were elements in a grand design. Both those efforts were frustrated by the United States, but there was no reason to believe the Soviets had given up the idea.

Egypt was interested not so much in an alliance as in getting arms and equipment for the fight against Israel and when the western powers stipulated that an assault on Israel would not be tolerated, Egyptian leaders turned their backs on the west. Not even Britain's agreeing, in July of 1954, to surrender all rights under the Anglo-Egyptian treaty of 1936 to keep troops in the Suez Canal zone, would soften Egypt's stand. The decision was then made in London and Washington to move ahead on defense arrangements without Egypt. John Foster Dulles had, from the first days of the Republican administration, begun to line up the countries constituting the "northern tier" of Middle Eastern states along the Soviet southern border as the participants in the system. The first step was a treaty between Turkey and Iraq signed on February 18, 1955; the second was the adhesion of Great Britain, Pakistan, and Iran to it in October. So the Baghdad Pact came into being; its name derived from the place chosen to serve as headquarters for the Middle East Treaty Organization, the agency created to implement the Pact. The United States did not become a party to the agreement for fear of offending Nasser; still, Washington was clearly the force behind it and promised to be the chief provider of the materiel to make it work. Further, the treaty was an element in America's policy of containing the Soviet Union in that it filled the geographical gap between NATO and SEATO. Indeed, it might be viewed as the coupling pin linking the two: Turkey being at the same time the easternmost member of NATO and western anchor of METO and Pakistan being the most westerly signatory of SEATO and the most easterly partner of METO. As the years went on, the United States moved closer to the organization. In November of 1956, assurance was given the signatories that a threat to their territorial integrity and political independence "would be viewed . . . with the utmost gravity" and the following June, the United States actually joined the military committee of the organization. In January of 1958, following a meeting of the member nations, the United States promised to provide a "mobile power of great force."

The price paid for the creation of the pact was high—angering Egypt and providing her the occasion to turn to the Soviet Union for help. What irritated Egypt was, of course, the reintroduction of the old imperial master, Britain, into the region and the weakening of Arab unity by Iraq's membership in the pact. That Nasser would do all in his power to repay the west for its rashness went without saying and that the Soviet Union would be his ally was not unexpected. The opportunity came in September of 1955 when the Soviets contracted to buy Egyptian cotton, for which Egypt had been having trouble finding a market, for themselves and for their satellites. As part of the payment, Egypt took a supply of arms—tanks, aircraft, weapons—chiefly of Czechoslovakian manufacture.

The deal was more political than economic. Russia became the military patron of Egypt and got a foot in the Middle Eastern door while Egypt received the wherewithal to strengthen her position vis-à-vis Israel. In that same fall of 1955, Nasser went about solidifying his relations with other Arab states and pulling the Soviet Union deeper into them. There was the formation of a Syrian–Saudi Arabian–Egyptian joint military command, a Lebanese–Syrian defense agreement, a Soviet–Syrian trade treaty, and a Yemen–Soviet treaty of friendship. At the same time, Nasser stepped up his raids on Israeli territory using Arab refugees from Palestine.

Both Britain and the United States meanwhile began making efforts to placate Nasser. The last thing they wanted was an Egyptian-led Arab coalition acting as a Soviet cat's paw in the Middle East. Aware of Nasser's deep interest in a high dam on the Nile at Aswan (about 800 miles south of Cairo) to irrigate 32 million acres of arid land, the two powers jointly offered him a loan of $70 million to get the project started and a promise of more to come. Before long, however, the United States had second thoughts about the matter. Nasser's flirtations with Russia, his arms build-up, his recognition of Red China, all led Dulles to reconsider the loan for the dam. Why give Nasser the money if it would enhance his position and enable him to pursue his wayward course? On July 19, 1956, the secretary of state informed the Egyptian government that the United States would not join in the financing of the dam. At the same time, Britain withdrew her offer. Six days later, Nasser struck back by nationalizing the Universal Suez Canal Company which owned and operated the canal. Henceforth, he announced, the Egyptian government would collect the tolls using the proceeds to pay off the stockholders and build the dam.

Britain and France were thunderstruck. The waterway was crucial to their oil supply and, further, their nationals were the principal stockholders. They could not trust the Egyptian ruler to guarantee the flow of traffic through the canal nor to reimburse their citizens. The alternative, clearly, was to get rid of him and Anthony Eden, the British prime minister, let President Eisenhower know, on July 27, that he was ready to use force. How much he must have regretted evacuating the British stronghold in the canal zone the previous month (pursuant to the 1954 treaty)! The French, on their part, were eager to join their friends across the channel in an Egyptian adventure. They had an additional grievance against Nasser. He had been funnelling Soviet arms to the Algerian nationalists in revolt against French rule and giving them other forms of aid and comfort. Paris was even more bellicose than London.

The United States shared the concern of the allies but was not willing to go as far as military action and Dulles' aim was to effect a peaceful settlement of the problem. He suggested the creation of a Suez Canal Users Association that would oversee the canal's operation collecting tolls, paying off the stockholders, and maintaining the waterway. Nasser, of course, rejected the idea. For him, the canal was a decisive element in the exploitation of Egyptian nationalism. The waterway will be "run by Egyptians, Egyptians, Egyptians," he shouted to a wildly cheering crowd of supporters.

France and Britain were now ready to move. There is evidence that the two powers were deep in conversations with Israel in the late summer of 1956 hatching a plan to invade Egypt. Israel had plenty of reason to join the conspiracy, Egypt's arms build-up, Nasser's unabashed and loudly heralded aim of destroying Israel, the support given him by Syria and Jordan, and increasingly ferocious raids on her border settlements were enough to cause her leaders to look to a military solution to the problem. Exactly what the three nations talked about is not known. It is, however, reasonable to conclude, if the recollection of Anthony Nutting, a participant, is to be believed, that the decision was taken for Israel to launch an attack following which Britain and France would intervene. That is precisely what happened on October 29, 1956. That morning, Israeli tanks swept across the Sinai peninsula right up to the canal, occupied the Gaza strip and several key islands in the Gulf of Aqaba, and captured vast stores of armaments. The next day, Britain and France issued an ultimatum to the two belligerents that they halt the fighting and withdraw to a point ten miles from the canal. The refusal to heed the demand led to a swift attack by France and England on Egyptian airfields and to seizure of Port Said.

President Eisenhower was alarmed. Here were the ingredients of a really large-scale war. The Soviet Union was standing behind Egypt threatening the invaders with retaliation and Khrushchev spelled out the details—armed volunteers and even guided missiles. Acting with courage and determination, Eisenhower took action to halt the war. In concert with the Soviet Union—a strange alliance—he went before the United Nations Security Council with a resolution ordering a cease-fire. An expected veto by France and Britain led to the president taking the case to the General Assembly. There the vote was overwhelmingly for the resolution. All the nations save Britain, France, Israel, New Zealand, and Australia were ranged on the side of peace. The three warring allies had no choice but to accept the decision. Saddened (and angered) by the American failure to understand and appreciate their problem, they withdrew. On November 6, the war ended.

The lessons of the crisis were clear to Eisenhower. The Soviet threat of intervention in the Middle East had been more than a scare; it had been a real possibility and the president felt some action to forestall it was necessary. The gravity of the situation was underscored by his unprecedented appearance before a joint session of Congress on January 5, 1957. He spoke of the danger to the security of the whole world—Africa, Asia, Europe, the western hemisphere—"if the nations of that area [Middle East] should lose their independence by alien forces hostile to freedom . . ." and asked for authority to use armed force to aid any country requesting military help for resisting "armed attack from any country controlled by international communism." He also requested $200 million for military and economic aid to nations desiring such aid. Congress did not at once grant the president his wishes. There was some questioning of the real source of insecurity in the region with some legislators believing it to be local instability and the conflict between the conservative traditional morarchies like Iraq, Saudi Arabia, and Jordan and the revolutionary nationalist republics like Egypt and Syria. Nonetheless, the authority was granted by a very safe margin (72–19 and 350–60) and on March 9, 1957, the president signed the "Eisenhower Doctrine" into law. The United States was now protector of Middle Eastern freedoms. For Dulles, the Doctrine was but another element in worldwide containment. "Gradually," he said, "one part of the world after another is being brought into it [containment network] and perhaps we may end up with a, what you might call, universal doctrine reflected by multilateral treaties or multilateral worldwide authority from Congress." Egypt, of course, denounced the whole business calling it an "imperialist plot" while Russia labelled it "colonialism" and "gross interference." Not to be outdone, Russia announced support for any Middle East nation facing aggression.

The action came none too soon, for one month later, in April, a movement engineered by left-wingers with Nasser's support threatened to overthrow King Hussein of Jordan and bring that country into the Egyptian–Syrian pro-Soviet antiwestern camp. Hussein appealed at once to the United States under the Eisenhower Doctrine and the president, stating that Jordan's independence was vital to the United States, ordered elements of the Sixth Fleet based in the Mediterranean, including the carrier *Forrestal* with 1,800 marines, to the eastern end of the sea. The Jordanian monarch, immeasurably bolstered, was able to crush the rebels and his kingdom was saved—for the west.

But more trouble was to come. In August, a group of pro-Nasser left-wing army officers in Syria seized the government and the consequences were considerable. One was the introduction into the country of large quantities of Soviet arms and equipment and technical personnel. Another was the merger of Syria and Egypt into a single state—the United Arab Republic—in February of 1958 that threw the Middle East into a serious state of political and military imbalance. A tremor of fear swept through the region as nations contemplated the possibility of a spread of Nasser-inspired resolutions. Their fears were not ungrounded. The UAR was the lodestar of pro-Nasser leftist elements in almost every country and they were restless. In May of 1958, they opened a rebellion in Lebanon against the Christian and prowestern government of President Camille Chamoun and in July they overthrew the prowestern regime in Iraq, assassinating the king, crown prince, and premier in the process. Chamoun lost no time in appealing to the United States for aid under the Eisenhower Doctrine before the rebels had the chance to mete out to him the same treatment his fellow ruler of Iraq had gotten. At the same time, King Hussein, fearful that he would be the next victim of the revolutionary virus called on the British for help. President Eisenhower responded promptly. On July 15, one day after the Iraqian upheaval and the Lebanese call, American marines from the Sixth Fleet landed in Beirut, Lebanon's capital, to be followed by an airborne brigade from the Seventh Army stationed in Germany. Britain answered the call, too, dropping paratroopers into Amman, Jordan's capital.

It should not be surprising that Moscow cried "imperialism" and "aggression." Khrushchev's response was to send troops to the Soviet–Turkish and Soviet–Iranian borders and to threaten intervention. But the Anglo-Americans did not frighten easily. They would not withdraw until the United Nations could make provisions for maintaining the peace. After several weeks of maneuvering by the powers at the UN and of grave tension, the General Assembly passed a resolution, unanimously, pledging the nations to refrain from interfering in one another's internal affairs and calling on the Secretary General to carry out that principle in relation to Lebanon and Jordan. Satisfied that the danger had passed and that Nasser had called off his agents, the Anglo-American forces began their withdrawal. By October, the last of the United States forces had left and by November all Britain's soldiers had departed.

So peace had been restored but it did not prove to be permanent. The intervention had contributed nothing to a long-term solution of Middle Eastern problems. The Arab-Israeli conflict was still intense; Nasser yet aspired to marshal the Arab world against the west and the Soviet Union was no less the willing provider of the wherewithal; and political and social upheavals in the Arab countries as well as rivalry amongst them kept the region in the usual turmoil. A revolt by pro-Nasser elements in Yemen in September of 1962 set in motion all the contending forces. Nasser at once sent troops to help the rebels whereupon Saudi Arabia and Jordan provided aid for their fellow monarch who had fled his capital. The Soviet Union, unwilling to lose an opportunity to insinuate itself into the area, shipped arms and equipment to the rebels. The following spring, an extremist political group called the Arab Socialist Renaissance Party or *Baath* and led by army officers overturned the regimes in Iraq and Syria. The two new governments, thereupon, joined in a unified military and economic union and had no trouble getting large-scale military aid from Russia. Iraq had, itself, since 1959 been the recipient of generous assistance in the form of tanks and guns from the Soviet Union as a reward for quitting the Baghdad Pact. That defection had forced the United States to shift the METO headquarters to Turkey and to change the name to Central Treaty Organization. There was no question that the move weakened the alliance and as compensation, Washington had, in the same year, signed bilateral defense pacts with Turkey, Pakistan, and Iran.

Whatever separated the Arab states was insignificant compared with what brought them together—a passionate hatred for Israel and a sworn resolve to destroy that fledgling republic. Whenever their bickering and rivalry threatened to lead to open warfare there was always the common enemy to face. Implacable rivals like Jordan and Syria or Egypt and Saudi Arabia found common ground in the great crusade. In 1964, there were two summit conferences of Arab leaders dealing with the Israeli problem at which substantial agreement was reached on several important measures—creation of a unified military command, diversion of the waters of the Jordan river to deprive Israel of water, and organization of a Palestine Liberation Army to spearhead raids on Israel. At the same time, the Soviet Union was pouring all kinds of military equipment into Egypt— fighters, bombers, submarines, destroyers, torpedo boats, missiles—and Nasser was not concealing the use he expected to make of them. "Liberate the Arab nation from the perils of Zionism," he cried.

Little wonder Israel was alarmed. Desperately, that little nation surrounded on all sides by hostile neighbors, appealed to the Soviet Union, the United States, and the United Nations for guarantees of security. No help could be expected from the Soviet Union, the Arab's friend; nor from the UN where the Soviet Union had support from the satellites and from the emerging African nations who considered Israel an imperialist tool of the western capitalist and colonial nations. The Anglo–French– Israeli joint action in 1956 against Suez was not easily forgotten. Further, France was a steady supplier of combat aircraft to Israel—the France who had for so long refused to let Moslem Algeria go free. Unexpectedly, no support came from Washington. Despite a large reservoir of public sympathy for Israel, the new Democratic Administration of John F. Kennedy tread warily in the Middle East. Willing to alienate neither the Arab states nor the Jews (at home as well as abroad), the president favored not one side nor the other. His policy was one of balance and fairness. His reception of Premier David Ben-Gurion in Washington in 1961 was followed by a letter to all the heads of the Arab states assuring them of his country's friendship and pledging support in their efforts to maintain their independence. At the same time, he expressed the hope that no state would hinder any other from living in peace, thereby making clear his opposition to any campaign to destroy Israel. On the thorny question of the nearly 1 million Arab refugees displaced from their Palestine homes in 1948, Kennedy suggested a compromise—the Jews would provide them compensation and opportunities to resettle in their former areas in return for recognition of Israel's "rights to live" by the Arab states. An Israeli plea in May of 1963 for a bilateral defense pact was refused as was the request for large-scale military aid although Kennedy did authorize the sale of ground-to-air missiles for defense against an Arab aerial attack.

Meanwhile, raids on Israel's borders were ceaseless. From Egypt, from

Jordan, and from Syria, members of the underground terrorist organization, Al Fatah, and of the Palestine Liberation Army penetrated Israel's settlements spreading death, destruction, and terror. And always they received encouragement from the Soviet Union. The Israelis, of course, retaliated. In May of 1965, their forces hit deep into Jordan; in July 1966, their jets destroyed a concentration of Syrian antiaircraft positions; in August, they engaged in an air battle over the Sea of Galilee with Arab fighter planes. In February of 1966, the situation grew tenser when a military coup in Syria brought to power a radical Pan-Arab group that demanded the total destruction of Israel and promised a stepped-up campaign of terrorism. In November, the new Syrian leaders, with Soviet blessing, joined Egypt in a unified military command. Vainly, Israeli officials pleaded with President Johnson, who had succeeded the assassinated President Kennedy in November of 1963, for a guarantee. Johnson, completely distracted by the war in Vietnam, had no intention of getting involved in another theatre of warfare.

The pot was at the boiling point in the Middle East and in April of 1967, it almost boiled over when Israeli jets smashed into Syria, blowing up military installations sixty miles from the capital at Damascus. The next month, Nasser closed the Strait of Tiran to Israeli shipping, thereby closing off the approach to Israel's only southern gateway, the port of Elat on the Gulf of Aqaba. The Arab world rejoiced at the bold move, which they hoped would wound Israel mortally. The United States and the western powers branded the act illegal. Israel responded on June 5 with a savage military attack on three fronts. Smashing into Egyptian territory, air units destroyed most of the Egyptian air force before it had the chance to take to the air while armored forces cleared the Sinai peninsula of enemy troops pushing them to the western bank of the Suez Canal. To the north, Israeli tanks captured the strategic Golan Heights from Syria, and to the east, Israeli columns drove Jordanian soldiers out of western Jerusalem and onto the east bank of the Jordan river. In the bargain, an estimated $1 billion of arms and equipment, chiefly of Soviet origin, was either captured or destroyed. On June 10, the fighting ended. The Six-Day War was over. It was an Arab disaster of gigantic proportions. Their forces had been routed decisively and ignominiously. Russia had not lifted a finger. The Arabs were not worth the risk of a world war.

Israel was now in a more secure position with buffer territory between herself and her three contiguous enemies and there was no question of surrendering her conquests. Indeed, her policy was to integrate the new possessions—the Sinai peninsula, Golan Heights, west bank—into the political and economic life of the country. Egypt and the other Arab states renewed their cry of revenge and restoration but it was hollow. The Soviet Union began again to furnish arms and equipment and financial personnel to Egypt and the other countries to replace the great losses, but it would be a long time before these nations would be in a position to fight. Meanwhile, the truce was uneasy. It was, in fact, an armed peace with raids across the borders virtually a daily affair. American policy after the war was geared to bringing about an Israeli withdrawal from the conquered land in exchange for Arab recognition of the existence of the Jewish state to be followed by direct negotiation on other issues. President Johnson could see no justice in the position of the United Nations shared by the Soviet Union and the Arab world that withdrawal be a prelude to negotiation. By the time the Democrats left office in January of 1969, the state of affairs in the Middle East was precarious. Arabs faced Israelis and behind the one stood the Soviet Union and behind the other was ranged the United States. It must be noted that although Americans regretted the absence of peace in the Middle East, their sympathies lay with the plucky, brave, outnumbered, and efficient Jews fighting to secure for "the remnant of Israel" a sanctuary.

A NOTE ON AFRICA

In Africa, too, the United States and the Soviet Union found themselves on opposite sides of most issues and in a contest for gaining preponderant influence. The chief issue was the movement of the natives for freedom from rule of their European masters. At the end of the war, there were only four independent nations on the continent—Egypt, Liberia, Ethiopia, South Africa. By 1968 the number had jumped to forty-two. Only Portugal retained significant holdings.

For the United States, African nationalism presented a cruel dilemma. There was sympathy for the natives yearning to be free especially among the American blacks who, quite naturally, had an affinity for their African brothers. More and more, they were seeking to reclaim their connection with the place from which their ancestors had come. On the other hand, there were the obligations to the European colonial masters—France, Britain, Belgium, Portugal—on whose cooperation and good will the Atlantic alliance so heavily depended. The Soviet Union faced no such quandary. It could stand four square on the side of freedom, independence, and anticolonialism as the United States equivocated and vacillated. Washington never failed to grasp the opportunity to urge the European allies to let the colonies go but, at the same time, the demands were never insistent. Inevitably, the colonial peoples came to look upon the republic across the Atlantic as neither true friend nor dependable benefactor.

Particularly depressing to the Africans was the American attitude toward the Republic of South Africa and Southern Rhodesia. Both nations practiced segregation and discrimination—apartheid—in the cruelest and most shameless way. The African bloc repeatedly sought to punish both countries by United Nations action. The American delegate did in August of 1963 join in a vote instructing member states to withhold arms from South Africa, but his instructions forbade him from going beyond that point to support expelling South Africa from the UN or taking punitive action against her. Similarly, the United States has refused to abide by a UN resolution to boycott Rhodesian chrome. As for Portugal, the last of the colonial powers on the continent, a motion in the UN in April of 1961 urging that country to reform her policy in her Angola colony received American support but two years later, Washington abstained on a resolution calling on members to refuse to sell arms to Portugal.

The most important American policy for Africa and one which had beneficial consequences was the establishment of the Peace Corps in March of 1961. Sprung from the fertile mind of President Kennedy, it was designed to be the vehicle for people-to-people diplomacy. The members of the Corps, mostly young men and women recently out of college, were assigned to an underdeveloped country to bring their skills directly to ordinary people to help to improve their daily lives. They were teachers, artisans, agricultural specialists, and they went into the village living with the people whom they were aiding on their own level. They worked in South America, Asia, and Africa and they were almost always successful earning the gratitude of the people for their selflessness and kindness.

Actually, Soviet-American rivalry on the "dark continent" did not, as in Europe, mean direct confrontation except in the tangled events in the Congo, the former Belgian colony, from 1960–1965. There the Soviet Union attempted to extend its influence by helping one side in the long and bloody civil war following independence as the United States helped the other. The rivalry was indirect with the Russians beaming propaganda broadcasts to the newly liberated nations and providing military and economic aid with the United States attempting to outdo them. It is worth noting that the Chinese communists entered the field in the 1960s and made significant inroads with economic and technical help.

BIBLIOGRAPHY

John S. Badeau, *The American Approach to the Arab World* (1968).
Rupert Emerson, *Africa and United States Policy* (1967).
Herman Finer, *Dulles over Suez: The Theory and Practice of his Diplomacy* (1964).
J. C. Hurewitz, *Soviet-American Rivalry in the Middle East* (1969).
William R. Polk, *The United States and the Arab World* (1965).
Nadav Safran, *The United States and Israel* (1963).
Benjamin Shwadran, *The Middle East, Oil, and the Great Powers* (1959).
Hugh Thomas, *The Suez Affair* (1966).

Fidel Castro (Wide World Photo).

Latin America

AFFAIRS in Europe and in Asia in the years following the close of the war occupied the attention of the American people and their leaders so completely that other parts of the world suffered neglect. Latin America was one of those places despite the fact that its problems were grievous and its position in the struggle against international communism crucial.

During the war, Washington was very much aware of the neighbors to the south. Their raw materials were essential to the war effort and their ports and harbors were useful as bases for American warships. Mexico, Cuba, and Brazil even took part in the fighting. High prices were paid for their products, and money, both as loans and grants, was poured into their economies. Besides, almost a half billion dollars worth of lend-lease material went south. Close relations were maintained by means of inter-American conferences and committee meetings. Then came the war's end and the problems raised by the Soviet Union's intransigence in Europe and Red China's victory in Asia demanded that the greatest part of America's resources—financial, diplomatic, emotional—be allotted to their solution. The threat lay in those two hemispheres, not in Latin America. Typical of the order and extent of the priorities was the fact that in the fiscal year 1952–1953, out of $6 billion of Mutual Security funds only $75 million went to Latin America. The whole matter was summed up neatly and accurately by a Brazilian diplomat in the words: "In the last twelve years [1946–1958], the Department of State had only two patterns of action: the Marshall Plan dedicated to Europe and the John Foster Dulles Plan dedicated to Asia and the Middle East."

The irony of the matter was that conditions in Latin America after the war were such as to make that region susceptible to communism and potentially dangerous to American security. As the *Buenos Aires Herald* noted, "Social unrest in this part of the world is the crucible out of which the Communists intend to produce new subversive movements even where this unrest is hardly discernible on the surface." The unrest was, as a matter of fact, more obvious than the newspaper made out. Low life expectancy, high rate of infant mortality, poverty, pitiable standard of living for all but the few, maldistribution of property and of the good things of life, illiteracy (as high as 90 per cent in some areas), crowded cities and squalid slums—all of those constituted the hallmark of Latin American life. Then there were the economic ills resulting from the halt in the demand for products as the war ended and the accompanying drastic drop in prices. And almost every country produced only one crop; thus they could find no refuge in diversification. Finally, there were the political evils characterized by the rule of dictators, military juntas, and oligarchs. Democracy was a rarity in Latin America. That an ex-president of Venezuela was present by invitation at the inauguration of his successor was so exceptional an event as to elicit widespread comment.

The Soviet Union was, of course, interested in Latin America and stood prepared to take advantage of any unrest and dissatisfaction. The existence of masses of "have-nots" provided fruitful soil. The principal vehicle for penetration was trade and economic assistance. As put in an official statement from Moscow, "The Soviet Union in its foreign policy is guided by the principle of offering support to the countries seeking national and economic independence from the colonial powers. On that basic principle the Soviet Union is building its economic relations with the countries . . . which are seeking independent development of their own." The political purpose of the trade and aid was never forgotten. Credit, technical assistance, loans for development were lavishly spread around the continent. By the mid 1950s, the Soviet Union and its satellites had made trade agreements with eighteen of the republics, and trade with them had increased significantly in the preceding five years. Cultural exchange was also heavily used by Moscow to bring Russia closer to Latin America. And while the Communist Party was legal in only eight countries, there were communists in every republic. The party membership was small—about 300,000 was estimated for the whole of Latin America—but the infiltration into labor, the press, students, and teachers was deep and wide.

The Truman administration viewed Latin America at the end of the war as an element in the military defenses against the Soviet Union and was not particularly interested in helping the conversion of the economy to a peacetime footing. When President Truman assured the southern republics that the United States would continue to be a "good neighbor," he meant that the doctrine of nonintervention would be respected; he did not mean that a neighborly helping hand containing money would be extended. There was no Latin American counterpart of the Marshall Plan; there *was* a Latin American counterpart of NATO. Indeed, the Latin American version antedated the European treaty by two years and served as a model for the latter. It was in September of 1947 that the

Inter-American Treaty of Reciprocal Assistance was signed by the twenty-one American republics, pledging each state to help resist an attack upon another and to consult in the event of any danger short of an armed attack. The consummation of such a defense treaty was so important that Secretary of State George Marshall himself headed the delegation to the conference at Rio de Janeiro and President Truman himself journeyed to the Brazilian capital to close the meeting. The Senate gave its approval by 72–1 on December 8, 1947. The treaty was the first in the worldwide network of agreements to contain the Soviet Union.

The Truman administration, the next year, took a second logical step in bringing Latin America into the western orbit by taking the lead in institutionalizing the Pan-American movement and by providing a constitution and permanent structure for the inter-American system. At the Ninth Inter-American Conference held in Bogotá from April 30 to May 2, 1948, the Organization of American States came into being. Its supreme organ was the Inter-American Conference, which would meet every five years. It had, also, an executive council sitting in Washington and consisting of one representative of each republic, a cultural council, an economic and social council, and a secretariat which took the place of the Pan-American Union. There was a provision for meetings of foreign ministers in times of crisis. The heart of the charter lay in three articles: renunciation of intervention in the internal affairs of any member state; recognition that an attack upon a member nation is considered an attack upon all; acceptance of procedures for settling disputes peaceably among signatories. The Senate approved the document in August of 1950 and the following December it went into force. It was a landmark event designed to put relations of the twenty-one American republics on a permanent and equal footing. Thus, the year 1948 takes its place alongside other great years in the history of western hemisphere relations. Once again, Secretary of State George C. Marshall headed the United States delegation to underline the significance of the meeting. The issues of the cold war were not neglected at Bogotá. The fight against communism was joined to hemispheric solidarity in a resolution that branded international communism or any other totalitarian doctrine incompatible with freedom.

Bogotá could not be considered an unqualified success. While delegates deliberated, demonstrators outside the building rioted and the object of their outburst was the United States. Some observers saw the communists as the source of the trouble, but it would be more nearly correct to ascribe it to disappointment with the contribution of the powerful northern neighbor to the solution of economic and social problems of the region. It was true, of course, that the Truman Administration, focusing on Europe and Asia, was not paying much attention to Latin America.

President Eisenhower, succeeding to office in January of 1953, seems to have realized that although for the United States the problem of Latin

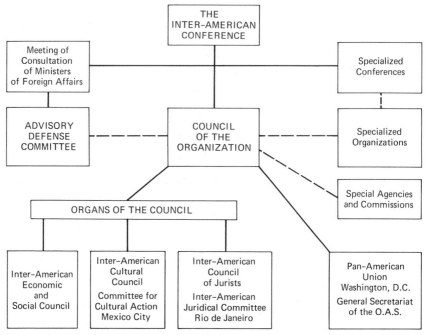

Organization of American States.

America was political, military, and ideological, for Latin Americans, economic and social development lay at the heart of the matter. In June of that same year, he sent his brother, Milton, president of Johns Hopkins University, to South America to determine exactly what needed to be done. Visiting ten republics, the distinguished educator soon discovered that the key to the region's well-being was in diversification, industrialization, stabilization of prices of the principal products, and promotion of exports. In his report, submitted in November, he recommended that loans, both public and private, be granted, and technical assistance be provided to improve the industrial output and aid diversification. He suggested, too, that steps be taken to maintain the price level of exports, which until then were subject to the vagaries of the world market. The president responded with some constructive measures. At a meeting of ministers of economics (or finance) of the twenty-one republics held at Petropolis (Brazil) in November and December of 1954, there was some implementation of Milton's recommendations, chiefly in the area of technical aid and loans. Politely, the Mexican finance minister labelled the meeting "not sterile." More bluntly, the Colombian delegate declared it "did not go far enough" in the matter of stabilizing prices and providing international banking facilities. As a matter of fact, the conference ought to be judged significant and successful in that it faced, for the first time since the war, the problems of development for Latin America. A real achievement of the meeting was that it inventoried the problems and made plans for their detailed study.

Eisenhower's move in the direction of attacking Latin America's social and economic problems was, in part, prompted by the events in Guatemala. There communists had become intrenched in the government of Jacobo Arbenz Guzmán who had become president in March of 1951. With Arbenz's blessing, communists had come to occupy the key posts in the country and took over the direction of a social revolutionary movement. Under their influence, Arbenz turned more and more to the left. He nationalized industries, including the giant United Fruit Company, without compensation, and moved closer to the Soviet Union. He hewed to the Soviet line in the United Nations and accepted the dictation of Moscow for his domestic and foreign policies. Central to the latter was his hostility to "Yankee imperialism" and his efforts to foment trouble in neighboring countries. Agents from the Guatemala Communist Party penetrated El Salvador, Honduras, and Nicaragua with propaganda and plans to subvert the governments there.

The prospect of the success of communism in Central America alarmed Eisenhower and Dulles. The words of the Monroe Doctrine sprang at once to mind—"we should consider any attempt on their part to extend their system to any portion of this hemisphere as dangerous to our peace and safety." That something would have to be done to dislodge Soviet influence was unquestioned. The most expeditious course would have been to dispatch a battalion of marines to the troubled area, but in 1954 that was not a viable course. Eisenhower was not free to do what the first Roosevelt or Wilson had done. The pledge not to intervene was not yet two decades old. So, the president laid the matter before the other American republics who were to convene in Caracas for the Tenth Inter-American Conference on March 1, 1954.

Dulles sought strong actions against Guatemala, but he could arouse little enthusiasm among his fellow delegates. The menace he saw did not seem so frightful to them and they rather sympathized with the revolution there, believing it ought to be permitted to run its course. The American secretary of state had to content himself with a milder resolution than the one he wanted, which condemned the domination of the political institutions of an American state by the international communist movement. The vote was 17–1 with Guatemala opposing and Mexico and Argentina abstaining. Many of the delegates who voted for the resolution maintained they had been pressured by the big northern republic and they were resentful. That resentment was nothing compared to their feelings three months later aroused by the collusion of the United States in the overthrow of President Arbenz. Washington, alarmed by the report that arms and ammunition from Czechoslovakia were en route to Guatemala, sent military equipment to Nicaragua and Honduras to shore up the defense of those countries against their communist neighbor. That equipment got to Carlos Castillo Armas, an exiled Guatemalan colonel, then in Honduras preparing to move with a small force against Arbenz. On June 18, he crossed the border, succeeded in toppling the government, and became president.

It was no secret that American arms had equipped the rebels. There were even reports that American diplomats and Central Intelligence Agency agents had fomented the revolution. Further, when Guatemala took its case to the UN and the OAS, the United States did everything possible to make things difficult. No wonder there was an outbreak of anti-United States feeling all over Latin America. The northern colossus had intervened once again in the affairs of a sister republic, however indirectly, and so soon after pledging to quit that nefarious practice. A revival of big-stick diplomacy was not a pleasant thing.

Memories are long and when Vice-President Richard Nixon journeyed to South America on a good will visit in April of 1958, one of the reasons for the hostile reception by people in Lima and Caracas was the recollection of the Guatemala affair. There were other causes for the mob assailing him—resentment of American neglect, Eisenhower's granting of the Legion of Merit award to two dictators (of Peru and Venezuela), restrictive American trade policies, and communist incitement—but the intervention was high on the list.

The shock of the second-highest official in the land being the target of eggs, spit, verbal abuse (including "Death to Nixon"), and attempts to break the glass of his automobile was very great and not without effect on the president. He knew that something more had to be done to assuage the deep hostility that gave rise to such extravagant conduct. Once again, in July, he sent his brother south, this time to Central America, to investigate conditions and to suggest remedies. Once again, Milton recommended bold economic measures to cure the region's basic ills and the president acted to "battle against the festering sore of underdevelopment." The task of formulating a program for social and economic reform was entrusted to a Committee of Twenty-One (one for each of the republics) under the aegis of the OAS.

Meanwhile, the president had let it be known that the United States would underwrite an inter-American lending institution and one was quickly created. A charter was drawn up and signed in April of 1959. In December, the new Inter-American Development Bank came into existence. It was capitalized at $1 billion, of which the United States subscribed $450 million. At once, loans began flowing to the republics for all sorts of projects. But Eisenhower's aim was greater than the establishment of a bank. As he stated on July 11, 1960, not long after returning from a tour of Argentina, Brazil, Chile, and Uruguay, he wanted his country to join with the other nations of the hemisphere to get basic social and economic reforms under way. In the same month, he secured from Congress an appropriation of $500 million as capital for a new inter-American development fund and sent the under-secretary of state, C. Douglas Dillon, to Bogotá in September of 1960 to lay before the Committee of Twenty-One his ideas for reform and development. Out of that meeting came the Act of Bogotá which was an agreement among the republics to take measures to improve social and economic conditions —to make reforms in taxation and land tenure, to erect schools and houses, to improve education, and the like. Financial support would come from the United States, but Washington made clear that help would be given only if real and true reforms were undertaken. Ruling elites would no longer be able to squander American money on pet projects designed to improve their lives while leaving untouched the welfare of the masses. Aid with strings attached was a new concept but a good one.

The speed with which the president acted was intimately connected to events in Cuba. There, on January 1, 1959, Fidel Castro, a thirty-two-year-old lawyer of middle-class origin, overthrew the government of Fulgencio Batista after long years of guerrilla warfare. In the revolution the United States took no part but it was, nonetheless, not displeased by Castro's victory. Batista's regime had been corrupt and authoritarian; it was prosperous but the riches were confined to the few. Castro, on the other hand, had given promise of instituting democratic and social reforms. Eisenhower extended recognition to the new government within one week of its establishment, but he was not prepared for the new leader's sharp turn to socialism and totalitarianism and his embracing of Moscow.

Americans received their first shock when Castro indulged in wholesale execution of Batista supporters. Next came the betrayal of his pledge to hold free elections, the gagging of the press, the dissolution of trade unions, the prohibition of assembly, the throttling of academic freedom, and the abolition of political parties save his own. He also expropriated all foreign-owned property, including American valued at $1 billion, without compensation. Meanwhile, he was drawing closer to the Soviet Union and linking Cuba's economic life inextricably with Russia's. In February of 1960, Soviet Deputy Premier Anastas Mikoyan arrived in Havana to negotiate a trade agreement exchanging 5 million tons of sugar over a five-year period for oil, military equipment, and technical help. Five months later, in another trade pact, Russia agreed to buy a half million tons of sugar annually to be paid for by products mostly from Red China. Castro had, in fact, pledged, virtually, the entire sugar crop to the Soviets. He became further enmeshed with the Soviets as a result of accepting a $100 million credit at 2.5 per cent interest. By 1961, 75 per cent of Cuba's foreign trade was with Russia.

The Cuban-Soviet romance was not only economic. Russia was the "big brother" militarily and ideologically as well. Castro surrounded himself with communists like Aníbal Escalante, secretary general of the national party; Antonio Nuñez, head of the National Agrarian Reform Institute; his own brother, Raul Castro; and Ernesto Guevara. He applauded every act of the Soviet Union and even once publicly and ostentatiously hugged Khrushchev at the UN. The Soviet Premier rewarded such loyalty with the announcement that Russia would protect Cuba against any invasion by the United States. And all the while, a steady supply of Soviet tanks, guns, jets, and military advisors was reaching Havana.

Castro was not content to socialize only his own country. He wanted to export the revolution. On July 26, 1960, the fourth anniversary of the beginning of his war against Batista, he proclaimed his promise "to continue making the nation the example that can convert the Cordillera of the Andes into the Sierra Maestra [his mountain headquarters in early revolutionary days] of the hemisphere." Cuba soon became, indeed, the training ground for aspiring saboteurs, propagandists, and subversives from all over Latin America. Whether Castro really intended to include the United States in his revolutionary net is difficult to determine. He did, however, spread propaganda leaflets among American blacks in the Harlem section of New York City, where he stayed while attending a UN session in 1960, and in the south.

The dilemma confronting President Eisenhower was acute: how to deal with a Soviet satellite 90 miles from American shores without violating the doctrine of nonintervention. He found the formula in an appeal to the principle of collective action under the Rio Pact of 1947 and in levelling economic pressures against Cuba. The president struck at Cuba's vulnerable point—sugar, her chief export crop. In July of 1960, he cancelled 95 per cent of American imports of sugar remaining for the year. Next, he cut off all sugar from Cuba for 1961. Finally, he embargoed all American exports to Cuba save for food and medical supplies. But those measures proved fruitless. They only drove Castro deeper into the Soviet orbit. Nor did the appeal to the other republics produce the desired result. At Washington's call, the foreign ministers of all the republics met for consultation under the terms of the Rio Pact in Santiago (Chile) in August of 1959 and in San Jose (Costa Rica) in August of 1960. But there was a marked reluctance to act against Cuba. Eisenhower's sense of danger and urgency was not shared by the others. They wanted to let the Cuban revolution follow its own course and were, in any event, opposed to intervening in the domestic affairs of a sister republic. The most the president could get were resolutions condemning totalitarianism and interference in the Americas by an extracontinental power plus an affirmation of confidence in democracy. No mention was made of Cuba.

Little wonder that Eisenhower, frustrated in his efforts, succumbed to the urgings of Cuban exiles in the United States, strongly supported by the Central Intelligence Agency, that the United States provide them the materiel and equipment for an invasion of the homeland. It was an unwise decision and not consistent with the caution and moderation that had characterized Eisenhower's foreign policy. He left office before the assault was mounted, but in the last few months of his administration rebel groups began to train under CIA auspices and with American equipment in several places—Florida, Texas, Louisiana, Panama, Guatemala, Nicaragua—in preparation for the great adventure. Before quitting the White House, Eisenhower made one last move against Cuba. He severed diplomatic relations with her. That act hardly phased Castro who felt secure nestling under the wing of the Soviet Union and who could brazenly defy that man he called "the senile White House golfer."

The new president, John F. Kennedy, no less disturbed by the Cuban situation and no more disposed to intervene unilaterally, did not reverse his predecessor's decision to aid the rebels. They continued their training and the United States continued the support. Finally, on April 17, 1961, all was ready and the invasion was launched in the Bay of Pigs on the southern coast of the island. It was a disaster. Castro met the 1,500 rebels with a superior force and cut them to pieces. Twelve hundred of them were taken prisoner and were held in Cuban jails until ransomed some eighteen months later by the United States for about $50 million worth of food and medicines.

The failure of the expedition may be ascribed to several factors—Castro agents in the rebel ranks who sent word to Havana of invasion plans, thus destroying the element of surprise; miscalculation by the CIA, which had predicted an uprising of dissidents coming to the rebel aid; the bad choice of landing place; and Castro's success in rounding up rebel sympathizers. The invaders, themselves, blamed the United States for the defeat in not having rushed men and aircraft to insure the landing's success. The pressure on Kennedy to commit American troops had been very great but he had pledged before the assault that the United States would not intervene. He might as well have intervened because most Latin Americans viewed the whole affair as a purely American matter. They knew that without American arms, equipment, money, training facilities, and ships, there would have been no attack. "Invasion by proxy" was invasion none the less. The CIA, which was widely believed to have fomented and engineered the whole business, was commonly referred to as the "Cuban Invasion Authority."

The United States emerged from the fiasco tarnished and discredited. Castro, on the other hand, found his position immeasurably strengthened and his prestige enhanced by his successful repelling of an invasion from the Colossus of the North. He was more defiant than ever. On May 1, at a great May Day celebration, he proudly announced that "Cuba is a socialist state" and later in the year, he boasted, "I am a Marxist-Leninist and will be one until the day I die." He was, of course, confident of Soviet support. Khrushchev had only just issued a warning that any attack by the United States on Cuba would find Russia at her ally's side.

Kennedy's refusal to aid the rebels did not mean that he intended to abandon Cuba to communism. He had said as much in a speech on April 20, 1961. "Our restraint is not inexhaustible" he had said and went on to warn that "This government will not hesitate in meeting its primary obligations, which are the security of our nation" if the nations of the hemisphere do nothing against outside communist penetration. As a matter of fact, he could not muster a great deal of support among the nations of the hemisphere for an anti-Cuban policy. A call for a consultative meeting of foreign ministers was opposed by Argentina, Brazil, Bolivia, Chile, Ecuador, and Mexico. Nonetheless, a conference did convene at Punta del Este in Uruguay on January 22, 1962, but it was with difficulty that Secretary of State Dean Rusk gained the votes for strong action against Cuba. All twenty republics agreed that the principles of communism were incompatible with the inter-American system and identified the Castro regime as a Soviet ally. When it came, however, to levying sanctions, a number of the nations were reluctant to act. On a resolution suspending trade with Cuba in arms and military equipment, the vote was 16–1 with four abstentions (Mexico, Brazil, Chile, Ecuador) and on the more significant proposal to exclude Cuba from the OAS, only a bare two-thirds majority could be mustered. A declaration that Cuba was a threat to the peace and safety of the hemisphere was not even attempted by the United States. The fact was that for most Latin Americans the rights of revolution and self-determination were crucially important, and they refused to impede or censure Cuba's efforts to realize her destiny.

The timing of the Cuban invasion was unfortunate for the Kennedy administration because it came precisely at the time the president was embarking on a bold new program for Latin America that he called the Alliance for Progress. It was built on the Act of Bogotá of 1960 but went beyond it. First announced in his inaugural address, it was elaborated in a talk to the Latin American members of the diplomatic corps on May 13, 1961 and to Congress the following day. Its objective was "to bring a better life to all the peoples of the continent" by achieving social justice and economic development in a framework of democracy. Kennedy envisioned the alliance as a vehicle for fundamental change, for the transformation of the economy and of society, and for the eradication of disease, hunger, and illiteracy. Houses and hospitals and schools would be built, production would be increased, new industries created, and farms modernized. All the people, not just the privileged few, would share in the benefits of the growth and prosperity of the nation. Each of the countries would be responsible for effecting reforms—levelling land ownership by redistribution and income by taxation—and for using an increasing share of its income for development. The United States, in turn, pledged $1 billion a year for at least twenty years. It was expected that eventually $100 billion would be needed, of which $80 billion would be generated in Latin America.

At Punta del Este on August 17, 1961, representatives of the twenty-one republics (Cuba included) met to draw up a formal charter for the Alliance. A Declaration of the Peoples of America, accompanying the charter spelled out the Alliance's purpose: ". . . to enlist the full energies of the peoples and governments of the American republics in a great co-operative effort to accelerate the economic and social development of the participating countries of Latin America, so that they may achieve the maximum levels of well-being, with equal opportunities for all, in democratic societies adapted to their own needs and desires." The Alliance was in part, a response to the Cuban revolution but, said the *New York Times*, it was more than that. "It is an attempt to answer one of the most momentous and menacing problems of our times, which is how the economically underdeveloped areas of the world can meet the insistent popular demand for social justice and economic development [in the framework of democracy]."

Much was expected of the Alliance but the achievement did not measure up to the promise. In the first twenty-seven months, the United States had provided $2.5 billion in loans and grants to the Alliance, but the accomplishment was cruely disappointing. All sorts of reasons have been advanced for the dismal performance of which two seem most significant. One was in the unwillingness of the moneyed and propertied class to surrender their preferred status and to subscribe to a social and economic revolution that would, in large measure, dispossess them. Second was the frequency of revolution and the general instability of the political climate. Between 1961 and 1963, six elected governments were overthrown by military juntas. The upheavals attendant upon violent political change and the rule of dictators were hardly conducive to reform and to the increase of people's well-being. Whether greater success would have been realized eventually had President Kennedy lived to complete his term and have another, no one can tell. It is true that, despite the Bay of Pigs, his stock in Latin America was high. His election had been received by the southern neighbors much as Franklin D. Roosevelt's had been twenty years earlier. Great things were expected of Kennedy as they had been of Roosevelt, especially when he said, shortly after gaining office, "I regard Latin America as the most critical area in the world today." There was confidence in his ability and in his intentions, and it is just possible that he would have made of the Alliance something more than it was at his death in November of 1963.

Before he fell to the assassin's bullets that sad day in Dallas, he had yet to face another hemispheric crisis—the greatest up to that time. It began in the late summer of 1962 with a great increase in Soviet shipments to Cuba of arms and military equipment. Further, aerial reconaissance showed missiles sites under construction on the island. Americans were, quite naturally, nervous and President Kennedy hastened to reassure them, at a press conference on September 4, that there was no evidence of Soviet combat troops or offensive missiles in Cuba. On the 13th, two days after receiving from Khrushchev assurance that Soviet equipment in Cuba was purely defensive, the president again calmed the people. Still, there was sufficient alarm for Congress to pass a resolution, on October 3, 384–7 in the House and 86–1 in the Senate, announcing American determination to take all measures to block the expansion of Cuba in the hemisphere.

Meanwhile, a Soviet military build-up in Cuba was unquestionably continuing. On October 14, aerial photos got clear shots of offensive missile sites near Cristobál in western Cuba. They were emplacements for both medium-range (1,100 miles) and intermediate-range (2,200 miles) missiles, capable of striking targets from Hudson's Bay to La Paz, thus posing a danger to American security of incalculable and unprecedented proportion. There was evidence, too, of the existence of forty-two missiles and of forty-two Soviet IL-28 (light) bombers. Never in its history had the United States been so menaced. For the president, the time to act had come. Despite further assurances from Soviet Foreign Minister Andrei Gromyko and Soviet Ambassador Anatol Dobrynin on October 18 that the military equipment was defensive only, Kennedy went before the American people on October 22 to announce his decision to face the Soviets. Pressure to destroy the sites by bomber aircraft or by invasion had been exerted on the president for some time, but he had rejected those solutions for fear they would lead to a Soviet–American war, and a nuclear one at that. His method of coping with the problem, he told the people on a national radio and television network, was to blockade Cuba to prevent the further importation of offensive weapons into that country. At the same time, he called upon the Soviet premier to halt his reckless course and warned that the United States would "regard any nuclear missile launched from Cuba against any nation in the western hemisphere as an attack by the Soviet Union on the United States requiring a full retaliatory response upon the Soviet Union."

Now, the world waited. Several Soviet vessels were at the moment en route to Cuba. Would they force their way through the naval blockade Kennedy had erected? And if they tried, what would the American response be? Not since the Soviet blockade of Berlin in 1948 had the world stood so precariously on the brink of war. Whatever would happen, Kennedy had the virtually unanimous support of the other American republics.

To them the threat was very real. The proximity of Soviet missiles made even leftists quake. The president of Brazil reflected continental sentiment when he said, "The Soviet Union had taken advantage of the struggles of the Cuban people for its own ends, to aid it in the cold war." On October 23, the Council of the OAS approved (19–1, Uruguay abstained, not having received instructions) a resolution calling for the immediate withdrawal and dismantling of the missiles and removal of the jet bombers. The member states were further enjoined to take measures to prevent the introduction into Cuba of additional offensive weapons. The American blockade received full support.

Happily, the crisis abated. The Soviet premier backed down. Two Soviet surface ships and one submarine turned back when challenged by American naval vessels. That took place on October 24. Two days later, Khrushchev, in a conciliatory message to Kennedy, offered to dismantle the missile sites and withdraw the weapons for an American pledge to lift the blockade and renounce any plan for invading Cuba. The next day, he added another condition—removal of American missiles from Turkey. Kennedy replied on the same day, accepting the Soviet offer except for the Turkish proviso. On October 28, Khrushchev announced "the discontinuance of further work on weapons construction sights [and the dismantling of] the arms considered offensive." The world could now breathe more easily, but it had gone through a week's experience which no one would care to relive. True to his word, Khrushchev removed the missiles and bombers and dismantled the sites. Still, Soviet troops remained and the build-up of an arsenal of defensive weapons continued. Cuba was no less solidly in the Soviet camp. Communism in the hemisphere was a fact of life.

There was not much President Kennedy could do about Cuba. Some groups in the United States would have been pleased to support an invasion to destroy Castro, but Kennedy had had his fill of brinksmanship and of the prospect of a Soviet military confrontation. He put his hope in the economic weapon. He would bring Cuba to her knees by cutting off her trade with the rest of the hemisphere and by isolating her in other ways. At several meetings in 1963 of OAS foreign ministers and one of presidents, measures were adopted banning travel and halting the flow of money to and from Cuba (both designed to stop Castro's propaganda and subversive activities) and limiting trade to food and medicines. Such steps, however, were not very effective in view of the fact that Russia and her satellites satisfied most of Cuba's economic needs and that some of the American republics, sympathizing with Cuba's revolution, ignored the prohibitions.

Lyndon B. Johnson, who came to the White House on November 22, 1963, followed his predecessor's policy toward Cuba and the rest of Latin America, as well. He continued the embargo on trade, maintained the aerial surveillance of military installations and weapons, sought to get the other republics to observe the trade strictures, and eschewed military interven-tion. Five days after assuming office, he pledged the "best efforts of this nation toward fulfillment of the Alliance for Progress" and later, on May 11, 1964, in an address to Latin American ambassadors in Washington, announced his dedication to "a peaceful, democratic, social revolution across the hemisphere."

Those words were welcome to many Latin Americans for they had feared that the new president would not pay much attention to their region. Said one Latin American diplomat on May 11, "With today's speech, the United States has returned to the political leadership that Kennedy had initiated." There was relief, too, at Johnson's emphasis on democracy and social reform, for he had recently extended recognition to two dictators who had come to power at the head of military juntas after turning out constitutionally elected governments. The president had, in fact, pushed the Alliance. In January of 1964, he had established an Inter-American Committee for the Alliance for Progress charged with determining each country's needs and in the first six months of his ad-ministration had provided close to $0.5 billion for projects. In the years that followed, he continued his support for the Alliance although his preoccupation with Vietnam prevented paying much attention, in general, to Latin America.

He did make a special effort to resolve one of the thorniest problems of the hemisphere—control and operation of the Panama Canal. Agita-tion by Panama for a revision of the treaty of 1903 was insistent, and President Johnson, appreciating the anomaly of holding an enclave within the borders of a sovereign nation, showed a willingness to negotiate. Over the years, the United States had voluntarily surrendered some of its treaty rights. In 1936, the guarantee of Panamanian independence and the right to intervene were given up. In 1955 control over sanitary conditions was turned over to Panama and the annual subvention was increased. None of those concessions satisfied Panama. It wanted nothing less than complete withdrawal by the United States from the Canal Zone and the turning over of the Canal to Panama. In 1959, riot-ters attacked the American embassy. To assuage the national feeling, President Eisenhower in 1961 had ordered that Panamanian and Ameri-can flags be flown together in a park in the Zone. Hardly satisfied, Pana-manians moved again, this time because some American students, upon returning in early January from Christmas vacation and finding a Panamanian flag flying atop their high school, tore it down. A bloody fight ensued whereupon American soldiers were sent in to stop the fighting. In the process, twenty-one Panamanians and three Americans were killed, and damage to property reached $2 million.

The seriousness of the situation led Johnson to consent to a review of all outstanding issues between the two powers. At the same time, he established a committee made up of the United States Ambassador to Panama, the governor of the Canal Zone, and the commander of American forces to meet regularly with Panamanian representatives for a discussion of pressing problems. Meanwhile, talks on treaty revision continued, but the disagreement on basic matters prevented any real progress. The United States was willing to relinquish sovereignty over the zone to Panama but wanted to retain control of the canal and maintain forces there to defend the waterway. Panama wanted the United States out completely and totally.

Whatever good Johnson hoped to accomplish in hemispheric matters was viewed by Latin America through the prism of American action in the Dominican Republic in 1965. That action turned the clock back to the "good old days" of Theodore Roosevelt and Woodrow Wilson and dragged the "good neighbor" concept in the dust. It was a bold and shameless intervention in the affairs of the republic. A series of revolutions touched off by the overthrow of the long-time dictator Rafael Trujillo in 1961 culminated, in April 1965, in a struggle between conservative elements and a leftist group that contained communists and whose leader had the makings of a Castro. Ostensibly to protect American lives and property but clearly to prevent a second Cuba, the president, on April 28, sent in some 25,000 marines, soldiers, and sailors. The outraged reaction by Latin Americans was immediate and so great that Johnson quickly searched for a face-saving device, which was to get OAS to take over the duty of policing the country. By a vote of 14–5, the Organization approved creation of an international American force that moved into the republic on May 28, permitting United States troops to leave.

Johnson's action violated every hemispheric agreement on intervention since Montevideo in 1933 and most particularly Article 15 of the Bogotá treaty of 1948, the Charter of the Americas. The president's credibility, and the nation's, too, sank justifiably to the lowest point since 1920. The case was best stated in a letter to the editor of the *New York Times*, dated May 17, 1965, from the noted Mexican novelist Carlos Fuentes. After comparing Khrushchev in Hungary in 1956 with Johnson in the Dominican Republic in 1965 and labelling both "unequivocally brutal and unlawful," he continued, "the consequences of Mr. Johnson's shortsighted action will be disastrous: We have reverted to the law of the jungle in Inter-American relations and, left without orderly legal process, these relations are wrecked on a stormy sea of self-interest, hubris, fear, suspicion, improvisation, and violence. Today only the most antisocial military regimes can feel secure under the protection of the Johnson Doctrine. All civilian governments can only suspect that any further national problem will be promptly labelled subversive to United States interests and resolved at bayonet point by United States marines. In the name of responsibility President Johnson has torn to shreds not only what was left of the inter-American system but also the patient, long-sighted work of Franklin Roosevelt and John Kennedy . . . no one must feel surprised if in the future Latin America . . . appeals to the only protection left: that of revolution."

In April of 1966, the Argentina president suggested a meeting of the presidents of all the republics to restore the confidence destroyed by the intervention. Such a meeting did come about in April of the next year and some gains were made (chiefly, an agreement to create a Latin American common market in fifteen years), but it would be untrue to conclude that one of the gains was a restoration of complete confidence. By the time Johnson left office in January of 1969, Latin America's problems were still grievous (economic distress, many military dictatorships, not much social justice or economic development) and the northern neighbor was still eyed with suspicion and hostility.

A NOTE ON CANADA

Canada was not a party to the inter-American structure. No representatives from that country attended the conferences and meetings of the republics of the hemisphere or joined the consultative sessions of foreign ministers during the various postwar crises. It was the fervent wish of the other nations that Canada would become one of them and it is said that a chair, the 22nd, is kept in the basement of the Pan-American Union for the most northern hemispheric country.

Canada's aloofness from the inter-American system is rooted in many factors. One is her orientation westward toward Europe (witness her role in NATO) and her membership in the worldwide British Commonwealth of Nations. Another lies in her fear that the OAS would turn out to be a colonial office of the United States and a cloak for American hegemony. Further, Canada did not wish to be in a position to oppose the United States in the conferences and meetings nor, on the other hand, to be a dutiful supporter of American policy.

With the United States, however, relations were intense and extensive in the postwar period. The close connection dated back to the coordination of the defense efforts of the two countries in the years immediately preceding the war. In 1938, President Roosevelt, in Kingston, Ontario, had given his "assurance that the people of the United States will not stand idly by if domination of Canadian soil is threatened by any other empire." Two years later, there were created a Permanent Joint Defense Board, a Joint Economic Committee, and a Joint War Production committee to intermesh the industrial and military capabilities of the two powers. After the war, those joint efforts were maintained and enlarged upon as both countries stood together to face the Soviet menace as they had the Axis danger. The Joint Defense Board continued to exist and there was begun an exchange of military personnel and equipment. Maneuvers in which units of both countries coordinated their operations became a regular feature of their military training. In 1957, the North American Air Defense Command (NORAD) was created with headquarters at Colorado Springs under the command of an American general and a Canadian deputy. It consisted of aircraft from both countries and was charged with the mission of fighting off a Soviet aerial attack on the continent. The same year saw the completion of an elaborate three-tier system of radar stations stretching across Canada from ocean to ocean to detect enemy aircraft—one, Pinetree, was situated a bit north of the Canadian–American border; a second, Mid-Canada, straddled the 55th parallel; a third, Distant Early Warning, was located in the Arctic circle. In 1958, there was established a Canada–United States Committee of Joint Defense made up of the secretaries of defense, finance, and foreign affairs to oversee the common defense effort. One year later, the great St. Lawrence seaway project was completed. It had been talked about for years but always American opposition, from railroad interests mainly, had held up congressional approval. Finally, in 1954, President Eisenhower succeeded in getting a bill through Congress authorizing construction of the waterway and its joint control with Canada. It was a magnificent achievement enabling sea-going vessels to reach ports of both countries on the St. Lawrence River and the Great Lakes. In 1959, too, an agreement was reached to equip Canadian aircraft and missiles with American nuclear warheads. The plan foundered, however, on the insistence by the United States that it control the atomic weapons as required by law.

That difficulty reflected a wider problem—Canada's feeling of inferiority and dependence in the relationship. The sentiment had some historic roots in the voluble clamor by American political leaders for a century, beginning in the time of the American revolution, to annex Canada to the Union and in two military invasions—1775 and 1812. But the chief source of the attitude was in more recent times and was more of a cultural and economic than political and military problem. The fact was that the Canadian economy was very largely controlled by Americans. United States citizens, with an investment of about $13 billion, own 51 per cent of Canada's industry—46 per cent of pulp; 74 per cent of gas and oil; 88 per cent of rubber; 96 per cent of motor vehicles. One result was a kind of industrial extraterritoriality enjoyed by the American firms of their Canadian subsidiaries that seriously impaired Canadian independence. Thus, for example, Ford of Canada refused to sell trucks to Red China because of the American embargo on trade with Mao's government although Canada had placed no such restrictions on its citizens. Similarly, when the United States government instituted antitrust suits against General Electric and Westinghouse, their Canadian affiliates were included.

Canadians were rankled, too, that Canadian subsidiaries were frequently discouraged from exporting to third countries so that the home office could capitalize on the trade. In the same way, the research and development functions are performed in the United States, which weakens Canadian technology. And because the greatest part of Canada's raw materials goes south to supply the American industrial machine, the profit from processing and fabricating is kept in the United States. The Canadians then turn around and buy their manufactured goods from the United States, which puts the Canadian economy in a colonial status reminiscent of the position of the American colonies in the mercantilist British empire in the eighteenth century. One Canadian summed up the relationship by designating his country as the "hewer of wood and drawer of water" for the United States. The Canadian balance of trade with the United States runs at an annual deficit of about $1 billion.

Not only the material products used by Canadians are made in America, Canadian culture is imported as well. American books, magazines, films, radio, television, art, and music swamp Canada, and the invasion by academicians from across the border has loaded major Canadian universities with an excessive number of American professors. Canada's postwar growth and importance in world affairs have made incongruous its relationship to the United States and has aroused Canadian resentment. A national election in 1958 had, as the principal issue, Canadian–American relations. Conservatives led by John Diefenbaker accused the Liberals in power of surrendering the country's independence to the United States. They campaigned on the platform of a new and greater Canada economically, culturally, and politically independent of the southern neighbor and were elected. Five years later, Liberals regained power in an election dominated again by the American issue. Indeed, no campaign can avoid the problem, for it touches almost every aspect of Canadian life. Nor can it be expected to disappear so long as the two nations are locked in so symbiotic a relationship, which is, at the same time, an unequal one.

BIBLIOGRAPHY

ELIE ABEL, The Missile Crisis (1966).

ROBERT J. ALEXANDER, Communism in Latin America (1957).

THEODORE DRAPER, Castro's Revolution: Myth and Realities (1962).

JOHN C. DREIER, The Organization of American States and the Hemisphere Crisis (1962).

DAVID GREEN, The Containment of Latin America (1971).

JEROME LEVINSON AND JUAN DE ONÍS, The Alliance That Lost Its Way (1970).

EDWIN LIEUWEN, *United States Policy in Latin America: A Short History* (1965).

RAMON E. RUIZ, *Cuba: The Making of a Revolution* (1968).

ROBERT F. SMITH, *The United States and Cuba: Business and Diplomacy, 1917–1960* (1960).

John F. Kennedy (*courtesy of the National Portrait Gallery, the Smithsonian Institution, Washington, D.C.*).

The 1960s—Europe and Asia

THE 1960s, governed for eight of the ten years by the Democrats, did not differ from the preceding decade and a half as far as American foreign policy was concerned. Containment continued to be the guiding principle, and both John F. Kennedy and his successor in November of 1963, Lyndon B. Johnson, followed closely in the footsteps of their two postwar predecessors, Democrat Harry S Truman and Republican Dwight D. Eisenhower. That the American people approved such a foreign policy was evident in the fact that each of the two candidates for election in 1960, Kennedy and Richard M. Nixon, in their speeches, press conferences, policy statements, as well as in their four nationally televised debates, strove to convince the electorate that he was better suited than his opponent to stand up to the two hostile powers, Russia and China, to deal with the menace to the hemisphere of Castro, and to keep America's defenses strong. Kennedy won but by the slenderest margin of 120,000 votes. The electorate had not been given real alternatives, and it seems to have been Kennedy's charm, wit, and grace, his lofty rhetoric and his youth and vigor that tipped the scales in his favor.

His inaugural address made clear his position. "Let every nation know," he said, "whether it wishes us well or ill, that we shall pay any price, bear any burden, meet any hardship, support any friend, oppose any foe to assure the survival and the success of liberty. I do not shrink from that responsibility—I welcome it." It was a defiant message and neither the "friends" nor the "foes" had any reason to be uncertain of where the new forty-three-year-old chief executive stood. One of those "foes," Nikita Khrushchev, had the opportunity very quickly to test the president's mettle. In June of that year, he met Kennedy in Vienna in a sort of informal summit. There the two leaders traded verbal blows on all the usual issues separating the two powers: Germany, Berlin, disarmament, security, nuclear testing. Neither budged, neither yielded, neither would compromise. The Soviet premier then put Kennedy to the supreme test by pulling his Berlin ploy. He informed the president that if the western allies did not complete a peace treaty with the German Democratic Republic and quit Berlin in six months, he would make a separate peace and end the occupation of the city. Kennedy did not even flinch. His reply was prompt and firm. "We cannot and will not permit the communists to drive us out of Berlin," he informed the American people and the world in a speech on July 25, "either gradually or by force . . . we do not want to fight, but we have fought before." Nor could his words be taken as a bluff. Eight days earlier, he had called up 250,000 reservists and had asked Congress for a $3.25 billion increase in the defense budget to strengthen the armed forces by 25 per cent. At the same time, he dispatched an additional 45,000 men to Europe to beef up the NATO forces. Khrushchev did not seem willing to test Kennedy's resolve any further and contented himself with a dramatic move to seal physically and structurally East Berlin from West Berlin by erecting a wall of brick and mortar on the borderline between the two parts of the city. Eventually, he was to extend the wall along the boundary between East and West Germany and a curtain of concrete was added to the one of "iron."

Meanwhile, President Kennedy was keeping pace with Soviet advances in space science and in missile technology. On April 12, 1961, in one of history's greatest and most awesome moments, the Russians put a man into space. Flight Major Yuri A. Gagarin circled the earth in outer space in 108 minutes. One month later, the United States sent its first astronaut aloft when Navy Commander Alan B. Shepard was hurled 115 miles into space in fifteen minutes. The space race was on. In August, a Soviet astronaut orbited the earth seventeen times in 25.3 hours and in the following February, an American followed suit, circling the earth 3 times in 4.9 hours. After the first Soviet success, Khrushchev had challenged "the capitalist countries [to] try to catch up with our country." Kennedy made certain that one of them did.

There was a race, also, between the two superpowers in nuclear weaponry. On September 1, 1961, the Soviets began a series of tests that was to go on for several months and was to detonate bombs 3,000 times more powerful than the ones used by the United States over Japan. Kennedy, deploring the violation of a moratorium on testing that both nations had agreed upon, resumed American testing. Thus unchecked, both nations indulged in a chilling contest for supremacy in the most deadly of weapons for the next two years. Luckily, events conspired to bring about some understanding to check the reckless course. A serious Soviet–Chinese rift developed in the summer of 1963 that altered significantly the Soviet outlook on international affairs. Hitherto secure on the Asiatic front, Soviet diplomats and leaders could concentrate their attention on Europe. But, as relations with the Chinese deteriorated and the ideological difference widened, they sought an amelioration of the tension with the capitalist nations. A bad year for Russia economically plus the thaw following the Soviet-American missile crisis in Cuba in the fall of 1962 led to a softening of the Russian position on nuclear testing. In April and again in June of 1962, Kennedy had appealed to Khrushchev to consent to limiting or banning nuclear testing, and in July the Soviet leader indicated his willingness to negotiate. Out of the ensuing conversations there came a treaty signed by the two nations and by Great Britain on August 5, 1963 that banned nuclear explosions in the atmosphere, in outer space, and under water. Nothing was said about underground testing. Eventually, most of the nations of the world adhered to the treaty except Red China, Cuba, and France.

France presented a very special problem to President Kennedy and her president, Charles de Gaulle, was as difficult to deal with as was Nikita Khrushchev. His policies and his ambitions tended to weaken the western alliance and to frustrate much of what the United States was trying to accomplish in regard to Europe. He had very little use for NATO. Before coming to power, he had said, "I would quit NATO if I were in power; it is against our independence . . . it is no longer an alliance; it is a subordination." He had meant, of course, that it was dominated by the United States and that France and the other members had to accept Washington's leadership. To him, such a state of affairs was anathema. He was a passionate and near-psychotic patriot who dreamed of restoring France to the glory and grandeur of the days of Louis XIV and Napoleon with himself the instrument. He wanted France to replace the United States as Europe's chief power. Further, he did not believe the United States would reply to a Russian attack on Europe with nuclear weapons for fear of inviting retaliation on American cities. Hence, he went about building a nuclear capability, a *force de frappe*, in France. "France must rely on herself," he had said as early as October of 1949. The Suez crisis of 1956 had taught him that France must be militarily independent of the United States.

As for the European Economic Community and European integration, in general, he opposed the concept, shared by the other five member states, of a politically and economically unified Europe speaking with one voice in foreign and defense policies. His idea was not integration but confederation—a federated Europe consisting of sovereign states, each retaining its independence of action but working together. And at the head of such a "Europe of fatherlands" would stand France, first among equals.

He came to power in May of 1958 and lost no time putting his ideas into practice. In February of 1960, France exploded her first atom bomb and de Gaulle then proceeded to build his own nuclear strike force. Then on January 14, 1963, he vetoed Britain's application to enter the Common

Market. His reason was that "England is insular, she is maritime . . . she has in all her doings very marked and very original habits and traditions . . . the very nature and structure of Great Britain differ profoundly from those of the continental countries." But those words fooled no one; the reasoning was spurious. What lay really at the root of his position was England's refusal to join France in creating a missile defense that would free Europe from dependence upon Washington. What infuriated him was Prime Minister Harold Macmillian's acceptance of American Polaris missiles for England's defense. France had rejected the same American offer, and Britain's choice of the United States over France made her unfit for entry into Europe.

As for NATO, de Gaulle moved unhesitatingly to impair it. Gradually, he reduced France's participation in the alliance. First, there was the withdrawal of French staff officers from the various naval commands, then came their removal from NATO headquarters. In 1966, de Gaulle removed French forces from the integrated allied armies and stopped participating in NATO maneuvers. In the same year, he ordered all American military units and all NATO commands and forces out of France. In a curious and typically Gaullist statement, he insisted that France's loyal adherence to the North Atlantic Treaty was untouched by her separation from the military organization created to implement the treaty's terms.

President Kennedy could do nothing to influence the French leader's conduct. His only weapon was to make public and categoric the determination of his country to stand by the allies in the defense of Europe and to reiterate the American position that the political integration of Europe was absolutely necessary for the well-being of the western world. In June of 1963 he journeyed to Europe and, in speeches before large crowds, sought to refute de Gaulle's contentions. At Frankfurt he said, "We look forward to a Europe united and strong . . . a world power capable of meeting world problems as a full and equal partner . . . a fully cohesive Europe that can protect us all against fragmentation of our alliance. With only such a Europe can we have a full give and take between equals, an equal sharing of responsibility and an equal level of sacrifice. . . . The choice of the paths to the unity of Europe is a choice Europe must make. But . . . you should know that this European greatness will not be an object of fear, but a source of strength for the United States of America." Already, one year earlier in a famous July 4 address in Philadelphia, he talked of a "declaration of interdependence . . . a concrete Atlantic partnership, . . . between the new union now emerging in Europe and the old American Union. . . ."

Kennedy's reception in Europe was enthusiastic. All the nations, save France, put their faith and trust in the United States as protector of Europe and many Frenchmen disagreed with their leader on that point. Most dramatic was Kennedy's performance in Berlin. There, at the center of the east-west confrontation, he uttered the words that since have became famous—"Ich bin ein Berliner" (I am a Berliner). A Boston-Harvard accent did not obscure the meaning of the remarks and the crowd in Berlin went wild. And in Frankfurt, he was equally dramatic and positive when he vowed that the United States "will risk its cities to defend yours because we need your freedom to protect ours." The German chancellor reflected a popular and widely held view when he observed, apropos of an effort by de Gaulle to wean Germany away from the alliance, "We will not trade the American umbrella for a French parasol."

Kennedy did not succeed, however, in selling his idea of establishing an allied naval force equipped with nuclear missiles and manned by international crews. The multilateral force (MLF) would consist of twenty-five ships each carrying eight polaris missiles whose use would be subject to an American veto with the proviso that control would pass to Europe after it unified. De Gaulle, as expected, would have none of the plan. For him, it was a further manifestation of European subservience. But even the friendly allies, Belgium, Holland, England and Italy, felt uneasy at the prospect of Germans using nuclear weapons and the plan was allowed to die.

Kennedy faced serious problems not only in Europe but in Asia as well. The situation in Indochina was menacing indeed. Ngo Dinh Diem, who had become prime minister in the government of Bao Dai in June of 1954, forced a plebiscite on the country that resulted in Bao Dai's overthrow. Diem then became president of the Republic of Vietnam. That was October 28, 1955 and it did not take much time for Diem to demonstrate the bankruptcy of his administration. The reforms he had promised were only nominally undertaken; the best land was in the hands of a small number of people (2.5 percent of the landlords owned 50 per cent of the land in the rich Mekong delta region); peasants were saddled with high rentals and usurious rates of interest; dictatorial power had been given the president in a new constitution in 1956 and only the forms of democratic government remained; press censorship and assaults upon the freedom and the rights of individuals were commonplace; and nepotism and corruption were rife. Diem's family, occupying prominent positions in the government, was ruthless and insatiable in exploiting the country. Meanwhile, Diem was moving to clean the communist guerrilla forces, the Viet Cong, out of the areas they controlled and to destroy them and their operations. In late 1959, the struggle took on a new character when North Vietnamese elements began moving south over the Ho Chi Minh trail to join the Viet Cong. A real war now replaced the guerrilla fighting. The truce of 1954 had ended. The second Indochina war had started and would go on for fourteen years.

There was never any question that President Kennedy was committed to keeping South Vietnam out of communist hands. He believed as firmly as did Eisenhower in the domino theory. Shortly before his death in November of 1963, when talking of his determination to give aid to Diem in his fight against the communists, he said, "For us to withdraw from that effort would mean not only a collapse of South Vietnam but southeast Asia." Upon coming into office, he had continued the financial subsidy and the supply of arms and equipment that Eisenhower had begun. In September of that first year, he sent Vice-President Lyndon B. Johnson to Saigon to assure Diem of his support and in October, he commissioned two trusted advisors, Walt W. Rostow and General Maxwell Taylor, to investigate conditions in Vietnam and recommend measures to be taken. Their advice was to increase the number of military advisors and to provide a military force of 10,000 American soldiers to close off the routes used by the North Vietnamese to funnel troops and supplies to the south. Kennedy rejected the second part of the recommendation but accepted the first. Throughout his administration he resisted the pressure to commit American troops to combat. On September 2, 1963, he remarked to CBS correspondent Walter Cronkite, "In the final analysis, it is their war. They are the ones who have to win or lose it. We can help them, give them equipment, send our men out there as advisors, but they have to win it. . . ."

The president did, however, significantly increase the advisory personnel. When Eisenhower left office, there were 1,000 American advisors. By the end of 1961, that figure had reached 1,364; by mid-summer of 1962, there were 8,000; by November of 1963, American forces numbered 15,500. They not only trained troops in tactics and in the use and maintenance of weapons and equipment; they also transported them to combat. In December of 1962, an American aircraft carrier docked in Saigon and unloaded thirty-three helicopters that were flown by American pilots and used to move Vietnamese troops from one operation to another.

Meanwhile, serious trouble was brewing in neighboring Laos where on August 9, 1960, a coup led by military officers of the communist Pathet Lao overthrew the conservative pro-western government. A struggle had been going on in that little country between the two factions since 1954 with the United States supporting one side and the Soviet Union the other. Despite massive American aid, the conservatives could not hold out and the Pathet Lao took over, forming, in November of 1960, a new government consisting of neutralist and communist elements. Kennedy gave up any hope of restoring the prowesterners. Instead, he sent 5,000 soldiers to Thailand to keep the Pathet Lao from invading that country. He did succeed in convincing Khruschev at their meeting in Vienna of the wisdom of settling the Laotian business. The result was a conference in Geneva of 14 interested powers in June of 1962 where the neutrality and independence of Laos was guaranteed and provision made for admitting prowestern conservative elements into a new coalition government along with neutralists and Pathet Lao. It did not prove to be a permanent solution but, at least, it permitted the president to concentrate on Vietnam.

There Diem was making small headway against the Viet Cong and their North Vietnamese allies, mainly because of popular dissatisfaction with his oppressive and dictatorial regime. Kennedy tried to prevail upon him to effect reforms and change policy and personnel but to no avail. The problem solved itself when on November 1, 1963, a coup carried out by dissident army officers killed Diem and his brother and took over the government. The revolution was not unwelcome in Washington. Indeed, it was rumored that Americans had had a hand in the plot. But President Kennedy was not able to take advantage of the change for in three weeks he lay dead by the hand of an assassin.

Lyndon B. Johnson who succeeded to office inherited all the problems his martyred predecessor had faced and had left unresolved. As for Europe, he mentioned them all in a speech in October of 1966 in which he pledged "America's best efforts to achieve new thrust for the Atlantic alliance, to support the movement toward Western European unity, to bring about far-reaching improvement in relations between East and West." It cannot be said that the new president succeeded in realizing those goals. The Atlantic alliance was in disarray, but not only because de Gaulle continued to keep French forces separate from those of the allies. There seemed to be, also, a general diminution of the feeling of fear among the allies concerning Soviet intentions and a slackening in their defense efforts. Many of them, for example, were reducing the term of military service for their conscripts. Then there was the final defeat of the multilateral force in which Kennedy and Johnson had placed so much hope. As for the Common Market, it, too, was foundering. De Gaulle continued to blackball Britain's entry and to block every step the Community tried to take to achieve real unity and integration. It limped along doing what could be done by a confederation of sovereign states.

With the Soviet Union, some progress toward improving relations was achieved. In June of 1964, the two powers signed a convention providing for consular offices in several cities of both countries, for cultural exchanges, and for protection of tourists. Most important, however, was the agreement on the necessity of limiting the production of atomic weapons in the world. On October 15, 1964, Khrushchev was ousted from the Kremlin to be replaced by Aleksei N. Kosygin as premier and Leonid I. Brezhnev as first secretary of the Party. The next day, the Red Chinese announced the explosion of their first atomic bomb. The Soviet Union and the United States needed no sharper impetus to drive them to action. They went to work, along with Great Britain, which shared their interest in the question, to draft a nonproliferation treaty. For several years various versions were exchanged, products of each of the three countries.

At last, following an amiable visit by Kosygin with Johnson in a small college town in New Jersey, the powers reached an agreement on a treaty. That was in June 1969. Two months later, each presented to the UN Disarmament Committee separate but identical drafts of a treaty. On July 1, 1968, the United States, Great Britain, and the Soviet Union, together with fifty-six other nations that possessed no nuclear weapons, signed a nonproliferation treaty. It was, practically speaking, not a very significant matter. It provided for limited inspection of the nonnuclear countries to stave off their production of nuclear weapons. It said nothing about those countries already possessing nuclear weapons limiting their production or reducing their stockpile. Further, the principal nonnuclear powers that aspired to join the club such as Japan, Italy, India, and West Germany and those nations who had some and wanted more, such as China and France, did not sign the treaty. Whatever value it had was moral which, as a matter of fact, counted for little in the international climate of the 1960s.

The Johnson administration faced yet another serious and disheartening problem in Europe—the Soviet invasion of Czechoslovakia in 1968. It all began when Alexander Dubçek was elevated by the Czech Communist Party Central Committee to the position of first secretary. Dubçek was a "good" communist, loyal and devoted to the Soviet Union, but he soon began to push for reforms in his country—free speech, democratization of the party apparatus, free press. Such a move threatened the stability of the communist world by loosening the bonds of discipline and encouraging dissent. Fear swept through the Party leadership of the satellites and when students and workers in Prague demonstrated against the republic's president, an old-line communist, they decided to act. The result was the invasion of Czechoslovakia by soldiers from the Soviet Union and the other members of the Warsaw Pact on August 20. Order was quickly brought to the wayward communist state, and party control and discipline were soon restored. Out of the experience came the Brezhnev Doctrine, pronounced by the Soviet Union, that sanctioned intervention by Russia in the internal affairs of a communist country to save it from slipping out of the satellite orbit.

The reaction of the world to the brutal suppression of the aspirations of the Czech people was vehement. The United States and other western powers denounced Moscow but nothing more was done. As in 1956 in Hungary, no one was willing to challenge Russia in her sphere of influence. One positive result for the west was a drawing together, at least for the moment, of the European allies in the face of the Soviet action.

Johnson's problems in Europe may have been troublesome, but they were nothing compared with the difficulties he faced in Vietnam. The military government that had replaced Diem made no move to institute reforms and proved no less corrupt and authoritarian than Diem's. Meanwhile, the Viet Cong were building an effective fighting force supported by the local population who looked to the communists for economic and social justice. Like Kennedy, Johnson was determined to save South Vietnam from the communists. "I am not going to lose Vietnam," he said shortly after coming to the White House, "I am not going to be the president who saw southeast Asia go the way China went." But, again like Kennedy, he had no thought of committing American troops. The American contribution would be massive aid. Little did the president realize that there could be no victory in Vietnam without direct American military support and that circumstances would soon draw America into the war.

August 2, 1964 was a crucial date on the road to that involvement. On that day three North Vietnamese torpedo boats attacked the American destroyer *Maddox* on patrol in the Gulf of Tonkin. *Maddox* was one of several vessels keeping an eye on the movement by water of troops and supplies from North Vietnam to the south. Johnson reacted by increasing the number of ships on patrol and ordering them, in the event of another attack, to drive off and to destroy the enemy. Two days later, the president learned of a second attack on *Maddox* and on another destroyer, *C. Turner Joy*, and of the destruction of two North Vietnamese vessels. That same night, he told the American people on television of the incident and that he had ordered retaliatory action in the form of bombing by aircraft of enemy gunboats and naval bases. The next day, August 7, he requested Congress to approve what he had done and to authorize him to take further action as he deemed necessary.

It was an excited and seething Congress which received the president's message. Eager to avenge the attack on United States ships, it passed, virtually without debate, the Gulf of Tonkin resolution, 416–0 in the House and 88–2 in the Senate, which gave the executive the right "to take all necessary measures to repel an armed attack against the forces of the United States and to prevent further aggression." It also designated southeast Asia as vital to the national interest of the United States and charged the president with helping any state in that area to retain its freedom. Many of those enthusiastically voting for the resolution were soon to regret their action for it was that resolution that the president used as a "blank check" to escalate American involvement without further congressional approval.

Yet it must be said that at the time, Johnson did not contemplate the use of American forces or aircraft in the war. During the Tonkin Gulf crisis he had said that the United States "seeks no wider war" and in the election campaign in the summer and fall of 1964, he stood as the moderate in opposition to the Republican candidate, Senator Barry Goldwater, who was advocating an all-out attack on North Vietnam including low-yield atomic bombs. "We are not about to send American boys nine or ten thousand miles away from home to do what Asian boys ought to be doing to protect themselves," Johnson said. "We don't want . . . to get tied down in a land war in Asia." After his election, he continued to resist pressure from his military advisors to bomb North Vietnam. Then came the attack on February 7, 1965 on an American Special Forces camp at Pleiku in central South Vietnam. Seven Americans were killed and 109 wounded. And the floodgates opened. Lyndon Johnson, tough Texan politician and true-blue American, was not one to dismiss lightly an assault on a United States installation. That was a presumptuous and dangerous game to play. Promptly, he ordered American bombers to hit North Vietnamese military installations and supply routes to the south. Then came the fateful decision in March when he ordered 4,000 marines and soldiers into combat. It was an American war now and the greatest weight in the fighting would henceforth be carried by United States forces. Australia, New Zealand, the Philippines, South Korea, and Thailand provided some units, but they constituted a token contribution. On the other side, Red China and the Soviet Union poured supplies of all kinds to the North Vietnam–Viet Cong effort.

Lyndon Johnson was sure of his ground. South Vietnam's freedom had to be saved at all costs, so he told an audience at Johns Hopkins University on April 7. If North Vietnam would accept that fact, he said, he would welcome "unconditional discussions" for peace. To prove his good intentions, he offered aid of $1 billion to help southeast Asia, including North Vietnam, improve conditions. The next day, the North Vietnamese came back with their own version of a peace program. It contained four points: withdrawal of United States troops; reunification of the peninsula by the Vietnamese themselves; acceptance of the program of the National Liberation Front (the political arm of the Viet Cong) as the basis for settling South Vietnam's destiny; neutralization of the country. Those terms were, of course, totally unacceptable to Johnson and so the war went on.

In July of 1965, 50,000 more American troops joined the fighting and, gradually, as the war raged, more and more of them entered combat— 184,000 by the end of 1965; 380,000 by the end of 1966; 450,000 by the end of 1967; 540,000 in 1968. And the number of dead and wounded mounted: 16,000 killed and 100,000 wounded between 1961 and 1967, that figure to reach 59,000 dead and 300,000 wounded by the end of the war in 1973. The cost ran high, too, $7 billion for the year 1966; $30 billion for 1968; and on and on. Despite the great sacrifice of men and money and the heavy and constant saturation bombing of enemy bases, supply lines, and centers of production and distribution (to the very outskirts of Hanoi, the capital, and Haiphong, the chief port), there was no American victory. Supplies kept moving south, the Viet Cong still held large areas, and corruption and authoritarianism yet characterized the

South Vietnam government. And all the while, American commanders were predicting an early victory as they called for more and more troops.

It was ironic and tragic that the war caused more injury to the American people than to the enemy. It did nothing less than tear the country apart. Large numbers of Americans—mostly students, teachers, and civil rights workers but also others from all walks of life—considered the war senseless and cruel. The country that was "being saved" was being laid waste by bombing and by defoliation; the people to be "saved" were being burned by napalm and killed by gunfire, bombing, and booby traps; the democracy that was to be preserved was in the hands of an authoritarian and dictatorial president who liquidated the political opposition and ran uncontested for re-election. The protests took the form of demonstrations on campuses and in Washington and in other major cities, of draft evasions, of obstructing troop trains, of teach-ins, and of strikes and parades. Opponents of the war rejected the administration's claim that the war was part of the Cold War and a phase of the containment of communism and that to abandon South Vietnam would be another Munich and result in the loss of all of southeast Asia. They saw the struggle as a civil war fought for economic and social justice and for freedom from oppressive landlords and venal politicians. These "doves" were appalled at the "hawks" among Americans who favored bombing North Vietnam "back to the stone age."

As the war went on, the president lost more and more of the confidence of the people. Early in 1967, polls showed a majority of those interviewed opposed his handling of the war and, later that year, only 23 percent approved his Vietnam policy. He had trouble with the Congress, too. Many senators and representatives believed his conduct of the war violated the war-making clause of the Constitution. They aired their criticism in congressional committee hearings, where they interrogated administration spokesmen and heard testimony from critics of the president. Johnson's stock dropped internationally, also, Allies, neutrals, and Soviet bloc nations alike were aghast at the murderous bombing of a defenseless people and horrified by the destruction American arms visited on a small country. The Swedish government and people were particularly hostile and welcomed deserters from America's forces as well as draft evaders. Canada, too, gave deserters and evaders a safe haven.

January and February of 1968 constituted a turning point in the war. At that time, the Vietnamese Lunar New Year, North Vietnamese and Viet Cong troops launched a gigantic and simultaneous surprise attack all over South Vietnam. They struck at almost every provincial capital and at five of the six chief cities, including Saigon. They penetrated even into the American embassy compound seizing one of the buildings. They inflicted tremendous damage on American installations and personnel. General William C. Westmoreland, the American commander, called the

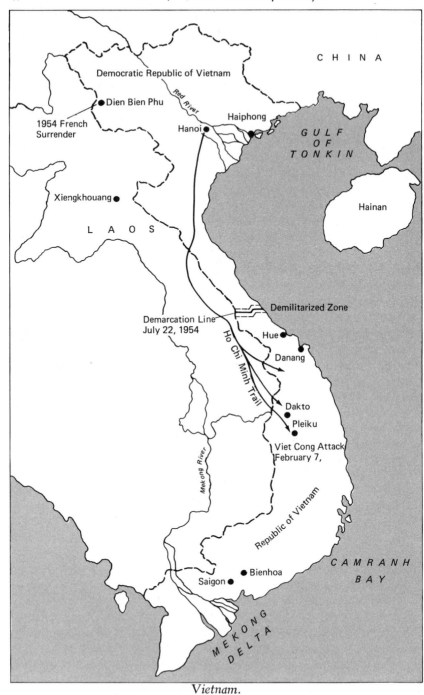

Vietnam.

assault the "last gasp" of the enemy. They had exhausted themselves and could be destroyed, he said, and called for 200,000 more men to administer the death blow. He would have been more nearly correct had he said the assault was the "last straw" for the American people. They had had enough and the clamor for ending the war reached a new crescendo. It touched even Lyndon Johnson. His shrewd political sense grasped the full meaning of the first presidential primary for the 1968 election, in New Hampshire on March 12. There Senator Eugene McCarthy of Minnesota, long a leader of the antiwar movement, won 42.4 percent of the Democratic vote and garnered twenty delegates.

On March 31, the president went on television to say, "I am taking the first steps to de-escalate the conflict." He announced also that the bombing would end except for some small sectors and that he would not stand for re-election. He knew defeat when he met it. To Westmoreland, he sent only 13,500 soldiers. In May, the North Vietnamese agreed to come to the conference table but refused to engage in serious talks until all acts of war ended. The United States delegates insisted that the infiltration of troops and supplies stop before negotiations commence. Neither side would budge and the conference ended. It remained for the next administration to take up the task of ending the war. The new president was Richard M. Nixon, who had defeated Vice-President Hubert H. Humphrey. Humphrey's chances for victory were slim. The Democratic party was badly split as their convention in Chicago unmistakably showed. Opponents of the war and of the Johnson policies—the followers of Senator McCarthy and of Robert Kennedy, who was assassinated on June 6—could not gain control of the party. Humphrey, supporter of his chief's war policies, had the backing of the party regulars and won the nomination but he lost many of the votes of long-time Democrats. It remained to be seen whether Nixon, who said he had a plan for ending the war, would, in fact, succeed in the task.

BIBLIOGRAPHY

CHESTER COOPER, *The Lost Crusade: America in Vietnam* (1970).
FRANCES FITZGERALD, *Fire in the Lake: The Vietnamese and the Americans in Vietnam* (1972).
DAVID HALBERSTAM, *The Best and the Brightest* (1972).
ROGER HILSMAN, *To Move a Nation* (1967).
LYNDON B. JOHNSON, *Vantage Point* (1971).
ARTHUR M. SCHLESINGER, *A Thousand Days: John F. Kennedy in the White House* (1965).
NEIL SHEEHAN, et al., *The Pentagon Papers* (1971).
THEODORE SORENSON, *Kennedy* (1965).

Epilogue—A Diplomatic Revolution

P RESIDENT Nixon ended the Vietnam war on January 27, 1973, or, to put the matter more correctly, he terminated America's role in the conflict, for after the withdrawal of United States forces, the fighting continued as fiercely as before. Between January of 1973 and February of 1974, South Vietnamese deaths in action numbered 13,136 and the Communists lost 41,668.

The president did not end American participation in the war until four years after he came to office. He did not quit the fight until his policy of "Vietnamization" was completed; that is, until he felt assured that the Vietnamese could handle their own defense. No intelligent observer really believed that the Vietnamese could defend themselves without American military aid, thus "Vietnamization" must be viewed, at worst, as a Nixonian hoax or, at best, as a means of assuaging the American conscience. The withdrawal of American forces was gradual and geared, so it was said, to the increasing Vietnamese military capability. The peak figure of 543,000 troops in 1969 dropped to 425,000 in mid-1970, to 275,000 in June of 1971, and to 27,000 by the end of 1972. The last soldier left Vietnamese soil in March of 1973.

Meanwhile, conversations were taking place in Paris between North Vietnamese and American representatives concerning terms. At the same time, Nixon was carrying on the war much to the consternation of many Americans. They had expected him to stop the fighting at once upon assuming office. He, however, maintained that more punishment would soften the communists at the peace table. So, he ordered the aerial bombing of North Vietnam, destroying parts of Hanoi, and Haiphong, blockaded Haiphong with mines, sent American troops into Cambodia (in April of 1970), thereby opening a new front, and used American helicopters to transport Vietnamese troops to Laos (in January of 1971).

Frustration and anger were widespread among the American people over "Nixon's war" and antiadministration demonstrations were almost daily affairs. They ranged from mild picketing of the White House to huge parades and marches such as the one involving 250,000 people on November 15, 1969, on a walk from Arlington National Cemetery on the outskirts of Washington to the White House. And blood was shed on the campus of Kent State University in Ohio on May 4, 1970 when National Guardsmen opened fire on protesting students, killing four of them. The reaction in Congress was hostile, too. The presumptuousness of the executive in continuing to conduct a war that Congress never declared infuriated most of the legislators. They disagreed violently with his contention (which was Lyndon Johnson's as well) that the Tonkin Gulf resoultion was "a functional equivalent of a declaration of war" (the words were actually those of Johnson's attorney general). Various moves were made in the Senate and in the House to force a cessation of the war by cutting off funds for its prosecution, but none succeeded. The Tonkin Gulf resolution was repealed in January of 1971, but it did not affect the president's conduct of the war. He easily fell back on his constitutional powers as commander-in-chief and on his insistence that his military operations were necessary to protect the lives of American servicemen. Finally, in November of 1973, a major constitutional breakthrough occurred when Congress overrode a presidential veto of a war powers act. That act provided that the executive must notify the Congress when he commits United States forces in an action and that he must seek the legislature's approval within sixty to ninety days if he wished to continue the fighting. Some congressmen opposed the measure because it permitted the president to *start* a war without a congressional declaration but the majority felt that, at least, another Vietnam could not occur without the sanction of the representatives of the people.

That it took the president four years to end America's role in the war must not obscure the wider significance of that action—as an element in what may properly be called an American diplomatic revolution of the 1970s. All the evidence seems to point to the fact that the decade of the 1970s marks the close of a period in the nation's diplomatic history that opened with the enunciation of the Truman Doctrine in 1947—a period of playing the role of world banker and policeman, of protector and guarantor of the nations of the free world.

The revolution may be said to have had its beginnings in a widespread movement over the last several years calling for reassessing and revising the Cold War policies. From all quarters—students and teachers, labor and capital, the churches, the professions, the press, fraternal organizations, and the legislatures of the states and of the nation—there has been a demand for a change. For the first time since the end of World War II, except for a brief and ineffectual flurry in the winter of 1950–1951 when the Red Chinese took part in the Korean war, there was a serious questioning of the country's role in international affairs. Typical was the observation by Professor Henry S. Commager that, "It is not our duty to keep peace throughout the world, to put down aggression wherever it occurs, to stop the advance of isms we do not approve. . . ." and by former Attorney General Nicholas Katzenbach that "our involvement must be less widespread and more selective than has been characteristic over the last twenty years." *New York Times* columnist James Reston more graphically described the mood of the country as one which wished to substitute for the slogans "no more appeasement" and "no more Munichs" that had underlaid the foreign policy of the period 1947–1970, the watchwords "no more involvement" and "no more Vietnams."

Large numbers of Americans agreed with the view of Senator John Stennis of Mississippi that "there are limits to what we can do in manpower and in money" and of columnist Walter Lippmann that those limits have been reached. They would agree, too, that the United States is overcommitted and overextended; that it does not have "the resources—material, intellectual, moral—to be at once an American power, a European power, and an Asiatic power," to use Professor Commager's words. The time had come to lay aside the extravagant and inflated slogans of the previous twenty-five years that guided America's international policy: "The free peoples of the world look to us for support in maintaining their freedom" (Harry S. Truman); "We are concerned with the destiny of free men everywhere" (Dwight D. Eisenhower); "I am a Berliner" (John F. Kennedy); "The United States will provide all the resources needed to combat aggression throughout the world" (Lyndon B. Johnson).

There is a feeling in the country that after $143 billion expended and twenty-five years of free-world leadership, the time has come to pursue a more modest and more restrained foreign policy. "Half-speed astern" rather than "full speed ahead" should be the rule, said James Reston. America ought to begin to look inward, to think of itself and of its pressing domestic needs. As John Connally said on December 17, 1971, in an address to the Houston Chamber of Commerce, "at long last, we've reached the point where we can no longer be completely and entirely generous, giving of ourselves, of our material resources, of our strength, and of our money that other nations may prosper. We have reached the point where, to a greater extent than ever, we must speak for ourselves; defend ourselves. . . ."

Central to the transformation of the public view on America's international role is the experience of the Vietnam war. The relationship was most aptly put by Senator Frank Church of Idaho in 1969. "Vietnam," he said, "is the culmination of our post-war policy of maximum intervention abroad. That policy lies shattered today in the jungles of Vietnam where we learned that there are limits to what we can accomplish in a foreign land. It required a calamity of those proportions to awaken us from our dreams of omnipotence."

There seems to be no question that the Nixon administration is committed to carry out the diplomatic revolution. By both word and deed the president has made his intention clear. At Guam, on July 25, 1969, he set forth a new American foreign policy—the Nixon Doctrine, whose "central thesis is that the United States will participate in the defense and development of allies and friends, but that America cannot—and will not—conceive *all* the plans, design *all* the programs, execute *all* the decisions and undertake *all* the defense of the free nations of the world." And, again, in his second inaugural address, he made the same point. "We shall do our share in defending peace and freedom in the world," he said. "But we shall expect others to do their share. The time has passed when America will make every other nation's conflict our own, or make every other nation's conflict our responsibility, or presume to tell the people of other nations how to manage their own affairs. . . . We have lived too long with the consequences of attempting to gather all power and responsibility in Washington."

The Nixon administration's aim, it appears, is to "decrease America's visibility" and lower its profile abroad, to use the president's own words, and to stop acting the role of "the cop on the beat," to use the words of Defense Secretary Melvin R. Laird. There is a determination not to make big wars out of little ones. Nixon said on June 20, 1972, "future conflicts which are peripheral to the central interests of the great powers should not directly involve the great powers themselves."

The withdrawal from Vietnam is only one piece of evidence, albeit a supremely important one, of the change in the country's postwar role. There is, also, the return of Okinawa to the Japanese in May of 1972 and the move to establish friendly relations with the People's Republic of China. The president's visit to Peking in February of 1972 was a historic occasion. That the American politician most closely identified for almost thirty years with vehement anticommunist sentiments should be the first to open relations with the great Asian communist nation to many people seemed unbelievable. Old-time Nixon supporters considered him a traitor; old-time Nixon-haters suspected some ulterior motive. None could deny, however, that the step constituted an important element in a changing American foreign policy. Coming to terms with one of the two chief Cold War enemies in itself was a diplomatic revolution. Following the cordial presidential visit was the relaxation of American opposition to Red China's admission to the United Nations that led to the ousting of the Republic of China and the seating of the People's Republic of China. Shortly thereafter came the exchange of diplomats between the two countries and the beginning of trade and of visits by Americans to the mainland.

Three months after visiting Peking, Nixon went to Moscow to seek a détente with the second principal Cold War opponent. His meeting with the Soviet leaders was warm and friendly and made possible some significant accomplishments in the relations of the two powers. An increase in trade followed as well as agreements on the limitations of strategic arms. Talks had been in progress, between representatives of Russia and the United States since November of 1969, first in Helsinki and then in Vienna, on strategic weapons and in the fall of 1972 a treaty was signed, fixing for each power a maximum number of land- and sea-based missiles. The Soviet Union was given a numerical advantage compensated for by America's superiority in guidance technology and in manned bombers. A second phase of the discussions is now (February of 1974) in progress with a view to making further cuts in nuclear weapons. There is, also, underway a multinational conference attended by NATO and Warsaw Pact members to effect a balanced reduction of forces in Europe as part of a general security agreement. Although that meeting is bogged down in various technicalities, Nixon and Brezhnev did sign, in November of 1973, an agreement on the prevention of nuclear war, which pledges the two countries to consult in the event of a threat of war anywhere in the world that might involve them in a nuclear fight.

Basic to the demonstration of America's international role has been the demand by the Nixon administration that the European allies assume a greater share of the burden of their defense in men and in money so that the American load could be lightened. That idea was not a new one; it antedated Nixon's coming to office. For some years Senator Mike Mansfield, representing a not-inconsiderable number of his colleagues, had been proposing a reduction in America's troop commitments to NATO and financial contribution to the alliance's defense budget. His resolutions never did gain the Senate's approval but in November of 1973, an amendment proposed by Senators Henry M. Jackson (Washington) and Sam Nunn (Georgia) to the military procurement bill did pass both Senate and House as a kind of substitute for the Mansfield proposal. It provided for the withdrawal of as many American soldiers from Europe as would wipe out any deficit in the American balance of payments incurred in participation in NATO. The legislation was designed, of course, to increase the European contribution.

Quite apart from congressional action, the Nixon administration sought to find a formula for shifting the burden of the defense of Europe to a more equitable basis. Henry A. Kissinger, the President's Special Advisor in National Security Affairs, made such a suggestion in a speech on April 23, 1973 in which he called for a new "Atlantic Charter." Its purpose, he said, was to revitalize the alliance and to redefine it in the light of changed conditions since the end of the war. By changed conditions he meant the tremendous growth in the prosperity of the Western European nations and their greatly increased capacity to provide for their own defense as well as the relaxed international climate accompanying the détente with Russia. He had in mind, too, the development of the European Community as the world's largest trading bloc which posed severe problems for American international commerce.

Europe did not, however, respond to Kissinger's overtures. Its reception of his call was, according to one commentator, "frosty." Nixon had, at a news conference on January 31, 1973, proclaimed 1973 as the "year of Europe" by which he meant that with the cease-fire in Vietnam and the accords with China and Russia, the United States could turn to European matters long neglected. But Europe was wary. The Nixon administration had not only neglected the Atlantic partners; it had ignored them. It had not consulted them on the crucial foreign policy decisions such as those concerning China and the Soviet Union. And as 1973 progressed there was further evidence that Washington played a lone hand when it suited American interests. The June 1973 agreement with the Soviet Union on preventing nuclear war was a well-kept Soviet-American secret until two days before the signing when British Prime Minister Edward Heath and German Chancellor Willy Brandt were informed of its contents. The other allies got word of it only six and one-half hours before the signing. Again in October, at the time of the so-called Yom Kippur War between Israel and the Arab nations, the allies were not consulted by President Nixon prior to his announcement on October 25 of a worldwide alert of American armed forces in the face of some Soviet saber-rattling. To many European statesmen, Kissinger's address in London on December 12, 1973 calling for a special relationship between Western Europe and the United States and suggesting that Europe consult with Washington before taking any action that touches American interests was somewhat gratuitous.

The European response did not come until the end of 1973. A formal reply had been planned for the early fall, but the Middle Eastern war followed by the crisis created by the drastic reduction of Arab oil exports to the West as a form of political blackmail deflected the powers. Indeed, European reaction to the oil crisis constituted *a* reply in that the western allies each scrambled to make the best deal possible with the Arabs, despite Washington's call for a solid front. Another indirect reply may be said to have come out of the meeting of the European Community at Copenhagen in December of 1973, where a virtual declaration of independence from American tutelage was adopted. The representatives of the nine member states (the original six had been augmented on January 1, 1973 by Great Britain, Ireland, and Denmark) proclaimed their "common will" that the Community speak with one voice in foreign affairs and strengthen its political unity.

When an official and formal response to the new "Atlantic Charter" came, it was in a form unsatisfactory to Washington for it consisted of two separate documents—one covering defense; the other trade, thereby ignoring Kissinger's linking of the two as interdependent. Further, its contents made no significant contribution to the American problem of shifting the defense burden. There is no reason to believe, however, that the United States will not continue to press for a shifting of a greater share of the defense burden onto the backs of the European allies.

Nixon's foreign, economic, and defense policies offer additional proof of the diplomatic revolution. The defense budget for 1974, although greater than for any previous year since the war's end in total dollars, is actually the lowest in ten years by $8 billion when the rate of inflation is considered. There is, also, the move to reduce the army by three divisions and the total armed forces numbers from 1.5 million to 790,000. Finally, the several devaluations of the dollar beginning in August of 1971, the surcharge on imports, and the establishment of import quotas are all designed to enhance America's own international economic position by pushing exports, protecting domestic industries, and restoring a favorable balance of trade.

It is not surprising that the new direction of American foreign policy has sent shock waves through nations all over the globe who in the last quarter century have come to depend on the United States for military and financial support. Will the United States, they wonder, retreat into an isolationist position and renounce its treaty commitments and obligations? The resolution introduced by Senator J. William Fulbright on February 8, 1974 to end all major foreign-aid programs (save for military assistance to a few countries and social programs) presented a frightening prospect. It seems safe to say that the country will not again practice the neutralism of the post-World War I period. The experience in two wars has taught Americans that liberating a continent is costlier and more difficult than preventing its being overrun. America can be depended on. It will not again serve notice to would-be aggressors that they may attack a free nation without fear of reprisal. It *will* expect an equitable sharing of the burden with those nations that have the wherewithal. Rolf Pauls, the German Ambassador in Washington, stated the case aptly when he remarked, in November of 1971, in reply to the question, will American extreme globalism turn into the other extreme of a new isolationism, "The more decided Europeans are to take care of themselves, the greater will be American preparedness to remain committed to their cause."

BIBLIOGRAPHY

Henry A. Kissinger, *The Necessity for Choice: Prospects of American Foreign Policy* (1960).

Richard Nixon, *United States Foreign Policy: A Report to the Congress* (1970–1973).

Garry Wills, *Nixon Agonistes* (1970).

The Presidents
and Their Secretaries of State

President	Political Party	Secretary of State	Dates of Service
Continental Congress		John Jay	Dec. 21, 1784–Mar. 22, 1790
George Washington	Fed.	Thomas Jefferson	Mar. 22, 1790–Dec. 31, 1793
		Edmund Randolph	Jan. 2, 1794–Aug. 20, 1795
		Timothy Pickering	Dec. 10, 1795–
John Adams	Fed.	Timothy Pickering	–May 12, 1800
		John Marshall	May 12, 1800–Feb. 4, 1801
Thomas Jefferson	Rep.	James Madison	May 2, 1801–Mar. 3, 1809
James Madison	Rep.	Robert Smith	Mar. 6, 1809–Apr. 1, 1811
		James Monroe	Apr. 6, 1811–Mar. 3, 1817
James Monroe	Rep.	John Quincy Adams	Sept. 22, 1817–Mar. 3, 1825
John Quincy Adams	Rep.	Henry Clay	Mar. 7, 1825–Mar. 3, 1829
Andrew Jackson	Dem.	Martin Van Buren	Mar. 28, 1829–May 23, 1831
		Edward Livingston	May 24, 1831–May 29, 1833
		Louis McLane	May 29, 1833–June 30, 1834
		John Forsyth	July 1, 1834–
Martin Van Buren	Dem.	John Forsyth	–Mar. 3, 1841
William Henry Harrison	Whig	Daniel Webster	Mar. 6, 1841–
John Tyler	Whig	Daniel Webster	–May 8, 1843
		Abel P. Upshur	July 24, 1843–Feb. 28, 1844
		John C. Calhoun	Apr. 1, 1844–
James Knox Polk	Dem.	John C. Calhoun	–Mar. 10, 1845
		James Buchanan	Mar. 10, 1845–Mar. 7, 1849
Zachary Taylor	Whig	John M. Clayton	Mar. 8, 1849–July 22, 1850
Millard Fillmore	Whig	Daniel Webster	July 23, 1850–Oct. 24, 1852
		Edward Everett	Nov. 6, 1852–Mar. 3, 1853
Franklin Pierce	Dem.	William L. Marcy	Mar. 8, 1853–Mar. 6, 1857

President	Political Party	Secretary of State	Dates of Service
James Buchanan	Dem.	Lewis Cass	Mar. 6, 1857–Dec. 14, 1860
		Jeremiah Black	Dec. 17, 1860–Mar. 5, 1861
Abraham Lincoln	Rep.	William H. Seward	Mar. 6, 1861–
Andrew Johnson	Rep.	William H. Seward	–Mar. 4, 1869
Ulysses Simpson Grant	Rep.	Elihu B. Washburne	Mar. 5, 1869–Mar. 16, 1869
		Hamilton Fish	Mar. 17, 1869–Mar. 12, 1877
Rutherford Birchard Hayes	Rep.	William M. Evarts	Mar. 12, 1877–Mar. 7, 1881
James Abram Garfield	Rep.	James G. Blaine	Mar. 7, 1881–
Chester Alan Arthur	Rep.	James G. Blaine	–Dec. 19, 1881
		Frederick T. Freylinghuysen	Dec. 19, 1881–Mar. 6, 1885
Grover Cleveland	Dem.	Thomas F. Bayard	Mar. 7, 1885–Mar. 6, 1889
Benjamin Harrison	Rep.	James G. Blaine	Mar. 7, 1889–June 4, 1892
		John W. Foster	June 29, 1892–Feb. 23, 1893
Grover Cleveland	Dem.	Walter Q. Gresham	Mar. 7, 1893–May 28, 1895
		Richard Olney	June 10, 1895–Mar. 5, 1897
William McKinley	Rep.	John Sherman	Mar. 6, 1897–Apr. 27, 1898
		William R. Day	Apr. 28, 1898–Sept. 16, 1898
		John Hay	Sept. 30, 1898–
Theodore Roosevelt	Rep.	John Hay	–July 1, 1905
		Elihu Root	July 19, 1905–Jan. 27, 1909
		Robert Bacon	Jan. 27, 1909–Mar. 5, 1909
William Howard Taft	Rep.	Philander C. Knox	Mar. 6, 1909–Mar. 5, 1913
Woodrow Wilson	Dem.	William Jennings Bryan	Mar. 5, 1913–June 9, 1915
		Robert Lansing	June 24, 1915–Feb. 13, 1920
		Brainbridge Colby	Mar. 23, 1920–Mar. 4, 1921
Warren Gamaliel Harding	Rep.	Charles E. Hughes	Mar. 5, 1921–
Calvin Coolidge	Rep.	Charles E. Hughes	–Mar. 4, 1925
		Frank B. Kellogg	Mar. 5, 1925–Mar. 28, 1929
Herbert Clark Hoover	Rep.	Henry L. Stimson	Mar. 28, 1929–Mar. 4, 1933
Franklin Delano Roosevelt	Dem.	Cordell Hull	Mar. 4, 1933–Nov. 27, 1944
		Edward R. Stettinius, Jr.	Dec. 1, 1944–
Harry S. Truman	Dem.	Edward R. Stettinius, Jr.	–June 27, 1945
		James F. Byrnes	July 2, 1945–Jan. 20, 1947
		George C. Marshall	Jan. 21, 1947–Jan. 20, 1949
		Dean G. Acheson	Jan. 21, 1949–Jan. 20, 1953
Dwight David Eisenhower	Rep.	John F. Dulles	Jan. 21, 1953–Apr. 15, 1959
		Christian A. Herter	Apr. 22, 1959–Jan. 20, 1961
John Fitzgerald Kennedy	Dem.	Dean Rusk	Jan. 21, 1961–
Lyndon B. Johnson	Dem.	Dean Rusk	–Jan. 20, 1969
Richard M. Nixon	Rep.	William P. Rogers	Jan. 21, 1969–Sept. 3, 1973
		Henry A. Kissinger	Sept. 22, 1973–
Gerald R. Ford	Rep.	Henry A. Kissinger	

INDEX